Islandica

A Series in Icelandic and Norse Studies

Cornell University Library

PATRICK J. STEVENS, MANAGING EDITOR

VOLUME LVIII

New Norse Studies

Essays on the Literature and Culture
of Medieval Scandinavia

EDITED BY

JEFFREY TURCO

New Norse Studies

Essays on the Literature and Culture of Medieval Scandinavia

EDITED BY

Jeffrey Turco

ISLANDICA LVIII

CORNELL UNIVERSITY LIBRARY
ITHACA, NEW YORK
2015

First published 2015 by Cornell University Library
Distributed by Cornell University Press

Printed in the United States of America
Design and composition: Jack Donner, BookType

A complete version of this book is available through open access
at http://cip.cornell.edu/Islandica

ISBN: 978-0-935995-23-7

Cloth printing 10 9 8 7 6 5 4 3 2 1

Contents

Preface

It is a pleasure to welcome as *Islandica* 58 the twelve thoughtful (and thought-provoking) papers gathered in this volume of *New Norse Studies: Essays on the Literature and Culture of Medieval Scandinavia*, edited by Professor Jeffrey Turco of Purdue University.

The *Islandica* series, whose engagement with the evolving nature of Norse and Icelandic Studies owes so much to the foresight of Daniel Willard Fiske and Halldór Hermannsson, has included but few volumes of essays, and all of these within the twenty-first century. It is to be hoped that this format—a vessel lighter and swifter by nature on the scholarly currents but necessitating therefor exquisitely sturdy structure and craftsmanship—will figure regularly alongside the bibliographic studies, academic monographs, and definitive translations that have long populated this venerable series.

I am most appreciative of the time and reflection all the authors devoted to their contributions, and congratulate them on this publication. Thanks without measure go to Jeffrey Turco for his unstinting effort, so often in times of stressful and unceasing commitments, to bring this volume to the pages now before you.

Patrick

Patrick J. Stevens, Curator of the Fiske Icelandic Collection, Cornell University Library and Managing Editor of the *Islandica* Series

Introduction

New Norse Studies: Essays on the Literature and Culture of Medieval Scandinavia is the third volume of collected essays to appear in *Islandica*, the series inaugurated in 1908 by Halldór Hermannsson, first curator of the Fiske Icelandic Collection at Cornell University. This long-lived series in Icelandic and Norse Studies was founded with a bequest from Willard Fiske (1831–1904), far-faring and passionate collector of rare books and manuscripts and professor of North European Languages as well as Cornell's first university librarian and Gilded-Age man of letters.[1] Limiting oneself to Fiske's wide-ranging *bibliophilic* interests—indicated only in part by the most famous collection that bears his name—one would have to mention an array of subjects extending from Iceland to the Italy of Dante and Petrarch, to Rhaeto-Romanic language and literature, and (as another of his collections, housed at the National and University Library of Iceland, still attests) to chess. Fiske's desire to furnish an already rapidly expanding scholarly world with "an annual volume relating to Iceland and the [Fiske] Icelandic Collection" has been realized in diverse forms in the series' one-hundred-seven-year history: first, primarily as a venue for

---

1. The curious reader is invited to consult the online exhibition devoted to Fiske's life and work in 2005, *The Passionate Collector: Willard Fiske and his Libraries*, at http://rmc.library.cornell.edu/collector/index.html. Kristín Bragadóttir has published an extensive study of Fiske's relationship with Iceland and the Icelanders in *Willard Fiske: vinur Íslands og velgjörðamaður* [friend and benefactor of Iceland] (Reykjavík: Háskólaútgáfan, 2008), of which an English translation is forthcoming.

bibliographical studies; then, with increasing frequency, as an organ for the publication of scholarly monographs and translations. Since its centenary in 2008, *Islandica* has also served as a forum for the publication of selected essays of interest to the scholar and student of Old Norse-Icelandic literature. This evolution was introduced by a gathering of articles on *Romance and Love in Late Medieval and Early Modern Iceland* (Islandica 54) in honor of Marianne Kalinke, edited by Kirsten Wolf and Johanna Denzin. That collection was preceded by a culling of critical studies by Joseph Harris, *"Speak Useful Words or Say Nothing"* (Islandica 53), bound with love in a single volume (to quote from one of Fiske's aforementioned passions) by Susan E. Deskis and Thomas D. Hill.

The present collection of contributions by an international cohort of scholars is addressed primarily to the specialist (both fully fledged and *in ovo*) in the field of Old Norse-Icelandic Studies and adjacent habitats; nonetheless it is devoutly to be wished that many of the items gathered here will in addition be of use not only to the academic non-specialist but also to the patient general reader who alights on our field in some number. With the latter in mind, the authors have endeavored to render their essays (to borrow a phrase apocryphally attributed to Einstein), "as simple as possible, but not simpler." Such a book can hope only to present a cross-section, not to document fully, the richness and vitality of a discipline that has burgeoned in recent decades. Its title means to suggest the scope of inquiry within its compass, whereas its claim to "newness" is twofold: certain of the authors open up new, or relatively unexcavated, fields of inquiry; others suggest fresh approaches to persisting problems. One contributor gently insisted that there is nothing "new" about him, but if the reader of these pages is occasionally reminded of the truth of Hegel's dictum—that what is well known is not necessarily known well—this volume will have served its purpose.

It is not unusual for a gathering of articles destined for primarily academic consumption to be organized around a single, unifying theme. I alert the academic fellow traveler that no attempt has been made here to jigsaw the assembled essays onto the Procrustean bed of a solitary idea. While the volume thereby gains in breadth, this procedure admittedly runs the risk of pleasing no one: To the curious, perhaps gazing in from outside the academy, a compilation of studies on "*The Literature and Culture of Medieval Scandinavia*" may already seem overspecialized (if not quite to the satisfaction of the scholar in the Nietzschean parable, who dares not speak of the leech as a whole but only of the *brain* of the leech); scholars of Old Norse literature, on the other hand, may wonder why such a book has not focused on some exciting new disciplinary subfield (if we are candid, most likely our own). Anyone inclined to digest these pieces as a whole, however, will notice intersecting and complementary—though, happily, not always *concurring*—approaches, interests, and themes at work among twelve scholars from six countries on three continents, all focused on diverse aspects of the medieval Scandinavian tradition. While it seems best to let these essays speak for themselves (lest their number swell to a *de facto* baker's dozen due to a protracted introduction), a few words regarding the gist and drift of these studies, in the order in which they appear, will be welcome.

The first three chapters focus on the "background," in various senses of the term, of saga narrative (although, one should note, not on a traditional quest for "origins"). Andy Orchard's "Hereward and Grettir: Brothers from Another Mother?" makes the case for viewing the latter hero of the first half of his title and his eponymous saga in an Anglo-Latin context that, from a more conventional viewpoint, would be regarded by many as "in the wrong language and from the wrong period." In "'Jafnan segir inn ríkri ráð': Proverbial Allusion and the Implied Proverb in *Fóstbrœðra saga*," Richard L. Harris, our foremost student of the Icelandic proverb, advances the state of our thinking on the complex relationship between saga narrative and the many "idioms and saws" that readers have long noted therein. Torfi H. Tulinius, in "Seeking Death in *Njals saga*," applies the insights of modern psychoanalysis to the grandest of the medieval Icelandic sagas, and (one might claim, although he does not) *vice versa*—thus illuminating both.

The four essays that follow are conjoined by marriage, if not by blood. Guðrún Nordal's "Skaldic Poetics and the Making of the *Sagas of Icelanders*" and Russell Poole's "Identity Poetics among the Icelandic Skalds" are both concerned with the fraught nexus of skaldic poetry and saga narrative—each in turn emphasizing what the formal characteristics of the former reveal about the cultural milieu of saga writing and skaldic poetry, respectively. My own "Loki, *Sneglu-Halla þáttr*, and the Case for a Skaldic Prosaics" reexamines the relationship of skaldic poetics and medieval Icelandic prose narrative, with a marked shift in focus towards the latter. Writing in a similar vein, Thomas D. Hill, in his *tour de force*, "Beer, Vomit, Blood, and Poetry: *Egils saga*, Chapters 44–45," reveals an analogue to the myth of Kvasir (told in Snorri's *Edda*) that informs the saga in question, thus likewise addressing the confluence of mythic and mundane narratives in saga literature.

The next two studies deal with issues of gender in the medieval and post-medieval period. Shaun F. D. Hughes, in "The Old Norse *Exempla* as Arbiters of Gender Roles in Medieval Iceland," examines the thorny problem of arriving at a definition of the *exemplum* in a medieval Icelandic context, before proceeding to take up the matter raised in his title. In "Performing Gender in the Icelandic Ballads," Paul Acker considers whether that (putatively) originally medieval genre can be regarded as a kind of "women's poetry."

The final three selections are *sui generis* as far as this volume is concerned, although not in and of themselves. Joseph Harris advances the state of the runological art in "The Rök Inscription, Line 20." Sarah Harlan-Haughey's "A Landscape of Conflict: Three Stories of the Faroe Conversions" adds to emerging bodies of scholarship on Old Norse literature from eco-critical and post-colonial perspectives. Rounding out the volume, Kirsten Wolf's lexical study of "Non-Basic Color Terms in Old Norse-Icelandic" will likely be the definitive reference on its subject for years to come.

A few words on technical matters should also prove useful: In view of the "double life" of *New Norse Studies* both in print and now online, individual bibliographies have been appended to each essay with an eye toward their independent electronic circulation. Full citations are provided in the footnotes as well as in the appended bibliographies in order to allow the digital medievalist to avoid what might ironically be considered excessive "scrolling." Medieval and ancient primary texts of known (or attributed) authorship are listed by author, anonymous works by title, translations of anonymous works by translator, and anthologies and compilations by their editors' names. A formal division between primary and secondary sources has been adopted only when the tally of the former is prodigious. As is customary, Icelandic personal names are listed alphabetically by given name rather than by patronym. As editor, I have striven for the greatest possible uniformity except when this would have been indistinguishable from a lapse into pedantry. The contributors have thus been given leeway regarding certain perennial scholarly bugbears, such as the decision whether or not to anglicize foreign names, or whether to normalize or modernize the orthography of texts cited. With the interest of the broadest possible audience in mind, the authors have been encouraged to cite from published translations when these are suitable for their purposes. In lieu of an index, the reader can search the electronic edition of this volume on the webpage of the *Islandica* series (http://cip.cornell.edu/Islandica) for any name or term; it is hoped that the absence of the former will be more than made up for by the increased functionality of the latter.

For his invaluable assistance with various aspects of this volume, I would like to thank Ellert Þór Jóhannsson of the University of Copenhagen. For her cold counsel on all things Faroese, I am grateful to Randi Ward. Patrick J. Stevens, present curator of the Fiske Icelandic Collection, has my heartfelt thanks for matters too myriad to mention, but foremost for his graciousness and patience, both on full display when fielding queries from afar that were best answered by delving into the irreplaceable collection whose untiring steward he is. Finally, I would like to thank the assembled contributors for their persistent faith in a project that has accompanied its editor to more postal codes and across more time zones than he could ever have foreseen.

J.T.
Chicago, Easter Sunday, 2015

Hereward and Grettir

Brothers from Another Mother?

Andy Orchard
UNIVERSITY OF OXFORD

Old Norse–Icelandic literature and Anglo–Saxon literature have customarily been seen as close cousins, notwithstanding the great gaps in time and space that are sometimes silently elided in asserting the family connection.[1] The continuing debate over the nature of the connections that seem to link *Beowulf* and *Grettis saga Ásmundarsonar* highlights how fraught such a notion can quickly become.[2] This paper again focuses on *Grettis saga*—which in its current form dates from the early fourteenth century but seems based on an earlier account by Sturla Þórðarson (1214–84)[3] that itself draws on earlier oral material—and seeks to try to bridge those gaps by considering a body of evidence, most of it seen from traditional and nativist points of view as being in the wrong language and from the wrong period: namely a series of Latin texts, generally written within 150 years of the Norman Conquest, that strongly serve to underline the family ties that bind Old Norse and Anglo-Saxon literature in sometimes

---

1. The literature is vast; see, for example, focusing only on *Beowulf*, Theodore, M. Andersson, "Sources and Analogues," in Robert E. Bjork and John D. Niles, *A "Beowulf" Handbook* (Lincoln: University of Nebraska Press, 1997), 125–48; Andy Orchard, *A Critical Companion to "Beowulf"* (Cambridge: Brewer, 2005), 98–129.

2. See Andy Orchard, *Pride and Prodigies: Studies in the Monsters of the "Beowulf" Manuscript*, revised paperback edition (Toronto: University of Toronto Press, 2003), 140–68; Magnús Fjalldal, *The Long Arm of Coincidence: The Frustrated Connection between "Beowulf" and "Grettis saga"* (Toronto: University of Toronto Press, 1998).

3. Sigurður Nordal, *Sturla Þórðarson og Grettis saga*, Studia Islandica 4 (Reykjavík: Mál og menning, 1938).

surprising ways. The aim here is to highlight the complex series of
interrelationships that connect these texts both with each other and
with Old Norse, and specifically Old Icelandic, literature. It will also
be suggested that still further parallels with both Anglo-Norman
and Franco-Scandinavian traditions make it possible to suggest both
a conduit and a milieu (to use suitably French terms) for such interchange to take place.

At least four Anglo-Latin texts are at issue, if we use the term
Anglo-Latin to mean Latin texts likely written in England or by
an Englishman; they are given here in a chronological order that
accounts for their final form, but does not preclude the high likelihood that one or more of them may well rely on earlier documents
or oral traditions, as indeed several claim:

1. *Encomium Emmae reginae* ("In praise of Queen Emma,"
   composed ca. 1041–42);[4]
2. *Gesta Herwardi incliti exulis et militis* ("The exploits of Hereward, the famous outlaw and warrior," composed ca. 1107–31);[5]
3. *Vita et passio Waldeui comitis* ("The life of and death of Earl
   Waltheof," composed at some point in the twelfth century);[6]
4. *Vita Haroldi* ("The life of Harold," composed ca. 1205–15).[7]

As far as the only clearly pre-Conquest text is concerned, we know
that the *Encomium Emmae* was written by a monk of Flanders, albeit

4. *Encomium Emmae Reginae*, ed. Alistair Campbell, Camden Classic Reprints 4
(Cambridge: Cambridge University Press, 1998).

5. The late Paul Gerhardt Schmidt and I were collaborating on a new text of the *Gesta
Herwardi* for Oxford Medieval Texts; here I quote from Schmidt's transcription and
edition, which is far superior to that found elsewhere, with parenthetical cross-references
(noted as such only in the first instance below) to the corresponding page numbers in
De Gestis Herwardi: Le gesta di Ervardo, ed. and trans. Alberto Meneghetti (Florence:
Edizioni ETS, 2013); cf. also *De Gestis Herwardi Saxonis*, ed. S. H. Miller and W. D.
Sweeting, in *Fenland Notes and Queries* 3 (1895): 7–72; *Hereward, together with De
Gestis Herwardi Saxonis*, ed. Trevor A. Bevis (Thorney: Westrydale Press, 1982); Michael
Swanton, trans., *Three Lives of the Last Englishmen* (New York: Garland, 1984), 45–88;
and Swanton, trans., "The Deeds of Hereward," in *Medieval Outlaws: Twelve Tales in
Modern English Translation*, ed. Thomas H. Ohlgren (West Lafayette: Parlor: 2005),
29–99.

6. *Vita S. Waldevi, Chroniques anglo-normandes*, ed. Francisque Michel, 3 vols.
(Rouen: E. Frère, 1836–40), 1:104–20.

7. *Vita Haroldi: The Romance of the Life of Harold King of England*, ed. Walter de
Gray Birch (London: Stock, 1885).

in England, while from its *Preface* we can infer that the author of the *Gesta Herwardi* was uncomfortable with English.[8] But each text has clear English connections, as well as emphatic Anglo-Norman interest, an aspect enshrined in the closely intertwined biographies of their respective protagonists. Queen Emma was born in Normandy, and was successively English queen to the Anglo-Saxon King Æthelred ("the Unready," who ruled 978–1014) and the Danish King Cnut ("the Great," at least as he was known in Scandinavia, who ruled 1016–35), while Hereward ("the Wake," ca. 1035–72) was outlawed by Emma's son King Edward ("the Confessor," who ruled 1042–66), but returned to fight the Norman King William ("the Conqueror" or "the Bastard," depending on one's point of view, who ruled 1066–87), being reconciled with the king and apparently ultimately buried at Croyland Abbey.[9] Waltheof was deprived of his father Siward's earldom of Northumbria by King Edward, who substituted Tostig Godwinson. Waltheof married William's niece, Judith, in 1070, but was beheaded six years later after taking part in a revolt against William; he too is said to have been buried at Croyland Abbey, which has a fifteenth-century statue of him.[10] King Harold Godwinson (who

---

8. See James Dunbar Pickering, "The Legend of Hereward the Saxon: an Investigation of *De Gestis Herwardi Saxonis*, Its Historical Basis, Its Debt to Saga and Early Romance, Its Place in English Literary History" (PhD diss., Columbia University, 1964), 60–61, who bases his arguments mainly on Martin, who suggests that the sole surviving manuscript of the *Gesta* was copied by "a scribe . . . comparatively ignorant in Latin, and the author was probably not much his superior in that respect." *Lestorie Des Engles*, ed. Thomas D. Hardy and Charles T. Martin, Rolls Series 91 (Nendeln: Kraus Reprints, 1966), lii. Martin goes on to suggest that Richard was not a native speaker of English, given his apparent difficulty with understanding terms like Old English *utlah* or *utlag* (he gives Hereward's cook the name Utlamhe and Utlac); likewise, he seems to have confused Old English *feax* ("hair") with Latin *facies* ("face") in describing the unkempt Hereward as being *prolixa facie* ("with a long face"), when more likely it is the traditionally long hair of the Anglo-Saxons that is at issue (373).

9. See the following: Edward Augustus Freeman, *The History of the Norman Conquest of England*, 6 vols. (Oxford: Clarendon Press, 1867–79); Cyril Hart, "Hereward the Wake," *Proceedings of the Cambridge Antiquarian Society* 65 (1974): 28–40; *Hereward, Bevis*; John Hayward, "Hereward the Outlaw," *Journal of Medieval History* 14 (1988): 293–304; Cyril Hart, "Hereward the Wake and his Companions," in his *The Danelaw* (London: Hambledon Continuum, 1992), 625–48; Victor Head, *Hereward* (Stroud: Alan Sutton, 1995); Peter Rex, *The English Resistance: The Underground War Against the Normans* (Stroud: Tempus, 2004), esp. 139–64; Rex, *Hereward: The Last Englishman* (Stroud: Tempus, 2005).

10. See F. S. Scott, "Earl Waltheof of Northumbria," *Archaeologia Aeliana* 30 (1952): 149–215; Robert M. Stein, *Reality Fictions: Romance, History, and Governmental Authority, 1025–1180* (Notre Dame: University of Notre Dame Press, 2006), 91–103.

ruled for most of 1066), famously fell at Hastings on October 14, 1066, attempting to oppose William's invasion, after having successfully seen off the earlier attempt to seize the crown by King Haraldr harðráði of Norway (1047–66; he was also king of Denmark until 1064). King Haraldr was accompanied by Harold's own brother, the aforementioned Tostig Godwinson, who died alongside him at the Battle of Stamford Bridge on September 25, 1066.

While the *Encomium Emmae* is the only one of these texts to predate the Norman Conquest, it nonetheless seems to be the result of profound Anglo-Scandinavian influence, notwithstanding the self-proclaimed provenance of its author, an influence most easily explained by composition at the Anglo-Scandinavian court of Cnut and his sons in England rather than in a religious house in Flanders.[11] So, for example, the descriptions of the invasion fleets of both Cnut and his father Svein seem to nod toward accounts of the so-called *landvættir* who protected Iceland against the invasion fleet of Harald Bluetooth (Svein's father and Cnut's grandfather, who died in 985 or 986), a tale told most fully by the Icelander Snorri Sturluson (1178/79–1241; he was the uncle of the aforementioned Sturla) in chapter 33 of his *Óláfs saga Tryggvasonar*.[12] Elsewhere, we find a passage in the *Encomium* which describes a miraculous raven banner:

> Erat namque eis uexillum miri portenti, quod licet credam posse esse incredibile lectori, tamen, quia uerum est, uerae inseram lectioni. Enimuero dum esset simplissimo candidissimoque intextum serico, nulliusque figurae in eo inserta esset imago, tempore belli semper in eo uidebatur coruus ac si intextus, in uictoria suorum quasi hians ore excutiensque alas instabilisque pedibus, et suis deuictis quietissimus totoque corpore demissus. (bk. 2, ch. 9)

> Now they had a banner of wonderfully strange nature, which though I believe that it may be incredible to the reader, yet since it is true,

11. See Simon Keynes, "Cnut's Earls," in *The Reign of Cnut, King of England, Denmark, and Norway*, ed. A. R. Rumble (London: Leicester University Press, 1994), 56–58; Andy Orchard, "The Literary Background to the *Encomium Emmae Reginae*," *Journal of Medieval Latin* 11 (2001): 157.

12. *Heimskringla*, ed. Bjarni Aðalbjarnarson, 3 vols., Íslenzk fornrit 26–28 (Reykjavík: Hið íslenzka fornritafélag, 1941), 1:271–72; see Orchard, "Literary Background," 163–65.

I will introduce the matter into my true history. For while it was woven of the plainest and whitest silk, and the representation of no figure was inserted into it, in time of war a raven was always seen as if embroidered on it, in the hour of its owners' victory opening its beak, flapping its wings, and restive on its feet, but very subdued and drooping with its whole body when they were defeated. (All translations mine)

Other texts likewise contain references to similar raven banners, always in a Norse or Anglo-Scandinavian context.[13]

In the case of the *Vita et passio Waldeui comitis*, an unusual text surviving in a single manuscript and perhaps written at Ramsey, the raven banner in question appears in the course of a prefatory portion of the text separately titled "Gesta antecessorum" (The exploits of the ancestors); this preface offers in its full form an interesting analogue for the mixture of literary elements from disparate traditions of exactly the kind found in all the texts under discussion:[14]

Tradunt relaciones antiquorum quod vir quidam nobilis, quem Dominus permisit, contra solitum ordinem humane propaginis, ex quodam albo urso patre, muliere generosa matre, proceari, Ursus genuit Spratlingum; Spratlingus Ulsium; Ulsius Beorn, cognomento Beresune, hoc est filius ursi.

Hic Beorn Dacus fuit natione, comes egregius et miles illustris. In signum autem illius diversitatis speciei ex parte generantium, produxerat ei natura paternas auriculas, sive ursi. In aliis autem speciei materne assimilabatur. Hic autem, post multas virtutis ac milicie experiencias filium genuit fortitudinis et milicie paterne probum imitatorem.

Nomen autem huic Siwardus (cognomento Diere, id est grossus); qui, quasi supra se elatus pre gratia probitatis ei innate, natale solum

13. See C. E. Wright, *The Cultivation of Saga in Anglo-Saxon England* (London: Oliver and Boyd, 1936), 126–33; Nils Lukman, "The Raven Banner and the Changing Ravens: A Viking Miracle from Carolingian Court Poetry to Saga and Arthurian Romance," *Classica et Mediaevalia* 19 (1958): 133–51; Orchard, "Literary Background," 168–69.

14. See also Christine Rauer, *Beowulf and the Dragon: Parallels and Analogues* (Cambridge: Boydell and Brewer, 2000), 126–32; Orchard, "Literary Background," 169–72.

habuit contemptui, patri suo jure hereditario succedere vilipendens, jussitque navem sibi magnam et fortem preparari et bene muniri in cunctis necessariis, tam in armamentis navis, quam in victualibus et armaturis corpori humano congruentibus. Quo facto, eandem ingressus, cum quinquaginta militibus probis et preelectis sibi associatis, mare conscendit, velaque ventis applicans tandem apud Orkaneiam portum invenit salubrem.

In insula autem illa habitabat draco quidam, qui erat non solum in bestiis, verum et in populo, strages maxima. Cujus fama ad aures Siwardi rerum gesta deferente, cum eo pugnam inire satatgebat; non operas locans arenariorum more, sed robur corporis et animi virtutem in hoc declarans, eum devicit et ab insula effugavit. Reversusque, navem ingressus, aquas remis sollicitans, processu temporis Northumberlandiam applicuit, ibique alterius draconis fama ad aures ejus convolavit.

Quem cum quereret ut eum similiter vel effugaret vel interficeret, videt collem quemdam arduum, et hominem quemdam senem in summitate sedentem; ad quem cum se divertisset ut rumores de dicto dracone inquireret, in colle residens, eum nomine suo proprio salutans, sic allocutus est: "Siwarde, bene novi qua de causa iter istud proficisceris: videlicet ut vires cum dracone experiaris; sed in vanum laboras: eum enim invenire non poteris; sed revertere ad socios tuos, et dicam tibi quid accidere fatatum est. Cum navem fueris ingressus, statim aura tibi dabitur grata; et prospero cursu cum vela ventis applicueris, portum invenies saluberrimum in fluvio quodam cui nomen Tamisia; quem cum conscenderis, tandem reperies civitatem quamdam cui applicabis, nomen autem ejus Londonie; ibidemque regem illius regni invenies, qui te in servicio suo retinebit, et terram sine magna mora dispendio tibi conferet."

Siwardus autem respondit se non adhibere magnam fidem sermonibus ejus, et si sic reverteretur, socii sui illud tanquam figmentum arbitrarentur. Senex autem a sinu suo vexillum quoddam extraxit et ei tribuit, quo facilius socii ejus ei fidem adhiberent. Nomen autem vexillo imposuit idem senex Ravenlandeye, quod interpretatur corvus terrae terror. Quo accepto, Siwardus ad socios suos rediens, navem ingressus est, et juxta senis vaticinia, post multas maris fluctuandis inundaciones, demum Londonias applicuit. (*Vita S. Waldevi*, Michel, 104–7)

The traditions of men of old relate that a certain noble man, whom the Lord allowed, contrary to the customary rule of human procreation, to be produced by a white bear as father and a high-born lady as mother, was known as Ursus ["bear"]. Ursus begot Spratlingus; Spratlingus begot Ulsius; Ulsius begot Beorn, nicknamed "Beresune," that is "Bear's Son."

This Beorn was a Dane by race, a distinguished nobleman and a renowned warrior. But as a sign of that diversity of species amongst his ancestors, nature had produced in him his father's tiny ears, those of a bear; in other things, however, he was like his mother's kind. This man, moreover, after many demonstrations of might and military prowess, begot a son, a splendid match for his father's strength and military prowess.

His name was Siward, nicknamed "Diere," which is to say "the Stout"; and he, as if inflated beyond himself because of his innate splendor, held the land of his birth in contempt, despising to succeed his father by hereditary right, and ordered a large and mighty ship to be prepared for him and properly equipped with all essentials, both as far as what was fitting for the ship's armament and the men's provisions and armor. Having done this, he boarded that ship, with fifty tried and tested warriors and comrades hand-picked by himself, and put to sea; setting his sails to the winds, he finally made safe harbor in Orkney.

But in that island there lived a certain dragon, which caused the greatest damage not only to animals, but also to the people. When the news of what had happened reached Siward's ears, he was keen to enter combat against it, not renting out his efforts after the fashions of gladiators, but simply showing thereby the power of his body and the strength of his resolve. He defeated it and forced it from the island. Returning, boarding ship, and churning up the waters with his oars, in due course he reached Northumbria, where news of a second dragon reached his ears.

When he went looking for it, to drive it away or kill it in the same way, he saw a certain steep hill and a certain old man sitting at the top; and when he turned toward him to ask for information about said dragon, the man sitting on the hill addressed him by his own name and spoke as follows: "Siward, I know full well for what reason you have made this journey, namely to test your strength against the dragon.

But you are wasting your time: you won't be able to find it. Go back to your comrades instead, and I will tell you what is fated to happen to you. When you have boarded the ship, you will straightaway get a fair wind, and when you set your sails to the winds on a favorable course, you will find a very safe harbor in a certain river called the Thames; and when you follow it upstream, you will reach at last a city, where you will land, and its name is London. There you will find the king of that kingdom, and he will keep you in his service and quite soon he will grant you land as a gift."

But Siward answered that he did not have much faith in his words, and that if he returned like this, his comrades would reckon it so much hogwash. But the old man took from his bosom a certain banner and gave it to him, so that his comrades would have more faith in him. The same old man gave the banner the name "Ravenlandeye," which means "Raven, Land's Terror." Having taken it, Siward went back to his comrades, boarded ship, and, just as the old man had foreseen, after many swelling surges of the sea, he finally reached London.

One might note that the appearance of the mysterious old man seated atop "a certain steep hill" (*collem quendam arduum*) resembles closely the appearance of the god Odin to Siward's Norse namesake, the dragon-slaying Sigurðr, in a prose passage following stanza 16 of the Norse Eddic poem *Reginsmál*. Sigurðr and his foster-father "met a great storm and sought shelter by a rocky promontory; a man stood on the rocks" (*Þeir fengo storm mikinn oc beitto fyrir bergsnǫs nacqvara. Maðr einn stóð á bergino*).[15] That the old man in the "Gesta antecessorum" addresses Siward by name without being told it, that he exhorts him to kill a dragon, and that he gives him a raven banner all attest to his Odinic qualities.[16] It may be significant here that the old man is introduced with a notably alliterative phrase ("senem in summitate sedentem") that may point to a Germanic poetic source, where such alliteration is structural. The relationship of this text to Norse literature (and

---

15. Andy Orchard, trans., *The Elder Edda: A Book of Viking Lore* (London: Penguin Classics, 2011), 158; Gustav Neckel and Hans Kuhn, eds., *Edda: Die Lieder des Codex Regius nebst verwandten Denkmälern*, vol. 1, *Text*, 5th ed. (Heidelberg: Winter, 1983), 177.

16. See, for example, *Grímnismál* 20 (Neckel, *Edda: Lieder*, 61); Orchard, *Elder Edda*, 53 and 297n.

specifically to Eddic poetry) has been the subject of surprisingly little debate; it will be clear, however, that in its ready incorporation of apparently Scandinavian material, the *Vita Waldeui* provides a useful analogue to the *Encomium Emmae*.

The bilingual genealogy provided for Beorn ("bear") makes one suspect that the name Ulsius masks the name Ulf ("wolf"), especially since warriors fighting in the guise of both wolves and bears are again indicative of Odinic practice,[17] as Snorri Sturluson reports (*Ynglinga saga*, ch. 6):

> Óðinn kunni svá gera at í orrustu urðu óvinir hans blindir eða daufir eða óttafullir, en vápn þeira bitu eigi heldr en vendir, en hans menn fóru brynjulausir ok váru galnir sem hundar eða vargar, bitu í skjǫldu sína, váru sterkir sem birnir eða griðungar. Þeir drápu mannfólkit, en hvártki eldr né járn orti á þá. Þat er kallaðr berserksgangr.
> (*Heimskringla*, Bjarni Aðalbjarnason, 1:17)

> Odin could make his enemies in battle blind, or deaf, or panic-struck, and their weapons so blunt that they could cut no better than a willow-wand; but his own men dashed forward without armor, and became as frenzied as dogs or wolves. They chewed their shield-rims, and became as strong as bears or bulls, and slaughtered people at a single stroke, but neither fire nor iron could touch them. It was called "going berserk."

In the context of Norse and Anglo-Saxon interchange, it may be significant that Siward's own name is a compromise between the Norse form Sigurðr (the principal hero of the Volsung family so favored by Odin), and its Old English equivalent, Sigeweard. Certainly, the historical Siward may have been related to that historical Earl Ulf (d. 1027) who is generally held to have married Cnut's sister Estrith,[18] and was the father of King Svein Estrithsson

---

17. See Stephan Grundy, "Shapeshifting and Berserkergang," in *Translation, Transformation, and Transubstantiation*, ed. Carol Poster and Richard Utz (Evanston: IL: Northwestern University Press, 1998), 104–22.

18. M. K. Lawson, *Cnut: The Danes in England in the Early Eleventh Century* (London: Longman, 1993), 97n53, says that the identification of Ulf with the husband of Estrith (Estrid) is commonly made but not certain.

(reigned 1047–74), as well as the son of Thorgils (or Thorkell) Sprakling, whose name presumably underlies the form *Spratlingus* (a scribal error for *Spraclingus?*) here. Saxo Grammaticus (ca. 1150–1220) in his *Gesta Danorum* ("The deeds of the Danes") names him Thurgillus Sprageleg and likewise reports he was the son of a bear, and died at the Battle of Svöld, ostensibly alongside King Óláfr Tryggvason.[19] Ulf's sister, Gytha Thorkelsdóttir, is said to have married Godwin, Earl of Wessex, and together they produced (among others) Tostig, Harold, and Edith (who was married to Edward the Confessor). The interpenetration of all these four Anglo-Latin texts is extraordinary in terms of the *dramatis personae* alone; the implicit connection of Siward to Thorgils Sprakling, who perhaps perished alongside Óláfr Tryggvason, links the *Vita Waldeui* to the next text under discussion.

A more ambivalent relationship between an Anglo-Latin text and a Norse tradition is witnessed in the *Vita Haroldi*, which turns on the notion that Harold Godwinson survived the Battle of Hastings, and depicts his later life in ways strongly parallel to Norse accounts of the supposed survival of Óláfr Tryggvason after the Battle of Svöld, which predates Hastings by sixty-six years. The notion that Óláfr Tryggvason jumped ship at the disastrous battle and survived has a long history, beginning with a rumor first mentioned and then dismissed by his own poet Hallfreðr Óttarsson vandræðaskáld, but persisting in the *Historia de antiquitate regum Norwagiensium* of Theodoricus (written ca. 1180), which also mentions that Óláfr traveled to distant lands for the sake of his soul.[20] The same tale is retold in different versions from the twelfth to the fourteenth centuries in the sagas of Óláfr Tryggvason by Oddr Snorrason (usually dated ca. 1190), Gunnlaugr Leifsson (written shortly after that of Oddr, and incorporated into the

---

19. See Axel Olrik, "Siward den digre, en vikingesaga fra de danske in Nordengland," *Arkiv för filologi* 19 (1903): 218–19, 234; *Chronicle of John of Worcester*, ed. R. R. Darlington et al., 2 vols. (Oxford: Clarendon, 1995), 2:548–49; Eric Christiansen, trans., *Saxo Grammaticus: Danorum regum heroumque historia, Books X–XVI*, 3 vols. (Oxford: B.A.R., 1980–81), 1:28–30 and 189–91. For the Latin text, I rely on *Gesta Danorum*, ed. Jørgen Olrik and Hans Ræder, 2 vols. (Copenhagen: Munksgaard, 1931–57).

20. See Gustav Storm, ed., *Monumenta Historica Norvegiæ: Latinske kildeskrifter til Noregs historie i middelalderen* (Kristiania [Oslo]: Brøgger, 1880), 24 and 68–71. Translated as Theodoricus Monachus, *The Ancient History of the Norwegian Kings*, trans. David and Ian McDougall, Viking Society for Northern Research Text Series 9 (London: University College London, 1998), 18, lines 12–18 (ch. 14) and 74n112.

anonymous *Longest Saga of Óláfr Tryggvason* in Flateyjarbók (*Óláfs saga Tryggvasonar en mesta*), a manuscript written in the last decades of the fourteenth century), and Snorri Sturluson.[21] Oddr and the *Longest Saga* give the fullest accounts, noting that Óláfr traveled to Jerusalem, and ended his days in a monastery in Greece, Syria, or Egypt sometime during the reign of Edward the Confessor in England. Indeed, the *Longest Saga* has the curious detail that Edward the Confessor used to read to his court the tale of Óláfr Tryggvason out of a book which Óláfr himself sent from Jerusalem to Edward's father Æthelred.[22]

Just as stories of Óláfr's survival were circulating, so too similar tales were being recycled about the survival of Harold Godwinson, Edward's successor. In the longest and most developed of these versions, the *Vita Haroldi*, Harold survived Hastings, after being cared for by a mysterious Saracen lady, and went on to live as a pilgrim and hermit. The tale of Harold's survival also appears in the fourteenth-century Icelandic *Játvarðar saga*, and the notion that the survival-tales of Óláfr and Harold are connected is in fact stated explicitly in Oddr Snorrason's aforementioned *Óláfs saga Tryggvasonar*, as well as in *Hemings þáttr*.[23] In the case of the survival-tales of both Óláfr and Harold, however, it has been argued, most powerfully by Paul White, that the direction of borrowing is in fact from the south, and that Oddr Snorrason in

---

21. See *Saga Óláfs Tryggvasonar af Oddr Snorrason munk*, ed. Finnur Jónsson (Copenhagen: Gad, 1932), chs. 73(61)-75(63); *Óláfs saga Tryggvasonar en mesta*, ed. Ólafur Halldórsson, Editiones Arnamagnæanæ A1–2 (Reykjavík: Stofnun Árna Magnússonar, 1958–61), chs. 267–69, 271, 283, and 286; *Hemings þáttr Áslákssonar*, ed. Gillian Fellows-Jensen, Editiones Arnamagnæanæ B3 (Reykjavík: Stofnun Árna Magnússonar, 1962), chs. 57–58; *Heimskringla*, Bjarni Aðalbjarnason, 1:367–70 (ch. 112). See also Theodore M. Andersson, trans., *The Saga of Olaf Tryggvason by Oddr Snorrason*, Islandica 52 (Ithaca: Cornell University Press, 2003), 126–34.

22. See *Óláfs saga Tryggvasonar en mesta*, Ólafur Halldórsson, 349 (ch. 286).

23. See further Margaret Ashdown, "An Icelandic Account of the Survival of Harold Godwinson," in *The Anglo-Saxons: Studies in Some Aspects of their History and Culture*, ed. Peter Clemoes (London: Bowes and Bowes, 1959), 122–36; Marc Cohen, "From Throndheim to Waltham to Chester: Viking and post-Viking Attitudes in the Survival Legends of Óláfr Tryggvason and Harold Godwinson," in *The Middle Ages in the North-West*, ed. Tom Scott and Pat Starkey (Oxford: Leopard's Head Press, 1995), 143–53; Alan Thacker, "The Cult of King Harold at Chester," in *The Middle Ages in the North-West*, 155–76; Gillian Fellows-Jensen, "The Myth of Harold II's Survival in the Scandinavian Sources," in *King Harold II and the Bayeux Tapestry*, ed. Gale R. Owen-Crocker (Woodbridge: Boydell, 2005), 53–64; Stephen Matthews, "The Content and Construction of the *Vita Haroldi*," in Owen-Crocker, *King Harold II*, 65–73.

particular was using one or more of the documents underlying the
Vita Haroldi.[24] Whatever the direction of borrowing, the fact of
these shared survival tales only underlines the permeability of the
Old Norse and early English traditions.

Against such a fully-fledged background of apparent interchange
between Anglo-Latin and Scandinavian sources, albeit with the
former generally anticipating the latter sometimes by several centuries, one might turn to the extraordinary *Gesta Herwardi*, which
in this context appears very much as a kind of proto-outlaw saga,
considerably predating Icelandic equivalents such as *Gísla saga
Súrssonar, Grettis saga Ásmundarsonar, Harðar saga ok hólmverja*, and *Áns saga bogsveigis*, all of which are first witnessed
in manuscripts from the thirteenth and fourteenth centuries.[25]
Just as Paul Gerhard Schmidt has described the *Gesta Herwardi*
as a "historical adventure novel,"[26] so too the great Icelandic
manuscript collector, Árni Magnússon (1663–1730), noted that
"*Grettis saga* approaches closer to story than to history."[27] Previous
discussion has certainly focused on perceived parallels between the
Gesta Herwardi and *Grettis saga*, although the scattered nature
of such scholarship has precluded a general perspective.[28] A more

---

24. See Paul A. White, *Non-Native Sources for the Scandinavian Kings' Sagas* (New
York: Routledge, 2005), 75–78.

25. See *Grettis saga Ásmundarsonar*, ed. Guðni Jónsson, Íslenzk fornrit 7 (Reykjavík:
Hið íslenzka fornritafélag, 1956); *Gísla saga Súrssonar*, in *Vestfirðinga sǫgur*, ed. Björn
K. Þórólfsson and Guðni Jónsson, Íslenzk fornrit 6 (Reykjavík: Hið íslenzka fornritafélag,
1943), 3–118; *Harðar saga*, ed. Þórhallur Vilmundarson and Bjarni Vilhjálmsson,
Íslenzk fornrit 13 (Reykjavík: Hið íslenzka fornritafélag, 1991); *Áns saga bogsveigis*, in
Fornaldar sögur Nordrlanda, ed. Carl Christian Rafn, 3 vols. (Copenhagen, 1829–30),
2:323–62; *Áns saga bogsveigis*, in *Fornaldar sögur Norðurlanda*, ed. Guðni Jónsson, 4
vols. (Reykjavík: Íslendingasagnaútgáfan, 1954): 2:365–403; Anthony Faulkes, ed. and
trans., *Three Icelandic Outlaw Sagas* (London: Everyman, 2001); Shaun F. D. Hughes,
trans., "The Saga of Án Bow-bender," in Ohlgren, *Medieval Outlaws*, 290–337. See also
Gabriel Turville-Petre, "Outlawry," in *Sjötíu ritgerðir helgaðar Jakobi Benediktssyni 20
júlí 1977*, ed. Einar G. Pétursson and Jónas Kristjánsson, 2 vols. (Reykjavík: Stofnun Árna
Magnússonar, 1977): 2:769–78; Shaun F. D. Hughes, "The Literary Antecedents of *Áns
saga bogsveigis*," *Mediaeval Scandinavia* 9 (1976): 198–235; Jesse Byock, trans., *Grettir's
Saga* (Oxford: Oxford World's Classics, 2009), see esp. the useful Appendix, "Grettir's
Journey through Outlawry," 239–48.

26. P. G. Schmidt, "Biblisches und hagiographisches Kolorit in den Gesta Herwardi,"
in *The Bible in the Medieval World*, ed. K. Walsh and D. Wood, Studies in Church History, Subsidia 4 (Oxford: Blackwell, 1985), 94–95.

27. "*Grettis saga* gengr nær fabulae en historiae." Quoted in *Sturlunga saga*, ed. Gudbrand Vigfusson, 3 vols. (Oxford: Clarendon, 1878), 1:1n1.

28. Connections between the *Gesta* and various saga-outlaws are asserted in broad

comprehensive overview of the structure of the *Gesta Herwardi* chapter by chapter, with parallels to *Grettis saga* highlighted in italics, might look as follows:[29]

A Comparison of the *Gesta Herwardi* and *Grettis saga*

Chapter	Summary
Preface	Sources and background
1	*Hereward as a child: has problems with his father; sent into outlawry;* [cf. *Grettis saga*, chs. 15–16]
2	*Hereward kills a giant bear;* [cf. *Grettis saga*, ch. 21]
3	*Hereward kills a bully and takes his sword;* [cf. *Grettis saga*, chs. 18–19, 40]
4	Hereward gains fame in Ireland by killing an opposing leader;
5	Hereward goes in disguise to a wedding and carries off the bride;
6	*Hereward is shipwrecked* returning from Ireland, and goes anonymously to Flanders; [cf. *Grettis saga*, ch. 17]
7	*Hereward fights incognito* in Flanders; [cf. *Grettis saga*, chs. 63, 72]
8	*Hereward defeats a famous warrior;* [cf. *Grettis saga*, chs. 21, 22, 24]
9	Hereward is beloved by a girl, and fights on her behalf;

terms by Henry Goddard Leach, *Angevin Britain and Scandinavia* (Cambridge, MA: Harvard University Press, 1921), 342–50, and Joost de Lange, *The Relation and Development of English and Icelandic Outlaw-Traditions* (Haarlem: Willink, 1935), 3–32. There is also a rash of relevant doctoral dissertations, such as Pickering, "Legend of Hereward"; Richard Howard Baum, "The Medieval Outlaw: a Study in Protest" (PhD diss., University of Utah, 1972), 11–51—these pages repeat verbatim those of Maurice Keen, *The Outlaws of Medieval Legend* , 3rd ed. (London: Routledge, 2000), 9–38, originally published in 1961; Timothy Scott Jones, "Redemptive Fictions: the Contexts of Outlawry on Medieval English Chronicle and Romance" (PhD diss., University of Illinois at Champaign-Urbana, 1994), 97–140; Timothy J. Lundgren, "Hereward and Outlawry in Fenland Culture: A Study of Local Narrative and Tradition in Medieval England" (PhD diss., Ohio State University, 1996), 48–170; Bernard I. Lumpkin, "The Making of a Medieval Outlaw: Code and Community in the Robin Hood Legend, 1400–1600" (PhD diss., Harvard University, 1999)·

29. Chapter-numbers here refer to the forthcoming OMT edition referred to in note 5 above (numbering is identical in the edition of Meneghetti, also cited there); chapter-numbers in square brackets refer to those of *Lestorie des Engles*, Hardy, which are identical to those employed in Swanton, "The Deeds of Hereward."

Chapter	Summary
10 [9]	Hereward comes to a girl and is recognized by her;
11 [10]	Hereward goes to fight in Zeeland;
12 [11]	Hereward manages the Zeeland wars;
13 [12]	*Hereward gets a swift horse;* [cf. *Grettis saga*, ch. 47]
14 [12]	Hereward returns from the Zeeland wars and divides up the spoils;
15 [13]	*Hereward returns from abroad and finds his brother dead;* [cf. *Grettis saga*, ch. 47]
16 [14]	Hereward panics the local Norman inhabitants, and gathers forces;
17 [15]	Hereward is made a knight in the English fashion;
18 [16]	*Hereward attacks a man who is plotting against him;* [cf. *Grettis saga*, ch. 59]
19 [17]	Hereward returns to Flanders, and performs heroic acts;
20 [18]	*Hereward returns to England, and gathers his outlaw band;* [cf. *Grettis saga*, ch. 69]
21 [19]	*Hereward heads for an island-refuge* (Ely); *is ambushed en route;* [cf. *Grettis saga*, ch. 69]
22 [20]	Hereward's enemy (William) attempts to take the island (Ely), and nearly loses his entire army;
23 [21]	William's sole surviving soldier is well treated by Hereward, and returns to William with a glowing report;
24 [22]	William is minded to make peace, but is dissuaded by some of his men;
25 [23]	Hereward enters William's court disguised as a potter;
26 [24]	Hereward enters William's court disguised as a fisherman; *a witch is used to try to dislodge the besieged outlaws from the island;* [cf. *Grettis saga*, chs. 78–80]
27 [25]	Hereward is betrayed by the people of Ely, who want to make peace with the king;
28 [26]	Hereward in dire straits is forced to kill his own horse;
29 [27]	Hereward pre-empts the arrival of the Abbot of Peterborough, and plunders his church;
30 [28]	Hereward has a vision of St Peter and returns the plunder; his journey back is miraculous, with will o' the wisps and a white wolf;

Chapter	Summary
31 [29]	*Hereward hunts down an enemy, and corners him in a toilet;* [cf. *Grettis saga*, ch. 19]
32 [30]	Hereward's wife becomes a nun at Crowland;
33 [31]	Hereward overcomes an eminent knight in a duel;
34 [32]	Hereward goes openly to the king, and pays him homage;
35 [33]	Hereward is attacked by one of the court, jealous at his treatment;
36 [34]	Hereward is accused by Robert de Horepol and put into prison;
37 [35]	Robert de Horepol praises Hereward to the king and receives his favor.

Previous analyses have tended to consider the *Gesta Herwardi* as a somewhat broken-backed text, containing both legendary and historical elements, with the former generally held to focus on Hereward's early life and his first period of outlawry abroad (chs. 1–15 [13]), and the latter dealing mainly with the time after return to England, his second period of outlawry at home, and the revolt against the Normans (chs. 20 [18]-37 [35]).[30] The above analysis suggests rather that elements shared with *Grettis saga* are scattered throughout the text, albeit that, as we shall see, the closest parallels are found with Hereward's first period of outlawry.

The prefatory letter (*Praefatio*) is confused and confusing, but contains a number of striking features:

NONNULLIS apud nos scire desiderantibus opera magnifici Anglorum gentis Heruuardi et inclytorum ejus, et auribus percipere magnanimitates illius ac gesta, nuper nostræ parvitati vestra insinuavit fraternitas, interrogans si aliquid in illo loco ubi degebat de tanto viro conscriptum aliquis reliquerit. De quo enim cum nos quodam in loco

---

30. Typical is Lumpkin, who notes that: "the biographical romance can be divided into three sections: Hereward's *enfance* and his exile from England; his leadership as an outlaw of the Saxon rebellion against the invading Normans; and his defeat and the subsequent alliance he makes with the conquering king" ("Making of a Medieval Outlaw," 35). See too Pickering: "The second half of the *Gesta* (divided into twenty-two chapters) is based on tales of the past told by countrymen around Ely" ("Legend of Hereward," 178).

audisse modicum Anglice conscriptum professi fuimus subito coegit
uestra dilectio illud ad presens perquiri et mox in Latinam linguam
transferri subiungens etiam et ea que a nostris audire contigerit cum
quibus conuersatus est ut insignis miles magnanimiter uiuens. Quibus
quidem uestris desideriis satisfacere cupientes multis in locis perqui-
rendo manus conuertimus et penitus nichil inuenimus preter pauca et
dispersa folia partim stillicidio putrefactis et abolitis et partim absci-
sione diuisis. Ad quod igitur dum stilus tantumdem fuisset appositus
uix ex eo principium a genitoribus eius inceptum et pauca interim
expressimus et nomen, uidelicet primitiua insignia preclarissimi exulis
Herwardi editum Anglico stilo a Lefrico diacono eiusdem ad Brun
presbiterum. Huius enim memorati presbiteri erat studium omnes
actus gygantum et bellatorum ex fabulis antiquorum aut ex fideli
relatione ad edificationem audiencium congregare et ob memoriam
Anglie litteris commendare. In quibus uero licet non satis periti aut
potius imperiti exarare deleta incognitarum litterarum ad illum locum
tamen de illo usque collegimus ubi in patriam et ad paternam domum
reuersus fratrem occisum inuenit; uestre prudencie rudi stilo relin-
quentes crudam materiam uel alicuius exercitati ingenii studio minus
dialecticis et rethoricis enigmatibus compositam et ornatam. (cf. *De
Gestis Herwardi*, Meneghetti, 74)

When some of us were keen to know about the exploits of the mighty
Englishman Hereward and those of his famous men, and to hear with
our ears of his generous deeds and doings, your brotherliness recently
aided our slender means, asking if anyone had left anything in writing
about such a great man in the place where he once lived. When we
said that we had heard somewhere of a short account of him written in
English, your generosity swiftly had it identified and soon translated
into Latin, also adding those details which we heard from our own
folk, with whom he spent time while living boldly as a mighty warrior.
So, wishing to satisfy your keenness, we made efforts to enquire in
many places, and found almost nothing beyond a few scattered leaves,
which had partly rotted and decayed with damp and partly torn by a
rip. So when a pen had been as much applied to it, we scarcely took
anything from it beyond his birth and beginnings from his parents
and a few intervening details and his name, which is to say the early
famous exploits of the most outstanding outlaw Hereward, produced

in English by Leofric the Deacon, his priest at Bourne. For it was the habit of this well-known priest to assemble all the acts of giants and warriors from the tales of old, or from some reliable source, for the enlightenment of listeners, and to set them in English writing for posterity. Although we were not familiar enough or rather unfamiliar with the alien writing to replace what was damaged, nonetheless we gathered from it that when he returned to his homeland and his father's house he found his brother slain; leaving this raw material in a rough style to your discretion or to the application of someone's trained skill to be set out and arranged with fewer complicated and puzzling passages.

The anonymous author clearly distinguishes two groups, namely his own people (characterized by first-person plural references) and those of his addressee (characterized by second-person plural references).[31] It is tempting to think of the former as English and the latter as Norman, although there is a clearly Anglo-Scandinavian slant. A reference to *uestra . . . fraternitas* (your brotherliness) seems to point to a shared monastic milieu, but one with split perspectives and different motivations for telling the tale. Leofric the Deacon of Bourne is perhaps not to be confused with Leofric of Bourne, whom the *Gesta Herwardi* names as Hereward's father, although there is a suspicion that some confusion of the term "father" (Latin *pater*, Old English *fæder*) in a secular and ecclesiastical context may have led to an unfortunate conflation. In any event, it is striking that Leofric the Deacon should feature not only at the beginning of the *Gesta*, but also in the middle and near the end. In *Gesta Herwardi*, chapter 20 [18], Leofric the Deacon is named first in the final tally of Hereward's gang, where he features as one of those who "in militia probatissimi adhuc computati sunt" (are still reckoned best proven in war), and in *Gesta Herwardi* 36 [34], he again appears as one "qui astutus semper erat in omni suo opere et stulticiam simulare loco docti et sapienter agere" (who was always smart in everything he did, able to pretend to be stupid instead of clever, and able to do that wisely).[32]

---

31. See also R. M. Wilson, *The Lost Literature of Medieval England*, 2nd ed. (London: Methuen, 1970), 124–26.

32. *De Gestis Herwardi*, Meneghetti, 126 and 168.

The *Gesta Herwardi* (the title in the single manuscript is *De gestis Herwardi*—"Concerning Hereward's Deeds") is usually ascribed to one Richard of Ely, who, it is suggested, composed it at the request of Hervey, first bishop of Ely, 1107–31.[33] The *Gesta Herwardi* was certainly used as a source by the anonymous compiler of the mid-twelfth-century *Liber Eliensis*,[34] who is the first to name the then-dead Richard as its author, in a passage that introduces several chapters evidently drawing on the earlier work:

> In libro autem de ipsius gestis Herwardi, dudum a venerabili viro ac doctissimo fratre nostro beate memorie Ricardo edito, plenius descripta inveniuntur. (*Liber Eliensis*, Blake, 188)

> But in a book about the deeds of Hereward himself, long ago produced by that venerable and most learned man, our brother Richard of blessed memory, these things are found described more fully.

The close relationship between *Gesta Herwardi*, chapters 21–25, and the *Liber Eliensis*, book 2, chapters 104–7, is documented in detail by Pickering,[35] but it is important also to note those parts of the *Liber Eliensis* that are *not* derived directly from the *Gesta Herwardi*, especially in so far as they seem to figure Hereward as a type of Judas Maccabaeus (*Liber Eliensis*, bk. 2, ch. 102),[36] or to provide an independent account of the siege of Ely (ibid., chs. 109–11).[37]

What also seems striking is the extent to which other lore and traditions attaching to Hereward's name are also echoed in *Grettis saga*, a phenomenon that necessitates a closer look at the *Gesta Herwardi* and the other extant texts from around the same period that also discuss Hereward's deeds, some of which seem to rely

---

33. See further the detailed account in *Liber Eliensis*, ed. E. O. Blake, Camden Third Series 92 (London: Royal Historical Society, 1962), xxxiv-xxxvi.

34. See *Liber Eliensis*, Blake, xxxvi; Janet Fairweather, trans., *Liber Eliensis: A History of the Isle of Ely from the Seventh Century to the Twelfth* (Woodbridge: Boydell and Brewer, 2005), 209–22.

35. See Pickering, "Legend of Hereward," 41–55; Fairweather, *Liber Eliensis*, 209–22.

36. *Liber Eliensis*, Blake, 174; Fairweather, *Liber Eliensis*, 204–6. See Lundgren, "Hereward and Outlawry," 140–44.

37. *Liber Eliensis*, Blake, 189–94; Fairweather, *Liber Eliensis*, 223–31.

on the *Gesta Herwardi* itself, and others that offer apparently independent perspectives. That Norse tales should thrive in Ely is unsurprising not only in a pre-Conquest context, given the prominent position of Ely within the Danelaw, but also and especially in an immediately post-Conquest context that involves the outlaw Hereward himself.[38] As the *Peterborough Chronicle* most fully explains, in the spring of 1070 the Danish King Svein Estrithsson (perhaps the grandson of the Earl Siward discussed above), arrived at the mouth of the Humber, and was locally expected to make a bid for the crown:

Her se eorl Walþeof griðede wið þone cyng. þæs on lengten se cyng let hergian ealle þa mynstra þe on Englalande wæron. Þa on þam ilcan geare com Swegn cyng <of> Denmarcan into Humbran, þet landfolc comen him ongean griðedon wið hine, wændon þet he sceolde þet land ofergan. Þa comen into Elig Cristien þa densce biscop Osbearn eorl þa densca huscarles mid heom, þet englisce folc of eall þa feonlandes comen to heom, wendon þet hi sceoldon winnon eall þet land.[39]

In this year Earl Waltheof made peace with the king, and at Lent the king had all the monasteries in England attacked. In the same year, King Svein came from Denmark into the Humber, and the locals came to meet him and made peace with him; they expected that he would take over the country. Then Christian the Danish bishop came to Ely, together with Earl Osbern and the Danish housecarls too, and the English folk from all the fenlands came to them; they expected that they should conquer the whole country.

The same source goes on immediately to recount the activities of "Hereward his genge" (Hereward and his gang), thereby implicitly linking Hereward to a local expectation of a Danish takeover that is twice emphasized:

---

38. Notable in this context is the careful use of the *Gesta Herwardi* as a source for the Ely rebellion in Ann Williams, *The English and the Norman Conquest* (Woodbridge: Boydell and Brewer, 1995), 45–57.

39. *The Peterborough Chronicle 1070–1154*, ed., Cecily Clark, 2nd ed. (London: Oxford University Press, 1970), 2, lines 1–7.

Þa herdon þa munecas of Burh sægen þet heora agene menn wolden
hergon þone mynstre, þet wæs Hereward his genge. Þet wæs forðan
þet hi herdon sæcgen þet se cyng heafde gifen þæt abbotrice an
frencisce abbot, Turolde wæs gehaten. þet he wæs swiðe styrne man
wæs cumen þa into Stanforde mid ealle hise frencisce menn. Þa wæs
þære an cyrceweard, Yware wæs gehaten; nam þa be nihte eall þet he
mihte—þet wæron Cristes bec mæsse hakeles cantelcapas reafes swilce
litles hwat, swa hwat swa he mihte—ferde sona ær dæg to þone abbot
Turolde, sægde him þet he sohte his griðe, cydde him hu þa utlages
sceolden cumen to Burh. Þet he dyde eall be þære munece ræde. Þa
sona on morgen comen ealle þa utlaga mid fela scipe woldon into þam
mynstre; þa munecas wiðstoden þet hi na mihton in cumen. Þa lægdon
hi fyr on forbærndon ealle þa munece huses eall þa tun buton ane
huse. Þa comen hi þurh fyre in æt Bolhiðe geate, þa munecas comen
heom togeanes. beaden heom grið. Ac hi na rohten na þing—geodon
into þe mynstre; clumben upp to þe halge rode, namen þa þe kynehelm
of ure Drihtnes heafod eall of smeate golde, namen þa þet fotspure þe
wæs undernæðen his fote, þet wæs eall of read golde; clumben upp
to þe stepel, brohton dune þet hæcce þe þær wæs behid, hit wæs eall
of gold of seolfre. Hi namen þære twa gildene scrines ix seolferne, hi
namen fiftene mycele roden, ge of golde ge of seolfre. Hi namen þære
swa mycele gold seolfre swa manega gersumas on sceat on scrud on
bokes swa nan man ne mæi oðer tællen—sægdon þæt hi hit dyden for
ðes mynstres holdscipe. (*Peterborough Chronicle*, Clark, 2–3, lines
9–36)

Then the monks of Peterborough heard tell that their own people
wanted to plunder the minster—namely Hereward and his gang—
because they had heard tell that the king had given the abbacy to a
French abbot called Thorold; that he was a very strict man; and that
he had at that time come into Stamford with all his Frenchmen. There
was a sacristan called Yware, who at night took away everything he
could: testaments, cassocks, copes, and vestments, and other such
small things, whatever he could; and he went just at day-break to the
Abbot Thorold, and told him that he sought his protection, and let
him know that those outlaws were coming to Peterborough, and that
he was wholly acting on the monks' advice. Early in the morning all
the outlaws came with many ships, and wanted to enter the minster;

but the monks held them back, so that they could not come in. Then they set a fire, and burned down all the monks' houses, and the whole enclosure except one house. Then they came in through the fire at the Bolhithegate, and the monks met them, and asked them for a truce, but they paid no attention. They entered the minster, climbed up to the holy cross, took the crown from our Lord's head, all of pure gold, and took the foot-rest that was underneath his feet, which was all of red gold. They climbed up to the steeple, brought down the crozier that was hidden there, which was all of gold and silver, seized two golden shrines, and nine silver ones, and took away fifteen large crucifixes, of gold and of silver. They took from there so much gold and silver, and so many treasures, in tribute, in vestments, and in books, that no one could describe it; they said that they did it out of their devotion to the minster.

While the emphasis in the *Anglo-Saxon Chronicle* paints Hereward and his gang as very much against the Normans as a whole and acting as one might expect Anglo-Scandinavians broadly supportive of a Danish claim, a striking feature of the *Gesta Herwardi* is that although Hereward is depicted as an implacable foe of the Normans in general, King William himself is depicted in a somewhat sympathetic light,[40] while the historical role of the Danes is wholly downplayed. Given that Hereward's family holdings would have been squarely within the Danelaw, as were Bourne and Ely, some significant Scandinavian input into any account of his life would seem likely.[41] In such a light, the fact that the only explicitly Scandinavian reference in the whole of the *Gesta Herwardi* is, as we shall see, to a Danish bear of human descent who turns out to be a potential rapist seems significant indeed.[42]

Frank Stenton describes Hereward as "a Lincolnshire thegn of moderate estate,"[43] but perhaps more significant in respect of

---

40. See Jones, "Redemptive Fictions," 111. Hugh M. Thomas notes that "William is always respectfully referred to as *rex*." "The *Gesta Herwardi*, the English and their Conquerors," *Anglo-Norman Studies* 21 (1998): 229.

41. See Pickering, "Legend of Hereward," 83.

42. See Lundgren, "Hereward and Outlawry," 130.

43. Frank M. Stenton, *Anglo-Saxon England*, 3rd ed. (Oxford: Oxford University Press, 1971), 605; see David Roffe, "Hereward 'the Wake' and the Barony of Bourne: A Reassessment of a Fenland Legend," *Lincolnshire History and Archaeology* 29 (1994): 7–10.

what looks unnervingly like a Viking raid on Peterborough (albeit that the church-building itself appears to escape unscathed) is the comment by Hugh Candidus in his *Chronicle*, written between 1155 and 1175, that "Hereward himself was a man of the monks."[44] Certainly, the *Gesta Herwardi* is contained in the thirteenth-century Peterborough Cathedral MS 1, currently held at Cambridge University Library; the *Gesta* has been incorporated into one of Peterborough's most important cartularies, assembled by Robert of Swaffham, the cellarer of the Abbey, around the year 1256. Ingrid Benecke has argued that in its current form the *Gesta Herwardi* was written down between 1227 and 1250, based on references to Robert de Horepol in the final chapters, though her conclusion is not universally accepted; most commentators support the notion of an original composition between 1107–31, as discussed above.[45] An unpublished shortened version of the *Gesta* is also found in the margins of Walter of Whittlesey's continuation of Robert of Swaffham's extension of Hugh Candidus' *Chronicle*, written about 1330.[46]

In such a context, with an originally twelfth-century tale possibly based on eyewitness records and local legends (perhaps rewritten in the thirteenth century and redacted into the fourteenth), the overlap between aspects of Hereward's story and that of the Icelandic outlaw Grettir Ásmundarson seems intriguing, to say the least; the fact that such an overlap involves not only the *Gesta Herwardi* but other accounts of what can only be called the legend of Hereward makes the connection still more compelling. So, for example, like Grettir, Hereward has two periods of outlawry, at home and abroad.[47] The first is prompted by the irascible, stubborn, and ungovernable nature of them both. Grettir's troubled childhood, his extraordinary strength, and his overbearing and

44. "ipse Herewardus homo monachorum erat." *The Chronicle of Hugh Candidus*, ed. W. T. Mellows (London: Oxford University Press, 1949), 79.

45. See Ingrid Benecke, *Der Gute Outlaw* (Tübingen: Niemeyer, 1973), 13–21; Jones, "Redemptive Fictions," 102; Schmidt, "Biblisches und hagiographisches Kolorit," 87.

46. See Lundgren, "Hereward and Outlawry," 58; *The Chronicle of Hugh Candidus*, Mellows, xviii-xix.

47. Cf. Byock who provides a useful pair of chronologies covering both periods (*Grettir's Saga*, 239–48). See too Lumpkin, "The Making of a Medieval Outlaw," 37.

uncompromising attitude, even in games, are portrayed in detail (*Grettis* saga, chs. 4–15); the account with regard to Hereward is briefer, but nonetheless no more positive (*Gesta Herwardi*, ch. 1):

> sed crudelis in opere et in ludo seuerus libenter inter coetaneos commouens bella et inter maiores etate in urbibus et in uillis sepe suscitans certamina nullum sibi in ausibus et fortitudinum executionibus parem nec maiores etiam etate relinquens. (78)

> Yet he was rough in work and tough in play, always picking fights among his peers and often stirring up strife among his elders in towns and villages; he had no match in deeds of daring and courageous acts, not even among his elders.

Hereward is rough and tough or, literally, "cruel" and "severe" (*crudelis . . . seuerus*); his character is a problem for those closest to him. Likewise in the case of Grettir his juvenile delinquency (which includes extreme cruelty and physical violence, culminating in a killing when he is only fifteen) is attributed to paternal negligence or hostility (*Grettis saga*, ch. 14): "Ekki hafði hann ástríki mikit af Ásmundi fǫður sínum, en móðir hans unni honum mikit" (He did not have much love from Ásmundr, his father, but his mother loved him greatly).[48] Hereward too has no love from his father, who indeed is held directly responsible for his son's first period of outlawry (*Gesta Herwardi*, ch. 1):

> Qua de re pater eius a rege Edwardo impetrauit ut exul a patria fieret patefactis omnibus quecunque in patrem et contra parentes uel que contra prouinciales egerat. Et factum est. Vnde statim agnomen exulis adeptus est in decimo octauo etatis anno a patre et patria expulsus. (80)

> And for that reason his father, after describing all that he had done against his father, and his parents, and the local folk, asked King

---

48. *Grettis saga*, Guðni Jónsson, 36. Note that practically the same thing is also said of the outlaw Án bow-bender: "Lítit ástríki hafði hann af feðr sínum, en móðir hans unni honum mikit" (Guðni Jónsson, *Fornaldar sögur*, 2:368). See Lange, *English and Icelandic Outlaw-Traditions*, 115.

Edward that he be banished from his homeland. And so it happened. Because of that he was at once called "Outlaw," since he was cast out from his father and his homeland when he was eighteen.

This passage is remarkable for the intensity of alliteration on "p" (*pater . . . impetrauit . . . patria . . . patefactis . . . patrem . . . parentes . . . prouinciales . . . patre . . . patria*), emphatically highlighting the role of Hereward's own father in the imposition of his outlawry, a political weapon Edward the Confessor seems to have used more than his predecessors.[49]

Hereward's first adventure after being condemned to outlawry occurs at the court of Giseberht de Ghent in Northumberland. His host has a custom at various festivals of testing young men by pitting them against wild beasts (*Gesta Herwardi*, ch. 2):[50]

Cum quibus Herwardus in primordio sui aduentus, uidelicet in Natale Domini, associatus rogauit sibi unum e feris aggredi licere aut saltim illum maximum ursum qui aderat; quem incliti ursi Norweye fuisse filium ac formatum secundum pedes illius et capud ad fabulam Danorum affirmabant sensum humanum habentem et loquelam hominis intelligentem ac doctum ad bellum; cuius igitur pater in siluis fertur puellam rapuisse et ex ea Biernum regem Norweye genuisse. (80)

Hereward was with them at the start of his visit, around Christmas, and since he was there he asked to be allowed to take on one of the wild animals, specifically the enormous bear that was there, and according to Danish legend was supposed to be the son of famous Norwegian bear with a human head and feet as well as human intelligence, one who understood the speech of men and was trained for battle. Its own father was said to have raped a girl in the forest and with her to have fathered King Beorn ["Bear"] of Norway.

---

49. See Frank Barlow, *Edward the Confessor* (Berkeley: University of California Press, 1970), 80. In the context of Hereward's family background, it seems relevant to mention a further curious document, *Excerptum de familia Herwardi* (Excerpt Concerning the Family of Hereward) in J. A. Giles, ed., *Vita [sic] Quorundam Anglo-Saxonum: Original Lives of Anglo-Saxons and Others who Lived before the Conquest* (London: 1854), 31–33.

50. See Jones, "Redemptive Fictions," 126–28.

This bear is evidently related to the one mentioned above in the *Gesta antecessorum* section of the *Vita Waldeui*. Hereward is initially refused the conflict, but when the bear escapes and goes on a rampage, he encounters it on his own. The key moment of Hereward's meeting with the bear reads as follows (*Gesta Herwardi*, ch. 2):

Interim Herwardus feram cruentatam ad thalamum domini sui propter voces trepidantium revententem, ubi uxor illius et filiæ ac mulieres timide confugerant, obvium habuit, ac in illum confestim irruere voluit; ipsum iste prævenit, gladium per caput et ad scapulas usque configens, atque ibi spatam relinquens, bestiam in ulnis accepit, et ad insequentes tetendit. Quo viso plurimum mirati sunt. (Ibid.)

In the meantime, Hereward came upon the blood-spattered wild animal as it was heading back to the lord's bedroom because of the screaming of the scared, where the lord's wife and daughters and the women had fled in fear, and the bear wanted to attack him at once, but he beat it to it, slicing his sword through its head right up to the shoulder-blades, and leaving the blade there, while he lifted up the beast in his arms and held it out to those who came after him; and they were completely astonished at the sight.

Quite what the bear is doing heading towards the lord's bed-chamber, where the womenfolk were, is unclear, but the potential for bestial rape, apparently a trait to which the beast's breeding has predisposed it, seems very clear.

Such a combat characterizes the figure found widely elsewhere of an irascible and anti-social young man who makes a name for himself as a monster-slayer, but who also has to exist outside the norms of human society, a tale-type known as "the bear's son's tale."[51] Examples include *Beowulf*, *Grettis saga*, and above all the accounts of the hero Bǫðvarr Bjarki (his nickname means

---

51. See especially Oscar L. Olson, *The Relation of the Hrólfs Saga Kraka and the Bjark-arímur to Beowulf* (Chicago: Chicago University Press, 1916); J. Michael Stitt, *"Beowulf" and the Bear's Son: Epic, Saga, and Fairytale in Northern Germanic Tradition*, Albert Bates Lord Studies in Oral Tradition 8 (New York: Garland, 1992); Jesse L. Byock, trans., *The Saga of King Hrolf Kraki* (London: Penguin, 1998), xxv–xxviii.

"little bear"), as it features in Scandinavian sources in *Hrólfs saga kraka*,[52] as well as in the *Gesta Danorum* of Saxo Grammaticus.[53] The fact that Bǫðvarr Bjarki's fame spread to England is confirmed rather strikingly by the appearance of one *Boduwar Berki* in the Durham *Liber Vitae*.[54] The same book also contains the name *Biuulf*, likely a reflection of another hero, Beowulf, who is also often identified as part of the same "bear's son" motif.[55] The former entry has been dated to the beginning of the twelfth century, with the latter to the beginning of the ninth. Pickering makes eight points of comparison between the tale of Bǫðvarr Bjarki and the *Gesta Herwardi*:[56]

1. An untried youth arrives from abroad at the court of an important lord;
2. A fierce beast is at the court, that tests the mettle of young warriors there;
3. The contest takes place at Christmas or Yuletide;
4. The young hero is forbidden from fighting the beast;
5. The beast in question is a white bear (*Gesta Herewardi*) or a bear of unspecified color (*Gesta Danorum*);
6. The young hero meets the bear in unexpected circumstances requiring single-handed action;
7. The young hero slays the bear with a single sword-stroke;
8. The young hero gains fame and respect from the deed.

In the case of the respect that Hereward gains from killing the bear, it is again striking that he is celebrated first and foremost by the local ladies (*Gesta Herwardi*, ch. 2):

52. See Guðni Jónsson, ed., *Fornaldar sögur Norðurlanda*, 4 vols. (Reykjavík: Íslendingasagnaútgáfan, 1954), 1:55–69; Byock, *Saga of King Hrolf Kraki*, 43–52.

53. See *Gesta Danorum*, Olrik, 51–61; Saxo Grammaticus, *The History of the Danes, Books I–IX*, ed. and trans., Hilda Ellis Davidson and Peter Fisher, 2 vols. (Cambridge: Brewer, 1979–80), 1:54–63, 2:47–49.

54. See R. D. Fulk et al., eds., *Klaeber's "Beowulf" and "The Fight at Finnsburg,"* 4th ed. (Toronto: Toronto University Press, 2008), xlii.

55. *The Durham Liber vitae: London, British Library, MS Cotton Domitian A. VII*, ed. David and Lynda Rollason, 3 vols. and CD-ROM (London: British Library, 2007): 2:11, 94, 218.

56. See Pickering, "Legend of Hereward," 94–97.

Qua de re prouinciales eum in laudibus preferebant et mulieres ac
puelle de eo in choris canebant. (82)

And in that regard, the locals began to shower him with praise, and
women and young girls began to sing about him in their songs.

The passage echoes the biblical 1 Samuel 18:7–9, where the women
of Israel inspire Saul's jealousy by singing that Saul has killed thousands but David tens of thousands; likewise, just as David's fame
incites resentment in Saul, who tries to kill him with a javelin, so too
Hereward is immediately attacked by a jealous assailant with a javelin
(*Gesta Herwardi*, ch. 2):[57]

Hoc autem Herwardo per seruum suum pene tarde comperto in ictu
iaculi lancea inuasorem suum transfodit. Hiis igitur domine sue patefactis et tantas denique insidias declinans discessit. At illa lacrimans
et multum deprecans ut saltim suum expectaret dominum aut filii sui
languentis exitum; si non euaderet ipse adoptiuus filius heres illorum
fieret. Quod impetrare non potuit. (Ibid.)

But when he learned of this plot at the last moment from his servant,
Hereward speared his attacker just as he was trying to throw a javelin.
When he described this to his lady, he departed, to escape such schemes.
In tears, she kept on asking that he would at least wait either for her
lord to return or for the death of their ailing son; if he didn't leave, he
could become their adopted son and heir. But she couldn't sway him.

The unfulfilled request from the lady of the house to wait for the
return of the absent lord, and Hereward's blunt and abrupt departure
find several parallels in Old Norse-Icelandic literature, notably in
Grettis saga, which, as we shall see, also has an account of its own
outlaw hero slaying a vicious bear at another's home.

---

57. See Elisabeth van Houts, "Hereward and Flanders," *Anglo-Saxon England* 28
(1999): 217; Schmidt, "Biblisches und hagiographisches Kolorit," 91–92; Jones, "Redemptive Fictions," 129. Van Houts gives the fullest account of Hereward's expeditions to
Flanders, highlighting the historical aspects of this part of the *Gesta*, including the fame
and availability of fine horses from the area, as well as the fact that a charter of Bishop
Lietbert of Cambrai (1051–76), dated to early 1065, is witnessed by one *miles Herivvardi*
("Hereward and Flanders," 201–23, esp. 209 and 210–13).

The parallel sequence of the bear-slaying in *Grettis saga*, however, while it removes entirely the sexual element underpinning the equivalent passage in *Gesta Herwardi*, adds other details (*Grettis saga*, ch. 21).[58] At this point in his outlawry, Grettir has already left his home in Iceland and traveled to Norway, where after several adventures he has arrived at the home of one Þorkell at Sálfti in Hálogaland. While he is warmly received by his host, there is another less welcoming guest, a distant relative of Þorkell's named Bjǫrn ("bear"), who is both brash and loud, and prone to provoke Grettir. When a wild bear breaks out of its cave and causes great damage, there are two attempts to kill it by Þorkell and Bjǫrn and others, both of which are failures. Then Grettir makes an attempt on his own (*Grettis saga*, ch. 21):

> Hann gekk þegar í einstigit, ok er dýrit sá manninn, hljóp þat upp með grimmð mikilli ok í móti Gretti ok laust til hans með hramminum, þeim er firr var berginu. Grettir hjó í móti með sverðinu, ok kom á hramminn fyrir ofan klœrnar ok tók þar af. Þá vildi dýrit ljósta með þeim fœtinum sem heill var, skaukz á stúfinn, ok varð hann lægri en hann ætlaði, ok fell þá dýrit í fang Gretti. Hann þrífr þá meðal hlusta dýrinu ok helt því frá sér, svá at þat náði eigi at bíta hann. Svá hefir Grettir sagt, at hann þóttist þá aflraun mesta gǫrt hafa, at halda dýrinu. En með því at dýrit brauzk um fast, en rúmit lítit, þá ruku þeir báðir ofan fyrir bjargit. Nú var dýrit þyngra, ok kom þat fyrr niðr á urðina; varð Grettir þá efri, en dýrit lamðisk þá mjǫk þeim megin, sem niðr vissi. Grettir þrífr þá til saxins ok lagði bjǫrninn til hjartans, ok var þat hans bani; eptir þat fór hann heim ok tók feld sinn, ok var hann allr rifinn í sundr. Hann hafði með sér þat, er hann hafði hǫggvit af hramminum. (*Grettis saga*, Guðni Jónsson, 76–77)

He went straight along the narrow path, and when the bear saw him, it ran at him ferociously and lashed at him with the paw that was farther away from the cliff. Grettir struck with his sword, hit the paw above the claws and chopped it off. Then the bear tried to strike him with its good paw, and shifted its weight to the stump; but because that paw was shorter than it had expected, the bear toppled into Grettir's

---

58. Guðni Jónsson, 73–78.

arms. Grettir grabbed the bear by the ears and held it at arm's length to prevent it from biting him. He said later that holding off that bear was his greatest feat of strength. Because the bear thrashed about and the path was so narrow, they both toppled over the edge of the cliff. The bear was heavier than Grettir, so it hit the boulders first, with him on top of it, and was badly injured by the fall. Grettir grabbed his short-sword, drove it through the bear's heart and killed it. Then he went home, taking his cloak with him, which was ripped to shreds. He also took the piece of the paw that he had cut off.

Note that this episode in *Grettis saga*, which takes place early in winter, complies with seven of the eight points of comparison between and the tales of tale of Bǫðvarr Bjarki and the *Gesta Herwardi* made by Pickering above. The detail of keeping the beast at arms' length links the feats of both Grettir and Hereward, and strengthens the general sense of similarity. Moreover, just as Hereward is celebrated for his bear-slaying, so earning the jealousy of another warrior whom he kills trying to attack him, so too Grettir ends up killing Bǫrn, who had so provoked him during his stay (*Grettis saga*, ch. 22). Nor is Bjǫrn the only human enemy of Grettir's to be associated with bears, nor indeed with the whole bear-slaying episode in the *Gesta Herwardi*.

The sexual element absent in the account of Grettir and the bear (although it is certainly implied in the parallel account in the *Gesta Herwardi*) is, however, much to the fore in the account of Grettir's dealings with berserks during the first period of his outlawry; the berserks, who as a type are of course implicitly and customarily identified with bears,[59] are described as follows (*Grettis saga*, ch. 19):

Þeir gengu berserksgang ok eirðu engu, þegar þeir reiddusk. Þeir tóku á brott konur manna ok dœtr ok hǫfðu við hǫnd sér viku eða hálfan mánuð ok fœrðu síðan aptr þeim, sem áttu; þeir ræntu, hvar sem þeir kómu, eða gerðu aðrar óspekðir. (Ibid., 62)

---

59. See especially Gerard Breen, "Personal Names and the Re-creations of *berserkir* and *úlfheðnar*," *Studia Anthroponymica Scandinavica* 15 (1997): 5–38.

They went berserk and spared no one, when their blood was up. They took away men's wives and daughters, and kept them for a week or two, and then sent them back to their husbands and fathers; they plundered wherever they went, and did other wicked deeds.

An immediate Anglo-Saxon analogue for such peremptory sexual appropriation can be found in the C-text of the *Anglo-Saxon Chronicle* for 1046, where Earl Swein Godwinson, the brother of Harold and Tostig, blots his own copy-book in a similarly shocking fashion:

> Her on þysum geare for Swegn eorl into Wealan Griffin se norþerna cyng forð mid him, him man gislode. Þa he hamwerdes wæs, þa het he feccan him to þa abbedessan on Leomynstre hæfde hi þa while þe him geliste let hi syþþan faran ham.[60]

In this year Earl Swein went into Wales, and Grufydd the Northern king went with him, and hostages were given them. When he was on his way home, he had the abbess of Leominster brought to him, and kept her with him as long as he liked, and then let her go home.

Such sexual predators are commonplace in the Icelandic sagas; an evidently parallel episode, again taking place at Christmas (Yuletide) happens later in *Grettis saga*, ch. 40:

> At jólum kom Grettir til þess bónda, er Einarr hét. Hann var ríkr maðr ok kvæntr ok átti dóttur gjafvaxta, er Gýríðr er nefnd; hon var fríð kona ok þótti harðla góðr kostr. Einarr bauð Gretti með sér at vera um jólin, ok þat þá hann. Þat var þá víða í Noregi, at markarmenn ok illvirkjar hljópu ofan af mǫrkum ok skoruðu á menn til kvenna eða tóku á brott fé manna með ofríki, þar sem eigi var liðsfjǫlði fyrir. Svá bar hér til, at þat var einn dag á jólunum, at kómu til Einars bónda illvirkjar margir saman. Hét sá Snækollr, sem fyrir þeim var; hann var berserkr mikill. Hann skoraði á Einar bónda, at hann skyldi leggja upp við hann dóttur sína eða verja hana, ef hann þœttisk maðr til; en bóndi var þá af œskuskeiði ok engi styrjaldarmaðr. (*Grettis saga*, Guðni Jónsson, 135)

---

60. *The Anglo-Saxon Chronicle 5: MS. C*, ed. Katherine O'Brien O'Keeffe (Cambridge: Brewer, 2001), *s.a.* 1046.

At Christmas, Grettir came to the house of a farmer called Einarr. He was a rich man, married, and had a daughter of marriageable age, who was called Gýríðr; she was a beautiful woman, and was thought a good match. Einarr asked Grettir to stay with him over Christmas. It happened then widely in Norway, that outlaws and mischief-makers came suddenly out of the woods and challenged men for their women-folk and took away men's property with overbearing force, wherever there were few folk around. So it happened one day at Christmas that many mischief-makers came together at farmer Einarr's. Their leader was called Snækoll; he was a mighty berserk. He challenged farmer Einarr, that he should either hand over his daughter or defend her, if he thought he was man enough; but the farmer was past his prime, and was not a fighter.

Grettir steps in, kicks the berserk's shield up into his jaw, and finally decapitates him. In such ways does Grettir establish himself as a defender of women against unwanted male aggression, in a fashion not unlike Hereward.

In the case of the first description of the berserks in *Grettis saga* (ch. 19), these sexual predators come to the home of Þorfinnr Kársson inn gamli at Háramarsey, where Grettir has been staying and has already made a name for himself, while Þorfinnr and most of the men are away, leaving Grettir and eight other men together with Þorfinnr's wife and daughter and the other women of the household. The twelve berserks in question arrive at Yuletide and make it clear that they intend to rape the women. Grettir tricks and eventually traps the berserks in a store-house adjoining a toilet, a humiliating position from which they attempt to extricate themselves by breaking through the partition wall and exiting via the toilet.[61] When the leader of berserks first emerges, Grettir spears him dead, and eventually kills ten of the twelve berserks himself; two more perish of cold while attempting to escape. Given the odd detail of a trapped enemy holed up in a toilet, it is striking that Hereward too hounds an enemy into a similarly humiliating situation (*Gesta Herwardi*, ch. 31):

---

61. There is a useful illustration of the relative layout of the buildings in Byock, *Grettir's Saga*, 54.

Et cum non haberet ibi ubi se uerteret imminente semper super eum
Herwardo in interiorem domum fugiens discessit ubi in foramine selle
super latrinam capud imposuit misereri sibi exorans. (160)

And since he did not have anywhere to turn, with Hereward always so
hard on his heels, he left the building in flight to where he placed his
head through the hole in a toilet-seat and begged for mercy.

Likewise, *Gesta Herwardi* (ch. 3) relates the story of Hereward's
conflict with a bully called Ulcus Ferreus ("Iron Sore"), whom he
encounters at the court of a Cornish prince called Alef. One wonders
whether the villain's first name *Ulcus* masks an original *Ulfus* ("wolf")
or even *Ursus* ("bear"): both "Iron Wolf" and "Iron Bear" would
be very suitable names for a berserk.[62] At all events, this character
certainly behaves like a berserk, being described as "unum nephandis-
simum uirum et ualde superbum" (one of the most wicked men, and
extremely arrogant), and "promereri sibi jam diu expectans ob forti-
tudinum merita reguli pulcherrimam filiam" (for a long time expecting
to earn for himself the very beautiful daughter of the prince through
his mighty strength).[63] Part of this bully's swaggering is the boast that
he has killed numerous opponents; Hereward's answer drips with cool
contempt (*Gesta Herwardi*, ch. 3):[64]

"Quoniam illos uiros quos a te dicis interfectos in mente tua concepisti
et ex corde tuo illos non a matre natos genuisti dignum est ut uno ictu
oris interfecti sint." (84)

Since those men you say you slew you made up in your own mind, and
they came from your heart and not from any mother, it's only right that
they should be slain by a single breath out of your mouth!

Inevitably, and following the same pattern described above, Hereward
encounters the bully in single combat, and initially pierces his enemy

---

62. See Breen on names relating to iron ("Personal Names," esp. 25).

63. *De Gestis Herwardi*, Meneghetti, 82.

64. "This is just the sort of retort that gets saga outlaws such as Egill Skallagrímsson
and Gunnlaugr ormstunga into trouble" (Jones, "Redemptive Fictions," 130).

through the thigh with his javelin, while his wounded foe bemoans the lack of his favored weapon, which he had earlier apparently given to the prince's daughter (*Gesta Herwardi*, ch. 3):

> "O utinam spata pre manibus quam sero mee sponse future tradidi unde tantos oppressi mihi adesset uno ictu semianimis saltim uindicaturus quam a quodam tyranno dimicando accepi." (84–86)

> If only I had in my hand the blade I just handed over to my future wife and with which I fought such great men, that I won in battle with a bully; I would, even though half-dead, avenge myself with a single blow.

That very blade, we infer, causes his own death with a single blow, while the favor of the prince's daughter toward Hereward is made explicit after he has killed the bully, even though in so doing he is detained by her disapproving father (*Gesta Herwardi*, ch. 3):

> Filia uero eius in euentu ualde exilarata formidolosum hominem et incompositum membris quoniam nimium uerita est Herwardo plurimum prouide in custodia ministrauit et in fine datis muneribus ac predicto ense sibi tradito clam decedere fecit rogans inmemor sui ne fieret. (86)

> Indeed, [the prince's] daughter was utterly delighted by the outcome, since she was very much afraid of that terrifying man misshapen in his limbs, and took the greatest care of Hereward while he was detained; eventually, having showered him with gifts, including giving him the aforementioned sword, she caused him to leave in secret, begging him not to forget her.

The ugliness of berserks is a byword, although the Latin phrase in question (*incompositum membris*) might equally refer to other kinds of deformity also associated with their kind.[65] The fact that Hereward also acquires an apparently special weapon once owned by his inhuman enemy can likewise be matched in cognate tales.[66]

---

65. See Breen, "Personal Names," 25–27.
66. See Orchard, *Pride and Prodigies*, 144–47.

In this context, there is again a parallel with a pair of episodes involving Biarco (Bǫðvarr Bjarki) in Saxo's *Gesta Danorum*.[67] In the first of these incidents, Biarco retaliates against the boisterous activity that occurs at the wedding of one Agner, son of Ingel, to Ruta, the sister of King Rolf (Hrólfr kraki). Agner, affronted, challenges Biarco to a duel, at the climax of which he is fatally wounded through the midriff. In the second incident, already mentioned above, Biarco confronts a huge bear, which, as in the analogues, he spears to death:

> Talibus operum meritis exsultanti novam de se silvestris fera victoriam praebuit. Ursum quippe eximiae magnitudinis obvium sibi inter dumeta factum iaculo confecit comitemque suum Hialtonem, quo viribus maior evaderet, applicato ore egestum beluae cruorem haurire iussit. Creditum namque erat hoc potionis genere corporei roboris incrementa praestari. (*Gesta Danorum*, Olrik, 51)

> While he was rejoicing in such prizes for his deeds, a wild beast from the forest provided him with a fresh victory. For he came upon a certain bear of an enormous size among the thickets and pierced it with a spear, and ordered his companion Hjalto to put his mouth to the wound and suck out the blood, because it was believed that an increase of bodily strength would be provided by this kind of drink.

Certainly, however, both Grettir and Hereward are unafraid of standing up to bullies and provoking their wrath. The relevant episodes involve a young man, already with a certain reputation for stubborn pugnacity, who is thrown into a foreign situation where as a recent arrival he is provoked by a bully who has designs on the lady of the house, but where he nonetheless manages not only to kill the bully with a sword-stroke, but also gain the favor of the lady and the esteem of the lord. Further schematic comparisons between (for example) the tales of Bǫðvarr Bjarki, as told in both Saxo's *Gesta Danorum* and *Hrólfs saga kraka* (where twelve berserks turn up to wreak havoc at Yuletide),[68] and that of Hereward in the *Gesta*

---

67. *Gesta Danorum*, Olrik, 51–61; Davidson, *History of the Danes*, 1:54–63 and 2:47–49.

68. *Hrólfs saga kraka*, Guðni Jónsson, 69–72; Byock, *Saga of King Hrolf Kraki*, 53–55.

Herwardi develop the points of contact, but the story remains essentially the same.[69]

Gerd Sieg has considered a whole series of such episodes spread throughout a range of sagas, in which a berserk demands the wife, daughter, or sister of a man of significant status, on penalty of a duel with that man or his representative, knowing full well that he cannot be killed by ordinary weapons, and is then surprised when the hero confronts him properly armed (often with the bully's own weapon), and then generally manages to lop off a limb before dispatching his victim.[70] Benjamin Blaney expands the paradigm dramatically, and notes no fewer than thirty-three examples from various sagas, including that from *Grettis saga*.[71] In any case, the wider tale-type, including Latin examples from both the *Gesta Danorum* and *Gesta Herwardi*, seems clear.

Other minor parallels link the *Gesta Herwardi* more specifically with *Grettis saga*, albeit that the routes of transmission remain opaque. So, for example, in one of the odder episodes in the *Gesta Herwardi*, our eponymous hero behaves rather badly, escaping the king's custody while the king is out hunting and killing a boy who bad-mouths him on his way (*Gesta Herwardi*, ch. 26):

Quo ascenso quidam de pueris regis uiso illo uocibus maledicis eum aggressus est monens sociis ut eum a ministris regis sequi repente facerent elapsum eum a uinculis asserens. Cuius obiurgantis uerba Herwardus non ferens cum autem illum contra seipsum offenderet gladio eum transuerberauit. (146)

When he had mounted [the horse], one of the king's lads spotted him and insulted him with foul language, telling his mates to chase him straightaway with the King's servants, crying out that he had slipped his chains. Hereward could not bear his inflammatory words, and when the boy got in his way, he struck him through with his sword.

---

69. See Pickering, "Legend of Hereward," 113–17.

70. See Gerd Sieg, "Die Zweikämpfe der Isländersagas," *Zeitschrift für deutsches Altertum* 95 (1966): 1–27; Jones, "Redemptive Fictions," 131.

71. See Benjamin Blaney, "The Berserk Suitor: the Literary Application of a Stereotyped Theme," *Scandinavian Studies* 54 (1982): 279–94; see also Blaney, "The *berserkr*: His Origin and Development in Old Norse Literature" (PhD diss., University of Colorado, 1972), esp. 140–73.

The parallel episode in *Grettis saga* takes place at a church, and again the king, this time Óláfr Haraldsson (995–1030) is close by, but not present to witness the provocation and its deadly outcome (*Grettis saga*, ch. 39):

> Þá hljóp fram piltr einn frumvaxta, heldr svipligr, ok mælti til Grettis: "Undarlegr háttr er nú hér í landi þessu, þar sem menn skulu kristnir heita, at illvirkjar ok ránsmenn ok þjófar skulu fara í friði ok gera þeim skírslur; en hvat myndi illmenninu fyrir verða, nema forða lífinu meðan hann mætti? Hér er nú einn ódáðamaðrinn, er sannreyndr er at illvirkjum ok hefir brennt inni saklausa menn, ok skal hann þó enn ná undanfœrslu, ok er þetta allmikill ósiðr." Hann fór at Gretti ok rétti honum fingr ok skar honum hǫfuð ok kallaði hann margýgjuson ok mǫrgum ǫðrum illum nǫfnum. Gretti varð skapfátt mjǫk við þetta, ok gat þá eigi stǫðvat sik. Grettir reiddi þá upp hnefann ok sló piltinn undir eyrat, svá at hann lá þegar í óviti, en sumir segja, at hann væri dauðr þá þegar. En engi þóttist vita, hvaðan sjá piltr kom, eða hvat af honum varð, en þat ætla menn helzt, at þat hafi verit óhreinn andi, sendr til óheilla Gretti. (*Grettis saga*, Guðni Jónsson, 133)

> Then a young lad leapt out, rather out of the blue, and spoke to Grettir: "It is an odd practice here in this country, where folk call themselves Christians, that criminals and robbers and thieves should be allowed to pass in peace and undertake ordeals: and what is a scoundrel to do but lengthen his life while he can? Here is a man of wicked deeds, who has been rightly convicted of crimes and has burnt innocent men inside a house, and yet is given the right to ordeal, and that is a huge scandal." He went up to Grettir and pointed his fingers at him and made faces and called him the son of a sea hag and many other bad names. Grettir totally lost it at that and could not control himself. Grettir raised up his fist and punched the lad under the ear, so that he was immediately knocked out flat unconscious, and some say that he immediately died. But no one could tell where the lad came from, or what became of him, and folk think is most likely, that he was an unclean spirit sent to damn Grettir.

Here the surprise appearance of the boy is given a rather otherworldly slant if, as has been suggested, the phrase "unclean spirit" (*óhreinn andi*) is intended to evoke the "unclean spirit" (*spiritus immundus*) who cries out against Jesus in the synagogue at Capernaum in the Vulgate (Mark 1:23–26).[72] Nonetheless Hereward and Grettir, in a pair of curiously similar episodes, are clearly guilty of assaulting and even killing a child, albeit after verbal provocation.

Similarly, several earlier scholars have noted the parallels that exist between the account of Hereward's retreat to the Isle of Ely in the *Gesta Herewardi* (ch. 22) and that of Grettir to the island Drangey in *Grettis saga* (ch. 69).[73] In the case of both outlaws, attempts are made to dislodge them by witchcraft, after all other means fail; the story in *Grettis saga* (chs. 78–79) involves the witch Þuríðr, the foster-mother of Grettir's arch-enemy Þorbjǫrn ǫngull, while that in *Gesta Herwardi* focuses on an unnamed witch who is brought in by William de Warenne, his own nemesis. In the Norse, Þuríðr bewitches a log and sends it to Drangey, where it causes Grettir to wound himself; in the Latin, the witch's behavior is rather more eye-popping (*Gesta Herwardi*, ch. 26):

> In octaua siquidem die cum omni uirtute eorum omnes aggressi sunt impugnare insulam statuentes illam predictam phitonissam mulierem in eminentiori loco in medio eorum ut satis undique munita libere sue arti uacaret. Qua ascensa contra insulam et habitatores eius diu sermocinata est, plurimas destructionis similitudines et figmenta subuersionis faciens posterioraque sua semper in fine sue orationis et incantationis detecta ostendens. (148)

> And then on the eighth day they all set out to attack with all their might, setting the aforementioned witch in a raised position in their midst, so that while she was properly protected on all sides so she might have every chance to practice her art. When she had been lifted up, she spoke out against the Isle and its inhabitants for a long time, setting up a whole stack of curses, images, and instruments of their demise, and showing her naked arse at them when her speeches and spells were over.

---

72. See Robert Cook, "The Reader in *Grettis saga*," *Saga-Book of the Viking Society* 21 (1984–85): 151; Orchard, *Pride and Prodigies*, 154.

73. See Jones, "Redemptive Fictions," 134–40.

While *Grettis saga* has no such stirring scene, the activities of the witch here can be closely matched in Norse sources. *Landnámabók* (The Book of Settlements), an early form of which is attributed to Ari Þorgilsson (1068–1148), but which in its current form seems to date from the late thirteenth century, lists accounts of more than four hundred settlers and their descendents into the twelfth century and tells briefly the story of the rather unpleasant Hrolleifr, and his still more unpleasant mother Ljót (whose name means "ugly": the masculine form of the name is also attested for berserks).[74] In a dispute with neighbors, she acts as follows (*Sturlubók*, ch. 180):

Þá var Ljót út komin ok gekk ǫfug: hon hafði hǫfuðit millum fóta sér, en klæðin á baki sér.[75]

Then Ljót came out, and walked backwards; she had her head between her legs, and her clothes over her head.

The scene is filled out still further in the fourteenth-century *Vatnsdæla saga* (ch. 26):

Ok er þeir brœðr kómu at, mælti Hǫgni: "Hvat fjánda ferr hér at oss, er ek veit eigi hvat er?" Þorsteinn svarar: "Þar ferr Ljót kerling ok hefir breytilega um búizk;" hon hafði rekit fǫtin fram yfir hǫfuð sér ok fór ǫfug ok rétti hǫfuðit aptr milli fótanna; ófagrligt var hennar augnabragð, hversu hon gat þeim trollsliga skotit.[76]

When the brothers approached, Hǫgni said: "What fiend is that coming towards us here? I do not know what it is." Þorsteinn replied: "That is Ljót the old witch, and she has made herself up strangely." She had pulled her clothes up over her head and was walking backwards, with her head shoved back between her legs. The look in her eyes was awful, since she could dart them about like a troll.

---

74. See Breen, "Personal Names," 25–27.

75. *Íslendingabók, Landnámabók,* ed. Jakob Benediktsson, Íslenzk fornrit 1 (Reykjavík: Hið íslenzka fornritafélag, 1986), 222.

76. *Vatnsdæla saga,* ed. Einar Ól. Sveinsson, Íslenzk fornrit 8 (Reykjavík: Hið íslenzka fornritafélag, 1939), 69–70.

In both the *Gesta Herwardi* and *Grettis saga*, the object of this magical behavior is to bring fate upon the heads of the respective heroes; in both cases, the rituals do indeed dislodge the intended outlaws, but with differing degrees of damage.

It is striking that while Grettir never lives to leave his island-refuge, Hereward does indeed escape to fight another day, and that the *Gesta Herwardi* ends with the outlaw fully reconciled with the king.[77] Other accounts do, however, describe the manner of Hereward's death in ways which look strikingly similar to what is found in *Grettis saga*. Of these, the so-called *Liber de Hyda* (ca. 1120–35, perhaps written at Lewes) has the following account:

> Post multas denique cædes atque seditiones, multa pacis fœdera cum rege facta et temerarie violata, quadam die cum omnibus sociis ab hostibus circumventus miserabiliter occubuit.[78]

> Finally, after many killings and treacherous attacks, many pacts of peace made with the king and rashly broken, one day when he was with all of his companions surrounded by his enemies, he died a wretched death.

This sparse description is considerably expanded in another source, the *L'Estorie des Engles* by the Anglo-Norman chronicler, Geffrei Gaimar, written in 1136–37, and comprising some 6500 lines of verse, of which the account of Hereward takes up 253 lines (5457–5710).[79] Gaimar's accounts of Hereward are "quite independent of the *Gesta*,"[80] and the death scene of Hereward is vividly described, from the moment

---

77. See further Rolf H. Bremmer, Jr, "The *Gesta Herwardi*: Transforming an Anglo-Saxon into an Englishman," in *People and Texts: Relationships in Medieval Literature*, ed. T. Summerfield and K. Busby (Amsterdam: Rodopi, 2007), 29–42.

78. *Chronica Monasterii de Hida juxta Wintoniam, ab Anno 1035 ad Annum 1121*, in Appendix A of *Liber Monasterii de Hyda*, ed. Edward Edwards, Rolls Series 45 (London: Longmans, 1866), 295; see Lundgren, "Hereward and Outlawry," 164–66.

79. *Lestorie des Engles solum la translacion Maistre Geffrei Gaimar*, ed. Thomas D. Hardy and Charles T. Martin, Rolls Series 91, 2 vols. (London: HMSO 1898–99; Kraus reprints, 1966), 1:339–404; cf. *L'Estorie des Engleis by Geffrei Gaimar*, ed. Alexander Bell, Anglo-Norman Texts 14–16 (Oxford: Blackwell, 1960). See Pickering, "Legend of Hereward," 65. For the date, see Ian Short, "Gaimar's Epilogue and Geoffrey of Monmouth's *Liber vetustissimus*," *Speculum* 79 (1994): 323–43.

80. *Lestorie Des Engles*, Hardy, xxxiv.

he is taken unawares when one of his companions lets him down, but another makes up for it by a stout defense:

> Si Hereward en fust guarni,
> Le plus haardi semblast cuard.
> Malement lagueitat Ailward,
> Son chapelein; le dust guaiter,
> Si sendormi sur vn rocher.
> Ke dirraie? suspris i fust;
> Meis gentement sen est contenuz,
> Si se content com vn leun,
> Il e Winter son compaignun. (lines 5618–26)

If Hereward had been warned / The bravest would have appeared a coward. / Ailward watched him ill / His chaplain. He should have watched, / But fell asleep upon a rock. / What shall I say? He was surprised, / But nobly he carried himself, / He carried himself like a lion, / He and Winter, his companion.

Such lines are typical of Gaimar's lengthy description of the death of Hereward, which can conveniently be summarized under the following eleven headings, with the relevant line-numbers also given here:[81]

A	Hereward is caught by surprise at his castle;	(5615–19)
B	Ailward is supposed to stand guard, but instead falls asleep;	(5620–22)
C	Hereward kills one of his assailants with his javelin;	(5650–55)
D	Hereward kills four of his assailants with his sword;	(5669–72)
E	Hereward's sword shatters on the helmet of a fifth assailant;	(5673–74)
F	Hereward kills two of his attackers with his shield;	(5675–76)
G	Hereward is stabbed through the back by four spears;	(5677–78)
H	Hereward is unable to get up off his knees;	(5678–81)
I	Hereward throws his shield at another attacker and decapitates him;	(5682–85)
J	Hereward dies at the same time as his last victim;	(5688–90)
K	Hereward is decapitated.	(5691–93)

---

81. See Lange, *English and Icelandic Outlaw-Traditions*, 30; Lundgren, "Hereward and Outlawry," 160–61.

By contrast, the death of Grettir at the hands of a band led by his arch-enemy Þorbjǫrn ǫngull (Guðni Jónsson, 258–64) might be similarly summarized as taking place in the following very similar nine-part sequence (*Grettis saga*, ch. 82):

1. Grettir is caught by surprise at his island-refuge;   [cf. Gaimar A]
2. Glaumr is supposed to stand guard, but instead
   falls asleep;   [cf. Gaimar B]
3. Grettir kills a man with his spear;   [cf. Gaimar C]
4. Grettir is unable to get up off his knees;   [cf. Gaimar H]
5. Grettir uses his *sax* and cuts a man in two;
6. Þorbjǫrn ǫngull stabs Grettir with a spear   [cf. Gaimar G]
   between the shoulders;
7. Þorbjǫrn ǫngull chops off Grettir's hand to gain the *sax*;
8. Þorbjǫrn ǫngull tries to use Grettir's own *sax*
   to cut off his head, but a piece breaks off;   [cf. Gaimar E]
9. Grettir is decapitated.   [cf. Gaimar K]

The death scene of the outlaw Gísli Súrsson (*Gísla saga*, chs. 34–36) also has some similarities to both of these accounts, but neither so many nor so close.[82]

Nor is Gaimar the only Anglo-Norman author linking the legend of Hereward in general, and the *Gesta Herwardi* in particular, with material other than in Old Norse-Icelandic or in Latin. Pickering quotes Nelles in pointing out ten points of similarity between chapter 5 of the *Gesta Herwardi*, which is set in Ireland, and the Anglo-Norman *Romance of Horn*, written around 1170 by an otherwise anonymous author who styles himself "Thomas," and is also responsible for (among other works) the *Romance of Tristan*:[83]

1. The young hero learns of a young woman being forced into marriage;
2. He travels secretly and in disguise;
3. At the wedding-feast, he takes his seat in a lowly position;
4. A woman recognizes the hero even through his disguise;

---

82. *Gísla saga Súrssonar*, Björn K. Þórólfsson, 109–16.

83. Walter R. Nelles, "The Ballad of Hind Horn," *Journal of American Folklore* 22 (1909): 54–55; cf. Pickering, "Legend of Hereward," 128–30. For further Anglo-Norman parallels, this time to the Tristan legend, see Thomas, "*Gesta Herwardi*," 217n19.

5. The betrothed woman makes the rounds with her female retinue, offering drinks, as is said to be the local custom;
6. The hero is particular about how he is served;
7. The betrothed woman recognizes the hero from his eyes, and gives him a ring;
8. The hero takes a harp and sings beautifully, to the amazement of all;
9. The hero appears to have given himself away by his behavior, and slips away from the feast;
10. The hero, with the help of his men, abducts the lady and takes her away to marry another.

In both the *Gesta Herwardi* and the Horn tradition, the hero then heads for home, learning from an old warrior of his father who fails to recognize him that the latter is dead (in the *Gesta Herwardi*, his brother) and that foreigners control the place; the old warrior laments the fact that the hero was not at home to protect it. The hero attacks the infiltrators, defeats them to the great joy of the locals, and takes back control of his home and family, of whom only his mother is left alive. Such a summary barely does justice to the complexity of the overlapping tales, though it does indicate the extent of the parallels.

Still further parallels between the *Gesta Herwardi* and French material are suggested by a lengthy anonymous poem of 3,207 octosyllabic rhymed couplets in Old French with traces of the dialect of Picardy on the life of the monk Eustache Busquet (ca. 1170–1217).[84] The poem itself, now entitled *Li Roman de Witasse Le Moine*, is found in only one manuscript, Paris, Bibliothèque nationale de France, fonds français 1553 (fols. 325v-338v); the manuscript is dated 1284, although the poem itself may be up to sixty years older.[85] In a series of episodes, Eustache, a Benedictine who becomes an outlaw after his father is murdered, evades capture by disguising himself successively as a Cistercian monk (430–543), a shepherd (578–619), a pilgrim (twice: 776–97 and 900–29), a man selling hay (854–99), a coalman (996–1041), a potter (996–1041), a prostitute (1242–83), a peasant (1322–58), a leper (1400–22), a cripple (1423–93), a carpenter (1546–1637), a fisherman

---

84. *Li Roman de Witasse Le Moine: Roman du treizième siècle*, ed. Denis Joseph Conlon (Chapel Hill: University of North Carolina Press, 1972); Kelly, "Eustache the Monk," in Ohlgren, *Medieval Outlaws*, 100–50.

85. Kelly, "Eustache the Monk," 100.

(1778–1819), a pastry cook (1820–81), a minstrel (2168–2216), and a messenger (2217–50). Eustache steals horses (three times: 544–77, 900–29, and 1466–93); in the last case, he steals the count's horse from outside a church, and is given away by the shouts of children, in a fashion that, without the concomitant violence, resembles the episodes involving Grettir and Hereward discussed above. In a further incident, Eustache fools his pursuers by reversing his horseshoes (1495–1545),[86] a trick also employed by Hereward (*Gesta Herwardi*, ch. 28 [26]):

> Interim ergo transuerso modo pedibus equorum suorum ferrum fecit imponere nec perciperetur e uestigiis eorum ubi pergere uellent aut ubi essent. Hoc etiam amicis et commilitonibus mandauit pro quibus tunc miserat ut sic facerent. (154)

> So meanwhile he had the shoes on his horses' feet reversed, so that it could not be determined from their tracks where they wanted to go or where they were. Hereward told his friends and fellow soldiers, for whom he had then sent, to do the same.

Tricks and disguises are associated more with the outlaw Gísli Súrsson (who disguises himself as an idiot out fishing in *Gísla saga*, ch. 26) than with the blunter and more direct Grettir, although Grettir does take on a disguise at the Hegranes-thing (*Grettis saga*, ch. 72), calling himself Gestr ("guest"). Neither Icelandic outlaw uses quite the same disguises of fisherman and potter in quite the same manner employed by Hereward (*Gesta Herwardi*, chs. 26–27).[87]

In yet another cunning stratagem, described in the *Liber de Hida*, Hereward plays dead in a way which again aligns him with both Norse and Norman sources:[88]

> Fertur denique quia semel cum quoddam castrum virtute vellet irrumpere, nec posset, mortuum se finxerat, feretroque impositum cum fallaci luctu ad ecclesiam ipsius castri incautis habitatoribus deferri

---

86. Pickering, "Legend of Hereward," 184.

87. One might note that a fisherman is also involved in Gaimar's account of Hereward and his men smuggling themselves past the surrounding Normans (lines 5504–23). See also Pickering, "Legend of Hereward," 182.

88. See Pickering, "Legend of Hereward," 71.

sepeliendum jusserat. Mox ut securus illatum animadvertit, feretro totus armatus exsiluit castrumque cum habitatoribus fallaciter subjugavit. (*Chronica Monasterii de Hyda*, Edwards, 295)

Finally, it is said that once when he wanted to take a certain castle by force, and could not, that he had pretended to be dead, and, when the inhabitants were caught unawares, had himself placed on a bier for burial inside the same castle. As soon as he knew that he had been carried in safely, he jumped off the bier fully armed, and by a trick conquered the castle and its inhabitants.

Lange speaks of the trick Hereward uses as being told of "the Viking Hasting [*recte* Hásteinn or Hafsteinn] at the siege of Luna," which he wrongly believed to be Rome.[89] The same thing is said twice about Frothi by Saxo Grammaticus in his *Gesta Danorum* (bk. 2, ch. 7, and bk. 3, ch. 8).[90] Haraldr harðráði is also described in several sources as having employed this deception.[91] Leach likewise notes that in a number of cases, "this game of possum was played by Normans or their kin,"[92] and in fact, there has been considerable discussion of the role that the Normans may have played in transmitting tales of this kind.[93]

89. Lange, *English and Icelandic Outlaw-Traditions*, 4.

90. *Gesta Danorum*, Olrik, 38 and 46; Davidson, *History of the Danes*, 1:42 and 50; see also 2:40n10.

91. See further White, *Non-Native Sources*, 100 and 148–50. The passages in question appear as follows: Snorri Sturluson, *Haralds saga Sigurðarsonar*, ch. 10, in *Heimskringla*, Bjarni Aðalbjarnason, 3:80–81; *Morkinskinna*, ed. Finnur Jónsson, Samfund til udgivelse af gammel nordisk litteratur 53 (Copenhagen: Jørgensen, 1932), 73–76; *Fagrskinna*, Bjarni Einarsson, 232–33. See Theodore M. Andersson and Kari Ellen Gade, trans., *Morkinskinna: The Earliest Icelandic Chronicle of the Norwegian Kings (1030–1157)*, Islandica 51 (Ithaca: Cornell University Press, 2000), 141–43; Alison Finlay, trans., "*Fagrskinna*," *a Catalogue of the Kings of Norway* (Leiden: Brill, 2004), 186–87. See also Sigfús Blöndal, *The Varangians of Byzantium*, trans. and rev., Benedikt A. Benediktz (Cambridge: Cambridge University Press, 1978), 72–73, and Klaus Rossenbeck, *Die Stellung der Riddarasǫgur in der altnordischen Prosaliteratur* (PhD diss., Universität Frankfurt, 1970), 70–74.

92. Leach, *Angevin Britain and Scandinavia*, 350.

93. See Frederic Amory, "The Viking Hasting in Franco-Scandinavian Legend," in *Saints, Scholars, and Heroes: Studies in Medieval Culture in Honour of Charles W. Jones*, ed. Margot H. King and Wesley M. Stevens, 2 vols. (Collegeville: Hill Monastic Manuscript Library, 1979): 1:265–86; Paul A. White, "The Latin Men: The Norman Sources of the Scandinavian Kings' Sagas," *JEGP* 98 (1999): 157–69; Jan de Vries, "Normannisches

Against the background of such obvious overlap between the legends of Hereward and Grettir, with other intertexts and parallels in a variety of different languages and texts of differing date, one might well conclude that a good tale well told bears repeating, and agree with the preface to the *Gesta Herwardi*:

> Propterea namque ut estimamus ad magnanimorum operum exempla et ad liberalitatem exercendam profectus erit Herwardum scire quis fuerit et magnanimitates illius audire et opera maxime autem miliciam exercere uolentibus. Vnde monemus aures aduertite et qui diligencius gesta uirorum forcium audire contenditis mentem apponite ut diligenter tanti uiri relatio audiatur qui nec in munitione nec in presidio sed in se ipso confisus solus cum suis regnis et regibus bella intulit et contra principes et tyrannos dimicauit quosque nonnullos deuicit. (76)

> So then it will be useful for us, considering examples of great-hearted exploits and the exercise of generosity, to know who Hereward was and to hear of his great-heartedness and especially for those who want to perform exploits and a warrior's deeds. So we urge you to listen carefully, particularly you who care to hear of the deeds of mighty men, and to pay close attention so that the tale may be told carefully of such a man, who, trusting not in a stronghold or in a fort but in himself alone with his own men waged war on kings and kingdoms, and fought against princes and bullies, and even defeated some.

In such a light, it has been said that "Hereward . . . has a brief life in history, and a long one in romance," and the same thing could surely be said of Grettir.[94] It certainly seems clear that there are numerous, specific, and intriguing parallels that link the *Gesta Herwardi* with Norse literature in general and with *Grettis saga* in particular. It seems also clear that both the *Gesta Herwardi* and *Grettis saga* have

---

Lehngut in den isländischen Königssagas," *Arkiv för nordisk Filologi* 3 (1931): 51–79; Elizabeth M. C. Van Houts, "Scandinavian Influence in Norman Literature of the Eleventh Century," *Anglo-Norman Studies* 6 (1983): 107–21; *The "Gesta Normannorum ducum" Orderic Vitalis, and Robert of Torigni*, ed. Elisabeth M. C. Van Houts, 2 vols. (Oxford: Clarendon Press, 1992–95), 1:xxxvi.

94. Charles Plummer, ed., *Two of the Saxon Chronicles Parallel*, 2 vols. (Oxford: Clarendon Press, 1899), 2:265.

similarly close connections with surviving Anglo-Norman and Franco-Scandinavian texts in both Latin and the Romance vernaculars, and that it is not madness to suppose that Normandy, glancing as it did both north and northwest, may have acted as fertile ground for such cross-pollination. Nor is the *Gesta Herwardi* the only Latin text with English links that bear witness to this kind of lively literary and cultural exchange. When it is recalled that all four of the Anglo-Latin texts considered here survive in no more than one or two manuscripts each, one can only speculate how many more such literary links have been lost. It seems likely that further scrutiny of other Latin texts might well yield still further results. If, in the final analysis, it cannot be said with certainty that Hereward's legend gave rise directly to that of Grettir, nor that the figure of Grettir immediately influenced the author of the *Gesta Herwardi*, the family ties that bind both outlaws, however defined, seem surely secure.[95]

Bibliography

Primary Sources and Translations

Ágrip af Nóregskonunga sögum, Fagrskinna—Nóregs konunga tal. Edited by Bjarni Einarsson. Íslenzk fornrit 29. Reykjavík: Hið íslenzka fornritafélag, 1984.

Andersson, Theodore M., and Kari Ellen Gade, trans. *Morkinskinna: The Earliest Icelandic Chronicle of the Norwegian Kings (1030–1157).* Islandica 51. Ithaca: Cornell University Press, 2000.

The Anglo-Saxon Chronicle 5: MS. C. Edited by Katherine O'Brien O'Keeffe. Cambridge: Brewer, 2001.

Bevis, Trevor A., ed. *"Hereward," Together with "De Gestis Herwardi Saxonis."* Thorney: Westrydale Press, 1982.

Byock, Jesse L., trans. *Grettir's Saga.* Oxford: Oxford World's Classics, 2009.

———— trans. *The Saga of King Hrolf Kraki.* London: Penguin, 1998.

The Chronicle of Hugh Candidus. Edited by W. T. Mellows. London: Oxford University Press, 1949.

Chronicle of John of Worcester. Edited by R. R. Darlington, P. McGurk, and J. Bray. 2 vols. Oxford: Clarendon, 1995.

---

95. I am grateful to both Morgan Dickson and Samantha Zacher for reminding me in different ways of the importance of old ties and of the French connection—the mistakes remain mine.

The Durham Liber vitae: London, British Library, MS Cotton Domi-tian A. VI. Edited by David and Lynda Rollason. 3 vols. and CD-ROM. London: British Library, 2007.

Encomium Emmae Reginae. Edited by Alistair Campbell. Camden Classic Reprints 4. Cambridge: Cambridge University Press, 1998.

L'Estorie des Engleis by Geffrei Gaimar. Edited by Alexander Bell. Anglo-Norman Texts 14–16. Oxford: Blackwell, 1960.

Lestorie Des Engles Solum La Translacion Maistre Geffrei Gaimar. Edited by Thomas D. Hardy and Charles T. Martin. Rolls Series 91. London: Her Majesty's Stationery Office, 1898–99. Repr. Nendeln: Kraus Reprints, 1966.

Fairweather, Janet, trans. *Liber Eliensis: A History of the Isle of Ely from the Seventh Century to the Twelfth.* Woodbridge: Boydell and Brewer, 2005.

Faulkes, Anthony, ed. and trans. *Three Icelandic Outlaw Sagas.* London: Everyman, 2001.

Finlay, Alison, trans. *"Fagrskinna": A Catalogue of the Kings of Norway.* Leiden: Brill, 2004.

Fulk, R. D., Robert E. Bjork, and John D. Niles, eds. *Klaeber's "Beowulf" and "The Fight at Finnsburg."* 4th ed. Toronto: Toronto University Press, 2008.

The "Gesta Normannorum ducum" of William of Jumièges, Orderic Vitalis, and Robert of Torigni. Edited by Elisabeth M. C. Van Houts. 2 vols. Oxford: Clarendon Press, 1992–95.

De Gestis Herwardi: Le gesta di Ervardo. Edited and translated by Alberto Meneghetti. Florence: Edizioni ETS, 2013.

De Gestis Herwardi Saxonis. Edited by S. H. Miller and W. D. Sweeting. *Fenland Notes and Queries* 3 (1895): 7–72.

Giles, J. A., ed., *Vita (sic) Quorundam Anglo-Saxonum: Original Lives of Anglo-Saxons and Others who Lived before the Conquest.* London, 1854.

Grettis saga Ásmundarsonar. Edited by Guðni Jónsson. Íslenzk fornrit 7. Reykjavík: Hið íslenzka fornritafélag, 1956.

Guðni Jónsson, ed. *Fornaldar sögur Norðurlanda.* 4 vols. Reykjavík: Íslendingasagnaútgáfan, 1954.

Harðar saga. Edited by Þórhallur Vilmundarson and Bjarni Vilhjálmsson. Íslenzk fornrit 13. Reykjavík: Hið íslenzka forn-ritafélag, 1991.

Hemings þáttr Áslákssonar. Edited by Gillian Fellows-Jensen. Editiones Arnamagnæanæ B3. Reykjavík: Stofnun Árna Magnús-sonar, 1962.

Hughes, Shaun F. D., trans. "The Saga of Án Bow-bender." In Ohlgren, *Medieval Outlaws,* 290–337.

Íslendingabók, Landnámabók. Edited by Jakob Benediktsson. Íslenzk fornrit 1. Reykjavík: Hið íslenzka fornritafélag, 1986.

Kelly, Thomas E., trans. "Eustache the Monk." In Ohlgren, *Medieval Outlaws,* 100–50.

Liber Eliensis. Edited by E. O. Blake. Camden Third Series 92. London: Royal Historical Society, 1962.

Liber Monasterii de Hyda: Comprising a Chronicle of the Affairs of England from the Settlement of the Saxons to the Reign of King Cnut and a Chartulary of the Abbey of Hyde in Hampshire, A.D. 455–1023. Edited by Edward Edwards. Rerum Britannicarum medii aevi scriptores 45. London: Longmans, 1866.

Michel, Francisque, ed. *Chroniques Anglo-Normandes: Recueil D'extraits Et D'écrits Relatifs À L'histoire De Normandie Et D'angleterre Pendant Les Xie Et Xiie Siècles.* 3 vols. Rouen: E. Frère, 1836–40.

Morkinskinna. Edited by Finnur Jónsson. Samfund til udgivelse af gammel nordisk litteratur 53. Copenhagen: Jørgensen, 1932.

Neckel, Gustav, and Hans Kuhn, eds. *Die Lieder des Codex Regius nebst verwandten Denkmälern.* Vol. 1, *Text.* 5th ed. Germanische Bibliothek. 4. Reihe, Texte. Heidelberg: Carl Winter, 1983.

Ohlgren, Thomas H., ed. *Medieval Outlaws: Twelve Tales in Modern English Translation.* West Lafayette: Parlor, 2005.

Óláfs saga Tryggvasonar en mesta. Edited by Ólafur Halldórsson. Editiones Arnamagnæanæ A1–2. Reykjavík: Stofnun Árna Magnússonar, 1958–61.

Orchard, Andy, trans. *The Elder Edda: A Book of Viking Lore.* London: Penguin Classics, 2011.

The Peterborough Chronicle 1070–1154. Edited by Cecily Clark. 2nd ed. London: Oxford University Press, 1970.

Plummer, Charles, ed. *Two of the Saxon Chronicles Parallel.* 2 vols. Oxford: Clarendon Press, 1899.

Rafn, Carl Christian, ed. *Fornaldar sögur Nordrlanda.* 3 vols. Copenhagen, 1829–30.

Li Roman de Witasse Le Moine: Roman du treizième siècle. Edited by Denis Joseph Conlon. University of North Carolina Studies in Romance Languages and Literatures 126. Chapel Hill: University of North Carolina Press, 1972.

Saga Óláfs Tryggvasonar af Oddr Snorrason munk. Edited by Finnur Jónsson. Copenhagen: Munksgaard, 1932.

Saxo Grammaticus. *Danorum regum heroumque historia, Books X-XVI.* Translated by Eric Christiansen. 3 vols. Oxford: B.A.R., 1980–81.

———. *Gesta Danorum.* Edited by Jørgen Olrik and Hans Ræder. 2 vols. Copenhagen: Munksgaard, 1931–57.

————. *The History of the Danes Book I-IX*. Edited and translated by Hilda Ellis Davidson and Peter Fisher. 2 vols. Cambridge: Brewer, 1979–80.

Snorri Sturluson. *Heimskringla*. Edited by Bjarni Aðalbjarnason. 3 vols. Íslenzk fornrit 26–28. Reykjavík: Hið íslenzka fornritafélag, 1941.

Sturlunga saga. Edited by Gudbrand Vigfusson. 3 vols. Oxford: Clarendon, 1878.

Swanton, Michael, trans. *Three Lives of the Last Englishmen*. New York: Garland, 1984.

————. "The Deeds of Hereward." In Ohlgren, *Medieval Outlaws*, 29–99.

Theodoricus Monachus. *The Ancient History of the Norwegian Kings*. Translated and annotated by David and Ian McDougall. Viking Society for Northern Research Text Series 9. London: University College London, 1998.

————. *Historia de antiquitate regum Norwagiensium*. In *Monumenta Historica Norvegiæ: Latinske kildeskrifter til Noregs historie i middelalderen*, edited by Gustav Storm, 1–68. Kristiania [Oslo]: Brøgger, 1880.

Vatnsdœla saga. Edited by Einar Ól. Sveinsson. Íslenzk fornrit 8. Reykjavík: Hið íslenzka fornritafélag, 1939.

Vestfirðinga sǫgur. Edited by Björn K. Þórólfsson and Guðni Jónsson. Íslenzk fornrit 6. Reykjavík: Hið íslenzka fornritafélag, 1943.

Vita Haroldi: The Romance of the Life of Harold King of England. Edited by Walter de Gray Birch. London: Stock, 1885.

Secondary Sources

Amory, Frederic. "The Viking Hasting in Franco-Scandinavian Legend." In *Saints, Scholars, and Heroes: Studies in Medieval Culture in Honour of Charles W. Jones*, edited by Margot H. King and Wesley M. Stevens, 2:265–86. 2 vols. Collegeville: Hill Monastic Manuscript Library, 1979.

Andersson, Theodore, M. "Sources and Analogues." In *A Beowulf Handbook*, edited by Robert E. Bjork and John D. Niles, 125–48. Lincoln: University of Nebraska Press, 1997.

Ashdown, Margaret. "An Icelandic Account of the Survival of Harold Godwinson." In *The Anglo-Saxons: Studies in Some Aspects of their History and Culture Presented to Bruce Dickins*, edited by Peter Clemoes, 122–36. London: Bowes and Bowes, 1959.

Barlow, Frank. *Edward the Confessor*. Berkeley: University of California Press, 1970.

Baum, Richard Howard. "The Medieval Outlaw: A Study in Protest." Ph.D. diss., University of Utah, 1972.

Benecke, Ingrid. *Der Gute Outlaw*. Tübingen: Niemeyer, 1973.

Blaney, Benjamin. "The Berserk Suitor: The Literary Application of a Stereotyped Theme." *Scandinavian Studies* 54 (1982): 279–94.

———. "The *berserkr*: His Origin and Development in Old Norse Literature." Ph.D. diss., University of Colorado, 1972.

Breen, Gerard. "Personal Names and the Re-creations of *berserkir* and *úlfheðnar*." *Studia Anthroponymica Scandinavica* 15 (1997): 5–38.

Bremmer, Rolf H., Jr. "The *Gesta Herwardi*: Transforming an Anglo-Saxon into an Englishman." In *People and Texts: Relationships in Medieval Literature*, edited by Thea Summerfield and Keith Busby, 29–42. Amsterdam: Rodopi, 2007.

Cohen, Marc. "From Throndheim to Waltham to Chester: Viking and Post-Viking Attitudes in the Survival Legends of Óláfr Tryggvason and Harold Godwinson." In Scott, *The Middle Ages in the North-West*, 143–53.

Cook, Robert. "The Reader in *Grettis saga*." *Saga-Book of the Viking Society* 21 (1984–85): 135–54.

Faulkes, Anthony. "The Myth of the Harold II's Survival in the Scandinavian Sources." In *King Harold II and the Bayeux Tapestry*, edited by Gale R. Owen-Crocker, 53–64. Woodbridge: Boydell, 2005.

Fjalldal, Magnús. *The Long Arm of Coincidence: The Frustrated Connection between Beowulf and Grettis saga*. Toronto: University of Toronto Press, 1998.

Freeman, Edward Augustus. *The History of the Norman Conquest of England*. 6 vols. Oxford: Clarendon Press, 1867–79.

Grundy, Stephan. "Shapeshifting and *Berserkergang*." In *Translation, Transformation, and Transubstantiation*, edited by Carol Poster and Richard Utz, 104–22. Evanston, IL: Northwestern University Press, 1998.

Hart, Cyril. *The Danelaw*. London: Hambledon Continuum, 1992.

———. "Hereward the Wake." *Proceedings of the Cambridge Antiquarian Society* 65 (1974): 28–40.

Hayward, John. "Hereward the Outlaw." *Journal of Medieval History* 14 (1988): 293–304.

Head, Victor. *Hereward*. Stroud: Alan Sutton, 1995.

Hughes, Shaun F. D. "The Literary Antecedents of *Áns saga bogsveigis*." *Mediaeval Scandinavia* 9 (1976): 198–235.

Jones, Timothy Scott. "Redemptive Fictions: The Contexts of Outlawry on Medieval English Chronicle and Romance." Ph.D. diss., University of Illinois at Champaign-Urbana, 1994.

Keen, Maurice. *The Outlaws of Medieval Legend.* 3rd ed. London: Routledge, 2000.

Keynes, Simon. "Cnut's Earls." In *The Reign of Cnut, King of England, Denmark, and Norway,* edited by A. R. Rumble, 44–88. London: Leicester University Press, 1994.

Lange, Joost de. *The Relation and Development of English and Icelandic Outlaw-Traditions.* Haarlem: Willink, 1935.

Lawson, M. K. *Cnut: The Danes in England in the Early Eleventh Century.* London: Longman, 1993.

Leach, Henry Goddard. *Angevin Britain and Scandinavia.* Cambridge, MA: Harvard University Press, 1921.

Lukman, Nils. "The Raven Banner and the Changing Ravens: A Viking Miracle from Carolingian Court Poetry to Saga and Arthurian Romance." *Classica et Mediaevalia* 19 (1958): 133–51.

Lumpkin, Bernard I. "The Making of a Medieval Outlaw: Code and Community in the Robin Hood Legend, 1400–1600." Ph.D. diss., Harvard University, 1999.

Lundgren, Timothy J. "Hereward and Outlawry in Fenland Culture: A Study of Local Narrative and Tradition in Medieval England." Ph.D. diss., Ohio State University, 1996.

Matthews, Stephen. "The Content and Construction of the *Vita Haroldi.*" In *King Harold II and the Bayeux Tapestry,* edited by Gale R. Owen-Crocker, 65–73. Woodbridge: Boydell, 2005.

Nelles, Walter R. "The Ballad of Hind Horn." *Journal of American Folklore* 22 (1909): 42–62.

Olrik, Axel. "Siward den digre, en vikingesaga fra de danske in Nordengland." *Arkiv för nordisk filologi* 19 (1903): 199–223.

Olson, Oscar L. *The Relation of the Hrólfs Saga Kraka and the Bjark-arímur to Beowulf.* Chicago: Chicago University Press, 1916.

Orchard, Andy. *A Critical Companion to Beowulf.* Cambridge: Brewer, 2005.

———. "The Literary Background to the *Encomium Emmae Reginae.*" *Journal of Medieval Latin* 11 (2001): 156–84.

———. *Pride and Prodigies: Studies in the Monsters of the Beowulf Manuscript.* Rev. ed. Toronto: University of Toronto Press, 2003.

Owen-Crocker, Gale R., ed. *King Harold II and the Bayeux Tapestry.* Woodbridge: Boydell, 2005.

Pickering, James Dunbar. "The Legend of Hereward the Saxon: An Investigation of *De Gestis Herwardi Saxonis,* Its Historical Basis, Its Debt to Saga and Early Romance, Its Place in English Literary History." Ph.D. diss., Columbia University, 1964.

Rauer, Christine. *Beowulf and the Dragon: Parallels and Analogues.* Cambridge: Boydell and Brewer, 2000.

Rex, Peter. *The English Resistance: The Underground War Against the Normans.* Stroud: Tempus, 2004.

———. *Hereward: the Last Englishman.* Stroud: Tempus, 2005.

Roffe, David. "Hereward 'the Wake' and the Barony of Bourne: A Reassessment of a Fenland Legend." *Lincolnshire History and Archaeology* 29 (1994): 7–10.

Rossenbeck, Klaus. *Die Stellung der Riddarasǫgur in der altnordischen Prosaliteratur.* PhD diss., Universität Frankfurt, 1970.

Schmidt, P. G. "Biblisches und hagiographisches Kolorit in den Gesta Herwardi." In *The Bible in the Medieval World: Essays in Memory of Beryl Smalley,* edited by K. Walsh and D. Wood, 85–95. Studies in Church History. Subsidia 4. Oxford: Blackwell, 1985.

Scott, F. S. "Earl Waltheof of Northumbria." *Archaeologia Aeliana* 30 (1952): 149–215.

Scott, Tom, and Pat Starkey, eds. *The Middle Ages in the North-West.* Oxford: Leopard's Head Press, 1995.

Short, Ian. "Gaimar's Epilogue and Geoffrey of Monmouth's *Liber vetustissimus.*" *Speculum* 79 (1994): 323–43.

Sieg, Gerd. "Die Zweikämpfe der Isländersagas." *Zeitschrift für deutsches Altertum* 95 (1966): 1–27.

Sigfús Blöndal. *The Varangians of Byzantium.* Translated and revised by Benedikt A. Benediktz. Cambridge: Cambridge University Press, 1978.

Sigurður Nordal. *Sturla Þórðarson og Grettis saga.* Studia Islandica 4. Reykjavík: Mál og menning, 1938.

Stein, Robert M. *Reality Fictions: Romance, History, and Governmental Authority, 1025–1180.* Notre Dame: University of Notre Dame Press, 2006.

Stenton, Frank M. *Anglo-Saxon England.* 3rd ed. Oxford: Oxford University Press, 1971.

Stitt, J. Michael. *Beowulf and the Bear's Son: Epic, Saga, and Fairytale in Northern Germanic Tradition.* Albert Bates Lord Studies in Oral Tradition 8. New York: Garland, 1992.

Thacker, Alan. "The Cult of King Harold at Chester." In Scott, *The Middle Ages in the North-West,* 155–76.

Thomas, Hugh M. "The *Gesta Herwardi,* the English and their Conquerors." *Anglo-Norman Studies* 21 (1998): 213–32.

Turville-Petre, Gabriel. "Outlawry." In *Sjötíu ritgerðir helgaðar Jakobi Benediktssyni 20 júlí 1977,* edited by Einar G. Pétursson and Jónas Kristjánsson, 2: 769–78. 2 vols. Reykjavík: Stofnun Árna Magnússonar, 1977.

Van Houts, Elisabeth M. C. "Hereward and Flanders." *Anglo-Saxon England* 28 (1999): 201–23.

———. "Scandinavian Influence in Norman Literature of the Eleventh Century." *Anglo-Norman Studies* 6 (1983): 107–21.

Vries, Jan de. "Normannisches Lehngut in den isländischen Königs-sagas." *Arkiv för nordisk Filologi* 3 (1931): 51–79.

White, Paul A. "The Latin Men: The Norman Sources of the Scandinavian Kings' Sagas." *Journal of English and Germanic Philology* 98 (1999): 157–69.

———. *Non-Native Sources for the Scandinavian Kings' Sagas*. New York: Routledge, 2005.

Williams, Ann. *The English and the Norman Conquest*. Woodbridge: Boydell and Brewer, 1995.

Wilson, R. M. *The Lost Literature of Medieval England*. 2nd ed. London: Methuen, 1970.

Wright, C. E. *The Cultivation of Saga in Anglo-Saxon England*. London: Oliver and Boyd, 1936.

"Jafnan segir inn ríkri ráð"

Proverbial Allusion and the Implied
Proverb in Fóstbrœðra saga

Richard L. Harris
UNIVERSITY OF SASKATCHEWAN

Fóstbrœðra saga is remarkable in its textual and literary-critical history as an object of several long-standing and generally inconclusive debates. The date of its most original, consciously composed form, and how that form is represented by its varied extant witnesses, are questions of primary interest. Agreement upon these matters would inevitably influence if not determine the resolution of a secondary problem: the point of the saga itself, its moral and ethical focus, its thematic force. However, in the absence of any foreseeable unanimity of opinion regarding questions of textual identity and origin, it might be helpful to search for the meaning of this saga by a purely internal method, using a phraseological approach to its texts, considering the value rendered them by proverbs and allusions to proverbs that can be seen to inform individual but crucial episodes of the narrative as a whole. Specifically, this paper is concerned with ways in which the traditional Old Icelandic proverb "Jafnan segir inn ríkri ráð" (The more powerful always decides)[1] is arguably illustrated and identified by allusion in *Fóstbrœðra saga*, imbuing that narrative as a whole with a paroemial force that embeds it in the communal wisdom of the saga's original audiences.

---

1. See Samuel Singer, ed., *Thesaurus Proverbiorum Medii Aevi*, 13 vols. (Berlin: de Gruyter, 1996–2002), henceforth TPMA, 4:460, and the *Appendix* below. For extensive attestation of this medieval proverb in Icelandic sources, and for proverbial materials in *Fóstbrœðra saga* generally, see also "Proverbs and Proverbial Materials in *Fóstbrœðra saga*" in my online *Concordance to the Proverbs and Proverbial Materials in the Old Icelandic Sagas*: http://www.usask.ca/english/icelanders/proverbs_FBRS.html.

1

Textual discussion of *Fóstbrœðra* first became complex in the 1930s, initiated by Vera Lachmann's observation that the Hauksbók version (ca. 1300) had some of the same stylistic features found in what had previously been assumed to be interpolations in the saga as it occurs in the obviously later Flateyjarbók (ca. 1400).[2] Thus was first called into question the traditionally held assumption that Hauksbók comprised the simpler and more authentic version, with the fuller saga, and its oddly floreate passages, combined as it is in Flateyjarbók with *Óláfs saga helga*, as a later and expanded redaction. Lachmann's views were developed further by Sigurður Nordal in the commentary accompanying his 1943 edition of the saga, with predictable reactions in succeeding decades when scholars noticed in Hauksbók what they took to be the relatively late stylistic features of the once presumed interpolations of Flateyjarbók, by this time generally accepted to have been expurgated from the now derivative Hauksbók.[3]

2

Jónas Kristjánsson's detailed meditation *Um Fóstbrœðrasögu*, with its various evidence for a later thirteenth-century date of composition, sees the stylistic peculiarities of the text as not inconsonant with features of the learned style of Old Icelandic prose, which in the fourteenth century came to be marked by florid style.[4] Of special pertinence to this paper are his conclusions regarding the first chapter of *Fóstbrœðra*, an episode in which Grettir Ásmundarson is saved from execution at the hands of some poor farmers in Ísafjǫrðr by intervention of the aristocratic Þorbjǫrg digra Óláfsdóttir pá, who rules the district when her chieftain husband, Vermundr inn mjóvi Þorgrímsson, is absent from home.[5]

---

2. See Vera Lachmann, *Das Alter der Harðarsaga*, Palaestra 183 (Leipzig: Mayer & Müller, 1932), 222–23.

3. See Sigurður Nordal, "Handrit. Aldur. Höfundur," in *Vestfirðinga sǫgur*, ed. Björn K. Þórólfsson and Guðni Jónsson, Íslenzk fornrit 6 (Reykjavík: Hið íslenzka fornritafélag, 1943), lxxii-lxxiii.

4. See Jónas Kristjánsson, *Um Fóstbrœðrasögu* (Reykjavík: Stofnun Árna Magnússonar, 1972), 251–91.

5. Ibid., 81–82.

The story is omitted from the otherwise longer Flateyjarbók redaction but occurs in its related manuscript, Membrana Regia Deperdita, as well as in Möðruvallabók, whose text, with that of Hauksbók, is seen by Jónas Kristjánsson as deriving from a source different from that of the former two books. The fragmentary witness to *Fóstbrœðra* in Hauksbók makes it impossible to know if it contained this episode of Grettir's narrow escape from hanging. Formerly regarded as an inexplicable interpolation indebted to chapter 52 of *Grettis saga*, the passage was now granted undisputed textual authenticity by Jónas Kristjánsson, who argued persuasively that the borrowing had worked in the other direction.

Earlier views of the Ísafjorðr episode's spurious existence at the start of the Möðruvallabók text were justified by its apparent irrelevance to anything that followed in the saga, since Grettir himself appears in it later only as a peripheral figure. However, the test of narrative consistency or coherence in medieval Icelandic literature has been shown to rely on more than mere linear progression. Ian Maxwell's study of *Njála* introduced a critical concept that seems useful here: "the principle of the integrity of episodes." "Sagas prefer to deal with whole episodes, not pieces or aspects or reflections of them."[6] Thus, the whole story of Grettir's brush with death forms the first chapter of *Fóstbrœðra saga*, in its entirety seeming irrelevant to the story that follows, unless one takes into account Maxwell's corollary of this concept, the "partial independence" of episodes. That is, although such scenes are recounted in a way that renders them whole in themselves, they are also part of the extended composition in which they occur: "Is there not also a rhetoric of narrative by which, without explicit comment, the author may keep his readers on track?"[7] The process of reading such episodes, then, involves seeking their thematic unity with the text in which they are embedded rather than attempting to place them in a logical and linear progression of narrative.[8] Let us

---

6. Ian Maxwell, "Pattern in *Njáls saga*," *Saga-Book* 15 (1957–61): 25.

7. Ibid., 26.

8. Maxwell's observations are similar in their critical impact to those of Adrien Bonjour, whose classic study of the digressions in *Beowulf* demonstrated how, separate and independent in themselves, they nevertheless can be read for the establishment of value in the main narrative in which they are embedded. See *The Digressions in Beowulf*, Medium Ævum Monographs 5 (Oxford: Basil Blackwell, 1950). Further to this, Jonathan D. M. Evans argued that the episodic character of medieval narrative cannot be studied

consider how the Ísafjǫrður episode, now generally accepted as part of the original text of the saga, can be read for its preludic value in a thematic rather than linear sense.

Such an undertaking has in fact already been accomplished by Giselle Gos in an essay concerned with certain women in *Fóstbrœðra saga*, whom she takes to be presented by the composer as wise mediators between outlaws and society—Grettir on the one hand, and the *fóstbrœðr* on the other. Thus, Gos would see the preludic quality of chapter 1 in *Fóstbrœðra saga* as constituting "the comparison between the foster-brothers and Grettir, their relationships to the communities, and the need for mediators in those relationships, as well as the large part women play in that social mediation in Iceland."[9] For Gos, the point of the saga is in part "the degree to which the women's roles in mediation parallel King Óláfr's."[10] This careful discussion of portions of *Fóstbrœðra* seems to touch upon a theme of interest to the composer of the saga. However, I will consider here the possibility that a shift in emphasis in our reading of elements of the first episode might suggest that the saga's composer had concerns of a broader and more comprehensive perspective than Gos has envisaged, and that these concerns are more clearly traceable through a wider range of the narrative.

A comparison of this episode with its presumably derived counterpart in chapter 52 of *Grettis saga* shows that the situation of Vermundr and his wife is established more fully in *Fóstbrœðra*. In addition, as the wise and stately woman takes up her viceregal duties on this occasion, she does so having first learned of the impending event at home, rather than more or less stumbling upon the gallows scene as she does in *Grettis saga*. Furthermore, in the latter saga she argues against his execution on the grounds that "executing Grettir will be more than you men of Isafjord can handle, because he is a man of renown and great family, even though fortune does not favor him" (*ofráð mun þat verða yðr Ísfirðingum, at taka Gretti*

---

productively in Aristotelian terms; this episodic tendency gives "evidence of the cultural patterns creating and sustaining them and investing them with meaning." "Episodes in Analysis of Medieval Narrative," *Style* 20 (1986): 128; see also 134.

9. Giselle Gos, "Women as a Source of *heilræði*, 'Sound Counsel': Social Mediation and Community Integration in *Fóstbrœðra saga*," *JEGP* 108 (2009): 288.

10. Ibid., 298.

af lífi, því at hann er maðr frægr ok stórættaðr, þó at hann sé eigi gæfumaðr).[11] Clearly, the primary rationale of her statement asserting her authority in *Grettis saga* is that Grettir, like Þorbjǫrg digra Óláfsdóttir pá herself, is of aristocratic background and that he is more than they can handle, both physically and socially. The rather comical scene prior to her entrance upon it has already demonstrated the incompetence of the captor farmers, with each excusing himself on ridiculously flimsy grounds from the responsibility of holding the dangerous *skógarmaðr* captive until Vermundr returned from his trip to the Alþingi. Nothing in this text shows Þorbjörg explicitly imposing her will upon the farmers—rather, modeling herself as a protective ruler of the neighborhood, she sternly extracts a promise from Grettir to cause no more trouble and take no vengeance upon his captors. Showing excessive restraint, he agrees and is immediately released.[12]

Þorbjǫrg's role is different in *Fóstbrœðra*, where the outlaw's privileged family background is also mentioned. Here, though, she adds, "His kinsmen will take his death badly, even though he is regarded as overbearing by many" (*mun frændum hans þykkja skaði um hann, þótt hann sé við marga menn ódæll*), calling attention to likely repercussions that could extend beyond his captors' control if they go though with the hanging. In response to her assertion of authority, "His life will not be forfeit on this occasion if I have any say in the matter" (*Eigi mun hann nú at sinni af lífi tekinn, ef ek má ráða*), they reply, "Right or wrong, you have the power to prevent him from being executed" (*Hafa muntu ríki til þess, at hann sé eigi af lífi tekinn, hvárt sem þat er rétt eða rangt*).[13] Gos sees as most important here the fact that "the verb used to describe Þorbjǫrg's

---

11. Translations of the sagas, unless otherwise noted, are from Viðar Hreinsson, ed., *The Complete Sagas of Icelanders*, 5 vols. (Reykjavík: Leifur Eiríksson, 1997), henceforth CSI, here: 2:131. The Icelandic original is cited from the *Íslenzk fornrit* editions (see Bibliography), here: ÍF 7:169, ch. 52. Page references to the aforementioned edtions apply to all subsequent quotations from the same until otherwise indicated.

12. For a perceptive psychological study of Grettir, see Robert Cook, "The Reader in *Grettis Saga*," *Saga-Book* 21 (1984–85): 133–54; "Reading for Character in *Grettis Saga*," in *Sagas of the Icelanders: A Book of Essays*, ed. John Tucker (New York: Garland, 1989), 226–40. The importance of familial background and social class to Grettir's motivation is elucidated in Kathryn Hume, "The Thematic Design of *Grettis Saga*," *JEGP* 77 (1974): 469–86.

13. CSI 2:330; ÍF 6:122, ch. 1.

actions is 'ráða' (judge/counsel/advise)."[14] In my argument I would
add to that the term "ríki," used by the poor farmers to denote
Þorbjǫrg's advantage by virtue of her power to control the situation
and its denouement. Throughout the saga there are incidents in which
reference is explicitly made to characters' possession and assertion of
their power to exercise their will to judge, to decide issues, to control
others, frequently with the term *ráð* or *ráða*, and sometimes with a
form of *ríki* in the text, or with situational description in which such
power is implied or contested. The point of this episode, in any case,
is clearly marked by the composer himself: "It can be seen from this
incident that Thorbjorg was a woman of firm character" (*Í þessum
atburði má hér sýnask, hversu mikill skǫrungr hon var*).

3

Indeed, readers even partially familiar with the traditional Icelandic
paroemial inventory cannot get very far in *Fóstbrœðra saga* without
the proverb "Jafnan segir inn ríkri ráð" intruding upon their consciousness. First attested for Old Norse in line 89 of *Málsháttakvæði*,[15] a
poem attributed to Bishop Bjarni Kolbeinsson, composed ca. 1200, this
proverb's force is often implicitly celebrated in the *Íslendingasögur*.
The saga figures' chronic obsession with asserting and maintaining
the right to decide, to have control over their social environment, was
carefully examined by Robert Cook in his 1971 paper, "The Sagas of
Icelanders as Dramas of the Will."[16] "Borrowing the medieval division
of the soul into three faculties—reason, emotions, will—we can say
that the saga treatment of character centers almost exclusively on the
will, to the neglect of the other two faculties."[17] Recounting examples
from a selection of several types of scenes in the sagas—whetting,
requests for aid, trickery, persuasion of reluctant persons, warnings,
obstinacy, and wise refusals—Cook elucidates ways in which "saga

---

14. Gos, "Women as a Source," 285.

15. Finnur Jónsson, ed., *Den norsk-isländske skjaldedigtning*, vols. B1–2, Rettet tekst (Copenhagen: Gyldendal, 1912–15), B2:138–45.

16. In *Proceedings of the First International Saga Conference, University of Edin-burgh, 1971*, ed. Peter Foote et al. (London: The Viking Society for Northern Research, 1973), 88–113.

17. Ibid., 91.

characters express themselves, and relate to each other primarily on the level of will."[18] With the development of feud theory, especially in the decades following Cook's paper, we might now see his observations, apt in themselves, as having reference to the competitive behavior of individuals in a society where resolution of conflict is sought in the processes of feud.

A pervasive social urge to assert control over territory would understandably be expressed in personal terms as one's insistence upon having one's way, in small matters as well as in larger ones. "Jafnan segir inn ríkri ráð" would then express communal wisdom regarding the anticipated outcome of any feud conflict. In any case, as Þorbjǫrg in chapter 1 of *Fóstbrœðra saga* makes clear to her farmers that it is not her will that they execute Grettir, and as they in turn make clear to her that, right or, as they believe, wrong, she has the power to impose her will upon them, the practical force of this unspoken proverb is abundantly evident in this integral preludic episode. That force is then echoed repeatedly by successive events and relationships treated by the composer throughout the saga, even though the proverb itself is never explicitly iterated in the narrative.

4

The idea that the stories of the *Íslendingasögur* are given thematic clarification by their composers' use of proverbs is nothing new. As Guðbrandur Vigfússon, in his commentary on *Hrafnkels saga,* observes of them, "These saws are to a Saga what the gnomic element is to a Greek play."[19] F. York Powell, in introducing his translation of *Færeyinga saga,* echoes these thoughts: "These idioms and saws, and such laconisms . . . are the very life-blood of a true Saga; where they abound, they are the infallible tests of a good tradition, ripened on the lips of good narrators; where they are absent, the story is the work of the scribe writing from his own head without the genuine impulses of the story-teller before his audience."[20] While, as today's readers will be

---

18. Ibid., 94.

19. Gudbrand Vigfusson and F. York Powell, eds., *Origines Islandicae,* 2 vols. (Oxford: Clarendon Press, 1905), 1:492.

20. Frederick York Powell, trans., *Færeyinga saga, or The Tale of Thrond of Gate,* Northern Library 2 (London: David Nutt, 1896), xxxix.

particularly aware, Powell's faith in the "true" results of what developed as the Free Prose understanding of oral saga traditions seems now without useful foundation, and while recently it has become more obvious that the composers themselves used proverbial material quite consciously and explicitly for their literary purposes, Powell's understanding of the importance of such texts to the narratives he studied is well justified by our own observations.

The process of proverbial allusion would be best understood in the context of a discussion of the definition of those texts we term "proverbs." In some respects, this discussion began rather early in Western society, with the coining of the words *paroemia* in Greek and *proverbium* in Latin. The former has roots that might be interpreted as "words by the road" and the latter's signified as "words put forth." B. J. Whiting summarized Aristotle's views of the proverb as "a short saying of philosophic nature, of great antiquity, the product of the masses rather than the classes, constantly applicable, and appealing because it bears a semblance to universal truth."[21] However, discussion subsequent to that of the Greek philosophers brought with it less certainty as to what constitutes those texts we call proverbs. In more recent times Archer Taylor complained, "The definition of a proverb is too difficult to repay the undertaking; and should we fortunately combine in a single definition all the essential elements and give each the proper emphasis, we should not even then have a touchstone."[22] In this absence of theoretical clarity, he concludes with a working definition: "Let us be content with recognizing that a proverb is a saying current among the folk."[23]

And yet, addressing that impossibility of strict definition, he says, most significantly, "An incommunicable quality tells us this sentence is proverbial and that one is not."[24] Many definers of the proverb since Taylor, and most before him, insist upon the attested currency of a text for it to be considered paroemial. Such a qualification, however, is one external to any universal structural understanding of what all

---

21. Bartlett Jere Whiting, "The Nature of the Proverb," in *When Evensong and Morrowsong Accord: Three Essays on the Proverb*, ed. Joseph Harris (Cambridge, MA: Harvard University Press, 1994), 56.

22. Archer Taylor, *The Proverb* (Cambridge, MA: Harvard University Press, 1931), 3.

23. Ibid.

24. Ibid.

such sayings must have in common, that is, the feature or features that project the "incommunicable" quality of which Taylor speaks. The actual existence of such a puzzling quality is clarified most usefully by Shirley Arora, who identifies a set of linguistic markers, the greater density of which in a text increases its chances of being perceived as proverbial in nature.[25] Her work indicates that we have the grammatical competence to generate and recognize such markers, whose structural and perhaps lexical features will signal that the content itself bears a burden of communal wisdom. In fact, as Arora's survey demonstrates, artificially manufactured proverbs, non-current texts containing the specified features, tend to be perceived as proverbs even when they are not so by virtue of use and currency. Thus, the definition of those texts we call proverbs need not require reference to currency, although we may naturally assume that they might be current, given their didactic value. Rather the "internal definition," here by analogy to Ferdinand de Saussure and his distinction regarding linguistics as the "internal" approach to language, involves the study of linguistic features that can be observed to accompany such texts.[26]

With this theoretical context of the proverb's definition established, we may proceed to consider proverbial allusion, how it functions, and its potential force in saga narrative. Such allusion is first discussed by Erasmus in the preface to his *Adages*, where he remarks that their use and appreciation in literature necessitate a comprehensive knowledge of proverbs in their base form in order to understand more fully what one is reading:

> Even if there were no other use for proverbs, at the very least they
> are not only helpful but necessary for the understanding of the best
> authors, that is, the oldest. Most of these are textually corrupt, and
> in this respect they are particularly so, especially as proverbs have a
> touch of the enigmatic, so that they are not understood even by readers

---

25. "The Perception of Proverbiality," *Proverbium* 1 (1984): 1–38.

26. Comparing the study of linguistics to a game of chess, Saussure distinguishes between that which is external and that which is internal to our understanding of the game: "In each instance one can determine the nature of the phenomenon by applying this rule: everything that changes the system in any way is internal." Ferdinand De Saussure, *Course in General Linguistics*, trans. Wade Baskin (New York: Philosophical Library, 1959), 23. Thus, the contextual use of the proverbial string is external to its nature, whereas the structure of the string is crucial to its generation and recognition.

of some learning; and then they are often inserted disconnectedly, sometimes in a mutilated state . . . . Occasionally they are alluded to in one word, as in Cicero in his Letters to Atticus: "Help me, I beg you; 'prevention,' you know," where he refers to the proverb "Prevention is better than cure."[27]

Clearly, competence in a culture's proverbial inventory is the best way to be prepared for an awareness, or understanding, of such allusions.

"Earlier scholars have overstated the fixity of proverbs," observes Wolfgang Mieder. "In actual use, especially in the case of intentional speech play, proverbs are quite often manipulated."[28] He refers us to Norrick's comments in *How Proverbs Mean*, where—speaking of the didactic quality of proverbs—the latter notes that "mention of one crucial recognizable phrase serves to call forth the entire proverb. Let us designate this minimal recognizable unit as the kernel of the proverb . . . . Proverbs bear much greater social, philosophical and psychological significance for speakers than do other idiomatic units."[29] The semantic density of proverbial material thus impresses such texts upon our consciousness. "Consequently a speaker can call forth a particular proverb for his hearer with a brief allusion to its kernel" (Norrick, 45). The kernel of the proverb in *Fóstbrœðra* operative in defining the saga's thematic coherence would then be composed primarily of (*segja*) *ráð*(*a*) with secondary qualification in the term *rík*(*ri*).[30]

5

The second chapter of the saga develops this theme as it introduces the two heroes and then a local chieftain, Þorgils Arason, as "powerful,

---

27. *Collected Works of Erasmus*, trans. M. M. Phillips and R. A. B. Mynors, vol. 31, *Adages Ii1 to Iv100* (Toronto: University of Toronto Press, 1982), 18.

28. Wolfgang Mieder, *Proverbs: A Handbook* (Westport, CT: Greenwood Press, 2004), 7.

29. Neal Norrick, *How Proverbs Mean: Semantic Studies in English Proverbs* (Berlin: Mouton, 1985), 45.

30. See Bjarni Vilhjálmsson and Óskar Halldórsson, *Íslenzkir málshættir*, 2nd ed. (Reykjavík: Almenna bókafélagið, 1982), 268, *s.v.* "ríkur," for variant forms of the proverb.

honest, wise and well-liked" (*vitr ok vinsæll, ríkr ok ráðvandr*).[31] The latter term, "ráðvandr," is defined by Guðbrandur Vigfússon as "'heeding one's *ráð*,' honest, upright."[32] In opposition to this mature wisdom, the composer goes on to describe the non-productive dynamic in the relationship between Þorgils' cousin, Þorgeirr, and Þormóðr, who are said to be "alike in temperament" (*í mǫrgu skapglíkir*). "Both also felt early on—and it later turned out to be true—that they would die fighting, since neither was the kind of man to back off from or give in to anyone he came up against" (*Snimmendis sagði þeim svá hugr um, sem síðar bar raun á, at þeir myndi vápnbitnir verða, því at þeir váru ráðnir til at láta sinn hlut hvergi eða undir leggja, við hverja menn sem þeir ætti málum at skipta*). On these grounds, the two undertake the, here emphatically pagan, ritual of declaring brotherhood: "They thus swore that whoever survived the other would avenge his death" (*Því tóku þeir þat ráð með fastmælum, at sá þeira skyldi hefna annars, er lengr lifði*).[33] The narrator clearly disapproves of this *ráð* from a Christian perspective: "Though people called themselves Christians in those days, Christianity was a new and very undeveloped religion and many of the sparks of heathendom still flickered, manifesting themselves as undesirable customs" (*En þó at þá væri menn kristnir kallaðir, þá var þó í þann tíð ung kristni ok mjǫk vangǫr, svá at margir gneistar heiðninnar váru þó þá eptir ok í óvenju lagðir*).[34]

Their subsequent unpopular behavior in the neighborhood upon their formalization of this agreement leads to complaints, and Vermundr, the powerful authority whose position was already conveyed to the saga audience in chapter 1 with the decisive actions of his wife, is called upon to intervene. Exercising his power by banishing Þorgeirr's family from Ísafjǫrðr, where they had settled without legal permission, he voices his anticipation of a quieter district: "and it is our hope that Thormod will be less unruly if he parts company with Thorgeir" (*væntum vér ok, at minni stormr standi af Þormóði, ef þeir Þorgeirr skiljask*).[35] Hávarr's acquiescence is expressed in terms

31. CSI 2:331; ÍF 6:124, ch. 2.
32. Richard Cleasby and Gudbrand Vigfusson, *An Icelandic–English Dictionary*, 2nd ed. (Oxford: Clarendon Press, 1957), henceforth CV, 487b.
33. CSI 2:331; ÍF 6:125, ch. 2.
34. CSI 2:331; ÍF 6:124, ch. 2.
35. CSI 2:332; ÍF 6:126, ch. 2.

recalling the proverb whose kernel is under discussion as he remarks, with some truculence, "Vermund, *you have the power to make me leave* Isafjord with all my belongings, but I expect *Thorgeir will want to decide* for himself where he stays" (*Ráða muntu því, Vermundr, at vér munum ráðask í brott ór Ísafirði með fé várt, en eigi veit ek, nema Þorgeirr vili ráða vistum sínum*). Vermundr thus has the power to force Hávarr's household from Ísafjǫrðr, but the wayfarings of Þorgeirr are another matter, for him to *ráða* as he wills, and thus beyond anyone's control, with the predictable result that "despite his youth, he was an unwelcome guest at most places he visited" (*ok var hann mǫrgum mǫnnum nǫkkurr andvaragestr, þar sem hann kom, þó at hann væri á ungum aldri*).

In the next episode the chieftain Jǫðurr of Skeljabrekka is the initiator in a horse-borrowing conflict with Þorgeirr's father. "*He had authority in the district*, but was ambitious and slew many man men while rarely paying compensation for the lives he took" (*ríkr í heraðinu ok stórráðr, vígamaðr mikill ok bœtti menn sjaldan fé, þótt hann vægi*). Hávarr allows him to take along one of his horses on a trip for flour but qualifies this permission, "*But I'd like you to return the horse* to me on your way back and take it no farther" (*ok vil ek, at þú látir hestinn hér eptir, er þú ferr aptr, ok hafir þú eigi lengra*). Upon the return journey, however, Jǫðurr decides to renege, despite the warning of his companions: "You *can* do that if you wish, but Havar has never looked kindly on broken agreements" (*Gera máttu þat, ef þú vill, en eigi hefir Hávari jafnan líkat, ef af því væri brugðit, er hann vildi vera láta*).[36] As they anticipated, Hávarr objects, "*I don't want the horse to go any farther*" (*Eigi vil ek, at nú fari hestrinn lengra*) and Jǫðurr asserts his own will, answering, "*We shall have the horse with or without your consent*" (*Þó munu vér hafa hestinn, þótt þú vilir eigi ljá*). "*That remains to be seen*" (*Svá mun vera, at þat sé*), comments Hávarr, who, proceeding to attack Jǫðurr, is then killed by him. When news of his father's slaying reaches Þorgeirr, he seeks redress at Skeljabrekka, where Jǫðurr advises him that he is not accustomed to pay compensation for his slayings. "'I did not know that,' says Thorgeir, 'but whatever the case, it is my duty to seek compensation from you now since I stand closest to the man you have slain'" ("*Ókunnigt er mér þat,*"

---

36. CSI 2:332; ÍF 6:127, ch. 2.

*segir Þorgeirr; "en hvat sem um þat er, þá kømr þetta til mín, at leita
eptir þessum vígsbótum, því at mér er nær hǫggvit"*).[37] When Jǫðurr
refuses to alter his discouraging custom, Þorgeirr delivers his ultimatum,
"*It's for you to decide how much you pay,* and *it's for me to decide
whether I accept it or not*" (*Þér munuð ráða, hvern sóma þér vilið
gera, en vér munum ráða þykkju várri*).[38] Having killed Jǫðurr in
vengeance, Þorgeirr reports back to his mother, Þórelfr, who tells him to
stay the night before seeking protection with Þorgils, since "Tomorrow,
men will come here looking for you and *we don't have the strength to
protect you* against a large party" (*Hér munu menn koma á morgin
at leita þín, ok hǫfum vér eigi ríki til at halda þik fyrir fjǫlmenni*).[39]

The lines quoted from dialogue in these two scenes contain lexical
evidence, which I have italicized, here as elsewhere in this essay,
of the main weight of their import—the conflicts over horse and
compensation are delivered in terms of "*vilja,*" "*ráða,*" and "*ríki,*" in
accordance with what we might expect from the rhetoric of feud and
its literary expression in Cook's dramas of the will. In commenting
on the skilled bravery of Þorgeirr, a lad of fifteen, taking vengeance
on a great chieftain for his father's death, the composer employs one
of those controversial *Fóstbrœðra* passages mentioned above, slipping
as they do into ecclesiastical rhetoric:

And yet it was no great wonder since the Almighty Creator had forged
in Thorgeir's breast such a strong and sturdy heart that he was as fear-
less and brave as a lion in whatever trials or tribulations befell him.
And as all good things come from God, so too does steadfastness, and
it is given unto all bold men together with a free will that they may
themselves choose whether they do good or evil. Thus Jesus Christ has
made Christians his sons and not his slaves, so that he might reward
all according to their deeds." (CSI 2:336)

En þó var eigi undarligt, því at inn hæsti hǫfuðsmiðr hafði skapat ok
gefit í brjóst Þorgeiri svá øruggt hjarta ok hart, at hann hræddisk ekki,
ok hann var svá øruggr í ǫllum mannraunum sem it óarga dýr. Ok af

37. CSI 2:334; ÍF 6:129–30, ch. 3.
38. CSI 2:334; ÍF 6:130, ch. 3.
39. CSI 2:335; ÍF 6:132, ch. 3.

því at allir góðir hlutir eru af guði gǫrvir, þá er ørugglleikr af guði gǫrr
ok gefinn í brjóst hvǫtum drengjum ok þar með sjálfræði at hafa til
þess, er þeir vilja, góðs eða ills, því at Kristr hefir kristna menn sonu
sína gǫrt, en eigi þræla, en þat mun hann hverjum gjalda, sem til vinnr.
(ÍF 6:130, ch. 3)

The composer thus comes forth from his story to comment upon it as
he has brought it to this point, directing the attention of his audience to
the long-ensuing narrative of the lives of the two *fóstbrœðr*, explaining
events so as to make clear the purpose of his whole story: people make
choices, exercising that *will* God gave them, and in doing so they
are thus self-defined and will themselves ultimately be judged on the
basis of those choices. Here, invoking the Christian doctrine of Free
Will, the composer calls God the "hǫfuðsmiðr," "*a chief workman,
the architect*" (CV 308b), the most powerful being, who exercises his
power to give all people free will, so they in turn may choose good or
evil for themselves and be rewarded accordingly.

Preben Meulengracht Sørensen considers at length the saga
composer's intentions at this moral level, noticing in particular that
the oddly learned, ecclesiastically flavored passages are ironically
humorous. Referring to Halldór Laxness' 1952 satirization of this
saga, he observes, "It can be said that since the appearance of *Gerpla* it
has been difficult not to see parody in *Fóstbrœðra*."[40] Yet that parodic
style had been in the narrative long before *Gerpla* and the critics who
have made much of it, in fact probably in the first layers of the saga's
written narrative, to judge by its occasional appearance throughout.
Humor at a cultural distance is especially difficult to recognize, let
alone interpret, but the tenor of this aspect of *Fóstbrœðra* reminds
one of passages in *Grettis saga* where its hero speaks lines that might
have been noble in his ancestral society of past generations and yet are
easily and humorously deflatable by his own time. For example, the
visit to Auðunn Ásgeirsson—a matching of heroes' strength motivated
by a past humiliation, with Grettir's challenge, "I want to fight you"
(*Ek vil berjask við þik*)—results in what must seem to readers now the

---

40. Preben Meulengracht Sørensen, "On Humour, Heroes, Morality, and Anatomy
in *Fóstbrœðra saga*," in *Twenty-Eight Papers Presented to Hans Bekker-Nielsen on the
Occasion of his Sixtieth Birthday*, ed. Michael Barnes et al. (Odense: Odense University
Press, 1993), 396.

humorous laconism, "I have to see to the food first" (*Sjá mun ek fyrst ráð fyrir mat mínum*).[41] Putting the misfit hero in his place, Auðunn affirms what matters in his world, the storing of food, responding not only to his old friend's unrealistic ambitions, but also more generally, for his audience, to the lack of viability of a heroic stance where there are only farmers—and merchants, as the composer makes clear elsewhere—trying to make a living.

As the humor of *Grettis saga* often punctures Grettir's attempts to impose the heroic mode on Christian Iceland, so too it might be seen as taking Twain-like jabs at the very notion of nobility in such behavior. Humor becomes a weapon in the hand of the composer, enabling him to challenge, by belittling, the values according to which some pre-Christians may have lived, and that certainly had once been admired and praised in the country's literature. The violence of the *fóstbrœðr* is as out of place in their society as Grettir's gratuitous aggressiveness is in his saga, and this conflict between peaceable communities and dangerous ruffians ostracized for their ways seems to be a thematic thread common to both works. The humor itself, in both cases, is derived from an abrupt contrasting of the behavior of two groups.

Similarly, Þorgeirr's courage is explained in high parodic style, using medical texts from the continent. The ludicrous explanation of his behavior occasions the ironically implied criticism we expect of this mode. Powerful and courageous because of God's gifts, he becomes ever more amoral in his unrestrained, violent actions, especially after his estrangement from his *fóstbróðir*, whereas Þormóðr's behavior is ameliorated with time and the influence of King Óláfr. The king's twice-voiced determination that Þorgeirr is not in every respect a lucky man can be interpreted at a spiritual level when he seems not altogether dead after he is killed. "Þorgeirr serves demonic powers after his death, and that is the saga-author's final judgement on his conduct in this life."[42] Thus, as Meulengracht Sørensen notices, traditonal Germanic heroism is reinterpreted and re-evaluated in Christian terms at the same time as the violence of pre-Christian times is ridiculed. The inevitability of the old pagan wisdom of feud—that the more

---

41. CSI 2:94; ÍF 7:96, ch. 28.
42. Meulengracht Sørensen, "On Humour, Heroes, Morality," 411.

powerful decides—remains true enough in the secular, physical world, but the Christian assumption of faith in God and his spiritual kingdom presents another plane on which such decisions take place; the final decision, that of the "hǫfuðsmiðr," has immensely greater impact than the secular *ráð* with which the old communal wisdom was solely concerned.[43] It seems clear that, although this saga has no introductory segment precisely identifiable as a Norwegian prelude, which we might anticipate in the *Íslendingasögur*, that portion of its narrative culminating in the stylistically remarkable and critically much-noticed passage on Free Will is preludic in a thematic sense, as I have suggested above.

6

This test of good or evil impulses in the exercise of power is studied through much of the rest of *Fóstbrœðra*—with the dark and subversive humor already identified intruding in passages where power is tried or challenged. Thus, in the home of the "rather faint-hearted" (*huglauss í hjarta*)[44] Þorkell at Gørvidalr, Þorgeirr finds himself in the company, at close quarters, of Vermundr's kinsman Butraldi, "a loner of no fixed abode": "He was a large, powerfully-built man with an ugly face, quick tempered and vengeful, and he was a great slayer of men" (*einhleypingr, mikill maðr vexti, rammr at afli, ljótr í ásjónu, harðfengr í skaplyndi, vígamaðr mikill, nasbráðr ok heiptúðigr*).[45] The association between two such figures in the fearful presence of their timid host already invites humorous observation. Butraldi crosses himself before the meal, at which "Neither of them

---

43. This elevation of secular, pagan ethical assumptions to the Christian spiritual level is no novelty in medieval Germanic literature. In Old English, for instance, in *The Wanderer* we see how the pre-Christian concept of *ár*, the protection granted a guest by the old code of hospitality, is translated at the beginning and more especially at the end of that poem into God's protective mercy, or Grace, when the speaker in the poem seeks the heavenly *fæstnes* (firmness, stability, stronghold). Similarly readers of the Old English *Seafarer* will remark how the old pagan aspiration for the praise of men is elevated to hope of accolades from the heavenly chorus itself: "ond his lof siþþan lifge mid englum / awa to ealdre, ecan lifes blæd, / dream mid dugeþum" (lines 78b-80a). For some studies on this subject, see Richard North, *Pagan Words and Christian Meanings*, Costerus New Series 81 (Amsterdam: Rodopi, 1991).

44. CSI 2:340; ÍF 6:142, ch. 6.

45. CSI 2:340; ÍF 6:143, ch. 6.

would share either the knife or the food with the other" (*Hvárrgi þeira vildi deila við annan kníf né kjǫtstykki*).[46] The tension of the scene, relying on the men's exaggerated preoccupation with their aggressive masculinity as opposed to Þorkell's fear of their violently disrupting his household, prepares the atmosphere for the ensuing robustly heroic battle. In a scene evocative of Skarpheðinn's acrobatic performance at Markarfljót, Þorgeirr slid down a snowy slope, axe raised, descending upon Butraldi, who "looked up, but before he knew what was happening Thorgeir struck him full on the chest with his axe and cut right through him and he fell back down the slope" (*lítr upp ok finnr eigi fyrr en Þorgeirr hjó framan í fang honum ok þar á hol; fellr hann á bak aptr*).[47] At the conclusion of this scene, in which Þorgeirr's superior power is conclusively demonstrated and then celebrated with a verse, the audience learns that no vengeance would be taken for Butraldi by his relatives, their reticence humorously explained: "they had no desire to be sent off to rest for the night by his [Þorgeirr's] weapons" (*því at þeim þótti illt at eiga náttból undir vápnum Þorgeirs*).[48]

In the last episode of killing before the *fóstbrœðr* part from each other, their conflict is with a respected member of the community, in circumstances where the righteousness of their involvement is especially questionable. Þorgils Másson, a relative of Grettir's father, Ásmundr Þorgrímsson, and a "big, strong man, skilful in the use of weapons and a good farmer" (*mikill maðr ok sterkr, vápnfimr, góðr býþegn*),[49] carving up a stranded whale, refuses to share with them the portion he has cut, and Þorgeirr observes that what he has already taken is considerable. Þorgils is not inclined to give in, and Þorgeirr responds with typical aggression, "Then *you will have to see how long you can hold us away from it*" (*Þat munu þér þá reyna verða, hversu lengi þér haldið á hvalnum fyrir oss*).[50] The fight between the two ends tragically for Þorgils, because "*Þorgeirr was the deadlier* of the two" (*Þorgeirr var þeira meir lagðr til mannskaða*),[51] a

46. CSI 2:341; ÍF 6:145, ch. 6. See TPMA 8:210.
47. CSI 2:342; ÍF 6:146, ch. 6.
48. CSI 2:343; ÍF 6:147, ch. 6.
49. CSI 2:343; ÍF 6:148, ch. 7.
50. CSI 2:343; ÍF 6:148–49, ch. 7.
51. CSI 2:343; ÍF 6:149, ch. 7.

blunt judgement in no way consonant with the heroic pattern, but rather humorously laconic in its conclusion on the skills of an experienced killer.

7

Outlawed for this slaying, Þorgeirr ranges with Þormóðr over Strandir—"and they prevailed over all things like weeds overtaking a field" (*ok gengu þeir einir yfir allt sem lok yfir akra*).[52] The composer uses the term *ofsi*, "overbearing, tyranny" (CV 464b), of their dominance in the region in the following scene, where he separates the *fóstbrœðr* both personally and morally through the subsequent narrative: "People say that at the height of their tyranny, Thorgeir spoke these words to Thormod: 'Do you know of any other two men as eager as we or as brave, or indeed anyone who has stood the test of his valour so often?'" (*Svá segir sumir menn, at Þorgeirr mælti við Þormóð, þá er þeir váru í ofsa sínum sem mestum: "Hvar veiztu nú aðra tvá menn okkr jafna í hvatleika ok karlmennsku, þá er jafnmjǫk sé reyndir í mǫrgum mannraunum, sem vit erum?"*).[53] Þormóðr responds thoughtfully, and drawing significantly upon the proverbial wisdom of his culture, "Such men could be found if they were looked for who are no lesser men than us" (*Finnask munu þeir menn, ef at er leitat, er eigi eru minni kappar en vit erum*).[54] At this Þorgeirr issues the hypothetical challenge that is to end the path of their life together: "*Which of us do you think would win if we confronted each other?*" (*Hvat ætlar þú, hvárr okkarr myndi*

---

52. CSI 2:344; ÍF 6:149–50, ch. 7.

53. CSI 2:344; ÍF 6:150, ch. 7.

54. CSI 2:344; ÍF 6:148–9, ch. 7. This conversation has its context in the proverbial wisdom deriving from the rhetoric of *mannjafnaðr*. The reasonableness of Þormóðr's response would have gained emphasis from the audience's awareness of a set of proverbial texts found in other sagas, presumably derived from *Hávamál* 64: "Ríki sitt / skyli ráðsnotra hverr / í hófi hafa; / þá hann þat finnr, / er með frœcnom kømr, / at engi er einna hvatastr." See TPMA 12:326. For attestations in prose, see *Hrólfs saga kraka* and *Vǫlsunga saga*, in *Fornaldar sögur Norðurlanda*, ed. Guðni Jónsson, 4 vols. (Reykjavík: Íslendingasagnaútgáfan, 1954), 1:153 and 1:71, respectively; *Morkinskinna*, ed. Ármann Jakobsson and Þórður Ingi Guðjónsson, 2 vols., Íslenzk fornrit 23–24 (Reykjavík: Hið íslenzka fornritafélag, 2011), 2:148; and the entirety of the first chapter of *Mágus saga*, in *Fornsögur Suðrlanda*, ed. Gustaf Cederschiöld (Lund: Berling, 1884), 1–2.

af ǫðrum bera, ef vit reyndim með okkr?).[55] Þormóðr answers, "I don't know, but I do know that *this question of yours will divide us and end our companionship*. We cannot stay together" (*Þat veit ek eigi, en hitt veit ek, at sjá spurning þín mun skilja okkra samvistu ok fǫruneyti, svá at vit munum eigi lǫngum ásamt vera*). Þorgeirr, realizing for once that he has gone too far, tries to retract, "I wasn't really speaking my mind—saying that I wanted us to fight each other" (*Ekki var mér þetta alhugat, at ek vilda, at vit reyndim með okkr harðfengi*). But the idea has been voiced: "It came into your mind as you spoke it and we shall go our separate ways" (*Í hug kom þér, meðan þú mæltir, ok munu vit skilja félagit*), counters Þormóðr. Here Þorgeirr's aggressive exuberance finally isolates him even from his *fóstbróðir*. The challenge, whimsical as he claims or more seriously motivated, differentiates him from Þormóðr in worldview, as he takes his closest associate as a possible competitor. The amorality of his expression initiates his permanent divergence from the fate of his old friend—they are now on different spiritual paths, exercising their power in opposing ways. In the immediately subsequent chapters we see the results of Þorgeirr's choice, and after that, Þormóðr's exaggeratedly energetic vengeance for his fallen associate, justified in the assignment of the task by King Óláfr himself.

8

As Þorgeirr goes his way, making himself an *andvaragestr*, "an unwelcome guest" (CV 21a), among the communities of Strandir, his cousins, Þorgils Arason and Illugi, have purchased a share in a ship for him to journey into his outlawry. Several stories of the time intervening, before his departure for Norway, accrue to the written text here. One of particular interest, about a horse conflict, is clearly intended to parallel the horse-borrowing incident that led to the death of his father, yet at the same time readers today are reminded also of the initial tragedy of *Hrafnkels saga* and its hero's foolishly arrogant killing of the young Einarr Þorbjarnarson. In this latter work, the folly of the owner's possessive treatment of a horse begins what can be seen as a narrative in which foolish behavior is a subject of primary

---

55. CSI 2:344; ÍF 6:151, ch. 7.

concern.[56] In addition, since the actual stealing of a horse was not an issue in either of these episodes of *Fóstbrœðra*, one might question the gravity of both situations in which the killings occur. In that case, humorous distortion of concepts of honor and exaggeration of violence both become matters for consideration. In this scene Þorgeirr discovers that Bjarni Skúfsson has taken his horse in order to catch some sheep and demands that Bjarni dismount: "I think *it would be a good idea for you to get down off that horse* and give it back to its owner" (*Þat sýnisk mér nú ráð, at þú stígir af baki ok látir hestinn koma í hendr eiganda*).[57] Upon Bjarni's refusal he persists, "*I want you to get down from the horse* immediately" (*Þat vil ek, at þú stígir nú þegar af baki*). And when Bjarni replies that the horse won't be hurt by his riding it, Þorgeirr delivers his ultimatum, "*I must insist that you ride no farther* at this present time" (*Ek vil þessu ráða, at þú ríðir eigi lengra at sinni*). He then imposes his power to decide the matter with a spear through Bjarni's middle, ending the confrontation and regaining his horse, after which he kills the servant Skúfr, for whom Bjarni had been collecting the sheep in the first place.

Two minor episodes in Flateyjarbók—whose theologically trained writer seems intent upon emphasizing the unbalanced, perhaps demonic, lack of restraint in Þorgeirr's determination to exercise his power—precede his departure from Iceland. In both cases his behavior is obviously indefensible and seals beyond doubt the judgment of Icelandic society as well as of the ecclesiastical institution from whose culture these stories seem to emerge on the page. In the former he kills Torfi bǫggull for not responding to his greetings, never realizing his victim could not hear him: "Thorgeir grew tired of calling out and his already bad mood turned to anger. He rode across the stream at Torfi and plunged his spear through him, killing him instantly" (*En er Þorgeiri leiddisk á hann at kalla, reiddisk hann við, er honum var áðr skapþungt. Hann ríðr þá yfir ána at Torfa ok leggr spjóti í gegnum hann. Torfi var þegar dauðr*).[58] This recklessly lethal mood is matched in a second passage, where riding down to the ship he kills

---

56. For a full development of this argument see my "The Proverbial Heart of *Hrafnkels saga Freysgoða*: 'Mér þykkir þar heimskum manni at duga, sem þú ert,'" *Scandinavian-Canadian Studies* 16 (2006): 28–54 (http://scancan.net/article.pdf?id=harris_1_16).

57. CSI 2:346; ÍF 6:155, ch. 8.

58. CSI 2:345; ÍF 6:153, ch. 8.

a resting shepherd: "Thus he was rather hunched over, with his tired legs bent and his neck sticking out. When Thorgeir saw this he drew his axe in the air and let it fall on the man's neck. The axe bit well and the head went flying off and landed some distance away" (*var hann nøkkut bjúgr, steyldr á hæli ok lengði hálsinn. En er Þorgeirr sá þat, reiddi hann upp øxina ok lét detta á hálsinn. Øxin beit vel, ok fauk af hǫfuðit ok kom víðs fjarri niðr*).[59] "He had committed no wrong against me. If you want the truth I couldn't resist the temptation—he stood so well poised for the blow" (*Eigi hafði hann nøkkurar sakar til móts við mik, en hitt var satt, at ek mátta eigi við bindask, er hann stóð svá vel til hǫggsins*). he explains with his usual blunt brutality. "One can see from this . . . that your hands will never be idle" (*Þat mun sýnask í því . . . at þú munt óhandlatr reynask*), observes his cousin as the outlaw leaves his country.

As a member of King Óláfr's court, Þorgeirr experiences some success. The king assigns him the task of seeking vengeance upon Þórir of Hrófá for having mistreated one of the his men: "I am asking you because I believe you will do my will in this matter" (*Því býð ek þér um þetta mál, at ek hygg, at þú munir minn vilja gera í þessu verki*).[60] He responds, "I am obliged to do as you bid me" (*Skyldr em ek til þess at gera þat, sem þú vill*). The composer thus makes clear that the venture is undertaken at the king's will, rather than at Þorgeirr's. At the scene of the king's assigned vengeance there is undeniable humor in Þórir's arrogant response to Þorgeirr's demand for compensation: "It may well be that you are here as the king's representative, but I seriously doubt that these are the king's words you speak" (*Vera má, at svá sé, at þú hafir hans umboð, en varla virðisk mér svá, sem ek heyra orð konungsins, þó at þú mælir*).[61] And Þorgeirr's responding threat in advance of the anticipated spear thrust matches his victim's belligerent tone as he rejects a peaceable resolution: "It is true that you do not hear him speak personally, but *it may well be that you feel his power*" (*Satt er þat, at þú heyrir eigi hann sjálfan mæla, en þó má vera, at þú reynir nøkkurt sinn hans ríki*). The violence of course is Þorgeirr's, as usual, but the *will* to violence comes at the king's bidding,

---

59. CSI 2:347; ÍF 6:157, ch. 8.
60. CSI 2:358; ÍF 6:183, ch. 13.
61. CSI 2:359; ÍF 6:185, ch. 13.

and the deed is one for which the king thanks Þorgeirr at their next meeting (CSI 2:362; ÍF 6:192, ch. 14).

It seems likely that the composer next purposely juxtaposes a strikingly different scene with this one, a scene that also reminds us emphatically of the first episode of *Fóstbrœðra*. In it Þorgeirr gives free reign to his own will to save the life of the smith Veglágr, who has turned out to be a thief and a forger of keys. When Þorgils Arason demands he be hanged, Þorgeirr, like Þorbjǫrg digra with a conceivably more just cause before him, exclaims, "Despite what you think is the right course of action, in this instance the man's price will be too costly for you. *He will not be executed if I have any say in the matter*" (Hvat sem yðr sýnisk rétt vera um þetta mál, þá mun yðr þó verða maðrinn dýrkeyptr í þessu sinni, ok eigi mun hann af lífi tekinn, ef ek má því ráða).[62] The composer has Þorgeirr use precisely the same words, here italicized, as those of Þorbjǫrg, inviting comparison and contrast. But whereas the farmers of Ísafjǫrðr are the ones to voice the qualification *"Right or wrong, you have the power to prevent him from being executed"* (Hafa muntu ríki til þess, at hann sé eigi af lífi tekinn, hvárt sem þat er rétt eða rangt),[63] here it is the acknowledged perpetrator of injustice himself who declares his lack of concern over, "what you think is the right course of action" (Hvat sem yðr sýnisk rétt vera).[64] Þorbjǫrg's evidence of being a *mikill skǫrungr*, a "great leader" (CV 565b), when she provides help for an aristocratic kinsman in temporarily humiliating difficulties, can have only contrastive associations with this episode, where Þorgeirr saves by threat of force the life of a proven thief. He has clearly used his power in the interests of injustice, forcing the audience to recall once again the admonitory explanation of his behavior and character after he has taken vengeance for the killing of his father.

Upon Þorgeirr's return to the Norwegian court, King Óláfr thanks him for carrying out his will in Iceland, but when Þorgeirr reasserts his desire to return to Iceland another time, the king reminds him of his earlier observation on his character, perhaps even referring to his spiritual flaw, "What I said to you the first time we met will now

---

62. CSI 2:360; ÍF 6:188, ch. 13.
63. CSI 2:330; ÍF 6:122, ch. 1.
64. CSI 2:360; ÍF 6:188, ch. 1.

come to pass—you will not be fortunate in all you do" (*Nú mun at því koma, sem ek sagða inn fyrsta tíma, er þú komt á várn fund, at þú myndir eigi vera gæfumaðr í ǫllum hlutum*).[65] Allowing him nevertheless to depart for home, the king cautions him, "we will not meet again if we part company now" (*eigi munu vit sjásk síðan, ef vit skiljum nú*). Þorgeirr, always determined in whatever venture, insists, "*I fully intend to return to meet you next summer*" (*þat ætla ek, at fara á yðvarn fund at sumri*). At this the king observes, "*You may well intend it, but it will not come to pass*" (*Vera má, at svá sé, at þú ætlir þat, en eigi mun svá verða*). King Óláfr, who, as is the way with Norwegian kings in their sagas, sees farther than his subjects, understands that despite the bent of Þorgeirr's own will, a Will beyond his by now has other designs for him and the character that he has made of himself. Just as later the king predicts that he and Þormóðr will be together after death, so here he predicts Þorgeirr's death, but with a different spiritual outcome as a result.

Ultimately it is the earlier, seemingly unjustified killing of Þorgils Másson over the stranded whale that leads to Þorgeirr's earthly demise. Gautr Sleituson, a relative of Þorgils, tries to provoke his killer into a lethal confrontation as they wait at the ship to leave again for Norway, but with the inevitable results: "he who does such deeds / often reaps a just reward" (*opt verðr rík, þeims rœkir, / raun*), observes Þormóðr in a verse celebrating Gautr's demise.[66] And then a relative of Gautr's, Þórarinn ofsi Þorvaldsson, in company with the Greenlander Þorgrímr trolli Einarsson, discovers the familial burden of taking vengeance for Gautr despite having previously made a truce with Þorgeirr. By means of a ruse they weaken his forces, and then after a long, gruesome battle, Þorgeirr is killed and Þórarinn ofsi mutilates his corpse, beheading him. The composer insists again that his courage was God-given: "It was the Almighty who touched Thorgeir's heart and put such fearlessness into his breast, and thus his courage was neither inborn nor of humankind but came from the Creator on high" (*Almáttigr er sá, sem svá snart hjarta ok óhrætt gaf í brjóst Þorgeiri; ok eigi var hans hugprýði af mǫnnum gǫr né honum*

---

65. CSI 2:362; ÍF 6:194, ch. 14.

66. CSI 2:365; ÍF 6:201, ch. 15, v. 13, lines 7–8. Guðni Jónsson glosses as follows: "sá kemst oft í harða raun, sem rækir slíkt" (ibid., note).

í brjóst borin, heldr af inum hæsta hǫfuðsmið).[67] It would seem all the more tragic, then, that he made the choices he did.

9

When Þormóðr presents himself at court, the king's first observation upon learning his identity is that he will pursue vengeance for the death of Þorgeirr. And it is with this purpose in mind that he seeks passage with Skúfr to Greenland, making his way to the home of the powerful chieftain, Þorkell Leifsson, at Brattahlíð in Eiríksfjǫrðr. He first sets himself at odds with his host in an episode pertaining to his unfortunate ways with and competition over women, which are not of concern in this essay. In doing so, however, he creates the atmosphere for adverse reaction among Greenland's most powerful people to his path of vengeance for Þorgeirr. In these latter passages of the saga, the composer casts Þormóðr in the roles of trickster and assumer of disguise. Humor is thus attached to most of these episodes, and although Þormóðr's pursuit of vengeance for his *fóstbróðir* and King Óláfr's *hirðmaðr* extends far beyond what was required, it does so with no noticeable signal of disapproval on the composer's part. Cloaked and hooded, he cleaves the head of Þorgrímr trolli at the Garðaþing in Einarsfjǫrðr, where the latter, in a moment perhaps anticipatory of Gunnarr Lambason's death scene in *Njála*, has been telling a slanted story of his triumph over a sympathetic victim.

The competition for power is treated ironically when Þormóðr, by now having killed not only Þorgrímr trolli but also his nephews, Þórðr, Þorkell, and Falgeirr, has thus incurred the wrath of their mother, Þórdís. When she searches for Þormóðr where he has been healed of his wounds and harbored, at the home of the benign sorceress Gríma, she does so in the company of Þorkell Leifsson, under whose protection Gríma and her husband, Gamli, inhabit their isolated farm at the end of Eiríksfjǫrðr. The search scene, where stereotypically the powerful and increasingly frustrated searchers are foiled by those hiding the quarry, is here enhanced by Gríma's resort to sorcery. Apparently relying on the power of Þórr, whose image is carved into the chair where she hides Þórmóðr, she objects to Þorkell about the

---

67. CSI 2:368; ÍF 6:208, ch. 17.

search upon their arrival, *"I am astonished that Thordis thinks me capable of harbouring an outlaw from people as powerful as those at Longunes* when there's only the two of us here" (*Undarligt sýnisk mér vera, at Þórdís ætlar, at ek muna halda skógarmann fyrir svá ríkum mǫnnum sem þau eru á Lǫngunesi, þar sem ek sit við annan mann í húsi*).[68] This covert insubordination escalates as she responds with powerful irony to Þórdís' comment upon observing the Þórr image ("Grima still keeps to some of the old ways. She has a figure of Thor carved on the arms of her chair"[69]):

I seldom go to church to hear the lessons of the wise because it is so far away and there's just the two of us here. What actually runs through my mind when I see the wooden figure of Thor is the thought that I can break it and burn it whenever I please. I also know that *the Creator of heaven and earth* and all things visible and invisible, who gives life to all things, *is far superior to Thor, and that no man may vanquish His power.* (CSI 2:385)

Ek kem sjaldan til kirkju at heyra kenningar lærðra manna, því at ek á langt at fara, en fámennt heima. Nú kømr mér þá heldr í hug, er ek sé líkneski Þórs af tré gǫrt, þat er ek má brjóta ok brenna, þegar ek vil, hversu miklu sá er meiri, er skapat hefir himin ok jǫrð ok alla hluti sýniliga ok ósýniliga ok ǫllum hlutum gefr líf ok engi maðr má yfir stíga. (ÍF 6:247, ch. 23)

When Þórdís asserts that without the protective presence of Þorkell she might come upon more of the truth, she is met only by Gríma's smug complacence, the sorceress's thoughts ironically couched at first in explicitly paroemial terms, and then moving toward spiritual advice leaving no doubt of the sorceress' real views and intentions:

It's just as the saying has it—"guessing often leads to error." And there's another saying, "if a man's time has not come, something will save him." What you sorely lack is a holy guardian so that the devil

---

68. CSI 2:385; ÍF 6:246, ch. 23.
69. CSI 2:384; Eptir er enn nǫkkut fyrnsku Grímu, er Þórs líkneski er skorit á stóls-brúðum hennar (ÍF 6:246, ch. 23).

lead you not into the evil you are contemplating. It's excusable when
people guess and are mistaken, but there's no excusing the man who
rejects the truth once it's proven.[70] (CSI 2:386)

Nú kømr at því, sem mælt er: Opt verðr villr, er geta skal, ok hitt
annars, at hverjum bergr nǫkkut, er eigi er feigr. En þér er nauðsyn,
þat er heilǫg gæzla er svá yfir þér, at fjándinn á ekki þik svá heimila til
illra hluta sem þú vildir gǫrt hafa. Því at þat er várkunn, at menn geti
stundum annars en er, en þat er engi várkunn, at hann trúi eigi því, er
satt er, þá er hann reynir sannleikinn. (ÍF 6:247–8, ch. 23)

Not only does Gríma, in the composer's humorously ironic way,
falsely contradict Þórdís' accurate assessment of the situation, but
also she does so in terms that subvert the status quo of Christianity
itself; her sorcery, derived from pagan powers, successfully defeats
the power of her human superiors, as well as that of their God. Here
as elsewhere in the sagas, the magic of powerless and marginalized
folk compensates for their social vulnerability, as they attempt to
defeat the plans of more powerful figures in their community. In this
episode, however, where the local establishment is at odds with King
Óláfr and his intentions, even pre-Christian forces are enlisted in the
latter's interests, and in a way that leaves this humorously portrayed
practitioner of pagan-motivated sorcery strangely innocent of evil. The
socially subversive aspect of Gríma's power in this episode is converted
to serve the interests of the Christian King Óláfr and his God.

The extension of royal power to Greenland is felt again as the
king appears in a dream to Þorgrímr í Vík í Einarsfirði telling him to
rescue Þormóðr. At this point he has become stranded on a skerry,
wounded and exhausted from swimming to escape forces seeking to
avenge his slaying of Ljótr, another of Þorgrímr trolli's nephews. To
confirm his identity and the validity of the dream, the king reveals
that one 'Gestr' staying with Þorgrímr í Vík is really the Icelander
Helgu-Steinar, come also to seek vengeance for the killing of Þorgeirr.
Upon his return to court, Þormóðr is eventually recognized for his
enthusiastic pursuit of vengeance for Þorgeirr, having gone to lengths
which might seem unreasonable to the modern reader were it not

---

70. For the paroemial texts in internal quotation, see TPMA 3:41 and 11:55, respectively.

that he undertook these projects at the insistence of his king, whose wishes are just. "It will be a long time before the ground you have scorched begins to grow again" (*Seint mun sá díli gróa, er þú hefir þar brennt*),[71] says the monarch, echoing the phrasing of an immediately preceding boasting-verse by Þormóðr and thus signaling his approval of this exaggeratedly extended spate of bloody vengeance.

A final demonstration of King Óláfr's divinely derived power to decide matters is clearly expressed in the last scenes of the saga, where asking why his faithful skald has become despondent, he is told, "Because, my Lord, I am not certain that we shall be resting in the same place tonight. Promise me now that we shall be and I will be glad" (*Því, herra, at mér þykkir eigi víst vera, at vit munum til einnar gistingar í kveld. Nú ef þú heitr mér því, at vit munim til einnar gistingar báðir, þá mun ek glaðr*).[72] The king reassures him, "*I don't know whether it is within my power to decide*, but if it is, then tonight you shall go where I go" (*Eigi veit ek, hvárt mín ráð megu um þat til leiðar koma, en ef ek má nokkuru um ráða, þá muntu þangat fara í kveld, sem ek fer*).[73] When Óláfr is struck and dies in battle, Þormóðr grieves for himself, surviving his king: "Since I shall not be resting in the same place as the king tonight, living seems worse than dying" (*Þat ætla ek nú, at eigi muna ek til þeirar gistingar, sem konungr í kveld, en verra þykki mér nú at lifa en deyja*).[74] But at that moment, "an arrow flew towards him and struck him in the chest. He knew not whence it came" (*er hann mælti þetta, þá fló ǫr at Þormóði ok kom fyrir brjóst honum, ok vissi hann eigi, hvaðan at kom*).[75] The episode is lengthened in Flateyjarbók, where the disappointed poet prays to the newly dead king, "Will you not, King Olaf, grant me the end you promised? You said you would not forsake me, if it were within your power" (*Hvárt muntu nú, inn heilagi Óláfr konungr, eigi ætla at enda við mik þat, sem þú hézt mér, at þú myndir mik*

---

71. CSI 2:392; ÍF 6:260, ch. 24. For a discussion of the proverbial phrase "Brenna e-m díla," see Halldór Halldórsson, *Íslenzk orðtök* (Reykjavík: Ísafoldarprentsmiðja, 1954), 151–52 and 156, as well as Halldór Halldórsson, *Íslenzkt Orðtakasafn*, 2 vols. (Reykjavík: Almenna bókafélagið, 1968–69), 2:109, *s.v.* "díli."

72. CSI 2:392; ÍF 6:263, ch. 24.

73. CSI 2:392; ÍF 6:263–64, ch. 24.

74. CSI 2:393; ÍF 6:268–69, ch. 24.

75. CSI 2:393; ÍF 6:269, ch. 24.

eigi fyrir róða láta, ef þín ráð mætti standa?).⁷⁶ And he rejoices at the subsequent shot, "very pleased at being wounded thus" (*þessu sári feginn harla*). Miraculously, his end is certain, and King Óláfr's *ráð* has proven consonant with that of *inn ríkri*, in this case God himself.

10

The moral contrast of the two heroes of *Fóstbrœðra saga* in the respective conduct of their lives, clearly delineated by Meulengracht Sørensen, is elucidated and informed by our recognition of the underlying proverbial allusion suggested at those moments in the text I have touched upon above. That "drama of the will" described by Robert Cook and present in many of the *Íslendingasögur*—and which indeed must have been essential to competitive social interactions from the very foundation of Icelandic culture—is epitomized and examined from a Christian theological point of view by the composer, or one of the composers, of *Fóstbrœðra*. It is in addition significant that in the portion of the narrative that could be specified as *Þorgeirs saga* the proverbial sub-text, more urgently operative, is more frequently alluded to than in the portion devoted to Þormóðr. Of the two, Þorgeirr is the spiritual *ógæfumaðr*, his will unrestrained and eventually in conflict with the Divine Will Itself. This conflict is what is examined in his story. Þormóðr, by contrast, in subjecting his will to that of the divinely appointed King Óláfr, thus exercises his Free Will by applying the extraordinary powers given him in accordance with the intentions of the Giver, or at least not in direct opposition to them.

A drama of the will similar to that which Cook noticed in the *Íslendingasögur*, and whose expression has significant phraseological similarities to the text of *Fóstbrœðra saga*, is found in *Sverris saga*. The date of this work is more certain than that of the former saga, but its composership is also much debated and with some textual indications as well as external evidence of there having been more than one writer at work. A portion of it was composed, according to internal evidence, by Abbot Karl Jónsson while "King Sverrir himself sat over him and decided what should be written" (*en yfir*

---

76. CSI 2:399; ÍF 6:269, ch. 24.

sat sjálfr Sverrir konungr ok réð fyrir hvat rita skyldi).[77] Its first task
is to trace the journey to the throne of this obscure Norwegian son
of one Gunnhildr and a comb-maker or smith, born around 1150
and sent to the Faroes at the age of 5 to be fostered and trained for
the priesthood by a paternal uncle, Hrói, Bishop of Kirkjunes. His
illegitimate royal paternity as a son of King Sigurðr munnr revealed
to him by his mother in 1176, he gives up the priestly calling for
kingly aspirations, a decision recalled disparagingly by the Church in
later conflicts between it and the throne. Calling him a *guðníðingr,*
or "a traitor to God, a renegade" (CV 219b), that institution sought
to neutralize his authority by asserting that as an ordained priest he
should never have undertaken the secular office of kingship, let alone
given up his sacerdotal duries. Whatever the genealogical validity of
his claim to the Norwegian throne, he had discarded prior and more
urgent spiritual commitments.

It is in the light of such ideologically based opposition to his
kingship that we may consider one of his several dreams reported as
justification of his seeking the crown with divine approval. In chapter
42, on the night preceding the Battle of Kalvskinnet, near Niðaróss,
in 1179, where Erlingr skakki jarl was to die, a man leads Sverrir
to a roasted male human corpse and tells him to eat. Regarding the
meal as unclean, the hero demures, but the dream man commands
him to obey, for it is God's will: "You will eat and you shall eat; *thus
wills he who decides all*" (*Þú vilt eta ok þú skalt eta; svá vill sá er
ǫllu rœðr*).[78] In deference to this superior will, he begins "to eat the
flesh from the bones, and every mouthful seemed difficult to swallow.
But the longer he ate, the less disgust he seemed to feel at eating the
remainder. Coming to the head, he was about to eat it also; but the
man who had led him there told him to cease eating, and took the
head himself" (*eta holdit af beinunum ok þótti hverr biti tregt niðr
ganga. Ok svá lengi sem hann hafði etit þá þótti honum því minna
fyrir er ofarr var. En er hann kom at hǫfðinu vildi hann þá ok eta
þat. Ok sá maðr er hann leiddi þangat tók hǫfuðit til sín ok kvað þá*

---

77. J. Sephton, trans., *The Saga of King Sverri of Norway*, Northern Library 4 (London:
David Nutt, 1899), henceforth Sephton, 1; *Sverris saga*, ed. Þorleifr Hauksson, Íslenzk
fornrit 30 (Reykjavík: Hið íslenzka fornritafélag, 2007), 3 ("Prologus").

78. Sephton 53; ÍF 30:66, ch. 42. For discussion of Sverrir's dreams, see Lars Lönnroth,
"Sverrir's Dreams," *Scripta Islandica: Isländska Sällskapets Årsbok* 57 (2006): 97–110.

hætta skyldu).[79] In Sverrir's interpretation, this dream anticipated the death in battle of Erlingr jarl and his most powerful barons, but also the escape of King Magnús, the leftover roasted head which he was instructed to leave uneaten. This passage is most meaningfully interpreted in the context of a proverbial allusion established in the reference to God as one who rules, or decides, all. Thus, Sverrir would contend, he has undertaken the pursuit of monarchy in deference to God's Will rather than following his own desires. At the same time as the dream admits Sverrir's joy in conquest, it also supports his contention that he was not, at least by intention, a guðníðingr but rather an initially reluctant follower of God's overwhelming Will, a point which is made often through the course of his biography, allusively using the force of the proverb whose literary significance is the subject of this essay.

On numerous occasions the piety of the king—who himself pauses to pray at precarious moments in battle, admonishes his soldiers to pray for the souls of those they have killed, and who grants clemency to even vaguely repentant enemies—is made indisputably clear. No matter what accusations the Church leveled against its renegade son, his biography asserts his faithful adherence, unusual among leaders of his time, to the moral demands of Christian teaching in his behavior. On his deathbed in 1202 he is reported to have observed, "The kingdom has brought me labour and unrest and trouble, rather than peace and a quiet life. But so it is that many have envied me my rank, and have let their envy grow to full enmity. May God forgive them all; and let my Lord now judge between me and them, and decide all my cause" (*Hefi ek meira starf, ófrið ok vandræði haft í ríkinu en kyrrsæti eðr mikit hóglífi. Er svá at minni virðingu sem margir hafi verit mínir ofundarmenn, þeir er þat hafa látit ganga fyrir fullan fjándskap við mik, sem nú fyrirgefi Guð þeim þat ollum. Ok dæmi Guð milli vár ok allt mitt mál*).[80] Even at his death, as he contemplated the many voices dubious of his paternal right to the throne, he left the question in the hands of "sá er ollu ræðr" (he who decides all).

Concomitant with what were meant to be viewed as signs of respect for his training and faith, however, readers notice the presence of a dark and malicious humor, whether emanating from the hand of the

79. Sephton 53; ÍF 30:66, ch. 42.
80. Sephton 231–2; ÍF 30:279, ch. 180.

nebulous biographer or represented by him as coming from the king's own mouth, or perhaps resulting from the collaborative dynamic of king and abbot in recounting the adventure. This humor had to do in every instance with that unavoidably prolonged exercise of power to obtain and keep his kingship that had taken up so much of his life and to which he alluded on his deathbed. The very titling of the earlier portion of his saga, the account of his ascent to power, *Grýla*, after the mythical monster, a traditional personified embodiment of that which threatens accepted social order, perhaps even the order of the pre-Christian universe, casts a viciously humorous perspective upon his long journey to power as it is described there.[81] Humorous references to the overwhelming effect of his assaults upon his enemies stress their aggressive nature to the point of their being troll-like. On three occasions the threat of the Birkibeinar is compared to that of "trolls at the door," or "between outhouse and home," emphasizing the chaotically destructive potential of the insurgent forces. Interestingly, the phrase, "troll fyrir durum," rarely occurring elsewhere in Old Icelandic literature, is found twice in *Fóstbrœðra saga*. It is used of Grettir's depredations upon the Ísafjǫrðr countryside in chapter 1, though not found in the corresponding chapter 52 of *Grettis saga* itself, and it appears also in chapter 9, where Þórdís' mother, Gríma, complains to Þormóðr of his importunate attentions to her daughter, saying that he may frighten more serious suitors away: "it's just that any man who might be thinking about proposing marriage to her will regard you as a troll on his doorstep" (*þeir menn, er til hafa gǫrzk at biðja hennar . . . má vera, at þeim sýnisk troll standa fyrir durum, þar sem þú ert*).[82]

The exercise of power in association with God's gift of Free Will, of primary concern in *Fóstbrœðra saga*, is thus also a matter of interest in *Sverris saga*, one of whose composers at least means to represent the priestly usurper's ascendance as the result of God's Will. In addition, such striking phraseological similarities between the two texts, as well as their stylistic sharing of a humor derived from situations of violence, might lead us to consider whether they share also, at some point

---

81. For useful information on *Grýla* see "Tröll og forynjur—Grýla," in Árni Björnsson, *Jól á Íslandi* (Reykjavík: Ísafold, 1963), 139–46, and more recently Terry Gunnell, "Grýla, Grýlur, 'Grøleks' and Skeklers: Medieval Disguise Traditions in the North Atlantic?" *Arv: Nordic Yearbook of Folklore* 57 (2001): 33–54.

82. CSI 2:349; ÍF 7:161, ch. 9.

in their respective literary development, a common compositional hand. While this is not the place for a detailed study of such matters, it is interesting to recall the connections of Abbot Karl Jónsson to Þingeyraklaustr as well as the conjecture of Guðni Jónsson, in an admittedly earlier critical era, that *Fóstbrœðra* "was probably written more than one time by the monks of Þingeyraklaustur between 1210 and 1380."[83] The composition of both works was imbued at some point with a transcendent spiritual vision of the ultimate source of the power to decide—that wielded by "sá er ǫllu ræðr."

Bibliography

Árni Björnsson. *Jól á Íslandi*. Reykjavík: Ísafold, 1963.

Arora, Shirley. "The Perception of Proverbiality." *Proverbium* 1 (1984): 1–38.

Bjarni Vilhjálmsson and Óskar Halldórsson. *Íslenzkir málshættir*. 2nd ed. Reykjavík: Almenna bókafélagið, 1982.

Bonjour, Adrien. *The Digressions in Beowulf*. Medium Ævum Monographs 5. Oxford: Basil Blackwell, 1950.

Cederschiöld, Gustaf, ed. *Fornsögur Suðrlanda*. Lund: Berling, 1884.

Cleasby, Richard, and Gudbrand Vigfusson. *An Icelandic-English Dictionary*. 2nd ed. Oxford: Clarendon, 1957.

Cook, Robert. "The Reader in *Grettis Saga*." *Saga-Book* 21 (1984–85): 133–54.

———. "Reading for Character in *Grettis Saga*." In *Sagas of the Icelanders: A Book of Essays*, edited by John Tucker, 226–40. New York: Garland, 1989.

———. "The Sagas of Icelanders as Dramas of the Will." In *Proceedings of the First International Saga Conference, University of Edinburgh, 1971*, edited by Peter Foote, Hermann Pálsson, and Desmond Slay, 88–113. London: The Viking Society for Northern Research, 1973.

De Saussure, Ferdinand. *Course in General Linguistics*. Translated by Wade Baskin. New York: Philosophical Library, 1959.

Erasmus, Desiderius. *Collected Works of Erasmus*. Vol 31, *Adages Ii1 to Iv100*. Translated by M. M. Phillips and R. A. B. Mynors. Toronto: University of Toronto Press, 1982.

Evans, Jonathan D. M. "Episodes in Analysis of Medieval Narrative." *Style* 20 (1986): 126–41.

---

83. "Líklega hefir . . . verið skrifuð upp oftar en einu sinni af Þingeyramunkum milli 1210 og 1380" (ÍF 6:lxxv-lxxvi).

Finnur Jónsson, ed. *Den norsk-isländske skjaldedigtning*. Vols. B1–2, Rettet tekst. Copenhagen: Gyldendal, 1912–15.

Gos, Giselle. "Women as a Source of *heilræði*, 'Sound Counsel': Social Mediation and Community Integration in *Fóstbrœðra saga*." *Journal of English and Germanic Philology* 108 (2009): 281–300.

Grettis saga Ásmundarsonar. Edited by Guðni Jónsson. Íslenzk fornrit 7. Reykjavík: Hið íslenzka fornritafélag, 1936.

Gudbrand Vigfusson and F. York Powell, eds. *Origines Islandicae*. 2 vols. Oxford: Clarendon Press, 1905.

Gunnell, Terry. "Grýla, Grýlur, 'Grøleks' and Skeklers: Medieval Disguise Traditions in the North Atlantic?" *Arv: Nordic Yearbook of Folklore* 57 (2001): 33–54.

Halldór Halldórsson. *Íslenzkt orðtakasafn*. 2 vols. Reykjavík: Almenna bókafélagið, 1968–69.

———. *Íslenzk orðtök*. Reykjavík: Ísafoldarprentsmiðja, 1954.

Harris, Richard L. *Concordance to the Proverbs and Proverbial Materials in the Old Icelandic Sagas*. http://www.usask.ca/english/icelanders/.

———. "The Proverbial Heart of *Hrafnkels saga Freysgoða*: 'Mér þykkir þar heimskum manni at duga, sem þú ert.'" *Scandinavian-Canadian Studies* 16 (2006): 28–54. http://scancan.net/article.pdf?id=harris_1_16.

Honeck, Richard P. *A Proverb in Mind: The Cognitive Science of Proverbial Wit and Wisdom*. Mahwah, NJ: Lawrence Erlbaum Associates, Inc., 1997.

Hume, Kathryn. "The Thematic Design of *Grettis Saga*." *Journal of English and Germanic Philology* 77 (1974): 469–86.

Jónas Kristjánsson. *Um Fóstbrœðrasögu*. Reykjavík: Stofnun Árna Magnússonar, 1972.

Lachmann, Vera. *Das Alter der Harðarsaga*. Palaestra 183. Leipzig: Mayer & Müller, 1932.

Lönnroth, Lars. "Sverrir's Dreams." *Scripta Islandica: Isländska Sällskapets Årsbok* 57 (2006): 97–110.

Maxwell, Ian. "Pattern in *Njáls saga*." *Saga-Book* 15 (1957–61): 17–47.

Meulengracht Sørensen, Preben. "On Humour, Heroes, Morality, and Anatomy in *Fóstbrœðra saga*." In *Twenty-Eight Papers Presented to Hans Bekker-Nielsen on the Occasion of his Sixtieth Birthday*, edited by Michael Barnes, E. W. Hansen, H. F. Nielsen, and R. Schützeichel, 395–418. Odense: Odense University Press, 1993.

Mieder, Wolfgang. *Proverbs: A Handbook*. Westport, CT: Greenwood Press, 2004.

Morkinskinna. Edited by Ármann Jakobsson and Þórður Ingi Guðjónsson. 2 vols. Íslenzk fornrit 23–24. Reykjavík: Hið íslenzka fornritafélag, 2011.

Norrick, Neal. *How Proverbs Mean: Semantic Studies in English Proverbs*. Berlin: Mouton, 1985.

North, Richard. *Pagan Words and Christian Meanings*. Costerus New Series 81. Amsterdam: Rodopi, 1991.

Powell, Frederick York, trans. *Færeyinga saga, or The Tale of Thrond of Gate*. Northern Library 2. London: David Nutt, 1896.

Sephton, J., trans. *The Saga of King Sverri of Norway*. Northern Library 4. London: David Nutt, 1899.

Singer, Samuel, ed. *Thesaurus Proverbiorum Medii Aevi: Lexikon der Sprichwörter des romanisch-germanischen Mittelalters*. 13 vols. Berlin: de Gruyter, 1996–2002.

Sverris saga. Edited by Þorleifur Hauksson. Íslenzk fornrit 30. Reykjavík: Hið íslenzka fornritafélag, 2007.

Taylor, Archer. *The Proverb*. Cambridge, MA: Harvard University Press, 1931.

Vestfirðinga sogur. Edited by Björn K. Þórólfsson and Guðni Jónsson. Íslenzk fornrit 6. Reykjavík: Hið íslenzka fornritafélag, 1943.

Viðar Hreinsson, ed. *The Complete Sagas of Icelanders*. 5 vols. Reykjavík: Leifur Eiríksson, 1997.

Whiting, Bartlett Jere. *When Evensong and Morrowsong Accord: Three Essays on the Proverb*. Edited by Joseph Harris. Cambridge, MA: Harvard University Press, 1994.

Appendix
Textual Data on the Proverb
"Jafnan segir inn ríkri ráð"
(The more powerful always decides)

The items assembled below attest in a compact fashion to the prevalence of the idea of the proverb "Jafnan segir inn ríkri ráð" in the medieval North. They are drawn from some of the philological tools available to those who might wish to undertake further paroemial studies of the Old-Norse Icelandic sagas. A key to the abbreviations employed by their various editors, as well as supplemental bibliography when more recent editions are available, is provided in footnotes. Explicit witnesses to oral paroemial tradition such as these likely constitute— like the extant narratives in which they are attested—only a minimal portion of the communal repositories of those societies from which they survive.

Excerpts from Collections Used

1. Bjarni Vilhjálmsson and Óskar Halldórsson, *Íslenzkir málshættir*, 2nd ed. (Reykjavík: Almenna bókafélagið, 1982), 268:

ríkur: jafnan segir enn ríkri ráð (*Málsháttakvæði*); ríkari verður að ráða (FJ); hinn ríkari verður ráð að segja (*Eimreiðin* 10. árg. 1904).[1]

2. Finnur Jónsson, "Oldislandske ordsprog og talemåder," *Arkiv för nordisk filologi* 30 (1913–14): proverb headword 334, p. 181:

ríkr (jfr heima): *jafnan segir enn ríkri ráð* (Mhk 23; jfr *Eirspennill* 47); "Altid er det den mægtigste (af to), der giver råd (med myndighed), hvis ikke *segja ráð* her er en blot omskrivning for *ráða* 'råde.' Det samma findes i prosa således: *hinn ríkari verðr* [*raað*] *at segja* (*Clár* ch. 15, lines 45–46). Sammenhængen her taler bestemt for den sidst anførte opfattelse. = GJ 276: *Ríkari verðr* (*hlýtr*) *að ráða*.[2]

3. TPMA 4:460, *s.v.* "Gewalt":

1. Der Mächtigere entscheidet (setzt seinen Willen durch). Nordic: *En sá réð, es ríkri vas* Aber derjenige entschied, der mächtiger war (Sólarljóð 36, 4 = Gering p. 11). *Jafnan segir enn ríkri ráð* Immer sagt der Mächtigere, was zu tun ist (wörtl.: "die Beschlüsse") (Málsháttakvæði 23, 1 = Jónsson, Arkiv 334; Jónsson 137). *Stare penes libitum satagit vis celsa quiritum—Ee wil waaldh sijn wiliæ haffwæ* Die hohe

---

1. *Málsháttakvæði* = Finnur Jónsson, ed., *Den norsk-isländske skjaldedigtning*, vols. B1–2, Rettet tekst (Copenhagen: Gyldendal, 1912–15), B2:138–145 [also Kock, ed., *Den norsk-isländske skaldediktningen*, 2 vols. (Lund: Gleerup, 1946–49), 2:73–78]; FJ = Finnur Jónsson, *Íslenzkt málsháttasafn* (Copenhagen: Gyldendal, 1920); *Eimreiðin* = "Íslenzkir málshættir og talshættir," *Eimreiðin* 10 (1904): 138–144.
2. Mhk = *Málsháttakvæði* (see previous note); *Eirspennill* = Finnur Jónsson, ed. *Eirspennill* (AM 47 Fol) (Christiania [Oslo]: Den Norske Historiske Kildeskriftkommision, 1913); *Clár* 15 = *Clarus saga, Clari fabella*, ed. Gustaf Cederschiöld (Lund: Gleerup, 1879) [also vol. 5 of *Riddarasögur*, ed. Bjarni Vilhjálmsson (Reykjavík: Íslendingasagnaútgáfan, 1949–1954), ch. 15, p. 38; Dennis Farrell Keeney, *Clarus saga: An Edition and Translation* (Ph.D. diss., University of Mississippi, 1990), ch. 15, p. 82]; GJ = Guðmundur Jónsson, *Safn af íslenzkum orðskviðum, fornmælum, heilræðum, snilliyrðum, sannmælum og málsgreinum, samanlesið of í stafrófsröð sett af Guðmundi Jónssyni prófasti í Snæfellsnessýslu og presti í Staðarstaðarsókn* (Copenhagen: Hið íslenzka bókmentafélag, 1830).

Gewalt der Quiriten will bei ihrer Willkür verharren—Gewalt will
immer ihren Willen haben (Låle 1017). *Hinn ríkari verðr ráð at segja*
Der Mächtigere kann sagen, was zu tun ist (wörtl.: "den Beschluss")
(Clári saga 15, 5 = Jónsson, Arkiv 334).[3]

The prevalence of the concepts underlying the proverb "Jafnan segir
inn ríkri ráð" is suggested by a related one, Dýrt er drottins orð (The
master's word is final [lit. "dear"]):

1. Finnur Jónsson, *Íslenskt málsháttasafn* (Copenhagen: Gyldendal,
1920), proverb word 74, p. 76:

dróttinn—dýrt er (mun verða; láta menn) dróttins orð Laxd 182, Bisk
1:484, 803, 2:51, Fms 2:269, 4:175, Isls 2:445, Alex 128 (honum væri
dýrt látanda *d. o.*), DraumJ. 5, Mhk. 5.[4]

---

3. Sólarljóð = Finnur Jónsson, ed., *Den norsk-isländske skjaldedigtning*, B1:635–648
[also Ernst A. Kock, ed., *Den norsk-isländske skjaldedigtning*, 1:308–16]; Hugo Gering,
"Altnordische Sprichwörter und sprichwörtliche Redensarten: eine nachlese zu *Arkiv för
nordisk filologi* 30, 61ff., 170ff.," *Arkiv för nordisk filologi* 32 (1915–16): 1–30 [also
Margaret Clunies Ross, ed., *Poetry on Christian Subjects*, 1: *The Twelfth and Thirteenth
Centuries*, Skaldic Poetry of the Scandinavian Middle Ages 7 (Turnhout: Brepols, 2007),
319]; Málsháttakvæði = see note 1 above; Jónsson, Arkiv = "Oldislandske ordsprog og
talemåder," *Arkiv för nordisk filologi* 30 (1913–14): 61–111, 170–217; Jónsson = Finnur
Jónsson, *Íslenskt málsháttasafn* (see note 1 above); Låle = Peder Låle, "Forndanska
och latinska ordspråk," vol. 1 of *Östnordiska och latinska medeltidsordspråk: Peder
Låles ordspråk och en motsvarande svensk samling*, ed. Axel Kock and Carl af Petersens
(Copenhagen: Samfund til udgivelse af gammel nordisk litteratur, 1889–94), 3–250;
Clári saga = G. Cederschiöld, ed., *Clári saga*, Altnordische Saga-Bibliothek 12 (Halle:
Niemeyer, 1907).

4. Laxd 182 = [edition unknown; see ÍF 5:147 (ch. 47)]; Bisk 1:484, 803, 2:51; Jón Sigurðsson and Guðbrandur Vigfússon, eds. *Biskupa sögur*, 2 vols. (Copenhagen: Hið íslenzka
bókmentafélag, 1858) [for *Lárentíus saga biskups* (1:803), see also *Biskupa sögur*, vol. 3,
ed. Guðrún Ása Grímsdóttir, Íslenzk fornrit 17 (Reykjavík: Hið íslenzka fornritafélag,
1998), 248]; Fms 2:269 = *Saga Ólafs konúngs Tryggvasonar*, in vol 2. of *Fornmanna sögur*,
ed. S. Egilsson and Þ. Guðmundsson (Copenhagen: Popp, 1826); Fms 4:175 [*sagði þeim
ráðinn sigrinn*] = *Saga Ólafs konúngs hins Helga*, in *Fornmanna sögur*, vol. 4, ed. Þorgeir
Guðmundsson, C. C. Rafn, et al (Copenhagen: Popp, 1829) [also *Heimskringla*, vol. 2,
ed. Bjarni Aðalbjarnarson, Íslenzk fornrit 27 (Reykjavík: Hið íslenzka fornritafélag), 126];
Isls 2:445 = *Kjalnesínga saga*, in Jón Sigurðsson, C. C. Rafn, et al., eds., *Íslendínga sögur*,
4 vols. (Copenhagen: Möller, 1843–89); Alex 128 = *Alexanders saga*, ed. C. R. Unger
(Christiania [Oslo]: Feilberg & Landmark, 1848) [also *Alexandreis, það er, Alexanders
saga á íslensku* (Reykjavík: Steinholt, 2002), p. 149, lines 4–5]; DraumJ. 5 = *Drauma-Jóns
saga*, ed. Hugo Gering (Halle: Buchhandlung des Waisenhauses, 1893) [also vol. 6 of *Riddarasögur*, ed. Bjarni Vilhjálmsson (Reykjavík: Íslendingasagnaútgáfan, 1949–1954), ch.
5, p. 164]; Mhk. = *Málsháttakvæði* (see previous note).

2. TPMA 6:41–42, *s.v.* "Herr":

5. Eigenschaften des Herrschers 5.1. Der Herr hat Macht und Autorität
5.1.3. Die Worte des Herrn haben Gewicht 5.1.3.1. Die Worte des
Herrn gelten viel

Nordic: *Dýrt er drottins orð* Das Wort des Herrn ist viel wert (Snorri,
Ólafs saga helga 82 → Fms 4, 175 [= Jónsson, Arkiv 74]; Snorri,
Heimskringla 248, 36 [Ólafs saga helga 85], 356, 13 [Ólafs saga
helga 165]; Grosse Ólafs saga Tryggvasonar 235 → Fms 2, 269 [=
Jónsson, Arkiv 74]; Biskupasögur 1:484, 803, 2:51 [→Jónsson, Arkiv
74]; Drauma-Jóns saga ch. 5, lines 48–49, ca. first half of the 14th
century [→ ZfdPh 26, 304 = Jónsson, Arkiv 74]; Kjálnesinga saga ch.
15, p. 35. *Dýrt láta menn dróttins orð* Man bezeichnet das Wort des
Herrn als etwas Kostbares (*Málsháttakvæði* 5, 5 = Jónsson, Arkiv 74;
Jónsson 31). *Dýrt mun mér verða dróttins orð* Das Wort des Herrn
soll mir gewichtig sein (Laxdœla saga ch. 19, p. 47 = Jónsson, Arkiv
74. Jónsson 31). *At honom vere sem auðrom dyrt latannda drottins
orð* Dass das Wort des Herrn für ihn ebensoviel bedeute wie für einen
andern (Alexanders saga 128 = Jónsson, Arkiv 74). *Jussio sueuit hero
celsi sublimis haberi—Høyt ær herræ bwdh* Der Befehl eines hohen
Herrn wird gewöhnlich hochgehalten—Hoch steht (wörtl.: "ist") das
Gebot eines Herrn (Låle, p. 58, no. 521).[5]

---

5. Snorri, Ólafs saga helga = Snorri Sturluson *Óláfs saga hins helga*, ed. P. A. Munch
and C. R. Unger (Christiania [Oslo]: Werner, 1853); Fms = see previous note; Heimskringla = Fms 4 (see previous note); Grosse Ólafs saga Tryggvasonar = O. A. Johnsen and
J. Helgason, eds., *Den store saga om Olav den hellige* (Oslo: Kjeldeskriftfondet, 1930–41);
Biskupasögur 2 = see "Bisk" in previous note; Drauma-Jóns saga = see "DraumJ" in
previous note; ZfdPh = *Zeitschrift für deutsche Philologie* 26 (1894): 289–308 [edition
of *Drauma-Jóns saga*]; Kjalnesinga saga = *Kjalnesinga saga*, ed. Jóhannes Halldórsson,
Íslenzk fornrit 14 (Reykjavík: Hið íslenzka fornritafélag, 1959) [see also previous note];
Málsháttakvæði (see note 1 above); Laxdœla saga = K. Kålund, ed. *Laxdœla saga*,
Altnordische Saga-Bibliothek 4 (Halle: Max Niemeyer, 1896) [also Einar Ól. Sveinsson,
ed, Íslenzk fornrit 5 (Reykjavík: Hið íslenzka fornritafélag, 1934)]; Alexanders saga =
see previous note [also Finnur Jónsson, ed., *Alexanders saga: Islandsk Oversættelse ved
Brandr Jónsson* (Copenhagen: Gyldendal, 1925); Jón Helgason, ed., *Alexanders saga: The
Arnamagnæan Manuscript 519a, 4to*, Manuscripta Islandica (Copenhagen: Munksgaard,
1966)]; Låle = see note 3 above.

Seeking Death in *Njáls saga*

Torfi H. Tulinius
UNIVERSITY OF ICELAND

In the last lines of *Njáls saga*, near the end of the 159th and ultimate chapter of this longest of the sagas about early Icelanders, we are told the following about Flosi, a noble man whose misfortune it was to commit a terrible crime:

> Þat segja menn, at þau yrði ævilok Flosa, at hann fœri utan, þá er hann var orðinn gamall, at sœkja sér húsavið, ok var hann í Nóregi þann vetr. En um sumarit varð hann síðbúinn. Rœddu menn um, at vánt væri skipit. Flosi sagði, at væri œrit gott gǫmlum ok feigum, ok sté á skip ok lét í haf, ok hefir til þess skips aldri spurzk síðan.[1]

> People say that the end of Flosi's life came when he had grown old and went abroad to find wood for building a house and spent the winter in Norway. The next summer he was late in his preparations. Men talked about the bad condition of his ship. Flosi said that it was good enough for an old man doomed to die, and he boarded the ship and put out to sea, and nothing was ever heard of the ship again.[2]

At this point Flosi has made compensation for the burning of Njáll and his family: "Hafði hann þá af hendi innt alla sætt sína bæði í

---

1. *Brennu-Njáls saga*, ed. Einar Ólafur Sveinsson, Íslenzk fornrit 12 (Reykjavík: Hið íslenzka fornritafélag, 1954), henceforth ÍF 12, 463.
2. Robert Cook, trans., *Njal's Saga* (London: Penguin Classics, 2001), 310.

utanferðum ok fégjǫldum" (He had then fulfilled all his part in the settlement, both the exile and the payments).[3] The settlement is not only with humans, but also with God, since Flosi has received absolution for his sins from the Pope himself. It is therefore noteworthy that the saga emphasizes that he pays no heed to warnings against putting out to sea on a damaged ship to go to Iceland. The ship disappears somewhere between Norway and Iceland and we must assume death by drowning. There is a strange peacefulness to Flosi's attitude, even though it might be qualified as reckless. Indeed, his decision not only puts his own life in danger, but also imperils that of his shipmates. However, the author takes care not to introduce his audience to these characters and therefore neutralizes any potential concern for them. Instead, Flosi's behavior can be seen as noble and detached. From a literary point of view, it is a fitting end for this tragic saga.[4] All passions have been spent and the characters can fade back into the past.

Flosi is only one of many characters in *Njáls saga* who seem to welcome their own demise, as will be shown in the following. Indeed, a willingness to die is an important structural and semantic feature of the saga. The desire of all living beings to "return to the quiescence of the inorganic world" is the troubling idea Freud proposes in his *Beyond the Pleasure Principle*, in which he introduces his concept of the death wish.[5] A psychoanalytic approach based on this concept can indeed enrich our understanding of the structure and meaning of this remarkable saga.

Psychoanalysis and the Sagas

In recent years, scholars have brought psychology to bear on literature of medieval Iceland. Ármann Jakobsson studies empathy as a key

---

3. Ibid., 309; ÍF 12:462.

4. Scholars have commented diversely on this ending over the years. Einar Ól. Sveinsson talks about Flosi's strength of character; he is ready to take whatever life brings him. See *Á Njálsbúð: Bók um mikið listaverk* (Reykjavík: Hið íslenska bókmenntafélag, 1943), 169. Richard F. Allen sees in it a parallel with the last voyage of the Danish king Scyld Scefing in *Beowulf*. See *Fire and Iron: Critical Approaches to "Njáls saga"* (Pittsburgh: University of Pittsburgh Press, 1971), 178.

5. Sigmund Freud, *Beyond the Pleasure Principle*, trans. James Strachey, Standard Edition of the Complete Psychological Works 18 (London: Hogarth Press, 1955), 62.

factor in his reading of *Egils saga* as a psychological drama, while Russell Poole, in an equally interesting article on *Grettis saga*, uses a broad spectrum of psychological theories to understand the saga's main character and his resonance for fourteenth-century Icelanders.[6] Poole focuses not least on Grettir's fear of the dark and other phobias which would have been easy to relate to in these times preceding the invention of gas or electric lighting. Neither scholar adopts a specifically psychoanalytic perspective, though Poole mentions Jacques Lacan's particular version of psychoanalysis as a possible key to aspects of Grettir's relationship with his father.

The tragic nature of *Njáls saga* as well as the sexual themes it contains invites a purer psychoanalytic approach, and I am not the first to attempt one. Richard F. Allen was inspired by C. G. Jung in his reading of the saga, and Carolyn Anderson has written a brilliant article in which she studies the construction of gender in the saga in light of the theories of Lacan.[7]

Applying psychoanalysis to the sagas is fraught with difficulties. Their authors are anonymous and we are not sure whether it is indeed correct to assume individual authorship of these works. Their texts vary from one manuscript to another, and the issue of to what extent and in what way they are based on oral tradition is still being discussed.[8] Moreover, it is not always obvious that the concepts of psychoanalysis can be of use in pursuing the aims of most literary historians, i.e., understanding the way the texts are structured, how they generate meaning, and how they relate to the social and historical reality in which they (in this case, the sagas) originate.

In a recent book on *Egils saga*, I try to show that the twofold structure that so characterizes that saga can be partly explained by using psychoanalysis. The first part of the saga, which deals primarily with Þórólfr Kveld-Úlfsson, stages a simple conflict between hero and

---

6. See Ármann Jakobsson, "*Egils saga* and Empathy: Emotions and Moral Issues in a Dysfunctional Saga Family," *Scandinavian Studies* 80 (2008): 1–18; Russell Poole, "Myth, Psychology and Society in *Grettis saga*," *alvíssmál* 11 (2003): 3–16.

7. See Allen, *Fire and Iron*; Carolyn Anderson, "No Fixed Point: Gender and Blood Feuds in 'Njals saga,'" *Philological Quarterly* 81 (2002): 421–440.

8. See esp. Gísli Sigurðsson, *The Medieval Icelandic Saga and Oral Tradition: A Discourse on Method*, Publications of the Milman Parry Collection of Oral Literature 2 (Cambridge, MA: The Milman Parry Collection of Oral Literature, Harvard University; distr. Harvard University Press, 2004).

king. In the second and longer part, in which Þórólfr's nephew, Egill Skalla-Grímsson, is the main character, this conflict is complicated by more or less hidden ones with the father and with God. This structure is engendered by a complex play of discreetly suggested parallels and connections between different characters of the saga, especially between kings, fathers, and pairs of brothers. It is possible to explain the way the text functions by using the concepts of condensation and displacement, which are in Freud's thought the way dreams both express and conceal from the reader what is going on in his unconscious mind.[9] In this sense, *Egils saga* both shows and hides that it deals with basic Oedipal conflicts, which it projects onto religious and political concerns. This approach explains many aspects of the saga, not the least the motivations of its main character, Egill, whose behavior can be understood in light of his conflicts with his father and brother. The psychoanalytic approach has explanatory value whether or not we choose to believe, as many do, that Snorri Sturluson authored the work, though it also brings an interesting perspective to that theory as well.[10]

In a series of articles on *Eyrbyggja saga*, I have endeavored to solve the problem of that saga's atypical structure in a similar way. In this saga, several father figures are systematically opposed. By combining the use of the narrative semiotics of A. J. Greimas with psychoanalysis, it is possible to show how this dispersion of the theme of the father is one of the factors that explain the meandering construction that characterizes the saga and that scholars have had trouble explaining. The problematic relationship with the father figure, and in a more general way, with inherited social status, can be seen as expressing an identity crisis of the chieftain class in mid-thirteenth century Iceland. How can young chieftains become what their fathers were, i.e., chieftains, when so many equally well-born and capable men are fighting for these positions?[11]

---

9. See *The Interpretation of Dreams*, trans. James Strachey, The Pelican Freud Library 4 (London: Penguin, 1976), 417.

10. See Torfi H. Tulinius, *Skáldið í skriftinni: Snorri Sturluson og "Egils saga"* (Reykjavík: Hið íslenska bókmenntafélag, 2004), 219–28.

11. See Torfi H. Tulinius, "Hamlet í Helgafellssveit: Samræður um samræður við söguöld," in *Greppaminni: Rit til heiðurs Vésteini Ólasyni sjötugum*, ed. Margrét Eggertsdóttir et al. (Reykjavík: Hið íslenska bókmenntafélag, 2009), 423–35.

I try to show that in both sagas the saga authors are communicating with their audiences subconsciously about issues that are important in their times. Indeed, if all acts of language are acts of communication, literature, and especially literary narrative, is a quite particular type of such communication. One reason for this is that it goes on through a "third party," the character or characters of the story. These imaginary beings are representatives of a sort; one could also call them agents. The author is working within a fictional world and the characters he manipulates are projections of his fantasy, desire, fears, and preoccupations—even those he does not know about, or in other words, of his Unconscious. The peculiar thing about literary narrative is that these characters are not only the author's agents but also the reader's, who likewise projects himself onto these characters and their adventures. If characters in a story are projections, they are projections of both the sender and the receiver of the particular type of message that literary narrative is.[12]

Literature has therefore the very special status of being both a type of mirroring—consciously or not, both reader and author mirror themselves in the tale told—and a form of communication between these two parties. One could call it "communicative mirroring" or "mirroring communication."

Jacques Lacan's famous mirror-stage becomes pertinent in this context. This theory was one of his earliest contributions to psychoanalytic theory. It is about the formation of the Self as a psychological construct. At a certain moment in its development, the infant is capable of seeing and recognizing itself in a mirror. The baby is filled with a feeling of pleasure and invests this pleasure, i.e., the libido, into its own image.[13] This primary narcissistic experience is central to the formation of the self, which is a construct, and—Lacan insists—never the reality of who we are. This reality, the "Real," as he calls it, remains forever outside the grasp of our conscious minds.

Both pleasurable and anxiety-ridden, like all libidinal experiences, the formation of the Self is a long and difficult process, always at the mercy of external attacks—the scolding mother, the angry sibling,

---

12. See Elizabeth Wright, *Psychoanalytic Criticism: A Reappraisal* (London: Polity Press, 1998), 112–19.

13. See Jacques Lacan, *Écrits: A Selection* (London: Tavistock Publications, 1977), 1–7.

the destructive father—or internal ones, either directly from the Unconscious or indirectly through the Superego. Describing the aim of psychoanalysis as a form of therapy, Freud said, "Where Id was, Ego must be." But that path is a rocky one, and in the end it leads nowhere because the Real—the strangest and most unsettling of Lacan's three basic concepts: the Symbolic, the Imaginary and the Real—prevails.[14] All the desperate meaning-making we have been engaged in throughout our lives comes to nothing when our mental lives disappear into oblivion, snuffed out one by one like candles, by a silent but inexorable wind.

But before that, there is the ceaseless task of becoming oneself; the unending construction of identity; the narcissistic engagement with the Symbolic, or who we are told we are; and with the Imaginary, or who we dream we are: sweet dreams of bliss that should go on forever and/or tearful, sudorous nightmares from which we are relieved to awaken.

Eros and Thanatos

The death drive appears rather late in Freud's work, his first major text about it being *Beyond the Pleasure Principle*, first published in 1920.[15] It is one of Freud's more difficult and speculative texts. In it he postulates that the goal of all life is to seek death (the "quiescence of the inorganic world") and that furthering this goal is an unconscious drive towards death which interacts constantly with the other main drive in our psyche, an equally unconscious life instinct. This theory led to a major reworking of Freud's conception of the psychic apparatus, with the development of the threefold scheme of the Id, the Ego, and the Superego.[16]

This development took some time and was expressed gradually in a series of Freud's works, where he speaks of these drives in the plural as two groups of drives, one aiming for death and the other for life.[17] On the one hand, the death drives are those of all living organisms, which at some point seek to end their existence. These drives are

---

14. See Wright, *Psychoanalytic Criticism: A Reappraisal*, 99–104.

15. See note 5 above.

16. Sigmund Freud, *The Ego and the Id*, trans. Joan Riviere, Standard Edition of the Complete Psychological Works 19 (London: Hogarth Press, 1953).

17. Ibid., 39–47.

exteriorized in the form of aggressiveness and internalized in the form of masochism. On the other, the life drives' role is to bind the destructive forces of the death drives. He calls the former group of drives Thanatos and the latter Eros. This model is not only dualistic but also dialectic: there is a constant struggle between two sets of drives, Eros trying to keep Thanatos in check. The result is that the two are intricately interwoven or blended, for example in sexuality, which calls for a certain dosage of each drive to be effective. Eros is the more apparent of the two drives while Thanatos is silently working behind the scenes, except at moments of crisis when passions are unleashed; then it appears, usually in the guise of aggressiveness, but sometimes as a willingness to die. This unbinding of the passions is associated with what Freud calls *Triebentmischung* or defusion of drives, i.e., a state which occurs when the binding of the death drive by Eros is deficient.[18]

Freud believes that, of the two sets of drives, Thanatos is both the stronger and the more fundamental to the living being. The role of Eros is merely to delay as long as possible the inevitable end. As Freud says, every living thing wants to die, but wants to do so on its own terms.[19]

The American literary critic Peter Brooks wrote a remarkable study in which he showed how Freud's theory of the death wish brings new insights into the workings of narrative. Expanding on the idea that every narrative is shaped in accordance with the way it ends, and basing his approach on Freud's *Beyond the Pleasure Principle*, he proposes to read narrative as intimately related to the death drive, reproducing the dialectic between Eros and Thanatos in its very form.[20]

Indeed, it is difficult to conceive of any story without an ending, and one can also say that each narrative is shaped by the way it ends, since the events narrated are chosen and ordered to lead to the ending the author has in mind. But Brooks sees additional characteristics of the death drive in literature, for example, the way the latter typically works with repetition (e.g., rhyme and alliteration in verse and epic triads in narrative).

---

18. Ibid., 42.

19. Freud, *Beyond the Pleasure Principle*, 39; see also Peter Brooks, *Reading for the Plot: Design and Intention in Narrative*, 1st Vintage ed. (New York: Vintage Books, 1985), 107.

20. Brooks, *Reading for the Plot*, 112.

Repetition is one of the ways in which the death drive manifests itself. Freud's discovery of this drive is related to his treatment of patients who suffered from shell-shock after the First World War. The way they would relive in their dreams the traumatic situations they had been exposed to did not conform to Freud's theory of the pleasure principle, and that is why he sought to replace it. In his new way of thinking, repetition was a way of achieving the illusion of mastery over the trauma. He gave an example of this in the story of his little grandson, who was extremely distressed whenever his mother left him, but seemed to deal with it symbolically by playing over and over again the strange game of throwing a toy under a bed and saying "fort!" (away) and then retrieving it and saying "da!" (here). By this repetitive behavior, Freud believed, the toddler was paradoxically reliving the anxiety of separation from his mother, but also gaining control over it by symbolically making the mother come back.[21]

Such repetition could be seen as a manifestation of the pleasure principle (relieving the anxiety), but the urge to repeat is deeper still. It allows the binding of energy which protects the psyche from too strong a stimulus (the trauma). It is therefore a sort of defense mechanism, and one could postulate that the more often one finds traces of this compulsion to repeat in a literary text, the greater the trauma it is dealing with. Brooks sees in Freud's theory of the death drive a sort of "master plot" for all narrative. I would argue, however, that in some stories it is more apparent than in others, and that in *Njáls saga* it is particularly so.

"Koma mun til mín feigðin . . . "

It is one of the distinctive features of the saga how many of its characters accept their death.[22] This is true of the main protagonists: Gunnarr decides to return to Hlíðarendi, despite Kolskeggr's and Njáll's previous warnings that it will bring about his death (ÍF 12:181–83);

---

21. Freud, *Beyond the Pleasure Principle*, 14–17.

22. I deliberately avoid the subject of fate and willing acceptance of it in this paper. Lars Lönnroth discusses the difficulties of disentangling Christian and pagan thinking on this matter in *Njáls Saga: A Critical Introduction* (Berkeley: University of California Press, 1976), 123–36. My interest here lies in how deeper psychological structures can be perceived in cultural constructs such as the saga in question.

Njáll, Bergþóra, and Skarpheðinn all show in some way that they are willing to die (ÍF 12:326–30), as does Flosi, as has already been noted. This is also true of many minor characters, such as Þjóstólfr; he obeys Hallgerðr when she tells him to go find Hrútr after he has killed her husband Glúmr, even though he suspects why she sends him there (ÍF 12:50). The same could be said of Kolr, Atli, Þórðr Leysingjason, and other characters involved in the series of vicarious murders committed by Hallgerðr and Bergþóra in their feud (ÍF 12:93, 99, 107). They all know what their involvement in the killings will bring upon them, but they nevertheless submit to the will of the women. This does not mean that they do not defend themselves when it comes to the actual fighting; however, it was within their power to avoid being in this situation in the first place.

This is also true of the Norwegian Þórir, who does not want to fight Gunnarr but, when prodded by his Icelandic hostess, goes to battle despite his knowledge that it will lead to his death (ÍF 12:155). Gunnarr's brother Hjǫrtr also chooses to fight though his death has been foretold in his brother's dream (ÍF 12:156). Not to be forgotten on this list is the young Þórðr Kárason, who prefers dying with his grand-parents to surviving them (ÍF 12:330).

This aspect of the saga is closely related to the stylistic feature of foreshadowing, which is one of its salient characteristics.[23] The fore-knowledge of one's death, as it has been predicted by somebody like Njáll who has the gift of prophecy, means that in some way one accepts it. This is particularly clear for Gunnarr. In a stimulating recent reading of the saga, Theodore M. Andersson remarks on the strangeness of Gunnarr's attitude throughout the saga: "It therefore seems difficult to believe that Gunnarr is not a partner, voluntary or involuntary, in his own undoing."[24] Though Andersson's approach to the saga is quite different from the one proposed here, he also has noticed that the saga seems to indicate that Gunnarr is collaborating in his own demise.

Closely connected to the ideas of foreshadowing and death are the noun "feigð" and the adjective "feigr." A study of the complete

---

23. See Günter Zimmermann, "Die Vorausdeutungen in der Njáls saga unter strukturellen Aspekt," in *Linguistica et Philologica: Gedenkschrift für Björn Colliner (1894–1983)*, ed. Helmut Humbach (Wien: Wilhelm Braumüller, 1984), 597–607.

24. Theodore M. Andersson, *The Growth of the Medieval Icelandic Sagas (1180–1280)* (Ithaca: Cornell University Press, 2006), 195.

corpus of the sagas about early Icelanders reveals that, in all of them except *Njáls saga*, it occurs at the most three times, and in many not at all. In our saga the noun and its adjectival form are found a total of ten times. Of course, this is the longest saga belonging to this particular genre. Nonetheless, the exceptional episodic density of these occurrences suggests that the author took a particular interest in the idea that the living were destined to die.

Gunnarr himself uses the noun in quite a remarkable way in chapter 68. His brother is warning of a possible danger and he replies, "Koma mun til mín feigðin . . . hvar sem ek em staddr, ef mér verðr þess auðit" (Death will come to me no matter where I am . . . if such is my fate).[25] What is unusual here is the choice of the expression *að vera einhvers auðit*. It is a positive word, suggesting good fortune, but here Gunnarr uses it with the word "feigð" which means "approach, or foreboding of death." This is the only occurrence of this word with this expression and it intensifies the impression that Gunnarr's attitude to death is quite positive.

One wonders why, and only a tentative answer can be proposed here. Gunnarr is a complex character. He is an outstanding warrior but also a peaceful man who does his best to avoid conflicts, though he will defend his honor when it is challenged, for example in the case of Otkell's and Skammkell's slandering of him (ÍF 12:136). He usually shows forbearance but he can also be carried away by his own ability to fight. Though he kills many men, he does not like it: "'Hvat ek veit,' segir Gunnarr, 'hvárt ek mun því óvaskari maðr en aðrir menn sem mér þykkir meira fyrir en ǫðrum mǫnnum at vega menn'" ("What I don't know," said Gunnarr, "is whether I am less manly than other men because killing troubles me more than it does them").[26]

Despite his self-control, Gunnarr is a man of strong emotions. He is often shown to be angry but he is also a true friend to Njáll as well as a loving brother to Kolskeggr and Hjǫrtr. Finally, he is open to feelings of lust, as can be seen in his brash and ill-fated decision to marry Hallgerðr. Hrútr calls it a *girndarráð* or "decision based on lust" (ÍF 12:87), and this seems to be the opinion of the author of the saga. Here we come to the famous scene, later in *Njáls saga*, when Gunnarr

---

25. ÍF 12:168; Cook, *Njal's Saga*, 114.
26. ÍF 12:139; Cook, *Njal's Saga*, 93.

changes his mind about leaving Iceland for a three-year exile, which was one of the terms of the settlement he agreed upon after the killing of Þorgeir Otkelsson. Gunnarr's horse has stumbled on its way from Fljótshlíð to the ship that will take him abroad and Gunnarr has dismounted. He turns back and sees his home and the surrounding countryside and says that it has never seemed more beautiful to him (ÍF 12:182).

This scene has been interpreted in different ways over the years. Quite a few think that Gunnarr is actually referring to Hallgerðr, who stayed behind at Hlíðarendi, and that the meadows and fields stand for her hair and other sexually charged attributes.[27] Several years ago, the late Hermann Pálsson brought to my attention the fact that what Gunnarr is watching is not only his farm but also the place where his grave-mound will stand, since it is believed to have been on the flat-land between Hlíðarendi and the sea (ÍF 12:192n). He also mentioned that the only other staging of a character contemplating the beauty of a landscape in the saga literature, which is in *Landnámabók*, is associated with death. Hallsteinn Þengilsson comes home, learns of his father's death, and interprets his mixed feelings with a verse which tells how the mountain which gives its name to the paternal farm is bowed with grief but that the slopes of his home welcome him with a laugh.[28]

Perhaps "mixed feelings" is the correct way to describe Gunnarr's emotions at this moment. Indeed, there is no reason to reject any of the interpretations of what is going through his mind. He could be feeling love for his home, and also want to stay with Hallgerðr, the object of his lust. He is also deliberately going against the advice of his two most trusted friends, Njáll and Kolskeggr, who both have said that he would certainly die if he does not honor his promise to leave the country for three years. Gunnarr is a man of strong and conflicting passions, but he does not like them and is never happier than when he has been freed from them and sings alone but content in his grave-mound.

27. Helga Kress, "'Óþarfar unnustur áttu': Um samband fjölkynngi, kvennafars og karlmennsku í Íslendingasögum," in *Galdramenn: Galdrar og samfélag á miðöldum*, ed. Torfi H. Tulinius (Reykjavík: Hugvísindastofnun, 2008), 40.

28. *Íslendingabók, Landnámabók*, ed. Jakob Benediktsson, Íslenzk fornrit 1 (Reykjavík: Hið íslenzka fornritafélag, 1986), 272.

It is indeed quite striking in this context that Gunnarr is never portrayed as particularly gay or joyful except when he is seen revelling in his grave mound after his death. Indeed, there he is "kátligr ok með gleðimóti miklu" (happy and had a very cheerful look).[29] There is one exception to this, and that is when he comes to the Alþingi after his successful journey abroad. Here he is "við alla menn léttr ok kátr" (light-hearted and merry with everyone),[30] but it is only a matter of hours or days before his fateful encounter with Hallgerðr, who goes out of her way to be attractive to him. Blinded by lust, he hastily decides to marry her, despite Hrútr's warnings. It is as if the saga is telling us that sexual passion can only bring tragedy, and that happiness is only achieved by steering clear of desire.

It is worthy of note that the saga on several occasions establishes a relationship between lust and a willingness to die. Both Þórir and Þorgrímr, the Norwegians who are killed by Gunnarr, know that they will die but accept to fight with him because of their desire for Egill's daughter Guðrún. She is the most beautiful (*kurteisust*) of women and called *náttsól* or "night sun" (ÍF 12:147, 155, 160), a cognomen which has connotations of death. It could therefore be significant that Þorgrímr is the first person Gunnarr kills during his last fight (ÍF 12:187), suggesting a link between the two characters that both have allowed themselves to be led into a deadly situation because of their passionate desire for a beautiful woman.

There is also a suggestion that Þjóstólfr is motivated by sexual passion for Hallgerðr when he kills Glúmr. Before that, Þjóstólfr had taunted Glúmr about "brǫlta á maga Hallgerði" (bouncing around on Hallgerd's belly).[31] That there are close links between exacerbated sexual passions and the death drive is in accordance with Freud's theory of the interweaving of life and death drives: Eros is serving Thanatos.

"Genginn út úr sjávarhǫmrum"

Nowhere is the ineluctability of programmed death in the saga more striking than in the famous Járngrímr episode, when Flosi dreams that an impressive figure steps out of the no less imposing mountain

---

29. ÍF 12:193; Cook, *Njal's Saga*, 130.

30. ÍF 12:85; Cook, *Njal's Saga*, 52.

31. ÍF 12:49; Cook, *Njal's Saga*, 32.

Lómagnúpr to the west of his home and calls Flosi's men to him (ÍF 12:346–48). The men are called in the order of their death, and also in clusters, showing that their deaths will occur at different moments in the future.[32] From the perspective of Freud's theory of the death drive, this is a particularly interesting scene for at least two reasons. The first is that it comes to Flosi in a bad dream, not a good one that fulfils his wishes as in Freud's earlier theory, where the pleasure principle prevails. In his nightmare Flosi is living the trauma to come, when so many of his followers will be killed, most of them by Kári. The second reason is that here the idea of future death is not presented as an expression of somebody's insight or foreknowledge, but as something which is inherently uncanny: a mysterious man, with a no less mysterious and intimidating name, coming out of a mountain.

It is no coincidence that Freud was working on his famous essay "The Uncanny" at the same time as he wrote *Beyond the Pleasure Principle*.[33] As Freud said himself, the death drive is in itself uncanny.[34] The idea of a force within us that is working toward our disappearance is not only counterintuitive but deeply unsettling. It is, however, also a fact of life, in the sense that we all grow old and die, that our own passing is already programmed. But Freud's theory is not a mere statement of this all-too-well-known reality. What troubles us, as in his theory of the Unconscious in a more general way, is that there is a force within us that we do not control and that we do not like. Not only are we not masters in our own house, as in Freud's famous formulation; there is also an enemy within.[35]

The figure of Skarpheðinn has long fascinated readers of *Njáls saga* as he obviously fascinated its author. He is indeed an unusual character, and in many ways unique in saga literature. In the first part of the saga, he stays in the background, obeying his father and supporting his friends. When he takes a leading role it is almost without exception to commit violent deeds, such as killing Þráinn

---

32. Lönnroth, *Njáls Saga*, 32. There is quite an extensive literature on Flosi's dream. It is enough in this context to refer to Einar Ólafur Sveinsson on its likely origin in an account in Gregory's *Dialogues*. See *Á Njálsbúð*, 10–11, 171.

33. See Nicholas Royle, *The Uncanny* (Manchester: Manchester University Press, 2003); Brooks, *Reading for the Plot*.

34. Freud, *Beyond the Pleasure Principle*, 21.

35. Sigmund Freud, *A Difficulty in the Path of Psycho-Analysis*, trans. James Strachey, Standard Edition of the Complete Psychological Works 18 (London: Hogarth Press, 1917), 143.

and later his son (ÍF 12:231, 280), but also to destroy his and his family's chances of garnering support for their cause after the slaying of Hǫskuldr Þráinsson, and finally to ruin the settlement that at last had been reached after much effort by many good people. As Síðu-Hallr says at this occasion, Flosi and he are obviously *ógæfumenn* (ÍF 12:314)—"men of misfortune." He also takes a lead when he decides to obey his father on the night of the burning and retreat into the farmhouse, though he knows it means their death (ÍF 12:326).

This would be sufficient to connect Skarpheðinn to the death drive in what could be called the psychodynamics of the saga, or in other words the way it speaks to the Unconscious. But there are other aspects of his character that add to this impression. He is in many ways an uncanny figure. He is very often described as pale, and he betrays strong emotions that he nevertheless does his best to repress (ÍF 12:114). One of his defining characteristics is his mysterious grin (*glott*) which he displays at numerous times in the saga (ÍF 12:96, 98, 114, 299, 304, 327). There is something strange about this grin, as if he is taking pleasure in negative things, but also being provocative.[36]

This is particularly true in his behavior at the Alþingi when he and his brothers are seeking support from major chieftains in the lawsuit that follows Hǫskuldr's slaying. This episode is of special interest in relationship to the death drive. It is a series of five scenes that are all structured in the same way and all repeat with variations the identification of Skarpheðinn (ÍF 12:297–306). As we have seen, repetition is closely related to the death drive, and though there are significant differences among the five scenes, it is the repetition that makes them remarkable as well as the fearsome and uncanny behavior of Skarpheðinn. This eeriness is suggested to the reader in several ways, among others in the way the four successive chieftains describe him. Of particular note is that Skapti Þóróddsson calls him *trǫllsligr* (like a troll) and Hafr inn auðgi says he is "svá illiligr sem genginn sé út ór sjávarhǫmrum" (so dreadful that it is as if he had walked out of a sea-cliff). During this episode, there is something out of the ordinary about Skarpheðinn that awakens a sense of unease in those who meet him, as if death itself were among them. Hafr's comparison

---

36. See Low Soon Ai, "The Mirthless Content of Skarphedinn's Grin," *Medium Aevum* 65 (1996): 101–107.

is particularly interesting because of the parallel between him and Járngrímr, who as we have seen announces the death of those whose names he calls. This is confirmed by the way people react to his body after his death. He had declaimed a skaldic strophe from within the ruins of the burned-down farm, suggesting to Grani Gunnarsson that he might already have been transformed into a revenant (ÍF 12:336–37). Everyone is pleasantly surprised that his dead body does not provoke fear (ÍF 12:344), suggesting that his acceptance of death and the sign of the cross that he burned himself across his chest may have prevented him from becoming one.

"Veg þú aldrei meir í inn sama knérunn": Repetition and the Death Drive

As in so many narratives, repetition is one of the ways in which the story is woven in *Njáls saga*. It is particularly present in passages such as Bergþóra's and Hallgerðr's vicarious killings of each other's men, in the story of Gunnarr's deceit of Hrútr early in the saga, as well as in the lengthy episodes of legal wrangling later on in the saga. It is of interest to note that the saga warns against repetition, as if the author sensed the links between repetition and the death drive. This is true of Gunnarr, who repeats the slaying of Otkell when he kills his son Þorgeir, despite Njáll's warning against killing again "í inn sama knérunn" (ÍF 12:139), i.e. in the same lineage. Tragic circumstances make this inevitable for Gunnarr. The same cannot be said for Skarpheðinn and his brothers, who allow themselves to be tricked by Mǫrðr, a person they should have distrusted, into killing Hǫskuldr, son of Þráinn, whom they had killed several years earlier. As in Freud's theory, repetition is the way in which the elusive death drive makes itself known. In the case of the slaying of Hǫskuldr Þráinsson, the saga obviously perceives it as causing the death of Njáll and all his sons (ÍF 12:281). It is as if some hidden force has taken over, both human and escaping the control of humans. The only way to stop it is to break the chain of revenge and counter-revenge as Gunnarr does after the killing of his cousin Sigmundr, but also as Síðu-Hallr does by renouncing compensation for his son's death. However, the death drive is unstoppable, and its destructive forces always prevail at the end.

Psychoanalysis can lead us to a better understanding of the dynamics of *Njáls saga*, as had already been shown by Carolyn Anderson in a previously mentioned article.[37] The present paper suggests that bringing the Freudian concept of the death drive into the analysis of *Njáls saga* can add new insights into this most remarkable and most studied of the sagas about early Icelanders. It is a saga deeply engaged in the struggle between the destructive impulses of the death drive and the efforts of survival instincts to keep Thanatos at bay. This engagement can be seen in the author's obvious preoccupation with chosen death, in the repetitive structure he gave to the story, but also in the way he takes the readers through his vast narrative, inviting them to experience the dangers of passions, to witness the efforts of good men to curb them and in the end return to the inorganic state as does Flosi in his peaceful death at sea. His life has run its course and he has ended it on his own terms. So has the saga.

Bibliography

Ai, Low Soon. "The Mirthless Content of Skarphedinn's Grin." *Medium Aevum* 65 (1996): 101–107.

Allen, Richard F. *Fire and Iron: Critical Approaches to Njáls saga.* Pittsburgh: University of Pittsburgh Press, 1971.

Anderson, Carolyn. "No Fixed Point: Gender and Blood Feuds in 'Njals saga.'" *Philological Quarterly* 81 (2002): 421–40.

Andersson, Theodore M. *The Growth of the Medieval Icelandic Sagas (1180–1280).* Ithaca: Cornell University Press, 2006.

Ármann Jakobsson. "*Egils saga* and Empathy: Emotions and Moral Issues in a Dysfunctional Saga Family." *Scandinavian Studies* 80 (2008): 1–18.

Brennu-Njáls saga. Edited by Einar Ólafur Sveinsson. Íslenzk fornrit 12. Reykjavík: Hið íslenzka fornritafélag, 1954.

Brooks, Peter. *Reading for the Plot: Design and Intention in Narrative.* 1st Vintage ed. New York: Vintage Books, 1985 [1984].

Cook, Robert, trans. *Njal's Saga.* London: Penguin Classics, 2001.

Einar Ólafur Sveinsson. *Á Njálsbúð: Bók um mikið listaverk.* Reykjavík: Hið íslenzka bókmenntafélag, 1943.

Freud, Sigmund. *A Difficulty in the Path of Psycho-Analysis.* Translated by James Strachey. Standard Edition of the Complete Psychological Works 18. London: Hogarth Press, 1917.

---

37. See "No Fixed Point."

———. *Beyond the Pleasure Principle*. Translated by James Strachey. Standard Edition of the Complete Psychological Works 18. London: Hogarth Press, 1955.

———. *The Ego and the Id*. Translated by Joan Riviere. Standard Edition of the Complete Psychological Works 19. London: Hogarth Press, 1953.

———. *The Interpretation of Dreams*. Translated by James Strachey. The Pelican Freud Library 4. London: Penguin, 1976.

Gísli Sigurðsson. *The Medieval Icelandic Saga and Oral Tradition: A Discourse on Method*. Publications of the Milman Parry Collection of Oral Literature 2. Cambridge, MA: The Milman Parry Collection of Oral Literature, Harvard University; distributed by Harvard University Press, 2004.

Kress, Helga. "'Óþarfar unnustur áttu': Um samband fjölkynngi, kvennafars og karlmennsku í Íslendingasögum." In *Galdramenn: Galdrar og samfélag á miðöldum*, edited by Torfi H. Tulinius, 21–48. Reykjavík: Hugvísindastofnun, 2008.

Íslendingabók, Landnámabók. Edited by Jakob Benediktsson. Íslenzk fornrit 1. Reykjavík: Hið íslenzka fornritafélag, 1986.

Lacan, Jacques. *Écrits: A Selection*. London: Tavistock Publications, 1977.

Lönnroth, Lars. *Njáls Saga: A Critical Introduction*. Berkeley: University of California Press, 1976.

Poole, Russell. "Myth, Psychology and Society in *Grettis saga*." *alvíssmál* 11 (2003): 3–16.

Royle, Nicholas. *The Uncanny*. Manchester: Manchester University Press, 2003.

Torfi H. Tulinius. *Skáldið í skriftinni: Snorri Sturluson og "Egils saga."* Reykjavík: Hið íslenska bókmenntafélag, 2004. Revised and Translated as *The Enigma of Egill: The Saga, the Viking Poet, and Snorri Sturluson*. Islandica 57. Ithaca: Cornell University Library, 2014.

———. "Hamlet í Helgafellssveit: Samræður um samræður við söguöld." In *Greppaminni: Rit til heiðurs Vésteini Ólasyni sjötugum*, edited by Margrét Eggertsdóttir, Árni Sigurjónsson, Guðrún Ása Grímsdóttir, Guðrún Nordal, and Guðvarður Már Gunnlaugsson, 423–35. Reykjavík: Hið íslenska bókmenntafélag, 2009.

Wright, Elizabeth. *Psychoanalytic Criticism: A Reappraisal*. London: Polity Press, 1998.

Zimmermann, Günter. "Die Vorausdeutungen in der Njáls saga unter strukturellen Aspekt." In *Linguistica et Philologica: Gedenkschrift für Björn Colliner (1894–1983)*, edited by Helmut Humbach, 597–607. Wien: Wilhelm Braumüller, 1984.

Skaldic Poetics and the Making of the *Sagas of Icelanders*

Guðrún Nordal
UNIVERSITY OF ICELAND
ÁRNI MAGNÚSSON INSTITUTE

1

The writing of the *First Grammatical Treatise* signals an important stage in the development of textual culture in the North. The author's reasons for the writing of the treatise are propounded in this often cited passage from the *Prologue*:

> til þess at hœgra verði at rita ok lesa sem nú tíðisk ok á þessu landi bæði lǫg ok áttvísi eða þýðingar helgar eða svá þau hin spaklegu frœði er Ari Þorgilsson hefir á bœkr sett af skynsamlegu viti þá hefir ek ok ritat oss Íslendingum stafróf . . . latínustǫfum ǫllum þeim er mér þótti gegna til várs máls.

In order that it may become easier to write and read, as is now customary in this country as well, both the laws and genealogies, or interpretations of sacred writings, or also that sagacious (historical) lore that Ari Þorgilsson has recorded in books with such reasonable understanding, I have composed an alphabet for us Icelanders as well . . . of all those Latin letters that seemed to me to fit our language well.[1]

---

1. *First Grammatical Treatise: Introduction, Texts, Notes, Translation, Vocabulary, and Facsimiles*, ed. Hreinn Benediktsson, University of Iceland Publications in Linguistics 1 (Reykjavík: Institute of Nordic Linguistics, 1972), 208.

This statement is significant for at least two reasons: it sets out a plan to adapt the Latin alphabet to the Icelandic language in order to regulate writing, and it lists examples of literary activity in Iceland in the period 1125–75. It is clear that the First Grammarian refers to works that have been written down already at the time of composition, but not to those transmitted orally at his time, such as skaldic poetry. He is describing *literary* culture, not *oral* culture.

The only known contextualizing of an indigenous stanza in the Latin alphabet prior to the writing of the treatise is indeed in one of the works mentioned in the Prologue. Ari fróði (the Learned) Þorgilsson refers in *Íslendingabók* (written ca. 1122–33) to a humorous ditty in Eddic meter recited by the recently converted Hjalti Skeggjason at the Alþingi in 999 or 1000. This stanza is not cited in the text to authorize Ari's account of the conversion of Iceland; rather, it is employed for humorous effect and to throw into relief Hjalti's relaxed and indifferent attitude toward his abandoned pagan faith at the sacred assembly. The First Grammarian presumably regarded the ditty as an integral part of Ari's narrative rather than as a separate entity worthy of Hjalti's authorship.

Judging from the numerous references to named poets from the ninth to the twelfth centuries, and subsequent testimonies to their verse-making in sagas and treatises after the composition of the *First Grammatical Treatise*, we can surmise that a large quantity of poems and stanzas from the preceding centuries was transmitted orally in the twelfth century.[2] A great deal of interpretation and scrutiny had to be exercised before oral poetry could be put to writing in the Latin alphabet, and exact rules of orthography and phonology were necessary to secure a faithful, or at least generally acceptable, presentation of the verse in the context of official historiography. It is tempting to argue for a link between the theorizing of the Icelandic language as early as the *First Grammatical Treatise* and the ingenious use of oral verse as source material in royal chronicles in the late twelfth and early thirteenth centuries. The *First Grammatical Treatise* would have

---

2. The existing skaldic corpus consists of sixteen thousand lines and some 5400 stanzas, the majority of which is composed after the conversion to Christianity; see Roberta Frank, "Skaldic Poetry," in *Old Norse-Icelandic Literature: A Critical Guide*, ed. Carol J. Clover and John Lindow, Islandica 45 (Ithaca: Cornell University Press, 1985), 161, and the website of the *Skaldic Edition of the Scandinavian Middle Ages*: www.skaldic.arts.usyd.edu.

admirably fulfilled the need for a solid foundation for the encoding of oral literature needed by the chroniclers, even though the author does not indicate that he wrote the treatise for that reason.[3]

Skaldic verse-making in the twelfth century was vibrant on at least four levels: (1) Skaldic poetry was used in everyday exchange between people in Iceland, if the evidence of the sagas in *Sturlunga* can be trusted. (2) Skaldic verse-making was actively practiced in the west Nordic region (Norway, Orkney, and the British Isles), and the poets dedicated their verse to kings and earls; this poetry was later used, or seen to be used, to authorize saga narratives of the patrons. (3) A number of narrative poems composed in the twelfth century, such as Einarr Skúlason's "Geisli" and the anonymous "Placitus drápa," reveal attempts to create metrical narratives of the past—though these experiments did not gain a following.[4] It is likely that both poems were written down early; "Placitus drápa" is preserved in a manuscript from ca. 1200 and "Geisli" was recited in the cathedral of Niðarós in the presence of three kings and a bishop in 1152/3 and possibly presented to these eminencies in written form as well. (4) The Icelandic-Orcadian poem "Háttalykill" from the middle of the twelfth century is an early sign of a systematic study of skaldic meter in the grammatical tradition, which was developed more fully in the thirteenth century. The First Grammarian is not untouched by this diverse skaldic activity. He cites skaldic couplets on two occasions in his treatise, and he was very likely influenced by the alliterative technique of the skalds in his application of minimal pairs in his analysis of the sound system. Skaldic verse was clearly not exclusively studied in the contexts of the royal court and royal historiography in

---

3. For a more detailed discussion of the *First Grammatical Treatise*, see Guðrún Nordal, "Metrical learning and the First Grammatical Treatise," in *Versatility in Versification*, ed. Tonya Kim Dewey and Frog (New York: Peter Lang, 2009), 23–38, where I argue that it is likely that the *First Grammatical Treatise* was written, or at least used, for this purpose. See also Guðrún Nordal, *Tools of Literacy: The Role of Skaldic Verse in Icelandic Textual Culture of the 12th and 13th Centuries* (Toronto: University of Toronto Press, 2001).

4. See Guðrún Nordal, "Samhengið í íslenskum fornbókmenntum," in *Sagnaheimur: Studies in Honour of Hermann Pálsson on his 80th birthday, 26th May 2001*, ed. Ásdís Egilsdóttir and Rudolf Simek, Studia Medievalia Septentrionalia 6 (Vienna: Fassbaender, 2001), 91–106, where I argue that the narrative poems are in fact early and unsuccessful attempts at saga writing, and that this thread was picked up again by the *rímur* poets in the fourteenth century.

the late twelfth and the beginning of the thirteenth centuries, but was practiced at different levels in society and in various social contexts in the west Nordic region.

The key question addressed in this paper is how we might set the cultural milieu of court poets and skaldic poetics, which underpinned royal vernacular historiography, against the making of the sagas of Icelanders in the same period. Theodore Andersson is correct in proposing a correlation between the writing of the kings' sagas and some sagas of the Icelanders in the thirteenth century, but he does not reflect on the importance of skaldic verse in the aesthetic and cultural relationship between these two genres.[5] I believe, on the other hand, that the first stages in the writing of the sagas of Icelanders cannot be fully elucidated unless we balance the literary production of the poets and the saga authors against the systematic study of skaldic poetry as well as the application of skaldic verse in royal historiography in the late twelfth and early thirteenth centuries. From the point of view of verse citations there are clear generic boundaries between the kings' sagas and the sagas of Icelanders. Bjarne Fidjestøl noted that even though the same poet figures in the kings' sagas and the sagas of Icelanders, there is little overlap between the stanzas cited by them in the kings' sagas on the one hand, and in the sagas of Icelanders on the other.[6] However, the gray area between the two genres is of great interest and will be explored below.

Skaldic verse played a pivotal role in contextualizing many of the early sagas of Icelanders, such as *Egils saga*, *Eyrbyggja saga*, and *Njáls saga*. Even though the dating of the sagas of Icelanders is less clear than that of the kings' sagas, I would argue that the way skaldic verse is cited in a saga and the identification of the poets can reveal the cultural milieu of the author, the intended audience, and possibly the time when the poetry was composed. Before I turn to the sagas of Icelanders, it will be necessary to draw up a picture of the cultural mobility of the poets and the saga authors in the early thirteenth century, as it will be one of the contentions of this essay that the

5. Theodore M. Andersson, *The Growth of the Medieval Icelandic Sagas (1180–1280)* (Ithaca: Cornell University Press, 2006).

6. Bjarne Fidjestøl, "On a New Edition of Skaldic Poetry," in *The Sixth International Saga Conference 28.7. – 2.8.1985: Workshop Papers*, 2 vols. (Copenhagen: Det Arnamagnæanske Institut, 1985), 1:319–35.

audience in Norway and the historical circumstances that inspired the writing of the large royal histories also motivated the writing of some of the *Íslendingasögur* (sagas of Icelanders).

2

Royal chronicles either written by Norwegian authors or patronized by Norwegian kings in the late twelfth century incorporate skaldic stanzas composed in a predominantly illiterate society, but it took time for the verse to be fully accepted as reliable source material in chronicle writing. The function of verse in the earliest kings' sagas before Snorri, such as in *Sverris saga*, Thedoricus's *Historia*, and *Ágrip*, can be judged to be aesthetic rather than historical. These three works are completely different in character. *Sverris saga* is a contemporary saga, written in the vernacular for the king himself, and references to verse composed for the king were not needed to authorize the account. In fact, the author makes little use of the numerous poems thought to have been composed for King Sverrir Sigurðarson (1151–1202; ruled 1177–1202), but interestingly he preserves a speech interlaced with two skaldic quotations by the king.[7] Theodoricus writes his Latin chronicle for Archbishop Eysteinn Erlendsson of Niðarós (?-1188; archbishop 1161–88); he refers to the existence of verse but makes no attempt to translate any in his narrative. The author of *Ágrip* does not use skaldic verse as source material, but rather as embellishment in the narrative. It seems therefore that the authoritative role of skaldic verse in the vernacular textual culture and the setting up of a hierarchy of verse by the court poets, in the context of *grammatica* and royal vernacular historiography, had not fully materialized in the late twelfth century.[8]

The creation of the skaldic canon was conditioned by historical circumstances in Norway in the first half of the thirteenth century,

---

7. *Sverris saga etter Cod. Am. 327 4to*, ed. Gustrav Indrebø (Kristiania [Oslo], 1920), 50–51.

8. See Preben Meulengracht Sørensen, "The Prosimetrum Form 1: Verses as the Voice of the Past," in *Skaldsagas: Text, Vocation, and Desire in the Icelandic Sagas of Poets*, ed. Russell Poole, Ergänzungsbände zum Reallexikon der germanischen Altertumskunde 27 (Berlin: de Gruyter, 2001), 172–90; see also Guðrún Nordal, "Attraction of Opposites: Skaldic Verse in *Njáls saga*," in *Literacy in Medieval and Early Modern Scandinavian Culture*, ed. Pernille Hermann, The Viking Collection: Studies in Northern Civilization 16 (Odense: University of Southern Denmark Press, 2005), 213–15.

the consolidation of royal power in Norway, and subsequent strengthening of the royal court as a cultural center. The subject matter of the verse reveals the intended audience of the kings' sagas, that is, the aristocratic milieu in Norway, Iceland, and Orkney, and most importantly the royal court; and the provenance of the verse suggests the places of writing of the early historical texts. Snorri Sturluson and his literary community in the first half of the thirteenth century are responsible for transmitting about one-sixth of the preserved skaldic corpus, or the greater part of the skaldic canon of the kings' sagas and *Snorra Edda*. Their mapping of the corpus was achieved in the first half of the thirteenth century, and was for the most part reproduced unchanged in the ensuing tradition of royal historiography and skaldic poetics until the end of the fourteenth century.

The writing of *Heimskringla*, Fagrskinna, and Morkinskinna commenced at a time of violent internal strife between the contenders for the Norwegian throne, resulting in the ascension of Hákon Hákonarson as the king in 1217 at the tender age of thirteen. After more than a twenty-year period of sharing his power with his father-in-law Earl (later Duke) Skúli Bárðarson, Hákon consolidated his sole rule of the country at Skúli's death in 1240, culminating in his coronation by the Pope's cardinal in 1247. The prologue to *Heimskringla* does not state that the work was written for the King or Earl Skúli, even though royal patronage is highly likely for a work of such a political nature. Snorri's "Háttatal" may be a guide in this direction; it is composed in honor of both Hákon and Skúli, indeed favoring Skúli.[9] Even though the writing of *Heimskringla* would have started and matured in Snorri's time, it is likely that the prototype was not finished till 1259, as Jonna Louis-Jensen has shown, and the version we regard as the archetype is the Kringla manuscript from ca. 1270.[10]

The encoding of skaldic verse in royal historiography served at least three purposes: first, to solidify the Icelanders' position as the carriers of the skaldic tradition and the collective memory of the Scandinavian past; second, to authenticate the verse, of pagan and

---

9. See Guðrún Nordal, "Skáldið Snorri Sturluson," in *Snorrastefna, 25.-27. júli 1990*, ed. Úlfar Bragason, Rit Stofnunar Sigurðar Nordals 1 (Reykjavík: Stofnun Sigurðar Nordals, 1992), 52–69.

10. Jonna Louis-Jensen, "*Heimskringla*: et værk af Snorri Sturluson?" *Nordica Bergensia* 14 (1997): 231–45.

Christian origin, as a foundation for the writing of royal vernacular historiography; and third, to strengthen Hákon's claim to the throne and to mythologize his royal lineage in line with other European royal families. The interlacing of verse by Icelandic poets in the sagas of the Norwegian kings, with whom a number of Icelandic chieftains at the time claimed kinship, was furthermore a highly political act in an Icelandic-Norwegian context. Theodoricus and Saxo both noted that the Icelanders preserved a wealth of oral poetry, but these oral riches were without value unless they could be converted into transferable goods in the new textual culture. The authorization of skaldic verse through royal chronology and the grammatical method seems to have been accepted by writers and audiences alike throughout the thirteenth century, and we would expect this preoccupation with skaldic verse to have influenced the way skaldic verse was incorporated into other saga genres, such as the sagas of Icelanders and the *fornaldarsögur*, particularly those sagas that can be associated with the same subject matter as that of the kings' sagas.[11] The translation of the verse from oral transmission to written texts, in all three indigenous saga genres, coincided with the first visible attempts of the Icelandic aristocracy at carving out a niche for themselves at court in Norway, and it was skaldic poetry that gave them the most significant advantage at the literary level.

Snorri Sturluson was the first powerful chieftain known to make this claim. Snorri was preoccupied with Norway all his life, and by Norway I mean the Norwegian aristocratic milieu, the court, the earls, and the king himself. Long before his first journey to Norway in 1218, probably during his formative years at Oddi before 1200, he sent a now-lost poem to King Sverrir Sigurðarson, which some argue may have been a memorial poem sent after Sverrir's death in 1202, though it could just as likely have been sent to Norway during Sverrir's reign. Some years later he bequeathed a poem to Earl Hákon galinn, Sverrir's nephew, and received precious presents from Norway in return: a shield, a sword, and armor—hence a complete knightly outfit—and a praising stanza by the court poet Máni, known from

---

11. See Guðrún Nordal, "Poetic Voices in the *fornaldarsögur*," in *The Legendary Sagas: Origins and Development*, ed. Annette Lassen et al. (Reykjavík: University of Iceland Press, 2012), 139–51.

Sverris saga. The icing on the cake was a generous invitation to stay with Hákon galinn. The author of *Íslendinga saga* comments deftly, "mjǫk var þat í skapi Snorra" (this was very much to Snorri's liking).[12] However, Earl Hákon galinn died in 1214 before he could receive the ambitious Icelander. In the year 1217 Snorri marched into the terrain at the Alþingi with six hundred (or seven hundred and twenty) men, and among those were eighty armored Norwegians.[13] Where did they and their costly armor come from? Why did Snorri maintain such a large Norwegian following in Iceland in the period before his first known journey to Norway? On this same occasion it is noted that he called his booth "Grýla," the same name that is associated with a part of the saga of Sverrir Sigurðarson. Is this a coincidence? These glimpses into Snorri's life are important clues to his disposition towards the court and courtly life before he arrives in Norway in 1218.[14] The young Snorri is eagerly imitating foreign aristocratic models, and thirsty for royal recognition.

The Sturlungar family was not the only one to seek royal favors through its literary creations. Icelandic chieftains began to identify themselves with European aristocrats in the twelfth century, but particularly in the thirteenth century, through the writing of royal histories, genealogies, myths of the settlement, and skaldic poetry. The Oddaverjar linked their lineage directly to the Norwegian dynasties. Jón Loftsson was the son of Þóra, Magnúss berfœttr's illegitimate daughter. The poem "Nóregskonungatal" (ca. 1180) composed for Jón Loptsson, Snorri Sturluson's foster-father, resembles a kings' saga in a nutshell. It is preserved only in the famous kings' saga manuscript Flateyjarbók. If scholars are right in associating works such as *Skjǫldunga saga* and *Vǫlsunga saga* with Oddi, it would be a further indication of the Oddaverjar's interest in the heroic and royal past of their family, which was in their view also that of the Norwegian King Hákon. Gizurr Þorvaldsson, the first earl of Iceland, had the privilege

---

12. *Sturlunga saga*, ed. Jón Jóhannesson et al., 2 vols. (Reykjavík: Sturlunguútgáfan, 1946), 1:269.

13. Ibid. The number of men depends on whether the author is intending long hundreds (120) or conventional hundreds.

14. On Snorri's use of cultural capital, see Torfi H. Tulinius, *Skáldið í skriftinni (Reykjavík: Hið íslenska bókmenntafélag, 2004)*; published in a revised translation as *The Enigma of Egill: The Saga, the Viking Poet, and Snorri Sturluson*, Islandica 57 (Ithaca: Cornell University Library, 2014).

of calling King Hákon Hákonarson his *frændi* (kinsman) due to his kinship with the Oddaverjar.[15] This blood association with King Hákon is emphasized in *Sturlunga saga*, probably due to endeavors on the part of the writer to substantiate the legitimacy of Gizurr's earldom.

The Oddaverjar, Haukdœlir, and Sturlungar were the three families most overtly engrossed in their relationship with the Norwegian royal house in the thirteenth century. The Haukdœlir in the south of Iceland and the Sturlungar in the west and northwest of Iceland were in direct competition for the earldom in Iceland. The fourth family was the Seldœlir in the Westfjords, the descendants of Hrafn Sveinbjarnarson. Hrafn Sveinbjarnarson was not considered of royal descent, but his saga depicts him as an overtly religious man, almost a saint-like figure, commanding the divine gift of healing presented to his great-grandfather through the mediation of King Óláfr Haraldsson, Saint Óláfr. Hrafn Oddsson, his grandson and Sturla Sighvatsson's son-in-law, became the most powerful man in Iceland after the death of Gizurr Þorvaldsson in 1268.

Snorri was the first of these influential chieftains, called *hǫfðingjar*, to go to Norway and to present to the earl or king his own poetry, and probably his knowledge of the old skaldic lore, but he was by no means the last. Other chieftains presented their poetry at the court; Gizurr Þorvaldsson was one. Sturla Þórðarson achieved the ultimate prize when Magnús lagabœtir, Hákon's son and Skúli's grandson, hired him to write the saga of King Hákon and then that of himself. There, Sturla follows Hákon's life in scrupulous detail, relying on eye-witnesses and written material at court, and even though he did not meet Hákon once in his life, he embeds in Hákon's chronicle 102 stanzas of his own making.

3

It is to be expected that these poets, authors, and courtiers, who were also fighting one another for the rule of Iceland on behalf of King Hákon, would not only focus their literary activity on the Norwegian royal family, past and present, but also have sagas written of their own

---

15. *Sturlunga saga*, Jón Jóhannesson, 1:493.

lineage and strengthen their claim to earldom by drawing attention to their families' roots in Norway and to the poetry respected and enjoyed by kings and earls in the west Nordic region. This was indeed the case. Skaldic verse was not only an important building block in the making of the kings' sagas in the first half of the thirteenth century, but also of other saga genres, such as the sagas of Icelanders and the *fornaldarsögur*, setting out the pre-history of many of the settlers of Iceland.

Two proposals will be put to test in the ensuing discussion of the *Íslendingasögur*: (1) Is it possible to link the subject matter of the sagas of Icelanders and their use of skaldic poetry to the same cultural milieu that fostered the study of skaldic poetry and the writing of the kings' sagas? (2) Further, were the authors of the kings' sagas and the known court poets, who were also courtiers and indeed kinsmen of the Norwegian king, likely patrons of the sagas, their intended audience, or indeed the writers of sagas about their own lineages and their history in Iceland?

The corpus of the sagas of Icelanders counts some forty texts. The sagas differ in length, subject matter, and use of stylistic devices, but they have three distinct features in common: the time frame of their narrative (from the settlement period to the establishment of the Icelandic church, ca. 870–1050), the main places of action (Iceland, Scandinavia, Greenland, and the British Isles), and the period in which they are written (thirteenth and fourteenth centuries). A precise dating of individual sagas within the two centuries in question is impossible, particularly in those cases where no early manuscript exists to provide a *terminus ante quem* for their writing. The process of dating is, however, *de facto* another way of describing the evolution or the growth of a *genre*. Scholars have sought to explain the making of the sagas of Icelanders from different viewpoints: from the saga authors' sense of realism;[16] from the sagas' interaction with other datable genres such as the kings' sagas and *fornaldarsögur*;[17] from the sagas' footing in their time of writing;[18] from the alternative ways in

---

16. See Sigurður Nordal, "Sagalitteraturen," in *Litteraturhistorie*, ed. Sigurður Nordal, Nordisk Kultur 8B (Stockholm: Bonniers förlag, 1953), 180–273.

17. See Andersson, *Growth*; see also Vésteinn Ólason, "The Fantastic Element in Fourteenth Century *Íslendingasögur*: A Survey," *Gripla* 18 (2007): 7–22.

18. See Torfi H. Tulinius, *Skáldið í skriftinni* (note 14).

which social, moral and political questions are treated in the sagas;[19] from the sagas' origin in oral story-telling;[20] and from the date of the earliest manuscript,[21] to name only few examples.

A skaldic stanza in a prose narrative represents the cultural footprint of the author. The practice and study of skaldic poetry in the thirteenth and fourteenth centuries changed over time, as we have noted, and left behind incomparable witnesses, treatises, textbooks and sagas, which testify to a flourishing tradition that provides a backdrop against which the *prosimetrum* form of the sagas of Icelanders must be set. The complex characteristics of skaldic verse, the intricacies of its diction and meter, imply furthermore that the citation of verse in a prose narrative is never straightforward, but lends ambiguity to the narrative, demands interpretation, and challenges the reader and listener to take a stand. The text and the chosen meter of the stanza are not only impregnated with meaning, but the identity of the poet, if known outside the boundaries of the text, and particularly if he is a respected court poet of the canon known in vernacular royal chronicles, suggests cultural connotations that reflect on the author of the saga and his cultural milieu.

In a paper published in 2007 I set out a division of the sagas of Icelanders depending on their citation of verse in the narrative and the origin of the poet, which I will use as a sounding board for the ensuing discussion. According to my yardstick eight groups emerge:

1. The sagas of the court poets (the skalds' sagas): *Bjarnar saga Hítdœlakappa*, *Egils saga*, *Fóstbrœðra saga*, *Gunnlaugs saga ormstungu*, *Hallfreðar saga*, and *Kormáks saga*.
2. Sagas where the main protagonist is a poet: *Gísla saga Súrssonar*, *Grettis saga*, *Harðar saga ok Hólmverja*, *Víga-Glúms saga*, *Hávarðar saga*, *Víglundar saga*, and *Þórðar saga hreðu*.
3. A saga with a strong royal or courtly emphasis: *Laxdœla saga*.

---

19. See Jesse L. Byock, *Feud in the Icelandic Saga* (Berkeley: University of California Press, 1982).

20. See Gísli Sigurðsson, *Túlkun Íslendingasagna í ljósi munnlegrar hefðar: Tilgáta um aðferð* (Reykjavík: Stofnun Árna Magnússonar, 2002); Tommy Danielsson, *Hrafnkels saga eller fallet med den undflyende traditionen* (Hedemora: Gidlunds förlag, 2002).

21. See Örnólfur Thorsson, "'Leitin að landinu fagra': Hugleiðing um rannsóknir á íslenskum fornbókmenntum," *Skáldskaparmál* 1 (1992): 28–53.

4. Two fourteenth-century sagas with a strong royal emphasis: *Vatns-dœla saga* and *Finnboga saga ramma*.
5. Sagas dated to the fourteenth century that display distinct learned interest in the past: *Bárðar saga Snæfellsáss*; *Flóamanna saga*; *Kjalnesinga saga*; *Króka-Refs saga*; and the two Vinland sagas, *Eiríks saga rauða* and *Grœnlendinga saga*. (Only a small quantity of verse is cited in these sagas.)
6. Moral tales: *Bandamanna saga*, *Hœnsa Þóris saga*, and *Hrafnkels saga*.
7. Sagas relating events in the Eastfjords and the northeast of Iceland: *Droplaugarsona saga*, *Fljótsdœla saga*, *Gunnars saga Keldugnúpsfífls*, *Vápnfirðinga saga*, *Þorsteins saga hvíta*, *Þorsteins saga Síðu-Hallssonar*, and *Ǫlkofra saga* in the Eastfjords; and *Ljósvetninga saga*, *Reykdœla saga* (the only stanza in the saga is also cited in *Víga-Glúms saga*), and *Valla-Ljóts saga* in the northeast of Iceland.
8. Sagas where verse is an integral part of the narrative while there is no principal poet: *Njáls saga*, *Heiðarvíga saga*, *Eyrbyggja saga*, and *Svarfdœla saga*.

In this paper I would like to revisit this division and focus on the handful of sagas where the narrative is interlaced with poetry by the canonized poets of royal historiography and skaldic poetics, i.e. the sagas in groups 1 and 8, and briefly note at the end *Víga-Glúms saga*, *Grettis saga*, and *Hávarðar saga* in group 2.

4

The six skalds' sagas are for obvious reasons most closely linked to the making of the kings' sagas and skaldic poetics, as they depict the lives and conquests of poets who traveled abroad and gained recognition for their skaldic verse-making at the courts of kings and aristocratic patrons.[22] Four of the sagas are especially pertinent in relation to the canonization of skaldic poetry in *Snorra Edda* and the kings' sagas: *Egils saga*, *Hallfreðar saga*, *Kormáks saga*, and *Fóstbrœðra saga*. Egill Skalla-Grímsson, Hallfreðr Óttarsson, and Kormákr Ǫgmundsson are among the most respected poets of the skaldic canon in *Snorra Edda* and "Skáldatal," but Egill stands out for not being cited in the kings'

---

22. See Poole, *Skaldsagas* (note 8 above).

saga corpus. Þormóðr Kolbrúnarskáld is ignored in *Snorra Edda*, notwithstanding his conspicuous presence at the court of King Óláfr Haraldsson.

Egill Skalla-Grímsson was not a court poet of the Norwegian kings, the reasons for which his saga makes abundantly clear. It can therefore be argued that the impetus for the writing of his saga in the middle of the thirteenth century was to secure his poetry a place within a narrative framework. It is of note that Egill is not listed in the "Skáldatal" version preserved in conjunction with *Heimskringla*, but his name is added to the version in the Uppsala *Edda* where he is listed as the poet of Arinbjǫrn hersis and King Athelstan. His verse would have been lost were it not for scattered citations in the poetical treatises. Egill's verse is cited in two works attributed to named chieftains and scholars of the Sturlungar family, Snorri Sturluson's *Edda* and Óláfr Þórðarson's *Third Grammatical Treatise*. The Sturlungar were the descendants of Egill Skalla-Grímsson's family, the Mýrarmenn, and there are strong reasons to place the writing of *Egils saga* in the Sturlungar's cultural milieu, even though it narrows the reading of this anonymous saga to attribute the saga to a named author.

Hallfreðr Óttarsson is the main poet of the saga of his name, and his verse is furthermore an important component in the saga of King Óláfr Tryggvason. Hallfreðr's verse is cited in *Snorra Edda* and in the *Third Grammatical Treatise*; and he is noted as King Óláfr's poet in both versions of "Skáldatal." *Hallfreðar saga* is preserved as an independent saga in only one manuscript, Möðruvallabók, written ca. 1330–70, but his life was so closely associated with that of the king that the saga was incorporated into the saga of Óláfr Tryggvason in the fourteenth century. The same can be said of Kormákr, though his saga is not preserved in conjunction with any of the fourteenth-century kings' sagas compilations. Kormákr's verse is cited in the kings's sagas, *Snorra Edda*, the *Third Grammatical Treatise*, and he is listed in both versions of "Skáldatal" as the poet of Earl Sigurðr. The saga is preserved complete in only one manuscript, again in Möðruvallabók, but in addition a fragment of the saga exists from the middle of the fourteenth century.

Fóstbrœðra saga is clearly a learned saga, preserved in Hauksbók and Möðruvallabók, and interwoven into the saga of King Óláfr helgi in Flateyjarbók.[23] It is of note that Þormóðr's verse is not cited in *Snorra Edda*, even though his verse is known from *Heimskringla*. A stanza attributed to Þormóðr in *Fóstbrœðra saga* is cited anonymously in *Third Grammatical Treatise* and he is noted in both versions of "Skáldatal" as the poet of Saint Óláfr. *Fóstbrœðra saga* stands out from most *Íslendingasögur* in using poetry as a vehicle to authenticate the depiction of events and characters. The method of citing "Þorgeirsdrápa," Þormóðr's praise-poem for his foster-brother Þorgeirr Hávarsson, as source material for the representation of Þorgeirr's fights and conquests in the first part of the saga gives the impression that the saga is based in part on the poem. This narrative technique, reminiscent of the citation of verse in the authorized kings' sagas, is also used in part of *Eyrbyggja saga*, as I will show below. The praise-poem genre seems to have been exclusive to royal or foreign aristocratic patrons, and only few praise-poems or memorial poems about Icelanders have been preserved before the thirteenth century: "Þorgeirsdrápa" in *Fóstbrœðra saga*, "Sonatorrek" in *Egils saga*, Arnórr jarlaskáld's lost *drápa* about Gellir Þorkelsson in *Laxdœla*, and "Hrafnsmál" by Þormóðr Trefilsson in *Eyrbyggja saga*. Þormóðr's loose stanzas, some cited on his journey to Greenland and the others with King Ólafr in Norway, are interlaced into the narrative in the second part of the saga, and some stanzas are the same as those cited in *Heimskringla*.

The other two skalds' sagas have a looser connection with the skaldic canon and vernacular royal historiography, which may indicate that they were either written later in the century in reaction to the established skaldic canon or that they serve different cultural ends. The two poets of *Gunnlaugs saga* do not belong to the canonized poets, even though they are represented in the saga as court poets. The verse of Hrafn and Gunnlaugr is cited neither in the kings' sagas nor in *Snorra Edda*, but Gunnlaugr, like Egill, is added to the list of poets in the version of "Skáldatal" in the Uppsala *Edda* as the court poet of King Aethelred II of England. It is likely that the saga of Gunnlaugr invited this addition. The introduction to *Gunnlaugs saga* in the fourteenth-century Stockholm manuscript (ca. 1300–25) puts

---

23. See Jónas Kristjánsson, *Um Fóstbrœðrasögu* (Reykjavík: Stofnun Árna Magnússonar, 1972), who dates the saga to ca. 1300.

a distance between the time of writing of the saga in that manuscript and the first half of the thirteenth century:

Saga þeira Hrafns ok Gunnlaugs ormstungu, eptir því sem sagt hefir Ari prestr inn fróði Þorgilsson, er mestr frœðimaðr hefir verit á Íslandi á landnámssǫgur ok forna frœði.[24]

This is the saga of Hrafn and of Gunnlaugr Serpent-Tongue, as told by the priest Ari Þorgilsson the Learned, who was the most knowledgeable of stories of the settlement and other ancient lore of anyone to have lived in Iceland.[25]

The writer of this manuscript implies that the saga is based on secondary evidence or the old lore of Ari fróði Þorgilsson, the most respected witness to the history of Iceland. He then goes on to describe the family of the Mýrarmenn, starting with Þorsteinn, Egill Skallagrímsson's son. Some men of the family are said to have been

menn vænstir, en þat sé þó mjǫg sundrgreiniligt, því at sumir í þeiri ætt er kallat, at ljótastir menn hafi verit. Í þeiri ætt hafa ok verit margir atgǫrvismenn um marga hluti, sem var Kjartan Óláfsson pá ok Víga-Barði ok Skúli Þorsteinsson. Sumir váru ok skáldmenn miklir í þeiri ætt: Bjǫrn Hítdœlakappi, Einarr prestr Skúlason, Snorri Sturluson ok margir aðrir. (*Gunnlaugs saga*, ÍF 3:51n3)

exceptionally good-looking men, whereas others are said to have been very ugly. Many members of the family were particularly talented in various ways, as were Kjartan Óláfsson, Víga-Barði, and Skúli Þorsteinsson. Some of them were also great poets, like Bjǫrn Hítdœlakappi, the priest Einarr Skúlason, Snorri Sturluson and many others. (*Saga of Gunnlaug*, 306)

---

24. *Gunnlaugs saga ormstungu*, in *Borgfirðinga sǫgur*, ed. Sigurður Nordal and Guðni Jónsson, Íslenzk fornrit 3 (Reykjavík: Hið íslenzka fornritafélag, 1938), hereafter *Gunnlaugs saga*, ÍF 3, 51n.

25. *The Saga of Gunnlaug Serpent-Tongue*, trans. Katrina C. Attwood, in *The Complete Sagas of Icelanders*, ed. Viðar Hreinsson, vol. 1 (Reykjavík: Leifur Eiríksson, 1997), hereafter *Saga of Gunnlaug*, 305. Here and subsequently, the translation has been modified to reflect the original orthography of Icelandic personal names.

The reference to Snorri Sturluson is of special note here. He is in the company of his kinsmen, Einarr Skúlason and Bjǫrn Hítdœlakappi, and the three of them are noted as the greatest poets (*skáldmenn miklir*) of the family. The court poet Skúli Þorsteinsson is listed with two well-known heroes of the sagas of Icelanders, Kjartan Óláfsson (*Laxdœla saga*) and Víga-Barði (*Heiðarvíga saga*). He was the foster-father of Bjǫrn Hítdœlakappi. The author links these descendants of Egill together, which indicates that the subject matter and kinship were used at the time to categorize sagas such as *Egils saga*, *Laxdœla saga*, *Heiðarvíga saga*, *Gunnlaugs saga*, and *Bjarnar saga Hítdœlakappa*. This connection between the descendants of Egill and the main heroes of these—Kjartan Óláfsson; Hallr Guðmundarson, Víga-Barði's brother; Gunnlaugr and Hrafn; and Skúli Þorsteinsson—is also brought out in the final chapter of *Egils saga*.[26] These five sagas are strongly associated with the skaldic tradition, even though the author of *Laxdœla saga* shows his deference to the skaldic canon and the poetic narrative technique in a negative manner.

The poetry of Bjǫrn Hítdœlakappi is not known outside the saga of his name, whereas his rival Þórðr Kolbeinsson was a known court poet in the kings' sagas for his *drápa* ("Eiríksdrápa") about Earl Eiríkr. *Bjarnar saga Hítdœlakappa* notes an additional poem by Þórðr devoted to Earl Eiríkr ("Belgskakadrápa") and a *drápa* about King Óláfr Tryggvason. Neither Þórðr nor Bjǫrn is noted in "Skáldatal" or *Snorra Edda*. *Bjarnar saga Hítdœlakappa* is notoriously poorly preserved. One fragment is preserved from the fourteenth century, but the complete saga has come down to us only in a seventeenth-century manuscript. A part of *Bjarnar saga Hítdœlakappa* (and also of *Laxdœla saga* and *Fóstbrœðra saga*) is preserved in Bæjarbók, a manuscript of *Óláfs saga* from ca. 1400, now lost except for four leaves but preserved in transcriptions from ca. 1700. The introductory words to the saga in Bæjarbók are noteworthy:

Nú skal segja nǫkkut af þeim íslensku mǫnnum, sem uppi váru um daga Óláfs konungs Haraldssonar ok hans urðu heimuligir vinir. Nefnir þar til fyrstan ágætan mann, Þorkel Eyjólfsson, er átti Guðrúnu

---

26. *Egils saga Skalla-Grímssonar*, ed. Sigurður Nordal, Íslenzk fornrit 2 (Reykjavík: Hið íslenzka fornritafélag, 1932), 299–300.

Ósvífrsdóttur, því at í þenna tíma var Þorkell í fǫrum ok var jafnan
með Óláfi konungi vel virðr, þá er hann var útanlands.[27]

Now some account is to be given of the Icelanders who lived in the days
of King Óláfr Haraldsson, and became his intimate friends. The first
of these to be mentioned was an excellent man, Þorkel Eyjólfsson, who
married Guðrún Ósvífrsdóttir. At that time Þorkell was on trading
voyages, and was always highly esteemed at King Óláfr's court when
he was abroad.[28]

The sagas of Gunnlaugr and Bjǫrn are personal in character, and
are not focused on the relationship with the king, like *Egils saga,
Hallfreðar saga,* and *Fóstbrœðra saga.*

The skalds' sagas are to varying degrees in dialogue with the kings'
sagas or the canonized skaldic corpus, yet their representation of the
poets' travels and interactions with foreign kings can profitably be
set against the backdrop of the kings' sagas. The three sagas most
closely associated with the Mýrarmenn, *Egils saga, Gunnlaugs saga,*
and *Bjarnar saga Hítdœlakappa,* depict the lives of poets who did
not achieve canonical status in the kings' sagas, and these sagas
serve to show the lives and failures of the poets, and highlight their
successes outside the Norwegian court. The three sagas from the
northwest of Iceland and the Westfjords, *Hallfreðar saga, Kormáks
saga,* and *Fóstbrœðra saga,* take their cue from the motive of the
love-sick skald who enjoyed the recognition of foreign dignitaries
and the freedom of his travels abroad. Hallfreðr's and Þormóðr's
destinies became intertwined with that of the king, just as their sagas
were incorporated into the vast subject matter associated with each
of the two Olafs.

The four sagas in group 8 cite verses by known poets of the skaldic
canon even though none of them is among the most respected of
the court poets. These sagas are not concerned with poets' recognition at the royal court or the fate of the poets; rather they are

27. *Bjarnar saga Hítdœlakappa,* in *Borgfirðinga sǫgur,* ed. Sigurður Nordal and Guðni
Jónsson, Íslenzk fornrit 3 (Reykjavík: Hið íslenzka fornritafélag, 1938), 111.

28. *The Saga of Bjorn, Champion of the Hitardal People,* trans. Alison Finlay, in *The
Complete Sagas of Icelanders,* ed. Viðar Hreinsson, vol. 1 (Reykjavík: Leifur Eiríksson,
1997), 255.

focused on events in Iceland and the workings of feud and vengeance. The subtle and nuanced use of skaldic poetry in the narrative of these sagas betrays the authors' intention of putting the genre of the sagas of Icelanders on a level with the kings' sagas. The authors of *Njáls saga*, *Heiðarvíga saga*, and *Eyrbyggja saga* cite verse by known poets in order to authenticate parts of their accounts, and *Svarfdœla saga* moreover contains stanzas attributed to the well-known poet Þorleifr jarlaskáld. There are twenty-three stanzas common to all manuscripts of *Njáls saga*, as well as the poem "Darraðarljóð" cited in the last section of the saga. The earliest manuscripts contain, however, additional stanzas which are mainly spoken by the two tragic heroes of the first half of the saga, Gunnarr Hámundarson (twelve stanzas) and Skarpheðinn Njálsson (ten stanzas). The stanzas are added to the narrative only in the pagan part of the saga (chapters 1–99). Skaldic poetry serves to change and modify the depiction of these figures in the saga, in a similar way as the stanzas by Kári Sǫlmundarson do in the final part of the saga. The author of the saga cites a poet outside the framework of the saga after the death of Gunnarr Hámundarson, and the full-length poem "Darraðarljóð."[29]

Fifteen stanzas are preserved in *Heiðarvíga saga*: two are found in the first part preserved only in the rendering of the lost text by Jón Ólafsson of Grunnavík; one stanza is by Leiknir (the same stanza is attributed to his brother Hallr in *Eyrbyggja saga*), and another by Gestr Oddleifsson (probably lifted out of the *Laufásedda* manuscript by Jón Ólafsson). The remaining thirteen stanzas are very cleverly and interestingly woven into the narrative. They are not used to draw attention to any particular characters in the saga; instead they emphasize powerful scenes and give credence to the subject matter. Þuríðr, the wife of Barði Guðmundsson and daughter of Ólafr pá, composes a stanza when she incites her husband to revenge. Þorbjǫrn Brúnason speaks two powerful stanzas when his wife serves him a bloody meal in order to incite him to action, and the following night he is visited by two dream-women who recite two stanzas. Gísli Þórgautsson speaks a stanza about his forebodings just before he is killed in Gullteigr. All

---

29. On Skaldic verse in *Njáls saga*, see further my "Attraction of Opposites," 211–36, and "Tilbrigði um *Njálu*," *Ritið* 3 (2005): 57–76.

of these stanzas are related, in one way or another, to the culminating battle, the Heiðarvíg.

The stanzas by Eiríkr víðsjá, who is also a known poet in the learned culture through a citation in the *Fourth Grammatical Treatise*, are cited as a commentary on the action and as a testimony to the accuracy of the saga's account of the killings. The writer uses skaldic poetry as source material, in similarity to the kings' sagas, and this technique is also at play in *Eyrbyggja saga*. Eiríkr víðsjá is not the only poet called as a witness to the Heiðarvíg in the saga. Tindr, the brother of Illugi svarti at Gilsbakki (the father of Gunnlaugr ormstunga), recites two stanzas relating to the battle. The authors of *Eyrbyggja saga* and *Heiðarvíga saga* use skaldic poetry to authenticate their account, and are careful in choosing respected poets for this purpose.

The author of *Eyrbyggja saga* takes a bolder step than the writer of *Heiðarvíga saga* toward using skaldic verse as source material. The two first stanzas cited in *Eyrbyggja saga* are from "Illugadrápa," composed by Oddr skáld about Illugi svarti, the father of Gunnlaugr ormstunga. The stanzas serve as documentary evidence, in the same way as verse in the kings' sagas does. Snorri goði is the focal point; his talent for leadership in the service of the good of the district is substantiated at this early stage in his life. The stanzas are not spoken as part of the narrative, but referred to as source material. With this formal introduction the audience of the saga is reinforced in the belief that Snorri goði is the main character in the saga, the person around whom the saga will evolve. The stanzas are not drawn from *lausavísur*, but from a longer, datable, and thus reliable poem.

Other verses of such formal character are the famous "Máhlíðinga-vísur," by Þórarinn Máhlíðingr, the nephew of Arnkell Þórólfsson, spoken in three dialogue scenes after the killing of Þorbjǫrn digri at Fróðá, the husband of Þuríðr Barkardóttir, Snorri goði's sister. Þórarinn's poetry was known in learned circles, at least in the Sturlungs' learned milieu; a half-stanza is cited in Snorri Sturluson's "Háttatal" in *Snorra Edda*.[30] Substantial research has gone into the dating of these stanzas. Russell Poole concludes that they were

---

30. Snorri Sturluson, *Edda*, ed. Finnur Jónsson, 2nd ed. (Copenhagen: Gad, 1926).

composed in the late eleventh or twelfth century in praise of Snorri goði's deeds, and other scholars concur with his assessment.[31]

Interlaced throughout *Eyrbyggja saga* are five laudatory stanzas by Þormóðr Trefilsson from a poem about Snorri goði (st. 20, ch. 26; st. 26, ch. 37; st. 33, ch. 44; st. 34, ch. 56; st. 35, ch. 62). The stanzas seem to belong to the same poem originally, even though they are all introduced in a different way. Þormóðr is known, from entries in Hauksbók and *Þórðarbók of Landnámabók*, to have composed in praise of Snorri goði. These sources post-date *Eyrbyggja saga*, and are not, therefore, of independent value.

Skaldic stanzas are used with precision in the saga to highlight and enlarge Snorri's character in relation to others. The stanzas are placed at strategic points in the saga. The verse is carefully chosen; sequences of verse, rather than occasional *lausavísur*, i.e. formal verse, rather than occasional stanzas, and the reference to praise poems in honor of Snorri goði all contribute to his aristocratic portrayal in the saga. His worthiness recounted in praise-poems invites implicit comparison with earls, or even kings, in other countries. This is no coincidence: Snorri goði Þorgrímsson was the forefather of the Sturlungs, and this portrayal may be their own. Another source may support such a "royal" reading of Snorri's life. One of the backbones of the saga is "The life of Snorri goði," a brief synopsis of his life, preserved in one of the manuscripts containing *Eyrbyggja saga* (Melabók).[32] This biographical outline has been attributed to Ari Þorgilsson, and if this is so, this short text would place writings about Snorri goði against the cultural backdrop of the beginnings of royal historiography in Iceland.

Three other sagas of Icelanders belonging to group 2 cite verses by poets mentioned in the skaldic canon. Víga-Glúmr is among the acknowledged poets of the canon in *Snorra Edda*, cited three times in *Skáldskaparmál* in the Codex Regius manuscript, and two of these

---

31. See Russell Poole, "The Origins of *Máhlíðingavísur*," *Scandinavian Studies* 57 (1985): 244–85. See also Vésteinn Ólason, "*Máhlíðingamál*: Authorship and Tradition in a Part of *Eyrbyggja saga*," in *Úr Dölum til dala: Gudbrandur Vigfússon Centenary Essays*, ed. Rory McTurk and Andrew Wawn, Leeds Texts and Monographs 11 (Leeds: School of English, University of Leeds, 1989), 187–203.

32. Appended to *Eyrbyggja saga*, ed. Einar Ól. Sveinsson and Matthías Þórðarson, *Íslenzk fornrit* 4 (Reykjavík: Hið íslenzka fornritafélag, 1935), 185–86.

examples are also cited in his saga. His verse is not found in the kings' sagas or in "Skáldatal." Grettir Ásmundarson and Hávarðr are cited only once each in *Snorra Edda*.[33] Grettir's stanza is cited in his saga—but Hávarðr halti's is not. None of these poets are known court poets, according to "Skáldatal," and are accordingly not cited in the kings' sagas.

5

I have noted above the importance of taking into account the historical circumstances in Norway at the time of the writing of the kings' sagas. Similarly, we need to consider the implications of unfolding political changes in Norway and the cultural transformations at its court for the development of the writing of sagas about the forefathers and foremothers of those Icelanders who were seeking the favor of the King Hákon gamli and other dignitaries in the thirteenth century. The use of skaldic verse in the early chronicles of the kings was not only fundamental to the authenticity of vernacular royal historiography, but also in the political interest of Hákon gamli. The cultural influences at his court were complex, and references to the canon of skaldic poets were fundamental to vouchsafe the authenticity of narratives concerning the royal lineage, but once they had been put to writing they had served their purpose. When King Hákon had secured the foundations of his lineage in well-documented vernacular royal chronicles, he could focus his ambition on molding his royal court after the European model, such as in France and England. The translation of courtly literature, most specifically from Anglo-Norman or French into Old Norwegian from 1225 onward, reveals these cultural endeavors.[34] Courtly values and emotions influenced not only Sturla Þórðarson's writing of *Hákonar saga Hákonarsonar*, but also the writing of the *Íslendingasögur*, as we can see most clearly in *Laxdœla saga*, which belongs to the same cultural milieu as many of the skalds' sagas.

---

33. See Guðrún Nordal, *Tools of Literacy: The Role of Skaldic Verse in Icelandic Textual Culture of the Twelfth and Thirteenth Centuries* (Toronto: University of Toronto Press, 2001), 78–79.

34. See Carolyne Larrington, "Queens and Bodies: The Norwegian Translated *lais* and Hákon IV's Kinswomen," *JEGP* 108 (2009): 506–27.

The authors of the thirteen sagas discussed above reveal the impact of the old skaldic model and the new imported models to varying degrees. It is likely, as was proposed above, that the Icelandic aristocracy, many of whom were courtiers of the Norwegian king, were the patrons of the sagas about their own lineages and their history in Iceland, their intended audience, or indeed the writers of sagas. The use of skaldic poetry in the narrative clearly depends on the subject matter and the identification of the poet and whether he is the main character of the saga or not, but the theme of the love-sick skald is regularly touched with borrowings from the world of romance. Both strands, the indigenous and the imported, are equally conditioned by the royal court.

Two of the best known skalds' sagas, *Fóstbrœðra saga* and *Hallfreðar saga*, are focused on the royal court; these sagas are interpreted in light of the king's saga and are later even understood to be an integral part of the king's life. The three skalds' sagas of the Mýrarmenn family and the descendants of Egill, *Egils saga*, *Gunnlaugs saga*, and *Bjarnar saga*, on the other hand, serve to glorify the poetic skills of the Sturlunga family, though none of them are known court poets, and thus boost the legitimacy and the poetic patrimony of the family at the time of writing. Notwithstanding *Heiðarvíga saga*'s and *Eyrbyggja saga*'s close affiliation with these three skalds' sagas, their authors measured their narrative against the model of the kings' sagas, and thus broadened the political and narrative scope of their sagas. The same is true of *Njáls saga*. These three sagas achieved a new standard in the way the narrative takes its cue from different narrative standards and the skaldic model.

Laxdœla saga is similarly a ground-breaking saga. It belongs to the same cultural milieu as that of *Eyrbyggja saga* and some of the skalds' sagas from the west of Iceland, yet the author shapes the subject matter and characters in an independent way. The author of *Eyrbyggja saga* constructs a "royal" portrayal of the main character, Snorri goði Þorgrímsson, by authenticating the account with formal skaldic verse[35] and punctuating the main events in his life with verse citations. The author of *Laxdœla saga* deliberately

---

35. See my discussion in "The Art of Poetry and the Sagas of Icelanders," in *Learning and Understanding in the Old Norse World*, ed. Judy Quinn et al. (Turnhout: Brepols, Belgium, 2007), 219–38.

avoids such references to skaldic verse in the narrative. Both sagas are preoccupied with Norwegian pre-history, and describe the flight of independently-minded Norwegian chieftains to Iceland via the British Isles because of the tyranny of Haraldr hárfagri.[36] The central characters are friends, Snorri goði and Guðrún Ósvífrsdóttir, and each plays a part in the other's saga. Both sagas are written in the second half of the thirteenth century but draw on opposite cultural reference points: *Eyrbyggja saga* is rooted in indigenous traditions, referring to local folklore, the power of the supernatural in the narrative, and supposedly authenticated skaldic verse, whereas *Laxdœla saga*, while also drawing on local story-telling, is indebted to the mannerisms or literary techniques of courtly romances and heroic legends.

The difference between these two sagas, written at the same time and possibly in the same cultural milieu and in the same family, must be explained in terms of different goals of the authors in their depiction of their main characters. Snorri goði Þorgrímsson is depicted as an Icelandic aristocrat, his actions serving as a prequel to those of his aristocratic descendants in the Sturlungar family in the thirteenth century, who most probably had a hand in shaping the saga in the mold of a king's saga, even underpinning the saga with a reference to a brief synopsis of his life.[37] The saga of Guðrún Ósvífrsdóttir is no less strikingly "royal" in its character descriptions and visual traits.[38] These aristocratic patterns are not, however, drawn from the indigenous traditions of royal historiography, but rather from the world of courtly romance and the heroic legends of Sigurðr, Guðrún and Brynhildr. The references to skaldic verse in the two sagas are most poignant in this respect, and bring home the significance of paying due notice to a saga's social and cultural context.

---

36. One strand in the interpretation of the "skaldic" sagas is their reference to the settlement and Iceland's pre-history; see my "Alternative Criteria for the Dating of the Sagas of Icelanders," in *Á austrvega: Saga and East Scandinavia, Preprint Papers of The 14th Saga Conference, Uppsala 9th – 15th August 2009*, ed. Agneta Ney et al., 2 vols. (Gävle: University of Gävle, 2009), 1:336–42.

37. This life of Snorri goði is only preserved in a late fourteenth-century manuscript (Melabók) and it has been attributed by some scholars to Ari fróði Þorgilsson. See *Eyrbyggja saga*, Einar Ól. Sveinsson, xxx.

38. See Ármann Jakobsson, *Staður í nýjum heimi: Konungasagan Morkinskinna* (Háskólaútgáfan: Reykjavík, 2002); see also "Svör Ármanns Jakobssonar við andmælaræðum," *Gripla* 14 (2005): 314–21.

Bibliography

Andersson, Theodore M. *The Growth of the Medieval Icelandic Sagas (1180–1280)*. Ithaca: Cornell University Press, 2006.

———, and Kari Ellen Gade, trans. *Morkinskinna: The Earliest Icelandic Chronicle of the Norwegian Kings (1030–1157)*. Islandica 51. Ithaca: Cornell University Press, 2000.

Ármann Jakobsson. *Staður í nýjum heimi: Konungasagan Morkinskinna*. Reykjavík: Háskólaútgáfan, 2002.

———. "Svör Ármanns Jakobssonar við andmælaræðum." *Gripla* 14 (2005): 314–21.

Bjarnar saga Hítdœlakappa. In *Borgfirðinga sǫgur*. Edited by Sigurður Nordal and Guðni Jónsson. Íslenzk fornrit 3. Reykjavík: Hið íslenzka fornritafélag, 1938.

Borgfirðinga sǫgur. Edited by Sigurður Nordal and Guðni Jónsson. Íslenzk fornrit 3. Reykjavík. Hið íslenzka fornritafélag, 1938.

Byock, Jesse L. *Feud in the Icelandic Saga*. Berkeley: University of California Press, 1982.

Danielsson, Tommy. *Hrafnkels saga eller fallet med den undflyende traditionen*. Hedemora: Gidlunds förlag, 2002.

Egils saga Skalla-Grímssonar. Edited by Sigurður Nordal. Íslenzk fornrit 2. Reykjavík: Hið íslenzka fornritafélag, 1932.

Eyrbyggja saga. Edited by Einar Ól. Sveinsson and Matthías Þórðarson. Íslenzk fornrit 4. Reykjavík: Hið íslenzka fornritafélag, 1935.

Fidjestøl, Bjarne. "On a New Edition of Skaldic Poetry." In *The Sixth International Saga Conference 28.7. – 2.8.1985: Workshop Papers*. Vol. 1, 319–35. Copenhagen: Det Arnamagnæanske Institut, 1985.

First Grammatical Treatise: Introduction, Texts, Notes, Translation, Vocabulary, and Facsimilies. Edited by Hreinn Benediktsson. University of Iceland Publications in Linguistics 1. Reykjavík: Institute of Nordic Linguistics, 1972.

Frank, Roberta. "Skaldic Poetry." In *Old Norse-Icelandic Literature: A Critical Guide*, edited by Carol J. Clover and John Lindow, 157–96. Islandica 45. Ithaca: Cornell University Press, 1985.

Gísli Sigurðsson. *Túlkun Íslendingasagna í ljósi munnlegrar hefðar: Tilgáta um aðferð*. Reykjavík: Stofnun Árna Magnússonar, 2002.

Guðrún Nordal. "Alternative Criteria for the Dating of the Sagas of Icelanders." In *Á austrvega: Saga and East Scandinavia, Preprint Papers of the 14th Saga Conference, Uppsala 9th – 15th August 2009*, edited by Agneta Ney, Henrik Williams, and Fredrik Charpentier Ljungqvist, 2 vols., 1:336–43. Gävle: University of Gävle, 2009.

———. "Attraction of Opposites: Skaldic Verse in *Njáls saga*." In *Literacy in Medieval and Early Modern Scandinavian Culture*, edited by Pernille Hermann, 211–36. The Viking Collection: Studies in Northern Civilization 16. Odense: University Press of Southern Denmark, 2005.

———. "Metrical learning and the *First Grammatical Treatise*." In *Versatility in Versification*, edited by Tonya Kim Dewey and Frog, 23–38. New York: Peter Lang, 2009.

———. "Poetic Voices in the *fornaldarsögur*." In *The Legendary Sagas: Origins and Development*, edited by Annette Lassen, Agneta Ney, and Ármann Jakobsson, 139–51. Reykjavík: University of Iceland Press, 2012.

———. "Samhengið í íslenskum fornbókmenntum." In *Sagnaheimur: Studies in Honour of Hermann Pálsson on his 80th birthday, 26th May 2001*, edited by Ásdís Egilsdóttir and Rudolf Simek, 91–106. Studia medievalia Septentrionalia 6. Vienna: Fassbaender, 2001.

———. "Skáldið Snorri Sturluson." In *Snorrastefna, 25.–27. júli 1990*, edited by Úlfar Bragason, 52–69. Rit Stofnunar Sigurðar Nordals 1. Reykjavík: Stofnun Sigurðar Nordals, 1992.

———. "Tilbrigði um *Njálu*." *Ritið* 3 (2005): 57–76.

———. *Tools of Literacy: The Role of Skaldic Verse in Icelandic Textual Culture of the Twelfth and Thirteenth Centuries*. Toronto: University of Toronto Press, 2001.

Gunnlaugs saga ormstungu. In *Borgfirðinga sǫgur*. Edited by Sigurður Nordal and Guðni Jónsson. Íslenzk fornrit 3. Reykjavík: Hið íslenzka fornritafélag, 1938.

Jónas Kristjánsson. *Um Fóstbrœðrasögu*. Reykjavík: Stofnun Árna Magnússonar, 1972.

Larrington, Carolyne. "Queens and Bodies: The Norwegian Translated *lais* and Hákon IV's Kinswomen." *Journal of English and Germanic Philology* 108 (2009): 506–27.

Louis-Jensen, Jonna. "Heimskringla: et værk af Snorri Sturluson?" *Nordica Bergensia* 14 (1997): 231–45.

Meulengracht Sørensen, Preben. "The Prosimetrum Form 1: Verses as the Voice of the Past." In *Skaldsagas: Text, Vocation, and Desire in the Icelandic Sagas of Poets*, edited by Russell Poole, 172–90. Ergänzungsbände zum Reallexikon der germanischen Altertumskunde 27. Berlin: de Gruyter, 2001.

Örnólfur Thorsson. "'Leitin að landinu fagra': Hugleiðing um rannsóknir á íslenskum fornbókmenntum." *Skáldskaparmál* 1 (1992): 28–53.

Poole, Russell. "The origins of *Máhlíðingavísur*." *Scandinavian Studies* 57 (1985): 244–85.

The Saga of Bjorn, Champion of the Hitardal People. Translated by Alison Finlay. In *The Complete Sagas of Icelanders*. Edited by Viðar Hreinsson. Vol. 1. Reykjavík: Leifur Eiríksson, 1997.

The Saga of Gunnlaug Serpent-Tongue. Translated by Katrina C.

Attwood. In *The Complete Sagas of Icelanders*. Edited by Viðar Hreinsson. Vol. 1. Reykjavík: Leifur Eiríksson, 1997.

Sigurður Nordal. "Sagalitteraturen" In *Litteraturhistorie*, edited by Sigurður Nordal, 180–273. Nordisk Kultur 8B. Stockholm: Bonniers förlag, 1953.

Snorri Sturluson. *Edda*. Edited by Finnur Jónsson. 2nd ed. Copenhagen: Gad, 1926.

Sturlunga saga. Edited by Jón Jóhannesson, Kristján Eldjárn, and Magnús Finnbogason. 2 vols. Reykjavík: Sturlunguútgáfan, 1946.

Sverrir Tómasson. "Ræða Sverris Tómassonar við doktorsvörn Ármanns Jakobssonar 1.2. 2003." *Gripla* 14 (2005): 285–300.

Sverris saga etter Cod. Am. 327 4to. Edited by Gustrav Indrebø. Kristiania [Oslo], 1920.

Torfi H. Tulinius. Skáldið í skriftinni: Snorri Sturluson og "Egils saga." Reykjavík: Hið íslenska bókmenntafélag, 2004. Revised and Translated as *The Enigma of Egill: The Saga, the Viking Poet, and Snorri Sturluson*. Islandica 57. Ithaca: Cornell University Library, 2014.

Vésteinn Ólason. "The Fantastic Element in Fourteenth Century *Íslendingasögur*: A Survey." *Gripla* 18 (2007): 7–22.

———. "*Máhlíðingamál*: Authorship and Tradition in a Part of *Eyrbyggja saga*." In *Úr Dölum til Dala: Guðbrandur Vigfússon Centenary Essays*, edited by Rory McTurk and Andrew Wawn, 187–203. Leeds Texts and Monographs 11. Leeds: School of English, University of Leeds, 1989.

Identity Poetics among
the Icelandic Skalds

Russell Poole

THE UNIVERSITY OF WESTERN ONTARIO

Famously, the skalds of Iceland successfully took over the mantle of court poet in tenth- and particularly eleventh-century Norway (and to an extent in England and other centers of Scandinavian diasporic populations as well). In this way they sustained a partial livelihood. In this paper I am going to propose that we can detect a sense of Icelandic (and to a lesser extent Orkney) identity in some of their verses. These markers might already have been symptomatic of an emerging ideology, to be more explicitly expressed in later prose texts, where "individual Icelanders, especially upwardly mobile young Icelandic men, are, on a case-by-case basis, represented as better, cleverer, and more gifted than any individual Norwegian, except perhaps the Norwegian king, against whom they frequently measure themselves. Their special talent thus enables them as individuals to be successful in Norwegian society, even though they come from the cultural margin."[1] That the sense of a community identity and the specification of markers for that identity should have evolved comparatively rapidly in the history of the Norse settlement in Iceland is hardly surprising. There might have

I would like to express my gratitude to Judy Quinn of the University of Cambridge, and Jeffrey Turco of Purdue University, for their invitations to present earlier versions of this paper at Cambridge and Cornell Universities respectively; I also thank other participants at these occasions and the anonymous reader for this volume for their comments. Funding support for the research embodied in the paper came from the Social Sciences and Humanities Research Council Canada and from the University of Western Ontario.

1. Margaret Clunies Ross, "From Iceland to Norway: Essential Rites of Passage for an Early Icelandic Skald," *alvíssmál* 9 (1999): 57. See also the essays by Guðrún Nordal and Jeffrey Turco in this volume.

been a communal impulse to actively cultivate—even fetishize—the distinctive identity that developed as a reflex of the genetic, cultural, and linguistic heritage of Icelanders and the specific set of livelihoods available for them to pursue. Among wider-world analogues for such rapid developments one could cite the case of settler identity politics in late eighteenth- and early nineteenth-century Australia.

I shall focus on the following textual features:

1. Allusions to and camaraderie with Icelanders;
2. Allusions to distinctive complexion and hair color, often explicitly linked to Icelandic affiliations;
3. Use of distinctive lexical items adopted into Icelandic (and Orkney Norse) from the Irish language.

The composition of settlement in Iceland was distinctive from the outset. While the bulk of the settlers of the main influx ca. 870 to 930 A.D. came from mainland Scandinavia, especially the western coast of Norway, significant numbers also came from the Viking settlements in Britain.[2] Ari's *Íslendingabók* emphasizes Norwegian settlement, but, as Hermann Pálsson points out, it is clear from *Landnámabók* and the sagas that many settlers must have come directly from the British Isles.[3]

Genetically speaking, the dominant elements in the population of early Iceland are a mix of Scandinavian and British. Studies of mitochondrial DNA variation indicate that contemporary Icelanders trace about 37 percent of their matrilineal ancestry to Scandinavia, with the remainder coming from the populations of Scotland and Ireland. In contrast, Y-chromosome analyses suggest that 75 to 80 percent of their patrilineal ancestry originated in Scandinavia.[4] It

---

2. See Jesse L. Byock et al., "A Viking-age Valley in Iceland: The Mosfell Archaeological Project," *Medieval Archaeology* 49 (2005): 203.

3. *Keltar á Íslandi* (Reykjavík: Háskólaútgáfan, 1996), 47.

4. See Byock, "A Viking-age Valley," 203; Agnar Helgason et al., "mtDNA and the origin of the Icelanders: Deciphering Signals of Recent Population History," *American Journal of Human Genetics* 66 (2000): 999–1016; Agnar Helgason et al., "Estimating Scandinavian and Gaelic Ancestry in the Male Settlers of Iceland," *American Journal of Human Genetics* 67 (2000): 697–717; Agnar Helgason et al., "mtDNA and the Islands of the North Atlantic: Estimating the Proportions of Norse and Gaelic Ancestry," *American Journal of Human Genetics* 68 (2001): 723–37.

has also been shown that ancient Icelandic mtDNA sequences are more closely related to sequences from contemporary inhabitants of Scotland, Ireland, and Scandinavia (and several other European populations) than to those from the modern Icelandic population: this appears to be due to genetic drift in the Icelandic mtDNA pool during the last 1,100 years.[5]

Irish place and proper names are plentifully attested in Icelandic.[6] Some proper names are attested only for the earliest phase of settlement whereas others became popular in the Middle Ages and in some cases have remained so down to the present day. Many are known only from Icelandic, not Norwegian,[7] and must therefore in themselves have been distinctive markers of Icelandic identity: examples are Bekan (Irish *Beccan*), Bresi (Irish *Bress*), Brjánn (Irish *Brían*), Butraldi (Irish *Putrall/Pudarill*—a nickname), Dufan (Irish *Duban*), Dufgus, sometimes partially Icelandicized as Dugfúss (Irish *Dubgus*), Dufþakr (Irish *Dubhthach*), Dungaðr/Dunkaðr (Irish *Donnchad*), Gilli (Irish *Giolla*), Gufa, as nickname of Ketill gufa (Irish *Gubha*), Kaðall (Irish *Cathal*), Kalman (Irish *Colmán*), Kjallakr (Irish *Cellach*), Kjaran (Irish *Ciaran*), Kjartan (cf. Irish *Muirchertach*), Kjarvalr (Irish *Cerball*), Kolka, attested in Icelandic as a nickname in Þorbjǫrn kolka (Irish *Colca*), Konáll (Irish *Conall*), Kormákr (Irish *Cormac*), Kýlan (Irish *Cuileán*), Melkorka (Irish *Mael Curcaig*), Myríðr (Irish *Muiriath*), Njáll (Irish *Níall*), and Patrekr (Irish *Patraicc*). The list is moderately impressive, even though by William Craigie's count under two percent of the names in Landnámabók are of "Gaelic" origin.[8]

The Irish element in the vocabulary of Icelandic, though not large, is equally unmistakable. Some of the lexical items have acquired special affective force, undergone semantic expansion, or entered into distinctive idioms. An instance is *máki/mákur*, which means "calf of the foot, foot, seal's flipper, [clumsy or flabby human] hand," from

5. See Agnar Helgason et al., "Sequences From First Settlers Reveal Rapid Evolution in Icelandic mtDNA Pool," *Public Library of Science Genetics* 5.1 (2009): DOI:10.1371/journal.pgen.1000343.

6. See, e.g., Hermann Pálsson, *Keltar á Íslandi*, 47–102.

7. See Hermann Pálsson, "Keltnesk mannanöfn í íslenzkum ørnefnum," *Skírnir* 126 (1952): 195–202.

8. "Gaelic Words and Names in the Icelandic Sagas," *Zeitschrift für Celtische Philologie* 1 (1897): 441.

Scots Gaelic *màg* "paw, claw, pejorative term for hand, seal's flipper"; probably the basic meaning "paw" has been extended in both Gaelic and Icelandic. It also occurs in a compound *slyttimákur* "idler," literally "slack hand" in a probably fourteenth-century verse in *Grettis saga*.[9] Another loanword, *lámi/lámr*, from Irish *lám* "hand,"[10] occurs in *Snorra Edda* as a *heiti* for "hand."[11] Its meaning is similar to *máki* and shows a parallel semantic development: in modern Icelandic it can mean "claw, paw, talon."[12] An exceptionally interesting example, from a cultural standpoint, is *gjalti*, from Irish *geilt* "madman," in the idiom *verða at gjalti* "go into a frenzy," especially in battle.[13] Another loanword that belongs in the context of "battle" is *kesja* "spear," from Irish *ceis* "spear."[14] Quite a few loanwords are attested only in later texts[15] but nevertheless were probably brought to Iceland by the first settlers;[16] further instances will be given presently. The notion of a wider Irish influence on Icelandic culture and literature has been extensively canvassed.[17]

Beyond these main founding ethnic groups, it has been suggested

---

9. Finnur Jónsson, *Den norsk-islandske skjaldedigtning*, vols. A1–2, Tekst efter håndskrifterne, vols. B1–2, Rettet tekst (Copenhagen: Gyldendal, 1912–15), henceforth *Skjaldedigtning*, B2:469; *Grettis saga*, ed. Guðni Jónsson, Íslenzk fornrit 7 (Reykjavík: Hið íslenzka fornritafélag, 1936), 150; Helgi Guðmundsson, "Máki, mákur," *Íslenzk tunga* 1 (1959): 53.

10. All citations of Irish words are taken from the *Electronic Dictionary of the Irish Language*, ed. Gregory Toner et al: http://www.dil.ie/index.asp.

11. Snorri Sturluson, *Edda: Skáldskaparmál*, ed. Anthony Faulkes, 2 vols. (London: Viking Society for Northern Research, 1998), 1:108.

12. Helgi Guðmundsson, "Máki, mákur," 50; see George Henderson, *The Norse Influence on Celtic Scotland* (Glasgow: J. Maclehose, 1910), vii.

13. See Einar Ól. Sveinsson, "Vísa úr Hávamálum og írsk saga," *Skírnir* 126 (1952): 173 and the references there given.

14. Alexander Bugge, *Vesterlandenes Indflydelse paa Nordboernes og særlig Nordmændenes ydre Kultur, Levesæt og Samfundsforhold i Vikingetiden*, Videnskabs-Selskabets Skrifter 2, Historisk-filosofisk Klasse 1 (Kristiania [Oslo]: Dybwad, 1905), 208.

15. See Hermann Pálsson, "Keltnesk mannanöfn," and *Keltar á Íslandi*, 150–207; Helgi Guðmundsson, *Um haf innan: vestrænir menn og íslenzk menning á miðöldum* (Reykjavík: Háskólaútgáfan, 1997), 121–99; Jan de Vries, *Altnordisches etymologisches Wörterbuch*, 3rd ed. (Leiden: Brill, 1977), xxi–xxii.

16. See Stefán Karlsson, *The Icelandic Language*, trans. Rory McTurk (London: Viking Society for Northern Research, 2004), 9.

17. See Gísli Sigurðsson, *Gaelic Influence in Iceland: Historical and Literary Contacts—A Survey of Research* (Reykjavík: University of Iceland Press, 2000), and "Þögnin um gelísk áhrif á Íslandi," in *Greppaminni: Rit til heiðurs Vésteini Ólasyni sjötugum*, ed. Margrét Eggertsdóttir et al. (Reykjavík: Hið íslenska bókmenntafélag, 2009), 153–64.

that Icelandic settlement probably contained a diversity of signifi-cant minority groups or singleton settlers. Most significantly for the purposes of this essay, Hermann Pálsson pointed to the importance of a group of immigrants stemming from Hålogaland, some of them apparently from north of the Arctic circle, and argued that there would have been a Saami element among them.[18] Close ties between Scandinavian and aboriginal inhabitants of Hålogaland are testified to by *Historia Norwegiae*.[19] Hermann also posited a contribution on the part of the related people of Permia/Bjarmaland, citing the *Landnámabók* episode where Hjǫrr konungr Hálfsson of Hǫrðaland has twins by the daughter of the king of Bjarmaland: "Hét annarr Geirmundr en annarr Hámundr. Þeir váru svartir mjǫk" (One was called Geirmundr and the other Hámundr; they were very dark).[20] From their dark coloring they acquired the nickname *heljarskinn*. Geirmundr settled in Iceland, where he lived in grand style, and later Icelanders were evidently proud to number him among their ancestors. Hermann further suggests that the Þórólfr heljarskinn galdramaðr mentioned in *Vatnsdœla saga* took both his complexion and his occult knowledge from Permian or perhaps Saami ancestry.[21] Evidently settlers with Hålogaland and Bjarmaland origins and affil-iations could assume positions of prestige and centrality in the newly forming network of Icelandic society.

Iceland was a challenging location in which to forge a livelihood. The archaeology indicates that settler livelihoods were predomi-nantly at no higher level than mere subsistence.[22] In the formation of Icelandic livelihoods the prevailing contacts with Norway and the experience settlers had with exploitation of the North Atlantic

---

18. See *Úr landnorðri: Samar og ystu rætur íslenskrar menningar*, Studia Islandica 54 (Reykjavík: Bókmenntafræðistofnun Háskóla Íslands, 1997).

19. Gustav Storm, ed., *Monumenta historica Norvegiae latine conscripta: Latinske kildeskrifter til Norges historie i middelalderen* (Kristiania: Brøgger, 1880), 78.

20. *Íslendingabók, Landnámabók*, ed. Jakob Benediktsson, Íslenzk fornrit 1 (Reykjavík: Hið íslenzka fornritafélag, 1968), 150. See *Geirmundar þáttr heljarskinns* in *Sturlunga saga*.

21. *Úr landnorðri*, 24; *Vatnsdœla saga*, ed. Einar Ól. Sveinsson, Íslenzk fornrit 8 (Reykjavík: Hið íslenzka fornritafélag, 1939), 46.

22. See Orri Vésteinsson, "Archaeology of Economy and Society," in *A Companion to Old Norse-Icelandic Literature and Culture*, ed. Rory McTurk (Oxford: Blackwell, 2005), 11–15.

environment played a dominant role. Where pastoralism was concerned, the settlers used the Norwegian transhumance model of cattle and sheep-raising.[23] Nevertheless, input from the British Isles also contributed, as indirectly indicated by the loanword *erg* (from Irish *airghe* "summer-grazing location")[24] for precisely the concept of "transhumance pasture" denoted by modern Norwegian *sæter*. Other loanwords in this semantic field are *tarfr* "bull" (from Irish *tarb* "bull"),[25] *des* "haystack" (from Irish *daiss* "heap, pile, rick, stack, especially of corn"),[26] and *kró* "enclosure" (from Irish *cró* "enclosure, fold, pen"). Gathering practices brought by colonists from the British Isles centered upon edible types of sea-weed: *slafak* "sea-lettuce" (from a Scots Gaelic form *slabhach*)[27] and *myrikjarni* (with by-forms) "badderlock, alaria esculentia" (from Scots Gaelic *mirceann* or similar).[28] Some related economic activities have their designations from Icelandic adaptations of Irish lexis: Modern Icelandic *sofn* (*hús*) "kiln for drying corn, lyme-grass," although formed in analogy with *ofn* "oven" (contrast Faroese *sornur*, with identical meaning), presupposes adoption of Irish *sorn* "oven, furnace, kiln."[29] The word *korki* "cudbear, lichen used for dying wool red" appears to represent an adaptation of Irish *corcair* "dye-plant, lichen (giving crimson dye)," ultimately from Latin *purpura*.[30]

Even when the privations of settlement are fully reckoned with and saga accounts that speak of settler affluence and munificence are subjected to all due skepticism, there do appear to have been some substantial magnates such as Óláfr pá (himself a classic example of mixed Norwegian/Irish descent) who practiced the kind of conspicuous consumption and patronage glimpsed in the *Húsdrápa* of Úlfr Uggason.[31] The sources of their wealth have remained somewhat of

---

23. See Byock, "A Viking-age Valley," 204.

24. Craigie, "Gaelic Words and Names," 442.

25. Bugge, *Vesterlandenes Indflydelse paa Nordboernes*, 259.

26. Ibid., 157.

27. s.v. "slabhacán" in Carl Marstrander, *Randbemerkninger til det norsk-irske spørsmål* (Oslo: Dybwad, 1928), 4n.

28. Oskar Bandle et al., *The Nordic Languages: An International Handbook of the History of the North Germanic Languages* (Berlin: de Gruyter, 2002), 328.

29. Stefán Karlsson, *The Icelandic Language*, 9.

30. Ibid.

31. *Skjaldedigtning* A1:136–39, B1:128–30. See also *Laxdæla saga*, ed. Einar Ól. Sveinsson, Íslenzk fornrit 5 (Reykjavík: Hið íslenzka fornritafélag, 1934), 80.

an enigma.[32] This may be in part because scholarship has taken its cue from Commonwealth-era Icelandic resentment of the Norwegian kings and thereby been blinded to the important contribution to the Icelandic economy made by mainland-based sources of income. From the outset a significant part of the social mix on Iceland were those who sailed there not as enemies of King Haraldr hárfagri but as his "envoys."[33] Óláfr Tryggvason and Óláfr Haraldsson are two subsequent kings who, despite never having Iceland within their power, could nevertheless keep it within their sphere of influence by dint of cultivating clients and agents.

A special case of this mix of clientship and agency was what has often been loosely termed the "profession" of the skald. It is a matter of record that *skáldskapr* had become firmly established in Norway somewhat prior to the time of the Icelandic settlement. If we are to put our trust in a stanza conventionally associated with the *Haraldskvæði* of Þorbjǫrn hornklofi,[34] we see Haraldr hárfagri as early as the ninth century cultivating a large entourage of poets and presenting them with gifts of distinction and affluence.[35] Most probably the stanza in question represents a late addition to the poem,[36] but it is clear that by the time of the tenth-century Norwegian kings and earls, with Hákon Hlaðajarl being perhaps the clearest example,[37] the practice of skaldic poetry had come to constitute a genuine "earner." From the era of the reigns of Sigurðr and Hákon, jarls of Hlaðir, and Haraldr gráfeldr, a king over part of Norway, we see a series of visits to the courts of Norwegian leaders on the part of Icelandic poets. Within a hundred years or so of the settlement, Icelanders had established themselves,

32. Jesse L. Byock, *Medieval Iceland: Society, Sagas, and Power* (Berkeley: University of California Press, 1988), 77–78.

33. Przemysław Urbańczyk, "Ethnic Aspects of the Settlement of Iceland," *Collegium Medievale* 15 (2002): 155–66.

34. Numbered as 19 in the standard edition: *Skjaldedigtning* A1:28, B1:24–25.

35. See Kari Ellen Gade, "Poetry and Its Changing Importance in Medieval Icelandic Culture," in *Old Icelandic Literature and Society*, ed. Margaret Clunies Ross (Cambridge: Cambridge University Press, 2000), 76.

36. See Klaus von See, "Studien zum Haraldskvæði," *Arkiv för nordisk filologi* 76 (1961): 96–111; Bjarne Fidjestøl, "'Have you heard a poem worth more?' A Note on the Economic Background of Early Skaldic Praise-Poetry," in *Selected Papers*, ed. Odd Einar Haugen (Odense: Odense University Press, 1997), 126–27, and "Kongsskalden frå Kvinesdal og diktninga hans," in *Rikssamlingstid på Agder: historie, diktning, arkeologi*, ed. Hans Try (Kristiansand: Studentbokhandelen, 1976), 7–31.

37. Fidjestøl, "Economic Background," 128.

in the words of Preben Meulengracht Sørensen, as "a kind of literary Swiss Guard"[38] and a communal pride was building up around this function.[39]

What these Icelanders stood to gain was probably twofold. One gain lay in an income stream that was not available or at least not so lucrative in their home base of Iceland, where kingship was non-existent and early chieftaincies may not, for the most part, have been particularly affluent. If these skalds could capitalize on their "intellectual property," to put it in modern terms, so as to make themselves a living embodiment of tradition and their poetics the poetics "of record," then the gifts and rewards in kind disbursed by Norwegian and other leaders would enable them and their families, and perhaps even their descendants back home, to obtain a variety of goods and services on a comparatively long-term basis. Strangely, Byock's study of Icelandic livelihoods does not take cognizance of this type of income, but contrast Bjarne Fidjestøl's study, where it is shown that Óláfr Haraldsson and Knútr inn ríki, among others, had the resources to fund skaldic incomes not merely on a piece-meal basis but sometimes even on a continuing one—a very expensive proposition.[40] A second gain for the skald and ultimately for Icelandic culture more broadly lay in the immaterials and intangibles of cultural capital and distinction formulated for modern times by Pierre Bourdieu and applied recently to Snorri Sturluson by Kevin Wanner.[41] Icelanders became the treasure house of tradition celebrated by Saxo Grammaticus, who states that he gathered a substantial part of his materials from Icelandic informants.[42]

---

38. Preben Meulengracht Sørensen, "Social Institutions and Belief Systems of Medieval Iceland (ca. 870–1400) and their Relations to Literary Production," in Clunies Ross, *Old Icelandic Literature and Society*, 13. See Margaret Clunies Ross, *A History of Old Norse Poetry and Poetics* (Woodbridge: D.S. Brewer, 2005), 104, and "Poets and Ethnicity," in *Á austrvega: Saga and East Scandinavia, Preprint papers of the 14th International Saga Conference Uppsala 9th-15th August 2009*, ed. Agneta Ney et al., 2 vols. (Gävle: University of Gävle Press, 2009), 1:186, 192.

39. See Margaret Clunies Ross, "From Iceland to Norway," and *History of Old Norse Poetry*, 96.

40. See Byock, *Medieval Iceland*; cf. Fidjestøl, "Economic Background."

41. Kevin Wanner, *Snorri Sturluson and the Edda: The Conversion of Cultural Capital in Medieval Scandinavia*, Toronto Old Norse-Icelandic Series 4 (Toronto: University of Toronto Press, 2008), 7–15.

42. Saxo Grammaticus, *Gesta Danorum/Danmarkshistorien*, ed. Karsten Friis-Jensen

Although some of the skalds may have been itinerant on a fairly long-term basis[43] and invited to make longish stays at one or other mainland political and cultural center,[44] none of them has the kind of corpus attached to his name that would suggest anything like a "full-time" occupation as a poet, and notoriously it could be a chancy livelihood. More plausibly, when Icelanders mounted intermittent forays overseas from their permanent home base, it was in the pursuance of a variety of income streams simultaneously or alternately, as opportunity arose and resources offered themselves. Activities as a trader could be particularly conveniently combined with functioning on an occasion-driven basis as a court eulogist. Trading ports were often also prestige centers. A telling example is Hlaðir (modern Lade), the location presided over by Hákon jarl and other Hlaðajarlar and probably the venue for some poetic performances in praise of the earl. The name means "loading place"; it was from there that the *finnskattr* "Saami tribute" was exported and trade conducted.[45] The Icelandic skald Einarr Skálaglamm puns on the name in such a way as to hint at the kind of luxury commodity traded or gifted there:[46]

Sjau fylkjum kom silkis
(snúnaðr vas þat) brúna
geymir grundar síma
grandvarr und sik (landi).[47]

"The guardian of the laces of silk of the ground of the eye-brows [HLAÐA (genitive plural form of *Hlaðir*) = *hlaða* (genitive plural form of *hlǫð* "ribbons")], wary of detriment, brought seven districts under him; that was an enhancement for the land."

---

and Peter Zeeberg, 2 vols. (Copenhagen: Det Danske Sprog- og Litteraturselskab & Gads Forlag, 2005), 1:74–77.

43. See Gade, "Poetry and its Changing Importance," 88.

44. See Fidjestøl, "Economic Background," 120.

45. Ibid., 131.

46. See Magnus Olsen, "Eldste forekomst av navnet Hlaðir (*Vellekla* str. 14)," *Maal og minne* (1942): 154–56.

47. *Vellekla*, st. 13, in Snorri Sturluson, *Heimskringla*, ed. Bjarni Aðalbjarnarson, 3 vols., Íslenzk fornrit 26–28 (Reykjavík: Hið íslenzka fornritafélag, 1941–51), henceforth *Heimskringla*, 1:241.

In a stanza to be cited later, Kormákr Ǫgmundarson records receiving a gift of just such a ribbon from Sigurðr jarl, doubtless for poetic services rendered.

The other obviously convenient "earner" for a skald was mercenary service. This activity has perhaps been insufficiently taken into account in analyses of the Icelandic economy before union with Norway, but would have combined nicely with the production of praise poetry for the war leader, since eyewitness accounts were at a premium, and could also link onwards to diplomacy and other forms of lieutenant-ship to the ruler, Sigvatr Þórðarson being the classic example. Saxo's listing of the war-bands that participated in the Battle of Brávellir, though no doubt anachronistic, shows that Icelanders could be regarded as contributing to overseas military expeditions: "A Tyle autem uenere Mar Ruffus, eo videlicet pago, qui Mithfirthi dicitur, ortus educatusque, Grombar Annosus, Grani Brundelicus, Grim ex oppido Skerium apud Scaha Fyrthi quidem provinciam satus. Deinde Berhgar vates advertitur, cui Brahi et Rankil comites adhibentur" (From Iceland came Mar the Red, born and bred in the district called Miðfjǫrðr; Grombar the Aged, Grani from Brynjudalr, Grim from the town of Skerjum in the district of Skagafjǫrðr. Next came Bergr the poet/priest/seer, accompanied by Bragi and Hrafnkell).[48] The *Berhgar vates* mentioned here could conceivably be a skald. On the other hand, the Brahi and Rankil mentioned by Saxo are suspiciously reminiscent of the Bragi and Hrafnkell associated with *Ragnarsdrápa*, warning us that we cannot place too much reliance on this testimony.

Fortunately, there is plentiful testimony from the Icelandic skalds themselves, an early instance being Vigfúss Víga-Glúmsson, who composed two verses placing himself among the combatants at the Battle of Hjǫrungavágr:

Oss es leikr, en lauka
liggr heima vinr feimu –
þryngr at Viðris veðri
vandar – góðr fyr hǫndum.

---

48. *Gesta Danorum*, Friis-Jensen, 1:514–15; Saxo Grammaticus, *Gesta Danorum: The history of the Danes*, ed. Hilda Ellis Davidson and trans. Peter Fisher (Cambridge: Brewer, 1979–80), 240 (modified).

Hlýs kveðk hælis bósa –
hann væntir sér annars –
vífs und vǫrmum bægi –
vér skreytum spjǫr – neyta.[49]

"We have a good play on our hands, but the friend of the woman of leeks[50] lies at home; the storm of Viðrir's staff [BATTLE] crowds in. I say that the scoundrel is enjoying cosy shelter under the woman's warm arm; he expects something different; we polish our spears."

Varðat hœgt, þás hurðir
hjǫrklofnar sák rofna
– hátt sǫng Hǫgna – Geitis,
– hregg – til Vagns at leggja.
Þar gingum vér, þrøngvir
þunníss, í bǫð, Gunnar
– strǫng vas danskra drengja
darra flaug – til knarrar. (*Skjaldedigtning* A1:120, B1:115; *Ágrip*, Bjarni Einarsson, 134)

"It was not easy to attack Vagn, when I saw the hurdles of Geitir [SHIELDS] broken, cleft by the sword. Loud rang the storm of Hǫgni [BATTLE]. There we went, thruster of the thin ice of Gunnr [SWORD], in the battle to the ship. Strong was the flight of spears of Danish lads."

Also in the tenth century, some of this poetry by itinerant skalds is beginning to foreground the poet's affiliation with the Icelandic community. *Sonatorrek* (st. 15) contains an early example:

Mjǫk's torfyndr,
sás trúa knegum,
of alþjóð
elgjar galga,

---

49. *Skjaldedigtning* A1:121, B1:115; *Ágrip af Nóregskonunga sögum, Fagrskinna – Nóregs konunga tal*, ed. Bjarni Einarsson, Íslenzk fornrit 29 (Reykjavík: Hið íslenzka fornritafélag, 1984), 132.

50. The exact workings of this kenning resist analysis but there may be obscene connotations.

þvít niflgóðr
niðja steypir
bróður hrør
við baugum selr.[51]

"It is hard to find anyone whom I can trust among all the people of the gallows of the elk [ICELANDERS], since a traitor to his kinsfolk, good [only] for Niflheim, sells his brother's corpse for rings."

The allusion comes in the shape of the riddle-like kenning *alþjóð elgjar gálga* (all people of the gallows of the elk), where the gallows of the elk is "ice" and the people of ice are Icelanders.[52] The *ofljóst*—a veiling of the referent via synonym substitution—depends upon the observation that elk can fall through weak ice and become suspended in the water below, thus becoming easy prey to wolves and other scavengers. By a typically skaldic flight of fancy, this plight is envisaged as analogous to the fate of the hanged man on the gallows, who becomes a source of food for ravens and other scavengers. Egill's "signature" on the stanza is twofold: play on the gallows motif, a favorite with him, combines with the allusion to Iceland.

A late allusion to not merely the ice of Iceland but also the fire occurs in a pair of stanzas in praise of an axe composed by the twelfth-century Icelandic skald Einarr Skúlason and tentatively grouped with other stanzas in the standard skaldic edition as *Øxarflokkr*.[53] The audience is presumed to be the Norwegian ruler who is presenting the poet with the axe. Einarr chooses base-words for his kennings so as to play on imagery of fire and snow, thus conjuring up the distinctively volcanic landscape of Iceland.[54]

---

51. *Egils saga*, ed. Bjarni Einarsson (London: Viking Society for Northern Research, 2003), 151.

52. Sveinbjörn Egilsson, *Lexicon poëticum antiquæ linguæ septentrionalis* (Copenhagen: Societas regia antiquariorum septentrionalium, 1860), *s.v.* "elgr." For other more conjectural interpretations see *Egils saga Skalla-Grímssonar*, ed. Sigurður Nordal, Íslenzk fornrit 2 (Reykjavík: Hið íslenzka fornritafélag, 1933), 252, and *Egils saga*, Bjarni Einarsson, 151.

53. *Skjaldedigtning* A1:478, B1:450–51, vv. 7 and 8.

54. See Russell Poole, "Ormr Steinþórsson and the *Snjófríðardrápa*," *Arkiv för nordisk Filologi* 97 (1982): 129–30.

Blóðeisu liggr bæði
bjargs tveim megin geima
sjóðs (ák søkkva stríði)
snær ok eldr (at mæra). (*Skjaldedigtning* B1:450–51, v. 7)

"Both gold and silver cover each side of the mountain of the blood-ember [BACK OF THE AXE]; I have reason to praise my benefactor."

The combination of a gold kenning *geima eldr* "fire of the ocean," a silver kenning *sjóðs snær* "snow of the purse," and the punning substitution of *bjarg* "crag" for *hamarr* (which can mean either "crag" or "back of an axe") builds up within the stanza a sequence of words—*liggr bjargs tveim megin snær ok eldr* (snow and fire lie on both sides of the rock)—that conjures up the image of a mountain enveloped in both snow and fire. In the fragment that follows Einarr continues the same line of imagery.

Dœgr þrymr hvert, en hjarta
hlýrskildir ræðr mildu
Heita blakks, of hvítum
hafleygr digulskafli.
Aldri má fyr eldi
áls hrynbrautar skála
– ǫll viðr folka fellir
framræði – snæ bræða. (Ibid., 451, v. 8)

"The gold is in its place there every day above the white silver—but the king has a generous heart. Never can the silver be melted by the gold; the warrior-prince performs every illustrious deed."

Here again a volcanic image is conjured up by the base-words of the kennings: *dœgr hvert þrymr leygr of hvítum skafli* (the fire is there every day above the white snow-drift).

In these words Einarr evokes what was probably in the Middle Ages, as now, the most salient aspect of his native land from the point of view of outsiders. Of Norwegian works, both *Historia Norwegiae* and *Konungs skuggsjá* make prominent mention of volcanism in their descriptions of the island.

In the verses of Sigvatr, in contrast with the apparently pejorative reference by Egill cited above, we notice a cozy camaraderie with fellow-Icelanders (*Nesjavísur*, st. 5):

Teitr, sák okkr í ítru
allvalds liði falla
(gerðisk harðr) of herðar
(hjǫrdynr) svalar brynjur;
en mín at flug fleina
falsk und hjalm enn valska
(okkr vissak svá, sessi)
svǫrt skǫr (við her gǫrva).[55] (*Heimskringla* 2:62)

"Teitr, I saw chill mailshirts fall over the shoulders of us both in the all-powerful one's noble war-band; a hard sword-din [BATTLE] was waged; and my black hair hid itself under the French helmet at the flight of javelins [BATTLE]; benchmate, I knew us both to be thus prepared against the opposing force."

In this verse Sigvatr apparently addresses or apostrophizes not his broader audience (with the king as its most eminent member) but instead an individual called Teitr, evidently one of Sigvatr's comrades, using the dual pronoun (*okkr*) rather than the plural seen consistently elsewhere in the poem. This Teitr is otherwise unknown. Erik Lind notes that the name is extremely common in Iceland from the earliest times but seldom encountered in Norway, except in very early attestations.[56] Sigvatr's benchmate was therefore probably a fellow Icelander. The poet's evident special empathy with him may be implied in his specification of his own dark hair color, a point to which I shall return presently. Another instance of Sigvatr addressing a specific comrade occurs in *Vestrfararvísur* (st. 1):

Bergr, hǫfum minzk, hvé, margan
morgin Rúðuborgar,

---

55. See Russell Poole, "The *Nesjavísur* of Sigvatr Þórðarson," *Mediaeval Scandinavia* 15 (2005): 173–74.

56. *Norsk-isländska dopnamn och fingerade namn från medeltiden* (Uppsala: Lundequist, 1905–15), *s.v.* "Teitr."

bǫrð létk í fǫr fyrða
fest við arm enn vestra. (*Heimskringla* 2:271)

"Bergr, we have recalled how on many a morning I left the ship secured
in the path of men at the western arm of Rouen."

This address to Bergr comes within a poem principally addressed to
the king and is again somewhat conspicuous, though it must be noted
that the poet addresses another man in stanza 5, using the nickname
Húnn, "Bear-cub." Information on Bergr is very limited; we have the
following from the prose narrative of *Heimskringla*: "Sigvatr skáld
kom þat sumar til Englands vestan ór Rúðu af Vallandi ok sá maðr
með honum, er Bergr hét" (Sigvatr the skald came west that summer
from Rouen in France to England and that man with him, who was
called Bergr).[57] Lind documents a similar distribution for the name
Bergr as for Teitr: highly prevalent in Iceland from the beginning of the
tenth century, whereas it apparently died out early in Norway.[58] Bergr's
father, according to *Landnámabók*, was Vigfúss Víga-Glúmsson.[59]
Stylistic and verbal resemblances between Vigfúss's two verses cited
earlier and Sigvatr's, particularly *Nesjavísur*, make it likely that Sigvatr
was aware of Vigfúss's narrative technique: Vigfúss's verses may have
encouraged Sigvatr in his self-presentation as a participant in battle.
We might infer that Sigvatr's special association with Bergr arose as
part of his wider affiliation, through his father Þórðr Sigvaldaskáld,
with Vigfúss and perhaps other poets attached to Sigvaldi Strút-Har-
aldsson, jarl of Jómsborg. *Liðsmannaflokkr*, a poem associated with
Sigvaldi's brother Þorkell inn hávi, is the example par excellence of a
poem that appears to emanate from the actively campaigning section
of the *drótt* and represent their point of view.[60]

In another verse Sigvatr addresses his fellow-poet and indeed
nephew Óttarr svarti ("the black"—note this probably significant
nickname) on the subject of a gift of nuts they have received from King
Óláfr Haraldsson (*lausavísa* 10):

---

57. *Heimskringla* 2:271.

58. *Norsk-isländska dopnamn*, *s.v.* "Bergr."

59. *Íslendingabók, Landnámabók*, Jakob Benediktsson, 253, 268–69n4.

60. Russell Poole, *Viking Poems on War and Peace* (Toronto: University of Toronto
Press, 1991), 86–115.

Sendi mér enn mæri
– man þengill sá drengi –
síð munk heldr at hróðri –
hnytr þjóðkonungr – snytrask.
Opt, en okkr bað skipta,
Óttarr, í tvau dróttinn –
endask mál – sem myndim
manndjarfr fǫðurarfi.[61]

"To me the renowned high-king sent nuts; this king is mindful of his men; it will be a long time before I devote more artistry to praise-poetry. But the lord, bold towards men, often bade us divide them in two, Óttarr, just as we would a father's legacy: my speeches are ended."

In a final example of this show of familiarity with a fellow-Icelander, and, as the verbal parallels would suggest, perhaps with a reminiscence of the Sigvatr *lausavísa* just cited, Arnórr Þórðarson in his praise-poem *Magnússdrápa* (st. 4) addresses or apostrophizes a man called Gellir:

Flœði fylkir reiði
framr þjóðkonungs ramma;
stǫkk fyr auðvin okkrum
armsvells hati, Gellir.
Létat Nóregs njóta
nýtr þengill gram lengi;
hann rak Svein af sínum
sókndjarfr fǫður-arfi.[62]

61. *Skjaldedigtning* A1:268, B1:248; Ernst Albin Kock, ed., *Den norsk-isländska skaldediktningen*, 2 vols. (Lund: Gleerup, 1946–50), 1:128. See Russell Poole, "Claiming Kin, Skaldic-style," in *Verbal Encounters: Anglo-Saxon and Old Norse Studies for Roberta Frank*, ed. Antonina Harbus and Russell Poole (Toronto: University of Toronto Press, 2004), 273.

62. *Skjaldedigtning* A1:339, B1:311–12; *Ágrip af Nóregskonunga sögum*, Bjarni Einarsson, 210; Diana Whaley, *The Poetry of Arnórr jarlaskáld: An Edition and Study* (Turnhout: Brepols, 1998), 119, and "Arnórr jarlaskáld Þórðarson, *Magnússdrápa*," in *Poetry from the Kings' Sagas 2*, ed. Kari Ellen Gade, Skaldic Poetry of the Scandinavian Middle Ages 2 (Turnhout: Brepols, 2009), 212.

"The bold leader fled the mighty rage of the high-king; the hater of the arm-ice [GENEROUS MAN] bolted from the treasure-friend of us both, Gellir. The doughty prince did not let the lord enjoy Norway for long; daring in assault, he drove Sveinn from his father's legacy."[63]

Other construals of the word *gellir* have been proposed,[64] but the present one is by far the most sensible and straightforward. The notion of the stanza containing a common noun *gellir* meaning "yeller" is far-fetched, whereas a proper name Gellir, deriving ultimately from a nickname, is both firmly attested and readily assignable to an appropriate historical personage. Aside from a couple of dubious attestations in place-names, the name occurs solely in Iceland, not in Norway.[65] The combination "Gellir Þorkelsson" appears three times: Arnórr reputedly composed a poem in memory of a man of that name; a man of that name is said in *Laxdœla saga* to have visited Magnús Óláfsson's court and to have received lavish gifts from him; a man of that name was the paternal grandfather of Ari Þorgilsson.[66] Considerations of chronology and the relative rarity of the given name combine to suggest that these three are identical and that the Gellir invoked by Arnórr in the stanza must surely also be the same individual: the expression *auðvin* "treasure-friend" can be taken as a pointed allusion to the gifts that both Arnórr and Gellir have received from the king. As with Sigvatr and Teitr, here is a pair of comrades who can testify to royal munificence. Given that Gellir Þorkelsson was clearly a well-known magnate, *lǫgsǫgumaðr*, and personality and that Bergr has a skaldic lineage, the likelihood increases that Sigvatr's Teitr was also a person from a prominent Icelandic family, and in that case quite conceivably a member of the kindred that produced the Teitr referred to by Ari Þorgilsson in his list of informants for *Íslendingabók*.[67] We might envisage a group of aristocratic families that played an instrumental part in the developing Christian institutionalization of Iceland. The address to Gellir, in the midst of an encomium to

---

63. Translation modified from Whaley, *Poetry of Arnórr jarlaskáld* (see previous note).

64. See ibid., 191.

65. Lind, *Norsk-isländska dopnamn, s.v.* "Gellir."

66. See, respectively, Whaley, *Poetry of Arnórr jarlaskáld*, 191–92; *Laxdœla saga*, Einar Ól. Sveinsson, 227–28; *Íslendingabók, Landnámabók*, Jakob Benediktsson, 20.

67. *Íslendingabók, Landnámabók*, Jakob Benediktsson, 1, 5, 7, 15, 17, 21.

the king, seems obtrusive to modern ears,[68] and that very feature of the rhetoric in itself may indicate how significant this kind of bond between Icelanders must have been. It may, inter alia, have served as an unmissable signal, transmitted via the poetic format, that Icelanders looked after each other as they pursued livelihoods abroad and had no need to rely exclusively on royal protection.

Characteristic of these verses is the use of the dual pronoun, seen for instance in Arnórr's phrase *auðvin okkrum* (our wealthy friend). Relating to two comrades as it does, it seems to carry some kind of affective load—companionability, coziness, intimacy. The implication of an identical social level can be paralleled in affective uses of the word *drengr*.[69] The emerging rhetoric of "Icelander-talking-to-Icelander" intimacy may have prompted a special adaptation of dual pronoun usage. Ultimately this adaptation developed so vigorously that the historical dual number of the first and second person is now used consistently in Icelandic at the expense of the plural, whose use is now confined to honorifics. Indeed Helgi Guðmundsson sees its honorific use in the medieval language as underlying this virtual extinction in the modern language.[70]

This developing sense of Icelandic identity also finds expression in the singling out of bodily characteristics that are purportedly distinctive of Icelanders. The references already seen in the stanza cited from Sigvatr's *Nesjavísur* have their precursor in the highly dramatic diction of Egill Skalla-Grímsson's *Arinbjarnarkviða*:

Hafðak endr
Ynglings burar,
ríks konungs,
reiði fengna.
Drók djarfhǫtt
of døkkva skǫr,
létk hersi
heim of sóttan. (*Egils saga*, Bjarni Einarsson, 156, st. 3)

---

68. See Whaley, *The Poetry of Arnórr jarlaskáld*, 119 and 191–92, and "Arnórr jarlaskáld Þórðarson, *Magnússdrápa*," 213.

69. See Judith Jesch, *Ships and Men in the Late Viking Age: The Vocabulary of Runic Inscriptions and Skaldic Verse* (Woodbridge: Boydell, 2001), 221.

70. *The Pronominal Dual in Icelandic* (Reykjavík: Institute of Nordic Linguistics, 1972), 98.

"In former times I had incurred the wrath of the son of the Ynglings, a powerful king. I put on the hat of courage over my dark hair and visited the war-leader."

Né hamfagrt
hǫlðum þótti
skaldfé mitt
at skata húsum,
þás ulfgrátt
við Yggjar miði
hattar staup
at hilmi þák. (Ibid., 157, st. 7)

"Nor did my reward for the poem at the abode of the munificent lord seem attractive to men, when I received from the king a wolf-grey stump of the hat [HEAD] in exchange for the mead of Óðinn [POETRY]."

Við því tók,
en tvau fylgðu
søkk sámleit
síðra brúna
ok sá muðr,
es mína bar
hǫfuðlausn
fyr hilmis kné. (Ibid., st. 8)

"I took it and there came with it two black-colored gemstones of broad brows [EYES] and the mouth that delivered my head-ransom at the king's knee."

Þar tannfjǫlð
með tungu þák
ok hlertjǫld
hlustum gǫfguð,
en sú gjǫf
golli betri
hróðugs konungs
of heitin vas. (Ibid., 157–58, st. 9)

"There I received a multitude of teeth with a tongue and listening tapestries [EARS], endowed with hearing, and that gift of the glorious king was deemed better than gold."

Thus the Egill who expresses a sense of betrayal on the part of fellow-Icelanders in *Sonatorrek* self-describes as "dark" in *Arinbjarnarkviða*. Particularly vivid and semiotically significant is the cluster of words constituting the kenning for "eyes" in st. 8/3–4: *søkk sámleit / síðra brúna* (literally, "black-colored gemstones of broad brows"). The element *sám-* appears in the version of this stanza contained in ms. W of *Snorra Edda* (Codex Wormianus); the other witness, ms. AM 132, reads *svart-* ("black").[71] While in principle *søkk* could instead be glossed as "cavities" (literally "sinkings"), in practice this is ruled out by the context in Wormianus.[72] As Sigurður Nordal points out, description of the speaker's eyes as *søkk sámleit*, "black-colored gemstones," serves to emphasize their rarity and value.[73] The comparison indicated by this base-word can only be with jet, a lustrous black semi-precious stone. It has nice local appropriateness to the setting for the episode in *Arinbjarnarkviða*, since the raw resource is found in Yorkshire near Whitby[74] and tenth-century working of jet has been detected at York.[75] The worked form of jet most closely similar to eyes would be beads, which can take eye-like shapes.[76] A prestigious Anglo-Scandinavian burial on St. Patrick's Isle at Peel, Isle of Man, included a wealthy female with necklace featuring Whitby jet beads among other stones.[77] Given the material-culture context, Egill may

---

71. *Skjaldedigtning* A1:44.

72. *Egils saga*, Sigurður Nordal, 261.

73. Ibid., 260–61n8.

74. See Barbara E. Crawford and Beverley Ballin Smith, *The Biggings, Papa Stour, Shetland: The History and Excavation of a Royal Norwegian Farm* (Edinburgh: Society Antiquaries Scotland, 1999), 173.

75. See D. M. Hadley, *The Vikings in England: Settlement, Society and Culture* (Manchester: Manchester University Press, 2006), 151.

76. See Johan Callmer, "Trade Beads and Bead Trade in Scandinavia, c.800–1000 A.D." *Acta Archaeologica Lundensia* 11 (Lund: Gleerup, 1971), 33–35.

77. See James Graham-Campbell and Colleen E. Batey, *Vikings in Scotland* (Edinburgh: Edinburgh University Press, 1998), 111; David M. Wilson, *The Vikings in the Isle of Man* (Aarhus: Aarhus University Press, 2008), 49. For finds in Norwegian contexts see Signe Horn Fuglesang, "Viking and Medieval Amulets in Scandinavia," *Fornvännen* 84 (1989): 20, and Charlotte Blindheim, "Kaupang," in *Medieval Scandinavia: An Encyclopedia*, ed. Phillip Pulsiano and Kirsten Wolf (New York: Garland, 1993), 350.

be conferring on the deep black color of his eyes connotations of preciousness and prestige. Meanwhile, the "broad brows" noted in the kenning are reminiscent of descriptions of Saami features as *breiðleit* and synonyms thereof.[78] A *lausavísa* (no. 6) ascribed to the Icelandic poet Kormákr (but not necessarily authentic) also elaborates on his dark complexion:

Svǫrt augu berk sveiga
snyrtigrund til fundar
(þykkik erma Ilmi
allfǫlr) ok lá sǫlva.
Þó hefk mér hjá meyjum,
mengrund, komit stundum
hrings við Hǫrn at manga
hagr sem drengr enn fagri. (*Vatnsdœla saga*, Einar Ól. Sveinsson, 211)

"I bring dark eyes to the meeting with the tidying-land of the head-dress [WOMAN]—I seem quite pale to the goddess of sleeves [WOMAN]— and a sallow appearance. Yet on occasion, land of the necklace [LADY], I have acquitted myself with maidens, to drive a bargain with a goddess of the ring [WOMAN], like a handsome warrior."

The characterization of the flirtatious speaker, as someone who in the past has successfully driven a bargain with a woman (or possibly women) and who now brings himself and his dark features to a new encounter, contains overtones of trading that we can recognize as neatly suited to the composite livelihood of skalds.[79] The word *manga* often carries a commercial meaning, in line with its ultimate source in Medieval Latin *mangonare*.[80] Guðbrandur Vigfússon's main gloss is "to barter, chaffer."[81] In Modern Icelandic *manga* equates to "bargain,

---

78. See Hermann Pálsson, *Úr landnorðri*, 164.

79. See Russell Poole, "Composition Transmission Performance: The First Ten Lausavísur in *Kormáks saga*," *alvíssmál* 7 (1997): 53.

80. de Vries, *Altnordisches etymologisches Wörterbuch*, s.v. See Johann Fritzner, *Ordbog over det gamle norske sprog*, 4th ed., 3 vols. (Kristiania [Oslo]: Den norske forlagsforening, 1883–96; repr. Oslo: Universitetsforlaget, 1973), s.v.

81. Richard Cleasby and Gudbrand Vigfusson, *An Icelandic-English* Dictionary, 2nd ed. (Oxford: Clarendon, 1957), s.v. See Finnur Jónsson, *Lexicon Poeticum Antiquae linguae septentrionalis: Ordbog over det norsk-islandske skjadesprog oprindelig forfattet af Sveinbjörn Egilsson*, 2nd ed. (Copenhagen: Möller, 1931), 126.

haggle, deal, hawk, peddle," though with an additional specialized sense of courting or wooing.[82]

Sigvatr, as we have already seen, rather dwells on his own dark complexion. A telling example comes from *Austrfararvísur* (st. 15), his account of a diplomatic journey to Götaland and Sweden:

> Oss hafa augu þessi
> íslenzk, kona, vísat
> brattan stíg at baugi
> bjǫrtum langt in svǫrtu.
> Sjá hefr, mjǫð-Nanna, manni
> mínn ókunnar þínum
> fótr á fornar brautir
> fulldrengila gengit. (*Skjaldedigtning* B1:224; *Heimskringla* 2:140)

"These dark Icelandic eyes have shown us, woman, a steep path a long way to the bright ring. This my foot, mead-Nanna [WOMAN], has gone most gallantly along ancient routes unknown to your man."

Here Sigvatr offers a self-characterization as a dark-eyed addresser of a woman and also as a guest whose performance as a traveler has qualities of the stereotypical *drengr*. The Kormákr and Sigvatr verses correspond in detailed lexis: *svartr*, *auga*, and *drengr*. Sigvatr's address to the unnamed woman, in collocation with the words *mjǫð* "mead" and *stíg* "path," contains key elements of the classic vignette of the woman of the hall awaiting the arrival of the warrior with horn of mead in hand: compare the Old English poetic compound *medostig* "mead-path."[83] In an extension of this playfulness, the reference to Nanna in Sigvatr's address might imply an alignment of her husband with Baldr, who is said in *Gylfaginning* to be quintessentially fair, bright, and white in complexion.[84] The speaker's reference to his foot (*fótr*) might trigger associations, in such a context, with the episode

---

82. Árni Böðvarsson, ed., *Íslensk orðabók*, 2nd ed. (Reykjavík: Bókaútgáfa Menningarsjóðs, 1983), *s.v.* My translation.

83. Seamus Heaney, trans., *Beowulf: A New Verse Translation* (New York: Norton, 2000), line 924.

84. Snorri Sturluson, *Edda: Prologue and Gylfaginning*, ed. Anthony Faulkes, 2nd ed. (London: Viking Society for Northern Research, 1988), 23.

in *Skáldskaparmál* (ch. 1) where Skaði hopes to identify and select Baldr on the basis of his fine feet but instead picks Njǫrðr. While such proposed associations are in their nature elusive and difficult to verify, we can infer that a witty play on the distinction between "dark" (the Icelandic skald) and "blond" (the Swedish husband) is going on in the verse.

In semiotic terms, black is the "marked" descriptor, as contrasted with fair, which is unmarked in virtue of the fact that fairness or blondness has traditionally been seen as a distinctive attribute of Nordic peoples. The Icelandic construction of identity evident here constitutes itself on the basis of the marked feature, perhaps in a gesture of exceptionalism. That could have happened as a cultural phenomenon, irrespective of the actual incidence of fair versus dark persons in the Icelandic population. In saga descriptions, one of the distinctive features of Saami people and people from Hålogaland and Arctic Norway more broadly is their possession of a dark complexion. The name of the founder of the dynasty of the earls of Hlaðir, Sæmingr, is most straightforwardly taken to mean "descendant of Sámr,"[85] and in turn *sámr*, "dark-colored," was liable to association with the ethnic descriptor *Saami*,[86] whether or not it was historically cognate with it.

How are we to explain this "cultural phenomenon"? It can be suggested that Hålogaland might have had a natural attractiveness and prestige for Icelanders in virtue of its long-enduring independence from the Norwegian kings. The tenth-century Hålogalanders were not Norwegians—a point vouched for inter alia by Sturla Þórðarson's mentions of Hålogaland as a separate entity in his redaction of *Landnámabók*—and they helped to galvanize opposition against the territorial ambitions of Norwegian rulers.[87] Representative of them, it seems, was Eyvindr skáldaspillir. Aside from his very public resistance to Haraldr gráfeldr, he had high-status Hålogaland affiliations[88] and

---

85. de Vries, *Altnordisches etymologisches Wörterbuch, s.v.* "sámr," "Sæmingr"; see Gro Steinsland, *Det hellige bryllup og norrøn kongeideologi: en analyse av hierogami-myten i Skírnismál, Ynglingatal, Háleygjatal, og Hyndluljóð* (Oslo: Solum, 1991), 217.

86. Hermann Pálsson, *Úr landnorðri*, 164, 57, and 68.

87. See Urbańczyk, "Ethnic Aspects," 159.

88. See Folke Ström, "Poetry as an Instrument of Propaganda: Jarl Hákon and his Poets," in *Speculum Norroenum: Norse Studies in Memory of Gabriel Turville-Petre*, ed. Ursula Dronke et al. (Odense: Odense University Press, 1981), 447.

spoke for those in the north who found themselves adversely affected by the reign of the Christian *Gunnhildarsynir*. When he records in a verse that the Icelanders have presented him with a cloak pin the implication is that he held significance for Icelanders, as someone whose favor they needed to gain or repay. He refers to his Icelandic benefactors by an *ofljóst*, like Egill before him in *Sonatorrek* (st. 15), as noted, and in this there is possibly an element of emulation or at least textual continuity:

Fengum feldarstinga
fjǫrð ok galt við hjǫrðu,
þanns álhimins útan
oss lendingar sendu.
Mest selda ek mínar
við mævǫrum sævar
(hallæri veldr hváru)
hlaupsildr Egils gaupna. (*Skjaldedigtning* A1:74, B1:65; Kock, *Den norsk-isländska skaldediktningen*, 1:40; *Heimskringla* 1:223–24)

"I received last year a cloak pin, which the channel-heaven's [ICE-] landsmen [ICELANDERS] sent to me from across the sea, and I spent it on livestock. For the most part I sold my leaping herrings of the palms of Egill [ARROWS] for the slender arrows of the sea [= HERRINGS]; the famine causes both things."

Additionally, as mentioned earlier, some leading settlers of Iceland in the ninth and tenth centuries had Hålogaland origins, notably the *heljarskinn* twins. It would hardly be surprising, in view of all this, if the marked feature of dark complexion associated with them likewise became prestigious in early Iceland. The emphasis on the dark coloring exhibited by some of the early skalds, described to some extent by themselves (as we have seen) and with great amplification in the sagas, might be consistent with respect and regard for the skalds as among the pivotal members and earners within their society. The ascription to them of melancholic and hostile personalities—dark minds to fit dark bodies—a topic extensively discussed by Margaret Clunies Ross,[89]

---

89. See, e.g., "The Art of Poetry and the Figure of the Poet in Egils saga," *Parergon* 22 (1978): 2–12; repr. in *Sagas of Icelanders*, ed. John Tucker (New York: Garland, 1989), 126–49.

may represent a secondary semiotic development of this distinctive feature, perhaps especially influenced by the malign self-presentation of Egill.

As already pointed out, the Icelandic skalds incorporated a number of special rhetorical and linguistic features in their work, namely direct address to and inclusion (via the first person dual pronoun) of individual comrades (who seem to be uniformly of Icelandic background), along with a tendency to Icelandic self-identification. As a further linguistic feature, we find a number of Irish lexical items that figure exclusively in attributions to early Icelandic and Orkney skalds, as distinct from Norwegian skalds, who do not appear on the available evidence to use them at all. In a loose analogy, we might be reminded of Seamus Heaney's application in his *Beowulf* rendering of the Anglo-Irish word *bawn* to refer to Hrothgar's hall. Heaney explains that in Elizabethan English *bawn* (from Irish *bó-dhún* "fort for cattle") referred specifically to the fortified dwellings that the English planters built in Ireland to keep the dispossessed natives at bay.[90] Putting a *bawn* into *Beowulf* appealed to him as a means by which an Irish poet could inscribe his signature on a composition and hint at a complex set of attitudes revolving around enforced colonial status.

One of these distinctive items is *gagarr* "dog." It appears to be linked to Old Irish *gaghar/gadhar* (where *gadhar* is the later form), "dog, hunting-dog, beagle." A frequent collocate is *milchu* "greyhound." That the sense in Icelandic and Orkney Norse was also primarily "hunting-dog" is suggested by three of the attestations to be considered below, where *gagarr* occurs as a base-word in kennings for weaponry, a slot normally occupied by synonyms for "wolf." In this instance, Irish has conventionally been seen as the borrower, not the lender.[91] That explanation to some extent has been encouraged by Finnur Jónsson's proposed etymology of ON *gaga*, for which, following Cleasby-Vigfússon (*s.v.*), he posits the meaning "to throw the neck back,"[92] comparing *gaghals* "with neck bent

90. Heaney, *Beowulf*, xxx.

91. See, e.g., George Henderson, *Norse Influence*, 130; Carl J. S. Marstrander, *Bidrag til det norske sprogs historie i Irland* (Kristiania: Dybwad, 1915), 112, 158; de Vries, *Altnordisches etymologisches Wörterbuch*, *s.v.* "gagarr."

92. *Lexicon Poeticum*, *s.v.* "gagarr."

back."[93] Finnur's logic is that the dog throws its neck back in order to bark or howl, making this an appropriate etymon, but in the one attestation of *gaga* the likelier gloss is "laugh, mock" (in accordance with Fritzner, *s.v.*), and altogether this suggestion smacks of over-ingenuity. More plausible would be an onomatopoeic origin, partly in view of the Orkney and Icelandic usage of the word to be discussed presently, but more broadly because it would be unsurprising for the name to be onomatopoeic when hunting dogs, including beagles, are specifically selected and bred for their barking propensities, which are functional for intimidating the prey and for communicating to hunters and other dogs over long distances or without a clear line of sight. Onomatopoeic words in the relevant semantic field, including *geyja, gagga, gaga*, and others, occur in the various dialects of Norse. On the other hand, attestations of *gaghar/gagarr* are richer and more widely distributed in Irish, and *gagarr* could readily be explained as a cultural or economic adoption into Icelandic and Orkney Norse, parallel to the pastoral and gathering terminology considered earlier in this essay. We may, on balance, have not so much a loanword here as a word that was more or less at home in both Irish and Norse parlance on the Atlantic islands.

The word is found in a series of poems, the anonymous *Darraðarljóð* possibly being the oldest:

Gengr Hildr vefa
ok Hjǫrþrimul,
Sanngríðr, Svipul
sverðum tognum;
skapt mun gnesta,
skjǫldr mun bresta,
mun hjalmgagarr
í hlíf koma.[94]

"Hildr goes to weave, and Hjǫrþrimul, Sanngríðr, Svipul, with drawn swords; the shaft will snap, the shield will break, the helmet hunting-dog [SWORD] will penetrate the armor."

93. *Norsk-islandske Kultur- og Sprogforhold i det 9. og 10. Århundrede* (Copenhagen: Høst, 1921), 60.

94. *Brennu-Njáls saga*, ed. Einar Ól. Sveinsson, Íslenzk fornrit 12 (Reykjavík: Hið íslenzka fornritafélag, 1954), 455; Poole, *Viking Poems*, 116–17, st. 3.

Darraðarljóð is uniquely preserved in an Orkney context in *Njáls saga*, which links it with the Battle of Clontarf, datable to 1014;[95] but the true occasion may be the Battle of Dublin of 919.[96] The image of weaving that provides the central trope for the poem appears to have been prompted by the expression *mórenglaim* "great weft," used in collocation with *claidib* "sword" in an Irish poem composed about 909 in praise of Cerbhall of Leinster, the king who expelled the Norse from the Dublin region in 902.[97] Equally, the occurrence of *gagarr* in *Darraðarljóð* may point to Viking contact with Irish-speaking communities under the aegis of the kingdom of Dublin.

Additional attestations occur in Tindr Hallkelsson's *Hákonardrápa*, a *lausavísa* attributed to [pseudo-] Egill Skalla-Grímsson (both authors are assumed to be Icelandic),[98] and *Málsháttakvæði* and *Krákumál* (both these anonymous poems are assumed to be of Orkney provenance).[99] Additionally, the word occurs as the nickname of one Þorgrímr gagarr Ljótsson, an Icelander.[100] This set of attestations is therefore exclusively Icelandic and Orkney. Competing for chronological first place with *Darraðarljóð* is Tindr's *Hákonardrápa*:

Vann á Vinða sinni
verðbjóðr Hugins ferðar,
– beit sólgagarr seilar –
sverðs eggja spor – leggi,
áðr hjǫrmeiðir hrjóða
– hætting var þat – mætti –
leiðar – langra skeiða –
liðs – hálfan tøg þriðja. (*Heimskringla* 1:286)

---

95. *Njáls saga*, Einar Ól. Sveinsson, 454–59.

96. See Nora Kershaw, ed. and trans., *Anglo-Saxon and Norse poems* (Cambridge: Cambridge University Press, 1922), 116; Poole, *Viking Poems*, 122–25; but cf. Máire Ní Mhaonaigh, *Brian Boru: Ireland's Greatest King?* (Stroud: Tempus, 2007), 92–93.

97. See Kershaw, *Anglo-Saxon and Norse poems*, 116.

98. *Skjaldedigtning* A1:603; B1:603.

99. See, respectively, Roberta Frank, *Sex, Lies and Málsháttakvæði: A Norse Poem from Medieval Orkney* (Nottingham: Centre for the Study of the Viking Age, University of Nottingham, 2004), 4, and Anne Heinrichs, "*Krákumál*," in Pulsiano, *Medieval Scandinavia: An Encyclopedia*, 368–69.

100. *Íslendingabók, Landnámabók*, Jakob Benediktsson, 184–85; Erik Henrik Lind, *Norsk-isländska personbinamn från medeltiden* (Uppsala: Lundequist, 1920–21), 96. I owe this reference to Richard L. Harris, fellow contributor to this volume.

"The offerer of a banquet of the company of Huginn [WARRIOR] set the mark of the [sword's] edges on the forces of the Wends—the hunting-dog of the sun of the strap [SHIELD > SWORD] bit their legs—before the mast of swords [FIGHTER] could clear twenty-five of the longships; that was a risk for the men of the expedition."

Here the skald plays upon the literal meaning of the base-word, to create the image of a biting dog. The example attributed to Egill Skallagrímsson (*lausavísa* 2) in *Egils saga* comes from a pair of stanzas that are treated as dubious by most if not all scholars,[101] and is in principle undatable (although see the suggestions made below):

Síþǫgla gaf sǫglum
sárgagls þría Agli
hirðimeiðr við hróðri
hagr brimrótar gagra,
ok bekkþiðurs blakka
borðvallar gaf fjórða
kennimeiðr, sás kunni,
kǫrbeð, Egil gleðja.
    (*Skjaldedigtning* A1:603, B1:602; *Egils saga*, Sigurður Nordal, 82, v. 5; *Egils saga*, Bjarni Einarsson, 44 and note)

"The adroit tending-tree of the wound-gosling [MAN] gave the talkative Egill three perpetually silent hunting-dogs of the sea-root [SEA-SNAILS] for his praise, and the knowing tree of the horses of the plank-plain [SEA-FARER], who knew how to make Egill glad, gave as the fourth gift the sickbed of the capercaillie of the stream [EGG]."

Here *gagarr* figures as the base-word in a whimsical circumlocution for "sea snail" that depicts this creature in riddle-style as a silent barker (compare the attestation from *Málsháttakvæði*). The verse as a whole describes the rewards—sea snails and duck eggs—presented to three-year-old Egill by his maternal grandfather in return for precocious skaldic virtuosity. The generic gifts it parodically alludes to are eggs and shells. Among eggs, the item of highest

---

101. Cf. *Egils saga*, Sigurður Nordal, vii.

prestige was the Resurrection egg, an Easter gift which stems from the East, with their center of production in Kiev. Eleventh-century examples are found at Sigtuna and on Gotland.[102] Among shells, the type of greatest prestige and thus the likeliest candidate for presentation was the cowrie, ultimately sourced from the Indian Ocean and widely distributed across the Viking world. Gotlanders brought whole shells back to their island and often placed them with the deceased in graves.[103] The name of Egill's benefactor, Yngvarr, coincides with that of the famed mid-eleventh-century expeditionary leader Yngvarr/Ingvarr, whose ventures on the "eastern way" are commemorated on numerous Swedish runestones[104] and form the subject of *Yngvars saga víðförla*. These distinctive motifs might point to composition of the stanza late in the eleventh century, consistent with the probabilities for other generic Viking stanzas in *Egils saga*.[105]

Málsháttakvæði provides our unique example of *gagarr* outside a kenning construction:

Ró skyldu menn reiði gefa,
raunlítit kømsk opt á þrefa,
gagarr er skaptr, þvít geyja skal,
gera ætlak mér létt of tal.
Verit hafði mér verra í hug,
var þat nær sem kveisu flug,
jafnan fagnar kvikr maðr kú,
kennir hins, at gleðjumk nú. (*Skjaldedigtning* B2:138–14, v. 4)

"Men should give their wrath a rest. Often a mere trifle leads to strife. A hunting-dog is formed because it must bark. I intend to make this recital light work for me. Worse intentions had been in my mind. It

---

102. See Margareta Attius Sohlmann, "Testimony from Gotland island of Viking Journeys East," Special issue, *Historiska Nyheter, Statens Historiska Museum: Olga & Ingegerd—Vikingafurstinnor i öst / Viking Princesses* (2004–05): 8–9.

103. See Gun Westholm, "Gotland and the Surrounding World," in *The Spillings Hoard: Gotland's Role in Viking Age World Trade*, ed. Ann-Marie Pettersson (Visby: Gotlands Museum, 2009), 146.

104. Jesch, *Ships and Men*, 102–04.

105. *Egils saga*, Sigurður Nordal, 81–82, v. 4; 100–101, v. 7; 119, v. 12.

was almost like the pain of a boil. The living man rejoices in a cow. It is apparent that I am enjoying myself now."[106]

Roberta Frank draws attention to the cheerful electicism, both stylistic and motivic, of this poem.[107] The choice of the word *gagarr* may have added to that sense of eclecticism.

The final attestation comes from *Krákumál*, a late pastiche supposedly spoken by Ragnarr loðbrók:

> Hjoggum vér með hjǫrvi.
> Herr kastaði skjǫldum,
> þás rægagarr rendi
> ræstr at gumna brjóstum;
> beit í Skarpa-skerjum
> skœru-bíldr at hjaldri;
> roðinn vas randar máni,
> áðr Rafn konungr felli;
> dreif ór hǫlða hausum
> heitr á brynjur sveiti. (*Skjaldedigtning* B1:649–56, st. 6)

"We strike with the sword. The army threw down their shields when the unleashed hunting-dog of the corpse [SWORD] dashed at men's breasts. In the Skarpa-skerries the war-iron [SWORD] bit in battle. The moon of the rim [SHIELD] was reddened before King Hrafn fell. Out from men's skulls the hot blood spurted on to the mailshirts."

Another distinctive word, *díar*, occurs in a stanza from Kormákr's *Sigurðardrápa* (st. 3), mentioned above, where the poet acknowledges the earl's gift of a headband:

> Eykr með enniðúki
> jarðhljótr día fjarðar
> breyti, hún sás beinan
> bindr; seið Yggr til Rindar. (*Skjaldedigtning* A1:79; *Skáldskaparmál*,
> Faulkes, 1:9)

---

106. Cf. Frank, *Sex, Lies and Málsháttakvæði*, 24.
107. Ibid., 17.

"The land-getter, who fastens the ?mast-top straight?, honors the
provider of the deities' fiord [POET?] with a headband. Yggr laid spells
for Rindr."[108]

Here, despite the irregularity of the kenning and the overall obscu-
rity of the *helmingr*, *díar* "gods, priests" is accepted by scholars as a
loanword from Irish *día*, also *dea*.[109] Senses of *día* are "[the Christian]
God" and "god, goddess, supernatural being, object of worship," the
latter often used of the pre-Christian gods in formulas such as *tongu
do dia toingthe hUlaid* "I swear by the gods whom the Ulstermen
swear by" and *atbiursa mo dee* "I swear by my gods."

The word *kelli* occurs as an apparent *hapax legomenon* in another
verse linked to Kormákr—albeit only in *Kormáks saga* and hence a
less reliable attribution. The relevant clause is as follows: *Fjǫll eru
fjarðar kelli / faldin* "The mountains are draped with the veil of the
fiord [ICE]."[110] A very similar word *kellir* occurs in a *þula* as a *heiti*
for "helmet."[111] Sophus Bugge saw the two words as independent
of each other, arguing that Kormákr's *kelli* lacks nominative -*r* and
originates in Irish *caille* "veil," ultimately from Latin *pallium*.[112] Most
scholars, however, have preferred to take them together, as derived
forms from ON *kollr* "head."[113] Falk went a different route, citing
alleged Irish *celbir*,[114] but as best I can determine the attested form is
actually *celbarr* (gen. sg. *celbairr*) "headpiece, helmet." Against the
majority viewpoint, it must be borne in mind that evidence from *þulur*
is not necessarily decisive: the *þulur* contain various layers of accretion and are not necessarily representative of pre-thirteenth-century

108. Cf. Anthony Faulkes, trans., *Edda* (London: Dent, 1987), 68.

109. Bugge, *Vesterlandenes Indflydelse paa Nordboernes*, 133; de Vries, *Altnordisches
etymologisches Wörterbuch, s.v.* "diar."

110. *Skjaldedigtning* B1:77–78, v. 34; *Vatnsdœla saga*, Einar Ól. Sveinsson, 266–67,
v. 53.

111. *Hjálms heiti* 2: *Skjaldedigtning* A1:667–68, B1:665–66.

112. "Om Versene i *Kormáks saga*," *Aarbøger for nordisk oldkyndighed og historie*
(Copenhagen: Thieles bogtrykkeri, 1889), 9; see also A. Bugge, *Vesterlandenes Indflydelse
paa Nordboernes*, 150.

113. See Frank Fischer, *Die Lehnwörter des Altwestnordischen* (Berlin: Mayer
und Müller, 1909), 198; Finnur Jónsson, *Norsk-islandske Kultur- og Sprogforhold*,
69; Jónsson, *Lexicon Poeticum, s.v.* "kellir"; de Vries, *Altnordisches etymologisches
Wörterbuch, s.v.* "kellir."

114. Hjalmar Falk, *Altnordische Waffenkunde* (Kristiania: Dybwad, 1914), 162.

skaldic usage;[115] indeed they may incorporate mistaken inferences from older skaldic usage. In light of this, derivation of *kelli* from *caille* remains the clearly most plausible solution. As the citations in the *Electronic Dictionary of the Irish Language* show, the reference is predominantly to a veil over the head: e.g., *sith-lais in uisci isin cuach tria chailli* "strained the water in the cup through her veil." The ecclesiastical content of this word, often used in funerary contexts in the original Irish, makes it a type of lexis especially likely to remain in active use in Iceland among people of Christian background, parallel with *bagall* "crozier" (from Irish *bachall* "crozier, pastoral staff," ultimately from Latin *baculum*), *kross* "cross" (from Irish *cros*, ultimately from Latin *crux*), *bjannak* "blessing" (from Irish *bennacht* "blessing," ultimately from Latin *benedictum* or *benedictio*), and of course *díar* "gods, priests."[116] These two attestations of Irish vocabulary in association with Kormákr are naturally all the more intriguing in view of Kormákr's transparently Irish name. Striking, but hard to explain, is the fact that both *kelli* and *día* occur in collocation with the Icelandic word *fjǫrðr* in their respective stanzas.

The lexeme *méil* is found uniquely in two stanzas by Icelandic skalds. The first is from *Vellekla* (st.10), ascribed to Einarr skálaglamm:

Rigndi hjǫrs á hersa
hríðremmis fjǫr víða
– þrimlundr of jók Þundi
þegns gnótt – méilregni,
ok hald-Viðurr hǫlða
haffaxa lét vaxa
Laufa veðr at lífi
lífkǫld Háars drífu. (*Heimskringla* 1:210–11, v. 99)

"The empowerer of the storm of the sword [WAR-LEADER] rained with a crushing rain far and wide upon the bodies of the chieftains; the bush of the battle [WARRIOR] added plenty of retainers for Óðinn. And the holding-Óðinn of the ocean-horses [SHIP-BORNE

---

115. See Elena Gurevich, "Zur Genealogie der *þula*," *alvíssmál* 1 (1992): 90–94, and "*Þulur* in *Skáldskaparmál*: An Attempt at Skaldic Lexicology," *Arkiv för nordisk filologi* 107 (1992): 36–37.

116. On these lexical items, see Fischer, *Die Lehnwörter des Altwestnordischen*, 18–19.

WARRIOR] caused the life-chilling tempest of Laufi (Bǫðvar-Bjarki's sword) [BATTLE] to swell with Óðinn's blizzard [SHOOTING OF SPEARS] to the detriment of their lives."

With this attestation we can compare the following from *Hákonardrápa* (st. 9), attributed to Hallfreðr vandræðaskáld:

Þaðan verða fǫt fyrða
(fregnk gǫrla þat) Sǫrla
– rjóðask bjǫrt í blóði
benfúr – méilskúrum.[117] (*Skáldskaparmál*, Faulkes, 68, v. 230)

"Thence men's garments of Sǫrli [ARMOR] are destroyed by crushing showers; bright fires of the wound [SWORDS] are reddened in blood."

Quite probably, as Marius Kristensen suggests, Hallfreðr is here borrowing from Einarr, who is fond of unusual kennings based on spears, arrows, and other thrown weapons.[118] Whatever the case, *méil* has proved rather a mystery.[119] Sveinbjörn Egilsson (followed by Finnur Jónsson) glosses it as "ferrum, telum,"[120] the sole unequivocal attestation being *mél* in Ingjaldr Geirmundarson's *Atlǫguflokkr* 6,[121] and compares it with OE *mæl*. Kristensen instead links with ON *-mal, melr, mælir* and glosses as "quiver."[122] Falk proposes that *méil* is synonymous with ON *malmr* "ore, metal" and posits an origin in *mihila, a derived form of Latin *mica* "crumb," in the sense of "gravel."[123] Holthausen posits linkage with Pers. *mex* (< **maixa-*) "stake."[124] Bjarni Aðalbjarnarson identifies with *mél* "bridle-bit" and

---

117. See Konstantin Reichardt, *Studien zu den Skalden des 9. und 10. Jahrhunderts* (Leipzig: Mayer & Müller, 1928), 61–63.

118. "Skjaldenes sprog: Nogle småbemærkninger," *Arkiv för nordisk filologi* 23 (1907): 236.

119. See Reichardt, *Studien zu den Skalden*, 59–64.

120. *Lexicon poëticum antiquæ linguæ septentrionalis* (Copenhagen: Societas regia antiquariorum septentrionalium, 1860), s.v. "mél"; see also Finnur Jónsson, *Lexicon Poeticum, s.v.*

121. *Skjaldedigtning* B2:100.

122. "Skjaldenes sprog: Nogle småbemærkninger," 240.

123. *Altnordische Waffenkunde*, 76.

124. Ferdinand Holthausen, *Vergleichendes und etymologisches Wörterbuch des*

glosses as "missiles" (*skotvopn*).[125] De Vries dismisses Falk's explanation but does not otherwise commit himself.[126]

All the above explanations seem strained or literally far-fetched. Could *méil* instead be connected with a disyllabic form of Irish *meilid* "to grind"? The entry for *meilid* in the *Electronic Dictionary of the Irish Language* includes the following: (a) of grain, etc., "grinds, crushes"; (b) of weapons, "grinds, sharpens": *ná melta riss . . . acht gaí* "that only spears should be whetted against it"; (c) of a person, "crushing, bruising," hence "overcomes, destroys"; III With abstract object and *for* of person, "wreaks, inflicts (on)": *a muilinn . . . ni bo chomailt far serbainn | [a] ro milt for uibh Cerbhaill* "it was not the grinding of oats thou didst grind on Cerbhaill's descendants"; *niconmela in fer-sa a baraind for Ultu* "that man shall not wreak his wrath on the Ulstermen." With object omitted: *amal melis milchu for mhil* "as a greyhound falls on a hare."[127]

As we see, *meilid* is often used in association with onslaughts and attacks involving weapons. If there is a relationship between this word and Icelandic *méil*, the two compounds with this element would mean respectively "grinding/sharp rain" and "grinding/sharp showers," or more broadly "destructive rain/showers," implying showers of weapons such as spears that are ground or sharpened or whetted and moreover have a grinding or mincing effect upon those whom they strike. Similar concepts are seen in OE poetry, e.g., *mylenscearpum* "sharp from the grinder," used of weapons, and *wundum forgrunden* "minced up with wounds" (of a person), both attested in *The Battle of Brunanburh*. At the same time, it must be acknowledged that the precise phonological relationship between the Irish and Icelandic forms of this word remains a difficulty.

Taking the four lexical items discussed above together, and admitting an element of uncertainty, it does look as if a select number of the most prominent of the *hǫfuðskáld* of Iceland, along with anonymous imitators in Iceland and Orkney, availed themselves of a small dash of distinctive Irish-derived vocabulary. While some Irish words did

---

Altwestnordischen, Altnorwegisch-isländischen, einschliesslich der Lehn- und Fremd- wörter sowie der Eigennamen (Göttingen, Vandenhoeck & Ruprecht, 1948), 193.

125. *Heimskringla* 1:211n.

126. de Vries, *Altnordisches etymologisches Wörterbuch, s.v* "méilregn."

127. See http://edil.qub.ac.uk/dictionary/search.php.

percolate into early Norwegian dialects, the uptake by Norwegian skalds on the basis of the available evidence is virtually nil: Bragi, for example, used the ship-*heiti lung*. The conspicuous piece of Irish lexis in a stanza (*lausavísa* 6) ascribed to the twelfth-century Norwegian king Magnús berfœttr Óláfsson probably owes its inspiration to a topical allusion:

Hvat skulum heimfǫr kvitta?
hugr's minn í Dyflinni,
enn til Kaupangs kvinna
kømkat austr í hausti.
Unik, þvít eigi synjar
ingjan gamans þinga;
œrskan veldr því's írskum
annk betr an mér svanna.[128]

"Why should we talk of a homeward voyage? My heart is in Dublin; I will yet again this autumn not return eastwards to the women of Kaupangr. I am enjoying myself because the girl does not deny me pleasurable trysts; youth is the cause that I love the Irish maiden better than myself."[129]

Here the word *ingjan* "girl, maiden" is a conspicuous cultural borrowing from Irish *ingen* "a daughter, girl, maiden, virgin; also frequently used of a (married) woman." While the identity of the particular *ingen* referred to remains uncertain, a plausible suggestion makes her the mother of Haraldr gilli, a claimant to be son of Magnús berfœttr.[130]

Camaraderie, complexion, lexis: these features combine to suggest an impulse on the part of some Icelandic (and Orkney) skalds, most prominently Egill, Kormákr, and Sigvatr, to individuate their poetic product by "branding" it with what were perceived as distinctive

---

128. *Skjaldedigtning* A1:433, B1:403; *Morkinskinna*, ed. Finnur Jónsson (Copenhagen: Jørgensen, 1928–32), 334; *Ágrip af Nóregskonunga sögum*, Bjarni Einarsson, 313–14.

129. Theodore M. Andersson and Kari Ellen Gade, trans., *Morkinskinna: The Earliest Icelandic Chronicle of the Norwegian Kings (1030–1157)*, Islandica 51 (Ithaca: Cornell University Press, 2000), 311.

130. Ibid., 488.

features of their insular communities. Indications of such a tendency show up a few decades after the initial settlement, with a cluster of instances in the decades immediately preceding and following the turn of the eleventh century and sporadic further imitations down into the thirteenth century.

Bibliography

Agnar Helgason, Carles Lalueza-Fox, Shyamali Ghosh, Sigrún Sigurðardóttir, et al. "Sequences From First Settlers Reveal Rapid Evolution in Icelandic mtDNA Pool." *Public Library of Science Genetics* 5.1 (2009): DOI:10.1371/journal.pgen.1000343.

——, E. Hickey, S. Goodacre, V. Bosnes, et al. "mtDNA and the Islands of the North Atlantic: Estimating the Proportions of Norse and Gaelic Ancestry." *American Journal of Human Genetics* 68 (2001): 723–37.

——, Sigrún Sigurðardóttir, J. R. Gulcher, R. Ward, et al. "mtDNA and the origin of the Icelanders: Deciphering Signals of Recent Population History." *American Journal of Human Genetics* 66 (2000): 999–1016.

——, Sigrún Sigurðardóttir, J. Nicholson, B. Sykes, et al. "Estimating Scandinavian and Gaelic ancestry in the male settlers of Iceland." *American Journal of Human Genetics* 67 (2000): 697–717.

Ágrip af Nóregskonunga sögum, Fagrskinna – Nóregs konunga tal. Edited by Bjarni Einarsson. Íslenzk fornrit 29. Reykjavík: Hið íslenzka fornritafélag, 1984.

Andersson, Theodore M., and Kari Ellen Gade, trans. *Morkinskinna: The Earliest Icelandic Chronicle of the Norwegian Kings (1030–1157).* Islandica 51. Ithaca: Cornell University Press, 2000.

Árni Böðvarsson, ed. *Íslensk orðabók.* 2nd ed. Reykjavík: Bókaútgáfa Menningarsjóðs, 1983.

Bandle, Oskar, Kurt Braunmüller, Lennart Elmevik, and Gun Widmark. *The Nordic Languages: An International Handbook of the History of the North Germanic Languages.* Berlin: de Gruyter, 2002.

Bjarni Einarsson. *Skáldasögur: Um uppruna og eðli ástaskáldsagnanna fornu.* Reykjavík: Bókaútgáfa Menningarsjóðs, 1961.

Blindheim, Charlotte. "Kaupang." In *Medieval Scandinavia: An Encyclopedia.* Edited by Phillip Pulsiano and Kirsten Wolf. New York: Garland, 1993.

Brennu-Njáls saga. Edited by Einar Ól. Sveinsson. Íslenzk fornrit 12. Reykjavík: Hið íslenzka fornritafélag, 1954.

Bugge, Alexander. *Vesterlandenes Indflydelse paa Nordboernes og særlig Nordmændenes ydre Kultur, Levesæt og Samfundsforhold i*

Vikingetiden. Videnskabs-Selskabets Skrifter 2. Historisk-filosofisk Klasse 1. Kristiania: Dybwad, 1905.

Bugge, Sophus. "Om Versene i *Kormáks saga.*" In *Aarbøger for nordisk oldkyndighed og historie.* Copenhagen: Thieles bogtrykkeri, 1889.

Byock, Jesse L. *Medieval Iceland: Society, Sagas, and Power.* Berkeley: University of California Press, 1988.

———, Phillip Walker, Jon Erlandson, Per Holck, Davide Zori, et al. "A Viking-age Valley in Iceland: The Mosfell Archaeological Project." *Medieval Archaeology* 49 (2005): 195–218.

Callmer, Johan. "Trade Beads and Bead Trade in Scandinavia, c.800–1000 A.D." *Acta Archaeologica Lundensia* 11. Lund: Gleerup, 1971.

Cleasby, Richard, and Gudbrand Vigfusson. *An Icelandic-English Dictionary.* 2nd ed. Oxford: Clarendon, 1957.

Clunies Ross, Margaret. "The Art of Poetry and the Figure of the Poet in Egils saga." *Parergon* 22 (1978): 2–12. Repr. in *Sagas of Icelanders,* edited by John Tucker, 126–49. New York: Garland, 1989.

———. "From Iceland to Norway: Essential Rites of Passage for an Early Icelandic Skald." *alvíssmál* 9 (1999): 55–72. http://userpage. fu-berlin.de/~alvismal/9sigvat.pdf.

———. *A History of Old Norse Poetry and Poetics.* Woodbridge: D.S. Brewer, 2005.

———. "Poets and Ethnicity." In *Á austrvega: Saga and East Scandinavia, Preprint papers of the 14th International Saga Conference, Uppsala 9th-15th August 2009,* edited by Agneta Ney, Henrik Williams, and Fredrik Charpentier Ljungqvist, 2. vols., 1: 185–92. Gävle: University of Gävle Press, 2009.

Craigie, William A. "Gaelic Words and Names in the Icelandic Sagas." *Zeitschrift für Celtische Philologie* 1 (1897): 439–54.

Crawford, Barbara E., and Beverley Ballin Smith. *The Biggings, Papa Stour, Shetland: The History and Excavation of a Royal Norwegian Farm.* Edinburgh: Society Antiquaries Scotland, 1999.

Egils Saga. Edited by Bjarni Einarsson. London: Viking Society for Northern Research, 2003.

Egils saga Skalla-Grímssonar. Edited by Sigurður Nordal. Íslenzk fornrit 2. Reykjavík: Hið íslenzka fornritafélag, 1933.

Einar Ól. Sveinsson. "Vísa úr Hávamálum og írsk saga." *Skírnir* 126 (1952): 168–77.

Electronic Dictionary of the Irish Language (eDIL). http://edil.qub. ac.uk/dictionary/search.php.

Eyrbyggja saga. Edited by Einar Ól. Sveinsson and Matthías Þórðarson. Íslenzk fornrit 4. Reykjavík: Hið íslenzka fornritafélag, 1935.

Falk, Hjalmar. *Altnordische Waffenkunde.* Skrifter og afhandlinger der Norske Videnskaps Akademi 2, Historisk-filosofisk klasse 6. Kristiania: Dybwad, 1914.

Fidjestøl, Bjarne. "'Har du høyrt eit dyrare kvæde?': Litt om økonomien bak den eldste fyrstediktinga." In *Festskrift til Ludvig Holm-Olsen*, edited by Bjarne Fidjestøl et al., 61–73. Bergen: Alvheim & Eide, 1984. Repr. as "'Have you heard a poem worth more?' A note on the economic background of early skaldic praise-poetry." In *Selected Papers*, edited by Odd Einar Haugen, 117–32. Odense: Odense University Press, 1997.

———. "Kongsskalden frå Kvinesdal og diktninga hans." In *Rikssamlingstid på Agder: historie, diktning, arkeologi*, edited by Hans Try, 7–31. Kristiansand: Studentbokhandelen, 1976.

Finnur Jónsson. *Norsk-islandske Kultur- og Sprogforhold i det 9. og 10. århundrede.* Copenhagen: Høst, 1921.

———, ed. *Den norsk-islandske skjaldedigtning.* Vols. A1–2, Tekst efter håndskrifterne. Vols. B1–2, Rettet tekst. Copenhagen: Gyldendal, 1912–15.

———, ed. *Lexicon Poeticum Antiquae linguae septentrionalis: Ordbog over det norsk-islandske skjadesprog oprindelig forfattet af Sveinbjörn Egilsson.* 2nd ed. Copenhagen: Möller, 1931.

Fischer, Frank. *Die Lehnwörter des Altwestnordischen.* Palaestra 85. Berlin: Mayer und Müller, 1909.

Frank, Roberta. *Sex, Lies and Málsháttakvæði: A Norse Poem from Medieval Orkney.* Nottingham: Centre for the Study of the Viking Age, University of Nottingham, 2004.

Fritzner, Johann. *Ordbog over det gamle norske sprog.* 4th ed. 3 vols. Kristiania [Oslo]: Den norske forlagsforening, 1883–96. Repr. Oslo: Universitetsforlaget, 1973.

Fuglesang, Signe Horn. "Viking and Medieval Amulets in Scandinavia." *Fornvännen* 84 (1989): 15–25.

Gade, Kari Ellen. "Poetry and its Changing Importance in Medieval Icelandic Culture." In *Old Icelandic literature and society,* edited by Margaret Clunies Ross, 61–95. Cambridge: Cambridge University Press, 2000.

———. *Poetry from the Kings' Sagas 2.* Skaldic Poetry of the Scandinavian Middle Ages 2. Turnhout: Brepols, 2009.

Gísli Sigurðsson. *Gaelic Influence in Iceland: Historical and Literary Contacts—A Survey of Research.* Reykjavík: University of Iceland Press, 2000.

———. "Þögnin um gelísk áhrif á Íslandi." In *Greppaminni: Rit til heiðurs Vésteini Ólasyni sjötugum,* edited by Margrét Eggertsdóttir, Árni Sigurjónsson, Guðrún Ása Grímsdóttir, Guðrún Nordal, and Guðvarður Már Gunnlaugsson, 153–64. Reykjavík: Hið íslenska bókmenntafélag, 2009.

Identity Poetics among the Icelandic Skalds 181

Graham-Campbell, James, and Colleen E. Batey. *Vikings in Scotland.* Edinburgh: Edinburgh University Press, 1998.

Grettis saga. Edited by Guðni Jónsson. Íslenzk fornrit 7. Reykjavík: Hið íslenzka fornritafélag, 1936.

Gurevich, Elena. "Zur Genealogie der *þula.*" *alvíssmál* 1 (1992): 65–98.

———. "*Þulur* in *Skáldskaparmál*: An Attempt at Skaldic Lexicology." *Arkiv för nordisk filologi* 107 (1992): 35–52.

Hadley, D. M. *The Vikings in England: Settlement, Society and Culture.* Manchester: Manchester University Press, 2006.

Heaney, Seamus, trans. *Beowulf: A New Verse Translation.* New York: Norton, 2000.

Heinrichs, Anne. "*Krákumál.*" In *Medieval Scandinavia: An Encyclopedia.* Edited by Phillip Pulsiano and Kirsten Wolf. New York: Garland, 1993.

Helgi Guðmundsson. "Máki, mákur." *Íslenzk tunga* 1 (1959): 47–54.

———. *The Pronominal Dual in Icelandic.* Reykjavík: Institute of Nordic Linguistics, 1972.

———. *Um haf innan: vestrænir menn og íslenzk menning á miðöldum.* Reykjavík: Háskólaútgáfan, 1997.

Henderson, George. *The Norse Influence on Celtic Scotland.* Glasgow: J. Maclehose, 1910.

Hermann Pálsson. *Keltar á Íslandi.* Reykjavík: Háskólaútgáfan, 1996.

———. "Keltnesk mannanöfn i islenzkum ørnefnum." *Skírnir* 126 (1952): 195–203.

———. *Úr landnorðri: Samar og ystu rætur íslenskrar menningar.* Studia Islandica 54. Reykjavík: Bókmenntafræðistofnun Háskóla Íslands, 1997.

Holthausen, Ferdinand. *Vergleichendes und etymologisches Wörterbuch des Altwestnordischen, Altnorwegisch-isländischen, einschliesslich der Lehn- und Fremdwörter sowie der Eigennamen.* Göttingen, Vandenhoeck & Ruprecht, 1948.

Íslendingabók, Landnámabók. Edited by Jakob Benediktsson. Íslenzk fornrit 1. Reykjavík: Hið íslenzka fornritafélag, 1968.

Jesch, Judith. *Ships and Men in the Late Viking Age: The Vocabulary of Runic Inscriptions and Skaldic Verse.* Woodbridge: Boydell, 2001.

Kershaw, Nora, ed. and trans. *Anglo-Saxon and Norse Poems.* Cambridge: Cambridge University Press, 1922.

Kock, Ernst Albin, ed. *Den norsk-isländska skaldediktningen.* 2 vols. Lund: Gleerup, 1946–50.

Kristensen, Marius. "Skjaldenes sprog: Nogle småbemærkninger." *Arkiv för nordisk filologi* 23 (1907): 235–45.

Laxdœla saga. Edited by Einar Ól. Sveinsson. Íslenzk fornrit 5. Reykjavík: Hið íslenzka fornritafélag, 1934.

Lind, Erik Henrik. *Norsk-isländska dopnamn och fingerade namn från medeltiden.* Uppsala: Lundequist, 1905–15.

———. *Norsk-isländska personbinamn från medeltiden.* Uppsala: Lundequist, 1920–21.

Marstrander, Carl J. S. *Bidrag til det norske sprogs historie i Irland.* Videnskabsselskabets Christiania skrifter. Historisk-filosofisk klasse. Kristiania: Dybwad, 1915.

———. *Randbemerkninger til det norsk-irske spørsmål.* Oslo: Dybwad, 1928.

Meulengracht Sørensen, Preben. "Social institutions and belief systems of medieval Iceland (ca. 870–1400) and their relations to literary production." In *Old Icelandic literature and society,* edited by Margaret Clunies Ross, 8–29. Cambridge: Cambridge University Press, 2000.

Morkinskinna. Edited by Finnur Jónsson. Samfundet til udgivelse af gammel nordisk literatur 53. Copenhagen: Jørgensen, 1928–32.

Ní Mhaonaigh, Máire. *Brian Boru: Ireland's Greatest King?* Stroud: Tempus, 2007.

Olsen, Magnus. "Eldste forekomst av navnet Hlaðir (*Vellekla* str. 14)." *Maal og minne* (1942): 154–56.

Orri Vésteinsson. "Archaeology of Economy and Society." In *A Companion to Old Norse-Icelandic Literature and Culture,* edited by Rory McTurk, 7–26. Oxford: Blackwell, 2005.

Poole, Russell. "Claiming Kin, Skaldic-style." In *Verbal Encounters: Anglo-Saxon and Old Norse Studies for Roberta Frank,* edited by Antonina Harbus and Russell Poole, 269–84. Toronto: University of Toronto Press, 2004.

———. "Composition Transmission Performance: The First Ten Lausavísur in *Kormáks saga.*" *alvíssmál* 7 (1997): 37–60.

———. "The *Nesjavísur* of Sigvatr Þórðarson." *Mediaeval Scandinavia* 15 (2005): 171–98.

———. "Ormr Steinþórsson and the *Snjófríðardrápa.*" *Arkiv för nordisk Filologi* 97 (1982): 122–37.

———. *Viking Poems on War and Peace.* Toronto: University of Toronto Press, 1991.

Reichardt, Konstantin. *Studien zu den Skalden des 9. und 10. Jahrhunderts.* Leipzig: Mayer & Müller, 1928.

Saxo Grammaticus. *Gesta Danorum/Danmarkshistorien.* Edited by Karsten Friis-Jensen and Peter Zeeberg. 2 vols. Copenhagen: Det Danske Sprog- og Litteraturselskab & Gads Forlag, 2005.

———. *Gesta Danorum: The History of the Danes, Books I–IX.* Edited by Hilda Ellis Davidson and Translated by Peter Fisher. Cambridge: Brewer, 1979–80.

See, Klaus von. "Studien zum Haraldskvæði." *Arkiv för nordisk filologi* 76 (1961): 96–111. Repr. in See, Klaus von. *Edda, Saga, Skaldendichtung: Aufsätze zur skandinavischen Literatur des Mittelalters*, 295–310. Skandinavistische Arbeiten 6. Heidelberg: Winter, 1981.

Snorri Sturluson. *Edda.* Translated by Anthony Faulkes. Everyman's Library. London: Dent, 1987.

——. *Edda: Prologue and Gylfaginning.* Edited by Anthony Faulkes. 2nd ed. London: Viking Society for Northern Research, 1988.

——. *Edda: Skáldskaparmál.* Edited by Anthony Faulkes. 2 vols. London: Viking Society for Northern Research, 1998.

——. *Heimskringla.* Edited by Bjarni Aðalbjarnarson. 3 vols. Íslenzk fornrit 26–28. Reykjavík: Hið íslenzka fornritafélag, 1941–51.

Sohlman, Margareta Attius. "Testimony from Gotland island of Viking Journeys East." Special issue, *Historiska Nyheter, Statens Historiska Museum: Olga & Ingegerd—Vikingafurstinnor i öst / Viking Princesses* (2004–05): 8–9.

Stefán Karlsson. *The Icelandic Language.* Translated by Rory McTurk. London: Viking Society for Northern Research, 2004.

Steinsland, Gro. *Det hellige bryllup og norrøn kongeideologi: en analyse av hierogami-myten i Skírnismál, Ynglingatal, Háleygjatal, og Hyndluljóð.* Oslo: Solum, 1991.

Storm, Gustav, ed. *Monumenta historica Norvegiae latine conscripta: Latinske kildeskrifter til Norges historie i middelalderen.* Kristiania: Brøgger, 1880.

Ström, Folke. "Poetry as an Instrument of Propaganda: Jarl Hákon and his Poets." In *Speculum Norroenum: Norse Studies in Memory of Gabriel Turville-Petre*, edited by Ursula Dronke, Guðrún P. Helgadóttir, Gerd Wolfgang Weber, and Hans Bekker-Nielsen, 440–58. Odense: Odense University Press, 1981.

Sveinbjörn Egilsson. *Lexicon poëticum antiquæ linguæ septentrionalis.* Copenhagen: Societas regia antiquariorum septentrionalium, 1860.

Urbańczyk, Przemysław. "Ethnic Aspects of the Settlement of Iceland." *Collegium Medievale* 15 (2002): 155–66.

Vatnsdœla saga. Edited by Einar Ól. Sveinsson. Íslenzk fornrit 8. Reykjavík: Hið íslenzka fornritafélag, 1939.

Vries, Jan de. *Altnordisches etymologisches Wörterbuch.* 3rd ed. Leiden: Brill, 1977.

Wanner, Kevin. *Snorri Sturluson and the Edda: The Conversion of Cultural Capital in Medieval Scandinavia.* Toronto Old Norse-Icelandic Series 4. Toronto: University of Toronto Press, 2008.

Westholm, Gun. "Gotland and the Surrounding World." In *The Spillings Hoard: Gotland's Role in Viking Age World Trade*, edited by Ann-Marie Pettersson, 109–54. Visby: Gotlands Museum, 2009.

Whaley, Diana. "Arnórr jarlaskáld Þórðarson, *Magnússdrápa*." In *Poetry from the Kings' Sagas 2: From c. 1035 to c. 1300, 1: Poetry by Named Skalds c. 1035–1105*, edited by Kari Ellen Gade, 206–28. Skaldic Poetry of the Scandinavian Middle Ages 2. Turnhout: Brepols, 2009.

———. *The Poetry of Arnórr jarlaskáld: An Edition and Study*. Westfield Publications in Medieval Studies 8. Turnhout: Brepols, 1998.

Wilson, David M. *The Vikings in the Isle of Man*. Aarhus: Aarhus University Press, 2008.

Loki, *Sneglu-Halla þáttr*, and the Case for a Skaldic Prosaics

Jeffrey Turco

PURDUE UNIVERSITY

In his 1993 novel, *Angels of the Universe*, Icelandic author Einar Már Guðmundsson recounts an episode in the life of his schizophrenic and ultimately suicidal protagonist, Páll: Born on the day of Iceland's domestically divisive entry into NATO, Páll sees no mere coincidence in the fact that his birthday is commemorated annually by massive public protests. The Icelandic parliament has split the country between the Eastern and Western Blocs, and as a consequence, it would seem, Páll's psyche now patrols its own tenuous borders—between reason and madness. The episode in question is a succinct and paradigmatic illustration of how allusions to the medieval sagas continue to create meaning for contemporary Icelandic audiences, many of whose members avidly trace their ancestry to the *dramatis personae* of narratives written largely in the thirteenth and fourteenth centuries. Páll recounts:

> Once I had been drinking with Rognvald and Arnor in the east of the city. On our way down to the town centre afterwards, by a building workers' shed on Miklatorg, we found a pickaxe. It was stuck in a half-frozen heap of earth and had clearly been forgotten when the tools were put away in the chest that stood beside it. Rognvald freed the pickaxe and walked along carrying it over one shoulder. We walked down to town like this and must have made a fairly sinister impression, the three of us, one carrying a pickaxe and Arnor seven feet tall to boot. On the corner of Laekjargata and Bankastraeti, we were stopped by the police. "And just what are you going to do with that pickaxe?"

asked one of the policemen, turning to Rognvald. "Kill one man and another," quoted Rognvald, in a malicious tone of voice. The police officer must have taken this otherwise innocent quotation ["höggva mann ok annan"] from *Egil's Saga* somewhat literally, because he jumped on Rognvald and they began fighting over the pickaxe. After they had skirmished for a good while, the three of us, Rognvald, Arnor, and I, were put in the back of the police van, and the pickaxe followed. On the way to the station, Rognvald said to the policemen: "You lot ought to piss off home and read the Sagas." "There's really not any need," said one of the officers.[1]

Rognvald can no doubt be forgiven for expecting the unexpectedly literally-minded (and apparently unliterary) policeman to recognize a celebrated moment in medieval Icelandic poetry—the famous verse composed by the temperamental warrior-poet Egill Skallagrímsson to honor the occasion of his first killing, committed at the tender age of seven:

My mother said	Þat mælti mín móðir,
I would be bought	at mér skyldi kaupa
a boat with fine oars,	fley ok fagrar árar,
set off with Vikings,	fara á brott með víkingum,
stand up on the prow,	standa upp í stafni,
command the precious craft,	stýra dýrum knerri,
then enter port,	halda svá til hafnar,
kill one man and another.[2]	hǫggva mann ok annan.[3]

The episode in Einar Már Guðmundsson's *Angels* effectively divides the Icelandic public into two distinct interpretive communities, one obtusely exoteric, the other esoteric and elusively allusive. The later, conspicuously, are disciplined by state powers on account of a penchant

1. Einar Már Guðmundsson, *Angels of the Universe*, trans. Bernard Scudder (Reykjavík: Mál og menning, 1995), 105–106. The original may be consulted in *Englar alheimsins* (Reykjavík: Mál og menning, 1993), 124–25.

2. Bernard Scudder, trans., *Egil's Saga*, in *The Complete Sagas of Icelanders*, ed. Viðar Hreinsson, 5 vols. (Reykjavík: Leifur Eiríksson, 1997), 1:77–78 (I have modified the ultimate line to correspond with Scudder's translation of Einar Már Guðmundsson's novel).

3. *Egils saga Skalla-Grímssonar*, ed. Sigurður Nordal, Íslenzk fornrit 2 (Reykjavík: Hið íslenzka fornritafélag, 1933), 100–101, ch. 40, v. 7.

for witty, seemingly harmless intertextual references that nonetheless subtly undermine the social hierarchy. While such tongue-in-cheek use of allusion may strike some readers as characteristically postmodern, this "weaponization" of narrative tradition, and the swift reaction it provokes, can (like most present-day Icelanders) readily trace a genealogy further back into the national past.

This essay examines analogous networks of allusion—not between the contemporary Icelandic novel and its saga intertexts, but rather between a medieval Icelandic prose narrative and the thirteenth-century mythographic tradition. To be sure, the "echoes" of mythic tradition in saga narrative are hardly a new object of critical attention.[4] Here, rather than simply adding to our catalogue of mythic analogues in Old Norse-Icelandic literature, I show (on the basis of a text where such analogues have escaped detection alto-gether) how mythic allusion can create a *sustained* secondary level of meaning that—contrary to prevailing notions of saga textuality—one might well call "allegorical." Such allusion, it seems, prompts similarly forceful reactions from state powers, be they modern-day Reykjavík police or medieval Norwegian royalty. In the seemingly mundane *Sneglu-Halla þáttr* (whose protagonist is a something of a counterpart to Einar Már Guðmundsson's snarky Rognvald), the

---

4. Several terms have been put forth since the 1950s to describe the workings of "myth in the saga" (Georges Dumézil), including "fictionalized mythology" (Dumézil), "Mythic overlays" (Haraldur Bessason), "prolonged echoes" (Margaret Clunies Ross), "mythic models" and "mythic elements" (John Lindow), and "mythic allusion" (Joseph Harris), albeit each term having somewhat different metaphorical implications. "Mythic elements" perhaps least prejudges the character and direction of the relationship between myth and saga, which, as Lindow notes, is not necessarily uni-directional, i.e., the myths themselves, at least in their extant form, may well have been influenced by the feud patterns evident in the sagas; see his "Bloodfeud and Scandinavian Mythology," *alvíssmál* 4 (1994 [1995]): 51–68. See further the following foundational studies: Georges Dumézil, *From Myth to Fiction: The Saga of Hadingus*, trans. D. Coltman (Chicago: University of Chicago Press, 1973); Joseph Harris, "*The Masterbuilder Tale in Snorri's Edda and Two Sagas,*" *Arkiv för nordisk filologi* 91 (1976): 66–101 [repr. in *"Speak Useful Words or Say Nothing": Old Norse Studies by Joseph Harris*, ed. Susan E. Deskis and Thomas D. Hill, Islandica 53 (Ithaca: Cornell University Library), 51–95]; Haraldur Bessason, "Mythological Overlays," in *Sjötíu ritgerðir helgaðar Jakobi Benediktssyni 20. júlí 1977, fyrri hluti* (Reykjavík: Stofnun Árna Magnússonar, 1977), 273–92, esp. 282. This line of inquiry has been reinvigorated more recently by Margaret Clunies Ross, *Prolonged Echoes: Old Norse Myths in Medieval Northern Society*, 2 vols. (Odense: Odense University Press, 1994–98). See additionally Torfi H. Tulinus, "The Prosimetrum Form 2: Verses as the Basis for Saga Composition and Interpretation," in *Skaldsagas: Text, Vocation, and Desire in the Sagas of Poets*, ed. Russell Poole (Berlin: de Gruyter, 2001), 191–217.

oblique citation of mythic tradition is mobilized by a disenfranchised medieval Icelandic poetic elite in order to negotiate a tenuously distinct Icelandic cultural identity vis-à-vis the political dominance of the Norwegian monarchy. In the *þáttr*, the Norse mythographic tradition is marshaled, in a manner reminiscent of the spirit of Germany's opposition to French domination in the early nineteenth century, to posit an Icelandic intellectual *Kultur* distinct from, or even superior to, the merely brute and administrative powers of a Norwegian *Zivilisation*.[5] And yet this movement is profoundly ambiguous in its—hardly uniformly hostile—relationship to Norwegian power, an ambiguity embodied in the *þáttr*'s eponymous hero and, I argue, in his persistent mythic analogue: the Norse god Loki.

Reading, Myth, and Monarchy: Skaldic Poetry and Saga Prose (Revisited)

Concerning the esoteric and exoteric dimensions of saga narrative, Torfi Tulinius has revived a useful hypothesis, first formulated in a 1959 article by Lee M. Hollander, which forms the starting point for this essay.[6] As Torfi notes, Hollander had suggested that "there could

---

5. In Germany, formulation of the distinction between *Kultur* and *Zivilisation* can be traced back at least to Kant's essay, *Idee zu einer allgemeinen Geschichte in weltbürgerlicher Absicht* (published in 1784, while one-fifth of Iceland was starving). The contrast of *Kultur* and *Zivilisation*, i.e., the positing of a disjuncture between "true" cultural achievement and the "merely" practical and technical prowess of the state and its veneer of courtliness, recalls the dilemma of Icelandic identity under Norwegian rule (dramatized in the *þáttr* in the interactions of the poet and his patron). See Norbert Elias, "Zur Soziogenese des Gegensatzes von 'Kultur' und 'Zivilisation' in Deutschland," in *Über den Prozeß der Zivilisation* (Berlin: Suhrkamp, 1997), 89–131, translated as *The Civilizing Process: Sociogenetic and Pyschogenetic Investigations* (Oxford: Blackwell, 2000), 3–30: "In German usage, *Zivilisation* means something which is indeed useful, but nevertheless only a value of the second rank, comprising only the outer appearance of human beings, the surface of human existence. The word through which Germans interpret themselves, which more than any other expresses their pride in their own achievements and their own being, is *Kultur*" (6). Further: "Whereas the concept of civilization has the function of giving expression to the continuously expansionist tendency of colonizing groups, the concept of *Kultur* mirrors the self-consciousness of a nation which had constantly to seek out and constitute its boundaries anew, in a political as well as a spiritual sense, and again and again had to ask itself: 'What is really our identity'" (7). And most relevantly for present purposes: "It is in the polemic of the stratum of the German middle-class intelligentsia against the etiquette of the ruling courtly upper class that the conceptual contraposition of *Kultur* and *Zivilisation* originated in Germany. But this polemic is older and broader than its crystallization in these two concepts" (10).

6. See Torfi H. Tulinius, "The Prosimetrum Form 2," 191.

be a relationship between the episodic, and seemingly rambling, structure of [*Eyrbyggja*] saga and the [structure] of skaldic verse. The author could trust his audience to link events narrated at a considerable distance from one another, because it was intellectually prepared for such linking by its experience in the interpretation of skaldic poetry."[7] Torfi also notes that the *fornaldarsögur* (ancient-legendary sagas) are marked with insertions of mythological poetry in Eddic verse, whereas the putatively historical *Íslendingasögur* are filled with quotations from skaldic poetry, that hermetic Nordic *Gelegenheitsdichtung* based on complex and sometimes impenetrable compound metaphors or kennings, often dense in allusion to mythic narratives. Torfi goes on to ask: "If the relative simplicity of the poetic language in Eddic verse is in accordance with [the simplicity] of the narrative of the *fornaldarsögur* . . . could [there] possibly also be a relationship between the narrative complexity of the *sagas of Icelanders* and that of the verse they contain? Could the latter sagas—or at least some of them—have been composed for a public which was capable of more sophisticated reading than that required for the simpler sagas of the former genre?" Torfi continues:

> This does not mean that the sagas of Icelanders were not intended for purely literal enjoyment, but that they could however allow for other levels of interpretation . . . . It makes sense to ask whether saga prose was composed in a way which might have been more accessible to a specific public [i.e., skilled in Skaldic and biblical hermeneutics] than to other readers, such as ourselves. ("The Prosimetrum Form 2," 192–93)

These questions have hardly received the attention they deserve.[8]

---

7. Quoted in ibid. See Lee M. Hollander, "The Structure of *Eyrbyggja saga*," *JEGP* 58 (1959): 227. Carol Clover appends the following comment to Hollander's discussion of *Eyrbyggja saga*: "The prose of the saga may be plain and natural, reflecting the patterns of an oral telling style; but the organization of the story is patently unnatural, closer in spirit to the sinuous patterns of skaldic diction." *The Medieval Saga* (Ithaca: Cornell University Press, 1982), 91.

8. Despite its suggestive title, Heather O'Donoghue's useful book-length study of *Skaldic Verse and the Poetics of Saga Narrative* (Oxford University Press, 2005) accounts for the relationship between prose and verse in the *Sagas of Icelanders* within a conventional formalist framework (e.g., how the prosimetrum form achieves "sophisticated stylistic and psychological effects"). Alois Wolf conceives of the relationship between saga prose and Skaldic poetry as an essentially *negative* one: the "erzählfremde Skaldik" necessitated the development of a new tradition of *Erzählprosa* better suited for continuous,

A re-investigation of the relation of skaldic *praxis* to saga prose seems especially timely upon the publication of a monumental new edition of the skaldic corpus, both symptom and cause of a minor renaissance of scholarly interest in skaldic poetry and poetics.[9] As I will attempt to illustrate, Torfi's question—at least as it regards the seemingly "prosaic" tale under discussion—must be answered in the affirmative.

While narratives that can be described, in various senses of the term, as "allegorical" are taken for granted in the literatures of other medieval European vernaculars, the literary dimension of medieval Icelandic prose is still something of a proverbial third rail in certain quarters. (Paradoxically, attention to complex literary artistry is the precondition of an ever-growing scholarship on the sagas' strange, prosimetric bedfellow—skaldic verse.) Recent criticism continues to echo romantic pronouncements that cast the writers of the sagas as the stenographers or (perhaps somewhat more generously) copy editors of oral tradition. A frequent assumption is that the sagas' murky oral origins (which one need not dispute) disallow them the sophisticated, "literary" qualities found in narrative traditions cultivated by secular and ecclesiastical elites in the court culture of continental Europe, which never developed in Iceland, even if Icelanders abroad participated in it. Despite renewed interest in the elite patronage of saga literature,[10] one routinely encounters a desire to view the sagas as overwhelmingly indebted to putatively simpler, popular traditions. The political implications of such a view of the past are clear enough, and scholars have been quick to offer romanticized portraits of the *Sitz im Leben* of medieval Icelandic literature that pit native oral traditions against the products of foreign-imposed literacy, rather than recognizing their frequent symbiosis.[11] (Indeed,

---

linear narration and commemoration of the indigenous past; see "Die Skaldendichtung—Wegbereiterin der Sagaprosa?" in *Studien zur Isländersaga*, ed. Heinrich Beck and Else Ebel (Berlin: de Gruyter, 2000), 288.

9. I refer to the monumental *Skaldic Poetry of the Scandinavian Middle Ages*, forthcoming in eight volumes under the general editorship of Margaret Clunies Ross (Turnhout: Brepols, 2007-). See further, e.g., Guðrún Nordal, *Tools of Literacy: The Role of Skaldic Verse in Icelandic Textual Culture of the Twelfth and Thirteenth Centuries* (Toronto: University of Toronto Press, 2001) and in the present volume; Margaret Clunies Ross, *A History of Old Norse Poetry and Poetics* (Woodbridge: D. S. Brewer, 2005); and Russell Poole in the present volume (see also his *Skaldsagas: Text, Vocation, and Desire*, cited in note 4 above).

10. See, e.g., Theodore M. Andersson, *The Partisan Muse in the Early Icelandic Sagas (1200–1250)*, Islandica 55 (Ithaca: Cornell University Library, 2012).

11. See Gísli Sigurðsson, *The Medieval Icelandic Saga and Oral Tradition: A Discourse*

one might be forgiven for mistaking competing analyses of *Snorra Edda*, for example, for a referendum on Icelandic membership in the European Union.) Under such conditions, literary tropes associated with "foreign" literatures, such as allegory, typological relationships, intertextual references, and allusion can safely be ascribed to the vagaries of manuscript or oral transmission, if not written off as figments of the scholarly imagination.

I would offer that we are still oddly comfortable with romantic commonplaces about the alleged "simplicity," "straightforwardness," and "objectivity" of medieval Icelandic narrative prose—as if one merely had to prick Icelanders to watch them bleed sagas.[12] Two ideological presuppositions underpin this view: first, that the sagas are closer to "the people" than are the medieval literatures of the European continent—imbued with a lingering whiff of *Volkspoesie* that masks the scent of a system of literary production fostered by elites and expressive of their values; the second, a corollary to the first, is the belief (largely axiomatic in Old Norse-Icelandic scholarship) that the *Íslendingasögur* are "decidedly anti-monarchical in outlook"[13] vis-à-vis the Norwegian royal powers that reasserted control over the so-called Icelandic "Free State" in the mid-thirteenth century. This is hardly to claim that scholars have neglected the sagas' ambiguous attitudes toward royal persons, as valorized and vilified portrayals of individual kings have been amply taken into account.[14] Indeed, medieval Icelanders' *ambivalence* towards the institution of monarchy has been the subject of increasing comment. What has been starkly underestimated, in my view, is the extent to which underlying attitudes

---

on Method (Cambridge, MA: The Milman Parry Collection of Oral Literature, Harvard University; distr. Harvard University Press, 2004).

12. For a classic formulation of this view of the sagas' allegedly "straightforward" style, see Dietrich Hofmann, "Vers und Prosa in der mündlich gepflegten Erzählkunst der germanischen Länder," *Frühmittelalterliche Studien* 5 (1971): 169–70.

13. "The Icelandic family sagas of the 13th and 14th centuries display a decidedly anti-monarchical point of view." Gerd Wolfgang Weber, "*Intellegere Historiam*: Typological perspectives of Nordic prehistory (in Snorri, Saxo, Widukind and others)," in *Tradition og Historieskrivning*, ed. Kirsten Hastrup and Preben Meulengracht Sørensen (Aarhus Universitetsforlag og Acta Jutlandica, 1987), 128n9. The sagas constitute "a form of resistance" according to Theodore Andersson, "The King of Iceland," *Speculum* 74 (1999): 932.

14. See esp. Ármann Jakobsson, *Í leit að konungi: Konungsmynd íslenskra konungasagna* (Reykjavík: Háskólaútgáfan, 1997).

towards foreign monarchy in saga literature are often positive, indeed *welcoming*.[15]

The adoption of the Icelandic sagas as a "national literature" in the nineteenth and twentieth centuries would hardly be the first time a modern state has made an ironic choice of texts, medieval or ancient, to embody its nationalist aspirations; Homer, Dante, Shakespeare, and the *Nibelungenlied* have all shared similar fates.[16] But only through a distorted national-romantic, anti-monarchical lens can the sagas be safely viewed as a wistful homage to a former state of freedom, reflected in a literary *Blütezeit* or "classical" period, followed by a period of literary decadence first redeemed by the rebirth of political independence in the twentieth century. The glorification of the national past inherent in what one might dub the romantic-nostalgic "snapshot" theory (i.e., saga writing as an attempt to capture the fleeting image of a formerly free, once proud society during its gradual disappearance) is, perhaps unsurprisingly, often taken for granted in Iceland today, but also no infrequent guest in critical studies, where somewhat more skepticism might be due.[17] Such a view naturally

---

15. For an exception to this rule, see Elizabeth Ashman Rowe, "Absent Mothers and the Sons of Fornjótr: Late-Thirteenth-Century Monarchist Ideology in *Þorsteins saga Víkingssonar*," *Mediaeval Scandinavia* 14 (2004): 133–60.

16. See Patrick J. Geary, *The Myth of Nations: The Medieval Origins of Europe* (Princeton: Princeton University Press, 2002).

17. A comprehensive list of scholarly expressions of the "snapshot" theory would require its own critical bibliography. For a succinct, representative formulation, consider the following passage from Vésteinn Ólason's *Dialogues with the Viking Age* (Reykjavík: Mál og menning, 1998), excerpted from a discussion of *Njáls saga* (tellingly titled "Retrospect"): "We have sought to analyse the thoughts and feelings of an individual looking back to the commonwealth period from the perspective of the new and different world order. For all that he recognizes the faults which led to the old world's demise and lives under a worthier moral system than that of the old world, he nevertheless looks back *nostalgically* [emphasis mine] to the human dignity and grandeur which seems to have perished with the fall of the old commonwealth" (206). See also Vésteinn Ólason, "Family Sagas," in *A Companion to Old Norse-Icelandic Literature and Culture*, ed. Rory McTurk (Oxford: Blackwell, 2005), 100–101, 111–12. See additionally Herman Pálsson, *Oral Tradition and Saga Writing*, Studia Medievalia Septentrionalia 3 (Vienna: Fassbaender, 1999): "All of the outstanding sagas are imbued with the same democratic spirit that inspired early Icelandic law makers. Collectively, the sagas constitute one of the great triumphs of medieval humanism. By liberating the Icelanders from *the restrictive bonds of absolute monarchy* [italics mine], the Althing created unique conditions for a new kind of imaginative literature. When Icelanders founded the Althing they were, unwittingly, taking the first step towards the creation of *Njáls saga* and other great prose works of the 13th century" (102). For further paradigmatic examples, see Kurt Schier, "Iceland and the Rise of Literature in 'terra nova'" *Gripla* 1 (1975): 80–81; Lars Lönnroth,

leaves little room for displays of literary sophistication and evidence of connoisseurship practiced by the elites that patronized the production of written texts—powerful farmers and clerics with a far more ambivalent relationship to royal powers on the Scandinavian continent than national-romantic literary historiography, or its heirs, can allow.

As Sigurður Nordal once wisely surmised, "All general statements about the Icelandic sagas must be regarded as so much hot air until those sagas which show themselves capable of being laid open to research are analyzed one by one."[18] With that in mind, I make the "case" here for the existence of both considerable literary sophistication, and the connoisseurship necessary to detect it, in a text that has received largely sparse, sporadic, and dismissive comment; I test Torfi's notion of "skaldic prose"[19] in order to elaborate a "skaldic prosaics"[20]—a poetics of saga prose, as it were—on the basis of a re-reading of the "episodic, and seemingly rambling"[21] *Sneglu-Halla þáttr.*[22] I show how this "misunderestimated" tale (to borrow a fortuitous malapropism) operates on multiple planes, literal and allegorical,

---

Njáls saga: A Critical Introduction (Berkeley: University of California press, 1976), 136: "Icelanders . . . revered the pagan era as a kind of Golden Age." This line of thinking has been cautiously tempered, but not challenged in its essentials, by a younger generation of scholars, see, e.g., Ármann Jakobsson, "Masculinity and Politics in Njáls saga," *Viator* 38 (2007): 191–215: "As a tragedy, *Njáls saga* might be seen more as a lament over the past than a celebration of the present or future, in the socio-political sense perhaps even nostalgic to a degree" (194).

18. Sigurður Nordal, *Hrafnkels saga Freysgoða*, trans. R. George Thomas (Cardiff: University of Wales Press, 1958), 3.

19. Torfi H. Tulinius, "The Prosimetrum Form," 198. Torfi's criteria for "skaldic prose" include "interlacing of plot lines" and "absent or inconspicuous connectors" in addition to the three I focus on here: "intertextuality," "unity," and "ambiguity."

20. I avail myself of the term *prosaics* in the sense employed by Gary Saul Morson and Caryl Emerson as "a theory of literature that privileges prose in general . . . over the poetic genres." *Mikhail Bakhtin: Creation of a Prosaics* (Stanford: Stanford University Press, 1991), 15. Morson and Emerson's further thoughts there are relevant for us here: "Critics have become so accustomed to using the term *poetics* as a virtual synonym for 'theory of literature' that they often overlook or underestimate the implications of the word *poetics* for an understanding of prose. For if literature is defined primarily with verse genres . . . in mind, then prose necessarily emerges as something less than fully literary, as literary only by association, or, perhaps, as not really literary at all."

21. Tommy Danielsson, "*Sneglu-Halla þáttr*," in *Medieval Scandinavia: An Encyclopedia*, ed. Philip Pulsiano and Kirsten Wolf (New York: Garland, 1993), 599.

22. Or "Tale of Sarcastic Halli," as it is titled in the translation by George Clark in Viðar Hreinsson, ed., *Complete Sagas*, 1:342–56. Page numbers hereafter refer to the more widely available *Sagas of Icelanders* anthology (London: Penguin, 2000), which reproduces the text of the "Tale" in the *Complete Sagas*, followed by the corresponding

before suggesting what the multivalence of Halli's seemingly simple tale allows us to infer about the social and political ambivalences of the milieu that produced, received, and—judging from a wide manuscript transmission down to the nineteenth century—rather thoroughly enjoyed it.

Halli *Agonistes*: Myth vs. Folklore

Sneglu-Halla þáttr is the unrelentingly raunchy tale of two Icelandic country boys, Halli and his envious rival Thjodolf, who compete for royal favor as skaldic poets at the court of Haraldr harðráði ("hard ruler") Sigurðarson in Norway.[23] As such, the tale belongs to the narrative type designated by Joseph Harris as "King-and-Icelander *þættir*," the short prose narratives sometimes also referred to as *Íslendingaþættir*.[24] With a story that ostensibly grew up around the skaldic verses it contains, it also shows an affinity with the so-called "Skald *þættir*," or short tales about the lives of the poets.[25]

But there is more at work in the *þáttr* than the sexual and gastronomic humor for which it is known. In the person of Halli, it features a figure whose one-upmanship and sexual defamation of his rivals (including his own royal patron) depend on a mastery and manipulation of generic conventions derived from Norse myth as represented in *Snorra Edda*, the poems of the *Poetic Edda*, and *Vǫlsunga saga*.[26] While practitioners of skaldic poetry depended on their knowledge of Norse myth and mastery of allusion to produce complex forms for

---

passage in *Eyfirðinga sögur*, ed. Jónas Kristjánsson, Íslenzk fornrit 9 (Reykjavík: Hið íslenzka fornritafélag, 1956), henceforth ÍF 9.

23. Unless making an argument from etymology, I henceforth generally employ anglicized forms of Icelandic proper names, more readily recognizable to readers of the aforementioned translation, e.g., *Þjóðólfr* = Thjodolf.

24. See Joseph Harris, "Þættir," in *Dictionary of the Middle Ages*, ed. Joseph R. Strayer, 13 vols. (New York: Scribner, 1989), 12:1–6. See also Elizabeth Ashman Rowe and Joseph Harris, "Short Prose Narrative (*þáttr*)," in McTurk, *Companion to Old Norse-Icelandic Literature*, 462–78.

25. See Rowe and Harris, "Short Prose Narrative," 463.

26. The agon between Halli and King Harald has a precedent in the figure of the skald Rögnvaldr kali, of whom Joseph Harris writes: "It seems that Rögnvaldr [in *Skjaldadigtning* BI, p. 478 (*lausavísa* 1)] is executing 'one-ups-manship' on his predecessor Haraldr harðráði (poem. c. 1040), for Haraldr's fragmentarily transmitted poem listed the king's *eight* accomplishments (*Skjaldadigtning*, BI, p. 320)," i.e., whereas Rögnvaldr's lists nine of his own. Harris, *"Speak Useful Words,"* 341n82.

simple meanings, Halli instead embodies this practice "in the flesh," i.e., in his own person, in a series of analogues to the mythic figure of Loki. The tale thus plays out the agonistic aspect of skaldic composition (which depends on the poet's "mythic competence") on the level of the prose narrative: Halli establishes his new social position as courtier by ensconcing himself within a sustained series of allusions to Norse myth, while framing his peers, and even his superiors, as the sexual deviants, low-lifes, and numbskulls of a déclassée "folktale" world.

The *þáttr* exists in a long version inserted into Flateyjarbók (1387–90) in the fifteenth century, on which I focus here, and a short version in Morkinskinna (ca. 1275). There is no general agreement as to which of the two stories is older (or rather, the two scholars who have addressed the question of dating have, respectively, occupied the two positions available on the matter.)[27] The later, and longer, version appears to be an elaboration; however, the shorter version could, according to Bjarni Aðalbjarnarson, be a reduction. It is perhaps least problematic to assume that the longer, later version is precisely that: *later*. There are indeed philological and stylistic grounds (though not unambiguous ones) for believing this to be the case.[28] The Flateyjarbók version exhibits a preoccupation with class stratification and unstable social identities that may indeed be reflective of later developments in medieval Icelandic society. Unlike the text in Morkinskinna, the Flateyjarbók version invokes "class consciousness," humble versus exalted origins, from the very beginning, contrasting King Harald Sigurðarson with his chief poet, Thjodolf, an Icelander of "humble origins" (*aettsmár*) who, like any *arrivista*, is "envious of newcomers" (*ǫfundsjúkr við þá, er til kómu*), and does not appreciate the arrival of Halli, a fellow farm boy turned poet.[29]

The *þáttr* does not introduce Halli with the genealogical excursus typical of saga narrative, but simply states that "His family was from Fljot" (*hann var ættaðr ór Fljótum*), a remote district in northern

---

27. See Tommy Danielsson, *Om den isländska släktsagans uppbyggnad* (Stockholm, Sweden: Almqvist & Wiksell, 1986), 74–75, and Bjarni Aðalbjarnarson, *Om de norske kongers sagaer* (Oslo: I kommisjon hos J. Dybwad, 1937), 156.

28. See note 56 below.

29. 695; ÍF 9:264.

Iceland.[30] In saga-ese, this means the character in question is a nobody. Yet even this limited account marks the beginning of a preoccupation with genealogy that is rare in the *Íslendingaþættir*, a literary form less concerned with lineage than the *Íslendingasögur*. Family ancestry is not only a recurring theme but a major source of contention in *Sneglu-Halla þáttr*. Halli may be a "nobody," but his bold words and ability to "speak with kings" belie this lack of social status. Thus when the king passes by in his dragon ship, striking Halli's shipmates dumb with a barrage of questions regarding their comings and goings, Halli nimbly replies, "We were in Iceland for the winter, and sailed from Gasir, and made land at Hitra, last night we lay up at Agdenes (Agdi's Ness), and our skipper is called Bard" (*Vér várum í vetr á Íslandi, en ýttum af Gásum, en Bárðr heitir stýrimaðr, en tókum land við Hítrar, en lágum í nótt við Agðanes*).[31] To this deft accounting the king provocatively replies, "Didn't Agdi fuck you?" (*Sarð hann yður eigi Agði?*) "Not yet" (*Eigi enna*), Halli retorts, setting off a ribald ship-to-ship repartee:

> The King grinned and spoke, "Is there some agreement that he will do you this service sometime later?" "No," said Halli, "and one particular consideration was crucial to our suffering no disgrace at his hands . . . . Agdi was waiting for nobler men than ourselves, and he expected your arrival there tonight, and he will pay you this debt fully." (695)

> Konungrinn brosti at ok mælti: "Er nǫkkurr til ráðs um, at hann muni enn síðar meir veita yðr þessa þjónustu?" "Ekki," sagði hann Halli, "ok bar þó einn hlutr þar mest til þess, er vér fórum enga skǫmm af honum . . . at hann Agði beið at þessu oss tignari manna ok vætti yðvar þangat í kveld, ok mun hann þá gjalda af hǫndum þessa skuld ótæpt." (ÍF 9:265)

This is the first of several sexually-barbed volleys the two will exchange, in effect accusing each other of *ergi*, that much-discussed Old Icelandic concept whose basic meaning is "effeminacy" or "passive" homosexuality, although *ergi* and its adjectival form *argr*

---

30. Ibid.
31. 695; ÍF 9:264–65.

extend to witchcraft, promiscuity, cowardice, and other Norse concepts of "unmanliness."[32] The term has legal standing in medieval Iceland; accusing another man of *ergi* is an actionable offence whose perpetrator can be slain with impunity.

If the scene between Halli and Harald seems familiar to readers of the sagas, that is as it should be; nearly identical accusations are made under strikingly similar circumstances in *Vǫlsunga saga* when Sinfjotli initiates a ship-to-shore insult match with the brother of a king whose land he is invading. Of Sinfjotli, we are wryly told, "This man knew how to speak with kings" (*Sá kunni at mæla við konunga*):

> You probably do not remember clearly now when you were the witch on Varinsey and that you wanted to marry a man and chose me for the role of husband. And afterwards you were a valkyrie in Asgard and all were on the verge of fighting for your sake. I sired nine wolves on you on Laganess, and I was the father of them all.[33]

> Eigi muntu glöggt muna nú, er þú vart völvan í Varinsey ok kvaðst vilja mann eiga ok kaust mig til þess embættis at vera þinn maðr. En síðan vartu valkyrja í Ásgarði, ok var við sjálft, at allir mundu berjast fyrir þínar sakar, ok ek gat við þér níu varga á Láganesi, ok var ek faðir allra.[34]

Sinfjotli's insult barrage culminates, "Do you remember when you were a mare with the stallion Grani and I rode you full speed at Bravoll?" (*Hvárt mantu þat er þú vart merrin með hestinum Grana, ok reið ek þér á skeið á Brávelli?*), thus linking his invasion of the king's realm with his imagined penetration of the king's brother's private regions. Halli is not merely "extremely impudent" (*orðhákr mikill*)[35] in his exchange with King Harald, nor simply displaying the knowledge of myth that qualifies him to be a skaldic poet; rather,

---

32. See, foremost, Preben Meulengracht Sørensen, *The Unmanly Man: Concepts of Sexual Defamation in Early Northern Society*, The Viking Collection: Studies in Northern Civilization 1 (Odense: Odense University Press, 1983).

33. Jesse Byock, trans., *The Saga of the Volsungs* (New York: Penguin, 2000), 49.

34. *Völsunga saga*, in Guðni Jónsson, ed., *Fornaldar sögur Norðurlanda*, vol. 1 (Reykjavík: Íslendingasagnaútgáfan, 1954), 131.

35. 695; ÍF 9:265.

he is shown, for the first but not the last time, to take a page from mythic-legendary history as a template for his own actions as a means of standing up to a social superior, despite, or rather because of, his own undistinguished origins. This resonance of *Vǫlsunga saga* is soon underscored by the introduction of Halli's benchmate ("Sigurd") and the recitation of a poem about Sigurd Fafnisbani and Fafnir, the respective dragon-slayer and slay-ee of the same tale.[36] By invoking Sinfjotli, the son of a king, the "genealogically-challenged" Halli implicitly asserts his own claim to a kind of nobility—but one grounded in *Kultur* rather than lineage. For any medieval Icelander who may have missed the point, the link between mythic competence and social status is made explicit in the next episode.

The tale tells how one day the king's entourage strolls by a blacksmith and tanner at fisticuffs. Harald commands his court poet Thjodolf to compose a verse on this street brawl. Thjodolf however considers the lowly subject matter, a fight between craft laborers, beneath his dignity, replying, "My lord . . . that's hardly suitable considering that I am called your chief poet" (*Herra . . . eigi samir þat, þar sem ek em kallaðr hǫfuðskáld yðvart*).[37] Such a common subject is—both literally and literarily—"too close to home" for Thjodolf, the former Icelandic farm boy who has worked his way up under royal patronage, and is perhaps unpleasantly reminded of his own "humble origins" (see note 29 above) by the lowly laborers, as well as by the arrival of a fellow *aettsmár* Icelandic wordsmith. But Thjodolf soon finds the task more befitting his station once the king orders him to recast this low topic in the mytho-heroic mold, transforming the blacksmith "into Sigurd Fafnisbani and the [tanner] into Fafnir, but nevertheless identify[ing] each one's trade" (*lát annan vera Sigurð Fáfnisbana, en annan Fáfni, ok kenn þó hvern til sinnar iðnar*).[38] Thjodolf promptly produces the poem made-to-order, followed by a second in which he poetically transforms the blacksmith into Thor and the tanner into the giant Geirrod—the opportunity to display his socially prestigious mythic learning obviously more in line with his own class aspirations. Thus when Halli later learns of Thjodolf's masterful poems, and is told that he could not produce their equal, he takes umbrage not

---

36. In Morkinskinna (ÍF 23:270) the name "Sigurðr" is borne by Halli's skipper.
37. 696; ÍF 9:267.
38. Ibid.

simply because Thjodolf has had the advantage of composing poetry in his absence; the more imminent threat to the status-seeking Halli is Thjodolf's command of mythic tradition per se.

Hence it comes as no surprise that Thjodolf continues to try to assert a monopoly on mythic discourse, attempting to shame Halli by contrasting, in full view the court, his own poetic productions with the unsophisticated juvenilia on rural themes once composed by his rival, known as Halli's "Polled-Cow Verses" or *Kolluvísur* (701; ÍF 9:276). Halli retaliates by informing the court of his antagonist's similar experiments in low genres, the so-called "Food-Trough Verses" or *Soðtrogsvísur* (701; ÍF 9:277) that Thjodolf composed back on the farm. Halli also tells the king's company how Thjodolf avenged his father more grimly than other men—namely by *eating* his father's killer: He relates the story of Thjodolf's father who "lived in Svarfadardal in Iceland . . . was very poor, and had many children" (*Hann bjó i Svarfaðardal á Íslandi, ok var hann fátœkr mjǫk, en átti fjǫlda barna*).[39] Thjodolf's poverty-stricken father, Thorljot, receives a calf out of charity and leads it home with a noose around its neck— the other end around his own. When the numbskull Thorljot attempts push the calf over the barnyard wall, both man and beast hang to their deaths. Thjodolf and his starving family then eat their father's "killer" (*fǫðurbana*).

According to medieval Icelandic law codified in the *Grágás*, a man had to own one cow for every one of his dependents in order to qualify to serve on a jury or accompany his chieftain to the Alþingi, i.e., to be considered an independent householder. Thus even with the gift calf, Thjodolf's father would still have been considered someone else's dependent. Thjodolf's father's inability to secure an existence for his family leads to his symbolic equation with an animal also (on account of its immaturity) unable to nurture others, except, like Thorljot, in death. Thorljot's bizarre, equilibristic hanging death conjures the image of a balance or scale, with the father on one side and the calf on the other, imputing to him the same dumb, animal nature as the beast whose fate he shares.[40] Moreover, the calf is considered a "cowardly" animal in medieval Iceland, as is suggested by the name

---

39. 703; ÍF 9:279.

40. See, e.g., Jacob and Wilhelm Grimm, *Deutsches Wörterbuch, s.v*: "[Das Kalb] gilt sprichwörtlich als dumm." http://www.dwb.uni-trier.de.

of the golem-like giant Mǫkkurkálfi (literally, "dust-calf") who wets himself before doing battle with Thor in *Snorra Edda*.[41] In other words, there is nothing heroic, much less "mythic" about Thjodolf's ancestry. The rural misadventure occasioned by Thjodolf's father's bestial stupidity stands in stark contrast to the world of myth, where the ability to transform oneself into an animal is reserved for figures whose power and cleverness are the opposite of Thjodolf's father's impotence and stupidity: Odin, to cite a well-known example, transforms himself into an eagle in order to steal the Mead of Poetry, and Loki famously becomes a seductive mare in order to lure away the Master Builder's work horse, having "such dealings" with the stallion that he later gives birth to Odin's eight-legged steed, Sleipnir.[42] Loki, on other occasions in the mythological tradition, transforms himself into a bird, a fly, a flea, a seal, and a fish.[43] Hence Halli, with his tale of the parodic "animal transformation" of Thjodolf's father, is not merely revealing a compromising story about Thjodolf and his kin; he is illustrating that they, unlike himself, do not belong in the world of myth (the province of the skaldic poet) but rather in a barnyard anecdote. Thus when Thjodolf flaunts his "mythic competence" by composing verses about Thor and Sigurd Fafnisbani in Halli's absence—and lampoons Halli's humble origins in Iceland to boot—Halli exacts literary revenge by transforming Thjodolf's family into the subjects of a folktale.

There is no Aarne-Thompson tale type that corresponds precisely with Halli's anecdote about Thjodolf's father, and yet the genre of the "anecdote," its status as oral narrative, its "there-once-was-a-poor-farmer" *incipit*, as well as its subject matter (i.e., the foolish man who accidentally causes the death of livestock) and barnyard setting all place it firmly within the confines of a folk tradition that will not be codified as such for centuries. Halli's malicious

---

41. See *Skáldskaparmál*, ed. Anthony Faulkes, 2 vols. (London: Viking Society for Northern Research, 1998), 1:21.

42. See ibid., 45; Snorri Sturlason, *Edda: Prologue and Gylfaginning*, ed. Anthony Faulkes, 2nd ed. (London: Viking Society for Northern Research, 1988), 35.

43. See, respectively, Gustav Neckel and Hans Kuhn, eds., *Edda: Die Lieder des Codex Regius nebst verwandten Denkmälern*, vol. 1, *Text*, 4th ed. (Heidelberg: Winter, 1962), 111–12 (st. 3–5 and 9); *Skáldskaparmál*, Faulkes, 1:24, 2, and 42; *Sǫrla þáttr*, in Guðni Jónsson, ed., *Fornaldar sögur Norðurlanda*, vol. 1 (Reykjavík: Íslendingasagnaútgáfan, 1954), 369; Úlfr Uggason's *Húsdrápa*, cited in *Skáldskaparmál*, Faulkes, 19–20; and *Gylfaginning*, Faulkes, 48–9.

association of Thjodolf (*Þjóðólfr*) with what the nineteenth-century folklorists would later call *þjóðsögur* (folktales) is supported by the anecdote's display of a complex of motifs found in Scandinavian and international tales. Particularly relevant from this perspective is type 1281a, "Getting rid of the man-eating calf," a variant of which is attested in nineteenth-century Iceland.[44] In continental Scandinavia this "numbskull" tale contains the elements of the hanged man, the man-killing calf, and the family's revenge on the bovine *fǫðurbani*, not to mention the generic figure of the poor, foolish father. In the folktale, the latter comes upon a hanged man and tries to take the deceased's shoes. The hanged man's feet, however, are so swollen that the shoes cannot be removed; thus the foolish man cuts off the feet and takes the shoes with the feet still in them. That night he sleeps in a room where a newborn calf has been sheltered. The man leaves early in the morning, taking the shoes but leaving behind the dismembered feet. His family discovers the calf and assumes that the newborn beast has devoured their father, leaving nothing but his feet. The family then slays their father's "killer." In other versions, the family members (or neighbors), rather than risk death in the maul of such a horrible creature, set the house ablaze and burn the calf inside. This burning might be considered loosely cognate with Thjodolf's family's eating of their father's "killer" (assuming, of course, that they cook the calf first). Versions of this tale are also attested in Norwegian, Danish, and Swedish.[45] (In Jón Árnason's Icelandic variant, the protagonist is a farm boy.) The story about Thjodolf's father in the *þáttr* could be related to these modern Scandinavian analogues, although the anecdote is also attested in Latin as early as 1508–12 in Heinrich Bebel's *Facetiae*.[46] While Bebel's anecdote or some variant thereof could be the proximate source of the nine-teenth-century Icelandic version, the evidence of *Sneglu-Halla þáttr*

---

44. See "Rauðskjöldóttur bolakálfur," in Jón Árnason, *Íslenzkar þjóðsögur og æfintýri*, 2 vols. (Leipzig: Hinrichs, 1862–64), 2:531–33; translated loosely and abridged in Adeline Rittershaus, *Die neuisländischen Volksmärchen: Ein Beitrag zur vergleichenden Mär-chenforschung* (Halle: Niemeyer, 1902), 363–65, no. 103.

45. See E. T. Kristensen, *Efterslæt til "Skattegaveren"* (Kolding, 1890), no. 166; Ørnulf Hodne, *Types of the Norwegian Folktale* (Oslo: Universitetsforlaget, 1984), no. 1739; Waldemar Liungman, *Die Schwedischen Volksmärchen* (Berlin: Akademie-Verlag, 1961), no. 1201; Eva Wigström, *Skånska Visor, Sagor och Sägner* (Lund, 1880), no. 26.

46. See Heinrich Bebel, "De quodam histrione," in *Facetiarum Heinrici Bebelii, poetae A.D. Maximiliano laureati, libri tres* (Bern, 1550), 62[r-v].

would suggest that this material was already familiar in medieval Iceland.

The tale of Thjodolf's "father's killer" has further motifs in common with international tale types represented in Scandinavian and other European folklore. In AT 1210 "Cow driven/hoisted to roof to graze, strangled," a cow is similarly pushed to its death by a fool. A Danish version of this well-attested tale features an industrious but poor man whose wife makes a disaster of everything. One day he asks her to tend to the family cow, with predictably dire results:

Således sagde han en dag til hende, at hun skulde give deres ko et godt skub ovenpå vandet. Det var hun også villig til. Da hun altså havde vandet koen, førte hun den ovenpå et jordhus, som brugtes til stald, og styrtede den ned, så den var død på stedet.⁴⁷

And so one day he said to her that she should give their cow a good "push" [an untranslatable pun which here means "en god del foder" or "extra portion"] on top of the watering. She was more than eager to do it. And so when she had watered the cow, she led it up onto an earth house, which they used as a stall, pushed it down off the top, and it was dead on the spot. (Translation mine.)

In other analogues, the cow is tethered, falls off the roof, and is strangled, more closely approximating the hanging death of Thjodolf's family calf. In another closely related tale, a "numbskull ties the rope to his leg as the cow grazes on the roof. The cow falls off and the man is pulled up the chimney."⁴⁸ Halli's account begins with the same scenario we find in the sixty-first tale of Grimms' *Kinder- und Hausmärchen*, "Das Bürle" (The Little Farmer):

---

47. Laurits Bødker, ed., *Folkeeventyr fra Kær herred* (Copenhagen: Akademisk forlag, 1963–67), 73. Also attested in Arthur Christensen, ed., *Molboernes vise gerninger* (Copenhagen: Det Schønbergske forlag, 1939), 89; Waldemar Liungman, *Die schwedischen Volksmärchen: Herkunft und Geschichte* (Berlin: Akademie-Verlag, 1961); Kristensen, *Efterslæt til "Skattegaveren,"* 209–10.

48. Stith Thompson, *Motif-Index of Folk Literature*, 6 vols. (Bloomington: Indiana University Press, 1955), 182 (J2132.2); cf. 214.

Es war ein Dorf, darin saßen lauter reiche Bauern und nur ein armer, den nannten sie das Bürle (Bäuerlein). Er hatte nicht einmal eine Kuh und noch weniger Geld, eine zu kaufen; und er und seine Frau hätten so gern eine gehabt.[49]

There once was a village full of rich farmers and only one poor one, whom they called "Little Farmer." He didn't even have a cow, much less money to buy one, though he and his wife would have been very happy to have one. (Translation mine.)

Related to Grimm's "Bürle" is the humorous eleventh-century Latin tale *Unibos*, which has a number of *Schwank* elements in common with *Sneglu-Halla þáttr*. *Unibos* tells the story of a wily peasant who, like Thjodolf's father, has but "one ox" (i.e., *uni-bos*), but who, like Halli, routinely outsmarts his superiors. Further elements paralleled in the *þáttr* (which I discuss more fully below) include the transfer of a horse to a new owner (ÍF 9:294–95), trickery involving silver (ÍF 9:286–87, 290–91) and other devious transactions (ÍF 9:293–94), a critique of feigned praise (ÍF 9:290–91, 292–93), and a bizarre under-water death (ÍF 9:291–92). Other tale types attest more broadly to the folkloric register of the Thorljot-subplot, such as AT 1122 "Stupid ogre hangs self" and 1681 "Stupid man kills animal."[50]

From the vantage point of "etymology as mode of thought," most famously associated with the Latin tradition codified by Isadore of Seville, but also attested in medieval Iceland,[51] the name "Thjodolf" (*Þjóð-ólfr*) is itself perhaps suggestive of the contrast of high and low social status implied by the generic distinction between myth and folktale. While one would not want to press the point, *Þjóð* is

---

49. *Kinder- und Hausmärchen gesammelt durch die Brüder Grimm*, Vollständige Ausgabe auf der Grundlage der dritten Auflage (1837), ed. Heinz Rölleke (Frankfurt am Main: Deutscher Klassiker Verlag, 1985), 296.

50. For further discussion of folktale elements in the *Íslendinga þættir*, see Joseph Harris, "Folktale and Thattr: The Case of Rognvald and Raud," *Folklore Forum* 13 (1980): 158–98.

51. See, for example, Snorri Sturluson's well-known explanation of the name of the gods (*Æsir*) as "men of Asia." Although *Sneglu-Halla þáttr* is not generally considered a "learned" text, Sveinbjörn Rafnsson argues that it was influenced by chapter 3 of the *Disciplina Clericalis*: "Exemplum de tribus versificatoribus"; see "Sagnastef í íslenskri menningarsögu," *Saga* 30 (1992): 92–95.

Icelandic for "people" in the dual sense of "nation" and "common people" (as in German *Volk*).[52] The *þáttr* arguably plays with this ambivalence. While the *Þjóð* element would presumably have had a positive connotation for a medieval Icelandic audience, *Sneglu-Halla þáttr* arguably inverts this meaning, turning the historical court poet Thjodolf into a *déclassé* "man of the people" in the pejorative sense. Further suggestive of class consciousness in the tale is the transformation in Flateyjarbók of Thjodolf's father's name from "Arnórr" to "Þorljótr." As Jónas Kristjánsson notes, "Thjodolf's father's name is correctly given as Arnórr in Morkinskinna (cf. *Skáldatal*), but Flateyjarbók gives his name as Thorljot [Þorljótr]."[53] The *Third Grammatical Treatise* and *Skáldatal* are the two sources for the "historical" Halli. While it is unknown whether *Skáldatal* served as a source for the writer of *Sneglu-Halla þáttr*, it seems unlikely, especially given medieval Icelanders' preoccupation with genealogy, that someone with the author's level of interest in the Halli figure would have been ignorant of this tradition. (The actual name of Thjodolf's father is irrelevant; what is important is the evidence of an onomastic tradition from which the text of Flateyjarbók diverges.) What at first appears a meaningless (perhaps originally oral) variant or simple error repays investigation as the product of conscious literary artistry. In light of the conflict of the genres of "myth" and "folktale" in this part of the *þáttr*, this variation may well be less incidental than it seems. The *Þor-* prefix in Thjodolf's father's name is of course derived from the Norse god Thor (*Þórr*), and is a frequent element in medieval Icelandic male personal names; *ljótr* is a common adjective meaning "ugly." I have argued that Halli contrasts his own "mythic" superiority with the imputed baseness of Thjodolf and his family, whom he casts as folkloric simpletons.[54]

---

52. See Einar Ólafur Sveinsson, *The Folk-Stories of Iceland*, Viking Society for Northern Research 16 (Exeter: Short Run Press, 2003), 15–16; originally *Um íslenzkar þjóðsögur* (Reykjavík: Hið íslenzka bókmenntafélag, 1940).

53. ÍF 9:cxi ("Formáli").

54. If one might speculate, the location of Thjodolf's family homestead in *Svarfaðardalr* (694; ÍF 9:263)—a detail not found in Morkinskinna—may also be suggestive of this contrast. The Icelandic verb *svarfa* (cognate to English *swerve*) can mean to sweep, swerve, or upset by overturning (in the sense of "upsetting the apple cart"); used reflexively (*svarfask um*) it can mean to cause a great tumult or havoc. Hence the root meaning of the name of Thjodolf's ancestral home might be suggestive of the lack of physical and affective restraint that typically characterizes the lower classes in medieval literature (and not least the behavior of Thorljot & son here); the *svarfa* element in the place-name of Thjodolf's

Thus the fact that "Thjodolf" (*Þjóð-ólfr*)—contrary to the evidence of *Skáldatal* and Morkinskinna—is turned into the son of "ugly Thor" (*Þor-ljótr*), would also (contrary to the historical evidence) not seem to bode well for Thjodolf's skaldic career, which depends in large measure on one's familiarity with mythic tradition. Hence I would suggest that the change of Thjodolf's father's name from "Arnórr" to "Þorljótr" in Flateyjarbók further underscores Thjodolf's family's "mythic incompetence."[55] The deliberate artistry implicit in this "variant" might be further suggested by Halli's unusual formulation, "*Þat hygg ek*, at Þorljótr héti faðir Þjóðólfs" (*I think* that Thorljot was the name of Thjodolf's father).[56]

A further measure of Thjodolf family's unreadiness for myth, exemplified in this barnyard anecdote, might be found in an implicit contrast between Thjodolf's unwise father and the all-wise *Alfǫðr*, Odin—both noted for the act of hanging, but for diametrically opposed reasons, and with opposite results. In *Hávamál*, Odin hangs from the tree Yggdrasil in order to acquire runes and wisdom, an act that contrasts starkly with Thjodolf's father's unwise hanging of

---

(fictive?) point of origin is perhaps suggestive (*nomen est omen*) of a certain rural boorishness contrasted with the refined etiquette of the court. In addition, a *svarf* (neuter singular) is a "hard fray" or "broil," such as the fight between the two craft laborers, which (recast as the battle of Thor and the giant Geirrod) serves as an allegory of the verbal brawling of Halli and Thjodolf. Such etymological resonances may seem far-fetched to us, but we must leave open the question as to whether such associations would have been unavailable to an audience schooled in skaldic poetics, particularly since Halli devotes considerable artistry to mocking Thjodolf's humble origins.

55. Naturally, the *ljótr* element in Icelandic personal names need not carry the resonance of its etymological meaning "ugly" any more than "Jeffrey" connotes "God's peace" to the native speaker of English. Still, Icelandic is etymologically more transparent to native speakers than English is to native speakers not fluent in a handful of languages, living and dead. Such etymological connotations would hardly have been unavailable to medieval readers and listeners schooled in deciphering skaldic poetry, i.e., from the perspective of a "skaldic prosaics."

56. 703; ÍF 9:279. See Jónas Kristjánsson, ÍF 9:cx: "Allar líkur eru til, að Sneglu-Halla þáttur hafi upphaflega verið sjálfstæð saga . . . . Í Flateyjarbók er mjög eindreginn heildarsvipur á þættinum, og bendir það til að hann sé þar verk eins höfundar" (All indications are that *Sneglu-Halla þáttr* was originally an independent story [*saga*] . . . . In Flateyjarbók there is a very distinct cohesiveness in the *þáttr*, which suggests that it is the work of a single author). The last line of the text in Flateyjarbók (ÍF 9:295) supports this conclusion: "Lýk ek þar sǫgu frá Sneglu-Halla" (Here I close the tale of Sneglu-Halli). Harris, however, calls the *ek*-narrator "a pre-classical stylistic trait," which would support an early origin of the Flateyjarbók version (see Harris, "Þættir," 3n18). Although this tag line could be a later addition, it is unlikely that this can be deduced on philological grounds.

himself back on the farm. Thorljot's accidental self-sacrifice, although it allows Thorljot to provide posthumously for his family, displays an utter lack of the wisdom that Odin acquires by sacrificing "himself to himself."[57] Halli's overarching argument about Thjodolf before the king's court seems to be that you can take the poet off the farm, but you can't take the farm out of the poet—unless, of course, the poet in question happens to be Halli himself.

This brand of "class warfare" by proxy of rapid-fire intertextual references is a pervasive feature of *Sneglu-Halla þáttr*. The closest "mythic analogue" to the noose that links Thjodolf's father and the calf is the tether Loki ties between his testicles and a nanny-goat's beard in Snorri's account of the myth of Skaði. Whereas Loki's testicular tug-of-war is funny (at least for those not personally involved), these very serious jests have deadly consequences for Thjodolf's father, and, by extension, for Thjodolf's pretense to a distinguished genealogy. As Einar Haugen once observed, Loki can be viewed as a "mediator" between the realms of Human and Animal.[58] As previously noted, Loki turns himself variously into a mare, a flea, a fish, a seal, a bird, and a fly (i.e., creatures of land, sea, and air—thus underscoring his indeterminate nature). The tale of Thjodolf's father and the calf might been seen as a failed "mediation" of this kind, an inability to successfully exist in between two orders, which is the character-istic talent of Loki and, as I shall argue, of Halli. Since Thjodolf's family lacks Halli's "mythic" stature (which he only begins to claim for himself in the first insult scene with the king), for them such a balancing act, i.e., between human and animal, can only end badly. Loki's animal transformations, by contrast, often rescue the family of the gods from cosmic catastrophes that dwarf the quotidian hunger faced by Thjodolf's kin, such as when he turns into a mare, foils the Master Builder's scheme, and bears Odin the fastest horse, the eight-legged Sleipnir. While Halli does not literally undergo any Loki-esque metamorphoses, he succeeds in demonstrating that Thjodolf's mastery of myth, as evinced in his stanzas on the blacksmith and

---

57. "Myself to myself" (*siálfr siálfom mér*). Neckel, Edda: Lieder, 40 (st. 138). Neckel, *Edda: Lieder*, 40 (st. 138).

58. See "The Mythical Structure of the Ancient Scandinavians: Some Thoughts on Reading Dumézil," in *Introduction to Structuralism*, ed. Michael Lane (New York: Basic Books, 1992), 170–83.

the tanner, is merely formal. Poetry, at least since Ovid (who was known in medieval Iceland),[59] has been conceived of as the art of transformation, an art Halli embodies in his personal transformation from Icelandic bumpkin to Norwegian courtier, and, as I will now show, from mundane wisecracker to "mythic" Loki-figure. Unlike his skaldic rival, Halli does not merely compose about the myths (in fact, he hardly composes about them at all); rather, he alludes to them in his own actions. In other words, Halli "lives them out," transforming himself literally into what Russell Poole (in this volume) calls "a living embodiment of tradition."

By casting Thjodolf in the lineage of "ugly Thor" (*Þorljótr*), the tale relocates the antagonism between Thjodolf and Halli within the paradigm of the antagonism between Thor and Loki, and between the gods and the giants more generally. Similar to the enforcer role played (albeit badly) by Thjodolf at King Harald's court, Thor maintains the tenuous exclusivity of divine society against would-be entrants from the "lower classes" (such as Hrungnir and the Master-Builder, i.e., "Hallis" of the giant world, who try to earn or conquer a place in divine society). In both the myths and the *þáttr*, the grounds for such exclusion on the basis of genealogy, as opposed to ideology, are tenuous at best; Thor and Loki are both half-giant, on their mother's and father's sides, respectively, just as Halli and Thjodolf are both sprung from the same humble Icelandic roots.

Previous scholarship has not taken note of any analogues between Loki and Halli, but they are in fact a pervasive, if overlooked, feature of the *þáttr*.[60] The *Tale* is indeed highly conscious of the thirteenth-century Icelandic mythographic tradition of Loki, which serves as a constant intertextual reference point, and furnishes meaning beyond the tale's literal sense, no less than *Egils saga* adds poignancy to Rognvald's actions in the episode recounted at the beginning of this essay.

---

59. See Guðrún Nordal, *Tools of Literacy*, 22, 37–38; Anne Holtsmark, "Ovid," in *Kulturhistorisk leksikon for nordisk middelalder*, ed. John Danstrup (Roskilde: Rosenkilde og Bagger, 1968), col. 65.

60. The only previous essay-length study of *Sneglu-Halla þáttr* addresses the status of the poet's "mouth"; see Ármann Jakobsson, "Munnur Skáldsins: Um vanda þess og vegsemd að vera listrænn og framgjarn Íslendingur í útlöndum," *Ritmennt: ársrit Landsbókasafns Íslands—Háskólabókasafns*, 10 (2005): 63–79.

Halli as a Loki Figure

As part of the "case" made here, I will now offer into evidence a series of thematic parallels and motivic analogues that link the figures of Halli and Loki. The three themes that are discussed first and more briefly are general in nature (and might pertain equally well to saga characters, e.g., Gísli Súrsson, who are not in any obvious sense Loki figures), but will take on greater significance in light of the highly specific character of the motifs later adduced.

"No Equal in Trickery"

Both Loki and Halli are noteworthy "trickster" figures, although this is not ultimately the defining characteristic of either. (The equation of Loki with "the trickster of primitive religions" is problematic; trickery is not Loki's essential function, although it is a key part of his toolkit, and he is arguably its unsurpassed mythic practitioner.) Similarly, the comment of Halli's benchmate that the poet has "no equal in trickery" (*Engum manni ertu líkr at prettum*)[61] is amply borne out in the series of episodes recounted below.

Ergi and Slander

Halli and Loki are arguably the two preeminent dispensers of sexual defamation in medieval Icelandic literature. The accusations of *ergi* and homosexuality which Halli lobs at his superiors are paralleled by Loki's sexual defamation of the gods in *Lokasenna*. Whereas Loki's slander takes place under the protection of Odin, King Harald likewise forbids his court to harm Halli for his outrages. A case in point is afforded by the following episode: "In the spring, King Harald went to the Gulathing Assembly. And one day the king asked Halli how he was doing for women at the assembly. Halli answered:

This Gulathing's great.	Gótt es Gulaþing þetta.
We fuck whatever we fancy. (710)	Gilju vit, hvat es viljum. (ÍF 9:293)

---

61. 707; ÍF 9:287.

The king then insultingly assigns Halli and Thjodolf the feminizing tasks of cooking and serving food, but the goldbricking Halli forces Thjodolf to perform these tasks alone. Since Thjodolf can no longer snub Halli socially, since he is now, like himself, a courtier of the King, Thjodolf, it seems, tries his own hand at sexual defamation—a form of verbal violence that knows no class boundaries, as Halli's exchanges with the king make evident. Spying Halli napping under a boat, Thjodolf lamely attempts to compose an insulting verse:

Sticking out from under the boat is a sole-bucket [shoe].[62] You're fucking now?[63] (Ibid).	Út stendr undan báti Ilfat. Muntú nú gilja? (Ibid.)

Thjodolf's verse, naturally, is hardly much of an insult to a man who avowedly "fucks whatever he fancies." This is a rather flatfooted comeback indeed, considering that Halli has just made Thjodolf culpable of *ergi* by forcing him to assume the role of female domestic. The setting of this incident at the Gulathing may be thematically

---

62. The folkloric connection between the human foot and wanton sexuality is seen, e.g., in the children's nursery rhyme, "There was an old woman who lived in a shoe / She had so many children, she didn't know what to do." (This association is presumably evident in more contemporary forms of foot-fetishism as well.) Since the foot is our primary means of "getting around," its association with sexual license may be rooted in well-documented male anxieties about unfettered female mobility leading to unrestrained female sexuality (fears that emerged full force in early-modern urban culture), as evinced by the figure of the airborne witch. In Snorri's mythography, the equation of sexuality with mobility is exemplified in the male sphere by the god Freyr, often interpreted as a fertility figure, whose golden boar Gullinbursti (in contemporary parlance, his "sweet ride") can convey him by both sky and sea, day and night, although the extant mythographic tradition does not depict this. The connection between the exposed foot and sexuality is evident in Snorri's account of Skaði's unintended betrothal to Njǫrðr: Skaði is allowed to choose for herself a husband from among the gods, but permitted only a preview of their feet. On the erotic potential of the "foot" in skaldic verse, see Russell Poole's discussion of *fótr* in the poetry of Sigvatr Þórðarson (*Austrfararvísur*, st. 15) in this volume.

63. "Muntú nú gilja?" might alternately be rendered as "So *this* is how you go about seducing?" So understood, Thjodolf would not be accusing Halli of having sex but of trying—ineptly—to solicit it. The human foot is associated with attempted seduction (or rather *ab*duction) in Bragi Boddason's kenning for "shield" in *Ragnarsdrápa*: "blað ilja Þrúðar þjófs" (the blade/leaf of the sole of the thief of Þrúðr [i.e., Hrungnir]). This reading would give Thjodolf's lame quip a firmer footing, but such a sudden display of sexually barbed wit might seem out of character with the portrayal of Thjodolf as an adept but otherwise uninspired and prudish technician. In either case, Thjodolf's response cannot withstand Halli's rebuttal (710; ÍF 9:293), reaffirming that Thjodolf, like whomever Loki targets, ultimately remains on the receiving end of sexual defamation.

relevant as well, since the laws of this particular Norwegian assembly made it a crime to accuse a man of behaving "like a woman."[64]

Having made short work of Thjodolf, Halli promptly avenges himself on the king for assigning him these unmanly kitchen duties. In the following episode, Harald spies Halli gazing covetously at an ornate axe and asks if him he will allow himself to be "fucked for the axe" (*Villtu láta serðask til øxarinnar?*). Halli nimbly replies, "I will not . . . but it seems understandable to me that you should want to sell the axe for the same price that you paid for it" (*Eigi . . . en várkunn þykki mér yðr, at þér vilið svá selja sem þér keyptuð*).[65] Forced to choose between a tacit admission of *ergi* and a display of royal munificence, Harald, with characteristic sagacity, opts for the latter, giving Halli the axe. Chided by the queen for being too lavish with commoners, especially ones who lambaste the royal couple with shameful obscenities, the king replies, "I don't wish to take in bad sense those words of Halli's which are *ambiguous*" (*vil ek eigi snúa orðum Halla til hins verra, þeim er tvíræði eru*),[66] a statement to which we will have ample cause to return.

Sexual Ambiguity

A third thematic parallel between Halli and Loki is Loki's ambiguous gender identity, as well as his well-attested bisexuality, e.g., as the mother of Odin's horse, and as father of the Midgard Serpent, Fenriswolf, and Hel. This sexual ambiguity is a trait shared by Loki and Odin, who in *Ynglinga saga* is said to practice *seiðr*, the "shameful" and "unmanly" form of sorcery associated with female sexuality.[67] The sexual ambiguity of Loki and Odin is playfully

---

64. "There are certain expressions known as *fullréttisorð* [actionable verbal offenses]. One is if a man says to another that he has given birth to a child. A second is if a man says of another that he is *sannsorðinn* (demonstrably used sexually by another man). The third is if he compares him to a mare, or calls him a bitch (*grey*) or a harlot, or compares him with a female of any kind of animal." Quoted in Meulengracht Sørensen, *The Unmanly Man*, 16 (see endnote 26); see also pp. 15–20, 28–31, and 38.

65. 711; ÍF 9:294.

66. 711 (modified); ÍF 9:294.

67. See Snorri Sturluson, *Heimskringla*, ed. Bjarni Aðalbjarnason, Íslenzk fornrit 26–28, 3 vols. (Reykjavík: Hið íslenzka fornritafélag, 1941), 1:19; Snorri Sturluson, *Heimskringla: History of the Kings of Norway*, ed. and trans. Lee Hollander (University of Austin Press, 1964), 11. See also Meulengracht Sørensen, *The Unmanly Man*, 19–20, 63–64.

recapitulated (though not without potentially serious consequences) in Halli's and Harald's reciprocal accusations of so-called "passive" homosexuality.

In addition, however, to the merely *thematic* parallels between Halli and Loki, Halli's deeds in the tale constitute nothing less than an extended series of motivic analogues to various exploits of Loki's depicted in the mythographic tradition. Deftly interwoven in the narrative strands of the *þáttr*, these analogues can now be picked out and recounted forthwith.

The Eating Contest in the King's Hall

When Halli accuses Harald of being stingy with food, Harald orders two men to carry a trough full of porridge onto the floor and commands Halli to eat from it until he bursts (700; ÍF 9:273–74). The eating contest in the royal hall and the trough (*trog*) arguably parallel the trough of meat that king Útgarðaloki has brought into his hall for Loki's eating contest in *Gylfaginning*, the first book of Snorri's *Edda*.[68] Both Loki and Halli compete against forces of nature: Loki against the ravenous element of fire, Halli against his own ravenousness and the limitations of the human stomach. Halli ultimately refuses to indulge the king's whim. Nonetheless, Loki's ability to consume massive quantities of food, while superhuman, is not supernatural either; Loki, too, has his limits and, unlike his rival Logi (fire), cannot continue eating indefinitely. Harald's apparent generosity can be understood as a snub at the poverty of medieval Icelanders, since porridge is the lowliest of medieval foodstuffs.[69] Halli's quip about porridge, that "buttered, it's the best of foods" (*Gǫrr matr es þat, smjǫrvan*), is proverbial in several Germanic languages and well attested in both Dutch and German around the time of the "younger" Flateyjarbók.[70] There is an undercurrent of

---

68. See *Gylfaginning*, Faulkes, 39–40.

69. See Melitta Weiss Adamson, *Food in Medieval Times* (Westport: Greenwood Press, 2004), esp. 3–5. Grimm's *Deutsches Wörterbuch* (see note 40 above), s.v. "Brei," provides ample illustration from medieval literary sources that "Brei ist eine einfache Lieblingsspeise des Volks."

70. "In den Brei gehört Fett." See "Brei" (s.v.) in *Thesaurus Proverbiorum Medii Aevi: Lexikon der Sprichwörter des romanisch-germanischen Mittelalters*, ed. Samuel Singer, 13 vols. (Berlin & New York: de Gruyter, 1996–2002), 2:85. Additionally, "Brei im Maul haben" is a well-attested idiom in *Frühneuhochdeutsch* meaning "to speak equivocally,"

irony in the king's gift insofar as the historical Harald was credited by Snorri (in *Heimskringla*) with saving Iceland from famine with shipments of wheat. By presenting his newest courtier with a trough of porridge, Harald puts the *arrivista* back in his place (i.e., on the farm); and by refusing to eat all of it, Halli reasserts his newfound position at court. The episode harkens back to the incident in which Halli accuses Thjodolf of having composed "Food Trough Verses" (*Soðtrogsvísur*) at home in Iceland—an insulting backstory that renders the double-edged nature of the king's magnanimity unambiguous.

Head Wagers

Loki and Halli are two of a select body of figures in the Old Norse-Icelandic corpus with a penchant for wagering their heads.[71] In *Snorra Edda*, Loki bets the dwarf Brokk that his brother Eitri cannot produce three treasures as good as those made for the gods by rival dwarf smiths: a head of golden hair for Sif; *Skíðblaðnir*, the folding ship that provides its own perpetual breeze; and Odin's spear *Gungnir*. Eitri indeed produces three superior treasures: the golden ring *Draupnir*, the golden boar *Gullinbursti*, and Thor's hammer *Mjǫllnir*.[72] Halli, for his part, wagers his head against his friend Sigurd's golden ring that he can obtain compensation for the death of a non-existent brother, who is in fact a complete stranger, killed by the king's irascible envoy Einar Fly, a classic saga "bad guy" or *ójafnaðarmaðr* (inequitable man) who "pays compensation to no one." Halli succeeds in securing compensation for the non-kinsman, but his deceit is not outrageous merely because the slain man is not Halli's brother. The episode must be viewed in the context of Halli's and Thjodolf's competing claims to genealogical preeminence. Without a

---

which is to say *ambiguously*, as in Luther: "wer sophistisch redet und brei im maul behelt" and "Sagt weder Ja noch Nein, wie der Leute Art is, gehen nicht gleich zu, behalten immer Brey im Maul" (Ibid., 2:86). In Norwegian folktales, failure to provide the mischievous *nisse* with properly buttered porridge invariably leads to malicious tricks played on the farmstead and its stingy inhabitants. See, e.g., Peter Christen Asbjørnsen, *Norske Huldreeventyr og Folkesagn*, 3rd ed. (Christiania [Oslo], 1870), 77.

71. The head wager is a mythic *topos*; alongside Loki, one might mention Odin, the giant Vafþrúðnir, and Snorri's fictive Swedish king, Gylfi, among its noteworthy practitioners.

72. *Skáldskaparmál*, Faulkes, 1:41–42.

genealogy to speak of and hailing "from Fljot" (695; ÍF 9:264), Halli is not simply a "nobody," but a nobody par excellence—a man with no business avenging *anyone*, much less a fictive kinsman. (Halli's fictive "brother" is indeed best viewed not just as a prank but in the context of the *Genealogie-Ersatz* constituted by Halli's ongoing self-mythologization.) Halli thus simultaneously appropriates and lampoons the revenge ethic of the class to which he aspires—in pointed counterpoint to Thjodolf's "avenging" of his father's bovine killer. Einar Fly, moreover, in contrast to Halli, can actually boast a distinguished genealogy, one that traces back to his grandfather, the famous poet Eyvindr skáldaspillir ("spoiler of poets") and his great-great-great-grandfather, King Harald Fairhair. Hence Einar Fly, descended from kings and poets, combines in one figure the social status of Halli's two previous antagonists: the poet Thjodolf and King Harald himself. Thus Halli's seemingly merely episodic conflicts are in fact progressive and cumulative, not arbitrary in their sequence.

Nor is the head wager the only Loki-ism at work in the Einar Fly episode. The student of Norse myth will readily recall Snorri's account in the *Edda* of how Loki transforms himself into a fly in order to sabotage the dwarf Eitri's attempt to produce treasure for the gods by stinging Eitri's brother three times as he works at the smith's bellows.[73] While threefold iterations are too common a literary and folkloric device as to be meaningful in themselves, in the context of the other Loki-motifs mentioned thus far it is difficult to ignore the fact that Halli tries exactly three times to trick Einar, who happens to be nicknamed "Fly," into paying compensation in the form of treasure (here, three marks of silver). Furthermore, in the case of both Halli and Loki, a "head wager" is at stake, making the list of allusions to Loki's ruse in Halli's dealings a rather complete one. In a further episode (707–8; ÍF 9:287–89), Halli once more wagers his head, this time against a gold ring, that he can silence an unruly mob, which he promptly accomplishes with an indecipherable but obscene-sounding public outburst. While in Morkinskinna the gold ring is wagered against Halli's *life*, in Flateyjarbók this deal is explicitly turned into a head wager.

---

73. Ibid., 1:42.

The Dwarfs' Treasures

The parallels between Snorri's myth of the gods' treasures and Halli's machinations, however, run deeper still: As mentioned previously, Loki acquires six treasures for the gods: Sif's golden hair, the magic ship *Skíðblaðnir*, Odin's spear *Gungnir*, the golden boar *Gullinbursti*, the golden ring *Draupnir*, and Thor's hammer *Mjǫllnir*. Not to be "out-Lokied" (as it were), Halli acquires a roast *piglet* in exchange for a swiftly composed poem, golden *rings* through a head wager, and passage on an overcrowded *ship* by scaring away all the German passengers with feigned premonitions of a watery grave. Finally, as a reward for a poem of pure gibberish, the English King Harold Godwinsson (whose knowledge of Old Norse is apparently not what it might be) grants Halli as much *silver* as will stick in his *hair* after it is dumped on Halli's head; this turns out to be a fair amount after Halli covertly coats his hair with tar. While this is not exactly a head of *golden* hair, a coiffure made of another precious metal is perhaps close enough.[74] One might also recall that in the myths Loki is represented as having mysterious powers of adhesion (as when he sticks to the eagle Thiassi or to the roof of the hall of the giant Geirrod). At this point, it might seem that Halli only receives *four* items, to Loki's six, making the parallel incomplete. But Halli also receives a belt and knife from King Harald, for a total of six objects. We might consider the belt a stand-in for Thor's hammer, since Thor is equally famous for his belt of strength. Halli's knife, like Odin's spear, is a pointed cutting weapon, on a scale more appropriate for its recipient. More significantly, the knife and belt are functionally identical with Odin's spear and Thor's hammer as emblems of status and strength, respectively. The formulaic "knife and belt" are well attested in the sagas as tokens of noble identity.[75] Hence, the gift of

---

74. In light of the ongoing agon between Halli and the king in the *þáttr*, there may be an ironic contrast implied here between Halli's easy success in England and Harald's harsh demise there in 1066.

75. For the formulaic *knífr ok belti* as tokens of noble identity, see (in the *Bibliography* below) *Laxdœla saga*: "En áðr en þau Melkorka skildisk, selr hon í hendr Óláfi fingrgull mikit ok mælti: 'Þenna grip gaf faðir minn [King Mýrkjartan] mér at tannfé, ok vænti ek, at hann kenni, ef hann sér.' Enn fékk hon honum í hǫnd kníf ok belti ok bað hann selja fóstru sinni: 'get ek, at hún dylisk eigi við þessar jartegnir'" (ÍF 5:51, ch. 20; also ÍF 5:241, ch. 84); as identifying tokens, see the slave Melkólfr in *Njáls saga* (ÍF 12:124, ch. 49; also

the knife and belt might be viewed a symbol of Harald's recognition of Halli's poetic sovereignty, just as Odin's spear is a symbol of his power, and Thor's belt the brute force with which that power is maintained.

Anyone unconvinced by these parallels is invited to consider the roasted piglet Halli receives from the king, which I have adduced as a parallel to the golden boar made by the dwarf smith Eitri. The piglet is not given to Halli by the King directly; rather, Harald has it brought to Halli *by his own personal dwarf* (700; ÍF 9:274).[76] In fact, it is as a reward for a well-crafted poem about the king's dwarf—made, like the gods' treasures, under time pressure and penalty of death—that Halli receives the knife and belt as well. Hence, three of the items Halli receives are obtained by means of a dwarf, as are the treasures Loki procures from Brokk, Eitri, and the Sons of Ivaldi. It is perhaps fitting that Halli's poetry should be rewarded in such a manner, since poetry—the vehicle of Halli's upward mobility—is, according to one

---

ÍF 12:121 ch. 47); as valuable gifts, see *Gísla saga* (ÍF 6:88, ch. 27) and *Hallfreðar saga* (ÍF 8:166, ch. 6; also ÍF 8:170–71, ch. 7); as supernatural gifts from kin, see *Gull-Þóris saga* (ÍF 13:184, ch. 3). The formula is also attested in *Droplaugarsona saga* (ÍF 11:156, ch. 8) as a gift after a premonition; in *Bjarnar saga hítdœlakappa* (ÍF 3:173, ch. 22) as a bribe; and in *Gǫngu-Hrólfs saga* (Guðni Jónsson, *Fornaldar sögur Norðurlanda*, 3:254, ch.32) as a supernatural gift. In *Norna-Gests þáttr* (ibid., 1:311, ch. 2), these items are not a gift, but are likewise mentioned in conjunction with a king and his follower. While the *knífr ok belti* (never, it seems, *belti ok knífr*) are typically bestowed in recognition of outstanding qualities, they may also be given to the outstandingly wicked (famously to Melkólfr in *Njáls saga*) or as a bribe to a person of low standing (in *Bjarnar saga hítdœlakappa*). Hence Harald's choice of gifts seems in line with his ambiguous treatment of Halli generally. Indeed, the fact that the king dresses up his dwarf with similar items ("gyrði hann sverði"; ÍF 6:270) in the preceding episode might well suggest a tongue-in-cheek gesture behind these gifts, and (as in the case of the potentially sodomitically acquired axe) serve to further underscore Harald's double-edged munificence.

76. The king's Frisian dwarf, Tuta, is Halli's physiognomic opposite, "thick-set" (*digrastr*) and "broad-shouldered" (*herðimestr*), whereas Halli is "a tall man, long-necked, with narrow shoulders and long arms" (*hár maðr ok hálslangr, herðilítill ok handsíðr*) [ÍF 9:264, 269]. Both are "ill-proportioned" in their limbs (*ljótlimaðr*), albeit for wholly opposite reasons. According to R. E. Kaske, Frisians had a reputation for being exceedingly tall in the Middle Ages (a "fact" known to Dante as well in *Inferno* 30, line 64). See R. E. Kaske, "The *Eotenas* in *Beowulf*," in *Old English Poetry: Fifteen Essays*, ed. Robert P. Creed (Providence: Brown University Press, 1967), 292–93. A Frisian dwarf is hence an ironic figure, not least in the court of a king reported in Snorri's *Heimskringla* (ÍF 28:187) to be some seven feet tall. A short Frisian is an anomaly, much as is a poor Icelander among foreign royalty, such as Halli, or his mythic analogue, Loki: a giant by descent who is nonetheless "reckoned among the gods." The poet's and the dwarf's status as aberrant outsiders who serve at the king's whim adds poignancy to the expressed sympathy of the king's shortest servant for his tallest (ÍF 9:274).

kenning central to Snorri's discussion of poetic language in the *Edda*, the *farkost dverga* or "ship of the dwarves."[77]

A Gift Horse "Fit for a King"

The remaining parallels between Halli and Loki, or examples of mythic allusion in the tale, can be recounted in brief. Let us recall once more Snorri's tale of the Master Builder and how Loki transforms himself into a mare in order to lure away the Builder's stallion from his labors, and how Loki ends up pregnant as a result. Although Halli lacks Loki's first-hand expertise in the finer points of equine courtship, Halli nonetheless shows that he knows a thing or two about horses having sex. When Thjodolf sends a horse from Iceland as a gift for king Harald, "The king went to see the stallion, and it was big and fat. Halli was there when the horse stuck out his prick" (*Konungrinn gekk at sjá hestinn, ok var mikill ok feitr. Halli var þar hjá, er hestrinn hafði úti sinina*). Halli then speaks this verse:

Always a young she-pig—	Sýr es ávallt,
Thjodolf's horse has	hefr saurugt allt
wholly befouled his[78] prick;	hestr Þjóðólfs erðr,
he's a master fucker. (711–12)	hann es dróttinserðr. (ÍF 9:294–95)

The "master fucker" of George Clark's translation rather masterfully captures the ambiguity of *dróttinserðr*.[79] Parsed as *dróttins-erðr* the word means something like "king-sized penis" (or, more apropos,

---

77. *Skáldskaparmál*, Faulkes, 1:4.

78. Clark's translation appears to maintain an ambiguity in the original as to whether "his" (i.e., *Þjóðolfs*) modifies "horse" (*hestr Þjóðolfs*) or "prick" (*Þjóðolfs erðr*), leaving open the question of who is being fucked by whom. In a further twist to this bawdy little verse, in addition to a "sow," *sýr* (line 1) is also the nickname of King Harald's father, Sigurðr sýr Hálfdanarson.

79. The Íslenzk fornrit edition of Jónas Kristjánsson gives *dróttinserðr* (i.e., sodomized by his owner, i.e., by Thjodolf, or—potentially—by the king); a few examples drawn from the rich later manuscript tradition of the *þáttr* serve to attest to the interpretive challenge posed by this *hapax*: AM 563 a 4° (1650–99) supplies *dróttinsserðr* ("the sodomizer of the king"); ÍB 384 4° (1799–1822) likewise reads *dróttinsserðr*; JS 259 4° (1825) supplies *dróttins sæti* [?] or "king's throne," which is either a misreading or a nonsensical bowdlerization.

"hung like a horse"). One could also read this *hapax legomenon* along with Finnur Jónsson as *dróttin-serðr*, which in his *Lexicon Poeticum* is interpreted with the passive meaning "sodomized by its owner" (from the verb *serða*, "to use a man sexually like a woman"). Michael Minkov argues that the word has the active meaning of "one that sodomizes or will sodomize his new master."[80] So understood, the king's rejoinder seems more on target: Harald chides Halli that Thjodolf's gift horse will never come into his possession "at this rate" (*at þessu*). Given the ambiguities of *dróttinserðr*, I would offer that the king's rejoinder can in fact be taken both ways: (1) the king is predicting that Thjodolf will be offended by the suggestion that the gift-giver has been sodomized by his own horse, or vice versa; or (2) the king understands Halli's prediction that the horse will sodomize his new master, the king—terms to which Harald will not bend.[81] True to form, Halli forces the king into the same dilemma as in the episode of the axe: Harald must either relinquish a valuable possession or admit to being *sorðinn*—used sexually by a man.

As previously recounted, Harald does not "wish to take in bad sense those words of Halli's which are ambiguous." Instead, fighting fire with fire, Harald counters Halli's ambiguity with his own counter-ambiguity, responding, "Tut, tut . . . he will never come into my possession at this rate" (*Tví, tví . . . hann kemr aldri í mína eigu at þessu*).[82] This could either mean that the king predicts that Thjodolf will take offense and revoke the gift, or the king may jokingly be saying "no, thanks, the horse is not my type." Suggestive of the king's awareness that he is engaged in a duel based on virtuoso displays of verbal ambiguity, Harald prefaces his ambiguous rejoinder to Halli's ambiguous slander with the exclamation "tut, tut" or in the Icelandic original "tví, tví." "Tví" is of course a common "expression to express disapproval"[83] in Old Norse, but it is also etymologically related to the word "two," and is the standard Icelandic prefix for "double" (cognate to German *zwie/zwei* and Latin *duo*). Thus Harald's

---

80. See Michael Minkow, "Sneglu-Halli, 2:11: Dróttinserðr," *Saga-Book* 22 (1988): 285–86.

81. Unlike King Harald, Minkow insists exclusively on the latter interpretation.

82. 711–12; ÍF 9:295.

83. According to Richard Cleasby and Gudbrand Vigfusson, *An Icelandic-English Dictionary*, 2nd ed. (Oxford: Clarendon Press, 1957), *s.v.*

exclamation could also be taken literally as "double, double"—an astute commentary on the double entendres of the aforegoing scene. In other words, the king jestingly lets Halli know that he gets the joke, and shows his poet that he can give as well as he can take. Either way, Halli should be pleased if Harald refuses Thjodolf's gift; anyone familiar with Snorri's tale of the Master Builder will recall that providing a steed fit for a sovereign, such as Odin's eight-legged horse Sleipnir, is a task properly left to a Loki figure.[84]

Halli and Loki: "Out of the Saga"

A final parallel with Loki can be seen in Halli's post-skaldic career and ultimate demise back in Iceland. When his fortunes back home have run out, Halli takes up fishing as a career of last resort. Similarly hard pressed at the tail end of mythic history, Loki transforms himself into a fish and even proceeds to invent the fishing net. The *þáttr* tells how one day, after a particularly strenuous row back to land, Halli takes a few bites of porridge and immediately drops dead. The king maintains that Halli "must have burst eating porridge," but the tale explicitly states that Halli eats only "a few bites," and it seems highly unlikely that a glutton of such mythic proportions could have died from overeating. This raises the question: Might there be something fishy about Halli's premature death? Surely Halli had a talent for making enemies, and the king's warning, "to go warily because of Einar Fly" upon his return to Iceland (712; ÍF 9:295), raises the prospect that a vengeful Einar may have poisoned the porridge. The fluga element in Einar's name is indeed attested as a nickname for an assassin.[85] More prosaically, it is equally possible that Halli dies from simple exhaustion after strenuous rowing, doubtless like many an Icelandic fisherman before him, without any cloak-and-dagger intrigue left over from his days as a courtier. The *þáttr* provides just enough evidence to invite us to speculate about, but not determine, the cause of Halli's death. Thus Halli even *dies* ambiguously. The fact that Halli perishes after eating only "a few bites" might indeed raise suspicions that

---

84. The well-known tale of Loki's brief equine liaison, resulting in the birth of Sleipnir, is recounted in the Master Builder episode in Snorri's *Edda* (*Gylfaginning*, Faulkes, 34–36).

85. See Cleasby-Vigfusson (note 83 above), 162; E. H. Lind, *Norsk-Isländska Person-binamn från Medeltiden* (Uppsala: 1920–21), col. 85.

Halli was poisoned. Such a poisoning motif would logically extend the association of Halli and Loki, since Loki is punished towards the end of his days with the dripping venom of a poisonous snake. It is notable, moreover, that the tales of Halli and Loki (in *Voluspá* and in Snorri's citation of the latter in his *Edda*) both conclude after their arrival at their final destinations—Iceland and the field of battle at Ragnarǫk, respectively—by boat.

The indeterminate manner of Halli's death—whether he is slain by an enemy or perishes mysteriously—is an apt, final ambiguity in a poetic career predicated on double meanings.[86] Halli's death poses an interpretive puzzle, and is thus a fitting (if ignominious) ending for a producer of skaldic verse. The indeterminate nature of his death is, however, also paralleled in two different traditions regarding the fate of Loki. According to *Snorra Edda*, Loki is killed by his adversary (Heimdallr); in *Vǫluspá*, however, Loki "just fades away" without explanation. Thus both possibilities—death at the hands of an adversary or death under ultimately mysterious circumstances—find their counterpart in the extant mythographic tradition. Harald's last words on Halli (i.e., that he must have burst eating porridge), can hence be read as a dismissal of Halli's attempts at self-mythologization (surely Loki, known for his ravenousness, would never have "burst" from overeating). Yet the king's final comment is at the same time a mythologization worthy of Halli himself; the king's jesting explanation—which he himself knows cannot possibly be true—itself constitutes a new "myth" about Halli.

The Companion of Thor(ljot's Son)?

The punctuation of Halli's quotidian follies with allusions to the figure of Loki compels us to ask: Does anything about Halli's antagonist and companion, Thjodolf, recall Loki's companion and antagonist, Thor? I have already discussed in passing the *Þor-* element

---

86. The "detective's question," i.e., *how* Halli dies, is perhaps secondary to the more fundamental observation that a court poet cannot survive in isolation from royal patronage. The fact that Halli runs out of money in Iceland (712; ÍF 9:295) underscores the economic dependency of the Icelandic skald on the Norwegian court (addressed by Russell Poole in this volume). Suggestively, we are not told of any compositions by Halli that post-date his return to Iceland.

in Thjodolf's father's name (unique to the Flateyjarbók version), and the generic resemblance between Thjodolf's agon with Halli and the fraught relationship between Thor and Loki. The answer is a reserved "yes"—an affirmation that must remain muted, for the reasons that follow.

A laundry list of resemblances between Thjodolf and Thor might read as follows: Like Thor and Loki, Thjodolf and Halli are antagonists *and* companions. Just as Halli debases Thjodolf sexually, forcing him to perform a woman's duties, Loki compels Thor to play a female role in *Þrymskviða*. Loki draws attention to Thor's lowly origins, just as Halli draws attention to Thjodolf's; in *Lokasenna*, Loki lampoons Thor's illegitimate parentage, addressing him as "jarðar burr" (Jǫrð's son)—that is, the son of his giantess mother—rather than his father's son.[87] Like Halli, Loki continually outmaneuvers his opponent but, in the end (after serving a brief stint as a fisherman), gets his comeuppance. In addition, Thor is associated with Thjodolf's ancestral home in Svarfaðardalr (see note 54 above), founded by Helgi the lean, who famously hedged his bets by worshipping both Christ *and* Thor as the occasion demanded.[88] Finally, Thjodolf composes about Thor in his poem about the blacksmith and the tanner. The resemblances between Thjodolf and Thor are hence perhaps palpable enough, but general and inchoate compared with Halli's feats and their analogues in mythic narratives of Loki. It would seem that the resemblances between Thjodolf and Thor exist in potentiality but that the *þáttr* fails to actualize this potential. This "failure," however, is a highly logical one, as a crucial aspect of the rivalry between Thjodolf and Halli lies in the fact that Thjodolf merely composes *about* mythic narratives but does not "live" them as Halli does. Thjodolf's mythologizing of the mundane, as in his poem about the blacksmith and the tanner, is restricted to his lifeless art, which the *þáttr* playfully contrasts with Halli's artful life.[89]

---

87. Neckel, *Edda: Lieder*, 108 (st. 58, normalized).

88. Helgi is reportedly guided to this area by Thor; see *Íslendingabók, Landnámabók*, ed. Jakob Benediktsson, Íslenzk fornrit 1 (Reykjavík: Hið íslenzka fornritafélag, 1968), 250. See further Jonas Wellendorf, "The Interplay of Pagan and Christian Traditions in Icelandic Settlement Myths," *JEGP* 109 (2010): 20–21.

89. In other words, what Margaret Clunies Ross in her brief summation of this episode calls "the mythological referencing potential of the kenning system" and "mundane subjects . . . presented as if they were subjects from myth and legend in order to

The mythological elements one would normally expect to find on display in skaldic verse are in fact almost entirely missing in Halli's poetry; they are instead transposed into the fictive persona of the poet himself. The relationship between the world of the myths and the world of the skald, which is typically only metaphorical, is realized literally in the story of Halli and his mythologized deeds. The substitution of one thing for another in skaldic poetry, translated into the realm of narrative, takes on the character of an indigenous form of reading distinct from but parallel to Christian allegory, and not unlikely shaped by it.[90]

The Case for a Skaldic Prosaics

Sneglu-Halla þáttr is what Torfi Tulinius, discussing the application of skaldic poetics to saga writing in general, has called a "multi-level prose narrative,"[91] a work whose interpretation depends on an audience well trained in teasing meaning out of obscure skaldic verses that allude to mythic narratives. When it came to the sagas, literary-minded Icelanders presumably did not leave their skaldic hermeneutics and mythological learning at the door like a pair of wet boots. When such expertise is lacking, the story, as with all but the most unreadable allegories, still makes sense to those who do not see beyond the literal meaning (its *sensus historicus* or *literalis*). Thus when the saga says Harald thinks "it was fun to set them [his Icelandic skalds] against each other" (*þótti honum gaman at etja þeim saman*),[92] we can take this statement both literally as a portrait of life at the king's court and/or as a commentary on the

---

have fun at the expense of the lower social orders" (*History of Old Norse Poetry*, 155, 117) transcends the agon between the two poets and is made an overarching feature of the *þáttr* itself.

90. As Thomas D. Hill notes in the present volume, recapitulation of mythic motifs in the sagas might be seen as cognate to the recapitulation of the life of Christ in medieval hagiography, or (one might add) to the secular appropriation of hagiographic *topoi* in courtly romance, such as in Wolfram's *Parzival*; on the latter, see esp. Arthur Groos, *Romancing the Grail: Genre, Science, and Quest in Wolfram's "Parzival"* (Ithaca: Cornell University Press, 1995), esp. 11, 37–38, 58, 168–69, 210, 211–12. Hence our penchant for locating the echoes of pagan myths in the sagas may, ironically, be predicated on a manner of reading that is decidedly Christian.

91. Torfi H. Tulinius, "The Prosimetrum Form 2," 193.

92. 702; ÍF 9:277.

Norwegian crown's practice of exploiting regional and family feuds in Iceland in order to consolidate royal power and influence over the island.

One final ambiguity in the conflict of Harald's poets worth mentioning is the status of the verses attributed to them: Halli bests Thjodolf in many ways, but is he actually the better poet? The evidence of *Sneglu-Halla þáttr* makes it difficult to answer this question in the affirmative. Halli's scant extant verses contain few kennings, none of which are mythological. Aside from one (unveiled!) reference to the sea goddess Rán, his work in fact displays none of the mythographic learning that characterizes skaldic verse, or for that matter his own behavior. His verses could easily be regarded as inferior to Thjodolf's *dróttkvætt* on both formal and thematic grounds: Halli's poems are mostly simple *lausavísur* addressing low topics, such as food, sex, and rural life. (Loki, of course, is not known for his poetry either.)[93] Nonetheless, Halli's amusing verses seem to have more life in them than Thjodolf's more workmanlike productions; Halli is at least witty, even going as far as to brag—in verse, no less—about his ability to produce bad poetry:

I composed a thula	Ortak eina
about an earl.	of jarl þulu,
Not among the Danes	verðrat drápa
has a poorer drapa appeared.	með Dǫnum verri.
Fourteen mistakes in metre	Fǫll eru fjórtán
and ten terrible rhymes.	ok fǫng tíu;
It's obvious to anyone,	opit es ok ǫndvert,
it goes upside down.	ǫfugt stígandi;
So he has to compose	svá skal yrkja,
Who knows how to—badly.	sás illa kann.
(709–10)	(ÍF 9:292–93)

---

93. Notwithstanding, I am sympathetic to Kevin J. Wanner's recent suggestion that Loki can in some sense be regarded as "a god of poets" (although I would rephrase this assertion less provocatively to read "an embodiment of the art of poetry"), insofar as skaldic poetry is—like its putative "god"—largely a locus of double meanings. My discussion of Halli and Loki might indeed provide grist for this particular mill. See Wanner, "Cunning Intelligence in Norse Myth: Loki, Óðinn, and the Limits of Sovereignty," *History of Religions* 48 (2009): 224–25.

The hero of this superficially simple yet multi-leveled tale at times reads as a rehabilitation of the "historical" Halli, whose poetry is less artful, less complex, and far less mythologically learned than Thjodolf's. Perhaps it is this very artlessness that makes Halli a fitting hero for a tale whose meta-subject is the complex, multi-leveled meaning of the seemingly prosaic and everyday. The only apparently artless Halli is indeed a fitting poster boy for saga narrative as a whole, whose style is outwardly straightforward, but whose surfaces often obscure depths of intricacy, learnedness, and—to recall three of Torfi's criteria for "skaldic prose"—unity, intertextuality, and ambiguity.

Happily, the skeptical critic need not take my word for it.[94] The presence of complex allegorical structures in the *þáttr*, the "skaldic prosaics" I make the case for here, is rendered explicit in the tale by no less an authority in matters of literary interpretation than King Harald himself. I have already recounted how one day the king strolls by a blacksmith and a tanner at fisticuffs, commanding Thjodolf to compose a verse and "make one of them into Sigurd Fafnisbani and the other into Fafnir, but nevertheless identify each one's trade." The king's final instructions to his poet are, I would now suggest, nothing less than the hermeneutic program of the *þáttr* itself. The "key" to the tale's allegory is provided in King Harald's words of advice to his "chief poet" (*hǫfuðskáld*): "It's more difficult than you think. You have to make them into altogether different people than they really are" (*Þetta er meiri vandi en þú munt ætla; þú skalt gera*

---

94. Such as Gísli Sigurðsson, who writes, "The Icelandic Sagas do not contain any key as to how they should be interpreted, such as we usually find in genuine medieval allegories" (*Discourse on Method*, 33). I would argue that "genuine medieval allegories" rarely contain such overt "keys" to their interpretation, or only in the most ham-fisted instances, but instead refer allusively to common cultural frames of reference, afforded in this case by the Norse mythographic tradition. *Sneglu-Halla þáttr*, however, seems to satisfy even the most onerous demand for an explicit hypogram, as King Harald's instructions supply precisely such a "key." See Vésteinn Ólason, *Dialogues with the Viking Age* (Reykjavík: Mál og menning, 1998), 10, for another expression of the anti-allegorical consensus. I readily agree that the sagas are not allegorical in the narrow sense (i.e., not in the manner of *Piers Plowman* or *Le Roman de la Rose*) that Vésteinn and Gísli seem to have in mind. Certain sagas, however, invite other forms of reading in the etymological sense of Greek αλληγορειν ("to speak otherwise"), and some, such as *Njáls saga*, were evidently written by authors steeped in the tropes and elliptical reading practices of Christian exegesis. My reading here is nonetheless fully compatible with Vésteinn's requirement that "the search for meaning [have] a visible path marked out for it in the text" (ibid).

af þeim alla menn aðra en þeir eru).[95] Indeed, it would be difficult
to think of a more succinct or programmatic elaboration of a skaldic
prosaics.[96]

The king is a fitting mouthpiece to espouse such artistic princi-
ples, as *Sneglu-Halla þáttr* is hardly the only tale where Haraldr
Sigurðarson's unrivaled interpretive skills are on display. In *Króka-
Refs saga* (whose crafty protagonist is cast from a mold similar to
Halli's), Harald is portrayed as a hyper-astute decipherer of cryptic
meanings, as evinced by his unraveling of Ref's seemingly nonsensical
proto-Joycean rantings (620–21; ÍF 14:153–56). Harald is in fact
routinely portrayed as the most sagacious of kings, chieftains, and
men in general in the northern lands.[97] The king might well serve
as an ideal "implied reader," a model of the kind of hermeneutically
sophisticated audience the tale requires (or at least invites), in contrast
to those, such as Thjodolf, the queen, and Einar fly, who prove inca-
pable of reading beyond the literal sense.

There is, however, at least one crucial distinction between how
skaldic poetry and skaldic prose function to produce meaning—a
difference that creates an inverse relationship between the poetic utter-
ance and the prose narrative in which it is embedded. In skaldic poetry
complex forms are used to produce simple meanings, as when Thjodolf
employs a kenning to refer to the "floor" as the "moor of socks" (*leista
heiði*), or a "shoe" as a "sole-bucket" (*ilfat*). (Thus the notoriously

---

95. 696; ÍF 9:267.

96. At another point in the narrative (during his ruse against Einar fluga) Halli describes
to the king a dream he has allegedly had, stating, "It seemed to me that I was quite another
man than I am" (*Ek þóttumk vera allr maðr annar sem ek em*) [ÍF 9:285; 706], in this
case the poet Þorleifr, whereas Einar appears in the dream as the target of Þorleifr's poetic
barbs, Earl Hákon Sigurðarson. Thus the multi-leveled reading I make the case for here is a
practice overtly illustrated in the *þáttr*—one that follows a "visible path marked out . . . in
the text," as required by certain readers (see note 94 above).

97. As the following passages attest: "þat er allra manna mál, at engi konungr hafi
verit vitrari á Norðrlöndum" (*Fagrskinna*, ÍF 29:261); "Haraldr konungr var . . . spekingr
mikill at viti, svá at þat er alþýðu mál, at engi höfðingi hafi sá verit á Norðrlondum,
er jafndjúpvitr hafi verit sem Haraldr eða ráðsnjallr" (*Heimskringla*, ÍF 28:118);
"Haraldr konungr var . . . spekingr at viti, ok þat (er) vitra manna mál at engi maðr
hafi verit djúpvitrari á öllum Norðrlondum en Haraldr konungr ok manna ráðsnjallastr"
(*Morkinskinna*, ÍF 23:204). Andersson and Gade translate from the text of Morkinskinna
as follows: "King Haraldr . . . had a profound intelligence, and it is the opinion of well-in-
formed men that no one in all the northern lands was more penetrating." *Morkinskinna:
The Earliest Icelandic Chronicle of the Norwegian Kings (1030–1157)*, Islandica 51
(Ithaca: Cornell University Press, 2000), 204.

long kenning "fire-slinger of storm of giantess of protection-moon of horse of ship-sheds," upon decryption, simply means "warrior.")[98] In "skaldic prose" this dynamic is inverted: complex meanings are produced by simple forms. Thus a tale that on the surface recounts the mundane antics of an Icelandic poet at court (e.g., Halli's "eating contest") alludes on a second level to mythic narrative (Loki's eating contest), which in turn suggests further levels of significance, both specific, such as Norway's relief of famine in Iceland with shipments of wheat, or the politically supplicant position of Iceland vis-à-vis Norway more generally.

Should any of the parallels I have adduced seem far-fetched, one need only recall how frequently saga literature invokes mythic paradigms in order to align or contrast characters with figures from the mythology as a form of commentary not otherwise afforded by the tight-lipped narration of a laconic "saga style."[99] The best-known illustration of this practice is perhaps afforded by the depiction of Egill Skallagrímsson as an often ironic Odin figure in *Egils saga*. Another ready example is found in *Vǫlsunga saga*, when Sigmund and his son Sigurd slay a wolf and a dragon respectively, thus recapitulating the battles of Odin and his son Thor against the Fenriswolf and the Midgard Serpent at Ragnarǫk. The list could readily be extended; the practice, an analysis of which has furnished one of the dominant paradigms of Old Norse-Icelandic scholarship of recent decades, has been investigated extensively.

The case for a skaldic prosaics, however, goes beyond the relatively uncontroversial assertion that medieval Icelandic audiences could recognize mythic analogues. There is a difference between occasional, interspersed allusions and "echoes" and the full-scale *Arbeit am Mythos* we encounter in a text such as *Sneglu-Halla þáttr*. I would venture to say that when allusion to mythic narrative constitutes a sustained secondary level of meaning—as in the case of Halli's Lokiesque dealings with royal authority—we have left the realm of the occasional mythic analogue and may speak of a "skaldic prosaics." Mindful of Sigurður Nordal's earlier-cited admonition, I do not

---

98. Found in a verse (here quoted in prose order) by the skald Þórðr Sjáreksson: "gimslöngvir drífu gífrs hlémána blakks nausta" (*Heimskringla*, ÍF 26:187).

99. See note 4 below.

consider this to be the case when- and wherever mythic elements are detectable in saga narrative. (Thomas D. Hill's contribution in this volume, for example, identifies a further instance of mythic allusion in *Egils saga*, where, however, such allusion provides periodic and occasional coloring rather than an ongoing secondary level of meaning.) Nonetheless, an examination of *Sneglu-Halla þáttr* would suggest that the saga corpus as a whole could benefit from more "close reading" than it has, for reasons perhaps more ideological than philological, traditionally received.[100] The *þáttr*, if nothing else, should cause us to question what Joseph Harris is careful enough to call "the obscure style of skaldic poetry and its *apparent* antithesis in saga prose" (emphasis mine).[101]

The foregoing discussion of narrative doubleness and rhetorical ambiguity returns us to my reading of Halli as Loki figure. As Andy Orchard puts it succinctly, "Loki [is] a wholly ambiguous figure."[102] Loki's ambiguity has long been the subject of critical comment. Jan de Vries long ago described Loki most aptly as a "problem."[103] But scholars have generally stopped short of the insight that it is ambiguity itself which constitutes Loki's essential nature; all other contradictory characteristics attributed to him—male or female, god or giant, helper or evildoer, man or animal—are merely functions thereof, not the products of a misleading identification of him with the "trickster" figure of comparative mythology.[104] (Loki's trickery, like all his

100. Scholars have tended to assume that the Norse obsession with what John Lindow calls "semantically charged word play," so evident in skaldic poetry, was left at the door when it came to saga prose. This view—which takes for granted substantially different audiences for the two (one originally courtly, the other domestic and humble)—is of course burdened by the fact that most of this poetry is ensconced in the *prosimetrum* of the sagas themselves. See Lindow's "Riddles, Kennings, and the Complexity of Skaldic Poetry," *Scandinavian Studies* 47 (1975): 319.

101. Joseph Harris, "Obscure Styles (Old English and Old Norse) and the Enigma of *Gísla saga*," *Mediaevalia* 19 (1996): 91. Harris continues: "Saga prose is open, informal, realistic, and accessible to any audience while skaldic poetry is involuted, stylized, used for ostentation rather than communication, and apparently, to test audiences." In the *þáttr*, the inverse is the case; Halli's poetry is simple and transparent by any standard (and certainly by the standards of skaldic versifying) but his actions, ensconced in myth, are "involuted, stylized," and almost certainly designed "to test audiences."

102. Andy Orchard, *Cassell's Dictionary of Norse Myth & Legend* (London: Cassell, 1997), 237.

103. Jan de Vries, *The Problem of Loki*, Folklore Fellows Communications 110 (Helsinki: Suomalainen Tiedeakatemia, 1933).

104. Ibid., 254–64. Although scholars have widely recognized Loki's ambiguity as essential to his character, this recognition is, even in the most sagacious analyses, often

double-edged actions, merely serves to maintain his fundamental ambiguity.) Ultimately, Halli and Loki are both figures of ambiguous sexual and social identities: Halli is a despised Icelandic bumpkin *and* an esteemed Norwegian courtier; Loki is counted "among the Æsir" despite the fact that his father was giant, a pedigree that should exclude him from the racially exclusive society of the Æsir; Loki's dual nature—man and animal, female and male, good (or at least helpful) and evil—is paralleled by Halli's own dual nature as a poor, porridge-eating Icelander who is also a slanderous yet esteemed praise-poet at the Norwegian royal court. Halli is furthermore accepted into an elite homosocial community and recognized as one of the king's men, but simultaneously accused by his own royal patron of "unmanliness" (*ergi*).[105] Thus, ultimately, both Loki and Halli strive to attain and maintain their privileged position in a foreign society whose values, rules, and order they simultaneously work to undermine.

The penultimate line of the *þáttr* suggests that the pervasive ambiguity of Halli and his mythic analogue has been thoroughly understood by the literary-minded king Harald. Upon hearing of Halli's death in Iceland, the king poetically exclaims in alliterative prose, "the *poor wretch* must have burst eating porridge" (*Á grauti myndi greyit sprungit hafa*).[106] The word translated here as "poor wretch" (*grey*) is ambiguous, since *grey* can also mean "bitch" in the sense of "female dog," as it does in Eddic poetry. The indeterminate biological gender of the word *grey* (which refers to either a "bitch" or a "poor fellow") is further underscored by the king's chosen epithet's neutral grammatical gender (*greyit*). *Grey* occurs only three times in the *Íslendingasögur*: in *Njáls saga*, *Gísla saga*, and *Flóamanna saga*.

---

preface to a more traditional view of him as a figure ultimately "hostile" to the gods. Cf., e.g., Jerold C. Frakes, "Loki's Mythological Function in the Tripartite System," in *The Poetic Edda: Essays on Old Norse Mythology*, ed. Paul Acker and Carolyne Larrington (New York: Routledge, 2002), 172. Such a view arguably precludes a more fundamental insight, i.e., that the only statement that can be made about Loki whose opposite cannot be asserted with equal validity is that he is fundamentally *ambiguous*.

105. This sexual ambiguity may be underscored by Halli's previously cited verse: "This Gulathing's great / We fuck whatever we fancy" (*Gótt es Gulaþing þetta. / Gilju vit, hvat es viljum*). Halli "fucks" whatever (*hvat*, neut. sg.) he fancies (not *hverja*, fem. sg., or *hverjar*, fem. pl.). While *hverja* would have violated the meter (presumably the poet could have chosen a different one), the use of the grammatically neuter (and sexually ambiguous) *hvat* potentially leaves the gender (or perhaps likewise à la Loki, even the species) of Halli's conquests open to multiple readings.

106. 712; ÍF 9:295.

228 New Norse Studies

Suggestively, in *Flóamanna saga* and *Gísla saga*, *grey* is not simply a "poor wretch" but a term of abuse specifically for a man who refuses to fight—an "unmanly man" (*argr maðr*) who, according to the sagas, behaves "like a woman."[107] Yet *grey* also occurs in the poetic meaning *bitch*, i.e., "female dog," throughout the Eddic corpus, specifically in *Hávamál*, *Þrymskviða*, *Helgakviða Hundingsbana in fyrri*, *Skírnismál*, and *Hamðismál*.[108] The word is famously and allusively linked to mythic tradition in the infamous verse allegedly composed by Hjalti Skeggjason at the Alþingi in 998AD, just before the conversion to Christianity—quite literally (or, at least, literarily) Iceland's "last word" on the pagan past:

In barking at gods I am rich:	Spari ek eigi goð geyja!
I think Freyja's a bitch;	Grey þykki mér Freyja;
One or the other must be:	æ mun annat tveggja
Odin's a bitch—or else she.[109]	Óðinn grey eða Freyja (ÍF 12:264)

Hjalti's intended blasphemy aside, this statement is an accurate reflection of both Freyja's mythic promiscuity as well as Odin's practice of the shameful, "unmanly" magic of *seiðr*, both of which are aligned with Norse concepts of the female.[110] Thus, in the space of a single word, Harald encapsulates the dual nature of Sneglu-Halli: the Icelandic bumpkin and "poor wretch," and the courtier and skald who performs and recapitulates mythic tradition for a living. In calling Halli "grey," Harald not only reaffirms Halli's status as a "poor fellow" and social inferior; he couches this slap in the same sexually

---

107. "Þat kemr til þess, at Sámr *greyit* þorir eigi at berjast við mik" (It appears that Sam is a cowardly dog and does not dare to fight me) [ÍF 13:317; Viðar Hreinsson, ed., *Complete Sagas*, 3:301]; "'Þat var ok líkara,' segir Gísli, 'at *grey* þitt mundi eigi þora við mik vápnum at skipta'" ("It comes as no surprise," says Gísli, "that a coward such as you would not dare to cross weapons with me") [ÍF 6:112; Viðar Hreinsson, ed., *Complete Sagas*, 2:45].

108. Stanzas 101, 6, 13, 11, and 29, respectively, in Neckel's 4th ed. (see note 43 above). See further Finnur Jónsson, *Lexicon Poeticum* (Copenhagen: Lynge, 1966), *s.v.*

109. Cited from Robert Cook, trans., *Njal's Saga* (New York: Penguin, 2000), 177 (modified), which reproduces the text from Viðar Hreinsson, ed., *Complete Sagas*, 3:124–25 (ch. 102).

110. See Meulengracht Sørensen (note 32 above). Like Loki, both of these *grey* (pl.), Odin and Freyja, practice animal shape-shifting. Hence all the gods and goddesses deemed culpable of *ergi*—defined either as feminized magic (Odin), "passive" homosexuality (Loki), or unrestrained sexuality (Freyja)—are animal shape-shifters. Thus if *grey* describes Odin and Freyja, it applies equally well to Loki and to a Loki-esque "bitch" like Halli.

defamatory terms that Halli had been so adept at dishing out in life.[111] In a display of ambiguity worthy of Halli himself, Harald bemoans the "poor fellow" while simultaneously reiterating his earlier accusations of *ergi*, promiscuity, and passive homosexuality. And yet, if Halli is a "bitch" in this sense, he is nonetheless in the company of mythic figures such as Odin and Freyja. Thus the term can also be read as the king's final, approving nod to Halli's attempt at self-mythologization. (It is as if Harald, not to be outdone in matters of double meaning, were saying to his departed poet, "Now how's *that* for ambiguity!")

The ambiguity of King Harald's last word on Halli—"poor fellow" or "bitch," male or female, sly compliment or overt insult—is indeed suggestive of the ambiguous social, sexual, and ethical status of the figure Halli has alluded to throughout the *þáttr*—Loki himself. Harald's closing words on Halli can be read as a final, posthumous, backhanded compliment, a nod to Halli's efforts to recast himself as mythic figure and thus figuratively outrank his own royal patron. Yet this homage is ultimately coupled with a reassertion of Norwegian sovereignty over its Icelandic subject. For not only does Harald display the wisdom and mythic competence necessary to detect Halli's poetic (or should I say "prosaic"?) game; he also manages to express himself ambiguously as to whether Halli is indeed a "Bitch" of mythic proportions, cousin to Loki, Odin, and Freya, or really just another "poor fellow" from Iceland who, like his rival, Thjodolf, would be better off in a barnyard folktale, stuffing himself with porridge, and leaving the realm of myth to those like King Harald, who actually trace their genealogy back to it. Harald's ability to reduce the social, sexual, and generic uncertainty that pervades the tale to a single, double-edged, ambiguously gendered, insult-slash-compliment is ultimately a reassertion of the wisdom that makes him (or Norway) fit to rule, and makes Halli (or Iceland) fit to be his subject or (in the language of contemporary American slang) his *bitch*.[112]

---

111. The king alone can tolerate Halli's sexual defamation since as royal "sire" he is the public heterosexual *par excellence* on whom no accusation of *ergi* can adhere. Because such a figure is lacking in Iceland, the slanderous Icelander can, paradoxically, only be tolerated in Norway. This may be suggested by the setting of Halli's mysterious death in Iceland (712; ÍF 9:295), where—one is left to wonder—perhaps Halli proved a little too sarcastic?

112. Joseph Harris rightly includes Halli among "a series of underdog heroes who assert themselves against Norwegian court prejudice and hold up their heads in the royal presence." However, a closer examination of this "projection of contemporary wishes

Hence the risqué *þáttr* is not simply a series of virtuoso vituperations peppered with sexual-cum-barnyard humor, nor "a series of episodes that could have been arranged otherwise as well," with "a looser and more paratactical construction than most other *þættir*."[113] On the contrary, it is a text that repays close attention, both for original audiences and for students and scholars of Old Norse-Icelandic literature. *Sneglu-Halla þáttr* presupposes considerable literary connoisseurship, detailed knowledge of mythographic tradition, and a consciousness of genre that reflects concerns of shifting social classes and political powers in Iceland from the thirteenth century onward. Halli's unflagging superiority within an imagined political reality in which Norwegian and other foreign courts are routinely trumped by the literary expertise of an Icelandic *Hinterwäldler* or "redneck" would have been no small wish-fulfillment to the literary elites that patronized such stories, faced with the task of reformulating Icelandic identity under conditions of encroaching foreign hegemony.[114] But, as I have argued, the tale lends itself with equal credibility to an opposite, more Norwegian-friendly interpretation as well.

Sneglu-Halla þáttr: Texts and Contexts

The ambiguities of Norwegian-Icelandic relations are a pervasive enough feature of the medieval Icelandic experience that the elusive problem of an exact dating of *Sneglu-Halla þáttr* has little immediate bearing on my reading here. Nonetheless the textual history of the *þáttr* raises questions about its precise *Sitz im Leben* that repay reexamination in the present context. The text of the *þáttr* follows *Magnúss*

---

onto stories set in the past," can, I argue here, also reveal the ambiguous nature of such "contemporary wishes." See "Saga as Historical Novel," in *"Speak Useful Words,"* 258; originally published in *Structure and Meaning in Old Norse Literature: New Approaches to Textual Analysis and Literary Criticism*, ed. John Lindow et al., The Viking Collection: Studies in Northern Civilization 3 (Odense: Odense University Press, 1986), 187–219.

113. Danielsson, "Sneglu-Halla þáttr," 599. Consonant with my arguments above about the ordering of episodes in the *þáttr*, Torfi Tulinius's first two criteria for "skaldic prose" (see note 19 above), "interlacing of plot lines" and "absent or inconspicuous connectors," might better account for the tale's apparently "looser and more paratactical" construction.

114. For more on this "identity crisis," see Torfi H. Tulinius, "The Matter of the North: Fiction and Uncertain Identities in Thirteenth-Century Iceland," in Clunies Ross, *Old Icelandic Literature and Society*, 242–65, esp. 261.

saga góða as the third of the seven additional *þættir* that constitute the late fifteenth-century addition or "younger" Flateyjarbók, which was made while the codex was in the possession of Þorleifr Björnsson.[115] As previously mentioned, there is no consensus on the relationship of the more complex Flateyjarbók version to the shorter text of Morkinskinna; while the text of Morkinskinna (ca. 1275) is roughly two hundred years older than that of Flateyjarbók, Tommy Danielsson aptly sums up the matter when he states that "which version is older has not been definitively settled."[116] In the preface to the *Íslenzk fornrit* edition, Jónas Kristjánsson cites (rather unconvincing) arguments by Bjarni Aðalbjarnarson that the Morkinskinna version is a reduction of Flateyjarbók, or alternately (as seems more intuitive) that the Flateyjarbók version is an expansion of Morkinskinna. Both Jónas Kristjánsson and Danielsson believe that Halli must have been a folk figure around whom humourous episodes accreted, and that the material of the *þáttr* is "very old" because of the inclusion of "authentic" skaldic verses. While we cannot know how old the Flateyjarbók version ultimately is, the text aligns closely enough with that of Morkinskinna that one must be based on the other, rather than drawing independently on a common oral tradition (which is not to say that none existed). To the best of my knowledge, no one has ever suggested that the Flateyjarbók version was first composed as late as the time of its recording, which would indeed require a radical rethinking of long-held assumptions about Icelandic literary history. Instead, I would simply offer that either the Flateyjarbók version is older, or its redactor was inspired by the text of Morkinskinna, which already contained a few Loki-motifs, and transformed and augmented these to create an integrated, mythically allusive prose narrative—a process parallel to the art of skaldic composition itself, in which scattered mythic allusions are fashioned into a comprehensive artistic product.[117]

---

115. Elizabeth Ashman Rowe does not treat these so-called *tillegs-þættir* ("additional tales") in her recent book, as her focus is on the social milieu of Flateyjarbók's original patron, Jón Hákonarson (ca. 1350–1416). See *The Development of Flateyjarbók*, The Viking Collection: Studies in Northern Civilization 15 (Odense: The University Press of Southern Denmark, 2006).

116. "Sneglu-Halla þáttr," 599.

117. Referring to the Morkinskinna version, Theodore M. Andersson remarks, "*Sneglu-Halla þáttr* is characterized by a series of farcical episodes at the Norwegian court,

Ultimately such philological questions may not be the most crucial ones. As Joseph Harris has rightly asked, "How can we tell what was an independant literary work, and wouldn't the notion of independence—so central to our conception of literature—be a historically relative one?"[118] The location of Halli among the additional *þættir* at the end of Flateyjarbók would seem to resist the kind of new-philological analysis of manuscript context that Elizabeth Ashman Rowe (see note 115 above) applies to the 1387–90 compilation. Aside from the tale's "King-and-Icelander" theme, it is difficult to see an editorial agenda at work in the placement of *Sneglu-Halla þáttr* between *Auðunar þáttr vestfirzka* and *Halldórs þáttr*. However, given the central importance of both family lineage and myth in *Sneglu-Halla þáttr*, it is perhaps noteworthy that it is included in Flateyjarbók in the first place, as the contents of this manuscript are organized around the principle of royal genealogy.

Flateyjarbók furthermore contains a single Eddic poem, *Hynd-luljóð*, in which two figures compare the nobility of ancestries, and Loki is mentioned explicitly in this context. One of the so-called "additional" Eddic poems not found in the Codex Regius, *Hyndluljóð* depicts the conflict between Freya and the giantess Hyndla ("little Bitch") as they examine the pedigree of Freyja's protégé, Óttarr, which must be established in order for him to win an inheritance claim against his opponent, Angantýr. The poem (which in the manuscript also contains the interpolated "shorter *Vǫluspá*") refers to mythic narratives about Loki as the mother of the wolf Fenrir, the horse Sleipnir, and the goddess Hel (st. 40), and as the (otherwise unattested) mother of all ogressess (st. 41). The lay (like the *þáttr?*) concludes with a poisoning motif (st. 49). Of greatest significance in the context of *Sneglu Halla þáttr*, however, is the poem's overarching thematic concern: Óttarr's ancestry is "mythologized"—his descent

---

in which the king plays the autocrat and Halli consistently has the best of it" (*Partisan Muse*, 121). If one assumes that the Morkinskinna text is indeed the earlier version, one might trace an evolution from a less flattering portrait of King Harald to a more ambiguous, Norwegian-friendly portrait in the longer version discussed here. Be that as it may, the Morkinskinna version seems already potentially ambiguous enough to complicate Andersson's reading of the *þáttr*.

118. Joseph Harris, "Gender and Genre: Short and Long Forms in the Saga Literature," in *The Making of the Couple: The Social Function of Short-form Medieval Narrative—A Symposium* (Odense: Odense University Press, 1991), 51.

ultimately traced to kings and the gods—recalling Halli's own efforts to ensconce himself in a network of allusions to a mythic figure, and thereby establish a distinguished "ancestry" for himself so he can better vie for status at court against his rivals. Hence one might say that the "poetization and mythologization of property relations"[119] evident in *Hyndluljóð* are applied to the "cultural capital"[120] of skaldic poetry in *Sneglu Halla þáttr*. Moreover, the Eddic poem refers to several of the mythical elements that I have argued are alluded to in the *þáttr*, i.e., the golden boar, Gullinbursti (st. 7, 45), the dwarf smiths (st. 7), and, again, Loki's bearing of Odin's horse Sleipnir (st. 40). The rivals Freya and Hyndla also exchange sexually defamatory insults that recall the king and Halli's sexually-barbed volleys. Moreover, *Hyndluljóð* (st. 3) draws a distinction—between those who posses riches, properly speaking, and those who merely possess the cultural capital of skaldic poetry— a distinction that defines the conflict between Harald and Halli. Hence the manuscript context of Flateyjarbók might well lend support to my reading of Halli's self-mythologizing at the court of King Harald as a kind of *Genealogie-Ersatz* for the kin-poor (*aettsmár*) Icelander.

Flateyjarbók also contains *Sǫrla þáttr*, another late insertion into the manuscript, which recounts one of Loki's adventures: his theft of Freya's gold necklace. The *þáttr* tells of four dwarfs who create a precious *gullmen* which Freyja acquires by sleeping with each of them on four subsequent nights. Loki, first transformed into a fly and later into a flea, steals this treasure from Freyja at Odin's behest. The tale contains several elements analogous to Halli's "Loki-isms" in his *þáttr*: the acquisition of prized possessions through dwarf middlemen; the "fly" element associated with Einar fly (and hence Halli's and Loki's previously discussed acquisition of treasures in episodes involving a "fly"); potions of sleep and forgetfulness also play a role in *Sǫrla þáttr*, which might, more tentatively, be suggestive of the poisoning motif that I locate at the end of *Sneglu-Halla þáttr*. Far

---

119. Aron Gurevich, "*Hyndluljóð*," in Pulsiano, *Medieval Scandinavia: An Encyclopedia*, 309.

120. See Kevin Wanner, *Snorri Sturluson and the Edda: The Conversion of Cultural Capital in Medieval* Scandinavia, Toronto Old Norse-Icelandic Series 4 (Toronto: University of Toronto Press, 2008).

more significant, however, is *Sǫrla þáttr*'s recasting of Loki as a wily, sharp-tongued peasant in the manner of a "folktale":

> Maðr hét Fárbauti. Hann var karl einn ok átti sér kerlingu þá, er Laufey er nefnd. Hún var bæði mjó ok auðþreiflig; því var hún Nál kölluð. Þau áttu sér einn son barna. Sá var Loki nefndr. Hann var ekki mikill vöxtum, orðskár var hann snemma ok skjótligr í bragði. Hann hafði fram yfir aðra menn visku þá, er slægð heitir. Hann var mjök kyndugr þegar á unga aldri, því var hann kallaðr Loki lævíss. (Guðni Jónsson, *Fornaldar sögur Norðurlanda*, 1:368)

> There was a man called Farbauti who was a peasant and had a wife called Laufey. She was thin and meagre, and so she was called "Needle." They had no children except a son who was called Loki. He was not a big man, but he early developed a caustic tongue and was alert in trickery and unequalled in that kind of cleverness which is called cunning. He was very full of guile even in his youth, and for this reason he was called Loki the Sly.[121]

The Loki of *Sǫrla þáttr* might indeed be viewed as an intermediary figure or bridge between the Loki of the mythographic tradition (whose exploits are referred to in Flateyjarbók in *Hyndluljóð*) and Halli's mundane reenactments of that god's exploits. The representation of Loki as a clever peasant (*karl*) in *Sǫrla þáttr* is neatly inverted in the manuscript context of Flateyjarbók by the representation of Halli, the clever but low-born Icelander, as a Loki figure in *Sneglu-Halla þáttr*.

Although the *þáttr* was not added until a generation later, it would hardly be difficult to imagine the appeal of the Flateyjarbók version for someone like the book's original, quasi-aristocratic patron, the wealthy Icelandic farmer Jón Hákonarson. Jón's grandfather, Gizurr galli (1269–1370), played an important role in the conflicts between Icelanders and the Norwegian king in the late thirteenth century, and had been a sworn follower of King Hákon. Gizzur even named his own sons after the Norwegian kings Magnús and Hákon in order to underscore his loyalty to Hákon háleggr. If Rowe is correct that the original agenda behind the Flateyjarbók compilation was to

---

121. Nora Kershaw, ed. and trans., *Stories and Ballads of the Far Past* (Cambridge: Cambridge University Press, 1921), 44.

inculcate a tolerance for persnickety Icelanders in the court of King Óláfr Hákonarson, it is not hard to imagine why *Sneglu-Halla þáttr* might have been left out of the earlier compilation; while its tale is ambiguous enough *in theory* on the question of Norwegian-versus-Icelandic cultural superiority to please even a foreign court, its compilers may have been wary of ascribing the sensitivity for detecting such nuances to *actual* royal persons, as opposed to their idealized fictional counterparts.[122] Be that as it may, if Rowe is correct that Flateyjarbók was designed to speak to the social-climbing ambitions of its original Icelandic patron, particularly vis-à-vis the Norwegian court, then the addition of the tale of the upwardly mobile Halli would seem a belated but ideologically fitting coda to Flateyjarbók as a whole.

Like Loki and Halli, medieval Icelandic patrons and audiences were confronted with their own ambivalence toward foreign powers that both threatened and guaranteed their existence, just as modern Icelanders have been confronted with their ambivalence toward the North Atlantic Treaty Organization, which has generated split feelings in Iceland ever since Páll's birthday on March 30, 1949.[123] For Einar Már Guðmundsson's schizophrenic Páll, the day of Iceland's entry into NATO is a day of public protest; privately, however, it remains an occasion to contemplate the possibilities of birth, survival, and artistic creation in a continued, if compromised, existence. Páll's case is a history of both exoteric and esoteric significance. Like the story of Halli, it tells one tale to the many, but another more meaningful one to an elite interpretive community—be they postmodern savants or skaldic poets—whose business it is to see beyond the literal sense of words and things. In the medieval Icelandic body politic, it is an analogous ambivalence that takes on literary flesh in the mythologized ambiguities of Sneglu-Halli and his tale.[124]

---

122. This does not, however, explain why *Magnúss saga góða* was left out of the original Flateyjarbók compliation in the first place; Rowe argues that the saga must have been part of the original plan (see *The Development of Flateyjarbók*, 21).

123. The intensity of feeling regarding this issue has largely subsided since the withdrawal of the United States' Iceland Defense Force from Keflavík in 2006, although passions have since been similarly roused since by referenda on the repayment of international banking debt and on membership negotiations with the European Union.

124. This essay was written in part at the *Stofnun Árna Magnússonar í íslenskum fræðum* in Reykjavík with funding from the Icelandic Fulbright Commission, and in part as a guest of the Fiske Icelandic Collection at Cornell University; the support of these institutions is gratefully acknowledged.

Bibliography

Adamson, Melitta Weiss. *Food in Medieval Times*. Westport: Greenwood Press, 2004.

Ágrip af Nóregskonunga sögum, Fagrskinna—Nóregs konunga tal. Edited by Bjarni Einarsson. Íslenzk fornrit 29. Reykjavík: Hið íslenzka fornritafélag, 1984.

Andersson, Theodore M. "The King of Iceland." *Speculum* 74 (1999): 923–34.

———. *The Partisan Muse in the Early Icelandic Sagas (1200–1250)*. Islandica 55. Ithaca: Cornell University Library, 2012.

———, and Kari Ellen Gade, trans. *Morkinskinna: The Earliest Icelandic Chronicle of the Norwegian Kings (1030–1157)*. Islandica 51. Ithaca: Cornell University Press, 2000.

Ármann Jakobsson. *Í leit að konungi: Konungsmynd íslenskra konungasagna*. Reykjavík: Háskólaútgáfan, 1997.

———. "Munnur skáldsins: Um vanda þess og vegsemd að vera listrænn og framgjarn Íslendingur í útlöndum." *Ritmennt: Ársrit Landsbókasafns Íslands—Háskólabókasafns* 10 (2005): 63–79.

Asbjørnsen, Peter Christen. *Norske Huldreeventyr og Folkesagn*. 3rd ed. Christiania [Oslo], 1870.

Austfirðinga sǫgur. Edited by Jón Jóhannesson. Íslenzk fornrit 11. Reykjavík: Hið íslenzka fornritafélag, 1950.

Bebel, Heinrich. *Facetiarum Heinrici Bebelii, poetae A.D. Maximiliano laureati, libri tres*. Bern, 1550.

Bjarni Aðalbjarnarson. *Om de norske kongers sagaer*. Oslo: I kommisjon hos J. Dybwad, 1937.

Bødker, Laurits, ed. *Folkeeventyr fra Kær herred*. Copenhagen: Akademisk forlag, 1963–67.

Brennu-Njáls saga. Edited by Einar Ól. Sveinsson. Íslenzk fornrit 12. Reykjavík: Hið íslenzka fornritafélag, 1954.

Byock, Jesse, trans. *The Saga of the Volsungs*. New York: Penguin, 2000.

Christensen, Arthur, ed. *Molboernes vise gerninger*. Copenhagen: Det Schønbergske forlag, 1939.

Cleasby, Richard, and Gudbrand Vigfusson. *An Icelandic-English Dictionary*. 2nd ed. Oxford: Clarendon, 1957.

Clunies Ross, Margaret. *A History of Old Norse Poetry and Poetics*. Woodbridge: D. S. Brewer, 2005.

———. *Prolonged Echoes: Old Norse Myths in Medieval Northern Society*. 2 vols. Odense: Odense University Press, 1994–98.

———, ed. *Skaldic Poetry of the Scandinavian Middle Ages*. 8 vols. (projected). Turnhout: Brepols, 2007–.

Cook, Robert, trans. *Njal's Saga*. New York: Penguin, 2000.

Danielsson, Tommy. *Om den isländska släktsagans uppbyggnad*. Stockholm: Almqvist & Wiksell, 1986.

———. "*Sneglu-Halla þáttr*." In *Medieval Scandinavia: An Encyclopedia*. Edited by Philip Pulsiano and Kirsten Wolf. New York: Garland, 1993.

Dumézil, Georges. *From Myth to Fiction: The Saga of Hadingus*. Translated by D. Coltman. Chicago: University of Chicago Press, 1973.

Einar Ólafur Sveinsson. *The Folk-Stories of Iceland*. Viking Society for Northern Research Text Series 16. Exeter: Short Run Press, 2003. Trans. of *Um íslenzkar þjóðsögur*. Reykjavík: Hið íslenzka bókmenntafélag, 1940.

Egils saga Skalla-Grímssonar. Edited by Sigurður Nordal. Íslenzk fornrit 2. Reykjavík: Hið íslenzka fornritafélag, 1933.

Einar Már Guðmundsson. *Angels of the Universe*. Translated by Bernard Scudder. Reykjavík: Mál og menning, 1995. Trans. of *Englar Alheimsins*. Reykjavík: Mál og menning, 1993.

Elias, Norbert. *The Civilizing Process: Sociogenetic and Pyschogenetic Investigations*. Oxford: Blackwell, 2000. Trans. of *Über den Prozeß der Zivilisation*. Berlin: Suhrkamp, 1997.

Eyfirðinga sögur. Edited by Jónas Kristjánsson. Íslenzk fornrit 9. Reykjavík: Hið íslenzka fornritafélag, 1956.

Frakes, Jerold C. "Loki's Mythological Function in the Tripartite System." In *The Poetic Edda: Essays on Old Norse Mythology*, edited by Paul Acker and Carolyne Larrington, 159–76. New York: Routledge, 2002.

Gísli Sigurðsson. *The Medieval Icelandic Saga and Oral Tradition: A Discourse on Method*. Cambridge, MA: The Milman Parry Collection of Oral Literature, Harvard University; distr. Harvard University Press, 2004.

Grimm, Jacob and Wilhelm Grimm. *Kinder- und Hausmärchen gesammelt durch die Brüder Grimm*. Vollständige Ausgabe auf der Grundlage der dritten Auflage (1837). Edited by Heinz Rölleke. Frankfurt am Main: Deutscher Klassiker Verlag, 1985.

Groos, Arthur B. *Romancing the Grail: Genre, Science, and Quest in Wolfram's "Parzival."* Ithaca: Cornell University Press, 1995.

Guðni Jónsson, ed. *Fornaldar sögur Norðurlanda*. 4 vols. Reykjavík: Íslendingasagnaútgáfan, 1954.

Guðrún Nordal. *Tools of Literacy: The Role of Skaldic Verse in Icelandic Textual Culture of the Twelfth and Thirteenth Centuries*. Toronto: University of Toronto Press, 2001.

Haraldur Bessason. "Mythological Overlays." In *Sjötíu ritgerðir helgaðar Jakobi Benediktssyni 20. júlí 1977, fyrri hluti*, edited by Einar G. Pétursson and Jónas Kristjánsson, 273–292. Reykjavík: Stofnun Árna Magnússonar, 1977.

Harðar saga. Edited by Þórhallur Vilmundarson and Bjarni Vilhjálmsson. Íslenzk fornrit 13. Reykjavík: Hið íslenzka fornritafélag, 1991.

Harris, Joseph. "Folktale and Thattr: The Case of Rognvald and Raud." Special issue: Folklore and Medieval Studies, *Folklore Forum* 13 (1980): 158–98.

———. "Gender and Genre: Short and Long Forms in the Saga Literature." In *The Making of the Couple: The Social Function of Short-form Medieval Narrative—A Symposium*, edited by Flemming G. Andersen and Morten Nøjgaard, 43–66. Odense: Odense University Press, 1991. Repr. in *"Speak Useful Words or Say Nothing": Old Norse Studies by Joseph Harris*, edited by Susan E. Deskis and Thomas D. Hill, 261–86. Islandica 53. Ithaca: Cornell University Library, 2008.

———. *"The Masterbuilder Tale in Snorri's Edda and Two Sagas." Arkiv för nordisk* filologi 91 (1976): 66–101. Repr. in Harris, *"Speak Useful Words,"* 51–95.

———. "Obscure Styles (Old English and Old Norse) and the Enigma of *Gísla saga." Mediaevalia* 19 (1996): 75–99.

———. "Saga as Historical Novel." In *Structure and Meaning in Old Norse Literature: New Approaches to Textual Analysis and Literary Criticism*, edited by John Lindow, Lars Lönnroth, and Gerd Wolfgang Weber, 187–219. The Viking Collection: Studies in Northern Civilization 3. Odense: Odense University Press, 1986. Repr. in Harris, *"Speak Useful Words,"* 220–60.

———. "Þættir." In *Dictionary of the Middle Ages*. Edited by Joseph R. Strayer. 13 vols. New York: Scribner, 1982–89.

Haugen, Einar. "The Mythical Structure of the Ancient Scandinavians: Some Thoughts on Reading Dumézil." In *Introduction to Structuralism*, edited by Michael Lane, 170–83. New York: Basic Books, 1992.

Hodne, Ørnulf. *Types of the Norwegian Folktale*. Oslo: Universitetsforlaget, 1984.

Hofmann, Dietrich. "Vers und Prosa in der mündlich gepflegten Erzählkunst der germanischen Länder." *Frühmittelalterliche Studien* 5 (1971): 135–75.

Hollander, Lee M. "The Structure of *Eyrbyggja saga." Journal of English and Germanic Philology* 58 (1959): 222–27.

Holtsmark, Anne. "Ovid." In *Kulturhistorisk leksikon for nordisk middelalder*. Edited by John Danstrup. Roskilde: Rosenkilde og Bagger, 1968.

Íslendingabók, Landnámabók. Edited by Jakob Benediktsson. Íslenzk fornrit 1. Reykjavík: Hið íslenzka fornritafélag, 1968.

Jón Árnason. *Íslenzkar þjóðsögur og æfintýri*. 2 vols. Leipzig: Hinrichs, 1862–64.

Kaske, R. E. "The *Eotenas* in *Beowulf." In *Old English Poetry: Fifteen Essays*, edited by Robert P. Creed, 285–310. Providence: Brown University Press, 1967.

Kershaw, Nora, ed. and trans. *Stories and Ballads of the Far Past.* Cambridge: Cambridge University Press, 1921.

Kjalnesinga saga. Edited by Jóhannes Halldórsson. Íslenzk fornrit 14. Reykjavík: Hið íslenzka fornritafélag, 1959.

Kristensen, E. T. *Efterslaet til "Skattegaveren."* Kolding, 1890.

Laxdœla saga. Edited by Einar Ól. Sveinsson. Íslenzk fornrit 5. Reykjavík: Hið íslenzka fornritafélag, 1934.

Lind, E. H. *Norsk-Isländska Personbinamn från Medeltiden.* Uppsala, 1920–21.

Lindow, John. "Bloodfeud and Scandinavian Mythology." *alvíssmál* 4 (1994 [1995]): 51–68.

———. "Riddles, Kennings, and the Complexity of Skaldic Poetry." *Scandinavian Studies* 47 (1975): 311–27.

Liungman, Waldemar. *Die Schwedischen Volksmärchen.* Translated by Elsbeth Umlauf. Berlin: Akademie-Verlag, 1961.

McTurk, Rory, ed. *A Companion to Old Norse-Icelandic Literature and Culture.* Oxford: Blackwell, 2005.

Meulengracht Sørensen, Preben. *The Unmanly Man: Concepts of Sexual Defamation in Early Northern Society.* The Viking Collection: Studies in Northern Civilization 1. Odense: Odense University Press, 1983.

Minkow, Michael. "Sneglu-Halli, 2:11: Dróttinserðr." *Saga-Book* 22 (1988): 285–86.

Morkinskinna. Edited by Ármann Jakobsson and Þórður Ingi Guðjónsson. 2 vols. Íslenzk fornrit 23–24. Reykjavík: Hið íslenzka fornritafélag, 2011.

Morson, Gary Saul, and Caryl Emerson. *Mikhail Bakhtin: Creation of a Prosaics.* Stanford: Stanford University Press, 1991.

Neckel, Gustav, and Hans Kuhn, eds. *Die Lieder des Codex Regius nebst verwandten Denkmälern.* Vol. 1, *Text.* 4th ed. Germanische Bibliothek. 4. Reihe, Texte. Heidelberg: Carl Winter, 1962.

O'Donoghue, Heather. *Skaldic Verse and the Poetics of Saga Narrative.* Oxford: Oxford University Press, 2005.

Orchard, Andy. *Cassell's Dictionary of Norse Myth and Legend.* London: Cassell, 1997.

Rittershaus, Adeline. *Die neuisländischen Volksmärchen: Ein Beitrag zur vergleichenden Märchenforschung.* Halle: Niemeyer, 1902.

Rowe, Elizabeth Ashman. *The Development of Flateyjarbók.* The Viking Collection: Studies in Northern Civilization 15. Odense: The University Press of Southern Denmark, 2006.

———. "Absent Mothers and the Sons of Fornjótr: Late-Thirteenth-Century Monarchist Ideology in *Þorsteins saga Víkingssonar.*" *Mediaeval Scandinavia* 14 (2004): 133–60.

———, and Joseph Harris. "Short Prose Narrative (*þáttr*)." In McTurk, *A Companion to Old Norse-Icelandic Literature and Culture,* 462–78.

Sigurður Nordal. *Hrafnkels saga Freysgoða*. Translated by R. George Thomas. Cardiff: University of Wales Press, 1958.

Singer, Samuel, ed. *Thesaurus Proverbiorum Medii Aevi: Lexikon der Sprichwörter des romanisch-germanischen Mittelalters*. 13 vols. Berlin: de Gruyter, 1996–2002.

Snorri Sturluson. *Edda: Prologue and Gylfaginning*. Edited by Anthony Faulkes. 2nd ed. London: Viking Society for Northern Research, 1988.

———. *Edda: Skáldskaparmál*. Edited by Anthony Faulkes. 2 vols. London: Viking Society for Northern Research, 1998.

———. *Heimskringla*. Edited by Bjarni Aðalbjarnason. 3 vols. Íslenzk fornrit 26–28. Reykjavík: Hið íslenzka fornritafélag, 1941.

———. *Heimskringla: History of the Kings of Norway*. Edited and translated by Lee Hollander. Austin: University of Austin Press, 1964.

Sveinbjörn Rafnsson. "Sagnastef í íslenskri menningarsögu." *Saga* 30 (1992): 81–121.

Thompson, Stith. *Motif-Index of Folk Literature*. 6 vols. Bloomington: Indiana University Press, 1955–58.

Torfi H. Tulinius. "The Matter of the North: Fiction and Uncertain Identities in Thirteenth Century Iceland." In *Old Icelandic Literature and Society*, edited by Margaret Clunies Ross, 242–65. Cambridge: Cambridge University Press, 2000.

———. "The Prosimetrum Form 2: Verses as the Basis for Saga Composition and Interpretation." In *Skaldsagas: Text, Vocation, and Desire in the Sagas of Poets*, edited by Russell Poole, 191–217. Berlin: de Gruyter, 2001.

Vatnsdœla saga. Edited by Einar Ól. Sveinsson. Íslenzk fornrit 8. Reykjavík: Hið íslenzka fornritafélag, 1939.

Vésteinn Ólason. *Dialogues with the Viking Age*. Reykjavík: Mál og menning, 1998.

———. "Family Sagas." In McTurk, *A Companion to Old Norse-Icelandic Literature and* Culture, 101–18.

Vestfirðinga sǫgur. Edited by Björn K. Þórólfsson and Guðni Jónsson. Íslenzk fornrit 6. Reykjavík: Hið íslenzka fornritafélag, 1943.

Viðar Hreinsson, ed. *The Complete Sagas of Icelanders*. 5 vols. Reykjavík: Leifur Eiríksson, 1997.

Vries, Jan de. *The Problem of Loki*. Folklore Fellows Communications 110. Helsinki: Suomalainen Tiedeakatemia, 1933.

Wanner, Kevin J. "Cunning Intelligence in Norse Myth: Loki, Óðinn, and the Limits of Sovereignty." *History of Religions* 48 (2009): 211–46.

———. *Snorri Sturluson and the Edda: The Conversion of Cultural Capital in Medieval Scandinavia*. Toronto Old Norse-Icelandic Series 4. Toronto: University of Toronto Press, 2008.

Weber, Gerd Wolfgang. "*Intellegere historiam*: Typological Perspectives of Nordic Prehistory (in Snorri, Saxo, Widukind and Others)." In *Tradition og Historieskrivning*, edited by Kirstin Hastrup and Preben Meulengracht Sørensen, 95–141. Acta Jutlandica 63.2. Aarhus: Universitetsforlag, 1987.

Wellendorf, Jonas. "The Interplay of Pagan and Christian Traditions in Icelandic Settlement Myths." *JEGP* 109 (2010): 1–21.

Wigström, Eva. *Skånska Visor, Sagor och Sägner.* Lund, 1880.

Wolf, Alois. "Die Skaldendichtung—Wegbereiterin der Sagaprosa?" In *Studien zur Isländersaga*, edited by Heinrich Beck and Else Ebel, 283–300. Berlin: de Gruyter, 2000.

Beer, Vomit, Blood, and Poetry
Egils saga, Chapters 44–45

Thomas D. Hill
CORNELL UNIVERSITY

Chapters 44 and 45 of *Egils saga*[1] concern the prequel of what Sigurður Nordal has described as one of the most understated love stories in the history of Western literature.[2] Egil's charismatic brother Thorolf has gone off to marry Asgerd, the young, beautiful, and intelligent girl who was fostered and raised in Egil's and Thorolf's home, but who was not related to them. The reader of the saga who is reading or listening to the saga for the first time can have no way of knowing what Egil feels for Asgerd. All the reader can know is that Egil became uncharacteristically sick just before his brother's wedding, that later after Thorolf's death in battle, Egil seeks Asgerd's hand in marriage with great determination, and that Egil becomes pitiably depressed when it appears that Asgerd has refused his suit.

The point of anticipating Egil's later wooing of Asgerd, however, is that Egil's swift recovery after his brother's departure and his emotional volatility during the adventures that ensue are well motivated, although only in retrospect. Egil is on the rebound, and as his friends might say, if saga men could use twenty-first-century idioms, he is in a funny mood. Thus when he encounters a bad and ultimately

---

1. All quotations from *Egils saga* are from the edition of Bjarni Einarsson (London: Viking Society for Northern Research, 2003) by page number. I have also consulted the editions of Sigurður Nordal, Íslenzk fornrit 2 (Reykjavík: Hið íslenzka fornritafélag, 1933), and Finnur Jónsson (Halle: Niemeyer, 1924). Translations of Old Norse-Icelandic are my own, but I have, of course, consulted previous translations and the comments of their various editors.

2. Sigurður Nordal, *Icelandic Culture*, trans. Vilhjálmur T. Bjarnar (Ithaca: Cornell University Library, 1990), 120.

murderous host, and the poisonous hostility of Queen Gunnhild, Egil responds with a combination of poetry, wit, and violence, which enables him to defy the king of Norway and his queen, respond to his host with memorable and elegant poetry, eventually take blood vengeance, and yet live to tell the tale.

The story, as it unfolds, seems almost random and anecdotal. Egil has recovered from his illness after the departure of his brother, and since he is bored and has nothing to do he joins Qlvir, one the stewards of the household, on a trip to collect rents. There is nothing planned or deliberate about this trip, and if Qlvir had been a more senior member of the household of his master Thorir Hroaldson, he would have presumably been included in the marriage feast. The trip Egil sets out on is thus a routine, rather low-level business trip, and the only reason Egil goes on this journey is that he has absolutely nothing to do at home. The beginning of the trip is again mundane enough. They run into bad weather, and although they make reasonable progress, they are tired, wet, and exhausted when they stop for the day and seek shelter from Bard, who is the supervisor of one of the king's estates. Here again, the story as it unfolds involves pure chance. If the weather had been better, they would presumably have gone farther; if the weather had been worse, they would not have gotten as far as they did. Their arrival at the estate Bard managed was a matter of pure luck; they did not plan to stay with Bard, and he could have had no way of knowing that they might arrive and need hospitality. And while Bard will, in the course of the evening, be commemorated in memorable and intricate verse as a bad host, his response to his unexpected guests is, it might seem, at least reasonably generous. He provides them with lodging and a good fire to warm them. And he also provides them with at least adequate provisions although they only have *skyr* and *afr*—"yogurt" and "buttermilk" to drink. It is difficult for a modern reader to gauge how grievous a breach of hospitality Bard's failure to provide alcoholic beverages was. From a common-sense point of view it is hard not to have some sympathy for Bard. He must have known that the king and his retinue were in the area and might arrive soon, as indeed they did. Fourteen thirsty sailors can drink a great deal of beer or ale,[3] and one would hardly

---

3. The terms "beer" and "ale" are to some degree ambiguous in modern usage and it

want to run out of ale when hosting King Eirik Bloodaxe and Queen Gunnhild. Keeping the provisions for the king's feast set aside was not a generous gesture, but it would hardly seem a mortal offense, and it is noteworthy that only Egil comments on the situation. But Bard had twice insisted that he did not have adequate provisions to provide for his unexpected guests, and so as the story unfolds and as the king arrives and tells Bard that he wants to share the royal feast with Ǫlvir and his men, Bard's stinginess is publicly exposed. Bard is at fault and he is shamed by the generosity of his master the king. It could be argued that Bard then overcompensates, as it were, and having formerly been a stingy host, he now insists on forcing his tired guests, who have already drunk a great deal of buttermilk and skyr, to drink massive amounts of ale. There is no suggestion that Ǫlvir or any other members of his party were deeply angered by Bard's behavior—they take Bard's churlishness in stride and accept the hospitality that is offered them. Egil, however, is more sensitive. His brother Thorolf, who has surpassed Egil in a variety of ways, is celebrating a marriage feast and marrying the girl whom Egil desires, and for Egil to have to drink ale on top of buttermilk is both annoying in itself and must remind Egil of the magnificent feast which he is missing, and more importantly of the occasion of that feast.

There is no direct way Egil can respond to Bard's churlishness; he has belatedly been invited to join the king's feast and the king has treated Ǫlvir and his companions honorably. It is saga convention, however, that poetry is often the mode that allows a speaker to address the emotional realities of a saga situation directly—in part because the intricate discourse of skaldic poetry is so indirect. So when Bard compounds his churlishness by forcing beer on the travelers whom he has already encouraged to drink buttermilk, Egil responds with a stanza that directly addresses Bard's behavior.

Sǫgðuð sverri flagða
sumbleklu þér, kumbla,
því tel ek, brjótr, þar er blétuð,

---

is not clear exactly whether what Egil and his friends were consuming was ale or beer; I use the term ale for convenience. The terms "ale," "beer," "wine," and "mead" were all used as "Grundwörter" in kennings for poetry. See Rudolf Meissner, *Die Kenningar der Skalden: ein Beitrag zur skaldischen Poetik* (Bonn: K. Schroeder, 1921), 427–30.

bragðvísan þik, dísir.
Leynduð alls til illa
ókunna þér runna,
illt hafið bragð of brugðit,
Bárǫðr, hugar fári. (58–59, v. 8)

You told the enemy of the giantesses [the man]
[there was] lack of beer for you
There where you sacrificed to the disir,
you desecrator of graves!
Therefore I reckon you cunning;
You concealed entirely
evil enmity of thought
to bushes [trees / men]
unknown to you.
Barðr, you played an evil trick.

Egil's insulting verse was concerned with Bard, but Bard takes advantage of his position as a trusted favorite of the king and queen and goes to queen Gunnhild to complain that Egil is mocking them all by drinking everything which is given him and claiming that he is still thirsty. Ǫlvir and most of his company are having trouble drinking beer on top of the skyr and buttermilk Bard gave them earlier in the evening, but Egil does not seem to be affected, so there is some justice to Bard's complaint. But Egil is mocking Bard, not the king or the queen, and so there is no reason for either of them to become involved.

Gunnhild, however, in keeping with her reputation as a sorceress and very dangerous opponent, accepts Bard's account of his quarrel with Egil and prepares a poisoned drink to give to this insolent guest. Egil responds by carving runes stained with blood on the drinking horn and reciting a verse that has strong affinities with the poetic charms. The drinking horn immediately bursts—thus proving the malign intentions of Bard and demonstrating Egil's poetic and magical abilities. This episode presents Egil in a markedly Odinic light—carving runes, performing magic, and reciting poetry—but some of the most striking parallels to Egil's magic feat are hagiographic. According to Christian legend, Benedict, the founder of the

Benedictine order, warded off poison drink with the sign of the Cross, just as Egil did with runes.[4] At any rate the evening, pleasant as it has been, is drawing to a close, and Egil and Ǫlvir, who is about to pass out, decide to head back to their lodgings. Bard comes to the doorway, asking Ǫlvir to drink one more toast. Egil takes the horn and throws it down, makes one more verse, and stabs and kills Bard with the sword he was holding. Bard collapses, bleeding and dying, and Ǫlvir vomits and passes out while Egil escapes, first to his lodging where he gets his weapons, and then eventually to another island from which he eventually escapes after further adventures.

This narrative strikes one immediately as a swash-buckling (i.e., shield-pounding) Viking adventure story. Neither Egil nor Bard is, technically speaking, a Viking, although Egil did go viking later in his career, but the account of drunken violence at a "Viking" feast accords well with what we would expect at such an occasion. Heavy drinking, vomiting, poison, and finally a killing seem appropriate. One problem with this view of these chapters in *Egils saga* is that *Egils saga* itself is a deeply ironic and to some extent comic work. If this account of Viking adventure seems like a comic-book version of such adventure, it is important to remember that we are not reading a contemporary account of life in the Viking Age, but a narrative by an author who lived approximately two hundred and fifty years later and whose view of tenth-century Icelanders and Norwegians was to some degree detached and ironic. Even if we accept *Egils saga* as historically true in broad outline (and I am myself sympathetic to this position), the details of what unfolded at a feast two hundred and fifty years before the saga was written are unlikely to have been preserved in oral tradition without elaboration and modification. If we see these chapters as a fictional construct (although perhaps based on real events), then we can perhaps read them and understand them as allusive and symbolic narrative.

---

4. Gregory the Great, *Dialogorum libri iv*, II, 4; for a convenient edition with good notes see *Grégoire le Grand, Dialogues*, ed. Adalbert Vogüé, trans. Paul Antin, 3 vols., Sources chrétiennes 251, 260, 265 (Paris: Les Éditions du Cerf, 1978–80), 2:143. This parallel was first noted by Régis Boyer, "The Influence of Pope Gregory's Dialogues on Old Icelandic Literature," in *Procedings of the First International Saga Conference: University of Edinborough 1971*, ed. Peter Foote et al. (London: The Viking Society for Northern Research, 1973), 1–27. In his notes on this episode in the *Dialogi*, Vogüè gives references to classical and Christian analogues.

In these chapters the young Egil Skallagrimsson emerges, for the first time, as an adult poet, Odinic figure, and opponent of royal authority in Norway. The relationship between Egil and Eirik and Gunnhild, and between Egil's family and the Norwegian royal family, is one of the central themes of the saga, and these chapters are important in the larger structure of the saga for that reason alone. But this is a richly detailed narrative, and it is appropriate to think about the saga author's emphases and about the possible implications of these details.

This is a story about beer (or ale—there is some question about the exact nature of the alcoholic drink involved), vomit, blood, and poetry, and these apparently diverse items in my list are in fact associated in Old Norse Icelandic mythology in that the divine being Kvasir is created from the spittle of the Æsir and the Vanir, and then killed for his blood, which is mixed with honey and made into mead. The mead comes into the possession of the giant Suttung, who guards it jealously until it is stolen by Odin (after various adventures), who drinks the mead and then flies back to Asgard in the shape of an eagle, where he vomits the mead into a cauldron. This mead is the inspiration of poets, and various kennings defining poetry as a kind of drink or liquid are quite common. Poetry is thus defined as the mead of Odin, or the blood of Kvasir, or other similar locutions.

Roberta Frank has questioned the authenticity of some portions of these myths.[5] I am more impressed by the evidence for the archaism of the myth or, to be more precise, this complex of myths than Professor Frank is, but even Professor Frank would grant that the equation of poetry and intoxicating drink is a genuinely old poetic figure in this tradition. In any case one can always make the somewhat reductive argument that *Egils saga* shows close stylistic and conceptual affinities with Snorri Sturluson's known work, and a number of scholars (including Torfi H. Tulinius, fellow contributor to this volume) have proposed that Snorri was in fact the author of *Egils saga*. Thus, whether the myth of Kvasir in all its baroque complexity was genuinely old or

---

5. Roberta Frank, "Snorri and the Mead of Poetry," in *Speculum Norroenum: Studies in Memory of Gabriel Turville-Petre*, ed. Ursula Dronke et al. (Odense: Odense University Press, 1981), 155–70. One argument for the archaism of the complex of myths involving Kvasir is that much of this material (the origin of Kvasir and the service of Odin to Baugi, etc.) does not serve as the basis for kennings, so it is hard to see why Snorri would or could make it up out of whole cloth.

not, the myth would have been known and presumably accepted by Snorri himself or the member of his circle or admirer of his work who wrote *Egils saga* as we have it.

At any rate, accepting for the moment the claim that the various myths about Kvasir are genuinely archaic, one immediate point to make about this traditional material is the way in which "poetry" and "poetic inspiration," two different but clearly related concepts, are associated with a wide variety of bodily fluids. Kvasir himself is created from the mixing of bodily fluids, the saliva of the various Æsir and Vanir. The gods then reshape these fluids into a being who epitomizes wisdom. Kvasir is soon killed, and his blood, mixed with honey, is made into mead. The curiously matter-of-fact way in which this killing is narrated—the dwarves who kill Kvasir are never punished for their crime and the gods accept their claim that Kvasir burst because of being too wise without question and apparently without comment—suggests that this step in the transformation of Kvasir is not regarded as all that dramatic a change. For a being who was once a cauldron's worth of mingled saliva to become a cauldron of mead is not apparently a wholly unexpected transformation. At this point, however, Kvasir has been identified with three kinds of fluid: saliva, blood, and mead. The next steps in the story involve other kinds of liquid. In order to obtain the mead, Odin seduces the giant's daughter Gunnloðr and wins three drinks of mead by sleeping with her three times. The mead of poetry is thus exchanged for the gift of semen, and the story of Odin bringing the mead to Asgard involves two further forms of human fluid: vomit and excretion. Odin vomits the mead he has stolen into a vat the other gods have prepared for him, and since he is closely pursued by a giant in the form of a bird, he excretes some of the mead behind, which is henceforth known as the "skáldfífla hlutr" or poetic mead of foolish poets. Since as a matter of biological fact birds excrete liquid and solid waste together, one does not have to identify the exact nature of Odin's excreted mead.

The only human fluid that is omitted from this list is sweat. For the sake of completeness I am tempted to point out that since Odin serves Baugi in the place of nine agricultural workers for a summer season, ample sweat is implicit in this exchange. But Snorri's text does not mention sweat, and it is probably best not to press this interpretation. At any rate, these stories involve various kinds of human liquid that are transformed or exchanged to produce the mead of poetry. Thus in terms of these myths there is a sense in which poetry is blood and poetry is vomit, and the mead or intoxicating drink of poetry is the fundamental metaphoric equation of this tradition.

In the story of Egil's encounter with Bard the narrative is essentially realistic, but this story is the story of Egil's first appearance as an adult poet, and beer, vomit, blood, and poetry are all emphasized, and the mixing and blending of these various intellectual and material substances are striking. In the conclusion of Egil's encounter with Bard, Bard follows his guests to the door and tries to force one final horn of ale on his drunken and reluctant guests. Egil takes the horn, recites one last stanza of poetry, and throws the horn and the beer it contains on the floor. He then stabs Bard, killing him immediately, and the blood pours out of the wound. At this point, Ǫlvir passes out, vomits, and falls to the floor. Ǫlvir's name may possibly derive etymologically from the phrase "to consecrate ale"—an etymology which seems relevant in this context,[6] and in any case Egil plays on the similarity of "ǫl" and "Ǫlvir" in the verse he recites before he kills Bard. At any rate, at this juncture in the narrative, Egil runs away. When the king's men go out to the entrance of the hall Bard and Ǫlvir are so completely covered with blood and vomit that the men think they have killed each other. It takes a while to realize that while Bard is truly dead and the blood all his, Ǫlvir is simply passed out, lying on the floor covered with blood and vomit and ale. The floor is covered with ale, blood, and vomit and the moment when these substances were mixed was commemorated with poetry. I would argue that this scene thus evokes and suggests the complex of myths about Kvasir; that just as we recognize Odinic allusion or echoes of the myth of Ragnarǫk in various sagas, we should similarly be aware of mythic allusion to the stories about Kvasir in this scene.

Up to this point my argument has been based upon close reading of the relevant chapters of *Egils saga* and underscoring the potential relevance of various stories about Kvasir. But it must also be admitted that this saga narrative is essentially realistic. People do drink too

---

6. See Jan de Vries, *Altnordisches etymologisches Wörterbuch*, 3rd ed. (Leiden: Brill, 1977), *s.v.* "Ǫlvér." De Vries says the etymology is disputed but mentions the phrase "alu vígja" as potentially relevant.

much at feasts and parties, particularly when pressured by friends or an importunate host. And all one has to do is glance at a police blotter in any town or city in either Scandinavia or the English-speaking world to see countless examples of how heavy drinking leads to violence that prudent and sober men would have avoided. My argument presumes—a skeptical critic might say—that the audience of *Egils saga* would be so steeped in Old Norse-Icelandic myth as to read realistic narrative in terms of myth. How can I be sure, or at least reasonably sure, that even the ideal reader (the literary critic's own mythical construct) would not have read this perfectly realistic and reasonable story as simply a realistic and reasonable story without the elaborate structure of mythological allusion I have suggested? I do not think this is a trivial objection—my own response to much "mythological" criticism of the *Íslendingasögur* is often skeptical. I would like the sagas (or at least some of the sagas) to be richly allusive in their use of myth. But how can one simultaneously avoid modern critical over-reading and still understand the more subtle instances of mythic allusion and patterning in the sagas?

The question is a difficult one, but in this instance I have an answer for my imagined critic. The last verse Egil speaks before he kills Bard, the poetry that prefaces the mingling of blood, vomit, and ale that concludes this scene, is as follows:

Ǫlvar mik, því at Ǫlvi
ǫl gervir nú fǫlvan;
atgeira læt ek ýrar
ýring of grǫn skýra;
ǫllungis kannt illa,
oddskýs, fyr þér nýsa,
rigna getr at regni,
regnbjóðr, Hárs þegna.[7] (60, v. 10)

I am getting drunk [literally: "It ales me"]
because ale now makes Ǫlvir pale.

---

7. Bjarni Einarsson (60n) suggests that a disyllabic form of the Odinic name Hárs, i.e., Háars would be metrically preferable. Sigurður Nordal and Finnur Jónsson also previously supported this emendation.

I cause the liquid of the spears of the auroch
[beer from the drinking horn]
to flow over [my] mustache
You [Bard] can peer around very badly
[you, Bard, are not careful]
point-cloud's rain-offer-er
[he who offers the rain of battle / warrior]
With the rain of the thegns of the high one,
It begins to rain.

In the last four lines of the poem, Egil is telling Bard that he (Bard) is not being careful, which is an extreme understatement. Egil is about to kill him, and adapting the intricate and allusive language of the skaldic tradition, Egil is saying that he is reciting poetry as he concludes the stanza. But he does not say directly that he is reciting poetry—he uses a mythological kenning for poetry; he speaks of poetry as the "regn Hárs þegna," the rain of the thegns of the high one. The high one is Odin; the thegns of the high one are poets, and so the rain of the thegns of the high one is poetry. But how and why can we think of poetry as rain? The answer involves myth. When Odin in the shape of a creature of the air, an eagle, vomited mead into the cauldron which the gods had set out for him, liquid fell from the air to the earth, so poetry can be described as the rain of the High one, i.e., Odin.

This is the interpretation of these verses as accepted by all editors and commentators, but to my knowledge no one has commented on how the kenning and the conclusion of this verse relate to the action of the saga. As Egil speaks the last words of the stanza, "rigna getr at regni, regnbjóðr, Hávars þegna" (oh man who offers rain, it begins to rain with the rain of the thegns of the high one), he throws down the horn of beer and thrusts his sword through Bard's stomach while Ǫlvir collapses, his vomit mixing with Bard's blood and the beer on the floor. In order to understand the literal meaning of the figurative language of the poem, one has to know the genealogy, as it were, of the mead of poetry. If for some reason one has forgotten what ale, blood, vomit, and poetry have to do with each other, the process of unraveling the kennings of the poem forces one to review the myths of Kvasir. These mythic associations are then literalized on the floor of King Eirik's hall.

The broad claim that the sagas of the Icelanders sometimes allude to Old Norse-Icelandic myth has been made before for a variety of sagas, and some of the parallels that have been suggested seem to me quite plausible.[8] There has been less discussion of the literary implications of such allusion, but it occurs to me that mythic allusion in the *Íslendingasögur* is rather similar to typology in hagiographic narrative. Egil is a drunken, violent, insolent young man in these chapters, but he is also a character who "bears the person" (to adapt the language of exegesis) of someone other than himself.[9] Just as Andreas in the Old English *Andreas* brings a flood upon the wicked Meremedonians, those archetypal bad hosts, which is both a mighty sign in itself, and which evokes the patristic and early medieval understanding of baptism as a flood that destroys and yet saves,[10] so Egil's adventures in Eirik's hall echo and suggest myths about the origin and dissemination of poetic inspiration and poetry itself, the product of that inspiration.

It is a critical commonplace that Egil Skallagrimsson, the protagonist of *Egils saga*, is a figure embodying extraordinary contrasts, brutal yet sensitive, violent when provoked, but a good friend and a good neighbor otherwise, drunken and insolent on occasion, but at the same time genuinely wise in both a political sense and in his knowledge of both poetic craft and runes. On first reading, this account of Egil's adventures at Eirik's court seems like a combination of adventure story and gross comedy, and of course it is. But the author of *Egils saga*, the man or woman who gave final shape to the text we have, tells the story of Egil's mad youthful adventures in Norway in a way that suggests that poetry and poetic madness (furor, or to use the Old Norse-Icelandic term, "óðr") is both a gift and a potentially dangerous blessing. The mead of poetry is an intoxicating drink, and those who drink it are often more than a little mad. As Egil begins his adult career as a poet and a warrior he reenacts, as it were, the history of poetry itself, and if his adventures seem grossly comic and violent, this saga is also the story of a man frustrated in love and asking nothing more than courtesy and justice. This odd

---

8. For a useful introduction and survey of this large topic see Margaret Clunies Ross, *Prolonged Echoes: Old Norse myths in Medieval Northern Society*, 2 vols. (Odense: Odense University Press, 1994–1998), and Clunies Ross, ed., *Old Norse Myths, Literature and Society* (Odense: University Press of Southern Denmark, 2003).

9. See further Jeffrey Turco, "Loki, *Sneglu-Halla þáttr*, and the Case for a Skaldic Prosaics," in this volume.

10. See Thomas D. Hill, "Figural Narrative in *Andreas*: The Conversion of the Meremedonians," *Neuphilologische Mitteilungen* 70 (1969): 261–73, for documentation.

blend of sensitivity and violence is in effect both a comment upon and a reiteration of the myth of Kvasir, the divine wisdom, who was sacrificed and yet lives; who is the embodiment of the highest divine wisdom, and yet realized in grossly physical liquid form. Egil is both sublime and gross—to some extent he *is* poetry—and if we are offended by his behavior, we must remember that both poetic and real intoxication can be a blessing and a curse at the same time.

Bibliography

Boyer, Régis. "The Influence of Pope Gregory's Dialogues on Old Icelandic Literature." In *Proceedings of the First International Saga Conference: University of Edinburgh 1971*, edited by Peter Foote, Hermann Pálsson, and Desmond Slay, 1–27. London: The Viking Society for Northern Research, 1973.

Clunies Ross, Margaret, ed. *Old Norse Myths, Literature and Society.* Odense: University Press of Southern Denmark, 2003.

———. *Prolonged echoes: Old Norse Myths in Medieval Northern Society.* 2 vols. Odense: Odense University Press, 1994–98.

Egils saga. Edited by Bjarni Einarsson. London: Viking Society for Northern Research, 2003.

Egils saga Skalla-Grímssonar. Edited by Sigurður Nordal. Íslenzk fornrit 2. Reykjavík: Hið íslenzka fornritafélag, 1933.

Egils saga Skallagrímssonar: nebst den grösseren Gedichten Egils. Edited by Finnur Jónsson. Halle: Niemeyer, 1924.

Frank, Roberta. "Snorri and the Mead of Poetry." In *Speculum Norroenum: Studies in Memory of Gabriel Turville-Petre*, edited by Ursula Dronke, Guðrún P. Helgadóttir, Gerd Wolfgang Weber, and Hans Bekker-Nielsen, 155–70. Odense: Odense University Press, 1981.

Gregory the Great. *Dialogues.* Edited by Adalbert Vogüé. Translated by Paul Antin. 3 vols. Sources chrétiennes 251, 260, 265. Paris: Les Éditions du Cerf, 1978–80.

Hill, Thomas D. "Figural Narrative in *Andreas*: The Conversion of the Meremedonians." *Neuphilologische Mitteilungen* 70 (1969): 261–73.

Meissner, Rudolf. *Die Kenningar der Skalden: ein Beitrag zur skaldischen Poetik.* Bonn: K. Schroeder, 1921.

Sigurður Nordal. *Icelandic Culture.* Translated by Vilhjálmur T. Bjarnar. Ithaca: Cornell University Library, 1990.

Vries, Jan de. *Altnordisches etymologisches Wörterbuch.* 3rd ed. Leiden: Brill, 1977.

The Old Norse *Exempla* as Arbiters of Gender Roles in Medieval Iceland

Shaun F. D. Hughes

PURDUE UNIVERSITY

1. Gender Roles and Ecclesiastical Reform 1262–1350

In 1262 what became known as the *Gamli sáttmáli* (Old Covenant) was verified at the Alþingi and Iceland became part of the Kingdom of Norway.[1] By the time the last of the Icelandic chieftains had confirmed it in 1264, Hákon Hákonarson, king of Norway 1217–63, had died, to be succeeded by his son, Magnús Hákonarson, later known as *lagabœtir* (law-reformer) who ruled until 1280. He turned away from the expansionist policies of his father and set about consolidating royal power throughout his extensive and far-scattered realm. Before his death King Hákon had initiated moves to reform and to unify the Norwegian legal system, which at that time had a separate law code for each of the four *þing*-districts of the kingdom. His son, Magnús, earned the credit due for making this plan a reality. In 1267 Jón rauði (the Red) was consecrated archbishop of Niðaróss (Trondheim). He set about to bring the legal standing of the Northern church in line

---

1. Dates and historical references here and elsewhere are drawn from Gunnar Karlsson, *The History of Iceland* (Minneapolis: University of Minnesota Press, 2000). Patricia Pires Boulhosa claims in her *Icelanders and the Kings of Norway: Medieval Sagas and Legal Texts*, The Northern World 17 (Leiden: Brill, 2005), esp. ch. 3, that the surviving documents relating to the *Gamli sáttmáli* are fifteenth-century forgeries. Chapter 3 has separately appeared as *Gamli sáttmáli: tilurð og tilgangur*, trans. Már Jónsson, Smárit Sögufélags (Reykjavík: Sögufélag, 2006). Helgi Skúli Kjartansson challenges her interpretation of the evidence in "Gamli sáttmáli—hvað næst?" *Saga* 49 (2011): 133–53, and Boulhosa defends her position in "A Response to 'Gamli sáttmáli—hvað næst?'" *Saga* 49 (2011): 137–51.

with the practices of the rest of Europe. In particular he argued that the Church was responsible for determining and administering its own legal responsibilities. Although the narrative of his ultimately fruitless struggle with royal authority lies outside this study, it did have consequences for Iceland. In 1268 Jón rauði consecrated Árni Þorláksson bishop of Skálholt, a position he held until his death in 1298.[2] As might be expected, Árni was as zealous as Jón rauði in pursuing policies that would bring the practices of the Icelandic Church more in line with then-current European norms as expressed in canon law.

In 1271 King Magnús, as part of his policy of legal reform, sent to Iceland a new legal code, which gained the nickname *Járnsíða* (Ironsides).[3] It was not particularly popular but was in force until 1280 when it was replaced by a revised version, which came to be known as *Jónsbók* after the lawman Jón Einarsson (d. 1306), who was instrumental in preparing it and presenting it to the Alþingi. The major innovation of *Járnsíða* compared to the previous code, *Grágás*, is that there is no section of laws concerning the church (*Kristinna laga þáttr*), only a *Kristindómsbálkr* containing seven paragraphs affirming the Christian faith and the rights of the king and bishops.[4] This omission is thought to have been the result of the influence of archbishop Jón, and it was rectified when in 1275 bishop Árni presented a new legal code to the Alþingi based on Canon Law for governing the Church in Iceland.[5] This *Nýi kristinréttr* or, as it became known, *Kristinréttr Árna*, concerned itself with the administration of the Church, and took a much more prominent role in the regulation of marriage than had previously been the case, making the consent of the bride obligatory along with the publication of the banns for three weeks before the marriage and outlining in detail the degrees of consanguinity

---

2. See Gunnar Kristjánsson, ed., *Saga biskupsstólanna: Skálholt 950 ára—2006—Hólar 900 ára* (Reykjavík: Bókaútgáfan Hólar, 2006), 35–36.

3. See *Járnsíða og Kristinréttur Árna Þorlákssonar*, ed. Haraldur Bernharðsson et al., Smárit Sögufélags (Reykjavík: Sögufélag, 2005), especially the introduction, 13–25. The surviving text of the law code is published on 61–141.

4. Ibid., 68–73.

5. Ibid., 143–90. Soon after his consecration bishop Árni had published in 1269 a detailed series of ordinances (*skipan*) dealing with the administration of ecclesiastical affairs in his diocese, significant portions of which dealt with regulating gender relations. See in particular Jón Sigurðsson et al., eds., *Diplomatarium Islandicum: Íslenzkt fornbréfasafn*, 16 vols. (Copenhagen and Reykjavík: Hið íslenzka bókmenntafélag, 1857–1972), henceforth DI, 2:23–37.

within which marriage was forbidden.[6] It was one thing to pass this law and another thing to enforce it. There seems to have been resistance to its provisions, particularly in the diocese of Hólar, but the reality was that the old practices eventually had to be put aside.[7] Bishop Árni's other major reform, which he achieved just before his death, was to wrest control away from the secular authorities who claimed ownership of those churches still in private hands and the revenues associated with them. Eiríkur Magnússon *prestahatari* (the hater of clerics), king of Norway 1280–99, Jørund, archbishop of Niðaróss from 1287 to 1309), and bishop Árni concluded this agreement at Qgvaldsnes in Norway in 1297, bringing to a close the long and bitter struggle known as the *Staðamál* (affair over church property).[8]

In addition to bishop Árni Þorláksson, among the bishops who were particularly committed to ecclesiastical reform and with aligning the practices of the Icelandic church with those current in the rest of Europe, were Þorlákr Þórhallsson, bishop of Skálholt 1178–93 and Jón Halldórsson, bishop of Skálholt 1322–39,[9] all of whom also

---

6. Canon Law did confirm that men and women were equal in the sexual act in marriage, although in general it stressed gender inequality. See James A. Brundage, "Sexual Equality in Medieval Canon Law," in *Medieval Women and the Sources of Medieval History*, ed. Joel T. Rosenthal (Athens: University of Georgia Press, 1990), 66–79.

7. See Agnes S. Arnórsdóttir, *Property and Virginity: The Christianization of Marriage in Medieval Iceland, 1200–1600* (Aarhus: Aarhus University Press, 2010), 87–94. Henric Bagerius has shown how the changes in Icelandic social and sexual identity after the unification with Norway are reflected in the Icelandic *riddarasögur*; see *Mandom och mödom: Sexualitet, homosocialitet och aristokratisk identitet på det senmedeltida Island* (Gothenburg: Göteborgs Universitet, 2009). Sigríður Beck, in *I kungens frånvaro: Formeringen av en isländsk aristokrati 1271–1387* (Gothenburg: Göteborgs Universitet, 2011), charts the development of an Icelandic aristocracy along European lines in Iceland in response to the loss of independence.

8. For a brief overview of this contentious episode in early Icelandic ecclesiastical history see Gunnar Karlsson, *History of Iceland*, 96–99; see also the sections "Hverjir áttu kirkjurnar" and "Staðamál og kirkjueignir" in Gunnar F. Guðmundsson, *Íslenskt samfélag og Rómakirkja*, Kristni á Íslandi 2 (Reykjavík: Alþingi, 2000), 79–102. For a more detailed investigation, see Magnús Stefánsson, *Staðir og Staðamál: Studier i islandske egenkirkelige og beneficialrettlige forhold i middelalderen* (Bergen: Historisk Institutt, Universitetet i Bergen, 2000). Orri Vésteinsson outlines how secular chieftains came to control so much Church property in *The Christianization of Iceland: Priests, Power, and Social Change* (Oxford: Oxford University Press, 2000), 93–132.

9. Jón Halldórsson had entered the Dominican monastery in Bergen as a child and studied at Dominican-run universities in Paris and Bologna. See vol. 3 of *Biskupa sögur*, ed. Guðrún Ása Grímsdóttir, Íslenzk fornrit 17 (Reykjavík: Hið íslenzka fornritafélag, 1998), henceforth ÍF 17, cii-iv, and Gunnar Kristjánsson, *Saga biskupsstólanna*, 36–37.

concerned themselves with attempting to correct what they saw as
inappropriate aspects of the relationships between the sexes and what
they must have perceived as the inappropriate freedom women had
to act on their own behalf. In the period before the submission to
Norway in 1262, Icelandic society was hardly a feminist paradise, but
scholars such as Agnes S. Arnórsdóttir and Jenny Jochens have shown
how women had considerable freedom in initiating divorce;[10] that they
enjoyed certain privileges in inheriting property because of a kinship
system that was "bilaterally organized with a patrilineal tendency";[11]
and that they exercised considerable freedom as widows.[12] Iceland did
not have any urban centers and its position on the inhabitable fringe
of Europe made gender cooperation more important than gender
hierarchies. Nevertheless reform-minded bishops did what they
could to bring the situation in Iceland in line with Canon Law, under
which any rights and privileges for women were severely restricted.

He was also renowned for his fluency in Latin. See Shaun F. D. Hughes, "*Klári saga* as
an Indigenous Romance," in *Romance and Love in Late Medieval and Early Modern
Iceland: Essays in Honor of Marianne Kalinke*, ed. Johanna Denzin and Kirsten Wolf,
Islandica 54 (Ithaca: Cornell University Library, 2009), 142 (the references there to both
citations in footnote 30 should be to ÍF 17:405–06 and 383). It has seemed natural to
conclude that he was Norwegian in origin but there is good evidence to suggest that this
may not be the case. The entry in *Flateyjarannáll* for 1323 begins: "Kom út Jón byskup
Freygerðarson" (Bishop Jón, the son of Freygerðr, arrived in Iceland). See Gustav Storm,
ed., *Islandske Annaler indtil 1578* (Christiania [Oslo]: Grøndahl, 1888), 395. "Freygerðr"
is a rare but distinctly Icelandic name, and decidedly not Norwegian as is shown by the
entry in E. H. Lind, *Norsk-Isländska Dopnamn och fingerade Namn från Medeltiden*, 3
vols. (Uppsala: Lundequistska Bokhandeln, 1905–31), 1:283, although his father's name,
Halldór, is common to both areas. See further the discussion in Hughes, "*Klári saga*,"
137–38.

10. Jenny Jochens, *Women in Old Norse Society* (Ithaca: Cornell University Press,
1995), 55–61.

11. Agnes S. Arnórsdóttir, *Property and Virginity*, 32. A bilateral system allows the
transferal of property in the same generation whereas a partrilineal system transfers
property from one generation to the next. See further Agnes S. Arnórsdóttir, *Konur og
vígamenn: Staða kynjanna á Íslandi á 12. og 13. öld*, Sagnfræðirannsóknir 12 (Reykjavík:
Sagnfræðistofnun—Háskólaútgáfan, 1995), 78–104. On the position of women in general
during the settlement period, see Jenny Jochens, *Old Norse Images of Women*, Middle
Ages Series (Philadelphia: University of Pennsylvania Press, 1996).

12. Jochens, *Women in Old Norse Society*, 61–64. In *High-Ranking Widows in
Medieval Iceland and Yorkshire: Property, Power, Marriage and Identity in the Twelfth
and Thirteenth Centuries*, The Northern World 49 (Leiden: Brill, 2010), Philadelphia
Ricketts has shown that "many Icelandic widows did not remarry; most Yorkshire ones
did. A significant portion of Icelandic women had extra-marital relationships . . . most as
widows; only one Yorkshire woman conducted a liaison and that was before widowhood"
(299–300).

The Church was not just interested in regulating the private lives of women; men too were to have their behavior strictly controlled. In 1178 bishop Þorlákur issued a *skriftaboð* (penitential) primarily concerned with regulating sexual behavior.[13] Long before his *Kristinréttr* of 1275, bishop Árni had issued a *skriftaboð* in 1269 almost immediately after having become bishop.[14] Bishop Jón Halldórsson issued his *Bannsakabréf* (Letter outlining the grounds for excommunication) in 1326. Most of the twenty-four grounds listed are concerned with preserving the status of the Christian religion and protecting the privileges of the church and its functionaries.[15] However, the twenty-first ground excommunicates those who perform marriages between couples who are fourth cousins *(fermenningar)* or more closely related, and in a clarificatory paragraph to the document bishop Jón reiterates the prohibition on secret engagements or marriages.[16] Furthermore he ordered his clergy not to dignify second marriages with a nuptial mass.[17] Jón Þorkelsson posits that in the same year, 1326, bishop Jón reissued an expanded version of bishop Þorlákur's *skriftaboð.*[18] But the Church did not rely solely on legislation in its attempt to regulate attitudes toward gender roles and sexual behavior. It also adopted a thirteenth-century innovation that had done much to

---

13. For Þorlákr's penitential see DI 1:237–44. This penitential is remarkably frank about a wide range of sexual issues opening with the penance required for acts of bestiality and singling out lesbian activity.

14. DI 2:37–42 (5 versions). Paragraphs 13–15 deal with adultery (41).

15. Ibid., 2:582–94. While some have taken the *Bannsakabréf* to indicate that Jón was particularly distressed about the low level of sexual morality discernable in his diocese, Lára Magnúsardóttir has argued that Jón was just following the directions of Eilífr korti Árnason, archbishop of Niðaróss, 1309–33. See her *Bannfæring og kirkjuvald á Íslandi, 1275–1550* (Reykjavík: Háskólaútgáfan, 2007), 393–99. Strictly speaking this indeed may have been the case, but like Árni Þorláksson before him, Jón was ever zealous in carrying out the archbishop's wishes, as witness his exertions on Eilífur's behalf (1326–28) during the so-called "Möðruvallamál," in which he struggled to enforce the archbishop's edict that the monastery at Möðruvellir be re-established against the wishes of bishop Lárentíus Kálfsson of Hólar (1267–1330), who had confiscated its lands and income after the drunken monks had burned the cloister to the ground in 1316. See Torfi K. Stefánsson Hjaltalín, *Eldur á Möðruvöllum: Saga Möðruvalla í Hörgárdal frá öndverðu til okkar tíma,* 2 vols. (Reykjavík: Flateyjarútgáfan, 2001), 1:31–35, 47–48. Indeed Jón may in fact have prodded the archbishop to do something in the belief that the decree would have more weight if it originated with the archbishop himself.

16. DI 2:590–91, 593.

17. Agnes S. Arnórsdóttir, *Property and Virginity,* 119.

18. The two surviving versions of Jón's re-issue of this decree are found in DI 2:596–606.

revitalize popular preaching on the continent of Europe, particularly in the hands of the Dominican Order, or the Order of Friars Preachers, which had been officially recognized in 1216.

2. The *Exempla* as a Preaching Tool

The Dominican order was committed to combating heresy and strengthening the faith of lay communities through vigorous preaching in the vernacular. One of the rhetorical strategies used by preachers to achieve this was to sprinkle their sermons with appropriate anecdotes.[19] During the twelfth and thirteenth centuries the number of such collections of short narratives known as *exempla* multiplied.[20] These stories were gathered together to serve as aids in preaching and assisting in the composition of homilies and sermons. They were often arranged thematically. For example, the *Tractatus de diversis materiis predicabilibus* of the Dominican Étienne de Bourbon (d. 1262) was planned as seven massive volumes, each one dedicated to one of the gifts of the Holy Spirit. As it was, Étienne lived long enough to complete only the first four volumes and the opening portion of the fifth, in the

---

19. Compilations of edifying narratives already existed even before the founding of the Dominican Order, and one of the most important and influential collections was that known as the *Disciplina Clericalis* ("Clerical Instruction"), by Petrus Alfonsi, which became one of the most important of the preachers' handbooks. See John V. Tolan, *Petrus Alfonsi and His Medieval Readers* (Gainesville: University Press of Florida, 1993), 139–54. The Icelandic versions of this text will be discussed in section four below.

20. Among the major collections from which stories seem to have made their way to Iceland in the fourteenth century are: Caesarius of Heisterbach (ca. 1180-ca. 1246), *Dialogus miraculorum: Dialog über die Wunder*, ed. and trans. Nikolaus Nösges and Horst Schneider, 5 vols., Fontes Christiani 86 (Turnhout: Brepols, 2009), and *Dialogue on Miracles*, trans. H. von E. Scott and C. C. Swinton Bland, intro. G. G. Coulton, 2 vols. (London: G. Routledge, 1929); Étienne de Bourbon (d. 1262), *Tractatus de diversis materiis predicabilibus: Prologus, Prima Pars: De Dono timoris*, ed. Jacques Berlioz and Jean-Luc Eichenlaub, Corpus Christianorum, Continuatio Mediaevalis 124 (Turnhout: Brepols, 2002), and *Tractatus de diversis materiis predicabilibus: Liber tertius de eis que pertinent ad donum scientie et penitentiam*, ed. Jacques Berlioz, Corpus Christianorum Continuatio Mediaevalis 124 B (Turnhout: Brepols, 2006); *Anecdotes historiques: Légendes et apologues tirés du recueil inédit d'Étienne de Bourbon dominicain du XIIIe siècle*, ed. Albert Lecoy de la Marche (Paris: Renouard, 1877); Jacques de Vitry (ca. 1160/70-1240), *The Exempla or Illustrative Stories from the Sermones Vulgares*, ed. Thomas Frederick Crane (London: D. Nutt, 1890; repr. New York: Burt Franklin, 1971); Jean Gobi (fl. 1330), *La "Scala Cœli" de Jean Gobi*, ed. Marie-Anne Polo de Beaulieu (Paris: Éditions de CNRS, 1991); Thomas de Cantimpré (1201-1272), *Les exemples du "Livre des Abeilles": Une vision médiévale*, trans. Henri Platelle, Miroir du Moyen Âge (Turnhout: Brepols, 1997).

process managing to amass a collection of more than three thousand *exempla*.[21] Markus Schürer has shown how *exempla* collections such as that by the Dominican Thomas de Cantimpré (1201–1272), *Bonum universale de apibus*, helped define the religious community and to give it a particular group identity by emphasizing the ideals of the Dominican order and by reinforcing the ideals of the *vita religiosa* such as chastity, obedience, asceticism, humility.[22]

While there have been numerous formal studies of the *exempla*,[23] there has not been much interest in examining them in the light of how they arbitrate gender roles. One study that does take such an

---

21. A complete edition is underway, but to date only volumes 1 and 3 have appeared. So far only one *exemplum* (from the not-yet-edited second volume) has been identified among the Icelandic *exempla* as coming from the *Tractatus*, namely XLIV: "Af tveimr munkum" (Of two monks) in Hugo Gering, ed., *Íslendzk æventýri: Isländische Legenden, Novellen und Märchen*, 2 vols. (Halle: Buchhandlungen des Waisenhauses, 1882–83), henceforth *ÍÆ*, 1:147–49 (here and following, Roman numerals refer to the number of the *exemplum* of Gering's edition, Arabic numerals to the volume number and page number followed by line number when needed). This also happens to be one of the *exempla* associated with Jón Halldórsson (for a Latin text see: *Anecdotes historiques, exemplum* 79, pp. 75–76).

22. Markus Schürer, *Das Exemplum oder die erzählte Institution: Studien zum Beispielgebrauch bei den Dominikanern und Franziskanern des 13. Jahrhunderts*, Vita Regularis 23 (Berlin: LIT, 2005), 129–47, 154–60, 300. There is no modern edition of Thomas' work, but a translation is available: *Les exemples du "Livre des Abeilles,"* trans. Henri Platelle. Gering notes that *exemplum* LXXXVI (which is another of those he attributes to bishop Jón Halldórsson): "Af konu einni kviksettri" (Of a woman buried alive) [*ÍÆ* 1:254–56; Gering's title] is based on no. 219 in Platelle's translation (252–53), and Gering notes similarities between what are Platelle's nos. 188 and 185 (222–23, 219–220) and his *exempla* XXXVI: "Frá prestakonu er tekin varð af djöflunum" (Of the priest's wife who became taken by devils) [1:124–26; Gering's title] and XXXIX: "Af konu er drýgði hórdóm við föður sinn" (Of the woman who committed adultery with her father) [1:129–33; Gering's title]—but see note 103 below.

23. See for example: Jean-Thiébaut Welter, *L'Exemplum dans la littérature religieuse et didactique du moyen âge*, Bibliothéque d'histoire ecclésiastique de France (Paris: Occitania, 1927; repr. New York: AMS Press, 1973); Suzanne Baumgarte, ed., *Summa bonorum: Eine deutsche Exempelsammlung aus dem 15. Jahrhundert nach Stephan von Bourbon*, Texte des späten Mittelalters und der frühen Neuzeit 40 (Berlin: Erich Schmidt, 1999); Jonathan Burgoyne, *Reading the Exemplum Right: Fixing the Meaning of "El Conde Lucanor,"* North Carolina Studies in the Romance Languages and Literature 289 (Chapel Hill: University of North Carolina Press, 2007); Fritz Kemmler, *"Exempla" in Context: A Historical and Critical Study of Robert Mannyng of Brune's "Handlying Synne,"* Studies and Texts in English 6 (Tübingen: Gunter Narr, 1984); Tolan, *Petrus Alphonsi*; and the relevant essays in Bernd Engler and Kurt Müller, eds., *Exempla: Studien zur Bedeutung und Funktion exemplarischen Erzählens*, Schriften zur Literaturwissenschaft 10 (Berlin: Duncker & Humblot, 1995); Walter Haug and Burghart Wachinger, eds., *Exempel und Exempelsammlungen*, Fortuna vitrea: Arbeiten zur literarischen Tradition zwischen dem 13. und 16. Jahrhundert 2 (Tübingen: Niemeyer, 1999).

approach is by Jacques Berlioz and Marie Anne Polo de Beaulieu.[24] In his part of the essay Berlioz observes: "Needless to say, the image of women conveyed in the collections of *exempla* as well as in the moral treatises is largely negative,"[25] and although he does concede there are some *exempla* that do portray virtuous women, he suggests that these stories are most useful for their details of everyday life and the glimpses they give of medieval gender relations. Marie Anne Polo de Beaulieu examines the use of the words *mulier* and *femina*, as well as other words for women, in the 972 *exempla* in the *Scala Cœli* by the Dominican Jean Gobi the Younger, compiled 1320–30. Again while there are some examples in the collection that portray virtuous women, Polo de Beaulieu is forced to conclude: "Gobi cannot find enough harsh words to denounce women's vices that stem not from passing temptation but from her sinful nature."[26]

Of the many thousands of *exempla* preserved in medieval collections, only a little over one hundred survive in Icelandic versions. These seem to have entered the country in two waves. The first was in the early fourteenth century, and many of these narratives are associated with Bishop Jón Halldórsson and are preserved in AM 657 a-b 4° (mid-fourteenth century). The second wave was in the fifteenth century, and the majority of these stories are translated from Middle English, particularly from the *Handlyng Synne* (finished 1303) of Robert Manning of Brunne,[27] itself translated from the anonymous thirteenth-century Anglo-Norman poem *Le Manuel des Péchés*.[28]

---

24. Jacques Berlioz and Marie Anne Polo de Beaulieu, "*Exempla*: A Discussion and a Case Study, 1: *Exempla* as a Source for the History of Women, 2: *Mulier* and *Femina*: The Representation of Women in the *Scala celi* of Jean Gobi," in Rosenthal, *Medieval Women*, 37–65. I have not seen the unpublished "Mémoire de maîtrise" (University of Paris IV) by Elizabeth Flüry-Hérard, "L'image de la femme dans les exempla, XIIIe siècle" (1975).

25. Berlioz and Polo de Beaulieu, "*Exempla*: A Discussion," 44.

26. Ibid., 60.

27. Robert Manning of Brunne, "*Handlyng Synne*" and its French Original, ed. Frederick J. Furnivall, Early English Text Society, o.s. 119, 123 (Millwood, NY: Kraus, 1988; first published 1901–03); *Handlyng Synne*, ed. Idelle Sullens, Medieval and Renaissance Texts and Studies 14 (Binghamton, NY: CMRS, SUNY, 1983).

28. There is no scholarly edition of this poem sometimes ascribed to a certain William of Waddington. Furnivall provides the relevant sections in his EETS edition (see previous note) and a somewhat fuller selection in Robert Manning of Brunne, "*Handlyng Synne*" (*Written A.D. 1303*) *with the French Treatise on which it is Founded*, "*Le Manuel des Pechiez*" *by William of Wadington*, ed. Frederick J. Furnivall (London: Roxburghe Club, 1862). See also E. J. Arnould, "*Le Manuel des Péchés*": *Étude de literature religieuse*

This period of activity in translating texts from English into Icelandic is probably to be associated with the time 1425–40 when English clerics were appointed as Bishops of Hólar.[29] Because they are for the most part translated from continental models, these short narratives have not excited much interest outside of the preparation of editions and associated source studies. Nor do the *exempla* leave many traces in subsequent Icelandic literary history, except for *Jónatas ævintýri* and *Af þrimr þjófum í Danmörk (Sagan af ill, verra og verst)*, both of which proved popular enough to be made into *rímur* and survive in subsequent prose retellings.[30]

Anglo-Normande (XIIIme siècle) (Paris: Droz, 1940). Arnould dates the poem to the second half of the fourteenth century (253) and concludes that the question of authorship remains open (245–49), it not even being clear which Waddington this William is associated with.

29.   These were John Craxton (1425–35) and John Bloxwich (1435–40). Robert Wodborn was appointed bishop in 1441, but never came to the country. See Gunnar Kristjánsson, *Saga biskupsstólanna*, 415–16. Einar G. Pétursson has edited the English-based *exempla* in *Miðaldaævintýri þýdd úr ensku*, Rit 11 (Reykjavík: Stofnun Árna Magnússonar á Íslandi, 1976). See also Peter A. Jorgensen, "Ten Icelandic Exempla and their Middle English Source," *Opuscula* 4, Bibliotheca Arnamagnæana 30 (Copenhagen: Munksgaard, 1970), 177–207; "Four Æventyri," *Opuscula* 5, Bibliotheca Arnamagnæana 31 (Copenhagen: Munksgaard, 1975), 295–328; "The Icelandic Translations from Middle English," in *Studies for Einar Haugen*, ed. Evelyn Scherabon Firchow et al., Janua linguarum, Series maior 59 (The Hague: Mouton, 1972), 305–20; Jonna Louis-Jensen, "Nogle Æventyri," *Opuscula* 5, Bibliotheca Arnamagnæana 31 (Copenhagen: Munksgaard, 1975), 263–77. Ólafur Halldórsson, in "AM 240 fol XV: tvinn úr handriti með ævintýrum," *Gripla* 18 (2007): 23–46, identifies a four-page fragment (AM 240 fol., XV) as coming from a manuscript containing *exempla* translated from English. Of the six whole or fragmentary stories, for the first see *Miðaldaævintýri þýdd úr ensku, exemplum* 27, p. 72, line 81, to p. 80, line 136; for the third, the last two lines of *exemplum* 4, p. 6, lines 13–14; and for the sixth, *exemplum* 4, p. 7, line 1, to p. 8, line 20. The second, an *exemplum* about the power of the Eucharist to punish wickedness, is found in several English manuscripts including British Library MS Royal 18 B xxiii (ca. 1450). See Woodburn O. Ross, ed., *Middle English Sermons: Edited from British Museum MS. Royal 18 B xxiii*, Early English Text Society 209 (London: Oxford University Press, 1940), 62. However, the version in Shrewsbury school MS 3, as retold by Beth Allison Barr, appears closer to the Icelandic fragment; see *The Pastoral Care of Women in Late Medieval England*, Gender in the Middle Ages 3 (Woodbridge: Boydell Press, 2008), 119.

30.   "Jónatas ævintýr," which is based on an English version of the *Gesta Romanorum*, was not edited by Gering. The *ævintýr*, the sixteenth-century *rímur* based on it, and the prose retelling of the *rímur* have all been critically edited by Peter A. Jorgensen, *The Story of Jonatas in Iceland*, Rit 45 (Reykjavík: Stofnun Árna Magnússonar á Íslandi, 1997). *Þjófarímur* (sixteenth century), based on Gering's *exemplum* XC: "Af þrimr þjófum í Danmörk" (*ÍÆ* 1:276–86; Gering's title), for which no direct source is attested although the story itself is widespread, remains unpublished. See Björn K. Þórólfsson, *Rímur fyrir 1600*, Safn Fræðafjelagsins um Ísland og Íslendinga 9 (Copenhagen: Möller, 1934), 453–54.

But there are signs that the Icelandic *exempla* did play a role in the Church's attempts to control gender relations on the island. However, before taking up this issue something needs to be said about the way in which medieval Icelandic authors and scribes refer to them.

3. Problems in defining the *Exempla* in Icelandic

As Thomas Frederick Crane states in the introduction to his edition of the *exempla* taken from the *Sermones vulgares* of Jacques de Vitry (ca. 1165–1240), the use of the word *exemplum* in the meaning "an illustrative story," first began to appear around 1200, and found its justification in section fifteen of the thirty-eighth homily of St. Gregory's *Forty Gospel Homilies*,[31] where Gregory states: "Sed quia nonnunquam mentes audientium plus exempla fidelium quam docentium verba convertunt" (The example of the faithful often transforms the hearts of listeners more than a teacher's words).[32] The term *exemplum* has proved difficult to define,[33] that is, to determine a definition for it that distinguishes it from similar short narratives such as *parabola* (parable), *fabula* (fable) and *similitudo* (analogy, parable),[34] and it has proven even more difficult to translate. From the point of view of modern scholarship, Claude Brémond et al. define the medieval exemplum as: "Un récit bref donné comme

---

31. Jacques de Vitry, *Exempla*, xviii. Crane's definition and discussion are referred to with approval by Welter, *L'Exemplum*, 1–3.

32. *Quadraginta homilarium in Evangelia libri duo*, ed. J. P. Migne, Patrologia Latina 76 (Paris: Migne, 1849), col. 1290; *Forty Gospel Homilies*, trans. Dom David Hurst, Cistercian Studies Series 123 (Kalamazoo, MI: Cistercian Publications, 1990), 351. Bruno Judic quotes this passage in his survey of the use of the word *exemplum* in Gregory's work as a whole. See "Grégoire le Grand et la notion d'*exemplum*," in *Le Tonnerre des exemples: Exempla et médiation culturelle dans l'Occident médiéval*, ed. Marie Anne Polo de Beaulieu et al., Collection "Histoire" (Rennes: Presses Universitaires de Rennes, 2010), 135.

33. For a survey of the issues involved, see ch. 1, "Définitions et problèmes," in Claude Brémond et al., *L'"Exemplum,"* 2nd ed., Typologie des Sources du moyen âge occidental, fascicle 40 (Turnholt: Brepols, 1996), 27–38.

34. See, for example, the first three essays in Haug, *Exempel und Exempelsammlungen*: Fritz Peter Knapp, "Mittelalterliche Erzählgattungen im Lichte scholastischer Poetik," 1–22; Peter von Moos, "Die Kunst der Antwort: Exempla und dicta im lateinischen Mittelalter," 23–57; Klaus Grubmüller, "Fabel, Exemple, Allegorese: Über Sinnbildungsverfahren und Verwendungszusammenhänge," 58–76. Especially useful is the diagram at the conclusion of Knapp's essay (22). Kemmler also refers to the *exempla* as "the evasive genre" (*"Exempla" in Context*, 154–68).

véridique et destiné á être inséré dans un discours (en général un sermon) pour convaincre un auditoire par une leçon salutaire" (A short account presented as factual and intended to be inserted into a narrative [usually a sermon] in order to persuade an audience through a salutary lesson).[35] However, when it came to providing a suitable translation for the word *exemplum* into Old Norse a number of problems presented themselves.

The roots of this difficulty lie in the fact that in his translation of the Greek New Testament into Latin, Jerome chose to render the Greek word παραβολή (comparison) as both *similitudo* (as for example in Luke 13:6) and *parabola* (as for example in Luke 15:3). Both of these verses were commented upon by St. Gregory in his *Forty Gospel Homilies*, and this work was among the very earliest patristic material translated into Icelandic, a task undertaken in the twelfth century. The Homilies on Luke 13:6 (Homily 31) and Luke 15:3 (Homily 34) are preserved and are found in AM 677 4°, a manuscript from the first half of the thirteenth century, although there are significant losses to the text of Homily 31.[36] What is interesting is that the translator chooses one word, *dæmisaga*, to render both *similitudo* and *parabola*.[37] We do not know how the

---

35. Claude Brémond et al., *L'"Exemplum,"* 37–38, translation mine. Kemmler (*"Exempla" in Context*, 155–66) gives a number of reasons why this definition "is not adequate enough" (166), but it is sufficient for the discussion here.

36. The surviving homilies in order of appearance are nos. 26 (incomplete), 29, 30, 40, 36, 34, 39, 38 (incomplete), 33 (incomplete) 31 (incomplete). They have all appeared in: Þorvaldur Bjarnason, ed., *Leifar fornra kristinna frœða íslenzkra* (Copenhagen: Hagerup, 1878), 19–86. For a discussion of AM 677 4°, see Konráð Gíslason, *Um frum-parta íslenzkrar túngu í fornöld* (Copenhagen: S. Trier, 1846), xciii-xcix. There (xciii-xciv) he says that the manuscript is "sjálfsagt snemma á fyrra hlut 15. aldar" (clearly early in the first part of the fifteenth century). "15. aldar" must be a misprint for "13. aldar," as that is how Þorvaldur Bjarnason quotes the passage (xiii), and when Konráð Gíslason edits the twenty-ninth homily in his *Fire og fyrretyve . . . prøver af oldnordisk sprog og literatur* (Copenhagen: Gyldendal, 1860), 459–67, it is introduced (viii) as being "efter den fortræffelige Membran, fra den første Halvdeel af det 13. Aarh., AM. 677 Qv" (taken from the splendid vellum manuscript from the first half of the thirteenth century, AM. 677 4°).

37. Þorvaldur Bjarnason, *Leifar*, 57 and 85, respectively. The word *dæmisaga* is used twice in an earlier text, the Old Icelandic Homily Book. See Andrea de Leeuw van Weenen, ed., *Lemmatized Index to The Icelandic Homily Book: Perg. 15 4° in the Royal Library Stockholm*, Rit 61 (Reykjavík: Stofnun Árna Magnússonar á Íslandi, 2004), 29. The Homily Book is preserved in a manuscript dated to around 1200. See Andrea de Leeuw van Weenen, ed., *The Icelandic Homily Book: Perg. 15 4° in the Royal Library Stockholm*, Íslensk handrit: Studies in Quarto 3 (Reykjavík: Stofnun Árna Magnússonar á Íslandi, 1993), 10. However, it is not possible to determine on the basis of these two usages, folio

translator rendered Gregory's *exemplum* in section 15 of Homily 38 mentioned above, because unfortunately there is a lacuna in AM 677 4° affecting much of this homily and the beginning of Homily 33. However, the word *exemplum* appears twice in the surviving text of Homily 33 and on both occasions it is translated by a form of *dæmi*.[38] Even though *dæmisaga* may have first been used with

---

63ᵛ, line 5, and folio 70ᵛ, line 33, what if any Latin word the author of the individual homilies was adapting. See Theodor Wisén, ed., *Homilíu-Bók: Isländska homilier eftir en handskrift från tolfte århundradet* (Lund: Gleerups, 1872), p. 139, line 14; p. 154, line 14, and Sigurbjörn Einarsson et al., eds., *Íslensk hómilíubók: fornar stólræður* (Reykjavík: Hið íslenska bókmenntafélag, 1993), 198 and 221. Matthew 25:14–30 is also referred to as a *dæmisaga* in *Stjórn: Gammelnorsk Bibelhistoria*, ed. C. R. Unger (Christiania [Oslo]: Feilberg and Landmark, 1862), 150; *Stjórn*, ed. Reidar Astås, 2 vols., Norrøne Tekster 8 (Oslo: Riksarkivet, 2009), 1:226.

38. Homily 33: "Cujus enim vel saxeum pectus illae hujus peccatricis lacrymae ad exemplum poenitendi non emolliant?" (*Quadraginta homilarium*, col. 1239), "Whose heart is so stony that this sinful woman's tears wouldn't soften it with her example of repentance" (*Forty Homilies*, 269), "því að tár þessar syndugrar konu hræra steinleg hjörtu úr til iðrunnar dæmis" (Þorvaldur Bjarnason, *Leifar*, 79—normalized); "et poenitentem peccatricem mulierem in exemplum vobis imitationis anteferte" (*Quadraginta homilarium*, col. 1245), "and bring before you the repentant sinful woman as an example for you to imitate" (*Forty Homilies*, 278), "og gáið eftir iðrunnar dæmum þessar syndugrar konu" (Þorvaldur Bjarnason, *Leifar*, 85). Note that Snorri Sturluson uses *dæmi* at least ten times in his *Edda* in places where it could without straining be translated as "story, example": *Edda: Prologue and Gylfaginning*, ed. Anthony Faulkes, 2nd ed. (London: Viking Society for Northern Research, 1988), ch. 34 (28.8) ("proofs," 28); ch. 41 (34.14) ("evidence," 34); *Edda: Skáldskaparmál*, ed. Anthony Faulkes, 2 vols. (London: Viking Society for Northern Research, 1998), ch. 1 (6.3) ("story," 65); ch. 2 (6.30) ("examples," 66); ch. 2 (8.22) ("example," 67); ch. 3 (14.19) (not translated as such, 72); ch. 7 (18.1) ("account," 75); ch. 17 (20.30) ("stories," 77); ch. 33 (41.13) ("in imitation," 95). Translations from Snorri Sturluson, *Edda*, trans. Anthony Faulkes, Everyman's Library (London: Dent, 1987). Hermann Pálsson finds in *Hrafnkels saga* "ýmis einkenni dæmisögu" (various characteristics of the *dæmisaga*) in *Úr hugmyndaheimi Hrafnkels sögu og Gretlu*, Studia Islandica 39 (Reykjavík: Menningarsjóður, 1981), 14. In chapter 4, "Forn dæmi," he translates "Fabula ostendit" as "Dæmisaga sýnir" (58), and it is clear that by *dæmisaga* he means the Æsopian *fabula* (a moral tale in which the chief protagonists are animals) with its *epimythium* or moral that comes after the narrative and comments on it; see also his *Sagnagerð: Hugvekjur um fornar bókmenntir* (Reykjavík: Almenna bókafélagið, 1982), 36–44, 91–92. Sverrir Tómasson, in "Helgisögur, mælskufræði og forn frásagnarlist," *Skírnir* 157 (1983): 154, rightly takes him to task for using *dæmisaga* in the sense of *fabula* since *exemplum* is a more appropriate translation—and in *Formálar íslenskra sagnaritara á miðöldum*, Rit 33 (Reykjavík: Stofnun Árna Magnússonar á Íslandi, 1988), 280–85, Sverrir discusses the particular use of *dæmi* in the historiography of Ari fróði Þorgilsson and Snorri. Possibly in response to Sverrir's criticism, Hermann later equates the *fabula* and the *exemplum* in the phrase "dæmisögur bæði klassískar og kristnar" (*dæmisögur* both classical and Christian), a conflation for which there is no evidence in Medieval Icelandic. See *Mannfræði Hrafnkels sögu og frumþættir*, Íslensk ritskýring 3 (Reykjavík: Menningarsjóður, 1988), 63. For example, Petrus Alfonsi in the *Disciplina clericalis* refers to his stories as *fabulae* three times: *Petri Alfonsi Disciplina clericalis*, ed. Alfons Hilka and Werner Söderhjelm, 3 vols., Acta societatis scientiarum Fennicae 38.4–5, 49.4

religious connotations, it was soon appropriated by secular writers for a short narrative without "a salutary lesson," at least in the moral sense (here translated as "anecdote"). For example, in the *Eirspennill* version of *Hákonar saga Hákonarsonar* (AM 47, fol., early fourteenth century), it states that "Eptir þat sagði hann [Hákon Hákonarson] dœmisǫgu þá er Sverrir konungr var vanr at segja" (After that Hákon Hákonarson told that anecdote that King Sverrir was accustomed to tell).[39] Therefore, when the *exempla* begin to appear in Icelandic in the early fourteenth century, their translators faced something of a dilemma in determining how to refer to them. Even though they were intended to have some kind of moral lesson, these short narratives must have been felt to have been qualitatively different from the similar stories found in the Gospels, in the same way that Oddur Gottskálksson (ca. 1514–1556) chose to abandon *dœmisaga* with its religious and secular connotations in his translation of the New Testament published in Roskilde in 1540.[40] Therefore, while the

(Helsinki: Druckerei der Finnischen Literaturgesellschaft, 1911–22), 1: *Lateinischer Text* 2.5; 9.17; 16.10. Only the last of these is translated into Icelandic in Sth. Pap. fol. nr. 66 (1690, but based on the lost vellum codex Ormsbók, ca. 1400), where *fabulas* is rendered as *sögur* (ÍÆ 1:180.2). And where Petrus on one occasion uses *exemplum* (*Disciplina clericalis*, Hilka, 1:15.14), the Icelandic translator uses *æventýr* (ÍÆ 1:178.21). Tolan discusses the particular sense of *fabula* in the *Disciplina clericalis* (*Petrus Alfonsi*, 82) and is of the opinion that the use of *exemplum* in the rubrics of stories present in many manuscripts did not originate with Petrus (*Petrus Alfonsi*, 235n36).

39. *Eirspennill: Nóregs konunga sögur*, ed. Finnur Jónsson (Christiania [Oslo]: Julius Thømte, 1916), 601 (normalized). The reference is to Sverrir's speech to his men before the battle at Íluvellir in chapter 47 of *Sverris saga*, ed. Þorleifur Hauksson, Íslenzk fornrit 30 (Reykjavík: Hið íslenzka fornritafélag, 2007), 72–73. Finnur Jónsson (vii) dates AM 47 fol. "uden tvivl til det 14 årh.s første fjærdedel, sikkert ikke senere" (without question to the first quarter of the fourteenth century, certainly not later). Similarly in reference to a secular event, the narrator of the AM 310 4° (late thirteenth-century) version of the Icelandic translation of the lost Latin life of Óláfr Tryggvason by the monk Oddr Snorrason (second half of the twelfth century) comments on the truth quotient of the account just given (ch. 45) of the battle between the hart that fled the dying body of Þórir hjǫrtr and the king's dog, Vígi, stating, "er ver segiom fra slicum lutum oc dômisogum. þa dômum ver þat eigi sannleik at sua hafi verit. helldr hyggiom ver at sua hafi synnz þui at fiandinn er fullr up flærðar oc illzku" (when we narrate such matters and anecdotes then we do not judge that to be the truth that so it has been, rather we think that so it may have seemed to have happened because the devil is filled up with falsehood and ill-will). *Saga Óláfs Tryggvasonar af Oddr Snorrason munk*, ed. Finnur Jónsson (Copenhagen: Gad, 1932), 142–43.

40. Oddur renders *similitudo* (Luke 13:6) and *parabola* (Luke 15:3) consistently as *eftirlíking*. Oddur Gottskálksson, *Nýja testamenti Odds Gottskálkssonar*, ed. Sigurbjörn Einarsson et al. (Reykjavík: Lögberg, 1988), 154, 158. Oddur made his translation principally from the Vulgate but with an eye to Martin Luther's translation among others. Luther follows the Greek and uses a single word, *Gleichnis* for παραβολή. See *Biblia, das*

268 New Norse Studies

term *dæmisaga* is occasionally applied to the *exempla*, a new term, *ævintýr* ("chance," "fortune," as well as "adventure," "happening"), came into use as a loanword from Middle Low German *eventür*.[41] While *ævintýr* continued to be used in the general sense of "adventure" even as late as the eighteenth century,[42] it soon came to refer specifically to the *exemplum* and then later in the form *ævintýri* to the folk-tale while *dæmisaga* was used to refer to the fable.[43]

ist, die gantze Heilige Schrift Deutsch, trans. Martin Luther (Wittenberg: Hans Lufft, 1534; repr. in 2 vols. Cologne: Taschen, 2004), vol. 2, folios 49ʳ, 50ᵛ. Jón Helgason in his analysis of Oddur's translation used a modern edition of Luther based on an edition of 1545. See Málið á Nýja Testamenti Odds Gottskálkssonar, Safn Fræðafjelagsins um Ísland og Íslendinga 7 (Copenhagen: Möller, 1929; repr. Rit um íslenska málfræði 4, Reykjavík: Málvísindastofnun Háskóla Íslands, 1999), 177. In his glossary to Oddur's work (240), he notes the use of eptirlíking with the comment: "Orðið 'dæmisaga' er ekki til" (The word dæmisaga does not exist). Eftirlíking is a word Oddur would have found in Stjórn, a text for which there is ample evidence he was familiar with, as for example in the paraphrase of "The Testament of the Twelve Patriarchs" inserted at the end of Genesis ("Testament of Zebulun"); see Unger, 243, and Astås, 1:366. Note that in both versions of the fifteenth-century translation of the Bible associated with John Wycliffe, similitudo is translated as lyknesse (Luke 13:6) and parabola as parable (Luke 15:3), a practice that had been abandoned by the time of the 1611 Authorized Version. John Wycliffe and his Followers, The Holy Bible, ed. Josiah Forshall and Frederic Madden, 4 vols. (Oxford: Oxford University Press, 1850), 4:193 and 198.

41. This was a borrowing from Old French *aventure* (something that must or might come to pass, an occurrence, adventure). See Pekka Katara, *Das französische Lehngut in mittelniederdeutschen Denkmälern von 1300 bis 1600*, Mémoires de la Société Néophilologique de Helsinki 30 (Helsinki: Société Néophilologique, 1966), 24–25, *s.v.* "aventür(e)." In Middle Low German are found both *aventür* and *eventür* (see Katara, *Das französische Lehngut*, 25) but it is the latter form that prevailed in the Scandinavian languages. Note the use of *ævintýr* in Stjórn (Unger, 7; cf. Astås, 1:13): "þeir uissu eigi sitt eptirkomanda æuintyr" (they did not know their future fortune); also (Unger, 64; cf. Astås, 1:95): "Jonithus saa fyrir nockur þau tidindi ok æuintyr er lǫngu sidarr komu framm" (Jonitus saw in the future those happenings and events that much later came to pass). Note as well how the doublet *tíðindi og ævintýr* here translates the Latin *eventus* (occurrence, event, good fortune, success): "Jonithus iste futuros quosdam eventus praevidit"; Petrus Comestor, *Historia scholastica*, ed. J. P. Migne, *Patrologia Latina* 198 (Paris: Migne, 1855), ch. 37, "*De dispersione filiorum Noe, et Nemrod*" (col. 1088C). Finally, note the translation of Genesis 41:13 (Unger, 202; cf. Astås, 1:304): "eptir þi sem huars ockars audna ok æuintyr gekk sidan" (according to how the fortune and good luck of each of us turned out later), where the doublet *audna ok æuintyr* translates the Vulgate's *eventus*: "audivimus quidquid postea rei probavit eventus." Standard definitions of *dæmisaga* and *ævintýri* can be found in Lauritz Bødker, *Folk Literature (Germanic)*, International Dictionary of Regional European Ethnology and Folklore 2 (Copenhagen: Rosenkilde and Bagger, 1965), 21–22, 65.

42. Steinunn Finnsdóttir (ca. 1641–1710) says in the eleventh stanza to the first fitt of *Hyndlu rímur*: "Ævintýr mun ei so leit / ef menn sér það kynna" (The "adventure" will not be so boring, if people familiarize themselves with it). Steinunn Finnsdóttir, *Hyndlu rímur og Snækóngs rímur*, ed. Bjarni Vilhjálmsson, Rit Rímnafélagsins 3 (Reykjavík: Rímnafélagið, 1950), 4.

43. The earliest surviving translations of the *fabulae* of Æsop into Icelandic are found

in the prologue to *Adonias (also Adonius) saga* (ca. 1400) found only in AM 593a 4⁰ (fifteenth century). See Agnete Loth, ed., *Late Medieval Icelandic Romances*, 5 vols., Editiones Arnamagnæanæ B20–24 (Copenhagen: Munksgaard, 1962–1965), 3:69–74, and Ole Widding, "Om Rævestreger: Et kapitel i Adonius saga," *Opuscula* 1, Bibliotheca Arnamagnæana 20 (Copenhagen: Munksgaard, 1960), 331–34. Here is found a version of "The Raven and the Fox," tale no. 124 as catalogued by Ben Edwin Perry, ed., *Aesopica: A Series of Texts Relating to Aesop or Ascribed to Him or Closely Connected with the Literary Tradition that Bears his Name*, new ed. (Urbana: University of Illinois Press, 2007), 381, although with details from an unidentified source, and a brief version of Perry 155 "The Wolf and the Lamb," in the version made popular by Phaedrus as the opening narrative to book 1 of his collection. See Sverrir Tómasson, "The 'Fræðisaga' of Adonias," in *Structure and Meaning in Old Norse Literature: New Approaches to Textual Analysis and Literary Criticism*, ed. John Lindow et al., The Viking Collection: Studies in Northern Civilization 3 (Odense: Odense University Press, 1986), 381–84, and Tómasson, *Formálar*, 292–95. The author of the prologue chooses not to employ Icelandic terminology to introduce these stories, but uses the Latin *fabula* instead (Loth, *Late Medieval Icelandic Romances*, 71 and 72): "Slikum grenum hæfa þær fabulas sem froder menn hafa vessad" (the fables that wise people have versified illustrate such particulars) and "segizt su fabula" (the fable declares). But by the time Guðmundur Erlendsson að Felli í Sléttahlíð (ca. 1595–1670) produced a translation of some 119 of Æsop's fables, they are referred to in JS 232 4⁰ (1688–1689) as *dæmisögur*: Guðmundur Erlendsson, *Dæmisögur Esóps í ljóðum*, part 1, ed. Grímur M. Helgason (Reykjavík: Æskan, 1967), xiii. Guðmundur, who also composed the as yet unpublished *Rímur af Esóp hinum gríska* in 14 fitts, had access to one of the many Latin editions of Æsop containing prose translations of the fables by William Hermansz of Gouda (ca. 1466–1510), Adriaan van Baarland (1486–1538), and others, volumes that had been appearing since at least 1509. The later editions often had the title *Fabularum quae hoc libro continentur interpretes*.

For more on the use of *dæmisaga* and *ævintýri*, see Einar Ólafur Sveinsson, *Um íslenzkar þjóðsögur* (Reykjavík: Hið íslenzka bókmenntafélag, 1940), 6–10; translated as *Folk-Stories of Iceland*, rev. Einar G. Pétursson, trans. Benedikt Benediktz, ed. Anthony Faulkes (London: Viking Society for Northern Research, 2003), 13–16. *Ævintýri* also became a synonym for a wide range of narratives known variously as *álagasögur*, *lygisögur*, *skröksögur*, *stjúpmæðrasögur*, and *yrkjusögur* (see Bødker, *Folk Literature*, 23, 184, 278, 288, 328). These and the related *kerlingasögur* and *kotasögur* are discussed by Jürg Glauser, *Isländische Märchensagas: Studien zur Prosaliteratur im spätmittelalterlichen Island*, Beiträge zur nordischen Philologie 12 (Basel: Helbing und Lichtenhahn, 1983), 17–22. Terje Spurkland discusses three of these terms in an attempt to determine the parameters of truth and fiction in the *fornaldarsögur*; see his "Lygisögur, skröksögur and, stjúpmæðrasögur," in *The Legendary Sagas: Origins and Development*, ed. Annette Lassen et al. (Reykjavík: University of Iceland Press, 2012), 173–84. Spurkland points out that "*skröksaga*" is also used in *Stjórn*, *Postola sögur*, and *Heilagramanna sögur* as a translation of "fabula" (see 176–77 and the references there), but this may be a particular religious use of the word in reference to stories that are at odds with the truth of scripture. He would take *stjúpmæðrasögur* as a translation of *fabulae aniles* ("old wives' tales"), a term more accurately translated as *kerlingasögur*. However, this appears to be a modern term although the expression *kerlingavilla* ("old wives error") in the prose epilogue to "Helgakviða Hundingsbana II" could also be translated as *fabula anilis*. Árni Magnússon in his Latin life of Sæmundr fróði refers to *aniles nugae*, which Gottskálk Jensson, "'Ævi Sæmundar fróða' á latínu eftir Árna Magnússon," in *Í garði Sæmundar fróða: Fyrirlestrar frá ráðstefnu í Þjóðminjasafni 20. maí 2006*, ed. Gunnar Harðarson and Sverrir Tómasson (Reykjavík: Hugvísindastofnun Háskóla Íslands, 2008), translates as *kerlingasögur* (168); see also Gottskálk's discussion of the word "fabula" in classical and early modern Icelandic contexts (140–42).

Unfortunately the usefulness of this term became further compromised in Modern Icelandic when it was also applied to folk literature in general[44] and to the International Folk Tale, the fairy tale, or *Märchen* in particular.[45] The question of how to refer to the *exempla* was never fully resolved by Icelandic authors and scribes. *Ævintýr* as a loanword has some claim as the most appropriate term for this imported genre. Perhaps the only observation to be made is that there

---

44. Magnús Grímsson and Jón Árnason used *ævintýri* this way in the first printed collection of Icelandic folklore, *Íslenzk æfintýri* (Reykjavík: E. Þórðarson, 1852; repr. Akureyri: Bókaútgáfan Edda, 1942), for the collection includes not only prose narratives but also verse including ballads and hymns. Note that Gering appears to translate "ævintýri" in a similarly broad fashion, as may be seen by the sub-title on the title-page to his collection of *exempla*: "*Íslendzk æventýri: Isländische Legenden, Novellen und Märchen*" (1:iii).

45. "A *Märchen* is not so vague a thing as a 'folktale' . . . Lüthi usually uses the term to refer to tales numbered 300–749 in the Aarne-Thompson *Type Index*, the so-called 'tales of magic.' The term 'wondertale' is not a bad equivalent." John D. Niles, "Translators's Preface," in Max Lüthi, *The European Folktale: Form and Nature*, trans. John D. Niles, Translations in Folklore Studies (Philadelphia: Institute for the Study of Human Issues, 1982), xxiv. Konrad Maurer used the term *Volkssagen* for his collection, *Isländische Volkssagen der Gegenwart* (Leipzig: Hinrich, 1860; repr. Rye Brook, NY: Elibron Classics, 2001), and Guðbrandur Vigfússon calqued this term as *þjóðsögur* (folk-stories) for the title of Jón Árnason's collection *Íslenzkar þjóðsögur og ævintýri*, 2 vols. (Leipzig: Hinrich, 1862–64), using the term throughout his "Formáli," 1:v-xxxviii. Jón Árnason on the other hand translated *Volkssagen* as *alþýðusögur* (popular tales, or literally "tales of the common people") in the "Formáli" to his collection, which arrived in Germany too late to be included in the published volumes and which was not printed until much later in the second edition, *Íslenzkar þjóðsögur og ævintýri*, 2 vols. (Reykjavík: Sögufélag, 1925–39), 2:715. *Alþýðusögur* had some currency in the middle of the nineteenth century but since then has dropped out of use. See Einar Ól. Sveinsson, *Um íslenzkar þjóðsögur*, 213–14; *Folk Stories*, 226–27, who also attempts to distinguish between *munnmælasögur* (oral narratives about odd behavior, witty retorts, etc., often centered on *lausavísur*), *sagnaþættir* (narratives associated with particular events, individual and families), and *þjóðsögur*. This latter category he divides into *þjóðsagnir* (folk-legends), which he defines as aetiological narratives associated with known people and places (what the Grimms classified as *Sagen*), and *ævintýri*, i.e., what the Grimms called *Märchen* (*Um íslenzkar þjóðsögur*, 10–19; *Folk Stories*, 16–23). See also Bødker, *Folk Literature*, 204, 261, 294–95, 295. However, these distinctions are far from universally followed. Sigfús Sigfússon used *Ævintýri og dæmisögur* as the title for the collection of *Märchen* in his folktale collection, *Íslenzk þjóð-sögur og -sagnir*, 16 vols. (Seyðisfjörður, Hafnarfjörður, and Reykjavík: Nokkrir Austfirðingar, Prentsmiðja Hafnarfjarðar and Víkingsútgáfan, 1922–1958), vol. 13 (1957); new ed., Óskar Halldórsson et al., 11 vols. (Hafnarfjörður: Þjóðsaga, 1982–1993), 10:1–177, although here just called "Ævintýri." The most recent major collection of folk stories uses a completely different system of organization in which the editors set out "að flokka þetta fjölbreytilega efni á nýjan hátt með það fyrir augum að það verði sem auðnýtanlegast fyrir nútímalesendur" (to classify this greatly diverse material in a new way with an eye toward making it so that it might be the most easily accessible to contemporary readers). Ólafur Ragnarsson et al., eds., *Íslenskt þjóðsagnasafn*, 5 vols. (Reykjavík: Vaka-Helgafell, 2000), 1:5–6.

was almost universal agreement that the *exempla* were different from the indigenous short narratives or *þættir*, and that term was almost never applied to them.[46]

4. Medieval Icelandic *Exempla*

There can be little doubt that the Dominican brother Jón Halldórsson played an important role in popularizing the use and distribution of *exempla*, and he may even have been responsible for their introduction into Iceland. Although there is no clear evidence to indicate what term bishop Jón used to refer to these narratives, by the time the earliest collections of them in Icelandic were put together, *ævintýr* seems well established as an appropriate term for them. Thus, in the preface to the collection of translated *exempla* in AM 657 a-b 4° (mid-fourteenth century),[47] the author states: "Til nytsemðar þeim sem eptir kunnu at koma sneru heimsins vitringar á latínu margskonar fræðum er mikil hullda lá á ok myrkvaþoka, fyrir alþýðu. En af því at eigi hafa allir þá gjöf hlotit af guði, at latínu skili, þá viljum vèr til norrænu færa þau ævintýr er hæverskum mönnum hæfir til skemtanar at hafa" (The world's wise men turned into Latin for the use of those they knew to come after that wisdom of various kinds in which much was hidden and concealed for ordinary people. And because not all have received that gift to understand Latin, then we wish to present in Norse those *exempla* [*ævintýr*] that are suitable for gallant people to have as entertainment).[48] There is a similar statement in the preface to the second collection of exempla in AM 624 4° (mid-fifteenth century): "Nú er

---

46. One exception is Gering's *exemplum* LXXXIX: "Trönuþáttr" (1:272–75). MS AM 624 4° (middle of the fifteenth century) reads only "Trönu . . ." for the heading and a later hand has added: "Trönu þáttr; Frá einum ríkum bóndasyni ok einni ekkju ok um þau brögð er þau beittuz við" (The Story of the Crane; concerning a rich farmer's son and a widow and about the tricks they played on each other). However, this story is more in the form of a *fabula* complete with the *epimythium* (1:275) " fylliz þat hèr, at hverr tekr þat at sèr sem hann veitir öðrum" (that is confirmed here, that everyone be prepared to experience that which they impose upon others"). There is no similar story listed under crane or stork in the 725 narratives catalogued in Perry's *Aesopica* or in Gerd Dicke and Klaus Grubmüller, *Die Fabeln des Mittelalters und der frühen Neuzeit: Ein Katalog der deutschen Versionen und ihrer lateinischen Entsprechungen*, Münstersche Mittelalter-Schriften 60 (Munich: Fink, 1987), and the source has not been identified.

47. A version of this preface is also found in Sth. Pap. fol nr. 66, as the preface to translation of the *Disciplina clericalis*.

48. ÍÆ 1:3. The preface is headed "Hèr byjar æventýrum nökkrum" (Here begin some *exempla*).

bert af þersum orðum ok greinum, at sá er samsetti bækling þenna
með ymsum æventýrum villdi dvelja oss frá illum umlestri, frá eiðum
röngum ok únýtri margmælgi" (Now it is revealed through these
words and reasons that he who assembled this booklet containing
various *exempla* ["æventýrum"] wished to hinder us from doing
wicked slander, swearing wrong oaths, and needless loquacity).[49] But
there must have continued some debate about whether or not *ævintýr*
was an appropriate term for these narratives, as the introduction in
AM 624 4° to Gering's *exemplum* LXXXV: "Af riddara ok álfkonu"
(Of a knight and an elf-woman), demonstrates: "Bæklingr sjá hinn
litli er samsettr af skemmtunarsögum þeim sem virðuligr herra Jón
biskup Halldórsson sagði til gamans mönnum. Má þat kalla hvárt
er vill, sögur eðr ævintýr" (This little booklet is composed of those
amusing stories that the worthy bishop Jón Halldórsson told to people
for entertainment. One can call that material whatever of the two
one wishes, stories or *exempla*).[50] And even though the preface to
the *exempla* in AM 657 a-b 4° quoted above unequivocally refers
to them as *ævintýr,* this is not at all the case in the opening section
of the *söguþáttur af Jóni Halldórssyni biskupi,* which appears in the
same manuscript. In his edition of *Íslendzk ævintýri,* Hugo Gering,
using stylistic criteria, identified thirty-six narratives (including the
söguþáttur) included in AM 657 a-b 4°, which he associated with
Jón Halldórsson and his circle.[51] Stefán Karlsson has convincingly
argued that these thirty-six narratives are in fact the work of Arngrímr
Brandsson (d.1361), better known as the compiler of *Guðmundar
saga biskups* (Version D).[52] In *Lárentíus saga biskups,* chapter 51 (A
Version), it is said that Jón Halldórsson considered Arngrímr "prest
þann sem hann helt fremstan í sínu byskupsdæmi" (That priest whom
he considered the foremost in his bishopric).[53] Arngrímr had received

---

49. Ibid., 1:4.

50. Ibid., 1:246.

51. *ÍÆ* 2:xxv–lxiv. The *exempla* attributed to an author designated α are: I–IV, VI,
IX, XV, XIX, XXII–XXV, XXVIII, XLVIII, LXXVIII, LXXXII, LXXXIII, LXXXVB,
LXXXVII–LXXXIX, XCVIII, CI in AM 624 4°; XLIIB from Stock. pap. fol nr. 66; and
X, XI XVI, XVII, XXVI, XXVII, XC–XCIII, XCV, XCVI from AM 647 a–b 4°.

52. Stefán Karlsson, "Icelandic Lives of Thomas à Becket: Questions of Authorship,"
in *Proceedings of the First International Saga Conference,* ed. Peter Foote et al. (London:
Viking Society for Northern Research, 1973), 236.

53. *ÍF* 17:412. In the B Version of *Lárentíus saga* (ibid.), Arngrímr is "einn sinn fremsta
prest" (one of his foremost priests).

the benefice at Oddi on Rangárvellir in 1334. He did not remain there long after bishop Jón's death, and in 1341 he became a monk, presumably at the monastery at Þingeyrar, because by 1350 he had become abbot there, a post he held, although not without controversy, until his death.[54] It is assumed it was during his time at Þingeyrar that Arngrímr undertook his literary activities, including writing the *sögupáttur* about his close associate bishop Jón and making a collection of *exempla* that he had heard or obtained from the bishop. It is interesting to note that Arngrímr is far from consistent in the *sögupáttur* in his use of terminology when referring to the *exempla*. It is as if for him this terminology is still in a state of flux compared to the introductory remarks from elsewhere in the same manuscript quoted above, which may or may not have originated with him. He opens by referring to these stories as *dæmisögur*[55] before switching to *frásögn* ("narratives"), itself a neutral term very frequently employed elsewhere in the collection,[56] and then turning to *ævintýr*:[57]

> En hverr man greina mega, hverr hans góðvili var at gleðja nærverandis menn með fáheyrðum dæmisögum er hann hafði tekit í útlöndum, bæði með letrum ok eigin raun, ok til vitnis þar um harðla smátt ok lítit man setjaz í þenna bækling af því stóra efni, því at sumir menn á

---

54. In 1357, on learning of the death overseas of the bishop of Hólar, Ormr Ásláksson, a synod of northern priests tried to remove Arngrímr from his posts as abbot and *officialis* (representative of the bishop during an overseas absence). At this point Arngrímr is said to have expressed the desire to become a Dominican and retire to their monastery in Bergen (reversing the journey of Jón Halldórsson). See Janus Jónsson, *Um klaustrin á Íslandi* (Reykjavík: Endurprent, 1980), 191, first published in *Tímarit hins íslenzka bókmenntafélags* 8 (1887): 174–265.

55. *Dæmisaga* appears again in the *sögupáttur* with the meaning *exemplum*. See ÍF 17:453; ÍÆ 1:92.247 (XXIII). *Dæmi* is also occasionally used where it might be translated as *exemplum*, for example: X, 1:31.32; XXII, 1:80.68; XXVIII, 1:109.46; XXXVI, 1:125.58.

56. *Frásögn* appears almost as often as *ævintýr* within the narratives to refer to themselves, for example: IV, 1:20.24; XXII, 1:77.1; XXII, 1:81.119; XXIII, 1:84.14; XXIII, 1:87.92; XXIII, 1:89.181; XXIV, 1:104.12; XLII, 1:146.211; LXXVIII, 1:207.90; LXXIX, 1:211.201; LXXX, 1:216.11; LXXXII, 1:234.43; LXXXIII, 1:244.129; LXXXVII, 1:256.8; LXXXIX, 1:275.92; XCI, 1:287.42; XCII, 1:291.130.

57. Among the places *ævintýr* appears in ÍÆ are Preface A: 1:3.5; Preface B: 1:4.27; X, 1:33.84; XXIII, 1:84.15; XXVII, 1:47.1; XXXII, 1:119.11; XXXVI, 1:125.54; XXXIX, 1:129.1; XLI, 1:134.1; XLIIB, 1:144.170; XLIV, 1:149.63; XLVI, 1:154.34; LXII, 1:185.11; LXV, 1:179.29; LXX, 1:190.69; LXXIX, 1:217.127; LXXXII, 1:236.100; LXXXV, 1:254.161; LXXXVII, 1:288.340. In LXXXIII, 1:243.102, *ævintýr* is used not in the sense of *exemplum* but rather as "adventure."

Íslandi samsettu hans frásagnir sér til gleði ok öðrum. Munum vér í fyrsta setja sín æfintýr af hvárum skóla, París ok Bolon, er gjörðuz í hans náveru.[58] (ÍF 17:445)

And everyone is capable of telling what kind was his benevolence to entertain people in the vicinity with rarely heard parables (*dæmisögur*) that he had picked up overseas, both in letters and as a result of his own experience, and as witness to this is assembled in this little book a very small amount and a little of that vast material, because some people in Iceland put together his narratives (*frásagnir*) for the pleasure of themselves and others. To begin with we shall assemble his *exempla* (*ævintýr*),[59] which happened in his presence, from each of the two schools, Paris and Bologna.

Likewise, the opening sentence to *Klári saga*, presumably written by Arngrímr, refers to the story that will follow as a *frásögn*,[60] one of the more frequent words used to introduce the *ævintýr*,[61] while in the colophon to the saga the narrator, presumably bishop Jón, states that the saga has served as a "ljós dœmi" (clear *exemplum*).[62]

This opening paragraph of the *sögubáttur* says that bishop Jón brought some of his narratives with him "með letrum" (in letters), that is, in written form, presumably in Latin. It is possible that he had made an anthology of *exempla* from various collections, possibly in Latin, but more plausibly in Icelandic. This would account for the appearance among the Icelandic *exempla* of narratives derived from the major anthologies, as there is no evidence that these collections circulated separately in Iceland.

One of the most important collections of *exempla* was the *Disciplina Clericalis* (Clerical Instruction) by Petrus Alfonsi.[63] It quickly

---

58. This text is based on AM 657 a-b 4°, and Gering prints the *sögubáttur* as *exemplum* XXIII but from AM 624 4°; see ÍÆ 1:84–94.

59. Here it would also be possible to translate *ævintýr* as "adventures" or "occurrences."

60. *Clári saga*, ed. Gustaf Cederschiöld, Altnordische Saga-Bibliothek 12 (Halle: Niemeyer, 1907), 1. Cederschiöld had edited the saga some thirty years earlier with a Latin translation by Samuel J. Cavallin as *Clarus saga, Clari fabella* (Lund: Gleerup, 1879).

61. See note 56 above.

62. *Clári saga*, Cederschiöld, 74.

63. Petrus Alfonsi (1062-ca. 1140) was born Moses Sephardi and had served as a rabbi in Huesca, in the Kingdom of Aragon, before converting to Christianity in 1106. He came

became popular and was translated into most of the European vernaculars, including Anglo-Norman.[64] As Sveinbjörn Rafnsson has argued, this text in whole or in part may have been known in Iceland before the arrival of Jón Halldórsson in Skálholt, because a translation of the conclusion to chapter 28, "Exemplum de Socrate et rege," to the end of the treatise is found at the beginning of folio 15[r] and ending at the top of 16[r] in AM 544 4° (early fourteenth century), i.e., in that part of Hauksbók written by a scribe described variously as Norwegian or Faroese in the employ of Haukr Erlendsson (d. 1334).[65] However, the evidence is equivocal as to whether this narrative was collected in Iceland or Norway and whether it was written down before or after Jón Halldórsson came to Iceland. What is unequivocal is that three tales derived from the *Disciplina clericalis* are found in AM 657 a-b 4°: "Af hálfum vin capitulum," "Hèr segir af öllum vin," and "Frá danska manni ok kerlingu."[66] They are among

---

to England a few years later and may have been personal physician to Henry I. It has been assumed that it was during this period (ca. 1110-ca. 1120) that he composed the *Disciplina Clericalis*. Fluent in Hebrew and Arabic as well as Latin, his collection of narratives served as a conduit for oriental stories into the Western tradition. For a general introduction, see "The Author and his Times," in Petrus Alfonsi, *The 'Disciplina Clericalis' of Petrus Alfonsi*, trans. and ed. Eberhard Hermes, English trans. P. R. Quarrie (London: Routledge, 1977), 1–99; Tolan, *Petrus Alfonsi*, 9–11; and Sveinbjörn Rafnsson, "Sagnastef í íslenskri menningarsögu," *Saga* 30 (1992): 81–121. Sveinbjörn Rafnsson surveys the translations into Icelandic of the *Disciplina Clericalis* and their influence on medieval and early modern literature.

64. There are two Anglo-Norman verse translations from the early thirteenth century both appearing with the title "Le Chastoiement d'un pere a son fils." Both have been edited in *Französische Versbearbeitungen* (1922) of the *Disciplina clericalis*, Hilka, part 3.

65. See Sveinbjörn Rafnsson, "Sagnastef," 81–85. The text is published in *Hauksbók udgiven efter de arnamagnæanske håndskrifter no. 371, 544 og 675, 40*, ed. Eiríkur Jónsson and Finnur Jónsson (Copenhagen: Thiele, 1892–96), 178, and in Sveinbjörn Rafnsson, 99–101. The text contains the concluding section of chapter 28: "Exemplum de Socrate et rege," to the end of the treatise (*Disciplina Clericalis*, Hilka, 1:41.1–1:46.11), omitting chapter 29: "Exemplum de prudenti consiliarii regis filio" (Ibid., 1:42.1–42.8). The translation is abbreviated but not drastically so, the occasional sentence being left un-translated, and the Latin is followed more closely than in the three *exempla* in AM 657 a-b 4°. Sveinbjörn argues that the quire now missing before 15[r] contained the rest of the *Disciplina Clericalis*. The situation is further complicated by the fact that it is not possible to determine whether AM 544 4° was written in Iceland or Norway (the latter seems more likely), nor is it possible to fix the manuscript, which may have been written any time up to 1334, the year of Haukur's death—fourteen years after Jón Halldórsson became bishop. The relationship of this text to the translation of the *Disciplina Clericalis* in AM 657 a-b 4° and Sth. Pap. fol nr. 66 (see below) is not clear, but for reasons I cannot go into here I believe they are unrelated.

66. XCI-XCIII in ÍÆ 1:286–92.

those texts that are presumed to have been collected by Arngrímr Brandsson from Bishop Jón Halldórsson. The first two narratives are based on the opening pair of *exempla* in the *Disciplina clericalis*: I: "Exemplum de dimidio amico" (The Half Friend) and II: Exemplum de integro amico" (The Perfect Friend), along with a version of no. XV: "Exemplum de decem coiris" (The Ten Chests).[67] The Icelandic versions have been "Europeanized," that is the references to Arabs, Mecca, and other features of the pluralistic society with which Petrus Alfonsi was familiar have been thoroughly "Christianized."[68] For example, in "The Half Friend" (*exemplum* XCI) the story of the dying Arab ("Arabs moriturus") has become a tale "af höfutspekingi gömlum" (of a certain aged chief-sage) who "lagðiz í banasótt" (lay on his death-bed), and the Spanish Muslim on a pilgrimage to Mecca by way of Egypt in the "Exemplum de decem coiris" (quidam Hyspanus perrexit Mech, et dum ibat pervenit in Aegyptam) becomes in *exemplum* XCIII "einn danskr maðr . . . at vitja heilagra staða" (a Danish man . . . visiting holy sites).[69] Because of changes like these in the Icelandic text, Gering speculates that these versions are based on oral retellings of these narratives by bishop Jón.[70] This may indeed be the case, but neither this translation nor the later versions of the *Disciplina Clericalis* have been extensively studied, so it is not possible to say from what language these texts have been translated.[71] These three

---

67. *Disciplina Clericalis*, Hilka, 1:2–4, 4–5, 20–22; *Disciplina Clericalis*, Hermes, 106–09, 128–30.

68. I employ the term "Europeanization" in the sense used by Lisa Lampert-Weissig: "This self-definition of 'modern Europe' has been shaped in part by a particular view of medieval Europe, a medieval Europe that is commensurate with Christendom and from which certain demons, such as the history of the Muslim presence on the Iberian peninsula from 711–1492, have been exorcised." *Medieval Literature and Postcolonial Studies*, Postcolonial Literary Studies (Edinburgh: Edinburgh University Press, 2010), 2. A similar process of "Europeanization" is also a feature of "Le Chastoiement d'un pere a son fils," where the Arab of the first narrative has been changed to "a wise man" (Tolan, *Petrus Alfonsi*, 125). The A version at line 229 has "uns saives hom . . . quant il sout que finer deveit" (*Disciplina Clericalis*, Hilka, 3:7). However, the A version of the opening of exemplum XV (lines 2209–13) follows the Latin text: "Li prodom ert d'Espaigne nez, / Or et argent aveit asez: / Parmi Egite tresspassout / Et tot dreit a Mech en alout / La ou Mahom ert henorez" (ibid., 3:40).

69. *Disciplina Clericalis*, Hilka, 1:3 and 20; ÍÆ 1:286, 292.

70. ÍÆ 2:229.

71. See James F. Caldwell, "On the Icelandic *Disciplina clericalis*," *Scandinavian Studies* 10 (1929): 125–35. Caldwell sets out to determine the particular Latin version used by the translator of the *Disciplina clericalis* found in Sth. Pap. fol nr. 66, and agrees with Gering that the three stories found in AM 657 a–b 4° represent a separate tradition

exempla must have been very popular and appear to have achieved a wide distribution, as elements from "Af hálfum vin capitulum"[72] turn up in chapters 13–15 of *Víga-Glúms saga*,[73] a narrative supposedly composed around 1230 but whose textual history is very complex.[74] Scholars assume the saga was written in Eyjafjörður and that the author was in some way connected with the monastery at Munka-þverá. However, a mid-thirteenth-century dating does not preclude the saga's being rewritten and "improved" along the way. While it is possible that a text of the *Disciplina Clericalis* was circulating in an Icelandic monastery before the bishopric of Jón Halldórsson, it is more likely that the episode involving Ingólfr and the calf was added to the text some time during the bishopric of Jón Halldórsson or soon afterward and so made its way into the Möðruvallabók version, as scholars agree that this episode and several others in the saga are extraneous to the main narrative involving Víga-Glúmr. This is the only example of an episode set in Iceland in the *Íslendingasögur* that can be directly traced to a non-native source.[75]

---

(127). However, his attempts to associate the later Icelandic translation with a particular Latin recension or manuscript prove inconclusive, although he does notice some evidence suggesting that the translator used a manuscript similar to Harley 3938 (130–35). However, Caldwell based his analysis strictly on the variants noted by Hilka and Söderhjelm in their critical edition of Petrus' work rather than checking the text in this or any other manuscript. H. L. D. Ward notes that Harley 3938, in which the *Disciplina clericalis* occupies folios 80–107b, is a sixteenth-century paper manuscript written in Italy. See H. L. D. Ward and J. A. Herbert, *Catalogue of Romances in the Department of Manuscripts in the British Museum*, 3 vols. (1883–1910; London: repr. British Museum, 1961–1962), 2:245. Because of the late date of the manuscript and its Italian provenance, even Caldwell's tentative conclusion and provisional stemma (135) will have to remain highly speculative until much more work is done in evaluating the texts of the surviving manuscripts; Tolan (*Petrus Alfonsi*, 201–04) identifies thirteen additional manuscripts not known to Hilka and Söderhjelm containing the *Disciplina clericalis* in whole or in part.

72. In the third translation of the *Disciplina Clericalis*, this story (Gering's *exemplum* L) is called "Frá lærisveini einum er freistaði vina sinna í nauðum staddr" (*ÍÆ* 1:164–65).

73. *Víga-Glúms saga*, ed. Gabriel Turville-Petre, 2nd ed. (Oxford: Clarendon Press, 1960), xxxiii–xxxviii.

74. John McKinnell, "Víga-Glúms saga," in *Medieval Scandinavia: An Encyclopedia*, ed. Phillip Pulsiano and Kirsten Wolf (New York: Garland, 1993), 691–92. One version of the saga that contains the episode based on the *Disciplina Clericalis* is found in the mid-fourteenth-century Möðruvallabók (AM 132 fol).

75. Although *Tristrams saga og Ísǫndar* (1226), the Icelandic translation of Thomas of Brittany's *Roman de Tristan*, left its mark on Icelandic vernacular literature, especially the *Riddarasögur*, even when motifs from it are incorporated into an *Íslendingasaga* such as in the "Spesar þáttr" of *Grettis saga* (chs. 63–93), they maintain an exotic distance in that the narrative there is set in Constantinople. In addition to a discussion of *Víga-Glúms saga*, Sveinbjörn Rafnsson ("Sagnastef," 92–95) argues for the influence of the

What appears to be a third translation of the *Disciplina Clericalis* (Gering's nos. XLIX–LXXVI) is found in Sth. Pap. fol. nr. 66.[76] This manuscript in the hand of Jón Vigfússon (d. 1692)[77] was completed

---

Disciplina Clericalis, chapter 3: "Exemplum de tribus versificatoribus" on *Sneglu-Halla þáttr* and of chapter 2: "Exemplum de integro amico" on chapters 56 and 62 of *Egils saga*, but interestingly enough only in the version found in Möðruvallabók. See *Egils saga*, ed. Bjarni Einarsson (London: Viking Society for Northern Research, 2003), 84, 106. However, apart from the appropriation in *Víga-Glúms saga*, none of these correspondences is particularly close. Episodes in *Grettis saga* that can be ultimately linked with the Old English poem *Beowulf* cannot be argued as demonstrating direct influence. See further, Susanne Kramarz-Bein, "Der *Spesar þáttr* der *Grettis saga*: Tristan-Spuren in der Isländersaga," in *Studien zur Isländersaga: Festschrift für Rolf Heller*, ed. Heinrich Beck and Else Ebel, Ergänzungsbände zum Reallexikon der Germanischen Altertumskunde 24 (Berlin: de Gruyter, 2000), 152–81, and Marianne Kalinke, "Arthurian Echoes in Indigenous Icelandic Sagas," *The Arthur of the North*, ed. Marianne Kalinke, Arthurian Literature in the Middle Ages 5 (Cardiff: University of Wales Press, 2011), 145–67.

76. ÍÆ 1:163–200. On this manuscript see ÍÆ 1:xxix-xxxi. In addition to the translation of Petrus Alfonsi, the collection contains the preface from AM 657 a-b 4°, as well as six versions of *exempla* also from AM 657 a-b 4° inserted between LXXI and LXXII but from the section written around 1400. Some of these narratives are found in other manuscripts as well: see XXV: "Af biskupi ok flugu" (ÍÆ 1:100–04; source unknown); LXXVIII: "Af dauða ok konungssyni" (1:204–11; source unknown although many post-medieval versions); LXXXII: "Af þrimr kumpánum" (1:232–39; source unknown); LXXXIII: Af rómverska dáranum" (1:239–44; Gering's title); XLIIB: "Af einum greifa" (1:139–46; ultimately from India), and LXXXIX: "Trönuþátttr" (1:272–75; see footnote 46 above). Where Gering did take his text from Sth. Pap. fol. nr. 66, he notes, "Die moderne Orthographie der Hs. habe ich natürlich nach Massgabe der Texte des 14. Jhs. geändert" (1:xxxi). The translation covers chapters 1–23 (of thirty-four) of the *Disciplina clericalis*, ending with the chapter 23: "Exemplum de arature et lupo iudicioque vulpis" (*Disciplina Clericalis*, Hilka, 1:32–33). Gering also prints as LXXVB (ÍÆ 1:197–98) a version of chapter 22: "Exemplum de rustico et avicula" (*Disciplina Clericalis*, Hilka, 1:30–31) found in Stock. papp. fol. nr. 67, from what is a fourth separate translation of the *Disciplina clericalis*. This manuscript contains in addition a version of chapter 2: "Exemplum de integro amico" and chapter 19: "Exemplum de duobus burgensibus et rustico" (*Disciplina Clericalis*, Hilka, 1:27–28; see LXXII: "Af tveimr burgeisum ok kotkarli," ÍÆ 1:192–94; Gering's title). Sveinbjörn Rafnsson edits all three narratives, "Sagnastef," 115–18. Stock. papp. fol. nr. 67 was written in Copenhagen in 1687 by Jón Eggertsson *klausturhaldari* (1643–1689). On Jón and his manuscript collecting see Vilhelm Gödel, *Fornnorsk-isländsk litteratur i Sverige*, Antiqvarisk Tidskrift för Sverige 16.4 (Stockholm: Kongl. Vitterhets Historie och Antiqvitets Akademien, 1898), 189–208, and Regina Jucknies, *Der Horizont eines Schreibers: Jón Eggertsson (1643–89) und seine Handschriften*, Texte und Untersuchungen zur Germanistik und Skandinavistik 59 (Frankfurt: Peter Lang, 2009)—on Stock. papp. fol. nr. 67 see 79–81. Since many stories from the *Disciplina clericalis* circulated independently, the translation of individual narratives in AM 657 a-b 4° and Stock. papp. fol. nr. 67 does not imply separate translations of the entire text (see Tolan, *Petrus Alfonsi* 132–58).

77. Jón Vigfússon became a scribe in the Swedish *Antiqvitetskollegiet* (College of Antiquities) in 1684 but otherwise little is known about him. See Gödel, *Fornnorsk-isländsk litteratur*, 194, 201.

in 1690 and contains mostly *riddarasögur*.[78] The translation of the *Disciplina Clericalis* is the last entry, taking up pages 323–417, and is headed by the following rubric: "Hèr hefjaz nökkur æventýr eðr vísra manna framsagnir ok holl ráð" (Here begin some *exempla* or the narratives and wholesome counsel of wise men).[79] There has been considerable speculation concerning the manuscript from which Jón Vigfússon made his copy of the *Disciplina Clericalis*. Knut Frederik Söderwall argued that the source was a medieval manuscript referred to in the edition of the Old Swedish *Um styrilsi kununga ok höfþinga* published by Johannes Thomae Bureus (1568–1652) in 1634.[80] However, Jonna Louis-Jensen has demonstrated that the Bureus reference and the source manuscript used by Jón Vigfússon were the lost vellum codex Ormsbók.[81] The translation covers

---

78. In addition to the translation of the *Disciplina Clericalis*, the manuscript contains versions of *Sigrgarðs saga frœkna, Vilhjálms saga sjóðs, Dámusta saga, Sigurðar saga fóts, Gunnars þáttr Þiðrandabana, Þorsteins þáttr sǫgufróða,* and *Stjǫrnu-Odda draumr.*

79. ÍÆ 1:163.

80. Knut Frederik Söderwall, *Studier öfver Konunga-styrelsen,* Lunds Universitets Årsskrift 15 (1878–1879), Afdelningen för philosophi, språkvetenskap och historia 4 (Lund: Fr. Berling, 1880), 55–56. See also ÍÆ 2:139. Bureus, in his list of sources to *En nyttigh Bok, om Konnunga Styrilse och Höfdinga* (Uppsala: Eskil Mattsson, 1634), Q1ᵛ, says that the phrase on page 15.4–7 introduced by: "Thi at svä är skriuat" (Because so it is written): "det fins i en äldre Swensk bok (som så börias: Enok heet madher) så lydandes. Annar späkinger sagdi: Sa är Gud ottaz ten rädhaz aller lutir: En sa är ey rädhiz Gud, sa rädhiz alla luti" (one finds that in an old Swedish book [that begins: a man is called Enoch] as follows. Another philosopher said: He who fears God, all things are afraid of him: But he who is not afraid of God is afraid of all things). This is close to but not exactly the same as the third sentence in XLIX: "Af ýmissa spekinga ráðum" (ÍÆ 1:163.5–8; Gering's title) and translates *Disciplina Clericalis,* Hilka, 1:2.18–19.

81. Ormsbók, the famous vellum codex in Bureus' possession as early as 1602, was either owned by or written for Ormr Snorrason from Skarð á Skarðströnd, lǫgmaðr sunnan og austan 1359–1368, 1374–1375 (d. after 1401). After Bureus' death it passed to the *Antiqvitetskollegiet* and was presumably destroyed in the fire that consumed Stockholm castle in 1697. See further, *Trójumanna saga,* ed. Jonna Louis-Jensen, Editiones Arnamagnæanæ A8 (Copenhagen: Munksgaard, 1963), xi-xv. The manuscript contained *riddarasögur,* among them *Bevis saga, Flóvents saga Frakkakonungs, Partalopa saga,* and the β version of *Trójumanna saga,* in *"Enoks saga," Opuscula* 5, Bibliotheca Arnamagnæana 31 (Copenhagen: Munksgaard, 1975), 225–37. Jonna Louis-Jensen argues that "Enok heet madher," or rather "Enoch hét maðr," the opening phrase of the *Disciplina Clericalis* translation found in Sth. Pap. fol nr. 66, along with other evidence from unpublished dictionaries and glossaries, confirm that this version of the *Disciplina clericalis* was one of the items included in Ormsbók. Lise Præstgaard Andersen assigns *"Enoks saga,"* i.e. the *Disciplina clericalis,* to foliation 86ᵛ-90ʳ⁻ᵛ in her hypothetical list of the materials in the second part of Ormsbók. See *Partalopa saga,* ed. Lise Præstgaard Andersen, Editiones Arnamagnæanæ B28 (Copenhagen: Reitzel, 1983), lxv, and Sveinbjörm Rafnsson, "Sagnastef," 86. If Ormr had been aware that there was a version of the

about two-thirds of the text and follows its Latin exemplar closely, although that does not preclude its having been translated from a vernacular version. The text has been "Europeanized," but not to the extent of Jón Halldórsson's versions.[82] Gering, in fact, does not bother to give a German translation for this part of his collection regarding such a task as "unnötig," and he provides a relevant Latin text in an appendix to volume 2.[83] The narratives in Sth. Pap. fol nr. 66 are handled very differently than those from the same text associated with Jón Halldórsson, and it is most unlikely that they were circulating in Iceland early enough to have been in a position to influence *Víga-Glúms saga*.

5. Icelandic *Exempla* as Arbiters of Gender Roles

It is hard to tell how the *exempla* were actually put to use in Iceland, since there are so few examples preserved and no complete collection surviving except the partial translations of the *Disciplina clericalis*. Nor do any collections of sermons survive outside the twelfth-century *Hómilíubók*. Neither the Dominicans nor the Franciscans had a strong presence in Iceland, where the monasteries were either Benedictine or Augustinian. On the other hand, the brief flurry of activity in the second quarter of the fifteenth century when a number of *exempla* were translated from English collections suggests that the utility of the form was still recognized. However, Bishop Jón Halldórsson had been raised in the Dominican monastery in Bergen and studied at Dominican-run universities in Europe, and his presentation of *Klári saga*, where various *exempla* are used to flesh-out a bare-bones narrative with a very specific moral purpose in mind, gives us, I think, the opportunity to see a master Dominican preacher in action.

Disciplina clericalis in Hauksbók, that might have inspired him to find or commission a version for his own collection (the concluding section of the translation may have already been lost by the time the manuscript came into Bureus' possession).

82. Thus in exemplum I, "arabs moriturus" (ÍÆ 1:164) is translated as "einn spekingr í helsótt sinni" (a sage during his fatal illness), and the Spaniard on a pilgrimage to Mecca (1:185) becomes: "kaupmaðr einn [af Spania] fór til Egiptalandz . . . ok . . . villdi fara um eyðimörk" (a merchant from Spain went to Egypt . . . and . . . wished to travel across the desert).

83. ÍÆ 2:139. The Latin may be found in the same volume (366–91).

I have argued elsewhere why I believe *Klári saga* is by Jón Hall-dórsson and why I think the claim that the narrative was translated from a Latin poem found in France is just a rhetorical ploy.[84] The saga is found in AM 657 a-b 4° (1350) and the copy is also assumed to be the work of Arngrímr Brandsson, but the style differs considerably from that of the *söguþáttur* and the *exempla* associated with Jón Halldórsson.[85] I would argue that this is because the saga, except for the opening sentence, is based on a manuscript version by Jón Halldórsson himself, while the *ævintýr* have been purged of the peculiarities of bishop Jón's style in the retelling, especially the Latin mannerisms and the plentiful and exotic vocabulary adopted from Low German, which was likely to have been a distinctive feature of Jón's Icelandic given his upbringing in the Hansa port of Bergen.[86] Although there is no evidence to point to any particular date for the composition of *Klári saga*, a case can be made that it was composed some time around 1326, the year bishop Jón issued his "Bannsak-abréf" and also perhaps reconfirmed bishop Þorlákur's penitential in

---

84. Hughes, "*Klári saga*," 147–48. To the references there should be added Roger Dragonetti, *Le mirage des sources: l'art du faux dans le roman médiéval* (Paris: Seuil, 1987). Because I argue the saga is an original work, not a translation, and closely bound with Skálholt (and Bergen), I would reject the argument by Peter Hallberg, *Stilsignalement och författarskap i norrön sagalitteratur: Synpunkter och exempel*, Nordistica Gothoburgensia 3 (Gothenburg: Acta Universitatis Gothoburgensis, 1968), 183–87, that the saga may be attributed to Bergr Sokkason (d. ca. 1345). I would also reject the argument of Karl G. Johansson that the origin of *Clári saga* should be assigned to the northern monastery of Þingeyrar, and the translation practices associated with it. See his "Bergr Sokkason och Arngrímur Brandsson—översättare och författare i samma miljö," in *Old Norse Myths, Literature and Society: Proceedings from the 11th International Saga Conference*, ed. Geraldine Barnes and Margaret Clunies Ross (Sydney: Centre for Medieval Studies, 2000), 181–97, as well as "A Scriptorium in Northern Iceland: Clárus saga (AM 657 a-b 4to) Revisited," in *Sagas and the Norwegian Experience—Sagaene og Noreg: Preprints of the 10th International Saga Conference, Trondheim 3.–9. August 1997*, ed. Jan Ragnar Hagland et al. (Trondheim: Norges Teknisk-naturvitenskapelige Universitet, Senter for Middelalderstudier, 1997), 323–31. Whatever role Arngrímr Brandsson may have had in having *Klári saga* and the *exempla* associated with bishop Jón committed to parchment during his tenure as abbot of Þingeyrar, he seems to have been careful about preserving Jón's vocabulary and style.

85. Gering (ÍÆ 2:xxviii-xxxi) examines the difference between the style of the saga and the *ævintýri* and comes to the conclusion that the saga is a work of the bishop's youth (2:xxx; i.e., presumably composed before 1300 when he was in France). This I believe is incorrect.

86. On the Low German influence in *Klári saga*, see Hughes, "*Klári saga*," 144–45, and Marianne Kalinke, "*Clári saga*: A Case of Low German Infiltration," *Scripta Islandica* 59 (2008): 5–25.

an expanded version and when he seems to have had issues of gender relations very much in mind.

Klári saga is considered to be the earliest of the surviving bridal-quest romances, initiating what became a distinctive Icelandic genre. It has been demonstrated that the medieval bridal quest narrative is a specifically German phenomenon with its roots in Merovingian historical accounts,[87] and bishop Jón was probably exposed to such stories during his time in Bergen. While the story has many features in common with the *riddarasögur*, it differs from them in that there is a strong didactic element in the story.[88] While the first half of the narrative chastises inappropriate female behavior, the second half extols wifely virtue in the face of overwhelming odds.[89] This is made abundantly clear in the epilogue to the saga:

---

87. Claudia Bornholdt, *Engaging Moments: The Origins of the Medieval Bridal-Quest Narrative*, Ergänzungsbände zum Reallexikon der Germanischen Altertumskunde 46 (Berlin: de Gruyter, 2005). On the motif in Icelandic literature see Marianne Kalinke, *Bridal-Quest Romance in Medieval Iceland*, Islandica 46 (Ithaca: Cornell University Press, 1990).

88. Not that the first half is free of such elements. During Klárus' first banquet with the princess Serena (*Clári saga*, Cederschiöld, 22), she offers to share a soft-boiled egg with him: "Ok nú býz hann at taka við egginu sem einn hofmaðr. En svá sem hann tekr við, þá fitlar hon til fingrunum. Ok allt saman af hálleika skurnsins ok hennar tilstilli verðr honum laust eggit ok steypiz upp í fang honum, svá at stropinn strýkr um bringuna ok kyrtilinn allt niðr at belti" (And now he prepares to take the egg as a courtier. But as he takes it then she fumbles it with her fingers. And all together as a result of the slipperiness of its shell and her connivance, the egg gets away from him and tumbles onto his breast so that congealed contents of the egg spill down his chest and his tunic all the way down to his belt). On this episode see Marianne Kalinke, "Table Decorum and the Quest for a Bride in Clári saga," in *At the Table: Metaphorical and Material Cultures of Food in Medieval and Early Modern Europe*, ed. Timothy J. Tomasik and Juliann M. Vitello, Arizona Studies in the Middle Ages and Renaissance 18 (Turnhout: Brepols, 2007), 51–72. Petrus Alfonsi has a whole section on the importance of good table manners embedded in chapter 26: "De modo comendendi," *Disciplina Clericalis*, Hilka, 1:37–38, a section that unfortunately is not preserved in any of the Icelandic translations. Tolan (*Petrus Alphonsi*, 155, 259) mentions that the fifteenth-century scribe of Vienna, Hofbibliothek 3530 at fol. 110ᵛ inserted a whole *exemplum* right before the epilogue on how to eat an egg properly (printed in *Disciplina Clericalis*, Hilka, Anhang II, 1:77).

89. The outline story for the saga can be found in *Beowulf* lines 1931b-62: a young woman living under the protection of her father behaves imperiously to any man who looks at her. She is given in marriage at her father's counsel and becomes a model wife. There has long been consensus that this woman is called Mōdþrȳð or Þrȳð, but the most recent editors opt for an earlier suggestion, that she is called Fremu. See R. D. Fulk et al., *Klaeber's "Beowulf" and "The Fight at Finnsburg,"* 4th ed. (Toronto: University of Toronto Press, 2008), 222–26, and R. D. Fulk, "The Name of Offa's Queen: *Beowulf* 1931-2," *Anglia* 122 (2004): 614–39. On the relationship of *Klári saga* to this material, see Hughes, "*Klári saga*," 150–52.

En hon [Serena] þolði allan þenna tíma angist ok armœðu fyrir ekki
vætta útan fyrir sína eiginliga dygð ok einfaldleik . . . ok þetta allt
lagði hon at baki sér ok þar með fǫður, frændr ok vini ok allan heimsins metnað, upp takand, viljanligt fátœki með þessum hinum herfiliga
stafkarli, gefandi svá á sér ljós dœmi, hversu ǫðrum góðum konum
byrjar at halda dygð við sína eiginbœndr eða unnasta. Fór þat ok
eptir verðugu í síðustu, at hon fekk þat, er hon var maklig fyrir sína
fáheyrða staðfestu . . . varð hon yfirdróttning allz Saxlands.[90] (*Clári
saga*, Cederschiöld, 73–74)

But she [Serena] endured all the time the misery and distress for
no other reason than her singular probity and simplicity. . . . And
she put absolutely everything behind her, including father, kin and
friends, and all the world's honor, taking up poverty willingly with
this miserable beggar, giving so by her behavior a clear *exemplum*,
how it befits other good women to maintain their probity with their
husbands or betrothed ones. That also turned out in due course as it
was deserved, that she received that which was fitting for her because
of her unheard-of steadfastness, that . . . she became sovereign queen
of all Saxland.

It is the period of the transition from haughty princess to model
wife that especially interests bishop Jón. To illustrate this process he
draws upon two *exempla* found only in later collections. The second
half of *Klári saga* takes elements from a narrative found in *El Conde
Lucanor* by Don Juan Manuel, the Infante of Castile (1282–1348), a
contemporary of the bishop's and someone with Dominican connections.[91] This narrative becomes later popularly known as "the taming

---

90. Given the tenor of this passage it seems more appropriate to translate *unnasti*
in its modern meaning "betrothed" rather than the more common medieval meaning,
"lover."

91. Juan Manuel founded a Dominican Convent in Peñafiel in 1318 where he was later
buried, and all through his life kept close connections with the Dominicans. For a succinct
introduction to Juan Manuel and his times, see David A. Flory, *"El Conde Lucanor":
Don Juan Manuel en su contexto histórico* (Madrid: Editorial Pliegos, 1995). Since the
final section of *El Conde Lucanor* was not completed until 1335, it is not a matter of
bishop Jón being aware of Jan Manuel's text, but of his being very much in tune with the
same traditions out of which the Spaniard composed his narratives. See also Jonathan
Burgoyne, *Reading the Exemplum Right: Fixing the Meaning of "El Conde Lucanor,"*

of the shrew."[92] It is combined with the narrative of the supremely patient wife later identified with the story of Griselda.[93]

Klári saga demonstrates that in the hands of a skillful storyteller, *exempla* could be successfully used to create a narrative that could play a role in the Church's attempt to bring Icelandic social behavior and gender relationships more in line with what it had been able to achieve on the continent of Europe. *Klári saga* promotes an extremely patriarchal version of social organization and permits only a very a limited role for women in its fictional society. Serena's "patience" in the face of the brutality and humiliation inflicted on her by a man she believes to be her husband is offered without qualification as a model of wifely behavior.

There are also among the surviving Icelandic *exempla* those that look as if they might have been selected because of their usefulness

---

North Carolina Studies in the Romance Languages and Literature 289 (Chapel Hill: University of North Carolina Press, 2007).

92. Tale type 901, "The Shrewish wife is Reformed," in Aarne-Thompson, *Types of the Folktale*, 310–12. Now called "The Obstinate Wife Learns to Obey" in the revised edition, Hans-Jörg Uther, *The Types of International Folktales: A Classification and Bibliography Based on the System of Antti Aarne and Stith Thompson*, 3 vols., FF Communications 133–35 [284–86] (Helsinki: Suomalainen Tiedeakatemia, 2004), 1:523–27. The Spanish version of the story is found in tale 35: "De lo que contesçió a un mançebo que casó con una muger muy fuerte et muy brava" (What happened to a young man who married a fierce and truculent woman), in Juan Manuel, *"El Conde Lucanor": A Collection of Medieval Spanish Stories*, ed. and trans. John England (Warminster: Aris and Phillips, 1987), 216–23. See also *El Libro de los Enxiemplos del Conde Lucanor et de Patronio*, ed. Hermann Knust and Adolf Birch-Hirschfeld (Leipzig: Seele, 1900), 154–61 and notes 368–79, as well as Renaldo Ayerbe-Chaux, *El Conde Lucanor: materia tradicional y originalidad creadora* (Madrid: José Porrúa Turanzas, 1975), 154–60, 309–19, as well as Hughes, *"Klári saga,"* 155–56.

93. Tale Type 887, "Griselda" (Aarne-Thompson, 302–03; Uther, 1:521–22). The earliest recognized appearance of this tale is Book 10, tale 10 of the *Decameron* (1350–1353) of Giovanni Boccaccio (1313–1375). Bishop Jón also appears responsible for introducing another story otherwise first recorded in *El Conde Lucanor*, tale 11: "De lo que contesçió a un Deán de Sanctiago con Don Illán, el grand maestro de Toledo" (What happened to a Dean of Santiago with Don Illán, the great sage of Toledo) [England, *El Conde Lucanor*, 84–91; *El Libro de los Enxiemplos del Conde Lucanor*, Birch-Hirschfeld, 45–51 and notes 324–34; and Ayerbe-Chaux, *El Conde Lucanor*, 98–104, 239–46]. In this story the Mage, Don Illan of Toledo, tests the ability of the Dean of Santiago to keep his word, although instead of partridges cooking in the kitchen, the Icelandic version substitutes a capon. This narrative, the third of the three stories associated with the Arabian magician Pérús published as LXXXI in *ÍÆ* (1:217–31) under the title: "Af meistara Pero ok hans leikum" (About Master Pérús and his games), is found in AM 657 a-b 4°, specifically from the second part of the codex designated by Gering as C1, dating from around 1400, as well as in AM 586 4° (ca. 1400) and in AM 343 4° from the same period.

in attempting to provide a model for what the Church considered appropriate male and female behavior. Markus Schürer's research has demonstrated the way in which the *exempla* collections helped to define the religious community, and all available evidence points to the Icelandic *exempla* being made for a monastic audience. Many of the stories tell of individuals with ecclesiastical connections, bishops, popes, and pious monarchs, or they deal with monastic life. A typical example would be Gering's XLIV: "Af tveimr munkum" (Of Two Monks),[94] in which two monks lost in a forest pray to Mary for assistance. They come to a well-appointed monastery, but at Matins all that the brothers sing is the opening verse from the Psalm 59 (Vulgate): "Deus, reppulisti nos et destruxisti nos; iratus es et misertus es nobis" (O God, you have cast us off, and have destroyed us; you have been angry, and have had mercy on us),[95] changing the last phrase each time to "et non misertus es nobis" (and have not had mercy on us). In the morning the elder monk is asked to preach to the brothers and he embarks on a sermon on the fallen angels during which the brothers in the congregation begin disappearing one by one until only the abbot and the two visitors are left. The monastery turns out to have been populated by devils who were forced against their will by Mary to give the two monks shelter and succor—but they could not bear to hear a sermon that focused on the shame and misery of their fall from grace. The story ends with the infernal monastery disappearing in a clap of thunder and the two monks finding themselves alone on a level field.[96]

---

94. ÍÆ 1:147–49. This is a story assigned by Gering to bishop Jón and adapted from Étienne de Bourbon's *Tractatus de diversis materiis predicabilibus*, book 2.

95. Ps. 59:3 (Douay-Rheims translation, modernized) from *The Vulgate Bible*, 6 vols., Dumbarton Oaks Medieval Library (Cambridge, MA: Harvard University Press, 2010–13).

96. ÍÆ 1:148: "Stóðu þeir úti á slèttum velli" (they stood outside on a level plain). This echoes the state of Þórr and his companions at the end of their visit to Útgarðaloki: "Þá sá hann þar vǫllu víða ok fagra en ǫnga borg" (Then he saw a wide and fair plain and no stronghold) [Snorri Sturluson, *Prologue and Gylfaginning*, 43 (slightly normalized)]. There is no corresponding phrase in the Latin text, which ends after the monastery has disappeared (Étienne de Bourbon, *Anecdotes historiques*, 76): "Dicti autem monarchi, se invenientes inter dumos et paludes vix ad viam redire potuerunt" (then the said monks, finding themselves among brambles and bogs, with difficulty were able to return to the road).

Among the stories translated from *Handlyng Synne*[97] is one of a woman who was a priest's concubine and who bore him four sons, all of whom became priests.[98] Despite her sons' urgings, she refuses to repent, and after her death, they cannot prevent the devils dragging her off to hell. Sacerdotal celibacy was never a strong point of the Icelandic clergy and even the most reform-minded bishop during Catholic times was forced to turn a blind eye to priestly concubinage. Nevertheless this *exemplum* was aimed at women listeners so that "allar konur skylldu varaz at falla í þersa synd þær sem heyra þvílík dæmi" (all women should be warned against falling into this sin, those who listen to such an *exemplum*).[99] So far as such priests who take concubines are concerned: "þeir vitu vel hvat þeir gjöra, en þat hefi ek heyrt sagt fyrir satt, at engi meistari væri svá góðr, þóat [hann] væri svá víss sem Salomon ok svá veltalaðr sem Aron, ok lifði til þers at hann væri þúsund ára gamall, þá kynni hann eigi at tala af þeirri sorg ok pínu er prestar skulu hafa er liggja í þersu saurlífi" (they know very well what they are doing, and I have heard it told for a fact, that no university scholar may be so learned, even though he be as wise as Solomon and as eloquent as Aaron, and even though he should live until he was a thousand years old, that he should be able to tell of the miseries and tortures that priests will have who indulge in this kind of immoral life).[100]

Another story from an unknown source found in AM 624 4°

---

97. Robert Manning of Brunne, *Handlyng Synne*, Furnivall, 253–58, lines 7987–8158; ÍÆ 1:124–26; Einar G. Pétursson, *Miðaldaævintýri þýdd úr ensku*, 51–56.

98. XXXVI in ÍÆ 1:124–26: "Frá prestakonu er tekin varð af djöflunum" (About the priest's wife who became carried away by devils; Gering's title). André Vauchez has shown how the problem of priests with concubines was a Europe-wide phenomenon in "La question du célibat ecclésiastique dans l'Occident médiéval: Un état de la recherche," in Lars Bisgaard et al., eds., *Medieval Spirituality in Scandinavia and Europe: A Collection of Essays in Honour of Tore Nyberg*, Odense University Studies in History and Social Sciences 234 (Odense: Odense University Press, 2001), 21–32. Certainly, this clerical celibacy was never effectively enforced in Iceland as the case of Jón Arason, last Catholic bishop of Hólar (1484–1550), testifies. He had six children with Helga Sigurðardóttir and his sons came to occupy important positions in the Icelandic administration. Two of them were beheaded with him at Skálholt on November 7, 1550. On concubinage in medieval Icelandic society, see Else Ebel, *Der Konkubinat nach altwestnordischen Quellen: Philologische Studien zur sogenannten "Friedelehe,"* Ergänzungsbände zum Reallexikon der Germanischen Altertumskunde 8 (Berlin: de Gruyter, 1993), and Auður Magnúsdóttir, *Frillor och fruar: Politik och samlevnad på Island, 1200–1400*, Avhandlingar från Historiska Institutionen i Göteborg 29 (Gothenburg: Historiska Institutionen, 2001).

99. ÍÆ 1:125.

100. Ibid., 1:126.

(mid-fifteenth century) tells of an unmarried woman who lived an immoral life.[101] The devil, becoming envious of her, plots to betray her and arranged it so that a young man falls in love with her and gets her pregnant. She gives birth to her baby in secret and then kills it. Even though she regrets this action, she does not go to confession. One night she prays to God for help and receives three drops of blood on the back of her hand. She does not know what this means and continues to pray until God appears to her and shows her his heart and the wound in his side. She then goes to confession and tell her sins with floods of tears. These tears fall on the marks left by the drops of blood and they disappear even though before this no amount of washing or rubbing had any effect on them. "Hèr af megum vèr hugsa, hversu guði er þat þægiligt, at vèr skriptumz rækiliga af öllum várum syndum ok leynum eigi með illvilja því er vèr munum at segja" (here we may contemplate how agreeable it is for God that we thoroughly confess all our sins and conceal not with ill-will that which we ought to say).[102]

In these narratives women are deprived of any agency. And if women do have agency, they use it to make decisions that are immoral and antisocial. Nowhere is this more reinforced outside of *Klári saga* than in a tale based on an English original also found in AM 624 4°, here set in France.[103] A rich man has a wife who is "góða ok fulla af miskunnsemi" (good and full of mercy) and a daughter who is "þá hina vænstu er verða mátti sköput af holldi ok blóði" (the most beautiful creature who might be fashioned of flesh and blood).[104] The father begins an affair with his daughter and she bears him three sons in secret, each one of whom she kills. One day the mother catches them out and says she is leaving. Facing the threat of the discovery of

---

101. Ibid., XXXVII, 1:126–27: "Af konu úgiptri er drap barn sitt" (Of the unmarried woman who killed her child; Gering's title).

102. Ibid., 1:127.

103. Ibid., XXXIX, 1:129–33: "Af konu er drýgði hórdóm við föður sinn" (Of the woman who committed adultery with her father; Gering's title). There are three surviving verse versions of this narrative in Middle English. *Altenglische Legende: Neue Folge*, ed. C. Horstmann (Heilbronn: Henninger, 1881; repr. Hildesheim: Olms, 1969), 334–38, prints one version with variants from a second. In *Miðaldaævintýri þýdd úr ensku*, 60–80, Einar G. Pétursson prints a third version not known to Horstmann in 1881 and discusses the relationship among the English versions and the Icelandic translation (xc-xci). For a history of incest in Iceland, see Már Jónsson, *Blóðskömm á Íslandi*, 1270–1870 (Reykjavík: Háskólaútgáfan, 1993).

104. *ÍÆ* 1:129.

288 New Norse Studies

their behavior, at the instigation of her father the daughter kills her mother. Sometime later the father one day at church is overcome with remorse and goes to the priest and openly confesses all his sins and promises to undertake the penance assigned. The father comes home and tells his daughter that he will have nothing more to do with her. He goes to bed early as he must begin a pilgrimage the next day. The daughter comes in on him, cuts his throat, and then goes with her three serving women taking with them all the valuables they can carry to another city where she uses her wealth to live a life of luxury and license as a courtesan. One day a famous bishop comes to town to preach and so many people go to hear him that there are no customers for the lady and her companions. She decides to go to the church to drum up some business. As she enters the bishop looks at her and it is as if she has an iron band around her neck and from it chains by which demons are leading her. The bishop is full of compassion for her plight and continues to preach of God's mercy. At that, "með almáttigs guðs miskunn fló ein ör í hennar hjarta . . . svá at tárin fellu niðr um hennar kinnr; ok brast þá festrin um hennar háls, en fjándinn varð hræddr ok flýði í brott" (through the mercy of almighty God an arrow flew in to her heart . . . so that the tears fell down on her cheeks; and then the band around her neck shattered, and the devil became afraid and fled away).[105] She now falls down and asks for God's help and mercy. She then confesses all her sins and asks the bishop for absolution. He says she must wait until the end of the sermon, but when it is finished and he goes to seek her out, he finds she is dead. The bishop now falls down and in tears begs God for a sign whether she has been saved or damned. A voice comes from heaven announcing that this formerly sinful soul now shines brightly in heaven, and the woman's body should be buried in sanctified ground, "því[at] þótt maðrinn hafi gjört allar þær syndir sem gjöraz mega í verölldinni ok vill hann skriptaz ok iðraz ok yfir bæta ok af láta ok lifa vel síðan, þá mun guð fyrirgefa honum" (because even though someone has done all those sins in the world that one might do, and such a person wishes to confess and repent and make redress and give up those sins and live well afterwards, then God will forgive that person).[106] This *exemplum*

---

105. Ibid., 1:132.
106. Ibid., 1:133.

is one of a number found in Gering's collection that emphasize the power of repentance and the infinite nature of God's mercy, but that also emphasize woman's sinful nature, which we have already seen was a feature of Jean Gobi's *exempla*. In such a world view, women only act on their own to do wrong. The sinful woman cannot make a move to address her sins but must first be struck by the arrow of God's mercy launched by the bishop. This leads her to confess her sins, but not to repent them or receive absolution. Nevertheless the intercession of the bishop on her behalf proves efficacious and according to the story she is enabled to be numbered among the blessed in heaven.

The preservation of the *exempla* in numerous manuscripts and fragments demonstrates that they did circulate, even if they may have left virtually no traces in Icelandic vernacular literature. This suggests that they were largely ineffective in influencing their target audience, except perhaps the one within monastery walls. Ironically, the kind of "reform" of gender relations that was at the heart of the social reforms attempted by the Church in the thirteenth and fourteenth centuries—and that lies behind the ideology of the *exempla*—would have to wait until the Reformation.

When the Reformation came to Iceland the Church lost its ability to legislate its own affairs, relinquishing control to the secular authorities. On 2 September 1537, Christian III, king of Denmark (1534–59) published an ordinance that abolished Roman Catholicism in his kingdom and its dependencies, including Iceland. This ordinance was translated into Icelandic by Gissur Einarsson, bishop of Skálholt (1540–48), and in 1541 the Alþingi confirmed it for the Diocese of Skálholt, although it would have to wait until 1551 to be confirmed in the Diocese of Hólar.[107] So far as the regulation of gender relationships is concerned, and in particular with respect to marriage, the ordinance represented a radical change from what was then the practice: "Med eckta personur hiuskaparins vegna hafa Gudz ordz þienarar ecki at giora, nema þad sem vidvijkur þeirra samteinging. og ad hugsuala þeirra sorgmæddar samuitzkur. enn allt annad heyrer til veralldligrar valldzstiornar" (The servants of God's word have nothing

---

107. DI, "Kirkjuordinanzía," 10:117–67 (Appendices 167–255; Latin text after the printed version of 1537, 256–338). See further Gissur Einarsson and Gunnar Kristjánsson, *Saga biskupsstólanna*, 50–52; on the reformation in Iceland in general, see Gunnar Karlsson, *History of Iceland*, 128–37.

to do with married people in terms of marriage, except that which concerns their joining together and to comfort their sorrow-stricken consciousnesses. But everything else is the province of the secular authorities).[108] Marriage is no longer a sacrament and the regulation of individual behavior has now become the concern of the State, not the Church. What this meant became clear a few years later when in 1564 the Alþingi passed the *Stóridómur*. This ordinance regulated individual sexual behavior in great detail and punished transgression by fines and other penalties, even stipulating the death penalty for the most severe offences and for repeat offenders.[109] A secular court of law now became the venue for regulating human behavior with its foibles and missteps, not the pulpit or the privacy of the confessional. Like many other things associated with Catholic practice in Iceland, there was no longer any place for the *exempla*. The State had taken over the regulation of personal relationships through the apparatus of the law and the courts, and was not inclined to trust in stories as a way of encouraging individuals to monitor or reform their behavior.

Bibliography

Primary Sources and Translations

Baumgarte, Suzanne, ed. *Summa bonorum: Eine deutsche Exempelsammlung aus dem 15. Jahrhundert nach Stephan von Bourbon.* Texte des späten Mittelalters und der frühen Neuzeit 40. Berlin: Erich Schmidt, 1999.

Biskupa sögur. Vol 3. Edited by Guðrún Ása Grímsdóttir. Íslenzk fornrit 17. Reykjavík: Hið íslenzka fornritafélag, 1998.

Caesarius of Heisterbach. *Dialogue on Miracles.* Translated by H. von

---

108. DI 10:143. The remainder of this section of the ordinance is three brief paragraphs indicating that marriage must not take place within the forbidden degrees of consanguinity, that the banns must be read three times, and the wedding ceremony will follow the form prescribed by Martin Luther. For a thorough survey of how the Church responded to its new and limited responsibilities, see Arngrímur Jónsson, *Fyrstu handbækur presta á Íslandi eftir siðbót: Handbók Marteins Einarssonar 1555, Handritið Ny kgl. Sam. 138 4to, Graduale 1594—Litúrgísk þróunarsaga íslenzkrar helgisiðahefðar á 16. öld* (Reykjavík: Háskólaútgáfan, 1992), 333–89.

109. "Stóri dómr um frændsemi- og sifjaspiell, hórdómr og frillulífi" (The great verdict concerning violation of the rules of consanguinity, incest, adultery and concubinage, June 30th, 1564; DI 14:271–76). Before it was repealed in 1870 twenty-five men and twenty-five women, mostly from the less privileged sections of society, had been executed in the enforcement of the law's harshest prescriptions.

E. Scott and C. C. Swinton Bland. Introduction by G. G. Coulton. 2 vols. London: Routledge, 1929.

———. *Dialogues miraculous: Dialog über die Wunder.* Edited and translated by Nikolaus Nösges and Horst Schneider. 5 vols. Fontes Christiani 86. Turnhout: Brepols, 2009.

Clári saga. Edited by Gustaf Cederschiöld. Altnordische Saga-Bibliothek 12. Halle: Niemeyer, 1907.

Clarus saga, Clari fabella. Edited by Gustaf Cederschiöld. Latin translated by Samuel J. Cavallin. Lund: Gleerup, 1879.

Egils saga. Edited by Bjarni Einarsson. London: Viking Society for Northern Research, 2003.

Einar G. Pétursson, ed. *Miðaldaævintýri þýdd úr ensku.* Rit 11. Reykjavík: Árna Magnússonar á Íslandi, 1976.

Eirspennill: Nóregs konunga sögur. Edited by Finnur Jónsson. Christiania [Oslo]: Julius Thømte, 1916.

Étienne de Bourbon. *Anecdotes historiques, légendes et apologues tirés du recueil inédit d'Étienne de Bourbon dominicain du XIIIe siècle.* Edited by Albert Lecoy de la Marche. Paris: Renouard, 1877.

———. *Tractatus de diversis materiis predicabilibus: liber tertius de eis que pertinent ad donum scientie et penitentiam.* Edited by Jacques Berlioz. Corpus Christianorum Continuatio Mediaevalis 124 B. Turnhout: Brepols, 2006.

———. *Tractatus de diversis materiis predicabilibus: Prologus, Prima Pars. De Dono timoris.* Edited by Jacques Berlioz and Jean-Luc Eichenlaub. Corpus Christianorum Continuatio Mediaevalis 124. Turnhout: Brepols, 2002.

Fulk, R. D., Robert E. Bjork, and John D. Niles, eds. *Klaeber's "Beowulf" and "The Fight at Finnsburg."* 4th ed. Toronto: Toronto University Press, 2008.

Gering, Hugo, ed. *Íslendzk æventýri: Isländische Legenden, Novellen und Märchen.* 2 vols. Halle: Buchhandlungen des Waisenhauses, 1882–83.

Gregory the Great. *Forty Gospel Homilies.* Translated by Dom David Hurst. Cistercian Studies Series 123. Kalamazoo, MI: Cistercian Publications, 1990.

———. *Quadraginta homilarium in Evangelia libri duo.* Edited by J. P. Migne. Patrologia Latina 76. Paris: Migne, 1849. Cols. 1075–312.

Guðmundur Erlendsson að Felli í Sléttahlíð. *Dæmisögur Esóps í ljóðum.* Part 1. Edited by Grímur M. Helgason. Reykjavík: Æskan, 1967.

Hauksbók udgiven efter de arnamagnæanske håndskrifter no. 371, 544 og 675, 4°. Edited by Eiríkur Jónsson and Finnur Jónsson. Copenhagen: Thiele, 1892–96.

Homilíu-Bók: Isländska homilier eftir en handskrift från tolfte århundradet. Edited by Theodor Wisén. Lund: Gleerups, 1872.

Horstmann, C., ed. *Altenglische Legende: Neue Folge*. Heilbronn: Henninger, 1881. Repr. Hildesheim: Olms, 1969.

Íslensk hómilíubók: fornar stólræður. Edited by Sigurbjörn Einarsson et al. Reykjavík: Hið íslenska bókmenntafélag, 1993.

Jacques de Vitry. *The Exempla or Illustrative Stories from the Sermones Vulgares*. Edited by Thomas Frederick Crane. London: D. Nutt, 1890. Repr. New York: Burt Franklin, 1971.

Járnsíða og Kristinréttur Árna Þorlákssonar. Edited by Haraldur Bernharðsson et al. Smárit Sögufélags. Reykjavík: Sögufélag, 2005.

Jean Gobi. *La "Scala Cœli" de Jean Gobi*. Edited by Marie-Anne Polo de Beaulieu. Paris: Éditions de CNRS, 1991.

Jón Árnason. *Íslenzkar þjóðsögur og ævintýri*. 2 vols. Leipzig: J. C. Hinrich, 1862–64.

———. *Íslenzkar þjóðsögur og ævintýri*. 2nd ed. 2 vols. Reykjavík: Sögufélag, 1925–39.

Jón Sigurðsson, Jón Þorkelsson, Páll Eggert Ólason, and Björn Þorsteinsson, eds. *Diplomatarium Islandicum: Íslenzkt fornbréfasafn*. 16 vols. Copenhagen and Reykjavík: Hið íslenzka bókmenntafélag, 1857–1972.

Jorgensen, Peter A. "Four Æventýri." *Opuscula* 5:295–328. Bibliotheca Arnamagnæana 31. Copenhagen: Munksgaard, 1975.

———. "Ten Icelandic Exempla and their Middle English Source." *Opuscula* 4:177–207. Bibliotheca Arnamagnæana 30. Copenhagen: Munksgaard, 1970.

———. "The Icelandic Translations from Middle English." In *Studies for Einar Haugen*, edited by Evelyn Scherabon Firchow et al., 305–20. Janua linguarum, Series maior 59. The Hague: Mouton, 1972.

———. *The Story of Jonatas in Iceland*. Rit 45. Reykjavík: Árna Magnússonar á Íslandi, 1997.

Juan Manuel. *"El Conde Lucanor": A Collection of Medieval Spanish Stories*. Edited and translated by John England. Warminster: Aris and Phillips, 1987.

———. *El Libro de los Enxiemplos del Conde Lucanor et de Patronio*. Text and Notes by Hermann Knust. Edited by Adolf Birch-Hirschfeld. Leipzig: Seele, 1900.

Loth, Agnete, ed. *Late Medieval Icelandic Romances*. 5 vols. Editiones Arnamagnæanæ B20–24. Copenhagen: Munksgaard, 1962–65.

Louis-Jensen, Jonna. "Nogle Æventýri." *Opuscula* 5:263–77. Bibliotheca Arnamagnæana 31. Copenhagen: Munksgaard, 1975.

Luther, Martin, trans. *Biblia, das ist, die gantze Heilige Schrift Deutsch*. Wittenberg: Hans Lufft, 1534. Repr. in 2 vols, Cologne: Taschen, 2004.

Magnús Grímsson and Jón Árnason. *Íslenzk æfintýri*. Reykjavík: Einar Þórðarson, 1852. Repr. Akureyri: Bókaútgáfan Edda, 1942.

Manning (Mannyng), Robert, of Brunne. *"Handlyng Synne" (Written*

A.D. *1303) with the French Treatise on which it is Founded, "Le Manuel des Pechiez" by William of Wadington.* Edited by Frederick J. Furnivall. London: Roxburghe Club, 1862.

———. *Handlyng Synne.* Edited by Idelle Sullens. Medieval and Renaissance Texts and Studies 14. Binghamton, NY: Center for Medieval and Renaissance Studies, SUNY, 1983.

———. *"Handlyng Synne" and its French Original.* Edited by Frederick J. Furnivall. Early English Text Society, o.s., 119, 123. 1901–03. Repr. Millwood, NY: Kraus, 1988.

Oddur Gottskálksson. *Nýja Testamenti Odds Gottskálkssonar.* Edited by Sigurbjörn Einarsson et al. Reykjavík: Lögberg, 1988.

Ólafur Halldórsson. "AM 240 fol XV: tvinn úr handriti með ævintýrum." *Gripla* 18 (2007): 23–46.

Ólafur Ragnarsson, Sverrir Jakobsson, Margrét Guðmundsdóttir, eds. *Íslenskt þjóðsagnasafn.* 5 vols. Reykjavík: Vaka-Helgafell, 2000.

Partalopa saga. Edited by Lise Præstgaard Andersen. Editiones Arnamagnæanæ B28. Copenhagen: Reitzel, 1983.

Petrus Alfonsi. *The "Disciplina Clericalis" of Petrus Alfonsi.* Translated and edited by Eberhard Hermes. English translation by P. R. Quarrie. London: Routledge and Kegan Paul, 1977. First published in German, 1970.

———. *Petri Alfonsi Disciplina clericalis.* Edited by Alfons Hilka and Werner Söderhjelm. 3 vols. Acta societatis scientiarum Fennicae 38.4–5, 49.4. Helsinki: Drukerei der Finnischen litteraturgesellschaft, 1911–22.

Petrus Comestor. *Historia scholastica.* Edited by J. P. Migne. *Patrologia Latina* 198. Paris: Migne, 1855. Cols. 1019–1722.

Ross, Woodburn O., ed. *Middle English Sermons: Edited from British Museum MS. Royal 18 B xxiii*, Early English Text Society 209. London: Oxford University Press, 1940.

Saga Óláfs Tryggvasonar af Oddr Snorrason munk. Edited by Finnur Jónsson. Copenhagen: Munksgaard, 1932.

Sigfús Sigfússon. *Íslenzkar þjóð-sögur og -sagnir.* 16 vols. Seyðisfjörður, Hafnarfjörður and Reykjavík: Nokkrir Austfirðingar, Prentsmiðja Hafnarfjarðar and Víkingsútgáfan, 1922–58.

———. *Íslenzkar þjóðsögur og sagnir.* Edited by Óskar Halldórsson et al. 11 vols. Hafnarfjörður: Þjóðsaga, 1982–93.

Snorri Sturluson. *Edda.* Translated by Anthony Faulkes. Everyman's Library. London: Dent, 1987.

———. *Edda: Prologue and Gylfaginning.* Edited by Anthony Faulkes. 2nd ed. London: Viking Society for Northern Research, 1988.

———. *Edda: Skáldskaparmál.* Edited by Anthony Faulkes. 2 vols. London: Viking Society for Northern Research, 1998.

Steinunn Finnsdóttir. *Hyndlu rímur og Snækóngs rímur.* Edited by Bjarni Vilhjálmsson. Rit Rímnafélagsins 3. Reykjavík: Rímnafélagið, 1950.

Stjórn. Edited by Reidar Astås. 2 vols. Norrøne Tekster 8. Oslo: Riksarkivet, 2009.

Stjórn: Gammelnorsk Bibelhistoria. Edited by C. R. Unger. Christiania [Oslo]: Feilberg and Landmark, 1862.

Storm, Gustav, ed. *Islandske Annaler indtil 1578.* Oslo: Grøndahl, 1888. Repr. Oslo: Norsk Historisk Kjeldeskrift-Institutt, 1977.

Sverris saga. Edited by Þorleifur Hauksson. Íslenzk fornrit 30. Reykjavík: Hið íslenzka fornritafélag, 2007.

Thomas de Cantimpré. *Les exemples du "Livre des Abeilles": Une vision médiévale.* Edited and translated by Henri Platelle. Miroir du Moyen Âge. Turnhout: Brepols, 1997.

Trójumanna saga. Edited by Jonna Louis-Jensen. Editiones Arnamagnæanæ A8. Copenhagen: Munksgaard, 1963.

Þorvaldur Bjarnason, ed. *Leifar fornra kristinna frœða íslenzkra.* Copenhagen: H. Hagerup, 1878.

Víga-Glúms saga. Edited by Gabriel Turville-Petre. 2nd ed. Oxford: Clarendon Press, 1960.

The Vulgate Bible. 6 vols. Dumbarton Oaks Medieval Library. Cambridge, MA: Harvard University Press, 2010–13.

Wycliffe, John, and his Followers. *The Holy Bible.* Edited by Josiah Forshall and Frederic Madden. 4 vols. Oxford: Oxford University Press, 1850.

Secondary Sources

Aarne, Antti, ed., and Stith Thompson, trans. and enlarg. *The Types of the Folktale: A Classification and Bibliography.* 2nd rev. ed. FF Communications vol. 75, no. 184. Helsinki: Suomalainen Tiedeakatemie, 1981.

Agnes S. Arnórsdóttir. *Konur og vígamenn: Staða kynjanna á Íslandi á 12. og 13. öld.* Sagnfræðirannsóknir 12. Reykjavík: Sagnfræðistofnun—Háskólaútgáfan, 1995.

———. *Property and Virginity: The Christianization of Marriage in Medieval Iceland, 1200–1600.* Aarhus: Aarhus University Press, 2010.

Arngrímur Jónsson. *Fyrstu handbækur presta á Íslandi eftir siðbót: Handbók Marteins Einarssonar 1555, Handritið Ny kgl. Sam. 138 4to, Graduale 1594—Lítúrgísk þróunarsaga íslenzkrar helgisiðahefðar á 16. öld.* Reykjavík: Háskólaútgáfan, 1992.

Arnould, E. J. *Le "Manuel des Péchés": Étude de literature religieuse Anglo-Normande (XIIIme siècle).* Paris: Droz, 1940.

Auður Magnúsdóttir. *Frillor och fruar: Politik och samlevnad på Island, 1200–1400.* Avhandlingar från Historiska Institutionen i Göteborg 29. Gothenburg: Historiska Institutionen, 2001.

Ayerbe-Chaux, Renaldo. *El Conde Lucanor: materia tradicional y originalidad creadora.* Madrid: José Porrúa Turanzas, 1975.

Bagerius, Henric. *Mandom och mödom: Sexualitet, homosocialitet och aristokratisk identitet på det senmedeltida Island.* Gothenburg: Göteborgs Universitet, 2009.

Barr, Beth Allison. *The Pastoral Care of Women in Late Medieval England.* Gender in the Middle Ages 3. Woodbridge: Boydell Press, 2008.

Berlioz, Jacques, and Marie Anne Polo de Beaulieu. "*Exempla*: A Discussion and a Case Study, 1: *Exempla* as a Source for the History of Women, 2: *Mulier* and *Femina*: The Representation of Women in the *Scala celi* of Jean Gobi." In Rosenthal, *Medieval Women*, 37–65.

Björn K. Þórólfsson. *Rímur fyrir 1600.* Safn Fræðafjelagsins um Ísland og Íslendinga 9. Copenhagen: Möller, 1934.

Bødker, Laurits. *Folk Literature (Germanic).* International Dictionary of Regional European Ethnology and Folklore 2. Copenhagen: Rosenkilde and Bagger, 1965.

Bornholdt, Claudia. *Engaging Moments: The Origins of the Medieval Bridal-Quest Narrative.* Ergänzungsbände zum Reallexikon der germanischen Altertumskunde 46. Berlin: de Gruyter, 2005.

Boulhosa, Patricia Pires. *Gamli sáttmáli: tilurð og tilgangur.* Translated by Már Jónsson. Smárit Sögufélags. Reykjavík: Sögufélag, 2006.

———. *Icelanders and the Kings of Norway: Medieval Sagas and Legal Texts.* The Northern World 17. Leiden: Brill, 2005.

———. "A Response to 'Gamli sáttmáli—hvað næst'" *Saga* 49 (2011): 137–51.

Brémond, Claude, Jacques Le Goff and Jean-Claude Schmitt. *L'"Exemplum."* 2nd ed. Typologie des Sources du moyen âge occidental, fascicle 40. Turnholt: Brepols, 1996.

Brundage, James A. "Sexual Equality in Medieval Canon Law." In Rosenthal, *Medieval Women*, 66–79.

Bureus, Johannes Thomae. *En nyttigh Bok, om Konnunga Styrilse och Höfdinga.* Uppsala: Eskil Mattsson, 1634. Repr. edition by Lennart Moberg. Sammlingar utgivna af Svenska fornskriftsällskapet 235, no. 69.1. Uppsala: Almqvist och Wiksell, 1964.

Burgoyne, Jonathan. *Reading the Exemplum Right: Fixing the Meaning of "El Conde Lucanor."* North Carolina Studies in the Romance Languages and Literature 289. Chapel Hill: University of North Carolina Press, 2007.

Caldwell, James F. "On the Icelandic *Disciplina clericalis.*" *Scandinavian Studies* 10 (1929): 125–35.

de Leeuw van Weenen, Andrea, ed. *The Icelandic Homily Book: Perg. 15 4° in the Royal Library Stockholm.* Íslensk handrit: Studies in Quarto 3. Reykjavík: Árna Magnússonar á Íslandi, 1993.

———. *Lemmatized Index to The Icelandic Homily Book: Perg. 15 4° in the Royal Library Stockholm.* Rit 61. Reykjavík: Árna Magnússonar á Íslandi, 2004.

Dicke, Gerd, and Klaus Grubmüller. *Die Fabeln des Mittelalters und der frühen Neuzeit: Ein Katalog der deutschen Versionen und ihrer lateinischen Entsprechungen.* Münstersche Mittelalter-Schriften 60. Munich: Wilhelm Fink, 1987.

Dragonetti, Roger. *Le mirage des sources: l'art du faux dans le roman médiéval.* Paris: Seuil, 1987.

Ebel, Else. *Der Konkubinat nach altwestnordischen Quellen: Philologische Studien zur sogenannten "Friedelehe."* Ergänzungsbände zum Reallexikon der Germanischen Altertumskunde 8. Berlin: de Gruyter, 1993.

Einar Ólafur Sveinsson. *Folk-Stories of Iceland.* Revised by Einar G. Pétursson Translated by Benedikt Benediktz. Edited by Anthony Faulkes. London: Viking Society for Northern Research, 2003.

———. *Um íslenzkar þjóðsögur.* Reykjavík: Hið íslenzka bókmenntafélag, 1940.

Engler, Bernd, and Kurt Müller, eds. *Exempla: Studien zur Bedeutung und Funktion exemplarischen Erzählens.* Schriften zur Literaturwissenshaft 10. Berlin: Duncker & Humblot, 1995.

Flory, David A. *"El Conde Lucanor": Don Juan Manuel en su contexto histórico.* Madrid: Editorial Pliegos, 1995.

Fulk, R. D. "The Name of Offa's Queen: *Beowulf* 1931–2." *Anglia* 122 (2004): 614–39.

Glauser, Jürg. *Isländische Märchensagas: Studien zur Prosaliteratur im spätmittelalterlichen Island.* Beiträge zur nordischen Philologie 12. Basel: Helbing und Lichtenhahn, 1983.

Gödel, Vilhelm. *Fornnorsk-isländsk litteratur i Sverige.* Antiqvarisk Tidskrift för Sverige 16.4. Stockholm: Kongl. Vitterhets Historie och Antiqvitets Akademien, 1898.

Gottskálk Jensson. "'Ævi Sæmundar fróða' á latínu eftir Árna Magnússon." In *Í garði Sæmundar fróða: Fyrirlestrar frá ráðstefnu í Þjóðminjasafni 20. maí 2006,* edited by Gunnar Harðarson and Sverrir Tómasson, 135–70. Reykjavík: Hugvísindastofnun Háskóla Íslands, 2008.

Grubmüller, Klaus. "Fabel, Exempel, Allegorese: Über Sinnbildungsverfahren und Verwendungszusammenhänge." In Haug, *Exempel und Exempelsammlungen,* 58–76.

Gunnar F. Guðmundsson. *Íslenskt samfélag og Rómakirkja.* Kristni á Íslandi 2. Reykjavík: Alþingi, 2000.

Gunnar Karlsson. *The History of Iceland.* Minneapolis: University of Minnesota Press, 2000.

Gunnar Kristjánsson, ed. *Saga biskupsstólanna: Skálholt 950 ára—2006—Hólar 900 ára.* Reykjavík: Bókaútgáfan Hólar, 2006.

Haug, Walter, and Burghart Wachinger, eds. *Exempel und Exempel-sammlungen.* Fortuna vitrea: Arbeiten zur literarischen Tradition zwischen dem 13. und 16. Jahrhundert 2. Tübingen: Niemeyer, 1999.

Helgi Skúli Kjartansson. "Gamli sáttmáli—hvað næst?" *Saga* 49 (2011): 133–53.

Hallberg, Peter. *Stilsignalement och författarskap i norrön sagalitteratur: Synpunkter och exempel.* Nordistica Gothoburgensia 3. Gothenburg: Acta Universitatis Gothoburgensis, 1968.

Hermann Pálsson. *Mannfræði Hrafnkels sögu og frumþættir.* Íslensk ritskýring 3. Reykjavík: Menningarsjóður, 1988.

——. *Sagnagerð: Hugvekjur um fornar bókmenntir.* Reykjavík: Almenna bókafélagið, 1982.

——. *Úr hugmyndaheimi Hrafnkels sögu og Gretlu.* Studia Islandica 39. Reykjavík: Menningarsjóður, 1981.

Hughes, Shaun F. D. "*Klári saga* as an Indigenous Romance." In *Romance and Love in Late Medieval and Early Modern Iceland: Essays in Honor of Marianne* Kalinke, edited by Johanna Denzin and Kirsten Wolf, 135–63. Islandica 54. Ithaca: Cornell University Library, 2009.

Janus Jónsson. *Um klaustrin á Íslandi.* Reykjavík: Endurprent., 1980. First published in *Tímarit hins íslenzka bókmenntafélags* 8 (1887): 174–265.

Jochens, Jenny. *Old Norse Images of Women.* Middle Ages Series. Philadelphia: University of Pennsylvania Press, 1996.

——. *Women in Old Norse Society.* Ithaca: Cornell University Press, 1995.

Johansson, Karl G. "Bergr Sokkason och Arngrímur Brandsson— översättare och författare i samma miljö." In *Old Norse Myths, Literature and Society: Proceedings of the 11th International Saga Conference*, edited by Geraldine Barnes and Margaret Clunies Ross, 181–97. Sydney: Centre for Medieval Studies, 2000.

——. "A Scriptorium in Northern Iceland: Clárus saga (AM 657 a-b 4to) Revisited." In *Sagas and the Norwegian Experience—Sagaene og Noreg: Preprints of the 10th International Saga Conference, Trondheim 3.–9. August 1997,* edited by Jan Ragnar Hagland, Jørn Sandnes, Gunnar Foss, Audun Dybdahl, 323–31. Trondheim: Norges Teknisknaturvitskaplege Universitet, Senter for Middelalderstudier, 1997.

Jón Helgason. *Málið á Nýja testamenti Odds Gottskálkssonar.* Safn Fræðafjelagsins um Ísland og Íslendinga 7. Copenhagen: Möller, 1929. Repr. in Rit um íslenska málfræði 4. Reykjavík: Málvísindastofnun Háskóla Íslands, 1999.

Jucknies, Regina. *Der Horizont eines Schreibers: Jón Eggertsson (1643–89) und seine Handschriften.* Texte und Untersuchungen zur Germanistik und Skandinavistik 59. Frankfurt: Peter Lang, 2009.

Judic, Bruno. "Grégoire le Grand et la notion d'*exemplum*." In *Le Tonnerre des exemples: Exempla et médiation culturelle dans l'Occident medieval*, edited by Marie Anne Polo de Beaulieu, Paul Collomb and Jacques Berlioz, 131–42. Collection "Histoire." Rennes: Presses Universitaires de Rennes, 2010.

Kalinke, Marianne. "Arthurian Echoes in Indigenous Icelandic Sagas." In *The Arthur of the North*, edited by Marianne Kalinke, 145–67. Arthurian Literature in the Middle Ages 5. Cardiff: University of Wales Press, 2011.

———. *Bridal-Quest Romance in Medieval Iceland*. Islandica 46. Ithaca: Cornell University Press, 1990.

———. "*Clári saga*: A Case of Low German Infiltration." *Scripta Islandica* 59 (2008): 5–25.

———. "Table Decorum and the Quest for a Bride in *Clári saga*." In *At the Table: Metaphorical and Material Cultures of Food in Medieval and Early Modern Europe*, edited by Timothy J. Tomasik and Juliann M. Vitello, 51–72. Arizona Studies in the Middle Ages and Renaissance 18. Turnhout: Brepols, 2007.

Katara, Pekka. *Das französische Lehngut in mittelniederdeutschen Denkmälern von 1300 bis 1600*. Mémoires de la Société Néophilologique de Helsinki 30. Helsinki: Société Néophilologique, 1966.

Kemmler, Fritz. *"Exempla" in Context: A Historical and Critical Study of Robert Mannyng of Brune's "Handlying Synne."* Studies and Texts in English 6. Tübingen: Gunter Narr, 1984.

Knapp, Fritz Peter. "Mittelalterliche Erzählgattungen im Lichte scholastischer Poetik." In Haug, *Exempel und Exempelsammlungen*, 1–22.

Konráð Gíslason. *Fire og fyrretyve . . . prøver af oldnordisk sprog og literatur*. Copenhagen: Gyldendal, 1860.

———. *Um frum-parta íslenzkrar túngu í fornöld*. Copenhagen: S. Trier, 1846.

Kramarz-Bein, Susanne. "Der *Spesar þáttr* der *Grettis saga*. Tristan-Spuren in der Isländersaga." In *Studien zur Isländersaga: Festschrift für Rolf Heller*, edited by Heinrich Beck and Else Ebel, 152–81. Ergänzungsbände zum Reallexikon der Germanischen Altertumskunde 24. Berlin: de Gruyter, 2000.

Lampert-Weissig, Lisa. *Medieval Literature and Postcolonial Studies*. Postcolonial Literary Studies. Edinburgh: Edinburgh University Press, 2010.

Lára Magnúsardóttir. *Bannfæring og kirkjuvald á Íslandi, 1275–1550*. Reykjavík: Háskólaútgáfan, 2007.

Lind, E. H. *Norsk-Isländska Dopnamn och fingerade Namn från Medeltiden*. 3 vols. Uppsala: Lundequistska Bokhandeln, 1905–31.

Louis-Jensen, Jonna. "'Enoks saga.'" *Opuscula* 5:225–37. Bibliotheca Arnamagnæana 31. Copenhagen: Munksgaard, 1975.

McKinnell, John. "Víga-Glúms saga." In *Medieval Scandinavia: An Encyclopedia*. Edited by Phillip Pulsiano and Kirsten Wolf. New York: Garland, 1993.

Magnús Stefánsson, *Staðir og Staðamál: Studier i islandske egenkirkelige og beneficialrettlige forhold i middelalderen*. Bergen: Historisk Institutt, Universitetet i Bergen, 2000.

Már Jónsson. *Blóðskömm á Íslandi, 1270–1870*. Reykjavík: Háskólaútgáfan, 1993.

Maurer, Konrad. *Isländische Volkssagen der Gegenwart*. Leipzig: J. C. Hinrich, 1860. Repr. Rye Brook, NY: Elibron Classics, 2001.

Moos, Peter von. "Die Kunst der Antwort: *Exempla* und *dicta* im lateinischen Mittelalter." In Haug, *Exempel und Exempelsammlungen*, 23–57.

Niles, John D. Translator's Preface to *The European Folktale: Form and Nature*, by Max Lüthi, xvii–xxv. Translated by John D. Niles. Translations in Folklore Studies. Philadelphia: Institute for the Study of Human Issues, 1982.

Perry, Ben Edwin. *Aesopica: A Series of Texts Relating to Aesop or Ascribed to Him or Closely Connected with the Literary Tradition that Bears his Name*. New ed. Urbana: University of Illinois Press, 2007.

Ricketts, Philadelphia. *High-Ranking Widows in Medieval Iceland and Yorkshire: Property, Power, Marriage and Identity in the Twelfth and Thirteenth Centuries*. The Northern World 49. Leiden: Brill, 2010.

Rosenthal, Joel T., ed. *Medieval Women and the Sources of Medieval History*. Athens: University of Georgia Press, 1990.

Schürer, Markus. *Das Exemplum oder die erzählte Institution: Studien zum Beispielgebrauch bei den Dominikanern und Franziskanern des 13. Jahrhunderts*. Vita Regularis 23. Berlin: LIT, 2005.

Sigríður Beck. *I kungens frånvaro: Formeringen av en isländsk aristokrati 1271–1387*. Gothenburg: Göteborgs Universitet, 2011.

Söderwall, Knut Frederik. *Studier öfver Konunga-styrelsen*. Lunds Universitets Årsskrift 15 (1878–1879), Afdelningen för Philosophi, Språkvetenskap och Historia 4. Lund: Fr. Berling, 1880.

Spurkland, Terje. "Lygisögur, skröksögur and stjúpmæðrasögur." In *The Legendary Sagas: Origins and Development*, edited by Annette Lassen, Agneta Ney and Ármann Jakobsson, 173–84. Reykjavík: University of Iceland Press, 2012.

Stefán Karlsson. "Icelandic Lives of Thomas à Becket: Questions of Authorship." In *Proceedings of the First International Saga Conference*, edited by Peter Foote, Hermann Pálsson, and Desmond Slay, 212–43. London: Viking Society for Northern Research, 1973.

Sveinbjörn Rafnsson. "Sagnastef í íslenskri menningarsögu." *Saga* 30 (1992): 81–121.

Sverrir Tómasson. *Formálar íslenskra sagnaritara á miðöldum.* Rit 33. Reykjavík: Stofnun Árna Magnússonar á Íslandi, 1988.

——. "The 'Fræðisaga' of Adonias." In *Structure and Meaning in Old Norse Literature: New Approaches to Textual Analysis and Literary Criticism,* edited by John Lindow, Lars Lönnroth, and Gerd Wolfgang Weber, 378–93. The Viking Collection: Studies in Northern Civilization 3. Odense: Odense University Press, 1986.

——. "Helgisögur, mælskufræði og forn frásagnarlist." *Skírnir* 157 (1983): 130–62.

Tolan, John V. *Petrus Alfonsi and His Medieval Readers.* Gainesville: University Press of Florida, 1993.

Torfi K. Stefánsson Hjaltalín. *Eldur á Möðruvöllum: Saga Möðruvalla í Hörgárdal frá öndverðu til okkar tíma.* 2 vols. Reykjavík: Flateyjatútgáfan, 2001.

Uther, Hans-Jörg. *The Types of International Folktales: A Classification and Bibliography Based on the System of Antti Aarne and Stith Thompson.* 3 vols. FF Communications 133–35 (284–86). Helsinki: Suomalainen Tiedeakatemia, 2004.

Vauchez, André. "La question du célibat ecclésiastique dans l'Occident médiéval: un état de la recherche." In *Medieval Spirituality in Scandinavia and Europe: A Collection of Essays in Honour of Tore Nyberg,* edited by Lars Bisgaard et al., 21–32. Odense University Studies in History and Social Sciences 234. Odense: Odense University Press, 2001.

Ward, H. L. D., and J. A. Herbert. *Catalogue of Romances in the Department of Manuscripts in the British Museum.* 3 vols. 1883–1910. Repr. London: British Museum, 1961–62.

Welter, Jean-Thiébaut. *L'Exemplum dans la littérature religieuse et didactique du moyen âge.* Bibliothéque d'histoire ecclésiastique de France 8. 1927. Repr. New York: AMS Press, 1973.

Widding, Ole. "Om Rævestreger: Et kapitel i Adonius saga." *Opuscula* 1:331–34. Bibliotheca Arnamagnæana 20. Copenhagen: Munksgaard, 1960.

Performing Gender in the Icelandic Ballads

Paul Acker
SAINT LOUIS UNIVERSITY

In his 1982 book-length study, *The Traditional Ballads of Iceland*, Vésteinn Ólason addressed the major philological questions regarding Icelandic ballads, principally concerning their origins.[1] First collected and preserved in seventeenth-century manuscripts,[2] could these ballads be considered medieval, and if so, when and from where did they first reach Iceland? Vésteinn argued the case in detail for each of the 110 ballads that had just been given their first modern edition by Jón Helgason.[3] By comparing Icelandic ballad stanzas with their close verbal parallels in Danish, Swedish, Norwegian, and Faroese ballads,[4]

---

1. See Vésteinn Ólason, *The Traditional Ballads of Iceland: Historical Studies* (Reykjavík: Stofnun Árna Magnússonar, 1982), henceforth *Traditional Ballads*.

2. The earliest ballad manuscript was copied by Gissur Sveinsson (1604–1683) in 1665. See the facsimile *Kvæðabók séra Gissurar Sveinsson: AM 147, 8vo*, Íslenzk rit síðari alda 2a-b (Reykjavík: Hið íslenzka fræðafélag, 1960). "Kvæði af Ólafi liljurós," discussed below, was first recorded in this manuscript, while "Elenar ljóð" was first recorded in a manuscript dated ca. 1680. See Jón Helgason, ed., *Íslenzk fornkvæði: Islandske Folkeviser*, 8 vols., Editiones Arnamagnæanæ B10-17 (Copenhagen: Munksgaard, 1962–1981), henceforth JH, 3:xiii. See also the facsimile of the page containing this ballad in Vésteinn Ólason, ed., *Sagnadansar*, Íslensk rit 5 (Reykjavík: Rannsóknastofnun í bókmenntafræði við Háskóla Íslands, 1979), henceforth *Sagnadansar*, 2.

3. See above. The first, nineteenth-century edition, *Íslenzk fornkvæði*, ed. Svend Grundtvig and Jón Sigurðsson (Copenhagen: det nordiske Literatur-Samfund, 1854–1885), henceforth ÍFk, is partly available online. Vésteinn Ólason compiled a one-volume edition with an introduction in 1979 (see previous note). For the sake of brevity I will typically refer to the ballads by their ÍFk numbers, given in Grundtvig and supplemented in JH.

4. Ballads in these languages are classified and grouped together in Bengt R. Jonsson et al., eds., *The Types of the Medieval Scandinavian Ballad: A Descriptive Catalogue* (Oslo: Universitetsforlaget, 1978).

he argued which of them might have come from Norway by about 1500, and which came from Denmark after the Reformation midway through the sixteenth century. Along the way, Vésteinn pointed toward some possible new directions for ballad study, such as a closer, more comprehensive linguistic analysis of the Danish element in ballad language, including (I would add) of the seventeenth-century literary translations of Danish ballads that were preserved alongside the putative oral-traditional ones.[5] Other kinds of new approaches, such as those incorporating postmodern theoretical concerns, had yet to be envisioned. One promising new direction, however, was adumbrated when Vésteinn and others following him asked whether the Icelandic ballads might in some sense have been a form of "women's poetry."[6]

Evidence for this hypothesis is found first of all in the preponderance of women cited as singers of ballads.[7] In 1708, Snæbjörn Pálsson had written a letter to the famous manuscript collector Árni Magnússon (1633–1730), commenting on an important ballad-book then owned by his wife, Kristín Magnúsdóttir:[8]

Fornkvæðabókin þykir mér ekki svo rík af fornkvæðum sem hjörtu og brjóst áttræðra kerlinga hef ég vitað, nær ég var barn, en þær með þeim fróðleik eru flestar í jörð grafnar nú.[9] (*Sagnadansar* 19)

---

5. These translated ballads are printed in a smaller font in JH. On linguistic importations, see *Traditional Ballads* 97–100, and *Sagnadansar* 23.

6. *Traditional Ballads* 24–25; *Sagnadansar* 82; See Helga Kress, "Searching for Herself: Female Experience and Female Tradition in Icelandic Literature," in *A History of Icelandic Literature*, ed. Daisy L. Neijmann (Lincoln: University of Nebraska, 2006), 510–11; Nína Björk Elíasson, "Eru sagnadansar kvennatónlist?" in *Konur skrifa til heiðurs Önnu Sigurðardóttur*, ed. Valborg Bentsdóttir et al. (Reykjavík: Sögufélag, 1980), 143–54.

7. We have no record of who sang (and first composed?) ballads in medieval times, nor does the earliest ballad MS in the seventeenth century (see above) mention its sources. Women performers of the (originally) oral-traditional ballads might compose or adapt them to their own tastes and concerns, although on the other hand later singers especially (male or female) might transmit much of the ballad texts memorially. See *Traditional Ballads* 25–29; *Sagnadansar* 40–50.

8. The manuscript, V, is now lost but known through two copies (V¹ and V²) located, respectively, in the Ny kongelig Samling, Royal Library, Copenhagen, Denmark (Ny kgl. sml. 1141 fol) and in the Jón Sigurðsson collection, National and University Library of Iceland, Reykjavík (JS 405 4°). The original manuscript was written down in 1699 and 1700 by Magnús Jónsson of Vigur (in the Westfjords) and two of his scribes. After Magnús died in 1702 the manuscript passed on to his daughter Kristín (d. 1712), who married Snæbjörn (see JH 1:ix, xviii–xx).

9. Normalized; quoted in the original orthography in JH 1:xx and *Traditional Ballads* 18.

The ballad-book does not seem to me as rich in ballads as the hearts and minds of eighty-year-old women I knew when I was a child, but most of them are now dead and buried, and their knowledge along with them.

Árni Magnússon for his part named only one ballad singer he collected from, a woman named Guðrún Hákonardóttir, who provided him with five ballads in the early eighteenth century.[10] In the next century (1858–9), scholar, scribe, and collector Gísli Konráðsson (1787–1877) transcribes seventeen ballads "eptir mynni gamalla kvenna" (from the memory of old women),[11] while Sr. Benedikt Þórarinsson in 1848–50 says he learned ballads from a woman named Björg Pétursdóttir (1749–1839), of whom he says "hún var fróð kona, minnug og óskreytin" (she knew much lore, had a good memory and did not alter anything).[12] Ballads in manuscripts collected in the nineteenth century are most often recorded by men from performances by women.[13] The named performers include Sigríður Jafetsdóttir (b. 1819, ÍFk no. 1, JH 6:150–51); Guðríður (Benediktsdóttir?, b. 1791; nos. 34, 38, 39, JH 7:6–10, 11–14); Helga Tjörvadóttir (b. 1781, no. 39, JH 7:10–11); Málfríður Jónsdóttir (who learned from her mother Þorbjörg Pétursdóttir, who learned from her mother Snjófríður Jónsdóttir; nos. 92, 60, 21, JH 7:14–19); Ingibjörg Pálsdóttir (1807–91, nos. 34, 39, 35, 60, 48, 37, 68, 61, JH 7:56–81); Gunnhildur Jónsdóttir (1787–1866, nos. 11, 39 and 61, JH 7:82–91); Anna Sigríður Pálsdóttir (b. 1845, no. 92, JH 7:98–99); and Guðrún Guðjónsdóttir (1816–1902, no. 60, JH 7:151–53). When ballads were recorded on tape in the 1960s and 1970s, fifty-one singers were women, and fifteen men.[14] For comparative purposes, one can

---

10. *Traditional Ballads* 22, citing JH 4:xli-xlvi. Other informants mentioned but not named by Árni were also women, including two old women from Álftanes in southwestern Iceland (*Traditional Ballads* 22; JH 4:xxxviii). Guðrún's ballads are ÍFk nos. 3, 47, 48, 72, and 82, edited in JH 4:156–77. Surprisingly, no. 82 is the lone copy of one of only two Icelandic ballads that have been classified as "heroic." The ballads recorded from "old women" are ÍFk no. 78 (a religious ballad) and no. 81 (the other heroic ballad), edited in JH 4:106–13.

11. JH 6:xviii.

12. JH 6:xxxi; translated in *Traditional Ballads* 22.

13. *Traditional Ballads* 23.

14. According to an unpublished handlist of recordings, Stofnun Árna Magnússonar. I thank Rósa Þorsteinsdóttir for providing me with this handlist and providing me with certain sound files.

mention that women were sometimes the sources for Scottish and Appalachian ballads and Norwegian ballads from Telemark.[15] In the Faroe Islands, on the other hand, men recite the famous heroic ballads about legendary male figures such as Sigurd the Dragonslayer, while the villagers dance. Nonetheless, one Faroese informant disclosed that while the men were resting after completing these long-winded performances, women would often sing their own sorts of ballads.[16] Similarly, Malan Marnersdóttir states that in the Faroes, the "lead singer most frequently was a man, but women, too, lead ballads" although they "have tended to lead shorter ballads."[17]

Within the ballad texts themselves, women often take on promi-nent roles as strong characters, something rather to be expected in a (putatively) medieval Icelandic genre, judging by women's roles in the sagas and Eddic poetry.[18] In his earlier and complementary study (*Sagnadansar* 68), Vésteinn had briefly mentioned as examples of strong women in the ballads the protagonists of "Ingu kvæði" (ÍFk 66) and "Kvæði af Kristínu og Ásbirni" (ÍFk 55). If we turn to the latter example, for instance, we find that Kristín makes fine clothes and sends them to Ásbjörn, who is so impressed he asks her to be his bride.[19] While she performs the heavily gendered activity of sewing and

---

15. *Sagnadansar* 82. The Norwegian ballad *Draumkvedet* (Jonsson, *Types*, B 31), for instance, was earliest copied down from a version sung by a Telemark woman, Maren Ramskeid. See Velle Espeland, "Oral Ballads as National Literature: The Reconstruction of Two Norwegian Ballads," *Estudios de Literatura Oral* 6 (2000): 1. For Scottish ballads, collector Robert Jamieson credited especially "Mrs Brown of Falkland," who "learnt most of them before she was twelve years old, from old women and maid-servants." Robert Jamieson, ed., *Popular Ballads and Songs* (Edinburgh: Constable, 1806), viii-ix.

16. The informant Jens Holm is quoted in a letter from Faroese scholar Mortan Nolsøe to Vésteinn Ólason (*Traditional Ballads* 24–25), who provides an English translation. Jens refers specifically to the Faroese analogue of ÍFk 14, "Margrétar kvæði," a chivalric ballad. Icelandic ballads are predominantly chivalric (62), followed by (among those clas-sified in Jonsson's *Types*) the supernatural (11), jocular (10), religious (5) and heroic (2).

17. "Women and Ballads: The Representation of Women in Faroese Ballad Tradition," *Scandinavica* 49 (2010): 29. Marnersdóttir (36–46) goes on to discuss the ballads collected from one female informant, Birte Sofie Jacobsdatter (1805–74), and how they differ from the heroic ballads typified by *Sjúrðar kvæði* (The Ballad/s of Sigurd the Dragonslayer).

18. See, e.g., Jenny Jochens, *Old Norse Images of Women* (Philadelphia: University of Pennsylvania Press, 1996).

19. JH 1:192–5, 3:252–4, 4:236–7, 5:3–6, 6:188–90, and fragments (see JH 8:179); *Sagnadansar* 126–28 (two versions). English-language summaries of each ballad in turn are provided in *Traditional Ballads*; for "Kristínu," see pp. 315–16. Briefer comparative summaries of Scandinavian ballads are provided in Jonsson's *Types*. For a bibliography of English translations of the Icelandic ballads, see Larry E. Syndergaard, *English*

embroidery, Kristín also takes on the customarily masculine role of initiating courtship. The contrast is clearer when we compare Danish versions, in which Ásbjörn asks for Kristín in marriage but insists that she first prove her ability to make clothes for him. Following up on Vésteinn's observations, Nína Björk Elíasson asks in an article from 1980, "Are the [Icelandic] Ballads Women's Poetry?" ("Eru sagnadansar kvennatónlist?"—see note 6 above). She surveys the ballads edited in JH volumes 6 and 7, collected in the nineteenth century by men from female singers (as noted above). She notes a focus on extramarital pregnancies, resulting from love trysts but also rape (often incestuous rape), in ballads such as "Ásu dans" (ÍFk 61), "Kvæði af Imnar og Elínu" (ÍFk 79), "Tófu kvæði" (ÍFk 35), "Kvæði af Loga Þórðarsyni" (ÍFk 88), "Ólöfar kvæði" (ÍFk 34 and 80), "Kvæði af syndugri konu" (ÍFk 77), "Þorkels kvæði Þrándar-sonar" (ÍFk 62), and "Ebbadætra kvæði" (ÍFk 30). As other topics that may indicate a particular (but of course not exclusive) interest for women, she discusses instances of young women's dreams for marriage ("Draumkvæði," ÍFk 39); of maternal or wifely compassion ("Stjúpmóður kvæði," ÍFk 11, and "Kvæði af Ingu lífstuttu, ÍFk 25); and of mockery of men in comic ballads ("Skeggkarls kvæði," ÍFk 99). Nína's survey begins to address a scholarly desideratum that Vésteinn in his 1982 monograph expressed thus:

> In no other type of poetry from the late Middle Ages or the subse-quent centuries do women play such a decisive role. Nor is their fate elsewhere described with as much sympathy as in the majority of the ballads. A detailed thematic study of ballads in relation to this is called for. (*Traditional Ballads* 24)

Helga Kress, writing on women in literary tradition for the 2006 *History of Icelandic Literature*, adds her own characterization, namely that "[the] ballads are mainly concerned with women's lives, and women mainly play a major role in these stories. Common themes are violence against women, forbidden love, rape and incest, and concealed childbirth and infanticide as well as women's solidarity and

---

Translations of the Scandinavian Medieval Ballads: An Analytical Guide and Bibliog-raphy (Turku: The Nordic Institute of Folklore, 1995), 161–66.

friendship, their concern for their children, and their revenge against evildoers."[20] She notes for instance that the daughters who are raped in "Ebbadætra kvæði" (ÍFk 30) go on to take their own revenge. One can add that one of the daughters had first said she wanted to kill herself in shame, but that she and her sisters instead conspired for seven weeks and then beheaded one of the brothers Judith-style by grabbing him by the hair, outside the church door.

In this article I take up on Vésteinn's call for further investigation of the role of gender in Icelandic ballads, focusing on the ballads numbered one and two in the standard collection (ÍFk). The first of these, "Kvæði af Ólafi liljurós" (The Ballad of Olaf Lily-Rose)," is the best-known ballad in modern Iceland, while the other, "Elenar ljóð" (The Song [or Ballad] of Elen) portrays its young heroine in a particularly exemplary way. (I append below my translations of these two ballads.) As my title suggests, I will modify Vésteinn's approach somewhat by invoking the idea advanced by Judith Butler and others of gender as a performance, not so much (in Butler's view) a freely chosen individual performance but a response to culturally repeated prior performances.[21] The idea has a particular relation to the ballads because the genre was itself performed, or so it is usually argued, on repeated occasions, as lyrics sung by a balladeer, with refrains sung perhaps by a community of dancers, or in other participatory ways.[22]

"The Ballad of Elen" in fact begins with a reference to just such a

---

20. "Searching for Herself," 510–11.

21. "As anthropologist Victor Turner suggests in his studies of ritual social drama, social action requires a performance which is repeated . . . gender is not a radical choice or project that reflects a merely individual choice, but neither is it imposed or inscribed upon the individual, as some post-structuralist displacements of the subject would contend . . . just as the play requires both text and interpretation, so the gendered body acts its part in a culturally restricted corporeal space and enacts interpretations within the confines of already existing directives." "Performative Acts and Gender Constitution: An Essay in Phenomenology and Feminist Theory," *Theatre Journal* 40 (1988): 526. Butler repeats some of her observations in her monograph *Gender Trouble: Feminism and the Subversion of Identity* (London: Routledge, 1990), but this prior article makes a few more explicit comparisons (and contrasts) between gender performance and other forms of artistic performance. Marnersdóttir ("Women and Ballads," 29), writing about women and Faroese ballads, similarly cites Butler, as well as Pierre Bourdieu (42), concerning "schemes of habitus that set the socially accepted gender roles which are constantly reproduced."

22. On the relation between ballad and dance, see *Traditional Ballads* 35–42 and *Sagnadansar* 79–80. Faroese ballads famously are still performed while villagers (or their equivalent) participate in a "chain dance"; Marnersdóttir ("Women and Ballads,"

ballad and dance event.[23] Elen asks her father if she can go to a *vaka* or "wake," an all-night entertainment where dancing and ballad singing would have figured prominently. Her father refuses permission on the grounds that Elen would be stared at by fools ("þig kann margur dárinn sjá"; st. 3), adding that her absent mother would never have behaved in such a way. Elen airily dismisses the imputation, stating that a fool will behave as he must ("Fari dárinn sem hann kann"; st. 4), and then she goes off to the dance. There she sings so loudly (while she dances—perhaps in a communal performance of ballads?) that she attracts the attention not just of (presumably) the gawking Icelandic locals, but also of a monstrous suitor, a *nykur* or creature of the deep, who abducts her, tying her to his horse (st. 8).[24] When she asks for a rest, the merman says he will grant it if she vows to wed him (st. 10), at which she makes, again, an utterly nonplussed refusal, saying "Eg því ekki nenni" (st. 11); that is, she does not "just say no" but rather something like "I can't be bothered" or "I'd rather not." In so doing she accidentally names the creature, since *nennir* is an alternate word for *nykur*,[25] which makes him magically vanish, as we learn also from later Icelandic folktales. Other Scandinavian versions of the ballad often end badly for the heroine.[26] In the Icelandic version, however,

---

28) quotes Christian Matras as saying that one cannot adjudge Faroese ballads without taking the dance into account.

23. My discussion follows version A in *Sagnadansar* 93–4, normalized from a text copied down ca. 1680 (see above); see JH 3:249–50. The only other copy, version C (version B records the first stanza only) was recorded ca. 1850, calls its heroine Kristín, and adds stanzas describing her retinue as she starts riding towards a *gleði* (party). The *nennir* hears her riding (rather than singing). She names him and he disappears.

24. In Icelandic folktales, the *nykur* is himself a kind of horse or centaur. See Jón Árnason, *Íslenzkar þjóðsögur og ævintýri*, 2nd ed., 6 vols. (Reykjavík: Þjóðsaga, 1954–1961), 1:129–32; Jacqueline Simpson, trans., *Icelandic Folktales and Legends* (Berkeley: University of California Press, 1972; repr. Stroud: Tempus, 2004), 110–14. "The nykr is the Proteus of the Northern tales, and takes many shapes," according to Richard Cleasby and Gudbrand Vigfusson, *An Icelandic–English Dictionary*, 2nd ed. (Oxford: Clarendon Press, 1957), *s.v.*

25. According to Cleasby and Vigfusson, *nennir* is "prob. an assimilated form, qs. Neknir . . . the popular name of the nykr"; there follows a reference to Maurer's *Isländ-dische Volkssagen* of 1860. Presumably the word is not attested in medieval sources (it is not to be found in the online *Dictionary of Old Norse Prose*); the online database of the Orðabók Háskólans (ed. Bjarni Einarsson) locates its earliest citation in the seventeenth century. *Elenar kvæði*, written down ca.1680 (JH 3:xiii), must have been composed fairly late if the word *nennir* is itself late (and not just unattested), given that the poem (or at least its ending) turns on a pun on that word.

26. Jonsson, *Types*, A 48.

Elen refuses any responsibility for the bad actions of aggressive males. In a more misogynistic version, she would have been punished, and indeed she is carried off under the water in the Danish version A.[27] Admittedly Elen is something of a comic figure, who succeeds in part because of her youthful innocence. But what is the gender lesson to be learned from this performance?

Vésteinn Ólason has hypothesized that in a danced version of the ballad, a young girl, impersonating Elen, might have been taken by the hand by a man, impersonating the merman, and led out of the ring of dancers (*Sagnadansar* 360). If we imagine further that the ballad is sung by a woman, with the girl perhaps singing Elen's stanzas, then the gender message embodied in her performance is not that girls who disobey their fathers inevitably get punished, but rather that women's words, in the magical world of the dance at least, have the power to make unwanted men simply disappear. The female and male dancers would return to the ring, to the safety and support of the community, which no doubt often did have the effect of ensuring that the romantic interludes at such occasions ended happily, even when young women danced in the company of men, or when physically aggressive males were rejected by the young women. Interestingly the Icelandic churchmen, like Elen's own father, were less sanguine about the effects of communal dances and actually did succeed in enacting the prohibition of dancing in the eighteenth century. In its later reception then, perhaps by a silent reader rather than a performer, "The Ballad of Elen" would have provided access to dancing as a private, perhaps even guilty pleasure.

Aðalheiður Guðmundsdóttir has in fact made a comparable argument recently for a related genre, Icelandic folktales, arguing that the dances of elves and of the *huldufólk* (hidden folk) in some of these tales represent a return of the repressed scene of communal dancing.[28] The other ballad I wish to consider, "Kvæði af Ólafi liljurós"[29]

---

27. Svend Grundtvig et al., eds., *Danmarks gamle folkeviser* (Copenhagen: Samfund til det danske literaturs fremme, 1853–1976), no. 39, 2.59–60. The Danish version B, which is not very closely related textually, ends with the advice that pretty young maids should not go to dances pridefully (2.60–63).

28. "How Icelandic Legends Reflect the Prohibition on Dancing," *Arv: Nordic Yearbook of Folklore* 61 (2005): 25–52.

29. ÍFk 1; Jonsson, *Types*, A 63.

(The Ballad of Olaf Lily-Rose), does in fact portray promenading if not dancing elves,[30] but unlike "The Ballad of Elen," it does not end happily. When I first began to formulate this study, I wrote (in an unpublished abstract) that this ballad, by contrast with "The Ballad of Elen," "follows a typical male quest pattern and is saturated with distrust for female sexuality." I have since considered that the ballad, even though it does follow the adventures of a young man and the elfin maids who "done him wrong," is not a typical quest romance in ballad form. Derek Brewer, writing on Middle English romances, has called them "symbolic stories" that reenact the psychosexual development of young men on the road to adult (hetero)sexuality and marriage.[31] "The Ballad of Olaf Lily-Rose" begins, it would seem, in such a way; "Ólafur reið með björgum fram" (Olaf rode out along the cliffs, st. 1) and stumbled upon a place where elves live (in the folklore, they are often said to reside in rocks, such as the rocky elfin "cathedral" at Tungustapi).[32] In the earliest version of the refrain to this ballad, Olaf has an errand and destination; he is on the way to a *byrðing* or merchant ship. Probably because the word *byrðing* was archaic, all other versions refer to *byrinn*, the breeze, which blithely blows, oblivious of the misadventures of Olaf and his kind.[33] In these versions, Olaf is riding aimlessly simply because

30. In a Swedish version, the elves are dancing: "Herr Olof rider för bergja, / finner en dans med elfver" (quoted in *Traditional Ballads* 117). So also in a Faroese version, Ólavur is invited to come into the dance and recite for the elf-maids (ibid). We might contrast this with the Icelandic version, st. 6, where Ólafur is invited to go into the elf-maids' dwelling and drink with them (version A) or go into the rock and dwell with them (version D). On elves and the hidden folk, see further Tom Shippey, "*Alias Oves Habeo*: The Elves as a Category Problem," in *The Shadow-Walkers: Jacob Grimm's Mythology of the Monstrous*, ed. Tom Shippey (Tempe: Arizona Center for Medieval and Renaissance Studies, 2005), 157–87.

31. *Symbolic Stories: Traditional Narratives of the Family Drama in English Literature* (London: Longman, 1988).Contrast also Olaf's experiences in the ballad with the accounts discussed by Ruth Mazo Karras of young men growing up as knights, as university students, and as craft workers. She concludes that "In all cases young men were training for a share in power, a place in the hierarchy from which they could be unlike women. In all cases they were competing against each other or their elders." *From Boys to Men: Formations of Masculinity in Late Medieval Europe* (Philadelphia: University of Pennsylvania Press, 2003), 151.

32. See Jón Árnason, *Íslenzkar þjóðsögur*, 1:32–35; *Icelandic Legends Collected by Jón Árnason*, trans. George E. J. Powell and Eiríkr Magnússon (London: Bentley, 1864), 35–41.

33. Version A has þar *lá búinn byrðing*, "there lay ready a ship"; B and C have þá *var /*

young men must do so, they ride forth (*fram*), heedless of danger.[34] Four elf maids come out in succession, revealing their ornamental attributes: a golden hairband, a silver pitcher, a silver waistband; the fourth one speaks and invites Olaf in (st. 6). He declines on religious grounds: "Eg vil ei með álfum búa, heldur vil eg á guð minn trúa" (I will not dwell with elves; rather I will have faith in my God; st. 7).[35] Christianity disapproves of the very belief in elfin maids, not to speak of sleeping with them, for that is what their invitation implies. The elf maid suggests Olaf can have it both ways, echoing (or twisting) his words (incremental repetition at its most effective): "Þó þú viljir með álfum búa / samt máttu á guð þinn trúa" (Though you might want to dwell with elves, you still can have faith in your God; st. 8). Any reply Olaf might have made is elided, and in the next stanza she asks him to wait while she goes into a green grove (a *græna lund*—never a good thing in Icelandic ballads).[36] She goes over to a chest and drapes a cloak over her shoulders, presumably to hide her intentions (st. 10). She next goes over to a coffer, grabs hold of and removes a keen-edged dagger (here the incremental repetition provides a hallucinatory doubletake on her evil errand). Famously (for anyone who knows the ballad—and *everyone* in Iceland knows the ballad),[37] she says he must spare her just one kiss (st. 12). When

---

þar lá búinn byrinn, "then was / there lay ready the breeze"; D and E have a different refrain (see *Sagnadansar* 92–3, version II); version F and the best known modern version, descending from A. P. Berggreen, *Folke-Sange og Melodier* (Copenhagen: Jaeger, 1845), have *Blíðan lagði byrinn*, "the breeze lay (or blew) gently." (Variant versions are labelled A-Z, and page references given for JH volumes, in *Traditional Ballads* 112.)

34. Thus in Grundtvig's paraphrase, "Olav rider *frem* langs med klipperne." In Icelandic, *með* can collocate with *fram* to mean simply "alongside," and some of my informants have suggested it be translated that way. However, with *fram* isolated at the end of the line and repeated again at the end of the refrain (emphatically, after a delay), I think the sense of "onward" is at the very least suggested. In performance, the word sounds almost like a drone, underscored by the stomping feet of the participants (I refer the reader to the version by Voces Thules mentioned below).

35. In Faroese and Norwegian versions, he declines because he is engaged to marry (quoted in *Traditional Ballads* 118).

36. Cf. "Kvæði af vallara systrabana" (ÍFk 15; *Sagnadansar* 246–47), st. 25, in which Ása says she is going to a green grove, when in fact she is going to fetch her father to seize the thief who raped and killed her sisters.

37. Icelanders often learn the ballad in elementary school, along with other folksongs; indeed, most Icelanders probably think of "Olaf" as a folksong, rather than as a ballad in particular. The ballad is the first to be have been printed in an anthology of Icelandic poetry. See Gísli Magnússon and Jón Þórðarson Thóroddsen, eds., *Snót: Nokkur kvæði*

he leans down from his horse to do just that (half-heartedly, in almost all versions, but whole-heartedly in the earliest version), she stabs him, the incremental repetition again making the action appear to happen twice (st. 14–15). To refuse the sexual invitation of the elves is to invite death, even a double death in successive stanzas.

Back home, Olaf knocks on his mother's door and asks her to let him in, to his proper abode rather than an elfin one, where he belongs and which in a sense he never should have left. His mother asks why he looks the way he does, as if the elves have had some sport with him ("sem þú hafir verið í álfaleik"; st. 20). He has to admit that indeed, the elf maid deceived him ("álfamærin blekkti mig"; st. 21); she "done him wrong." He asks his mother to get him a soft mattress, to return that is to the comfortable bed of his prepubescence. He asks his sister to bind his wound, the bloody token of his exogamous adventure. His mother leads him into bed and then kisses him, but by then he is dead. In the last line of the earliest version, we are told three bodies were buried the next day (st. 24); apparently Olaf's elfin adventure proves to be the death of every member of this fatherless family: mother, son, and sister.[38]

"The Ballad of Olaf Lily-Rose" is often sung by men's choirs, or by groups of young men waiting outside the dance clubs of modern-day Reykjavík. The final word of each stanza, *fram*, meaning "onward, ahead," recurs as a kind of bass drone urging the poem along to its conclusion. It may be in part because I had heard the poem performed in this way that I first associated it with men's voices. As a particularly noteworthy example, one might listen to the ballad as sung by members of the Icelandic folk group Voces Thules (currently available on YouTube).[39] One also hears the singers stamp their feet

---

eptir ýmiss skáld (Copenhagen: Kvisti, 1850), 200–206. From here it was reprinted in Icelandic school songbooks (see JH 7:lii-liii). "Olaf" is not unknown in English, having been translated in full four times (see Syndergaard, "*English Translations*," 162); part of the original was included in *Songs of the Philologists*, a collection of songs (thirteen of them by Tolkien) sung by faculty and students at Leeds University during the 1920s (see *An Illustrated Tolkien Bibliography* online: www.tolkienbooks.net).

38. In other versions in other languages, Olaf was engaged to be married; hence Vésteinn's comment that "it spoils the ballad that the impending wedding is left out" (*Traditional Ballads* 113). While I think it is often worthwhile and illuminating to consult other versions, my aim in this study has been to make sense of the first recorded Icelandic version on its own terms.

39. One can also hear on YouTube versions of the related Faroese ballad, Ólavur

in what I am told (by Shaun F. D. Hughes, fellow contributor to this volume) is more typical of the Faroese heroic ballad performance style.[40]

But Olaf Lily-Rose, his epithet suggesting perhaps some sort of floral panache, is not much of an emblem of questing masculinity. The one time he leaves home, intending to get some items off a merchant ship, he loses his way. He knows enough not to enter the rocky home of elves, from which he may never return; he has heard the relevant cautionary folk tales, perhaps from his own mother. But he is not experienced enough to know one cannot risk even a token kiss with these strange women; you never know where it might lead. One gender lesson this ballad imparts, then, is perhaps best understood as a mother's lesson, or a parental lesson at least: young men must be very careful when they first venture outside the domestic circle. There are other lessons, of course: a boy's best friend is his mother; there's no place like home; be careful when riding out among the rocks and lava plains of Iceland. There is even a misogynistic pleasure to be had in encountering beautiful *femmes fatales* in the safety of lyrical fiction.

Vésteinn (*Sagnadansar* 82) notes that some scholars have suggested that ballads might have been sung by mothers to their children "að stytta börnum stundir og fræða þau" (to pass the time for children and to instruct them); in his view, however, the subject matter was inappropriate and the ballads' more likely venue was the *kvöldvaka* or evening entertainment. Nonetheless, as Nína Björk has pointed out,[41] Hreinn Steingrímsson reported from nineteenth- and twentieth-century informants that they had learned the texts and melodies from their mothers, who had hummed the tunes to their children ("Það var raulað við krakka"), as Jakobína Þorvarðardóttir (b. 1886) says of "The Ballad of Olaf Lily-Rose."[42]

Riddararós, with heavy metal (or "folk metal"/"pagan folk") inflections, by the Faroese bands Týr and Valravn.

40. According to Marnersdóttir ("Women and Ballads," 28), the chain-dance "is simple, consisting of three steps: two to the right and one to the left."

41. "Eru sagnadansar kvennatónlist?" 150.

42. In Hreinn's *Appendix* to *Sagnadansar* (432); said of melody d, printed in *Sagnadansar* (406). Melody c of "Olaf" is the earliest recorded Icelandic ballad tune, printed by Berggreen in 1845 (*Folke-Sange og Melodier*, 12–13) as a parallel to Danish versions (Berggreen's first edition is rare and was not cited by Hreinn; I thank Susan

In contrast to the macho performance style of Voces Thules, then, one can listen to a number of older women performing the ballads *a cappella*. Their recordings are kept at the Arnamagnæan Institute in Iceland, and some of these are available online at Ísmús (Folkloric Sound Archive), including the one of "The Ballad of Olaf Lilyrose" by Jakobína, who makes the comment about *krakkar* (children) at the end.[43] The wavering voices of these singers, who sometimes forget where they are midway through the ballad, may provide some approximation of those eighty-year women in whom the ballad tradition lay for Snæbjörn Pálsson back in the seventeenth century. And while late medieval young men and women may well have had the gender lessons of the ballads imprinted on their very bodies as they performed like the other dancers around them,[44] they may first have felt the ballad tunes hummed into their infant ears, and heard the ballad lyrics spoken to them in their mother's voice.

Boynton for helping arrange for me to see a copy at the Royal Library, Copenhagen). Hreinn publishes all known melodies for ballads ÍFk 1, 15, 35, 39, 45, 60, 83, 86, 88, 92, and 98. Concerning female performers, cf. also p. 432, tune IIb, learned from an old woman, Rannveig Gísladóttir (d. 1899); c, performed by Andrea Jónsdóttir (b. 1902) who learned it from her mother; d, Guðný Jónsdóttir (b. 1884), who learned it from her mother (so also III, Vd, VIb, VIIb); e, Ástríður Thorarensen (b. 1895), who learned it from a housemaid; g, Hjaltlína Guðjónsdóttir (b. 1890), whose mother hummed the tune to her babies day and night; p. 433, tunes Ve and f, learned by a brother and sister (b. 1891) in childhood from their mother; j, Hulda Kristjánsdóttir (b. 1909), who learned it from her mother; VIa, Þórunn Bjarnadóttir (b. 1884), who learned it when she was eight from her fostermother; p. 434, VId, Stefanía Sigurðardóttir (b. 1879), who learned it at her father's and mother's home, where it was often performed for the children; e, Þórunn Ingvarsdóttir (b. 1888), who learned it from her mother; f, Kristín Pétursdóttir (b. 1887), who learned it from women at their spinning wheels; VIII, Þorbjörg Pálsdóttir (b. 1885), who learned it from her kinswoman Þorbjörg; X, Hildigunnur Valdemarsdóttir, who learned it from her mother; and p. 435, XIa, Björg Björnsdóttir (b. 1913), who learned it from Guðrún Sigurjónsdóttir.

43. In addition, two ballad recordings (ÍFk 35 and uncat., see *Sagnadansar*, no. 88) by a male singer (Brynjólfur Sigurðsson) appear on the 1998 CD *Raddir*. For a professional recording (by a female singer) of five traditional ballad melodies (and four new ones), see Anna Pálina, *Sagnadans* (2004).

44. Judith Butler emphasizes the relationship between gender and the body: "Consider gender, for instance, as a *corporeal style*, an 'act,' as it were, which is both intentional and performative, where '*performative*' suggests a dramatic and contingent construction of meaning . . . . The effect of gender is produced through the stylization of the body" (*Gender Trouble*, 139–40). Butler has less to say, however, about the occasions in which such bodily attitudes are apprehended and rehearsed (such as, in this case, Icelandic ballad dances), or about the particular mental attitudes that are assimilated concurrently (as in Icelandic ballad lyrics).

Appendix: Translations

"The Ballad of Elen"

Translated by Paul Acker
Source: *Elenar ljóð*, in Vésteinn Ólason, *Sagnadansar* 93–94 (also
see JH 3:249–50)

1. Little Elen sang so loud
(the leaf is on the linden)
a merman heard her 'neath the flood.
('tis harder to untangle than to bind)

2. Elen asked her father once:
"Let me step out to the dance."

3. "You shall not to this dancing go
where many a fool can ogle you."

4. "Let fare the fool as best he can,
I shall betake me to the dance."

5. Farewell, farewell, dear daughter mine;
your mother ne'er did such a thing.

6. Little Elen sang so loud
a merman heard her 'neath the flood.

7. The merman took his charger bold
set on it a saddle gold.

8. He took Elen by the hand,
tied her to his saddle-band.

9. As they rode beside a lake,
Elen craved a rest to take.

10. "I'll gladly grant a rest to thee
if thou will vow to marry me."

11. "Marry you, *mere man*? I'd rather not."
—The merman vanished from the spot.

12. Elen made her way back home,
(the leaf is on the linden)
thanked God she had escaped from harm
('tis harder to untangle than to bind).

"The Ballad of Olaf Lily-Rose"

Translated by Paul Acker
Source: *Kvæði af Ólafi liljurós*, in Vésteinn Ólason, *Sagnadansar*
91–92 (cf. Berggreen, 406; see also JH 1:24–28)

1. Olaf along the sea cliffs rode,
(the fire was burning red)
came upon an elves' abode.
(a ship lay ready waiting 'neath the sea cliffs ahead)

[Berggreen version:
Olaf along the sea cliffs rode
    (lost his way, found his way)
came upon an elves' abode
(where fire was burning red; a gentle breeze was blowing 'neath the
    sea cliffs ahead)]

2. There came out an elfin maid,
gold was woven in her braid.

3. Then came out a second one,
a silver pitcher in her hand.

4. Then came out a third young maid,
a silver sash about her waist.

5. Then came out a fourth young maid,
Straightaway these words she said:

6. "Welcome, Olaf lily-rose,
come inside and drink with us."

7. "I will not dwell among the elves
but rather trust in God himself."

8. "Though you dwell among the elves
you still may trust in God himself.

9. Wait for me a while or so
while I into the greenwood go."

10. She walked on over to a chest,
draped a cloak across her breast.

11. She reached into the coffer deep
took in hand a dagger keen.

12. "You must not ride away from us
until you spare me just one kiss."

13. Olaf leaned down from his steed
kissed the maid whole-heartedly.

14. She thrust the knife into his breast,
next his heart the blade did rest.

15. Much pain did Olaf then abide
when she stabbed him in his side.

16. Olaf saw his own heart's blood,
at his horse's feet it stood.

17. Olaf pricked his horse with spur
rode up to his mother's door.

18. He struck the door with open hand:
"darling mother, let me in."

19. "Where do you come from now, my son,
why are your cheeks so pale and wan?

20. You look so black, you look so blue,
as if the elves had sport with you."

21. "I cannot hide from thee for long;
an elfin maid has done me wrong.

22. Mother, lend me an eiderdown,
sister, a cloth to bind my wound."

23. She led her son up to his bed;
When she kissed him, he was dead.

24. There was more weeping than delight:
(the fire was burning red)
three dead were buried in one night.
(a ship lay ready waiting 'neath the sea cliffs ahead).[45]

Bibliography

Aðalheiður Guðmundsdóttir. "How Icelandic Legends Reflect the Prohibition on Dancing." *Arv: Nordic Yearbook of Folklore* 61 (2005): 25–52.

Andri Snær Magnason and Rósa Þorsteinsdóttir, eds. *Raddir* (Original Recordings of Icelandic Folk Music). Árni Magnússon Institute and Badtaste Records, 1998. CD.

Anna Pálína and Draupner. *Sagnadans*. Reykjavík: Dimma, 2004. CD.

Berggreen, A. P. *Folke-Sange og Melodier*. Copenhagen: Jaeger, 1845.

Bjarni Einarsson, ed. *Munnmælasögur 17. aldar*. Íslenzk rit síðari alda 6. Reykjavík: Fræðafélagið, 1955.

---

45. I would like to thank Vésteinn Ólason, Sif Ríkharðsdóttir, Jóhanna Katrín Friðriksdóttir and Gunnlaugur Ingólfsson for answering my queries about translating these ballads.

Bourdieu, Pierre. *Masculine Domination*. Translated by Richard Nice. Stanford: Stanford University Press, 2001.

Brewer, Derek. *Symbolic Stories: Traditional Narratives of the Family Drama in English Literature*. London: Longman, 1988.

Butler, Judith. "Performative Acts and Gender Constitution: An Essay in Phenomenology and Feminist Theory." *Theatre Journal* 40 (1988): 519–31.

———. *Gender Trouble: Feminism and the Subversion of Identity*. London: Routledge, 1990.

Cleasby, Richard, and Gudbrand Vigfusson. *An Icelandic-English Dictionary*. 2nd ed. Oxford: Clarendon, 1957.

Espeland, Velle. "Oral Ballads as National Literature: The Reconstruction of Two Norwegian Ballads." *Estudios de Literatura Oral* 6 (2000): 10pp. http://www.visearkivet.no/pdf_filer/diverse_artikler/english/oral_ballads_as_national_litterature.pdf.

Gísli Magnússon and Jón Þórðarson Thóroddsen, eds. *Snót: Nokkur kvæði eptir ýmiss skáld*. Copenhagen: Kvisti, 1850.

Grundtvig, Svend et al., eds. *Danmarks gamle folkeviser*. Copenhagen: Samfund til det danske literaturs fremme, 1853–1976.

———, and Jón Sigurðsson, eds. *Íslenzk fornkvæði*. Copenhagen: det nordiske Literatur-Samfund, 1854–85.

Hreinn Steingrímsson. "Lög við íslenzka sagnadansa." Apendix to Vésteinn Ólason, *Sagnadansar*, 395–435.

An Illustrated Tolkien Bibliography. http://www.tolkienbooks.net/

Ísmús: Icelandic Music and Cultural Heritage. http://www.ismus.is/.

Jamieson, Robert, ed. *Popular Ballads and Songs*. Edinburgh: Constable, 1806.

Jochens, Jenny. *Old Norse Images of Women*. Philadelphia: University of Pennsylvania Press, 1996.

Jón Árnason. *Icelandic Legends Collected by Jón Árnason*. Translated by George E. J. Powell and Eiríkur Magnússon. London: Bentley, 1864.

———. *Íslenzkar þjóðsögur og ævintýri*. 2nd edition. Edited by Árni Böðvarsson and Bjarni Vilhjálmsson. 6 vols. Reykjavík: Þjóðsaga, 1954–61.

Jonsson, Bengt R., Svale Solheim, and Eva Danielson, eds. *The Types of the Medieval Scandinavian Ballad: A Descriptive Catalogue (in collaboration with Mortan Nolsøe and W. Edson Richmond)*. Oslo: Universitetsforlaget, 1978.

Jón Helgason, ed. *Íslenzk fornkvæði: Islandske Folkeviser.* Editiones Arnamagnæanæ B10–17. Copenhagen: Munksgaard, 1962–81.

Karras, Ruth Mazo. *From Boys to Men: Formations of Masculinity in Late Medieval Europe.* Philadelphia: University of Pennsylvania Press, 2003.

Kress, Helga. "Searching for Herself: Female Experience and Female Tradition in Icelandic Literature." In *A History of Icelandic Literature*, edited by Daisy L. Neijmann, 503–51. Lincoln: University of Nebraska, 2006.

Kvæðabók séra Gissurar Sveinsson: AM 147, 8vo. Íslenzk rit síðari alda 2a-b. Reykjavík: Hið íslenzka fræðafélag, 1960.

Marnersdóttir, Malan. "Women and Ballads: The Representation of Women in Faroese Ballad Tradition." *Scandinavica* 49 (2010): 27–48.

Nína Björk Elíasson. "Eru sagnadansar kvennatónlist?" In *Konur skrifa til heiðurs Önnu Sigurðardóttur*, edited by Valborg Bentsdóttir, Guðrún Gísladóttir og Svanlaug Baldursdóttir, 143–54. Reykjavík: Sögufélag, 1980.

Shippey, Tom. "*Alias Oves Habeo*: The Elves as a Category Problem." In *The Shadow-Walkers: Jacob Grimm's Mythology of the Monstrous*, edited by Tom Shippey, 157–87. Tempe: Arizona Center for Medieval and Renaissance Studies, 2005.

Simpson, Jacqueline, trans. *Icelandic Folktales and Legends.* Berkeley: University of California Press, 1972. Repr. Stroud: Tempus, 2004.

Syndergaard, Larry E. *English Translations of the Scandinavian Medieval Ballads: An Analytical Guide and Bibliography.* Turku: The Nordic Institute of Folklore, 1995.

Vésteinn Ólason, ed. *Sagnadansar.* Íslensk rit 5. Reykjavík: Rannsóknastofnun í bókmenntafræði við Háskóla Íslands, 1979.

———. *The Traditional Ballads of Iceland: Historical Studies.* Reykjavík: Stofnun Árna Magnússonar, 1982.

The Rök Inscription, Line 20

Joseph Harris
HARVARD UNIVERSITY

In memory of Frederic Amory

The only severely damaged line on the Rök Stone is the one numbered 20 in the now standard treatment of Elias Wessén.[1] According to Wessén and most subsequent interpreters, line 20 was to be read after his 19 and before his 21–28; in two of my articles on Rök I have followed and defended this order (though ultimately calling for a reversal of 27–28), but I did not attempt in those articles to comment extensively on the damaged line.[2] The present small-scale study in memory of a large-minded friend essays a reconstruction and interpretation of line 20, building on the conclusions and utilizing the conventions of those two articles, as well, of course, as on those of my predecessors.[3] As previous scholars have noted, an understanding

---

1. Elias Wessén, *Runstenen vid Röks kyrka*, Kungl. vitterhets historie och antikvitets akademiens handlingar, filologisk-filosofiska serien 5 (Stockholm: Almqvist & Wiksell, 1958). Line 26, side D, suffered the total loss of its first rune (coordinates cipher), but completion of the word there is non-controversial.

2. See Joseph Harris, "Myth and Meaning in the Rök Inscription," *Viking and Medieval Scandinavia* 2 (2006): 45–109 (line 20 is discussed chiefly pp. 51–52), and "The Rök Stone through Anglo-Saxon Eyes," in *The Anglo-Saxons and the North*, ed. Matti Kilpiö et al. (Tempe, AZ: ACMRS, 2009), 11–45. These articles, especially "Myth and Meaning," constitute a necessary background to the present study and its terminology.

3. Among the "conventions" in "Myth and Meaning," 46n2: Vamoð's name; Wessén's line numbers and his normalizations of OSw (in most cases); but also the use of OWN forms following Ottar Grønvik, *Der Rökstein: Über die religiöse Bestimmung und das weltliche Schicksal eines Helden aus der frühen Wikingerzeit*, Osloer Beiträge zur Germanistik 33 (Frankfurt am Main: Peter Lang, 2003). Grønvik (at least in this work) uses angular brackets for the transcription of runes (41); I follow the bold usage instead, except when quoting from Grønvik. In addition, Grønvik writes oral /a/ as <A>, nasal as <a>; I prefer to follow the tradition of writing nasal as **ą**, oral as simple **a**. My references to "Section," "Question," and "Answer" are explained in the articles cited in note 2 above;

Rök Stone, side C (back), trimmed to highlight lines 18–20.
Riksantikvarieämbetet (Swedish National Heritage Board).
Reproduced by permission.

of this line depends heavily on an overall interpretation of the Rök inscription.[4] Philologically restrained speculation would seem to be the only method available.

A consensus description of the immediate context of line 20 might read as follows: Line 19, in "Rök runes" (or "Swedish-Norwegian" or "short-twig" runes) of a more or less uniform height about half that of more central lines, ends with a punctuating dot; its integrity of script and graphic definition are reinforced by its clear semantic unity as the concluding segment of Section 2's Answer. Below 19 (read as a modern text, actually vertical and to the right of 19) is line 20, written in the same runes and reading in the same left-to-right (i.e., upward) direction. The runes of line 20 were from the beginning slightly smaller than those of 19, and the size of these two lines would seem to reflect progressive crowding. The rune master did succeed in getting a complete sense unit on this extreme right edge of side C (the back of the stone), but vertical shrinkage of the runes and the placement of 20 in an exposed location along the edge were the price. We do not know when the damage to 20 occurred; scholars have speculated that it might have been when the village of Rök's old tithe barn was demolished in 1843 and the stone removed from its place. The rune stone was re-immured in the porch of the new church in the course of the same day and with the same

---

there I also discuss the meaning of *minni*, which I leave untranslated here. In general, I treat Wessén (note 1 above) as the edition of reference.

4. Hermann Reichert, "Runeninschriften als Quellen der Heldensagenforschung," in *Runeninschriften als Quellen interdisziplinärer Forschung: Abhandlungen des Vierten Internationalen Symposiums über Runen und Runeninschriften in Göttingen, 4–9 August 1995*, ed. Klaus Düwel et al. (Berlin: de Gruyter, 1998), 100; Grønvik, *Der Rökstein*, 68.

side, the front, exposed, but the brief revelation of the whole stone, with its previously (and subsequently) hidden inscribed back, top, and sides was time enough for a church official to make a complete drawing, including the hidden faces. The drawing clearly shows that the damage was already present on June 8, 1843, but whether it is "fresh damage," as von Friesen comments, is uncertain.[5] In any case, the damage sheered away the bottoms of most of the runes, and in some places the affected area rises to obliterate whole runes, even extending slightly into line 19. Nevertheless, a good many runes in line 20 can be identified with certainty or near certainty, and others can be deduced from the possibilities offered by the remnants (in comparison with the normal forms of Rök runes), together with estimates of the probable words (guided by the diction of the inscription elsewhere and the probable content according to each interpretation); finally, even where effacement is complete, we can still determine, more or less, the number of missing runes and make deductions or, ultimately, guesses based on overall content.

At the end of line 20 and extending up to the top of line 19 is a series of very legible, undamaged Rök runes spelling **ftiʀfra**, interepreted since Bugge's time as OSw *(a)ftiʀ fra*, ON *eptir frá*.[6] These runes are usually considered the conclusion of line 20, and their larger size (almost the size of the more standard lines of side C, such as line 18) explained as the rune master's exploitation of the empty space left after the dot ending line 19. The stone offers several (partial) graphic analogues: on side A, the front, the bottom framing line of line 1 is fixed, but the letters expand in height to fill the natural space offered by the stone; with line 6 it is the top framing line that is fixed while the letters of the second half of the line expand (but not so dramatically as in line 1) downward in length following the space offered by the stone; the same is true of line 7. But lines 6–8 offer a somewhat different situation from lines 19–20 since 8 is a sort of dwarfed line terminated by a downward curving frame and by the stone's shape,

---

5. "af allt att döma tämligen färska skadorna" (rather fresh damage, to judge by all indications). Otto von Friesen, *Rökstenen: Runstenen vid Röks kyrka Lysings härad Östergötland* (Stockholm: Kungl. Vitterhets- historie- och antivitets akademien, 1920), 1; see also 84. Further, see Wessén, *Runstenen vid Röks kyrka*, 10 and 92–97, for a reproduction of the drawing.

6. Sophus Bugge, *Der Runenstein von Rök in Östergötland, Schweden*, ed. Magnus Olsen, with contributions by Axel Olrik and Erik Brate (Stockholm: Hæggström, 1910), 82–83. Wessén normalizes to *æftiʀ*, but I follow Bugge for this word.

and 7's expansion occurs after (to the right of) the end of 8; similarly 7 is naturally shortened by the curve of the stone, reinforced by its frame, creating the conditions for the expansion of letters in the last half of line 6.[7] With the larger runes **ftiʀfra**, the shape of the stone is not a factor since the space offered there is purely a function of the ending of line 19's sense unit, and no analogous downward curving frame exists (or still exists) for line 20.

A variant explanation of **ftiʀfra**, based largely on the analogy with lines 6–8, has these runes standing in line 19, though unconnected semantically with the material before the dot; 19 therefore has an *a* and a *b* component. Line 19 proper is 19a, and **ftiʀfra** is 19b. In this explanation 19b is the beginning, semantically and syntactically speaking, of line 20 rather than its conclusion.[8] This situation could be paralleled several times on the stone; for example, a sense unit ends with a dot in 5, but the inscription line continues with the beginning of a new sense unit that spills over into 6 (**• þat sakum ana/rt**); similarly in lines 14 and 17. On the other hand, sense units apparently end and new ones begin within lines 24–25 without punctuation (**traki uilin is þat** and **[i]atun uilin is þat**), though also in these same lines punctuating crosses coincide with a shift into cipher (or into a different cipher) and a new sense unit. An important graphic objection to this variant reading would be that **ftiʀfra** foots with 20 at the edge of the stone so that the rune master would have had to have 20 fully planned or, better, already cut before the beginning of its sentence could be cut (but again cf. lines 6–8); in other words, if the rune master had set out to enter a sentence with the word order 19b-20, he could not have carved its beginning, the double-sized runes of 19b, first because he would not have known at the beginning that he would have that extra space for the large runes. Wessén states, very simply, another reason for his order 20–19b: "Vad ristaren nu har att tillägga är av annan art. Därför fortsätter han icke omedelbart i rad 19, utan

7. Lis Jacobsen, "Rökstudier," *Arkiv för nordisk filologi* 76 (1961): 15–20, offers a fine but ultimately unconvincing analysis of lines 6–8 in support of the "variant explanation" of **ftiʀfra** (see next note).

8. Jacobsen, "Rökstudier," is the main proponent of this argument; she labels 19a as 19.1, and 19b as 19.2, but I consider the use of letters a bit clearer. The order 19b–20 is followed by Niels Åge Nielsen, *Runerne på Rökstenen*, Odense University Studies in Scandinavian Languages 2 (Odense: Odense University Press, 1969), 37, without argument.

markerar det nya med ny rad (r. 20)" (What the rune carver now has to add is of another kind. Therefore he does not continue directly in line 19 but distinguishes the new material with a new line [line 20]).[9] Moreover, while **ftiʀfra** could be construed as the beginning of a sentence, it would require an **a** to yield *[a]ftiʀ fra*; this **a** cannot be supplied from the undamaged space between the dot and **f**, but it is easily imagined in the damaged space of 20.[10] This appears to be a strong argument against 19b-20, and on balance, it is more natural to imagine **ftiʀfra** coming at the end of 20.

In the history of the interpretation of Rök a third explanation for **ftiʀfra** is important. Von Friesen separated these seven runes from both 19a and 20, read them as shift cipher, and connected them to the end of line 25, the mysterious word **nit(i)**, which however is in numerical or coordinates cipher; rewritten as Rök runes and utilizing the frame as final **i**'s (normal on Rök), the sense unit so created read: **nit(i)ubafuks(i)**, ON *nyt upp af øxi* "may advantage grow up from it."[11] Criticism of the larger context constructed by von Friesen and of many details would lead too far afield here and can be read in earlier

---

9. Wessén, *Runstenen vid Röks kyrka*, 49.

10. Bugge had already captured this argument with admirable brevity and added a syntactic one: "Dafür, dass *ftiʀ fra nach* (nicht *vor*) *d* Z. 9 [= line 20] gelesen werden soll, spricht: 1) wir können dann die auffallende Form *ftiʀ* entfernen; denn *a* kann die letzte Rune in *d* Z. 9 gewesen sein, wodurch wir die erwartete Form **aftiʀ* erhalten. 2) *nuk* mit dem enklitischen *'k* steht am passendsten an der Spitze des Satzes; vgl. die entsprechende Stelle der Vafþr" [For the case that **ftiʀ fra** should be read *after* (and not *before*) line 20 speak the following arguments: 1) This way we can eliminate the surprising form **ftiʀ** because the last rune in line 20 can be the **a** by which we obtain the expected form **aftiʀ*. 2) **nuk**, with its enclitic *'k*, stands in the most suitable position at the head of the sentence: cf. the analogous passage of the *Vafþr*] (*Der Runenstein von Rök*, 85). The reference here is to *Vafþrúðnismál* 55.7, a (partial) parallel to line 20 discussed by Bugge (83). Jacobsen ("Rökstudier," 18) answered the first of these objections by pointing to three instances on Rök of omission on an initial **a** (lines 4, 15, and 22); but these are all instances of the preposition *at* as proclitic to a following noun and so quite different from the case at issue. For the syntactic matter raised by Bugge (and supported with the Eddic parallel) she cited an instance of somewhat similar syntax in Rök lines 7–8 (*ok dó með hann [um sakar]* "and died with [them] he"); but well before Jacobsen wrote, Otto Höfler had already improved this awkward passage with the reading *ok dœmir enn um sakar*; see *Der Runenstein von Rök und die germanische Individualweihe*, Germanisches Sakralkönigtum 1 (Tübingen: Niemeyer; Münster: Böhlau, 1952), 37–42. Since Jacobsen's day, Höfler's reading has been adopted by Nielsen, *Runerne på Rökstenen*, 28–29, and by Lars Lönnroth, "The Riddles of the Rök-Stone: A Structural Approach," *Arkiv för nordisk filologi* 92 (1977): 25–26. Grønvik, *Der Rökstein*, 53–55, adopted the new reading but with a different meaning.

11. von Friesen, *Rökstenen*, 64–65.

works beginning with Wessén's, but it is worth repeating from my earlier articles that von Friesen, Höfler, and Lönnroth are with this move guilty of an arbitrary linkage that ignores the graphic and runological routing directions. The probability of shift cipher yielding a coherent expression of longer words, as in **ftiʀfra** understood as *(a)ftiʀ fra,* would also seem slight if we judge by the undisputed shift-coded line 23 (**airfbfrbnhnfinbantfa̧nhnu**) and the end of 24 (**rhþrhis**): when an underlying message conceived in Rök runes has been disguised through shift cipher, a few of the resulting rune combinations may accidentally yield sensible individual words in OSw (for example, **nu**, **is**) or possible morphemes, but as a whole, it seems unlikely to produce extended, syntactically and semantically plausible discourse.[12]

Our rejection of the order 19b-20 is somewhat less conclusive than our rejection of von Friesen's move, but we are left, together with most post-Wessén writers on Rök, supporting the order 20–19b, that is, regarding **ftiʀfra** as the conclusion of 20. Grønvik's recent edition of Rök is an important witness for this order because Grønvik otherwise adopts many of the ideas of the school of Otto Höfler (which itself derives from von Friesen). We may use Grønvik's initial presentation of 20 (C9 in his numbering system) as the starting point for our own reading.[13] Grønvik's underdotting signifies an only partially preserved rune, but the degree of partial preservation varies radically:

> Bugge meinte, einige von ihnen [the damaged runes] bestimmen zu können, aber nicht alle, und liest (1910: 83–85) in heute geläufiger Transliteration:
> **C9 < n u k m i̧ ṇ i̧ m i̧ ʀ A l u ṣ A̧ k i A i n h u A ʀ [. . .] f t i ʀ f r A >**
> Nach den ersten 24 einigermaßen sicher identifizierbaren Runen steht eine Reihe zum größten Teil unbestimmbarer Runenreste (hier zunächst durch [. . .] angegeben). Es handelt sich wahrscheinlich um 10 Runen. Die 8. Rune in dieser . . . Reihe . . . wird jedoch von Bugge als ein deutliches <þ> erkannt, die Runen 1–3 [of this heavily damaged section] von Brate (1917 [sic]: 241) als <iþi>. (Grønvik, *Der Rökstein,* 67)

---

12. I have not come across a discussion of such cases in terms of mathematical probability. Of line 23, Bugge (*Der Runenstein von Rök,* 103) simply states that *diese Runen Wörter . . . nicht enthalten können* (these runes cannot contain words).

13. Grønvik's text-internal references are to Bugge, *Der Runenstein von Rök,* 83–85, and Erik Brate, *Östergötlands runinskrifter,* Sveriges runinskrifter 2 (Stockholm: Norstedt, 1911–18), 241.

Bugge thought that he could determine some of the damaged runes but not all; in 1910 (83–85) he read the following in today's current transliteration:

C9   < n u k m ị ṇ ị m ị ʀ A l u ṣ Ạ k i A i n h u A ʀ [. . .] f t i ʀ f r A >

After the first twenty-four moderately certainly identifiable runes stand a series of largely indeterminable rune remains (represented for the moment by [. . .]). It is a matter of probably about ten runes. The eighth rune in this series was however recognized by Bugge as a clear <þ>; and the runes 1–3 of this heavily damaged section are read by Brate (241) as <iþi>.

Such was the state of the art in reading of the fractured runes of this line in the time of Bugge and Brate, though a discrepancy in Grøn-vik's account with regard to the total rune space in the most heavily damaged area will be noted below (see note 16).

This consensus was built up gradually with contributions from Brate, Olsen, and von Friesen; I accept it as an accurate inventory of the runes still or once observable or partly observable in the line. When we look at the photograph accompanying this article and follow Bugge's discussion, most of the reconstruction appears possible or even probable, for example, the ịṇị of m[ini]; and the word before ainhuaʀ, spelled alu, is clear.[14] I see no trace in the modern photo of the m or the subsequent runes of miʀ (meðʀ), however, and here I rely on the 1907 autopsy by Bugge's three younger colleagues. Bugge wrote simply: "R. 8–10 sind von mir und Brate als... miʀ gelesen" (runes 8–10 are read by Brate and by me as miʀ). (Here Bugge is numbering the runes from the beginning of the line, not as in Grønvik above within the damaged area.) In the enhanced photo (Plate II) from 1910 these three letters appear clearly.[15] Within Grønvik's bracketed section, the area of most damage, it is certain that we can still read, with Brate, iþ as the first two runes after huaʀ; but of the third rune of Brate's group we can only be certain that its staff rose to the top of the line and that no twig branched from the top, certainly not to the left and very probably also not to the right. For the remaining fragment shows approximately the top third of the staff, and the damaged area

---

14. Bugge, *Der Runenstein von Rök*, 83–84.

15. Ibid. 83n1, 84, and Plate II. This would probably be the same photograph that appears in Brate's edition cited in note 13 above.

rises steeply up the right side, extending here into line 19. Thus the rune under discussion could not be **u, þ, r, t, m, l,** or **ʀ**; less certainly excludable would be **ą, b,** and **f** (the twigs, all right-branching, would have been erased, but the upper twig tends to start fairly high on the staff and might be expected to have left a trace in the remaining fragment). Besides Brate's **i,** the following would seem to be possible given the damage: **h, n, s** (perhaps less likely given the length of the remaining staff), and, crucially for my argument, **k.** In **k** (also in **a**) the right-branching twig tends to begin at a point on the staff that could well be below the end of the existing fragment and could have been completely erased in the damaged area. Anticipating my hypothesis about the content, I tentatively adopt **k** here. Subsequent discussion will help to justify that adoption.

   There follows space for perhaps four or five runes in the devastated area;[16] then in its midst we find (with Bugge) a clear **þ,** followed by space again for at least four or five runes before we arrive at the **f** of **ftiʀfra.** The rune before **f** must have been **a.** I therefore revise Grønvik's, i.e., "today's current transliteration," as our platform for interpretative hypotheses of 20:

nukmįņimįʀaluşąkiainhuaʀiþk̇|123(4,5)|þ|123(4)|(ȧ)ftiʀfra

Here the overdotted runes are my additions, **k̇** partly on the basis of detective speculation around a partially preserved staff, **(ȧ)** without any surviving traces but dictated by the word *aftiʀ.* With all due reservation about **k̇,** I believe this could be called the current corrected state of the art.

   The next level of interpretation entails segmentation into words

---

16. Brate estimates the lost runes between the second **i** of **iþi** and the lone **þ** at "about seven" (*Östergötlands runinskrifter*, 241); but if the second **i** was in fact a **k,** the discrepancy of perhaps one rune-space vanishes. Elsewhere Brate mentions that "etwa 10 Runen vollständig fehlen" (Bugge, *Der Runenstein von Rök*, 273); that would seem to be equivalent to an estimate of five lost runes before and five after the lone **þ.** Neither Bugge nor Brate explicitly estimates the rune-spaces of the obliterated area between the lone **þ** and **ftiʀfra,** though Brate does imply that the five runes of **suniʀ** in 19 above the second lacuna correspond to missing runes in 20 (*Östergötlands runinskrifter*, 241). Grønvik (quoted above) seems to estimate the whole space of his bracketed areas at ten runes, of which the first three were **iþi** and the eighth **þ;** he apparently, then, allowed for four missing runes before the lone **þ.** This seems about right to me, but the space to the right of **þ** cannot have contained only two runes.

and sense units, but a full review of my predecessors is beyond my remit. I begin with Wessén, who, however, follows, more or less, Bugge's segmentation and interpretation: **nuk m[ini] miʀ alu [sa] k[i] ainhuaʀ ... þ ... ftiʀ fra.**[17] Wessén's own transcription is more agnostic, but his normalization and translation put his understanding largely in line with Bugge's although he fills out the space preceding the lone þ to yield a relative pronoun: *Nu'k minni meðr allu sagi. Ainhvaʀʀ ... svað ... æftiʀ fra* "Nu säger jag minnena fullständigt. Någon ... det som han har eftersport" (Now I tell the memorials completely. Someone ... that which he has found out).[18] Jacobsen begins the sentence with 19b but agrees on **nu'k mini miʀ alu** (and on the isolated **ainhuaʀ**); Nielsen follows her but adds **saki** to yield **saki ainhuaʀ**; Lönnroth essentially follows Bugge's (Wessén's) segmentation but normalizes and interprets in accordance with his argument that 20 provides the concluding part of a structural frame of the whole inscription that balances lines 1–2.[19] In short, most or all of Bugge's segmentation just quoted is widely, if not universally, agreed on.

From the brief review above, we see a good deal of agreement on the line. Even in Lönnroth's version (though not in Jacobsen's) it seems semantically to constitute a variant of the inscription's *sagum*-formula, with *minni* appearing here uncompounded. I shall now discuss some details assuming the general understanding of *nu'k minni ... sagi*. I believe that the present tense and *nu* here refer forward to the last, the enciphered part of the inscription: "I shall now tell (a/some) *minni*," the neuter making the sg/pl distinction inoperative. Varin here speaks, as it were, in his own voice, using the pronoun *ek* (in contrast to the ceremonial third person of lines 1–2 in the traditional opening "formula") and the regular first-person singular inflectional form in *sagi* (instead of the apparently archaic *sagum*); uncompounded *minni*, elsewhere *mǫgminni*, may contribute to these less formal features.[20]

---

17. Wessén, *Runstenen vid Röks kyrka*, 50; Bugge, *Der Runenstein von Rök*, 85.

18. Wessén, *Runstenen vid Röks kyrka*, 26–7. Wessén may have drawn the suggestion of an **a** before **þ** in his *svað* from von Friesen; see note 37 below.

19. See Jacobsen, "Rökstudier," 18; Nielsen, *Runerne på Rökstenen*, 37; Lönnroth, "Riddles of the Rök-Stone," 50.

20. In my articles (see note 2 above), I accepted Grønvik's innovative suggestion that *sagum* (< **sagu-miz*) is an otherwise unattested mediopassive where an ancient first-person

Perhaps we may understand the tone as more personal, the language as more demotic, as Varin introduces Section 3, the climax of the inscription and the myth surely closest to his own feelings.

These features—*nu*, present/future tense, the forward thrust of the *sagum*-formula—argue against the Jacobsen/Nielsen retrospective focus whereby line 20 capped Sections 1 and 2, but Jacobsen is right to bring up the difficulty of *meðr allu* (normalized: *með ǫllu*) "completely" in the context of line 20 since that adverbial sense attached to the phrase in the dictionaries hardly describes the allusive and playful (or merely fragmentary) way the narrative material is conveyed on Rök.[21] (Jacobsen related "completely" more plausibly to the name-*þula* of Section 2, but that retrospective focus is unconvincing on other grounds.) In view of the prospective context, I propose to understand *með ǫllu* as "in completion," that is, "in conclusion, finally," with reference to the order of sections and to Section 3's sacred story, the story that will bring the inscription to its culmination with an allusion to the highest god on the top face of the stone.

The sentence may end with *með ǫllu sagi*, but **ainhuaʀ** introduces several possibilities. Most scholars interpret this as a single word, ON *ein(n)hverr* "someone, anyone" (earlier "each one").[22] Wessén writes the OSw as *ainhvaʀʀ* and translates as *någon* "someone"; Nielsen attaches the word (retaining the transliteration **ainhuaʀ**) as subject to the verb *sagi*: *En eller anden må sige* (one or another may say); Lönnroth similarly has "May each person...tell" [enough of the memories completely]: **nuk** = *nóg*.[23] Grønvik alone of recent scholars separates **ain** from **huaʀ**, applying **ain** to the first clause and **huaʀ**

---

singular inflection survives (*Der Rökstein*, 48–49); Bugge's first-person is similar but vague on the origin of *-um* (*Der Runenstein von Rök*, 11–13); Brate interpreted the form as first person plural imperative "let us say" (Brate, *Östergötlands runinskrifter*, 233, and Brate in Bugge, *Der Runenstein von Rök*, 267; also Bugge, *Der Runenstein von Rök*, 11n2); Wessén seems to straddle the fence with "'jag säger' (el. 'vi säga')" (33). This word still lacks a clear and historically inevitable explanation.

21. "Med linje 20 slutter den del af indskriften, der er ristet med svensk-norske runer" (With line 20 the part of the inscription in Swedish-Norwegian runes is closed) [Jacobsen, "Rökstudier," 21].

22. Richard Cleasby and Gudbrand Vigfusson, *An Icelandic–English Dictionary*, 2nd ed. (Oxford: Clarendon Press, 1957), henceforth Cleasby-Vigfusson, observe (*s.v.*) that *einn* and *hverr* are written and inflected separately in early texts.

23. See Wessén, *Runstenen vid Röks kyrka*, 27; Nielsen, *Runerne på Rökstenen*, 37; Lönnroth, "Riddles of the Rök-Stone," 50.

to the following subordinate clause: *Nu'k minni með ǫllu segi einn: hverr...* "Jetzt sage ich vollständig einen Spruch ganz allein: wer..." (Now I shall tell fully a saying, quite alone: who...). The remainder of Grønvik's interpretation here would lead too far into his theories about the whole, but I believe his separation of **ain** from **huaʀ** is important. Somewhat similarly, von Friesen makes this separation and regards **huaʀ** as the interrogative pronoun, though again his overall construction of the passage would lead us astray.[24]

In fact, the common distributive or indefinite pronoun ON *ein(n)-hverr* is itself suspicious; its only appearance in Peterson's register of words in all Swedish runic inscriptions is here in Rök; and it seems to occur only five or six times in poetry.[25] Moreover, with uncompounded **huaʀ**, the second sense unit in 20 would closely resemble other instances in Rök of the interrogative pronoun following the *sagum*-formula in a question or indirect question: lines 5–6 **þat sakum ana/rt huaʀ fur niu altum**; line 21 **sagwmogmeni [þ]ad hoaʀ...oaʀi goldin = sagum mogminni þat huaʀ...vaʀi guldinn**. We find the same construction a third time where **huaʀ** is in the dative case: lines 23–24 **sakum (m)ukmini uaim si burin [n]iþ/ʀ** (OSw *sagum mǫgminni, [h]vaim se burin niðʀ*).

The difference between an OSw equivalent of *(einn)hverr* and Rök's **huaʀ** is worth dwelling on for a moment longer. In the OWN paradigm of the interrogative pronoun, the original *huaʀ* was replaced by *hverr*; or as Grønvik, following Seip, puts it: the interrogative pronoun ONorw *huær, huar* has absorbed into itself both Proto-Nordic **hwaʀ* and Proto-Nordic **hwarjaʀ*.[26] The etymological distinction is clearly mirrored in Gothic *hwas* and *hwarjis*, and the Rök stone maintains that distinction with *huariʀ* (line 14, m. pl. nom.) and *huariaʀ* (line 3, f. pl. nom.), both attributive (adjectival) usages in contrast to the three substantival (pronominal) usages just rehearsed; the interrogative pronouns are all to be translated as "who" or "to whom" while the others translate as "which." If the **huaʀ** of **ainhuaʀ** had represented

---

24. See Grønvik, *Der Rökstein*, 68; von Friesen, 85–86.

25. See Lena Peterson, *Svenskt runordsregister*, Runrön 2 (Uppsala: Institutionen för nordiska språk, Uppsala universitet, 1989), *s.v.*; Finnur Jónsson, *Lexicon Poeticum* (Copenhagen: Lynge, 1966), *s.v.* "einhverr, einnhverr." Three skaldic instances date from the twelfth century or later; one is supposed to be from ca. 1025; the two Eddic occurrences (*Hávamál* 121; *Hárbárðslióð* 30) could be earlier.

26. Grønvik, *Der Rökstein*, 87.

the later ON *hverr*, it should, on Rök, appear as **huariʀ* because the vowels of final syllables are not yet lost after short stressed vowels in this text, for example, *sunu, sitiʀ*.[27] When Wessén writes *ainhvaʀʀ*, he would seem to be promoting before its time the syncope of -i- after a short stem (and also assimilation of a necessary medial stage **-hvarʀ*). I conclude that Grønvik must be right in assigning **ain** to the first clause and **huaʀ** to the second. I will discuss them in that order.

The syntax of **ain** is ambiguous. (1) It could conceivably modify *minni* as n. pl.: many of Cleasby-Vigfusson's citations of *minni* in its several relevant senses are plural, and Cleasby-Vigfusson gives the plural of *einn* "in a distributive sense" as "single," for example, *ein gjöld* (n. pl. nom./acc.) "a single wergild" as opposed to double, triple, or quadruple.[28] In our context this usage could yield: "I will say a unique *minni* [a pl. construction] in conclusion." The "singularity" of the *minni* could be justified in terms of the whole inscription: Section 3 embodies a myth in contrast to the two sets of non-sacred material from heroic legend in Sections 1 and 2; Section 3 is, as suggested above, the climax of the whole inscription and perhaps most fully embodies Varin's hopes; and Section 3, since its *minni* are unnumbered in contrast to Sections 1 and 2, may be drawn from a different repertoire. We could paraphrase the sense of *ein minni* (pl.) simply as "a special *minni*." (2) But perhaps a second construction will seem more probable: *einn* could be assigned to modify the subject *'k*. This syntax enjoys some support from distinguished predecessors: Grønvik does not discuss the matter, but his translation ("ich...ganz allein," quoted above) is appealing.[29] Von Friesen lends some indirect support by applying *einn* separately to a person, though not to *ek*.[30] This phrasing "ich...ganz allein" presumably accompanies Varin's use of the demotic verb form *sagi* and calls attention to his personal voice.

As nom. sg. of the interrogative pronoun, **huaʀ** is most immediately

---

27. Ibid., 86. Grønvik (69, 86–87) maintains this preservation in the form **niþiʀ** by using the framing line as the second -i-; Wessén (26–27) does not discuss the matter but transcribes **niþʀ**, normalized *niðʀ*.

28. Cleasby-Vigfusson (*s.v.*) gives postposed *einn* as a special usage which might apply here, but the time differential between Cleasby-Vigfusson's texts and Rök is great.

29. Technically Grønvik's German translation is ambiguous in the same way as the inscription, but his normalization to Old Norse with *einn* makes it clear that he refers this word to the subject.

30. von Friesen, *Rökstenen*, 85–86.

taken as the subject of the verb *frá* (<*frah*), past tense of the OSw equivalent of ON *fregna* (in dialects also *frega*). Most Rök commentators, starting with Bugge, have interpreted *frá* this way, however they have construed the syntax. Jacobson and Nielsen, but also Bugge and others, take *(a)ftiʀ fra* as equivalent to a verb that would in Old Norse be *fregna eptir* "ask after, investigate, research." Wessén, for example, translates *(han) har eftersport* (he has investigated). Proponents of this adverb-plus-verb combination seem to have taken it for granted on the basis of later Old Norse and synonyms like *spyrja eptir, frétta eptir* and perhaps on the basis of the modern languages. In any case, it has a modern feel and not much support in older sources; Peterson registers a very large number of instances of *æftiʀ* as a preposition, but only two (including this one) as an adverb, and this is her only instance of *fregna*; *Lexicon Poeticum* cites only one occurrence of *fregna eptir* (twelfth century). I shall offer alternatives for *eptir* further on, but it is tempting to interpret the verb *fregna* as belonging to the ancient formula of hearsay knowledge, as in the opening lines of *Beowulf*: *we... þrym gefrunon* "we have heard of the glory (of the Spear-Danes)."[31] Grønvik's translation *weiß ich (habe ich in Erfahrung gebracht)* "I know (I have experienced)" might rather refer to the wisdom connections of this verb, as are richly attested in *Hávamál*, for example. Touching *frá* as the past tense of *fregna*, one might raise the question whether the loss of final -*h* can have happened as early as Rök (generally dated to the first half of the ninth century); Noreen gives 980 as "der älteste Beleg des *h*-Schwundes im Auslaut" (the oldest evidence for h-loss in final position).[32] Within Rök we have **faþi** (line 2) from **faihjan*, but internal loss of *h* precedes loss in final position.[33] This problem, if it is a problem, exceeds my knowledge, and for now I take comfort in the long line of good scholars who have accepted *frá* as "learned," "heard tell," "asked," or the like.[34]

---

31. R. D. Fulk et al., eds., *Klaeber's "Beowulf" and "The Fight at Finnsburg,"* 4th ed. (Toronto: University of Toronto Press, 2008), 110nn to lines 1–3, as well as xcixn1; see also Teresa Pàroli, *L'elemento formulare nella poesia germanica antica*, Biblioteca di ricerche linguistiche e filologice 4 (Rome: Istituto di glottologia, Università di Roma, 1975).

32. See Adolf Noreen, *Altisländische und altnorwegische Grammatik*, Altnordische Grammatik 1, 5th ed. (Tübingen: Niemeyer, 1970), 168.

33. Ibid., 167.

34. It would be even more comforting if von Friesen had dealt with this problem, but he did not, taking **ftiʀfra** for cipher.

Whether **huaʀ** governs *frá* or a verb lost in the lacunas (as in Grøn-vik's reconstruction), line 20's second sense unit must be structured like the questions following the *sagum*-formula in 3–5 (*hværiaʀ valraubaʀ vaʀin*...), 5–8 (*hvaʀ fur niu aldum*...), 12–14 (*hvar hæstʀ se*...), 14–17 (*hvariʀ tvaiʀ tigiʀ kunungaʀ satin*...), 21–22 (*hvaʀ Inguldinga vaʀi guldinn*...), and 23–25 (*[h]vaim se burin niðʀ*...), and especially resembles the three questions beginning with *hvaʀ/ hvaim*. Thus, tentatively taking *frá* as the verb of the clause headed by *huaʀ* ("who has heard tell [of something yet to be determined]?"), we enter upon the first lacuna with the probability that it will contain a noun suitable to be the object of a verb, tentatively of *frá*, and having this structure: **iþk̇[123(4)]**. There is a very limited number of nouns that begin with *ið*, and one has already been hypothesized for this position by von Friesen: ON *iðgjald* (< Pr-N **gelda-*), occurring only as pl. *iðgjǫld*.[35] *Lexicon Poeticum* lists thirteen nouns that begin with *ið*, but only eight (including *iðgjǫld*) survive the runological test I described above.[36] Most of these eight are, of course, ill-suited to the context of 20. But *iðgjǫld* fits what has been reconstructed of the rune fragments and the space; its phonology is unimpeachable for Rök (for breaking cf. **iatun, fiaru, skialti, fiakura,** etc). Its choice by von Friesen appears, however, to be based less on such structural considerations than on some kind of analogy with *Sonatorrek*, st. 17.[37] Von Friesen here misinterprets Egill's idea in favor of his own

---

35. See Jan de Vries, *Altnordisches etymologisches Wörterbuch*, 3rd ed. (Leiden: Brill, 1977), *s.v.*; Rosemarie Lühr, *Die Gedichte des Skalden Egill* (Dettelbach: Röll, 2000), 208, 283.

36. The few words in Finnur Jónsson's *Lexicon Poeticum* beginning with *ið* appear in de Vries' *Wörterbuch* to be variants of words in *ið*.

37. Von Friesen does consider structural conditions when (85) he professes to see the top of a staff that might belong to a before the second þ, helping to justify the gen. pl. in his *iðgjalda*: "Insätta vi en form af iðgiǫld efter **huaʀ**, synes denna snarast böra, af spåren af toppen till en hufvudstaf före det sista þ och dessa båda teckens inbördes ställning att döma, vara gen. pl., alltså **iþ[kialta]**" (If we insert a form of *iðgjǫld* after **huaʀ**, it seems that this ought to be the gen. pl., namely **iþ[kialta]** to judge by the trace of the top of a main stave before the last þ and the position of these two signs relative to each other). In the modern photograph I can see a tiny tick where the top of a staff would be, but considering the destruction of the surface below the tick and to both sides, especially to its left, only the short rune ʀ could certainly be ruled out; t, which is needed for *iðgjǫld*, seems not to be ruled out. We may note also that the lone þ is quite a bit larger than the first þ; it looks as if the rune carver was beginning, somewhere in the first lacuna, to expand his letters as he saw enough space ahead. On the interpretation of this part of *Sonatorrek* generally, see Harris, "Myth and Meaning" and the articles cited there.

idée fixe, revenge (instead of mine: renewal of the family), but this word, which also appears in *Hávamál* and four more times in Cleasby-Vigfusson, is rich with probable reflections of the thought world of Rök.

After *iðgjǫld*, assuming that its last four runes adequately occupy the space to the right of **iþK**, we come next to the lone *þ*, followed by three, four, or perhaps five missing runes before the (invisible but inevitable) **[a]** of *aftiʀ*. Here the crossword-puzzle method we have been attempting fails before too many possibilities; the best I can do is to discuss some of these. I proceeded (above) tentatively on the assumption that the verb *frá* was governed by the subject **huaʀ**, but Grønvik instead took *frá* as first person (relating to, though not in syntactic connection with, the *ek* of the first clause) and having a summing-up sense, though technically the main clause, to which the **huaʀ** clause is subordinate. He found the verb for **huaʀ** in the first lacuna, thus with segmentation:

<huAR i þi[ki ni]þ[i A]ftiR> = ON *hverr [í (?) þiggi nið e]ptir.*
(Grønvik, *Der Rökstein*, 68, slightly improved)

In other words, he accepted Brate's **iþi** and worked the *þi* part into a verb *þiggja* "receive" (in 3rd sg. pres. opt.), counting four runes to the lone *þ*, which he worked into the object of the verb.

One problem is the meaning of the preposition/adverb *í* here; Grønvik concedes: "Die hier vorgeschlagene Übersetzung ist nicht ganz unproblematisch. Das unsicher belegte Adverb í (?) habe ich zuerst mit 'darin' überssetzt, was aber sehr unklar ist" (The translation suggested here is not totally without problems. I first translated the uncertainly attested adverb *í* as "therein," which however is very obscure). To improve the sentence Grønvik is driven to hypothesize a rune-cutting error:

Vielleicht ist hier ein Schreibfehler zu verzeichnen, indem eine s-Rune weggelassen und ursprünglich ein Ausdruck <huaR is> mit einer Relativpartikel /is/ geplant sein kann. Demnach würde der Satz folgendermaßen lauten: <*huAR is þiki niþi AftirR frA*>, awn. *hver es þiggi nið eptir frá*—"Wer den Verwandten nachher empfängt (empfangen wird), weiß ich." (Ibid., 69)

Perhaps we should reckon with scribal error here, where an s-rune could have been omitted and the expression ***huaʀ is**, with the relative particle **is**, could have been intended originally. Accordingly the sentence would take the following form: <*huAR is þiki niþi AftirR frA*>, OWN *hver es þiggi nið eptir frá* (Who will receive the relative hereafter, I know).

The content here reflects (and the argument is weakened by) Grønvik's idea that the latter part of the inscription deals with Vamoð's dedication as a kind of "relative" (*niðr*) to Thor, but the structural situation also seems unsatisfactory in that the space from the lone þ to the f is occupied in this reconstruction by only two runes, i (which takes up less room than most) and the obligatory a before **ftiʀ**. To my eye (and I am relying on photographs) the second lacuna is at least the same size as the first (where Grønvik has four runes, von Friesen five). If we judge by the parallel line, 19, the first lacuna could hold five runes, the second five or, with the space under the dot, six. I grant that line 19 cannot lay down a law for the restitution of 20, but the second lacuna surely needs more than two runes.

Von Friesen (although he disposed of **ftiʀfra** differently) pursues reasoning somewhat similar to Grønvik's for the stretch of text from **huaʀ** on, namely that he finds a verb and an object for the subject: **huaʀ iþ[kialta] þ[urbi]**. (The verb, here in pres. opt., takes a gen. object, hence the gen. pl. *iðgjalda*.) To paraphrase in von Friesen's sense: (Let him [the new son] consider, when he is alone [*einn*]), who might need *iðgjǫld* (revenge).[38] Five runes before the lone þ is perhaps a little crowded and four after the þ rather generous with the white space, but this reconstruction gets in all the knowns (i**þ̇k** + 4–5 spaces; þ + 4–6 spaces) and fits syntactically. The content is, as always, based on the larger—here unacceptable—understanding, but disregarding content, von Friesen's reconstruction is structurally plausible.

Before making my own guesses about the word or words beginning with the lone þ, I should comment on *aftiʀ*. In the memorial context generally (*Aft Vamoð . . . aft faigian sunu*, lines 1–2) and especially in the context of Section 3's version of the Baldr myth and the reference there (in a **huaʀ** question, lines 21–22) to a dead man who *vaʀi guldinn* "was compensated for," I think *aftiʀ* in 20 is most likely to

---

38. von Friesen, *Rökstenen*, 85, 87–88, 102–03.

carry a sense connected with death. Certainly it is very widespread in this general sense on rune stones, although Rök's usage appears to be either adverbial or as a preposition with implied object; this adverbial usage of *aftiʀ (æftiʀ)* is one of only two in Peterson's parsing of the Swedish runic corpus.[39] But one other sense should be mentioned, namely "left behind," because *eptir* in this sense is alliteratively collocated with *iðgjǫld* in a significant ancient text. *Hávamál* 105 reads: *Gunnlǫð mér um gaf . . . / drycc ins dýra miaðar; / ill iðgjǫld lét ec hana eptir hafa / síns ins heila hugar, / síns ins svára sefa* (Gunnlǫð gave me . . . a drink of the mead of poetry; I let her have *eptir* foul recompense for her generous mind, for her heavy heart). (*Hafa eptir* probably means "keep," rather than "in return.")[40]

The word *iðgjǫld* seems to occur six times in Old Norse. The verbs it is collocated with are limited to *geta* (*Sonatorrek* 17), *hafa eptir* (*Hávamál* 105) and, in prose, *hafa* (twice) and *fá* (twice). But the only synonym of *fá* and *geta* that might fit our puzzle is *þiggja*, and *Lexicon Poeticum* shows, among many occurrences in verse, a few that resemble our context, e.g. *Nú hefir hǫrð dœmi hildingr þegit* "Now the warrior has received a harsh destiny" (*Helgakviða Hundingsbana II* 3). If the sentence read *huaʀ iðgjǫld þa (a)ftiʀ* (with *frá* as "I know" as in Grønvik), the lacuna between the lone þ and f would be filled by only one rune since successive occurrences of the same rune are normally contracted in runic orthography, here hypothetically **þaftiʀ*.[41] A sense in this direction would, however, fit my understanding of Section 3: "who received recompense after [a death]." Compare lines 21–22 (Question 1) and 23–25 (Question 2). In the myth alluded to in these Questions and more openly in the Answer (25–28) of Section 3, an Odin figure, the Kinsman (*sefi*) who respected the shrines (*viavari*), sired at ninety a descendant to

---

39. Peterson, *Svenskt runordsregister*, s.v. "æftiʀ"; in Grønvik's translation (quoted above), *nachher* is also adverbial and favors a present or future sense of the verb.

40. Gustav Neckel and Hans Kuhn, eds., *Edda: Die Lieder des Codex Regius nebst verwandten Denkmälern*, vol. 1, *Text*, 4th ed. (Heidelberg: Winter, 1962), 33. See Beatrice La Farge and John Tucker, *Glossary to the Poetic Edda: Based on Hans Kuhn's Kurzes Wörterbuch* (Heidelberg: Winter, 1992), s.v. Cf. Carolyne Larrington, trans., *The Poetic Edda* (Oxford: Oxford University Press, 1996), 28; Patricia Terry, trans., *Poems of the Vikings: The Elder Edda* (Indianapolis: Bobbs-Merrill, 1969), 28; Andy Orchard, trans. *The Elder Edda: A Book of Viking Lore* (London: Penguin, 2011), 29—all with "in return."

41. One violation of this principle in Rök is found at the beginning of line 19 (**s suniʀ**).

replace his dead son, the Baldr-figure Vilin, killed by a *iatun*. In the local East Gautish myth the name of the replacement son is "Thor" (26). This reconstruction of 20 would be improved if we provided more filler for the second lacuna, such as a short adverb like *ár* "in ancient days," well known in mythological contexts; such speculation is gratuitous but would suit the myth and perhaps Varin's standpoint as commentator. But as pointed out above, the sequence *þá ár* would normally be spelled **þar*, and the space would be filled by only three runes. A longer form of *ár, árla*, is also attested for mythological time, but again the sequence *árla aftiʀ* would be contracted, yielding a total rune count in the lacuna of four: **þarlaftiʀ*. The clumping of adverbs (or preposition/adverbs) in *þa arla aftiʀ* might be thought syntactically objectionable, although as a whole the inscription is hardly a textbook case for Old Norse syntax.

An alternative space filler after *þa* might be to add a genitive qualifier for *iðgjǫld* such as *sunaʀ* (as in *Sonatorrek* 17) or *magaʀ*; every one of the six recorded instances of *iðgjǫld* in the dictionaries has a genitive qualifier, thus: *huaʀ iðgjǫld þa sunaʀ/magaʀ aftiʀ, fra* (I have heard who received compensation for his son after [death]). But either of these emotive words, both used elsewhere on Rök,[42] pushes the rune count in the second lacuna to seven. A possibly better speculation using these thematically weighted words might posit a preposed object of *aftiʀ* in the acc. (cf. *aft faigian sunu*),[43] thus: *huaʀ iðgjǫld þa sunu/magu aftiʀ* (who received recompense after [the death of] his son). This appealing filler raises the rune total for the second lacuna to a more plausible six and makes *aftiʀ* a preposition, a more securely

---

42. **sunu** (acc. sg. m.) appears in line 2 of the dead Vamoð and **suniʀ** (*synir*) four times in the *þula* of lines 17–19. As to *magu* (acc. sg. m.), in an earlier article I adopted Gun Widmark's explanation of **mukmini** as *mǫg-minni*, with the first evidence of apocope of -*u* after a stressed short vowel and the first *u*-umlaut appearing here medially in the environment of the compound. See "Varför ristade Varin runor? Tankar kring Rökstenen," *Saga och Sed: Kungl. Gustav Adolfs Akademiens årsbok* (1992): 29–31; Harris, "Anglo-Saxon Eyes," 39nn69–70. This explanation would, however, not forbid an uncompounded form *magu* (a poetic and emotional word that appears prominently in the early Norwegian inscription at Kjølevik). The form *mǫgminni* is independently supported by Alain Marez, "'sakumukmini'?—Une relecture de l'inscription de Rök," *Études germaniques* 52 (1997): 543–57.

43. Cleasby-Vigfusson (*s.v.*) generally assigns a locative meaning to *eptir* + dat. and a temporal one to *eptir* + acc., with the acc. usage very common in connection with death and succession and in runic contexts.

attested syntactic choice, to judge by Peterson's *Svenskt runords-register*. Finally, I would like to try out just one last speculation for the second lacuna, thus: **huaʀ iōg[iald] þ[egin a]ftiʀ frá**. This would mean "who has heard tell of recompense received after [a death]?" Five runes (counting **a**) are supplied, and the somewhat awkward appendage of *frá* as "ich weiß" is avoided; moreover this conjecture may match Varin's stance above the *greppaminni*-like inscription better with its reference to an audience, the audience's knowledge, and also more cryptically to the content of the myth.

Whichever necessarily speculative reconstruction we favor, line 20 stands somewhat outside the Question-Answer framework of most of the inscription, perhaps as a meta-level commentary on the inscription and an introduction to Section 3. Such an introduction has the effect of foregrounding this as the most important, climactic section, but it also fits into a picture of Varin as a sort of scholar. Wessén emphasized Varin's narrative repertory and his runic knowledge, suggesting that competitive display was one of his motives; Lönnroth generally follows this direction with more emphasis on play and wit; Widmark, modifying Wessén, also calls Varin a *þulr* but sees his cultivation of the cultural heritage as a social act of cultural preservation, perhaps born of resistance to the encroachment of the European behemoth or fears for the oral tradition following loss of his (only?) son.[44] There can be some degree of truth in all these efforts at empathetic interpretation, based as they can only be on the unique result, the inscription itself; what we can know for certain (besides his memorial purpose) is only the result of Varin's efforts: there is no comparable attempt to collect and preserve varied story material in a runic inscription.

Also unique is Varin's stance toward his medium. The inscription is artistically and complexly couched in different types of script: the standard Rök runes are graced in line 1 with the handsome **t**'s of the old futhark; after moving into shift cipher in 23, he tests the reader's alertness by sliding back into unshifted Rök runes in 24a, then again into shift cipher in 24b, turning unshifted Rök runes upside down in

---

44. Gun Widmark, "Tolkningen som social konstruktion: Rökstenens inskrift," in *Runor och ABC: Elva föreläsningar från ett symposium i Stockholm våre 1995*, ed. Staffan Nyström (Stockholm: Sällskapet Runica et Mediævalia, etc., 1997), 165–75. On Widmark's argument here, see Joseph Harris, "Philology, Elegy, and Cultural Change," *Gripla* 20 (2009): 257–75, esp. 267–73.

25a, and slipping over to coordinates cipher in 25b. His coordinates cipher is expressed in several (perhaps symbolic) forms (o's from the older futhark together with s's from the younger in 25b, a line which ends in a key-like sign that points the way to 26 with its two variants on the key-like sign), culminating in the great windmills of 27–28.[45] In 21–22 Varin begins his cipher section with two lines that are famously incised in the 24-character futhark. I do not have space to discuss Varin's displacements from the 24-character standard or his special signs; but if any substantial portion of the symbolic (and numerical) subtleties discussed by Hans Schwarz in "Varin und das ältere Futhark" is true, Varin's knowledge of ancient runic art was very extensive.[46] Schwarz belonged to the Höfler school and so found "magic" where now, post-Wessén, I am inclined to find "religion" and "art"; we would, however, agree on Varin's intentional and progressive mystification in the realization of the mythic material of Section 3. For Schwarz, Varin's knowledge was traceable to a dark but unbroken tradition of runic magic passed on in verse. The alternative offered by Brate appeals more to my sense of the inscription: Varin studied older inscriptions through the lens of his skill in the younger futhark.[47] Schwarz effectively mocks this position:

> Will man nicht mit Brate den Rökritzer für einen ausgekochten Paläo-graphen und Sprachwissenschaftler halten, der sich seine Weisheit auf autodidaktischem Wege durch mühsame Analyse älterer Runendenk-mäler angeeignet habe, so bleibt nur die Annahme übrig, daß er—wie andere Runenmeister—sein Geheimwissen aus lebendiger Überliefe-rung geschöpft hat. (Schwarz, "Varin und das ältere Futhark," 208)

If, unlike Brate, one does not wish to consider the inscriber of Rök to be a hardboiled paleographer and linguist who has acquired his

---

45. What I called "key-like signs" in "Myth and Meaning" (and here) should be iden-tified as *hahalruna* "Kesselhaken," "'cremacula,' i.e., a pothanger with a rack." See René Derolez, *Runica Manuscripta: The English Tradition* (Brugge: De Tempel, 1954), 133, and Klaus Düwel, "Geheimrunen," in *Reallexikon der Germanischen Altertumskunde*, ed. Heinrich Beck et al., vol. 10 (Berlin: de Gruyter, 1997), 567–8. I retain this amateur's mistake to facilitate reference across my articles.

46. Hans Schwarz, "Varin und das ältere Futhark," in *Wort und Welt: Aufsätze zur deutschen Wortgeschichte, zur Wortfeldtheorie und zur Runenkunde*, ed. Hartmut Beckers (Münster: Nodus, 1993), 197–225.

47. Brate in Bugge, *Der Runenstein von Rök*, esp. 283–91.

knowledge autodidactically by laborious analysis of older runic monuments, then there remains only the assumption that, like other rune masters, he drew his secret knowledge out of living tradition.

But were there any other rune masters of the ninth century comparable to Varin? Brate notes two Viking Age inscriptions that give evidence of "study" of some older inscriptions, but they pale in comparison to Rök.[48] Certainly no other inscription in the younger futhark makes extensive and self-conscious use of the older futhark. But the best conception of the sources of Varin's knowledge may lie somewhere between Schwarz's model of continuity through oral tradition and Brate's antiquarian revivalism through writing and may include elements of both.[49]

In connection with Varin's antiquarian learning, however, one is tempted to look back at **mini miʀ alu** and wonder whether the rune master might be using **alu**, the ancient runic word-sign for something like apotropaic "sacred power," to characterize the myth that will be featured in Section 3; such a unique usage would closely parallel his deployment and deformation of the older futhark. Undoubted attestations of *alu* range from ca. 200 to the Eggja stone of ca. 650–700, and no surviving instance of *alu* definitely situates the word-sign in a syntactic connection, with the result that it appears to have no inflection and so to hover between "word" and "sign." Many scholars have related **alu** to the sacred ale, *ǫl* (<*alu*), which, in Eddic verse, embodies the "strength of earth," is linked with death and burial (cf., for example, ON *erfiǫl* and modern Danish *gravøl*), and once is actually compounded with *minni*.[50] In our context, the ordinary ale word (**með ǫlvi*) can obviously not be inserted, and Varin, if he ever encountered inscribed **alu**, can only have understood it as we do.

---

48. Ibid., 287–88.

49. As his archaizing reading might suggest, Schwarz dates Rök quite early, "about 760" (197), a date he derives from Theoderic's birth in 456 plus nine generations by relying on Höfler's refutation of the Aachen connection and his interpretation of lines 6–7 as referring to Theoderic's birth (Höfler, *Der Rökstein von Rök*, 9–52). Höfler himself generally adhered to Bugge's dating in the first half of the ninth century.

50. The *alu* problem has generated a large bibliography. I find Peter Pieter, "Die Runenstempel von Spong Hill: Pseudorunen oder Runenformel?" *Neue Ausgrabungen und Forschungen in Niedersachsen* 17 (1986): 181–200, to be especially helpful. The Eddic references are to: *Guðrúnarkviða II*, 21; *Hávamál* 137; *Hyndluljóð* 38, 43 (*jarðar megin*); and *Hyndluljóð* 45 (*minnisǫl*).

There are good reasons why **alu** has never been considered for the **mini miʀ alu** of line 20.[51] Only about twenty-three certain instances of *alu* are recognized by runologists in all Germania; of these only four (but one of these located in Västergötland) are incised in stone, bracteates being the main medium to employ *alu*. The strongest reason for rejecting the ancient *alu* in line 20, however, is not that the audience of the inscription would not understand it—puzzling bait from an artistic-antiquarian rune master would not be out of place in this inscription—but that the reader would inevitably understand it as *með ǫllu*, the relatively well-attested adverbial phrase discussed above. The Varin I (and most of my predecessors) have constructed would be capable of alluding to *alu* in his text, but if we are to believe that there exist *des mots sous les mots*, a sober methodology seems to demand from the text a more distinct signal of its "hypogram."

Bibliography

Brate, Erik, ed. *Östergötlands runinskrifter*. Sveriges runinskrifter 2. Stockholm: Kungl. vitterhets- historie- och antikvitets-akademien, 1911–18.

Bugge, Sophus. *Der Runenstein von Rök in Östergötland, Schweden*. Edited by Magnus Olsen with contributions by Axel Olrik and Erik Brate. Stockholm: Hæggström, 1910.

Cleasby, Richard, and Gudbrand Vigfusson. *An Icelandic-English Dictionary*. 2nd ed. Oxford: Clarendon, 1957.

Derolez, René. *Runica Manuscripta: The English Tradition*. Werken uitgegeven door de Faculteit van de wijsbegeerte en letteren 118. Brugge: De Tempel, 1954.

Düwel, Klaus. "Geheimrunen." In vol. 10 of *Reallexikon der Germanischen Altertumskunde*, edited by Heinrich Beck, Dieter Geuenich, and Heiko Steuer, 567–68. Berlin: de Gruyter, 1997.

Finnur Jónsson. *Lexicon Poeticum: Antiquæ Linguæ Septentrionalis:*

---

51. The only exception seems to be Thomas L. Markey, "Studies in Runic Origins 7: The *alu*-Problem," an unpublished but widely circulated paper, where the occurrence of *alu* in Rök is considered "highly unlikely" (p. 1 of version of April 16, 1999). I agree, but Markey's analysis of *allu* as an "adverb... 'entirely, in all'... functionally equivalent... to OE *ealles*" seems mistaken; the n. dat. sg. *allu* is not to be separated from *með*. Markey's published discussion of the *alu* problem in "Studies in Runic Origins 1: Germanic *maþl-/*mahl-* and Etruscan **meθlum**," *American Journal of Germanic Linguistics & Literatures* 10 (1998): 188–89, does not mention Rök.

Ordbog over det norsk-islandske skjaldesprog. 2nd rev. ed. Copenhagen: Lynge, 1966.

Friesen, Otto von. *Rökstenen: Runstenen vid Röks kyrka Lysings härad Östergötland.* Stockholm: Kungl. Vitterhets- historie- och antivitets akademien, 1920.

Fulk, R. D., Robert E. Bjork, and John D. Niles, eds. *Klaeber's "Beowulf" and "The Fight at Finnsburg."* 4th ed. Toronto: Toronto University Press, 2008.

Grønvik, Ottar. *Der Rökstein: Über die religiöse Bestimmung und das weltliche Schicksal eines Helden aus der frühen Wikingerzeit.* Osloer Beiträge zur Germanistik 33. Frankfurt am Main: Peter Lang, 2003.

Harris, Joseph. "Myth and Meaning in the Rök Inscription." *Viking and Medieval Scandinavia* 2 (2006): 45–109.

———. "Philology, Elegy, and Cultural Change." In *Nordic Civilisation in the Medieval World*, edited by Vésteinn Ólason, special issue, *Gripla* 20 (2009): 257–75.

———. "The Rök Stone through Anglo-Saxon Eyes." In *The Anglo-Saxons and the North: Essays Reflecting the Theme of the 10th Meeting of the International Society of Anglo-Saxonists in Helsinki, August 2001*, edited by Matti Kilpiö, Leena Kahlas-Tarkka, Jane Roberts, and Olga Timofeeva, 11–45. Tempe, AZ: ACMRS, 2009.

Höfler, Otto. *Der Runenstein von Rök und die germanische Individualweihe.* Germanisches Sakralkönigtum 1. Tübingen: Niemeyer, 1952.

Jacobsen, Lis. "Rökstudier." *Arkiv för nordisk filologi* 76 (1961): 1–50.

La Farge, Beatrice and John Tucker. *Glossary to the Poetic Edda: Based on Hans Kuhn's Kurzes Wörterbuch.* Heidelberg: Winter, 1992.

Larrington, Carolyne, trans. *The Poetic Edda.* Oxford: Oxford University Press, 1996.

Lönnroth, Lars. "The Riddles of the Rök-Stone: A Structural Approach." *Arkiv för nordisk filologi* 92 (1977): 1–57.

Lühr, Rosemarie. *Die Gedichte des Skalden Egill.* Jenaer indogermanistische Texbearbeitung 1. Dettelbach: Röll, 2000.

Marez, Alain. "'sakumukmini'?—Une relecture de l'inscription de Rök." *Études germaniques* 52 (1997): 543–57.

Markey, Thomas L. "Studies in Runic Origins 1: Germanic *maþl-/*mahl- and Etruscan meθlum," *American Journal of Germanic Linguistics & Literatures* 10 (1998): 153–200.

———. "Studies in Runic Origins 7: The *alu*-Problem." Unpublished paper.

Neckel, Gustav, and Hans Kuhn, eds. *Die Lieder des Codex Regius nebst verwandten Denkmälern.* Vol. 1, *Text.* 4th ed. Germanische Bibliothek. 4. Reihe, Texte. Heidelberg: Carl Winter, 1962.

Nielsen, Niels Åge. *Runerne på Rökstenen.* Odense University Studies in Scandinavian Languages 2. Odense: Odense University Press, 1969.

Noreen, Adolf. *Altisländische und altnorwegische Grammatik.* Altnordische Grammatik 1. 5th ed. Tübingen: Niemeyer, 1970.

Orchard, Andy, trans. *The Elder Edda: A Book of Viking Lore.* London: Penguin, 2011.

Pàroli, Teresa. *Sull'elemento formulare nella poesia germanica antica.* Biblioteca di ricerche linguistiche e filologiche 4. Rome: Istituto di glottologia, Università di Roma, 1975.

Peterson, Lena. *Svenskt runordsregister.* Runrön 2. Uppsala: Institutionen för nordiska språk, Uppsala universitet, 1989.

Pieter, Peter. "Die Runenstempel von Spong Hill: Pseudorunen oder Runenformel?" *Neue Ausgrabungen und Forschungen in Niedersachsen* 17 (1986): 181–200.

Reichert, Hermann. "Runeninschriften als Quellen der Heldensagenforschung." In *Runeninschriften als Quellen interdisziplinärer Forschung: Abhandlungen des Vierten Internationalen Symposiums über Runen und Runeninschriften in Göttingen, 4–9 August 1995,* edited by Klaus Düwel and Sean Nowak, 66–102. Berlin: de Gruyter, 1998.

Schwarz, Hans. "Varin und das ältere Futhark." In *Wort und Welt: Aufsätze zur deutschen Wortgeschichte, zur Wortfeldtheorie und zur Runenkunde,* edited by Hartmut Beckers, 197–225. Münster: Nodus, 1993. Originally published in *Beiträge zur Geschichte der deutschen Sprache und Literatur* 78 (1956): 323–56.

Terry, Patricia, trans. *Poems of the Vikings: The Elder Edda.* Indianapolis: Bobbs-Merrill, 1969.

Vries, Jan de. *Altnordisches etymologisches Wörterbuch.* 3rd ed. Leiden: Brill, 1977.

Wessén, Elias. *Runstenen vid Röks kyrka.* Kungl. vitterhets historie och antikvitets akademiens handlingar, filologisk-filosofiska serien 5. Stockholm: Almqvist & Wiksell, 1958.

Widmark, Gun. "Varför ristade Varin runor? Tankar kring Rökstenen." *Saga och Sed: Kungl. Gustav Adolfs Akademiens årsbok* 47 (1992): 25–43.

———. "Tolkningen som social konstruktion: Rökstenens inskrift." In *Runor och ABC: Elva föreläsningar från ett symposium i Stockholm våre 1995,* edited by Staffan Nyström, 165–75. Stockholm: Sällskapet Runica et Mediævalia, Riksantikvarieämbetet, Stockholms Medeltidsmuseum, 1997.

A Landscape of Conflict

Three Stories of the Faroe Conversions

Sarah Harlan-Haughey

UNIVERSITY OF MAINE

There are eighteen islands with several mountainous peaks, steep green slopes and sheer basalt cliffs, alive with sea birds. No trees grow on them except where people have planted and tended them themselves. There is hardly an area of level ground, little foreshore, many fjords, bays and narrow passages between the islands, and everything seems exposed to the northern weather and currents of the sea. Erosion is the pervasive feature of the landscape, and the natural scenery is abrupt, awesome, and beautiful.[1]

Færeyinga saga, which tells the story of the partial colonization and conversion of the Faroe Islands by Norway around the year 1000, was written down in Iceland during the great period of saga production— around 1200—and is preserved in different texts, including *Óláfs saga Tryggvasonar* and Flateyjarbók.[2] Its narrative is dramatic and

I am grateful to Thomas D. Hill and Danielle Marie Cudmore of Cornell University, Larry Syndergaard of Western Michigan University, and Joseph Harris of Harvard University for their helpful comments, as well as to James Sears of the University of Montana, for insights into the geological formation of the Faroe Islands.

1. From George Johnston's introduction to his translation of *Færeyinga saga* in *Thrand of Gotu: Two Icelandic sagas from the Flat Island Book* (Erin, Ontario: Porcupine's Quill Press, 1994), hereafter Johnston, 7.

2. For a recent study of medieval perceptions of the Christianizing process carried out by Óláfr Tryggvason and Óláfr Haraldsson in Norway, Iceland and the Faroes, see Sverre Bagge, "The Making of a Missionary King: The Medieval Accounts of Olaf Tryggvason and the Conversion of Norway," *JEGP* 105 (2006): 473–513. See also Bagge's "Christianization and State Formation in Early Medieval Norway," *Scandinavian Journal of History* 30 (2005): 107–34.

masterfully structured, and it contains many literary and folkloric themes that could be studied extensively. Two such recurring themes in the text are (1) the perilous sea voyage due to the pagan sorcerer Þrándr's witchcraft and (2) the Norwegian crown's Christianizing emissaries' rocky and difficult entry to the Faroes. These motifs dramatize the central conflict of the saga: colonial or imperial power and its opposition to individualistic pagan powers that rely on the forces of nature. The saga's basic narrative, somewhat ambiguous in its loyalties because of these motifs, lends itself to an interesting comparative study of the colonial process as depicted in *Færeyinga saga* and its "spin-offs," in particular a Faroese ballad called *Sigmunds kvæði* that was collected from the Faroese folk tradition in the nineteenth century, and a modern stamp issued by the Faroe post office in 2000.

This essay will examine the depiction of the Faroese land- and seascape in these three works—the saga, the ballad, and the postage stamp—with the aim of demonstrating how the Faroe ecology serves as a complex symbol of political, economic, and religious conflict in three distinct periods of Faroese history. It will also reveal how these themes serve to unify the saga as a carefully constructed literary product, as well to dramatize its central narrative conflict: the tension between the Norwegian project of Christianization, on the one hand, and regional landscapes and identities, on the other.

In this saga we can note a complex discourse of imperialism at work, with oral and written sources in dialogue, and with different voices subverting one another. It is a testament to the artistry of the redactor that it remains easy for the audience to see both sides of the story, and to sense the multiplicity of voices bolstering a work that is ultimately written with one authorial intention. In *Færeyinga saga* there is no simple binary of colonizer and colonized; rather, protean, loosely defined categories of citizenship, landscape, and personality shift continually in a fluid narrative, and the author's deployment of land- and seascapes reflects this fluidity. Most importantly, the depiction of the natural world as fundamentally resistant to possession by Sigmundr and Óláfr is the most effective narrative device in the saga, subtly underlining the difficulties of conquest. Difficult entry to the Faroes due to storm, wind, and wave is a result of Þrándr's sorcery, but it is also a manifestation of the islands' distinctness and power. The earth itself is resistant to entry: even after Sigmundr successfully reaches land following his struggle with the waves, he usually has to scale great cliffs and earthworks in order to come ashore. Ultimately, the deaths of the main characters focus on the natural backdrop of the narrative.

What motivates the saga's Icelandic author to present the Faroe Islands in such a way? *Færeyinga saga* is an Icelandic text about a conflict between Faroe Islanders and the Norwegian crown. How can we unravel the complexities of this political constellation? A succinct description of Faroese economic circumstances makes the connection between the Faroes and Iceland quite clear: "The lack of wood, iron, and grain made the Faroese especially dependent on foreign trade. They bartered for these commodities with cloth (as the many loom stones suggest), wool, and feathers. The find at Sandur of ninety-eight coins from many devout countries (dated to 950–1050) proves wide commercial contacts."[3] Iceland and the Faroe Islands are siblings, with parallel landscapes, parallel economies and, to a certain extent, parallel histories. Like the Faroes, Iceland lacked wood, iron, and grain, and was forced into a supplicant position toward more resource-rich political entities. Both fiercely independent island populations struggled against the mainland Scandinavian powers, principally Norway. Their landscapes are, on the one hand, imposing symbols of the islanders' strength and uniqueness; on the other hand, they are the very element that forces them to remain dependent on inimical overlords. These landscapes are the root and source of their pride and their subsequently fierce desire for independence, yet they are also the cause of their equally intense need for commodities that these landscapes cannot produce.

The landscapes of the Faroes and Iceland are often portrayed as neither fertile nor nourishing, but imposing and destructive.[4] Take for example the sterility in this modern description of the Faroes: "The seventeen inhabitable [islands] offered no rich soils, no broad plains,

---

3. Hans Jacob Debes, "The Faroe Islands," in *Medieval Scandinavia: An Encyclopedia*, ed. Phillip Pulsiano and Kirsten Wolf (New York: Garland, 1993), 184.

4. See *Hrafnkels saga* for an example of a similarly malicious landscape. However, cf. Margaret Clunies Ross, "Land-Taking and Text-Making," in *Text and Territory: Geographical Imagination in the European Middle Ages*, ed. Sylvia Tomasch and Sealy Gilles (Philadelphia: University of Pennsylvania Press, 1998),162, for a contrasting reading of the Norse landscape as female. I consider both readings valid approaches to different texts, and sometimes to different moments within a given text.

no chance of wealth either from mineral resources or trade, no subject population, and no easy farming."[5] This explains to a large extent the Icelandic saga redactor's interest in the otherwise insignificant Faroes: their struggles imposed by landscape mirror Iceland's in many ways, and in 1200, around the time the saga was composed, these struggles were far from resolved. By 1152, the Faroe Islands became part of the archbishopric of Niðarós, and by the 1180s "the islands seem to have become a 'tax land' under the Norwegian Crown."[6] But the islands did not become part of Norway until 1270, a little under a century after the saga was written and two centuries after the action took place. Iceland and Greenland were also integrated into the Norwegian empire around this time. *Færeyinga saga* is not simply a history of a past, completed event; it documents a continuing struggle still taking place, not only in the Faroe Islands, but also in Iceland itself, and it is thus relevant not only as a piece of literary history, but also as a key to Icelandic authors' ambivalent attitude toward their own island in many other sagas. Thus understanding the attitudes at work in the portrayal of the land- and seascape of the Faroe Islands helps us better identify the sense in many of the *Íslendingasögur* of an island that both nurtures and destroys—a place that, although beautiful, can be monstrous in its sudden and dangerous movements.

The situation of the medieval Faroes in relation to Norway is also roughly analogous to the process of colonization in other northern European histories, such as the English colonization of Ireland, the subjection of Wales and Brittany by the English and French respectively, the (later) Danish colonization of Greenland, and other regional imperial expansions. All of these peoples of Northern Europe may in some way have shared a common European culture, but their structures of power were unequal. Some of the same structures of power and resistance were present when the energies of the relatively unified medieval Scandinavian kingdom—in this case the efforts of Óláfr Tryggvason and later Óláfr Haraldsson—were trained on converting and exacting tribute from the autonomous satellite nations that had left for the sake of independence in waves of flight and colonization,

---

5. See Eric Christiansen, *The Norsemen in the Viking Age* (Oxford: Blackwell, 2002), 217.

6. Ibid., 184.

followed by resistance and engulfment. Although this is not typical Saidian colonialism, in *Færeyinga saga* religion and tax create structures for "othering." Colonialism is not here as much a matter of race (although North Atlantic people are probably seen as more racially diverse than Norwegians) as it is about wealth, religion, and landscape. To see this more clearly, let us turn to the first text of interest in this cross-temporal comparative study.

Pagan witchcraft that controls the weather and the seas in particular is common in the Icelandic sagas.[7] In *Færeyinga saga*, this theme is sustained and developed until it becomes an important means of expressing both the plot and the meaning of the saga, as the wily protagonist, Þrándr, uses weather magic to hinder and subvert the Norwegian rulers' attempts to control the Faroese people, whom he leads. Generally, Þrándr uses his magic to slow down the Norwegian takeover, while conversely, the Christian hero Sigmundr does his best to complete that process. For example, Sigmundr attempts to reach the island, relying on the protection of the mighty King Óláfr Tryggvason, who is himself portrayed as a sort of sorcerer, but:

Nú rak á storm fyrir þeim, ok skilðusk þá skipin, ok hafa nú rekit mikit, svá at dœgrum skiptir. . . . Nú er at segja frá þeim Sigmundi at byrr kemr á fyrir þeim ok sigla nú at eyjunum, ok sjá þá at þeir eru komnir austan at Eyjum, ok eru þeir menn á með Sigmundi at kenna landsleg, ok eru þeir mjǫk komnir at Austrey. Sigmundr sagði at hann mundi þat helzt kjósa at fá vald á Þrándi. Ok er þá berr at eyjunni kemr á mót þeim bæði straumr ok stormr, svá at ekki er nálægt um at þeir næði eyjunni; fá tekit í Svíney, með því at menn váru kœnir ok liðgóðir.[8]

---

7. In his study of the figure of Thor as a wind god, Richard Perkins argues that "wind-magic may probably be said to be more common amongst pagan peoples than, say, Christians"; that wind and weather were seen as fickle, hard to predict, out of control, and a great mystery; and that wind magic used to the detriment of others appears often in the Icelandic saga corpus. See *Thor the Wind-Raiser and the Eyrarland Image* (London: Viking Society for Northern Research, 2001), 9–12. A. E. J. Ogilvie and Gísli Pálsson discuss episodes of weather magic in *Laxdœla saga, Njáls saga, Eiríks saga rauða, Eyrbyggja saga, Gísla saga Súrssonar, Fóstbrœðra saga, Vatnsdœla saga,* and *Víglundar saga* in "Mood, Magic and Metaphor: Allusions to Weather and Climate in the Sagas of Icelanders," in *Weather, Climate, Culture,* ed. S. Strauss and B. S. Orlove (Oxford: Berg, 2003), 264.

8. *Færeyinga saga, Ólafs saga Odds,* ed. Ólafur Halldórsson, Íslenzk fornrit 25 (Reykjavík: Hið íslenzka fornritafélag, 2006), hereafter ÍF 25, 51–52, chs. 23 and 24.

Now a gale came against them, and ships were separated and much tossed about, and so it went on for days. . . . Now it is to be told of Sigmund and his crew that a favourable wind comes for them, and they sail towards the Islands and see that they are approaching the islands from the east, and there are men with Sigmund to ken the lie of the land, and they have come in close to Eysturoy. Sigmund said that he would most choose to lay hands on Thrand. But when they bear up toward the island there come against them both current and gale, so that they did not come near to reaching the island; they do get ashore on Svinoy because the men were skillful and handy seamen. (Johnston 60)

Þrándr's ability to control the weather and the sea makes it next to impossible for Sigmundr and his men to reach the island. The only factors in their favor are their skill and perseverance. On Þrándr's side are the land- and seascapes of the Faroes, the powers of the pagan gods, and an equally tenacious human personality. Although the end of the tale—the eventual conversion of the Faroe Islands—is here foreshadowed, the narrator also appears to enjoy depicting the intractability of the land and its people and indulging in a bit of *Schadenfreude* at Sigmundr's inability to reach the shore. In the passage just cited, the cause of the storm (Þrándr's magic) is elided, but Sigmundr continues to have trouble getting to and from the Faroes, and it gradually becomes clear that Þrándr is calling down the storm upon his enemies. Þrándr's reliance on weather magic even extends to using it against *himself* in order to avoid having to leave his islands to swear fealty to a foreign overlord:

En er Þrándr verðr þess varr at Sigmundr ætlar at flytja hann á konungs fund, þá baðsk hann undan þeiri ferð. En Sigmundr lét þat ekki tjá, ok slógu landfestum þegar byr gaf. En er þeir váru eigi langt í haf komnir, þá hittu þeir bæði í strauma ok storm mikinn; urðu við þat aptrreka til Færeyja ok brutu skip í spán ok týndu fé ǫllu, en mǫnnum varð borgit flestum. Sigmundr barg Þrándi ok mǫrgum ǫðrum. Þrándr sagði at eigi mundi þeim ferðin takask slétt ef þeir léti hann nauðgan fara. Sigmundr sagði at hann skyldi fara allt at einu, þó at honum þœtti illt. Tók Sigmundr þá skip annat ok fé sitt at fœra konungi fyrir skattinn, því at Sigmund skorti eigi lausafé. Láta þeir í haf í annat sinn; komask nú lengra áleiðis en fyrr; fá þó enn mótviðri stór ok rekr þá aptr til

Færeyja ok lesta skipit. Sigmundr sagði at honum þótti mikit farbann
á liggja. Þrándr sagði at svá mundi fara hversu opt sem þeir leitaði til,
svá at þeir flytti hann nauðgan með sér. (ÍF 25:73–74, ch. 31)

When Thrand finds that Sigmund is planning to bring him before the
King he tries to beg off the voyage, but Sigmund was not persuaded,
and they cast off moorings as soon as they were given a fair wind. But
they had not gone far into the open sea when they met currents and a
bad storm and they were driven back by these, right back to the Faroes,
and smashed their ship to splinters and lost all their goods, but the men
were saved, most of them. Sigmund saved Thrand and many others.
Thrand said that they would not have a smooth crossing if they made
him go against his will. Sigmund said that he must go anyhow, never
mind that he did not like it. Sigmund took another ship then, and
money of his own to bring for the King's tribute, for Sigmund was not
lacking ready money. Again they put to sea, and make better headway
than before, but again they meet strong winds and are driven back to
the Faroes and damage the ship. Sigmund said that there seemed to be
a curse on the trip. Thrand said it was bound to go this way so long as
they tried to bring him against his will. (Johnston 68, ch. 30)

This episode causes considerable damage to all the humans involved—
even Þrándr must be saved from drowning—but Sigmundr bears
the brunt of this magic, as he loses all the goods and tribute he had
amassed to bring to Norway, and must pay the tribute himself, as well
as ready a new boat, which also becomes damaged. Sigmundr must
also rescue the very man who caused him such trouble because his new
belief system requires it of him, and he is not the kind of man who
shirks his duty, however unpleasant it may be.

This passage resembles an episode in *Laxdœla saga* where the
doomed Þórðr is sunk by the magician Kotkell. Þórðr, like Sigmundr,
struggles against a magical storm, but his ship is capsized and
destroyed. One wonders if the difference between the two heroes'
experiences is that Sigmundr has Óláfr's luck backing him talisman-
ically against Þrándr, and is thus able to make it out alive, unlike
his counterpart in *Laxdœla saga*, who has no such supernatural
powers behind him—permitting the sorcerer in that narrative to
easily destroy his enemy at sea from land. The sea is a space where

one becomes more vulnerable to attack, and the machinations of a practiced sorcerer would typically spell doom for his target. Yet Sigmundr survives, unlike Þórðr. The saga's contemporaries would likely have recognized this difference and wondered at Sigmundr's survival, aware as they were of other stories where resistance against a weather sorcerer proves futile. Sigmundr's survival is a miracle, and serves as evidence that his message has a higher power behind it, a power that can overcome the "diabolical" forces of nature.[9]

Disruptive natural phenomena can seem equivalent to magic in the saga's logic—or at least the two qualities are seen as cousins in the service of Þrándr's strong will. Opposed to nature and Þrándr's primal, pagan power are the forces of civilization, order, leadership (contrasted with an individualism that often borders on myopic self-ishness), and Christianity. In an article on the parallels between sagas and early historical novels, Joseph Harris argues that "the morphology of the historical passage [of the saga] is essentially stable; a mono-lithic new order overtakes an individualistic ancient one, empire, for example, succeeding provincialism." Such is the case in *Færeyinga saga:* "The balance of the two orders is, of course, never static, and a static presentation of the oppositions would in any case be ironically undermined by our knowledge that the new order, though modified in the dialectic of history, represents the way of the future, the writer's present."[10] In this saga, these oppositions are performed on the natural stage of the Faroe Islands, and the scenery adds a third order to the old and the new—that of nature itself, which problematizes the straightforward, human-centered dialectic of history.

Þrándr's environmental trickery persists throughout the saga, as he repeatedly uses his magic to impede the Christian heroes Sigmundr and Óláfr Tryggvason in their attempts to bring the Faroes under rein. Several times, Óláfr provides Sigmundr with special ships to transport

---

9. Perkins notes how in various sagas the superior power of the Christian god is often set in explicit contrast with weaker pagan forces (*Thor the Wind-Raiser*, 14).

10. Joseph Harris, "Saga as Historical Novel," in *Structure and Meaning in Old Norse Literature: New Approaches to Textual Analysis and Literary Criticism*, ed. John Lindow, Lars Lönnroth, and Gerd Wolfgang Weber, The Viking Collection: Studies in Northern Civilization 3 (Odense: Odense University Press, 1986), 187–219; repr. in *"Speak Useful Words or Say Nothing": Old Norse Studies by Joseph Harris*, ed. Susan E. Deskis and Thomas D. Hill, Islandica 53 (Ithaca: Cornell University Library, 2008), 227–60.

him to the Faroes, and more often than not, they are destroyed in the journey, as we see in chapter 23:

> Ferr Sigmundr til skipa sinna, ok er svá sagt at fimm tigir manna váru á hváru skipinu. Létu nú í haf, ok gaf þeim vel byri þar til er þeir hǫfðu fugl af eyjum, ok heldu samflota. Haraldr járnhauss var á skipi með Sigmundi, en Þórir stýrði ǫðru skipi. Nú rak á storm fyrir þeim, ok skilðusk þá skipin, ok hafa nú rekit mikit, svá at dœgrum skiptir. (ÍF 25:51, ch. 23)

> Sigmund goes to his ships, and there are said to have been 50 men on each ship. They put to sea and a fair wind held for them until they saw birds from the islands, and they were able to keep their ships together. Harald Ironskull was on the ship with Sigmund, and Thorir commanded the other ship. Then a gale broke on them, the ships were separated, and they were separated before the wind for many days. (Johnston 53, ch. 23)

Sigmundr has no difficulty until he nears Þrándr's domain, as signaled by the presence of seabirds. Then his luck changes, and despite having a good strong crew, he takes days to reach land. Later in the conflict, Þrándr successfully feigns illness to avoid going to Norway—apparently he can control his appearance of health as well the elements, thus underlining his status as a "force of nature" in his own right. Other Faroese leaders go to the meeting with Óláfr, but they do not trust the king's transparently self-interested plans for the Faroes, and while they manage to resist his demands for a time, his personality and power ultimately force their capitulation, and compel the Faroes to pay tribute. The question remains: had Þrándr been there, would things have turned out differently? Is he a match for Óláfr? In diametric opposition to Óláfr's overt assertion of his prerogative as a Christian monarch, Þrándr resists underhandedly, relying on his covert command of the disruptive energies of nature and eschewing direct human confrontation.

Right after the meeting with the capitulating Faroese, the ship sent to collect tribute is lost at sea, as is the second one dispatched. The continual loss of good ships and loyal crews irritates Óláfr, and conquering the islands economically and spiritually becomes something of a fixation. He seems unaccustomed to meeting resistance akin to Þrándr's:

> Þat var á einu húsþingi er hann átti at hann hafði þat mál í munni, sagði frá mannskaða þeim er hann hafði látit af Færeyjum, "en skattr sá," segir hann, "er þeir hafa mér heitit, þá kemr ekki fram. Nú ætla ek enn þangat menn at senda eptir skattinum." Veik konungr þessu máli nǫkkut til ýmissa manna at til þeirrar ferðar skyldu ráðask. En þar kómu þau svǫr í mót at allir menn tǫldusk undan fǫrinni. (ÍF 25:97, ch. 43)

> Next spring at a local court that King Olaf held he had this case on his mind, and he spoke about the losses in men he had suffered on account of the Faroes—and "that tribute," says he, "which they have pledged me, not an ounce of it comes. Now I am going to send men after that tribute again." The King put the proposal more or less to one man after another, that they should take on the voyage. But the answers that came back were that they all begged off the voyage. (Johnston 89, ch. 44)

All of Óláfr's tribute gatherers have grown afraid to go to the Faroes after the loss of vessel after vessel. This is potent magic indeed.

Only at the end of the saga, when all other major figures have been killed, does Þrándr's magic lose its potency, as he loses control of the very elements he previously commanded. He can no longer use water and storms to achieve his ends, and his other magical power—the ability to summon and control *draugar* and then dismiss them at will—fails him, and these same ghosts begin to haunt him. In this way, he is similar to another ambiguous protagonist who represents a moribund heroic value system, Grettir Ásmundarson, whose former strengths turn into weaknesses. We also find parallels in the account in *Njáls saga* of the magician Svanr who, as Ogilvie and Gísli Pálsson note, is ironically "said to have been drowned in a 'great storm,' his skills seemingly of no avail to him against this natural weather event."[11] Þrándr too is betrayed by the very nature whose forces he once marshaled, and the narrative hinges on this

---

11. Ogilvie, "Mood, Magic and Metaphor," 4.

pivotal change. When nature turns against those who previously wielded its powers, we know the fight is over, and arguably, that the land has lost its wild ally. For, as Harris puts it, "even though Sigmundr is slain three-fourths of the way through the saga and Þrándr lives on, it is clear that, like King Óláfr Tryggvason, the future belongs to Sigmundr and his ways; and this is worked out in the narrative of the second part of the saga where, during the reign of St. Óláfr, when Christianity was restored permanently in Norway and during that of Magnús Óláfsson, the heirs of Sigmundr stamp out the faction of Þrándr, and the old trickster dies, the saga says, of grief."[12]

Although the redactor of *Færeyinga saga* is a Christian, and presumably does not long for the heathen days of old, a certain ambiguity in his portrayal of the power and glory of Þrándr's sorcery and of the intractable roughness of the islands themselves, which seem to actively resist the various colonial impositions of tax, religion, and military levy—and the author's apparent sympathy with this resistance—do remain strong forces in the text and suggest a reading that focuses on a subversive landscape. Scholarly consensus further invites such a reading, describing *Færeyinga saga* as "an enormous accretion of oral material that must have circulated earlier"; the written narrative is a product of many people's voices, not all of which were necessarily sympathetic to the Christian colonial process.[13] The author "cites no verse and apparently had no written sources; the anecdotes he built on must have come from the Faroes, but he evidently did not know the islands at first hand," and Ólafur Halldórsson suggests that the author probably was confusing the islands out of ignorance of the topography of the archipelago.[14] Despite evidence of a single author's hand in the work, the material itself is at least partly from diverse Faroese accounts, that is, in the voice of a people who were in the process of being colonized.[15]

12. Harris, "Saga as Historical Novel," 250–51.

13. See Theodore M. Andersson, "Kings' Sagas," in *Old Norse-Icelandic Literature: A Critical Guide*, ed. John Lindow and Carol J. Clover (Ithaca: Cornell University Press, 1985), 221.

14. See Johnston 9 ("Introduction") and ÍF 25:xxxiv, respectively.

15. "Ólafur Halldórsson conjectures that he acquired this from Faroese tales and accounts, probably told by Faroese travelers" (Johnston 9).

Perhaps this is why the elements of conversion and imperialism, "two aspects of the new order," are so closely related in *Færeyinga saga*, "where Þrándr is identified with provincial resistance to the crown and Sigmundr's mission of conversion is closely bound up with the payment of tribute to Norway."[16] The author may have felt pressure to be fair to both camps that helped him write his story, for he sustains "a narrative that did equal justice to imposing missionary kings, Óláfr Tryggvason and Óláfr Haraldsson, and to their wily Faroese antagonist, Þrándr í Gǫtu, presented as a man of superb cunning and supernatural power, who detests the Christianity forced on him."[17] The multiplicity of voices that have influenced *Færeyinga saga* is such that the resulting narrative is a composite product—only the sustained presence of the natural elements so powerfully depicted throughout the saga can unify and ground it.

To demonstrate the saga's complex tone in terms of its depiction of both nature and of the actors in the story, we may consider Þrándr's status as one of the protagonists of the tale, perhaps a result of the Faroese saga informants' pride in their people and land. His ability to hinder sea crossings represents the remoteness of the Faroes and their isolation, as well as their power and "otherness." That this individual's resistance by means of magical storms and waters is a cipher for pagan resistance to Christianity generally is a first critical conclusion to draw, but I would argue for a more subtle reading of the forces at work here. According to saga and historical narratives of the settlement period, raiders and angry farmers leave increasingly untenable situations in Scandinavia and head westward into the insular North Atlantic—a place of cultural contact among Celtic, English, and Nordic cultures and a syncretic, shifting identity conditioned by settlement.[18] But soon enough, the Christian empire catches up with them, as Thomas DuBois aptly summarizes:

---

16. Harris, "Saga as Historical Novel," 258.

17. Peter Foote, "Færeyinga saga," in *Medieval Scandinavia: An Encyclopedia*, 222.

18. To call the Norwegian Christian rulers leaders of an empire is a controversial claim; Norway is a small and lightly populated country. I follow other scholars in my choice of words to describe the re-colonizing project carried out by the Norwegian kings around the turn of the millennium, since it stretches east and west over vast expanses of land and sea and arguably affects at least ten independent countries. See Christiansen, *The Norsemen*, 216–19, and Harris, "Saga as Historical Novel," 231.

By the end of the [saga era] the North had become transformed from a complex mosaic of interdependent non-Christian communities to an increasingly consolidated and religiously unified region, diminished in range from its earlier expanse and merged into a few large royal realms. Christianity had become installed as the fruit and agent of this unity and had begun to make inroads from its beachheads in Atlantic Scandinavia and the royal courts of the mainland outward toward the marginalized farmsteads and forest settlements of the region.[19]

This is a movement, painted in the broadest strokes, away from smaller, diverse ecoregions with distinct identities and toward satellites of a central Scandinavian monarchy. Þrándr, a deeply flawed, individualistic native of one of these western islands, may have represented the diversity of the pre-Christian past in the insular North Atlantic, thus explaining the saga's ambiguous tone where his mischief in concerned.[20] Þrándr is unique and difficult to categorize, like the region he represents.

In some ways, the saga writer's characterization of Þrándr is a familiar colonial depiction of an inferior, "defective" native; his red hair and freckles are genetic traits that require reining in or suppression. Other famous examples of freckled or red-headed men show the connection between archaic, regressive behavior and red hair to be a *topos*; Grettir Ásmundarson is freckled, as are Eric the Red and the unruly Thor himself. While Norwegians can also have red hair, Þrándr's appearance suggests he has been "othered" in some important way. As Joseph Harris observes, "Þrándr was clearly conceived as the shifty red-headed man of the medieval proverbs."[21] Johnston argues that his reddish coloring is meant to identify him as "foxlike," and I believe this is likely, especially since Þrándr seems blessed with the olfactory capacities of a canine, like a similarly marginal figure in the saga, the outlaw Úlfr, later identified as Þorkell

---

19. Thomas A. DuBois, *Nordic Religions in the Viking Age* (Philadelphia: University of Pennsylvania Press, 1999), 10.

20. Thus, as Linda Tuhiwai Smith argues, "stories of colonialism" that form a block of international experience similar from region to region are "part also of a very local, very specific experience." See "Imperialism, History, Writing, and Theory," in *Decolonizing Methodologies: Research and Indigenous Peoples* (London: Zed Press, 1999), 24.

21. Harris, "Saga as Historical Novel," 246.

þurrafrost ("Dryfrost").[22] Like Dryfrost, who is able to smell the presence of the fugitive youngsters Sigmundr and Þórir in his house before he sees them, and who is clearly blessed with an exceptional sense of smell, Þrándr is able to smell Sigmundr, and when he needs to he can track him like a hound, all the way to his hiding place in an earthen hole (ÍF 25:83, ch. 38; Johnston 76, ch. 36). Both Þrándr's and Úlfr's superb senses of smell align them more with nature than the human world, making each an uncanny blend of beast and man.

In other ways, however, Þrándr is portrayed as a wise, handsome man, who has borne up well against the continued marginalization of his way of life. The somewhat conflicting account of Þrándr's physical appearance might be evidence of the multiplicity of voices informing the saga, for at one point he is described as "fríðr sýnum" (handsome), while at another he is "heldr greppligr í ásjónu" (rather hard-faced).[23] Þrándr's actions are also ambiguous; at times he seems morally slippery, lying or taking false oaths in order to get Sigmundr and Óláfr off his island. For example, he promises under duress to visit Earl Hákon in person to deliver his tribute, but escapes this obligation, as we have already seen, by destroying the ships taking him over to Norway. When Sigmundr returns alone and presents himself before the Norwegian leader, Earl Hákon dryly comments on Þrándr's wiliness compared to Sigmundr's earnest simplicity: "Eigi hafi þit orðit jafnslœgir þit Þrándr; þœtti mér uggvíst at hann kœmi skjótt á minn fund" (You have not both been so sharp, you and Thrand. It seemed unlikely that he would be in a hurry to come to me).[24] On the other hand, Þrándr's use of weather magic could be seen more sympathetically as an act of passive resistance, a way to stall an unfair arrangement through a strategic alliance with the formidable natural situation of the Faroes.

Þrándr's behavior toward the representatives of Óláfr's power is indeed overt flattery veiling an implicit menace, as we see when he takes pains to flatter Sigmundr, and when he meets Norway's new representative, Karl mœrski (ÍF 25:60, ch. 25; Johnston 59, ch. 25).

---

22. Johnston argues that Þrándr's red hair suggests "that in other respects also he might be like a fox" (122n).

23. ÍF 25:4 and 7, respectively. For further discussion of this apparent disparity of appearance, see Harris, "Saga as Historical Novel," 246.

24. ÍF 25:58, ch. 24; Johnston 58, ch. 24.

Þrándr's dealings with Sigmundr's replacement are obsequious, even unctuous, as in this histrionic declaration:

> Litlu síðar kom þar Þrándr ok fagnaði vel Karli. "Em ek," segir hann, "feginn orðinn er slíkr drengr hefir komið hingat til lands várs með ørendi konungs várs, er vér erum allir skyldir undir at standa. Vil ek ekki annat, Karl, en þú farir til mín til vetrvistar ok þat með þér allt þíns liðs, er þinn vegr væri þá meiri en áðr." Karl svarar at hann var áðr ráðinn at fara til Leifs, "en ek munda elligar," segir hann, "fúsliga þiggja þetta boð." Þrándr svarar: "Þá mun Leifi auðit vegsmuna af þessu. En eru nǫkkurir aðrir hlutir þá, þeir er ek mega svá gera at yðr sé liðsemð at?" (ÍF 25:99, ch. 48)

> By and by along came Thrand and gave Karl a fine greeting. "I am overcome with delight," said he, "that such a man has come over to our land here on our King's task, which we are all duty bound to stand behind. I will have nothing else, Karl, but you will come to my place for winter quarter and as many of your crew as may do dignity to your honour." Karl answers that it was already arranged for him to go to Leif's—"but otherwise," said he, "I would gladly accept this invitation." Thrand answers, "The honour of this must be fated to Leif, then, but are there other things I might do that would be of help to you?" (Johnston 90–91, ch. 45)

In response to Þrándr's request to be of help, Karl makes him, ironically, the tax collector for Eysturoy and all the northerly isles. Unused to the way things are done in the Faroes, Karl has missed the veiled threat behind Þrándr's pretty words. His language is mocking, not sincere; a form of doublespeak. It seems likely that Karl mœrski would not have survived a winter stay at Þrándr's homestead. In many ways, Þrándr's mimicry of courtly language is in line with Homi Bhaba's formulation of the process of mimicry in postcolonial narratives—the suppressed colonial subject mimics the language, manners, and power structures of the colonizer while twisting them in a certain way, changing the meaning of the alien forms.[25] Throughout the saga Þrándr pretends

---

25. Homi K. Bhabha, "Of Mimicry and Man: The Ambivalence of Colonial Discourse," in *The Location of Culture* (London: Routledge, 1994), 85.

to take on the duties and responsibilities of Norwegian-style rule, only to twist or parody them: his production of a bag of bad silver as tax payment instead of a sincere tribute of good coin; the fact that his kinsmen establish a money-lending racket under his aegis in place of legitimate tribute-gathering; and of course, his famous twisting of the words of the Creed, are all travesties of imperial mechanisms of power.[26] His inversions of their meaning in his ironic performances are effective forms of passive resistance through mimicry.

But in the Norwegian view of things, Þrándr represents not only paganism, but also the pluralistic complexities of local squabbling and civil war. As a representative of the pagan Faroese who cannot make up their mind about tax or God, his behavior toward his own relatives—his willingness to use them as fighting pawns, to take their goods and money, and to sell his foster children—is a testament to the still-pagan isles' need for a unifying Christian ruler. According to the colonial narrative, Þrándr is a bad leader who counsels his people into things that "aren't good for them" according to the colonial authority, such as their revolt against taxes and proselytizing. When he takes his countrymen aside to talk them out of accepting the rule of King Óláfr and Christianity, his equivocal language places him in a liminal position between their multiformity on the one hand and a monolithic power structure on the other. "The saga's implicit comparison between Sigmundr and the other main character Þrándr is a good example of old and new interwoven in a feud plot. Þrándr is underhanded, treacherous (not least to his own kin), secretive, a great manipulator, a magician. An Odinic figure, he himself never fights but uses his three nephews and others in his feuds."[27]

In additon to his control of weather and ocean and his superior sense of smell that allows him to track down his enemies, Þrándr is intimately connected with other aspects of the natural world as well. He can summon ghosts from land and sea, and his intimate knowledge of the topography and waterscapes of the Faroes affords him strategic advantages. From the Norwegian perspective, Þrándr's control of nature points to the unknown menace of a hostile country and people;

---

26. See Peter Foote's classic studies of this latter moment: "Þrándr and the Apostles" and "A note on Þránd's *Kredda*," both reprinted in *Aurvandilstá: Norse Studies* (Odense University Press, 1984), 188–98 and 199–208, respectively.

27. Harris, "Saga as Historical Novel," 246.

his superior knowledge of and power over the landscape are enviable and threatening. His innate connection with his native land marks both his power and his status as "savage." But from the Faroese, and arguably Icelandic, perspective, his power over nature implies that he is useful to his allies and countrymen, much in the same way as that other sorcerer on a peripheral island, Þorbjörg, aids her countrymen in Greenland in times of dearth with weather magic in *Eiríks saga rauða*.[28] But ultimately, Þrándr is only an obstruction; as Valentin Mudimbe notes in his analysis of the politics of land ownership in colonial situations, "[N]on-Christians have no rights to possess or negotiate any dominion in the then-existing international context, and thus their land is objectively a *terra nullius*...that may be occupied and seized by Christians in order to exploit the richness meant by God to be shared by all humankind."[29] He is ultimately seen as but an extension of the land, not a person to the extent that Sigmundr is, as the forced conversion episode demonstrates; Sigmundr is prepared to execute him summarily should Þrándr choose to maintain his friendship with those he calls "fornum vinum minum" (my old friends).[30] His desire to maintain his loyalty to the gods of his forefathers is not respected as a valid choice, and to compound insult with injury, he is compelled to come along with Sigmundr as he forcibly converts the rest of the island's inhabitants.

While Þrándr is a complex, *allzumenschlich* figure, so too is his enemy, Sigmundr Brestisson. Far from being a simple pawn of Óláfr Tryggvason's, Sigmundr is an ambivalent, troubled, and heroic figure, who does his best in spite of factors that make his role as cultural translator and mediator difficult. Although he represents the "imperial" aspect of Norwegian interests (just as Þrándr stands for the idiosyncratic islanders), he remains a complex, human figure, and not a mere cipher.[31] Sigmundr is first backed by Earl Hákon as a tax

---

28. Reimund Kvideland and Henning K. Sehmsdorf note that "Fishermen and sailors employed the services of wise folk to make favourable sailing wind." *Scandinavian Folk Belief and Legend* (Minneapolis: University of Minnesota Press, 1991), 150.

29. Valentin Y. Mudimbe, "*Romanus Pontifex* (1454) and the Expansion of Europe," in *The Idea of Africa* (Bloomington: Indiana University Press, 1994), 30.

30. ÍF 25:73, ch. 31.

31. For an analysis of the "imperial aspect" of the sagas, see Harris, "Saga as Historical Novel," 254.

collector to the Faroes and as a peacekeeper elsewhere; and then by King Óláfr Tryggvason as a missionary and tribute collector to the Faroes. Sigmundr does his best to faithfully represent the interests of church and state, but he is only one man, however heroic he may be, and he cannot bear the weight of these institutions on his shoulders. Thus, he ultimately fails, dying in the line of duty after sowing the seeds of a more stable future in the Faroes. After his death during the interregnum in Norway, Þrándr and his followers relapse, but Sigmundr's project is completed at the end of the saga by his descendants, with support from Óláfr inn helgi overseas.

Sigmundr's initial reluctance to carry out his assignment in a recalcitrant and backward region might be seen to prefigure the "white man's burden" in modern colonial narratives.[32] Again, while the Faroese are ethnically identical to the Norwegians, they are characterized as uncouth, violent, temperamental, and aligned with threatening forces of nature. When Óláfr Tryggvason assigns him to convert the Faroese, "Sigmundr mæltisk undan því starfi" (Sigmund begged to be let off this work), not wanting to take on responsibility for so many contrary folk.[33] He knows their fighting spirit well, having been born in the Faroes and suffered their rough culture firsthand when his father was killed and he passed into slavery. Sigmundr's misgivings are well-founded: Þrándr's countrymen need little persuading to revolt against Sigmundr's "good news." Þrándr merely has to pull them aside at the *þing* and they return armed and ready to kill Sigmundr for trying to force Christianity and taxes on them (ÍF 25:72, ch. 30; Johnston 62, ch. 29). In spite of this frequent rough treatment, however, Sigmundr often sympathizes with the other side in this "clash of the relatively modern idea of the state with ancient liberties."[34] Faroese himself, he also identifies very strongly with outlaw figures. After his family is

---

32. "Take up the White Man's burden—
      Send forth the best ye breed—
      Go bind your sons to exile
      To serve your captives' need;
      To wait in heavy harness,
      On fluttered folk and wild--
      Your new-caught, sullen peoples,
      Half-devil and half-child."
   From Rudyard Kipling's poem, "The White Man's Burden," in *Rudyard Kipling's Verse* (New York: Doubleday, Page and Co., 1922), 371.

33. ÍF 25:71, ch. 30; Johnston 65, ch. 29.

34. Harris, "Saga as Historical Novel," 254.

murdered through Þrándr's conniving, he is fostered by Þrándr, who treacherously sells him and his cousin into slavery. He has the luck to be rescued from exposure and subsequently fostered by the outlaw Úlfr, or Þorkell Dryfrost. Later in life, however, Sigmundr becomes a sort of professional outlaw-hunter under orders from various Norwegian rulers. As someone rescued and fostered by an outlaw, he betrays his personal loyalties in doing so. But he remains ambivalent about these assignments, as attested by his readiness to reach a settlement with another outlaw, Haraldr járnhauss (Ironskull). He then becomes a negotiator for Haraldr Ironskull with Hákon, and, after some hard negotiation, he finally manages to ally Þorkell Dryfrost with Hákon (chs. 21 and 26). These actions further cement his role as a mediator between Norway and the remote fugitives on the margin of the (increasingly) centralized Norwegian state. In many ways, his fraught relationship with King Óláfr traces the general narrative pattern followed by exceptional Icelanders who go to court to prove their worth and gain riches, and who subsequently return to their homeland on political errands for Norwegian rulers, at times with disastrous consequences for their own lives and well-being.[35] Snorri Sturluson is another example of this type of figure, and in fact, his ultimate destruction in the line of "duty" closely parallels Sigmundr's. Again, the author is perhaps consciously paralleling Icelandic and Faroese heroes and their respective fortunes.

Sigmundr's assignments are not always attractive, but he typically manages to negotiate in such a way as to bring his far-flung quarry back to the Norwegian center. He succeeds until he is charged with bringing Þrándr back to Norway to meet with Hákon and later Óláfr. In his attempts to corral Þrándr, he consistently fails. The motif of heavy lifting identifies Sigmundr's emotional and physical burden, as well as his ambivalence toward his life's work. At a crucial point in the narrative, we learn that Sigmundr believes in nothing but his own might and main.[36] He will depend on that all-too-human

---

35. On this theme, see Vésteinn Ólason, "Den frie mannens selvforståelse i islandske sagaer og dikt," in *Medeltidens födelse*, ed. Anders Andrén, Symposier på Krapperups Borg 1 (Nyhamnsläge: Gyllenstiernska Krapperupsstiftelsen, 1989), 277–86.

36. "Þá mælti Hákon: 'Hvat segir þú mér til þess, hvern hefir þú átrúnað?' Sigmundr svarar: 'Ek trúi á mátt minn ok megin'" (Hakon said, "Tell me this, where do you place your trust?" Sigmund answers, "I believe in my own might and main") [ÍF 25:50, ch. 23; Johnston 53, ch. 23].

force throughout the saga, as Sigmundr works for the Norwegians against the Swedes as well as against the Faroese. Sigmundr mediates between the crown on the one hand and the treacherous human political landscape and the dangerous natural spaces it inhabits on the other. He mediates between outlaws and kings. He negotiates against, then for, then ultimately against the rights of the wilder lands and the individualistic men shaped by them. His sympathy for Úlfr the outlaw and Haraldr Ironskull—and arguably for the difficult Þrándr—as well as his quasi-familial ties with Úlfr make it hard for him to sign on wholeheartedly with Norway's ambitions. Collectively, the work of tax-gathering and converting adds up to a weighty burden for one man to bear, and the saga emphasizes this sense of encumbrance through repetition of the motifs of Sigmundr carrying another man while he himself struggles to survive, of lifting a rock too heavy for a man, and of taking on the yoke of missionary activity. The first instance of this "heavy lifting" motif appears in chapter 10 in Sigmundr's youth:

> Ganga nú ór Víkinni til Upplanda ok þannveg austan eptir Heiðmǫrk ok norðr til Dofrafjalls ok koma þar við vetr sjálfan, ok snjóvar þá á fyrir þeim ok vetrar. Ráða þeir þó á fjallit með litlu ráði, fara villt ok liggja úti svá at mǫrgum dœgrum skipti matarlausir, ok þá lagðisk Þórir fyrir ok biðr Sigmund þá hjálpa sér ok leita af fjallinu. Hann kvað at þeir skyldu báðir af koma eða hvárgi þeirra ella. En sá var munr krapta þeirra at Sigmundr leggr Þóri á bak sér, ok veit þá heldr fyrir ofan. Dǫsuðusk nú mjǫk báðir; finna nú eitt kveld dalverpi nǫkkut á fjallinu ok fóru nú eftir því, ok um síðir kenna þeir reykjarþef, ok því næst finna þeir bœ ok ganga inn ok finna stofu. (ÍF 25:22, ch. 10)

They make their way out of the Vik to Upplond, and from there east through Heidmork and north to Dofrafjall and they get there at the onset of winter, the ways are snowed up in front of them and it grows wintry. Nevertheless they start on up the mountain without much forethought, they go astray and lie out without much food, and for many days, and then Thorir lies down, and he tells Sigmund to look after himself and find his way down from the mountain. He replied that either they both should come down or else neither. And there was such difference in strength between them that Sigmund takes Thorir on his back; and it clears a little then, overhead. They both grow weaker and weaker; then one evening they come upon a narrow dale in the mountain, they go along it and at length they smell smoke; next thing they come upon a house and go in and come into the hearth-room. (Johnston 32, ch. 10)

As Sigmundr and Þórir are lost inland in a sea of wintry white, and are on the verge of death in the wilderness, Þórir lies down to die but Sigmundr carries him. His noble sacrifice and compassion seem to have an almost magical effect, as the sun appears and they soon come upon the lonely habitation of the beastlike outlaw Úlfr Dryfrost. But although Sigmundr survives and saves his cousin, we know that this expedition's outcome was resting on a knife's edge—things could have gone differently for these headstrong boys—and we recognize a foreshadowing of the risky adventures that will attract Sigmundr throughout later life. This episode is the first instance of Sigmundr as a heroic Christ-figure who bears crosses of loyalty and compassion in ensuring that his kinsman does not die of exposure in the sub-arctic winter. Shortly after this episode, Úlfr mentions in the context of his own life story a maxim that cautions against "lifting rocks too heavy for one's strength" (*taka stein um megn sér*), now explicitly establishing the notion of heavy lifting as a theme throughout the saga.[37] King Óláfr in turn charges Sigmundr with the task of bearing "the yoke of His service, to bring all your subjects to His glory."[38] In the course of this ultimate task Sigmundr bears the cost of lost ships, lost tributes, and lost lives. He sustains losses of his own time and energy as well. Sigmundr finally loses his battle against the Faroes and the sea in his great swim across the sound, and although he is able to survive the nightlong swim in the freezing waters, he must carry his cousin Þórir and his supporter Einarr across the sound. In spite of his Herculean—or Beowulfian—efforts, both of his companions ultimately succumb to exhaustion and drown. Sigmundr lands likewise exhausted and unable to move on hostile shores, where he is beheaded by a farmer who covets his gold jewelry. He battles the

37. Johnston 39, ch. 15; ÍF 25:32, ch. 32.
38. Johnston 64, ch. 28; ÍF 25:70, ch. 29.

hostile elements bravely and successfully, but in the end he cannot overcome the recalcitrant and at times monstrous inhabitants of this landscape. These two forces combine to bring about his demise (ch. 72). He is destroyed like a beached whale, and the resources he carries on his body are similarly harvested.[39] Underscoring this bestialization, he is denied the human gesture of a Christian burial. Sigmundr's death on the beach is a final marker of his liminality, his ultimate destruction by the sea, and the fundamental change in perception of what he is—no longer a hero, but a washed-up instrument of a greater power.

Thus, while Þrándr uses meteorological magic and trickery, Sigmundr relies on his own "might and main," on the force of human perseverance without the aid of magic; he is the figure of the intrepid explorer/adventurer. As a final note on Sigmundr's role in this story of colonization, I would append an analogy between Sigmundr and a later Scandinavian one-man colonizer/mediator: the nineteenth- to early twentieth-century explorer and writer Knud Rasmussen. Rasmussen was a Dane with some Greenlandic blood who conducted sled trips across the Arctic in an endeavor that was to provide much of the primary material on pan-Inuit culture.[40] He was seen by the Danes as a tragic figure who spoke for the Inuit and tried to preserve their culture, all the while knowing he was exploiting them and narrowing their horizons, as well as codifying and translating their cultural products in his own voice. Knud Rasmussen was a liminal figure like Sigmundr, torn between sympathies for the people he contacted (and changed), and his obligations to his state and nationality. Like Sigmundr, who, as we have seen, bore the burden of taxing and Christianizing the Faroe Islands, Rasmussen

> personally colonized the area, in the sense that he took care that Christianity was brought there, and established a trading station, the profits

---

39. I doubt that any Faroese storyteller—or Icelander, for that matter—would have failed to recognize the parallels between Sigmundr's tragic beaching, and the cyclic harvesting of whales stranded on the shores of North Altantic islands, an important event for the physical and economic wellbeing of island dwellers.

40. See Kristen Thisted, "Voicing the Arctic: Knud Ramussen and the Ambivalence of Cultural Translation," in *Arctic Discourses*, ed. Anka Ryall et al. (Newcastle-upon-Tyne: Cambridge Scholars, 2010), 59–81.

from which were used not only to cover his own living expenses, but also to finance the seven so-called "Thule Expeditions," carried out between 1912 and 1933. . . . With his own upbringing in Greenland and close relations to the Greenlandic people, Rasmussen saw himself more or less as "chosen" for the project. (Thisted, "Voicing the Arctic," 61–62)

Similarly, Sigmundr carries out tasks for the Norwegian crown, bringing unruly elements under Norwegian control, collecting tribute and spreading Christianity; but he is clearly "chosen" to bear the good news to the Faroes, as a Faroe Islander himself by birth with close relations to those living there. In Rasmussen's case a thousand years later, Thisted continues, "his double identity as both Greenlander and Dane is the key to understanding the special mission Knud Rasmussen took upon himself as an interpreter between two worlds, the Inuit and the European." Similarly, Sigmundr's double identity makes him a mediator between two opposed worlds, a pivotal figure who bridges them and changes the colonized culture permanently as a consequence.

Þrándr in contrast plays the role of a moribund icon of a dying culture akin to that played by some of the more memorable Inuit collaborators Knud Rasmussen meets along his journey. For example, "in Rasmussen's description Majuak [the Inuit storyteller who tells Rasmussen the best stories] is turned into an icon of a dying culture, and the story of the meeting on the island of Little Diomedes is turned into a *myth*, carrying a meaning that reaches far beyond the individuals acting in the story."[41] Þrándr's dramatic last stand, followed by his grief that his way of life has passed forever and by his death, shows similar contours. Moreover, Þrándr's shifting alliances and ever changeable and fickle moods characterize him as impetuous and sullen, the classic "half-devil, half-child" of Kipling's famous formulation of the identity of the colonized figure. As a "savage" he is by nature so closely aligned with the behavior of his environment that they form a symbiosis in the saga. So too does Rasmussen view the Inuit, albeit more sympathetically than in Kipling's language: they are "children" of the capricious, unpredictable Arctic climate. "The Eskimo's temperament can be bright and sunlit like the water on the

---

41. Ibid., 75.

deep fjords on a summer's day. But it can also be wild and merciless like the big ocean, which eats into his land" and "the temperament of the Netsilik Eskimo is like one of the many lakes that fill his land: easily put in motion, but just as easily regaining its calm."[42] It is the "service" of Knud Rasmussen to interpret and modify this wild nature for the benefit of civilization, just as it is Sigmundr's in the saga.

A final comparison between Sigmundr and Rasmussen is afforded through an intriguing inversion. Thisted tells us that "if Rasmussen was critical toward the Danish colonial administration, he was by no means against colonization as such."[43] Sigmundr is the reverse of this—he seems comfortable with Norwegian leadership, but critical of aspects of the colonial project, especially those that encroach on ancient freedoms. Thus even a brief appraisal reveals the profound ambivalence these cultural mediators manifested in their personal struggles with the task of colonization. Both perform firmly fixed roles, but they do so in ambivalent, nuanced ways.

For both sides represented in the saga, the Faroese landscape itself is intractable; even after Sigmundr converts the population by force, parts of the Faeroes keep slipping back into the old ways. In the end, both human protagonists are destroyed by the landscape of the Faroes—the islands themselves are the only clear winner in the epic conflict of human beings fighting for opposed value systems. Although the islands are marked by human struggle and buffeted by successive waves of peoples with different ideologies, they remain intractable, gorgeous, and harsh. I follow the foregoing discussion of the human characters Sigmundr and Þrándr with an in-depth analysis of two motifs central to the narrative of the saga: difficult sea crossings to and difficult entry into the Faroes. These motifs can take varying forms, but they uniformly emphasize the Faroese landscape itself as a formidable and damaging player in this great political drama.[44] The Faroe Islands are no exception to the rule of destruction they impose; in fact, their geography intensifies this disturbing quality. Tindhólmur, the highest mountain in the Faroes, is a volcanic island boasting five

---

42. Ibid.

43. Ibid., 78.

44. See Giles Deleuze and Félix Guattari, *Desert Islands and Other Texts, 1953–1974* (Los Angeles: Semiotext[e], 2004), 9–14, for whom the historical allure of "the island" resides in the fact that it creates a cyclic narrative of conquest played out *ad infinitum*.

spiky peaks. It is clearly a victim of erosion; half of the mountain or more has been eaten away by the sea, and it stands a spectacularly unbalanced half-mountain. From one angle, Tindhólmur looks like a whole mountain; from the facing perspective, it is just a very tall cliff; from a side perspective, it is exactly half a mountain. It is an unsettling, if beautiful, landform, because destructive processes are so visibly at work in its shape. One doubts that this geological reality would be lost on any human visitor or inhabitant of the Faroes.[45] The Faroe Islands are a broken series of igneous basalt formations cut by deep fjords and crevasses, and exist in the middle of the Norwegian Sea, far from everything else. The interior of the islands mimics the irregularity of the sea. A recent visitor writes in his travelogue: "The Faroe Islands are an archipelago of 18 upthrusted hunks of igneous rock in the middle of precisely nowhere, the stretch of North Atlantic halfway between Norway and Iceland. . . . The Faroes are easily the most moodily beautiful place I have ever been. Each island is a giant slice of elaborately tiered basalt, tilted to one side and covered in green, tussocky felt."[46] The choice of words to describe the landscape gives us a sense of precarious impermanence; the islands are "upthrusted hunks" or "giant slice[s]" of tilted basalt. Such descriptions hardly invoke the monolithic stability of more permanent-seeming mountain ranges such as the Rockies in North America. The sublimity of the Faroes, this author seems to intimate, lies in their very impossibility, their teetering on the edge of destruction, at least in a geological timeframe.

The sloping highlands, the fractured rocky landscape with its chasms and crevasses so manifestly dangerous for man and beast, and the monstrous and changeable ocean, which surges straight through the center and around the periphery of the landforms—all of these make human identification with this land difficult. The Faroese landscape mirrors its seascape in its brokenness, its peril, and its changeability, and it is frighteningly inadequate in terms of natural

---

45. A Faroese postage stamp illustrates this surreal mountain: "The cruise on 'Maria' 1854: Gáshólmur & Tindhólmur" by Anker Eli Petersen, issued March 26, 2004, and in the Public Domain: https://commons.wikimedia.org/wiki/Faroese_stamps_2004#media-viewer/File:Faroe_stamp_479_maria_cruise_-_tindholmur.jpg.

46. Metcalf, Steven, "Into the Mystical Unreal Reality of the Faroe Islands," *New York Times Travel Magazine*, March 25, 2007.

370 New Norse Studies

resources. Yet in spite of, if not because of this, a strong sense of proud nationalism infuses the saga, even more so in the later *Sigmunds kvæði*. The landscape is in a constant state of flux and negotiation with the sea, and is supremely liminal, as are the endless shifting, clashing, and merging of its human inhabitants. Their convoluted conflict becomes increasingly difficult to track, even by saga standards, as the story progresses. One party gains ground and the other loses it, only to see the advantage reversed in the next encounter; the ebb and flow of the sea underlie this narrative. As we will see, the motif of the perilous sea voyage is regularly followed by an easy one, a difficult entry into the Faroes followed by an easy escape, or vice versa. Thus the saga's rhythms of conflict follow those of the Faroes themselves.[47]

As a site of narrative, the Faroes are linked generically with both Iceland and Norway and other small island nations, yet special and unique. The resilience of the Faroes, along with their precarious position, draws attention to their power as a player in the stories taking place in their land- and seascapes. In terms of topography, human mapping, and history, it is difficult to transfigure the Faroes with human processes, although nature can work on nature in geological time as the sea carves out more and more of the islands. It seems likely the early settlers were aware of this process, and this geographical reality can have the effect of dwarfing the saga's human conflict at times. In his study of early medieval northern landscapes, Alfred K. Siewers argues that some literary descriptions of place function as "a nexus of connective energies—divine, human, and what might be called environmental—with ethical meaning." In his analysis of the Irish story *Tochmarc Étaíne*, he argues that "the otherworldly mounds in the landscape form a network of resistance to the objectifying military power of the high kingship."[48] Similarly, this Faroese archipelago of fjords, rocky passages among the eighteen islands, basalt, mountains, little or no flat land, and a punishing subarctic climate forms a multiplex network of resistance not only to political power, but also to the human making of meaning in general. It imposes a

---

47. For example, some of the deep-cut tidal channels that flow between individual islands change direction every six hours, much like a one-way street in a big city that responds directionally to traffic patterns; the Faroese must be unusually in tune with these natural habits of the islands in order to navigate their landscape without serious mishap.

48. Alfred K. Siewers, *Strange Beauty: Ecocritical Approaches to Early Medieval Landscape* (New York: Macmillan, 2009), 39.

higher ethic of nature onto a story of human conflict. Siewers argues for a reading of Early Irish materials in "the non-modern sense of ecoregion as story,"[49] and I advocate the same for *Færeyinga saga*. The ecocentric textuality of *Færeyinga saga*, applying the words of Siewers again, "implicates the mortality of human experience in a mix of alternate ecological temporality, regional landscape, and frameworks of multiple dialogues."[50] Now I will turn to the natural motifs of sea crossings and difficult entry to the islands that emphasize the ebb-and-flow quality of *Færeyinga* saga.

Beyond the specific moments where Þrándr uses weather magic to halt or destroy vessels crossing to and from the Faroes, there are many other instances in the saga where characters have difficulty making the sea crossing (chs. 23, 30, 35, 44). Sometimes friends of Þrándr have difficulty on the water, although it is unclear whether Þrándr is the ultimate cause of this difficulty (e.g., ch. 48). Most of these difficulties supervene in the context of shipwreck, a common enough occurrence in a land where ships can easily become misdirected.[51] Shipwrecks are, like whale beachings, a natural, economically consequential occurrence. Here again, it remains ambiguous whether Þrándr is the cause of his friends' and kinsmen's bad luck. After he has had some trouble controlling the behavior of his unruly and roguish kinsmen, they are conveniently shipwrecked, and then return as *draugar* to haunt him:

> Nú láta þeir Sigurðr í haf ok eru tólf menn saman á skipi, ok er þat orð á at þeir ætli at halda til Íslands. Ok er þeir hafa skamma stund í hafi verit, þá rekr á storm mikinn, ok helzk veðrit nær viku. Þat vissu allir þeir er á landi váru at þetta var þeim Sigurði í móti sem mest, ok sagði mǫnnum óvænt hugr um þeira ferð. Ok er á leið haustit fundusk rekar af skipi þeira í Austrey. Ok er vetr kom, gerðusk aptrgǫngur miklar í Gǫtu ok víða í Austrey, ok sýndusk þeir opt, frændr Þrándar, ok varð mǫnnum at þessu mikit mein: sumir fengu beinbrot eða ǫnnur meizl. Þeir sóttu Þránd svá mjǫk at hann þorði hvergi einn at ganga um vetrinn. Var nú mikit orð á þessu. (ÍF 25:103–104, ch. 49)

---

49. Ibid.

50. Ibid., 54.

51. Animals also succumb to the treacherous tides of the Faroes; every year, scores of pilot whales are slaughtered by the inhabitants when they are drawn into the bays.

So Sigurd and the others put to sea, twelve men all told on the ship, and the word is that they intend to make for Iceland, and when they have been at sea a short while a big storm comes up, the weather holds nearly a week. Everyone on shore knew this was dead against Sigurd and the rest of them and forebodings were gloomy about their trip. And when fall had passed, jetsam was found from their ship on Eysturoy, and when winter came there were mighty hauntings at Gotu and all over on Eysturoy, and Thrand's kinsmen often showed themselves and people suffered much hurt from it, some got broken bones or other hurts. They went after Thrand so much that he did not dare go alone anywhere during the winter. There was much talk about this. (Johnston 94–95, ch. 46)

In another episode, three Norwegian brothers are picked out of the wreckage by Þrándr's thuggish kinsmen, Sigurðr, Þórðr, and Gautr. They get a taste of their own medicine when the sailors turn out to be worse thugs than they are, causing trouble throughout the district, and making matters even more complicated for the conflict-prone trio (ÍF 25:107–13, chs. 50–55; Johnston 98–104, chs. 48–53). One suspects this, too, to have been a plan of Þrándr's. Thus an alliance with nature can impose ethical norms upon the most straightforwardly evil characters in the saga.

The motif of the supernaturally impeded sea crossing is also frequently reversed. Although a character like Sigmundr or Þrándr may easily cross the ocean, the redactor intimates that this facility is not due to natural causes, but rather to luck or supernatural power. Consider, for instance, the fact that Sigmundr has a good crossing after he reluctantly agrees to convert the Faroes. Likely lurking in the saga audience's mind is this question: Is Óláfr's good magic helping him (ÍF 25:71, ch. 30; Johnston 65, ch. 29)? In another instance good weather helps Þrándr's kinsman Sigurðr escape an ordeal by hot iron (ÍF 25:96, ch. 45; Johnston 88, ch. 44). The language of the passage makes the sudden clearing of the sea passage seem like more than a coincidence. This time, however, the supernatural aid is diabolical or at least pagan, helping Sigurðr escape the consequences of his evil deeds.

Another difficulty in sea-crossing is maritime ambush: a character leaves land in an attempt to reach another island in the Faroes, but is attacked at sea by his enemies. A spectacular ambush at sea leads to an equally spectacular fight on a cliff, and Brestir's fall off it leaves both Sigmundr and Þórir orphaned. In chapter 37 (Johnston 35), Þrándr attacks Sigmundr in a narrow island channel:

> Ok nǫkkuru síðar um sumarit fór Sigmundr á skipi ok þeir þrír saman at landsskyldum sínum. Þeir reru í eitt þrǫngt sund milli eyja nokkurra. Ok er þeir kómu úr sundinu, þá sigldi þar skip á móti þeim ok átti allskammt [til] þeira. Þeir kenndu menn þessa, ok váru þar Gǫtuskeggjar, Þrándr ok þeir tólf saman. (ÍF 25:81, ch. 37)

> Somewhat later in the summer Sigmund rowed off to collect his rents, the other two with him. They rowed through a narrow sound between some islands and when they came out of the sound a boat was sailing toward them and it was almost right on them. They recognized the men, they were the Gotu-men, Thrand and eleven with him. (Johnston 74, ch. 35)

In this surprise attack, Þrándr uses his intimate knowledge of the Faroe land- and seascape to gain a tactical advantage, while Sigmundr counters with his signature reliance on pure human strength. At this moment, when Sigmundr pushes over his enemies' boats, the author tells us his luck shifts. Perhaps Sigmundr, in his spectacular victory over his enemy against all odds, in a very tight situation, has used up the last of his luck; his might and main have run out. These motifs—a perilous sea crossing, a difficult entry into the Faroes, and the lifting of a weight too heavy for one human to bear—converge in Sigmundr's intense, condensed, emotional death. He must bear his kinsmen across a vast sound on his back, and he is too weak to secure safe entry to the islands. (These acts arguably portray Sigmundr, once more, as a sort of hybrid ship/whale/man.) He is surreptitiously buried on the seashore—a marginal place—without witnesses. We have the sense of two great powers at play, larger than any human players: a recalcitrant nature and God's civilizing process. People, no matter how strong, are ground up in the clash.

We have now seen the diversity of ways in which the saga explores the motif of the sea crossing, as pagan/natural and Christian/human forces help and hinder protagonists in their transits to and from the islands. Now let us look at a similar process that takes place once the ships have reached the shore, or nearly so: the journey has rarely ended at this point, for protagonists and antagonists alike must contend with the rocky landscape of the Faroe Islands, scaling cliffs or negotiating rough beaches. Once the vessels have been moored, they must be protected to prevent their destruction. Finally, the motif of the difficult entry, like that of the perilous sea crossing, can be reversed, as characters escape from land with trouble. This difficulty of entry is highlighted in the various approaches to Skuvoy. Skuvoy seems to be the focus of the saga's description of fortress-like landscapes, doubtless due to its imposing topography.[52] Skuvoy is explicitly described as a steep fortress, whose natural defenses of cliffs and raging coastline are augmented by man-made outworks in a strategic alliance between humans and landscape: "Skúfey er svá háttat, at hon er svá brǫtt at þar er hit bezta vígi; er þar ein uppganga, ok svá segja þeir at eigi mun eyin sótt verða ef fyrir eru tuttugu karlar eða þrír tigir, at aldri komi svá margr til at sótt verði" (Skuvoy is so steep-sided that it makes a good fortress: there is one cliff path on it and they say that the island will never be taken if it is manned by twenty or thirty fighting men; it will not be taken, however many men attack it).[53] The island is by nature a martial landscape, echoing the military structures of man, yet greater than any fortification. The outworks Ǫzurr (Faroese: Øssur) has built on top of the island are almost an insult to the superior natural defenses of the landform. In his attack on the island, however, Sigmundr is fortunate to find few guards on Skuvoy, and his men start breaking apart the earthworks in what resembles an accelerated erosive process, an echo of the waves breaking inexorably against the land below them. But while they can destroy the works of men, the island will yet expel them. In the chase and battle that ensue, Sigmundr is trapped on the other side of a land rift. Although his exceptional strength allows him, unlike allies and pursuers, to leap across the chasm, he lands on the edge of

---

52. Ólafur Hálldorsson argues that the geography is transposed, the author having confused Skuvoy with Dimun (ÍF 25:xxxiv). A cursory study of photographs of these respective islands makes this seem likely, but for the sake of this study, i.e., since we are dealing with saga narrative and not a geographical or geological survey, I take the author's descriptions at face value.

53. ÍF 25:48, ch. 22; Johnston 52, ch. 22.

the sea strand and is pushed into the sea—a fate that underscores his marginality.

The fortress-like structures of the smaller islands in the Faroes can of course be used just as effectively to keep people in as keep them out, as we see when Sigmundr imprisons Þrándr on an island after Þrándr attacks him there. Sigmundr manages to escape Þrándr and his companions, smash their boats, and row away. Desperation forces Þrándr to burn a signal fire: "Þeir Þrándr brenndu vita, ok var róit til þeira, ok fóru þeir heim í Gǫtu" (Thrand and his men burned a signal fire and were rowed out to, and they went home to Gotu).[54] His control of weather and the sea can do nothing for him now—he is in a natural jail. While larger islands with cliffs make a defender's position nearly unimpregnable, when boating to smaller islands one is vulnerable. Thus the landscape itself facilitates certain kinds of violence. The saga presents the islands variously as fortresses, open plains, or jails, depending on topography and other factors, such as luck. In spite of this focus on and sensitivity to landscape, the saga's geography is remarkably imprecise. Phrases such as til einnar eyjar, "to a certain island,"[55] hardly offer the detailed place-name descriptions found in many of the Icelandic sagas.

Færeyinga saga offers one of the most nuanced depictions of the difficulties and ambiguities of colonialism and conversion in Old Norse-Icelandic literature. Unlike Færeyinga saga, most of the kings' sagas place the pagan/Christian divide in much more starkly biased relief.[56] Other conversion narratives do not cast an inveterate enemy of the faith at the center of the story, making his perspective seem comprehensible, and even justifiable. Every step Þrándr takes in his one-man war against Christianity and Norwegian rule makes sense from his perspective. He never makes a move that is irrational or unreasoned. "His indefatigable scheming and play-acting are comical to the point of buffoonery, yet they are effective, and their comicality does not take away from the dignity at his core,"[57] and most importantly, Þrándr is granted the dignity of a choice. The redactor, with

---

54. ÍF 25:80, ch. 37; Johnston 74, ch. 35.
55. ÍF 25:112, ch. 55; Johnston 103, ch. 52.
56. See Harris, "Saga as Historical Novel," 234–35.
57. Johnston 13 ("Introduction").

his repeated collocation of religion and taxes, shows the conflict to be as much an economic as a religious one. This is important to our understanding of these struggles as occurring in a context of colonization, with economic as well as ideological ramifications.

In the first chapter of *Færeyinga saga*, a connection with Iceland is already made explicit; Auðr djúpúðga (the Deepminded) stops in the Faroes and leaves her daughter Ólǫf (whose name perhaps prefigures those of the great Christian kings) on the islands before moving on to "other empty lands."[58] This is part of the saga's selective interpretation of history—the islands are devoid of people, and no mention is made of signs of habitation by Irish monks known to have occupied the islands before Norwegian settlement. This seems noteworthy, since the sagas of the settlement of Iceland generally take pains to mention Christian monks who inhabited the land previously. Auðr makes a lasting impression on the Faroes, preparing them for colonization at the end of the saga by Christianity. Margaret Clunies Ross argues that the religious objects left behind by the Irish monks who lived in both Iceland and the Faroes—and I would add by extension Auðr's influence on the landscape of the Faroes—changed the landscape's meaning in the eyes of the Norsemen: "[T]hese religious objects were probably also thought of as imbued with spiritual force, so that, although Iceland did not become Christian again for over one hundred years, the land remained subject to their powers, and there was a sense in which the territory of Iceland itself remained Christian even though its human inhabitants for the most part did not."[59]

If Christianity and Icelandic connections are part of the fabric of the Faroes' history from the very beginning, so too is Norway. The settlers originated there, and the author takes care to mention that the islands were considered to be held "in fief" from Haraldr gráfeldr (Greycloak) (ÍF 25:3, ch. 1; Johnston 19, ch. 1). Moreover, both protagonists journey to Norway to prove their worth early in their careers. But although Iceland and Norway are influences, as are the traces of Christianity left in the Faroes, they are not the land itself, which has a tendency to ultimately resist any human meaning-making. It is, if anything, fickle and elemental, allying itself with one side or the other

---

58. ÍF 25:3, ch. 1; Johnston 19, ch. 1.
59. Clunies Ross, "Land-Taking and Text-Making," 174.

as long as luck holds, but just as quickly destroying either. Moreover, in contrast to the landbound stability and fixed identity of Norway as "Motherland," the western islands are different, paradoxically both exile and original, bearers of the original sin as well as the original power of paganism. Each island in the West Atlantic becomes a parable of the other, and so Iceland reiterates the history of the Faroes, Orkney, the Isle of Man, and England. Each becomes one instance in the repeated pattern of imperial colonization, as the Scandinavian kings, constrained by the Arctic Circle to the north and the great medieval states to the south, expand ever eastward and westward.

Færeyinga saga, with its incremental repetition of certain motifs such as sea voyages in storms, or the three men with a hand in Sigmundr's father's death, was structurally well suited for reinterpretation as a ballad. The vital tradition of Faroese balladry has produced many different versions of the stories first recorded in *Færeyinga saga*. A study of these ballads points to the same vexed issues of transmission and cultural perspective as in the saga, but the direction is arguably reversed—from Iceland back to the Faroes. In the Faroese ballads about Sigmundur's efforts, we find the series of incrementally repeated motifs gracefully transferred from one medium to another, regardless of time and place or political agenda. They are used to different effect, but the tensions they give voice to remain constant. Although Stephen Mitchell notes that in some cases "we can be confident that the Faroese ballad, although not collected until the 19th century, antedated all published versions of the Old Norse text," this is not the case here.[60] *Sigmunds kvæði eldra* follows the action of the saga too closely to be a different form of the story entirely. So in *Sigmunds kvæði* we have the highly oral byproduct of a literary text, a Faroese reworking of an Icelandic cultural document, instead of an Icelandic reworking of a product of Faroese culture. In the case of this later reshaping of this story, the ballad of Sigmundur (now in modern orthography) is motivated by direct, not oblique, nationalism; yet, perhaps due to the necessarily simplifying process of ballad-making, the moral issues become more black and white—pro Christianity via Norway, and contra paganism in the Faroes.

---

60. Stephen A. Mitchell, *Heroic Sagas and Ballads* (Ithaca: Cornell University Press, 1991), 148.

A conflict of wills expressed through the landscape is not uncommon in European balladry, but this instance is special in that it documents the ways in which a Faroese reader of the medieval text seized upon its motifs of the dangers of nature as a means of translating it into ballad form.[61] The two genres speak the same language of incremental repetition and pathetic fallacy. In the saga the motif of the difficult landscape is an intermittent if dominant sign of power. In the ballads, however, it becomes the focus, providing an example of the processes of transposing a literary narrative into ballad form. The ballad maker fixates on land- and seascapes in order to reduce the narrative to its bare essentials while maintaining, or even enhancing, its dramatic effect. He is also composing this version for the entertainment of his countrymen, who know the land- and seascape of the Faroes intimately, and uses these motifs to heighten their connection with the story.

The ballad maker retains the theme of arduously achieved control over the landscape, the motif of weather magic, and the ideal of human heroism in the face of the perilous natural world. In this passage, Sigmundur struggles to land while malevolent natural/magical power pushes against the boat:

Sjógvurin brýtur streyma strítt,
einki aktar Sigmund[ur] slíkt.
Sjógvurin brýtur sum boðafles,
"Haldum beint á Mjóvanes!"
Sjógvurin gerst nú gulur, nú blá,
sandurin uppi á tilju lá.
Tekur at rúka sandur og sjógvur:
"Nú er Tróndur vorðin óður."
Náttina eina, dagarnar tveir,
Sigmundur úti fyri Gøtu lá.
Tó ið vær kostum lív og lund,
vær náum ei á Gøtu sund.
Tó ið vær kostum lív og and,

---

61. For a general study of natural elements used to dramatic effect in balladry, see Edith Randam Rogers, *The Perilous Hunt* (Lexington: University Press of Kentucky, 1980).

náum vit ei á Gøtu sand.

Vær náum ei á Gøtu sand,

Tróndur ristir mót os gand. [62] (couplets lines 17–24)

The breaking waves, the strong currents / Sigmund never let such things deter him. / The breaking waves crashing so fierce, / "Keep the course for Mjóvanes!" / The sea suddenly turned yellow, then blue, / and swept sand across the ship's deck. / A furious blast of sand and sea: / "Now Þrándr's anger is roused." / One night and two days, / Sigmund weathered the storm, unable to advance. / "This could end up costing us body and soul. / Never shall we reach Gøta strand. / We shall never reach Gøta strand. / Þrándr is using sorcery against us."

The incremental repetition of the sea-wave motif lends a sense of menace and foreboding to the ship-launching prior to the sea voyages to the Faroes; in the first instance, we know it is a choppy sea because the waves break as they would on a reef on the sandy beach in Norway. As the ship pushes off from shore, the waves become more menacing as they reappear in the next few stanzas, turning from blue to yellow to black, making it clear that this storm is the result of sorcery. The water becomes so agitated that sand from the ocean floor weighs down the vessel. These events may terrify, but the heroic men on board hold their course, pushing through the rough weather in spite of the malicious enchantment. Soon, the waves break violently in the middle of the ocean—Sigmundr had never seen anything like it, we are told. When the sand begins to mix in equal parts with the ocean, clearly something is seriously amiss—the very fundament of the ocean has been aroused to anger by Þrándr's magic. When he notes the churning sand and sea, and especially the steaming water, Sigmundr declares in a litotes: "Now Þrándr is angry with us." The understated magic of the saga has been discarded in favor of a monstrous, unnaturally churning ocean. The ballad maker's exaggeration of the supernatural would likely appeal to the ballad's local audience, all of whom would

---

62. I cite the Version A text of "Sigmunds kvæði eldra," also known as F22, A, from *Føroya Kvæði: Corpus Carminum Færoensium a Sven Grundtvig et J. Bloch Comparatum*, ed. N. Djurhuus and C. Matras, 8 vols. (Copenhagen: Ejnar Munksgaard, 1941–2003), 1:453–55.

be used to this sort of struggle against the elements in their everyday lives in the harsh Faroes.

Later in the ballad, Sigmundur encounters another magical storm, and his ship's deck buckles like a hoop from the strain of trying to land while Þrándr's magic pushes the vessel away. The power of this motif is yet again enhanced vis-à-vis the saga, but gone are the mystery and ambiguity. The landscape is even more supernatural and spectacular in the ballad than in the saga, but the menace is only one-way: Þrándr is a pagan sorcerer and his magic is destructive—end of story. The double-edged nature of Þrándr's relationship to nature so carefully depicted in the saga is nowhere evident.

The ballad maker's highlighting of the environmental elements of the narrative can be viewed as a literary-critical reading of another text. He underscores the power of the water as a supernaturally dangerous force, and amplifies other natural elements, repeating them incrementally such that they gain in power and force as the ballad develops. In conjunction with the perilous supernatural sea crossing is the motif of the deadly rocks, a balladic reduction of the saga's theme of difficult entry. It is repeated many times in both saga and ballad, further emphasizing the natural menace of the Faroes. The narrow yet amenable beach is contrasted with the rocky danger nearby. In the ballad, the hero's difficult ascent to the island is also amplified, as the power and danger of the great cliffs on the island's shore are emphasized:

> Sigmundur tekur sín kaðal í hond,
> búgvið spjótið rennir á land.
> Hann skeyt upp í grønan vall,
> oddurin niður í grótið gall.
> Tríati favnar var bjørgið hátt,
> Sigmundur lesti seg við ein tátt.
> Á gøtuni lógu garpar tveir,
> bráðan bana fingu teir. (couplets 47–50)

Sigmund takes his rope in hand / and casts a ready spear toward land. / It shot up to the grassy cliff, / and its point lodged into the rock. / The cliff was thirty fathoms high, / Sigmund drew himself up along the line. / On the path there were two men, / they both quickly met their deaths.

Sigmundur, in keeping with his actions in the saga, fights nature with his might and main, but the meaning of this encounter has shifted significantly. His death-defying scaling of the cliffs is classic swashbuckling, and we urge him upwards, admiring his human ingenuity. The cliffs have lost a little of their menacing alterity and have just become another obstacle to be conquered. This motif of the rocky shore as a place of death reaches its fullest development in the most powerful moment of the ballad, when Sigmundur kills his opponent Øssur. Before Øssur dies, he and Sigmundur are some-what reconciled, and their burial agreement amplifies the emotional content of the narrative, creating a truly moving story of nobility and fate. In a typical balladic adaptation, which simplifies while maintaining the narrative's emotional core and its ability to move its audience, Øssur asks Sigmundur, his killer, to bury him near the seashore with his feet facing the ocean so he can "see" the waves crashing against his homeland from his grave (line 67): "Tað var Øssurs síðsta orð: / 'Høvdið skal venda mót Grønuskor'" (Øssur's last words were: "My head should point toward Grønaskor"). In the saga narrative, Qzzur is not buried at all; this section appears to be a balladic addition intended to lead the audience to the emotional core of the narrative, as the emphasis on the dying man's deep apprecia-tion of the wild land- and seascape of the Faroes invokes the listeners' patriotic pride in their homeland; his last words are an encomium of the beauty of his country. Again, his words mark the landscape as both beloved and murderous; both men end up dead on the rocks, Øssur because he is a part of the landscape and loves it, Sigmundur because he is fated to perish on his mission.

The menace and beauty of the Faroese landscape come even more to the fore in the distillation inherent in the process of ballad-making. The political message of the saga—the island's ambiguous political history—is lost as the ballad maker reduces the work to its emotional core: a supernatural tale of heroism, of good versus evil. We can see this clearly in the way the ballad begins with an invocation of King Óláfr as the catalyst of the story (lines 7–8): "Ólavur kongur kristnum býður, / Gud og milda[r] miskunnstíðir" (King Óláfr offers Christians / God and gentle times of mercy).

Thus the beginning of the ballad narrative is framed within a Christianizing context, leaving little room for sympathizers with Faroese independence such as is traceable in the saga. Musically, the ballad's major modality in lilting, positive-sounding major thirds and fourths creates one of the brightest chords of all and a comfortably resolving perfect cadence that terminates each stanza—musical elements that will place the ballad unambiguously in the service of nationalistic and nationwide celebration. The outcome of the conflict is thus known and prefigured in the melody itself. This is not a song of tragic loss and hard gain, but a cheerful tune for performance. In fact, since Faroese ballads are and were performed at times of celebration and holidays, it was likely performed, among other times, on the festival day of the other great Christianizing Óláfr, who appears at the end of the saga and arguably lies figurally behind his namesake in *Sigmunds kvæði*.

That saint Óláfr is the patron saint of the Faroes is significant in this context. If we trust the evidence of the ballad, the modern Faroese seem to fundamentally identify with and claim as theirs the stormy imperialism of the Norwegians. The past is past, and complex issues of colonialism, religion, and national identity versus regionalism have lost their poignancy, making it easier for the ballad maker to simplify the conflict as a strictly religious one. However, the ballad maker retains the saga's uncontrollable landscape, its weather magic, and its human heroism in the face of a beautiful yet malevolent nature.

This brief discussion of two versions of the story of the Norwegian conversion and political annexing of the Faroes has pointed out the importance of natural imagery in the furthering of the narrative. The saga and the ballad are similar accounts with a few major differences. One is an orally inspired, yet highly literate, heroic history, compiled and written down by a man from a country with a parallel history—another "fishing place" on the margins of Scandinavian culture; it is a sustained narrative of a perilous landscape, with an intimate, albeit inaccurate, portrait of the geography of the islands, themselves portrayed as an almost impregnable fortress. The other is a literarily-inspired oral creation, which after having been "frozen" by the ballad collectors, becomes literary again, only to be recreated once more orally in performance by the Faroese. This ballad expresses more than an oblique Icelandic interest in a "somewhere else" that is "like us" as in *Færeyinga saga*—it is a nationalistic account of the foundational history of "our land." Due in part to the simplifying process of ballad production and in part to the passage of time, the depiction of Þrándr as a villain and sorcerer retains no trace of pride in independent islands with a pagan past, as we find in the saga. The one aspect of the story that remains constant is the sense of awe and wonder at the force of the natural onslaught of water and waves.

As a postscript, as well as a micro-study of modern Faroese medievalism, I conclude with a brief discussion of a millennial-anniversary stamp produced by the Faroe post office. Its iconography, although ostensibly celebrating the islands' dual pagan and Christian heritage, betrays in its use of color and light the same ambiguity about a pagan past and a Christian present that we find in the saga. Þrándr stands on a rock as the waves he has summoned crash around him.[63] His profile is primitive, perhaps even a bit Neanderthal-like, and he holds Thor's hammer in the air as a prophylactic against the Christian magic coming from the sea, symbolized by ships with masts in the shape of crosses being pushed forward by streaming rays of light emanating from a hopeful dawning sun. Þrándr, in contrast to the brilliance of the seascape, is a dark figure standing on dark rocks—surrounded by brilliant waves that crash about him as they move in from the Norwegian ships—he is an icon of a dimly-remembered, benighted heathenism. In fact, his gesture of defiance could also be seen in his shielding his eyes to avoid being blinded (or to avoid "seeing the light," as it were); perhaps this is the artist's intention, as Þrándr, according to the saga, goes blind toward the end of his life, and this blindness seems intended as another sign of his spiritual perdition.

His land, the islands of the Faroes that the stamp ostensibly celebrates, is draped in darkness; the nature he inhabits looks chaotic and violent whereas the Christians' looks relatively controlled and brilliant. Out of some sense of ecumenism, however (and perhaps because neo-paganism is one of Europe's fastest-growing religions), the artist depicts the cross on the upper right corner of the stamp and the modern symbol of Odin's cross on the left-hand corner, as if celebrating both religions of the islands. But even the orientation

---

63. The stamp is first in a series dedicated to Christianity in the Faroes by Anker Eli Petersen, issued by the Postverk Føroya on February 21, 2000, and viewable in color in the Public Domain: https://upload.wikimedia.org/wikipedia/commons/f/f9/Faroe_stamp_360_arrival_of_christianity.jpg

of these symbols gives away the artist's—and the post-office offi-cials'—inclinations, as the sinister religion is on the left side, and the "right" one is, of course, on the right. The rectangular stamp is divided by a diagonal line running from the top left to the bottom right, creating two equal halves—the bottom left is dark, sinister, and organically structured; the top right is bright, glorious, and geometric. One is reminded of the equation of light with God's love. Hence, in the stamp, the course of Faroese history is aligned with the course of world and salvation history. Moreover, the choice of the Odinic cross as the symbol for the surely quite syncretic religion of the Faroe Islands simplifies a complex praxis and relates it to comprehensible, and potentially risible, modern pagan practice. The Odinic cross, a circle surrounding a cross, also contains within itself the symbology of the coming, conquering religion.

Even Þrándr's hammer, the only part of the pagan half of the composition that pushes into the Christian section, looks like an underdeveloped cross—decidedly puny and ineffectual in the face of so many crosses and other symbols of triumphant Christianity, but also a prefiguration to be fulfilled by the advent of the true cross. The mainsails appear to be furled (as they might well be when approaching shore), but also giving the impression that the ships are being propelled by divine (Christian) power rather than (pagan) forces of nature, i.e., wind and tide. On this stamp, the natural power Þrándr commands is at the forefront of the work of art, a symbol of the power and beauty of the Faroese landscape, while the Christian ships are "other"—newcomers with a different kind of power bolstering them. One detects, crossing behind the rays of light, a Faroese flag, which is itself a cross turned on its side, and a version of the Danish flag, the banner of the current protector of the islands. Thus the islands' distant political future is already present in an image that ostensibly provides a snapshot of an earlier cultural collision.

The artist has depicted Þrándr and his religion as moribund, doomed, and worth losing. This is a common move in colonial narra-tives and image-making, and I believe it would be useful to draw some connections between the depictions of the near-extinct pagan "native" and his archetypal relative, the doomed Native American. In his study of the iconography of the Native Americans produced by white settlers and artists, Nicholas Thomas writes, "The evocation of the native Americans has a conditional quality: not 'here they are,' but 'here is their passing.' As in E. S. Curtis's classic images of noble Indians vanishing into the mists, the landscape or their own melancholy, so also in . . . the many settler-colonial representations of 'The Last of the. . .' this fading to absence is determined by the presence of another figure, a white protagonist who is in some cases a settler, in others a writer able to record the truth of an extinguished culture."[64] This same powerful iconography applies in some ways to this image on the Faroe stamp, and, I would argue, to the ballad and the saga as well. Doubtless a large number of sagas contain similar snapshots of a moribund pagan past, similar scenes of passing written from the vantage point of a future where the outcome is clear.[65]

However the image of the native pagan may change throughout these three works—the saga, the ballad, and the postage stamp—the Faroese landscape remains a powerful player up to the present day; its human ally may lose his force and effectiveness, but the wild Faroe beach still remains, and the waves crash as violently as ever against its rocks. In the image on the stamp, the landscape is broken down into even more iconic chunks than in the ballad—just sea, rocks, and sand. The emotional—and ecological—core of the conflict is packed into the elements of this tiny image with tight, telegraphic intensity. The wonder of the Faroese stamp lies in the way it showcases a surprising narrative consistency from medieval saga, to modern ballad, to contemporary image—three works that testify to the persistence of the themes of the intractability and the resilience of the Faroe Islands, however else the focus on the interplay of their human inhabitants may shift.

Bibliography

Andersson, Theodore M. "Kings' Sagas." In *Old Norse-Icelandic Literature: A Critical Guide*, edited by John Lindow and Carol J. Clover, 197–238. Ithaca: Cornell University Press, 1985.

Bagge, Sverre. "Christianization and State Formation in Early Medieval Norway." *Scandinavian Journal of History* 30 (2005): 107–34.

---

64. Nicholas Thomas, "The Primitivist and the Postcolonial," in *Colonialism's Culture: Anthropology, Travel, and Government* (Princeton: Princeton University Press, 2002), 178.

65. The notion of the Norse pagan as a sort of noble savage has been widely discussed. See Harris, "Saga as Historical Novel," and Lars Lönnroth, "The Noble Heathen," *Scandinavian Studies* 41 (1969): 1–29. The parallel between the white American iconography of nostalgia and the overcoming of nature and paganism by imperial religion as represented in the sagas would be a topic ripe for further study.

————. "The Making of a Missionary King: The Medieval Accounts of Olaf Tryggvason and the Conversion of Norway." *Journal of English and Germanic Philology* 105 (2006): 473–513.

Bhabha, Homi K. *The Location of Culture.* London: Routledge, 1994.

Christiansen, Eric. *The Norsemen in the Viking Age.* Oxford: Blackwell, 2002.

Clunies Ross, Margaret. "Land-Taking and Text-Making." In *Text and Territory: Geographical Imagination in the European Middle Ages,* edited by Sylvia Tomasch and Sealy Gilles, 159–84. Philadelphia: University of Pennsylvania Press, 1998.

Debes, Hans Jacob. "The Faroe Islands." In *Medieval Scandinavia: An Encyclopedia.* Edited by Phillip Pulsiano and Kirsten Wolf. New York: Garland, 1993.

Deleuze, Gilles, and Félix Guattari. *Desert Islands and Other Texts, 1953–1974.* Los Angeles: Semiotext(e), 2004.

DuBois, Thomas A. *Nordic Religions in the Viking Age.* Philadelphia: University of Pennsylvania Press, 1999.

Færeyinga saga, Ólafs saga Odds. Edited by Ólafur Halldórsson. Íslenzk fornrit 25. Reykjavík: Hið íslenzka fornritafélag, 2006.

Foote, Peter. *Aurvandilstá: Norse Studies.* Odense: Odense University Press, 1984.

————. "*Færeyinga saga,* Chapter Forty." In *Aurvandilstá,* 209–221.

————. "A Note on Þránd's *Kredda.*" In *Aurvandilstá,* 199–208.

————. "Þrándr and the Apostles." In *Aurvandilstá,* 188–198.

Føroya Kvæði: Corpus Carminum Færoensium a Sven Grundtvig et J. Bloch Comparatum. Edited by N. Djurhuus and C. Matras. 8 vols. Copenhagen: Ejnar Munksgaard, 1941–2003.

Harris, Joseph. "Saga as Historical Novel." In *Structure and Meaning in Old Norse Literature: New Approaches to Textual Analysis and Literary Criticism,* edited by John Lindow, Lars Lönnroth, and Gerd Wolfgang Weber, 187–219. The Viking Collection: Studies in Northern Civilization 3. Odense: Odense University Press, 1986. Repr. in *"Speak Useful Words or Say Nothing": Old Norse Studies by Joseph Harris,* edited by Susan E. Deskis and Thomas D. Hill, 227–60. Islandica 53. Ithaca: Cornell University Library, 2008

Johnston, George, trans. *Thrand of Gotu: Two Icelandic sagas from the Flat Island Book.* Erin, Ontario: Porcupine's Quill Press, 1994.

Kipling, Rudyard. *Rudyard Kipling's Verse.* New York: Doubleday, Page and Co., 1922.

Kvideland, Reimund, and Henning K. Sehmsdorf. *Scandinavian Folk Belief and Legend.* Minneapolis: University of Minnesota Press, 1991.

Lönnroth, Lars. "The Noble Heathen." *Scandinavian Studies* 41 (1969): 1–29.

Mitchell, Stephen. *Heroic Sagas and Ballads*. Ithaca: Cornell University Press, 1991.

Mudimbe, Valentin Y. *The Idea of Africa*. Bloomington: Indiana University Press, 1994.

Ogilvie, A. E. J. and Gísli Pálsson. "Mood, Magic and Metaphor: Allusions to Weather and Climate in the *Sagas of Icelanders*." In *Weather, Climate, Culture*, edited by S. Strauss and B. S. Orlove, 251–74. Oxford: Berg, 2003.

Perkins, Richard. *Thor the Wind-Raiser and the Eyrarland Image*. London: Viking Society for Northern Research, 2001.

Rogers, Edith Randam. *The Perilous Hunt: Symbols in Hispanic and European Balladry*. Lexington: University Press of Kentucky, 1980.

Siewers, Alfred K. *Strange Beauty: Ecocritical Approaches to Early Medieval Landscape*. New York: Macmillan, 2009.

Smith, Linda Tuhiwai. *Decolonizing Methodologies: Research and Indigenous Peoples*. London: Zed Press, 1999.

Thisted, Kristen. "Voicing the Arctic: Knud Ramussen and the Ambivalence of Cultural Translation." In *Arctic Discourses*, edited by Anka Ryall, Johan Schimanski, and Henning Howlid Wærp, 59–81. Newcastle-upon-Tyne: Cambridge Scholars, 2010.

Thomas, Nicholas. *Colonialism's Culture: Anthropology, Travel, and Government*. Princeton: Princeton University Press, 2002.

Vésteinn Ólason. "Den frie mannens selvforståelse i islandske sagaer og dikt." In *Medeltidens födelse*, edited by Anders Andrén, 277–286. Symposier på Krapperups Borg 1. Nyhamnsläge: Gyllenstiernska Krapperupsstiftelsen, 1989.

Non-Basic Color Terms in Old Norse-Icelandic

Kirsten Wolf

UNIVERSITY OF WISCONSIN-MADISON

1. Introduction

In recent years, basic color terms in Old Norse-Icelandic have received considerable attention.[1] The consensus so far is that Old Norse-Icelandic has eight basic color terms: *blár, brúnn, grár, grœnn, gulr, hvítr, rauðr,* and *svartr.*[2] Non-basic color terms, which comprise terms that are hyponyms of basic color terms, contextually restricted, of infrequent use, and not psychologically salient for

---

1. See, e.g., Georg C. Brückmann, *Altwestnordische Farbsemantik,* Münchner Nordistische Studien 11 (Munich: Herbert Utz Verlag, 2012); Natalie M. Van Deusen, "The Matter of *blár* in *Tristrams kvæði,*" *Arthuriana* 22 (2012): 109–15; Kirsten Wolf, "Basic Color Terms in Old Norse-Icelandic: A Quantitative Study," *Orð og tunga* 15 (2013): 141–61; "The Color Blue in Old Norse-Icelandic Literature," *Scripta Islandica* 57 (2006): 55–78; "The Color Brown in Old Norse-Icelandic Literature," *NOWELE* [Forthcoming]; "The Color Grey in Old Norse-Icelandic Literature," *JEGP* 108 (2009): 222–38; "The Colors of the Rainbow in Snorri's *Edda,*" *Maal og minne* (2007): 51–62; "Reflections on the Color of Esau's Pottage of Lentils (*Stjórn* 160.26–161.9)," *Gripla* 16 (2005): 251–57; "Snorri's Use of Color Terms in *Gylfaginning,*" *Skandinavistik* 37 (2007): 1–10; "Some Comments on Old Norse-Icelandic Color Terms," *Arkiv för nordisk filologi* 121 (2006): 173–92; "Towards a Diachronic Analysis of Old Norse-Icelandic Color Terms: The Cases of Green and Yellow," *Orð og tunga* 12 (2010): 109–30; Anna Zanchi, "The Colour Green in Medieval Icelandic Literature: Natural, Supernatural, Symbolic?" in *The Fantastic in Old Norse/Icelandic Literature: Sagas and the British Isles, Preprint Papers of the Thirteenth International Saga Conference, Durham and York 6th-12th August, 2006,* ed. John McKinnell et al. (Durham: Durham University, 2006), 1096–1104.

2. See Brückmann, *Altwestnordische Farbsemantik;* Wolf, "Some Comments."

informants,[3] have received attention primarily from lexicographers, who have catalogued them and offered translations of them. This article is a synchronic study of the non-basic color terms attested in Old Norse-Icelandic. More specifically, it analyzes their formation, frequency, and semantic range. The data are drawn from Finnur Jónsson's *Lexicon Poeticum* (LP), Fritzner's *Ordbog over Det gamle norske Sprog* (ONS) including Hødnebø's supplement to the dictionary (ONS+), Cleasby and Vigfusson's *An Icelandic-English Dictionary* (CV) including Craigie's supplement to the dictionary (CV+), and the online edition of the Arnamagnæan Commission's *Dictionary of Old Norse Prose* (ONP).[4] Altogether, these reference works have yielded well over a hundred secondary color terms. Terms indicating a pattern (spotted, striped, speckled, dotted, etc.), such as *apalgrár, bláfáinn, blámeng(ja)ðr, blárendr, brúnmóalóttr, grárendr, grœnmenginn, hvítrǫndóttr, jarpskjóttr, rauðdropóttr, rauðflekkóttr, svartsblesóttr, svartflekkóttr,* and *svartsǫðlóttr,* many of which are restricted to describing the appearance of farm animals, have not been included. Nor have terms with the prefix *al-* (e.g., *algrár, algrœnn,* and *alhvítr*), since all they imply is that no other color is present, and terms with the prefix *í-* (e.g., *íblár, ígrœnn,* and *írauðr*), since the prefix merely conveys a diminutive notion, though in the case of *ígrœnn,* it may convey intensity or iteration in the same way that *eigrœnn, iðjugrœnn* and *sígrœnn* do. Finally, bynames (e.g., *kylnusvartr* and *skegg[s]hvítr,* etc.) have been excluded.

2. Non-basic color terms

The following presents a list and discussion of the individual non-basic color terms arranged in categories according to their formation.

---

3. The last criterion is not especially applicable to a dead language, and representation across a variety of genres may be a more suitable criterion. See Brent Berlin and Paul Kay, *Basic Color Term: Their Universality and Evolution* (Berkeley: University of California Press, 1969), 5–7; see also C. P. Biggam, *The Semantics of Colour: A Historical Approach* (Cambridge: Cambridge University Press, 2012), 44.

4. It should be noted that the excerpting of these dictionaries is selective, and only a small selection of the oldest texts was selected for ONP as if for a concordance. All references that follow, to these and other works, are to page, preceded by volume and followed by line (indicated after a period), when applicable.

2.1 Monolexemic color terms

Blakkr (LP: "mörk, sort"; ONS: "blakk, om Hestens Farve"; CV: "dusky black . . . pale"; ONP: "ɔ[blakket ɔ:] lys/bleg, gulbrun / ?pale, tawny") is attested four times in poetry.[5] The referents are *marr* (horse),[6] *kveldriðu stóð* (a kenning for a wolf),[7] *borð* (a *heiti* for a ship),[8] and *bjórr* (a *heiti* for blood).[9] In prose, it is used to describe the color of a horse ("hestr": *Diplomentarium Norvegicum* [hereafter DN] 4:196.29, the appearance of vellum ("þetta er blacktt bokfelle": Rask 72 26r, marginal note), and once the color of copper ("hon þ[otti] [Sua] [bera] [af] meyum sem <r>auda gull af [*var.* + blǫcku] eiri": *Sturlaugs saga starfsama* 8.8 [GkS 1006 fol. 33]).

Hárr (*hærr*) (LP: "gråhåret, gammel"; ONS: "graa . . . især graahaaret"; CV: "hoary") refers more to age than color,[10] and should maybe not be regarded as a color term.[11] It is found twelve times

---

5. The symbol "ɔ:" signifies "i.e." in ONP. *Blakkr* goes back to Indo-European *bh(e) leg-*, *bhleng-*. See Ásgeir Blöndal Magnússon, *Íslensk orðsifjabók* (Reykjavík: Orðabók Háskólans, 1989), 62. Jan de Vries maintains that "neben 'gelbbraun' bedeutet altnordisch *blakkr* gerade in der älteren Zeit auch 'dunkelbraun' oder 'grau' (vgl. shetländisch *blekk* 'eisenhaltige Erde, die als Farbstoff verwendet wird'). Die beiden Bedeutungen sind aus einer Grundbedeutung 'gebrennt' abgezweigt." *Altnordisches etymologisches Wörterbuch*, 3rd ed. (Leiden: Brill, 1977), 42.

6. "Beittu, Sigurðr, inn blacca mar" (*Guðrúnarhvǫt* 18.3–4). Gustav Neckel and Hans Kuhn, eds., *Edda: Die Lieder des Codex Regius nebst verwandten Denkmälern*, vol. 1, *Text*, 5th ed. (Heidelberg: Winter, 1983), 267.

7. "vinhróðigr gaf víða / visi margra Frísa / blǫkku brúnt at drekka / blóð kveldriðu stóði" (Hallfreðr vandræðaskáld's *Óláfsdrápa* 6.7; *Skjaldedigtning* 1:149).

8. "óðu blǫkk í blóði / borð fyr Útstein norðan" (Bjarni gullbrárskáld's *Kalfsflokkr* 2.3; *Skjaldedigtning* 1:363).

9. "fekk benþiðurr blakkan / bjór" (Þórmóðr Kolbrúnarskáld's *lausavísa* 22.7; *Skjaldedigtning* 1:265).

10. *Hárr* is derived from Germanic *hairu*. It is related to Old English *hār*, modern English *hoar*, and Old High German *hēr*. See Ásgeir Blöndal Magnússon, *Íslensk orðsifjabók*, 306; de Vries, *Altnordisches etymologisches Wörterbuch*, 212.

11. Cf. the observation made by William E. Mead on the use of the term in Old English poetry: "*Hār*, hoary, is used more conventionally than *grǣg*, and appears at times to be chosen more for the sake of the alliteration than for the sake of the color. *Hār* occurs twenty-seven times . . . . Seven times *hār* is applied to the hoary, gray stone, once to the gray cliff, four times to armor, once to a sword, once to the ocean, once to the gray heath, three times to the wolf, twice to the frost, and seven times to warriors, in each case with some conventionality and with an apparently slight feeling of color." "Color in Old English Poetry," *PMLA* 14 (1899): 190. See also Biggam (note 3 above), who claims that

in poetry. Examples include "at három þul" (*Hávamál* st. 134), "inn hára þul" (*Fáfnismál* st. 34), "hión . . . hár" (*Rígsþula* st. 2), "hárr . . . austrkonungr" (Þjóðólfr ór Hvini's *Ynglingatal* 16.9; *Skjaldedigtning* 1:10), and "hárir men" (Sigvatr Þórðarson's *Bersǫglisvísur* 12.3; *Skjaldedigtning* 1:237).[12] In all instances, the referent is humans or supernatural beings with the exception of Hallr Snorrason's *drápa* about Magnús Erlingsson, where it is a wolf ("hárr gylðir" 1.2; *Skjaldedigtning* 1:516). In prose, it always describes elderly humans.

Hǫss (LP: "grå"; ONS: "graa, graalig"; CV: "gray") is restricted to poetry.[13] In *Eiríksmál* (7.4; *Skjaldedigtning* 1:165) it is used about the color of a wolf ("ulfr enn hǫsvi"), and in Eyvindr Finnsson skáldaspillir's *Háleygjatal* (8.3; *Skjaldedigtning* 1:61), "hǫssvan serk hrísgrisnis" describes the appearance of an "úlfhéðinn." In Þjóðólfr Arnórsson's *Sextefja* (7.5; *Skjaldedigtning* 1:340), the referent is an eagle ("hvassar klœr hǫss arnar"), and in an anonymous eleventh-century *lausavísa* (2.1; *Skjaldedigtning* 1:394), it is an ox ("hǫss hjarðar vísi"). As a compound, it appears in the form of "enn hǫsfjaðri" (about a raven) in Þórbjǫrn hornklofi's *Haraldskvæði* (4.1; *Skjaldedigtning* 1:22).

Jarpr (LP: "rødbrun"; ONS: "brun"; CV: "brown") is attested four times in poetry and eleven times in prose.[14] In poetry, it is used

---

"from the late 10th century at least, it became possible to use *har* to indicate 'old,' with no colour element at all" (222).

12. Finnur Jónsson translates "riddari enn hári" (1.4; *Skjaldedigtning* 1:407) in a *lausavísa* by Eldjárn as "hårlange ridder," and in LP he offers the following translation: "med fyldig hårvækst." According to Ásgeir Blöndal Magnússon (*Íslensk orðsifjabók*, 307) and de Vries (*Altnordisches etymologisches Wörterbuch*, 212), fullness of hair is a secondary meaning of the adjective; the former notes that in this meaning it appears most commonly in compounds, such as *ljóshár(r)* and *laushár(r)*. It is possible, therefore, that a more accurate translation would be "gråhårede ridder."

13. *Hǫss* is derived from Germanic **haswa-*. It is related to Old English *hasu* (gray), Old High German *hasan* (blank, shiny), and Middle High German *heswe* (pale, dull) (de Vries, *Altnordisches etymologisches Wörterbuch*, 282). "Hǫsmagi," the name of a ram, appears in *Grettis saga* (259.18). Cf. the comment by Mead on the use of the color term in Old English poetry: "*Haso*, 'gray,' is found seven times. . . . *Haso* is used with an apparent definiteness of color-feeling, and is applied to the dove, to the eagle, to the curling smoke, to the leaves of plants, and even to the *herestræta*, the highways with their dusty dirty-white surfaces. The examples are not sufficiently numerous to enable us to decide whether is was often used conventionally, but there is certainly little evidence in the instances cited that such was the case" ("Color in Old English Poetry," 192).

14. Julius Pokorny reconstructs the proto-Indo-European root of *jarpr* as **ereb(h)-*,

exclusively about human hair with the exception of *Heiðreks gátur*, in which *enar jarpari* (13.4; *Skjaldedigtning* 2:242) refer to pieces in a board game. In prose, the referent is also human hair, the only exception being "eɴ iarpa hest" (*Flóvents saga* 146.43).[15]

Rjóðr (LP: "rød, rødmosset"; ONS: "rød"; CV: "ruddy . . . red") may be synonymous with *rauðr* or a hyponym of red.[16] Certainly, *rjóðr* is contextually more restricted than *rauðr*. In prose, where it is attested twenty times, it is used exclusively about facial color as in, for example, *Nitida saga*: "hun var bædi vitur og væn lios og riod j andliti þuillikast sem en rauda rosa væri samtemprad vid sniohuita lileam" (3.7), the only exception being "allr þeirra búnaðr var rjóðr [var. rauðr] af gulli" (*Karlamagnúss saga* 181.2). In poetry, where *rjóðr* is attested five times, it refers to facial color in stanza 21 of *Rígsþula* ("rauðan oc rióðan"), in a *lausavísa* by Kormákr Ǫgmundarson ("At emk . . . / ullar Svǫlnis fulli / of reiði-Sif rjóða": 22.3; *Skjaldedigtning* 1:74), and in a *lausavísa* by Þormóðr Kolbrúnarskáld ("Emka rjóðr": 24.1; *Skjaldedigtning* 1:266). Once the referent is a rose ("rósa rjóð": *Máríudrápa* 19.2; *Skjaldedigtning* 2:500), and once it is the Holy Cross ("krossinn rjóðann": *Heilagra meyja drápa* 5.4; *Skjaldedigtning* 2:583).

Finally, mention should be made of *ámr*, *bleikr*, and *fǫlr*. *Ámr* (LP: "mørk, mørkladen"; CV: "black or loathsome") appears only in poetry and does not indicate color but low lightness or high

---

"in Worten für dunkelrötliche Farbtöne." *Indogermanisches etymologisches Wörterbuch*, 2 vols. (Bern and Munich: Francke Verlag, 1959–69), 1:334. See also Ásgeir Blöndal Magnússon (*Íslensk orðsifjabók*, 430), who draws attention to the personal names Erpr and Irpa in Old Norse-Icelandic.

15. It is difficult to assess the precise hue(s) to which *jarpr* refers and to determine if it should be regarded as a color term. "Dark" would seem a reasonable candidate in the earliest compositions, for it appears that it was not until the late Middle Ages, when *brúnn* came to designate a more general brown hue (or black or dark brown when used about horses) rather than the reddish-brown hue suggested by the earliest occurrences, that *jarpr* began to attach itself more firmly to the brown spectrum and assumed a specific sense of reddish brown to fill the gap left by *brúnn*. This is evident from one of the occurrences listed by the *Orðabók Háskóla Íslands*: "ýmist er hesturinn einlitur, t. d. grár með ýmsum tilbrigðum, rauður, jarpur (rauðbrúnn)."

16. According to de Vries (*Altnordisches etymologisches Wörterbuch*, 449) it is a variant of *rauðr*. It is related to Old English *réod*.

saturation.[17] *Fǫlr* (LP: "bleg, hvidlig"; ONS: "bleg, gulbleg, graableg"; CV: "pale") is found in both poetry and prose, but, like *ámr*, it does not signify color but high lightness or low saturation.[18] *Bleikr* (LP: "bleg, hvid"; ONS: "bleg, hvid, lysgul"; CV: "pale, wan . . . fawn-coloured . . . auburn"), which also appears in both poetry and prose, is problematic.[19] As is evident from the definitions, the adjective denotes different hues according to its context. According to ONP, *bleikr* appears most frequently in the meaning "bleg (ɔ: med mindre intens farve end den naturlige, ?bleget), / pale (ɔ: of weak or reduced colour), wan, ?bleached," as in, for example, "gevr hon [sólin] af ser litit lios oc bendir firir með bleikum lit margs mannz feigð" (*Alexanders saga* 70.33) and "stundum var hann raudr sem blod en stundum bleikr sem bast edr blarr sem hel edr fólr sem nárr suo at ymsir þesser litir færduzst j hann suo bra honum vid" (*Flateyjarbók* 2:136.35). However, the term is also commonly used in the meaning "blond, lys / blond, fair, light-coloured" (translation offered by ONP), as in, for example, "Alexannder son Priami var huitr ahaurunnd hær madr herdimikill. sterkr oc storradr harid bleikt oc bla augun" (*Trójumanna saga* 66.12) and "Fǫgr er hlíðin, svá at mér hefir hon aldri jafnfǫgr sýnzk, bleikir akrar ok slegin tún" (*Njáls saga* 182.21). When used to describe the color of horses and cows, the term means, according to ONP, "lys, ?lys gråbrun, ?bleggul, ?skimlet (- fr. vair) / light-coloured, ?fawn, ?pale yellow dappled (- fr. vair)"; examples of the term being used to describe farm animals include "Því næst riðu fram or konungs fylking Riker ok Marant, annarr á bleikum hesti en annarr á grám" (*Karlamagnúss saga* 302.39) and "ek sá hér upp rísa at Hofi uxa bleikan" (*Vápnfirðinga saga* 48.18). For the suggestion in ONP that in *Stjórn* (161.5, 8) the term means "?(lys) rød / ?(light) red," see my article on "Esau's Pottage of Lentils."[20]

---

17. de Vries (ibid., 8) translates *ámr* as "rostrot, dunkel"; both he and Ásgeir Blöndal Magnússon (*Íslensk orðsifjabók*, 116) believe it is related to Old English *ōm* (rust). The latter is of the opinion that the original meaning of the word is rustbrown. He draws attention also to the names Ámr, Ámsvartnir, and Ámgerðir in Old Norse-Icelandic.

18. The Germanic form of *fǫlr* is **falwaz*. It is related to Old English *fealu*, Old Saxon *falu*, and Old High German *falo* (ibid., 150).

19. *Bleikr* is related to Old English *blāc*, Old Saxon *blēk*, and Old High German *bleih* (shining, light, pale, wan) (ibid., 43).

20. 254–57 (see note 1 above). The occurrences listed by *Orðabók Háskóla Íslands* indicate that it was not until the first half of the 20th century or maybe even the mid-20th century that the term appears in the meaning pink and that it continued to denote also pale until the late 20th century, though it is, of course, important to bear in mind that

Given its range, it is probable that *bleikr* should be considered a macrocolor or composite color covering, at least partly, a category of pale or light colors.[21]

2.2 Color terms with the prefix *døkk-* and the suffix *-døkkr.*

Døkkr, which is derived from Germanic **dankwia* and means "dark,"[22] is a tonal color word and unspecific as to hue. It appears as a prefix to five color terms and a suffix to one color term. Common to these terms is that they appear only in prose.

Døkkblár (ONS: "mørkeblaa"; CV: "dark blue"; ONP: "mørkeblå, mørk blåsort, ?sort [cf. blár adj. / dark blue, blue-black, ?black"]) describes a tunic ("kyrtill": *Sturlunga saga* 1, 518.13), the design of a dragon (*dreki*) on a shield (*Bragða-Mágus saga* 98.11), a mark (*mark*) on weapons (*Þiðriks saga* 1:338.7), and the color of a shield ("skjǫldr": *Þiðriks saga* 1:338.12).[23]

Døkkbrúnaðr/døkkbrúnn (ONS: "mørkbrun"; CV: "dark brown"; ONP: "mørkebrun [cf. brúnaðr adj.] / dark brown") is attested four times and describes a shield ("skjǫldr": *Vǫlsunga saga* 55.15), a dragon (*dreki*) on a shield (*Þiðriks saga* 1:346.15), and a tunic ("kyrtill": *Biskupa sögur* 2:55.28 and var).

Døkkgrœnn (ONS: "mørkgrøn"; CV: "dark green"; ONP: "mørk blågrøn / cerulean [ɔ: dark blue-green"]) is found once, in *Stjórn* (62.26), and describes one of the colors of the rainbow (*regnbogi*). The Latin gloss (*Speculum historiale*) is "cæruleum."

Døkkjarpr (ONS: "mørkbrun"; CV: "dark auburn"; ONP: "[om hår]

---

writers often have a tendency to archaize. Certainly in the spoken language, it seems that the adjective is no longer used in the meaning pale, but it continues to be used to describe the color of horses and cows.

21. Biggam defines a macrocolor as follows: "Not every language has a single colour lexeme per colour category, that is, a word such as N[ew] E[nglish] *green* for the green category. To Modern English speakers, red, orange, brown and purple are separate categories with separate lexemes denoting them, but speakers of other languages, although perfectly capable of seeing these four colours, may denote them with a single lexeme. Such a colour concept is a macrocolour." *Blue in Old English: An Interdisciplinary Semantic Study* (Amsterdam: Rodopi, 1997), 181. See also Biggam, *Semantics of Colour*, 61–62. I have suggested that "a . . . reason for the absence of *gulr* in the earliest Old Norse-Icelandic literary works is possibly the existence of *bleikr*, which, along with derivatives of *gull*, may have rendered *gulr* unnecessary" (Wolf, "Towards a Diachronic Analysis," 123).

22. de Vries, *Altnordisches etymologisches Wörterbuch*, 92.

23. For a discussion of *blár*, see Wolf, "Blue in Old Norse-Icelandic Literature."

mørkebrun, mørk kastanjebrun / [of hair] dark brown, deep chest-
nut-coloured") is attested twice, and in both instances the referent
is human hair ("hár": *Laxdœla saga* 234.15; "lokkar": *Alfrœði
íslenzk* 3:98.28).

Døkkrauðr (ONS: mørkrød"; CV: "dark red"; ONP: "mørkerød /
dark red") is used to decribe the color of a bear (*bjǫrn*) on a shield
(*Þiðriks saga* 1:339.12), the edge (*rǫnd*) of a shield (*Þiðriks saga*
1:339.13/26), and a stone ("steinn": *Sigurðar saga þǫgla* 191.19).
Rauðdøkkr is attested once, and the referent is the edge (*rǫnd*) of a
shield: "hefer hann skiolld ok vmm vtan rønd daukkrauda [var.
ʀaud døck]" (*Þiðriks saga* 1:339.25).

2.3 Color terms with the prefix *fagr-*.

While the etymology of *fagr* has been debated, it is agreed that it
means "beautiful," "bright," or "shining."[24] The adjective is therefore unspecific as to hue and refers to brightness or saturation.

Fagrgrœnn (ONS: "af en smuk grøn Farve"; CV: "light-green") is
attested twice. The referents are a tree stem ("leggr": *Heimskringla*
1:93.13; cf. "fagr ok grœnn" 1:162.9) and a field ("vǫllr": *Sǫgur
Danakonunga* 216.7).

Fagrrauðr (LP: "lyserød"; ONS: "af en smuk rød Farve"; CV:
"light-red") is found once in poetry, in *Vǫluspá*, about a cock
(*hani*).[25] It is attested three times in prose. Once the referent is
a horse ("hestr": *Blómstrvallasaga* 57.9), and twice it is a shield
("skjǫldr": *Þiðriks saga* 1:346.15; *Vǫlsunga saga* 55.16).

---

24. Biggam refers to the *Oxford English Dictionary*, which presents nine major
senses in which "bright" is used in modern English; she argues that two of the nine are
relevant to color studies: "1. Shining; emitting, reflecting, or pervaded by much light.
a. said of luminaries. b. of polished metals, precious stones, and other objects whose
surfaces naturally reflect light. c. of illuminated surfaces, of the day in sunshine, etc. d. of
transparent substances: Clear, translucent . . . 4.a. Of vivid brilliant color: used also with
names of color, as *bright red*." "The Ambiguity of *Brightness* (with Special Reference to
Old English) and a New Model for Color Description in Semantics," in *Anthropology of
Color: Interdisciplinary Multilevel Modeling*, ed. Robert E. MacLaury et al. (Amsterdam:
John Benjamins, 2007), 172. In her 2012 study, she does not use the terms "bright" or
"brighness," but instead "vivid" and "vividness" or the phrases "fully saturated" and
"full saturation" (*Semantics of Colour*, 5). Number 4.a above is relevant as far as *fagrgrœnn* and *fagrrauðr* are concerned.

25. "gólum um hánom í gaglviði / fagrrauðr hani, sá er Fialarr heitir" (st. 42).

2.4 Color terms with the prefix *glit-* and *heið-*.

Glit, which is related to Old High German *gliz* or *glīz*, meaning "glitter," and *heiðr*, a cognate of Old English *hādur*, Old Saxon *heder*, and Old High German *heitar*, meaning "bright" or "clear," are unspecific as to hue and refer to brightness or reflectivity.[26] This category comprises *glitrauðr* and *heiðblár*.[27] The former describes eyes ("augu": *Hjálmþérs saga* 491.12). The latter describes a sapphire: "hann [saffirus] er litr sem heidblár himin" (*Alfræði íslenzk* 1:77.13).[28]

2.5 Color terms with the prefix *ljós-* and the suffix *-ljóss*.

Ljóss, which is derived from Germanic **leuhsa* and means "light,"[29] is a tonal color word and unspecific as to hue. It appears as a prefix to seven color terms and a suffix to one color term.

Ljósblár (ONS: "lyseblaa"; CV: "light blue") is found only in Norwegian sources, and in all three instances the referent is cloth or clothing: *dýki* (DN 2:189.16), *kaprún* (DN 10:15.15), and *undirstakkr* (DN 4:423.14).

Ljósbleikr (ONS: "lysegul"; CV: "pale, fawn-coloured") is attested twice and describes the color of a horse ("hestr": *Grettis saga* 109.12, 221.3; *Sturlunga saga* 2:260.34).

Ljósbrúnleitr is attested once and used about human complexion: "Jacobus . . . [var] vndarliga biartleitr [var. medallagi lios brunleitr]" (*Maríu saga* 867.10–11).

Ljósgrœnn is attested once, and the referent is a topaz: "Hann [Topacius] hefir 2 myndir, 1 er rauda gulli likr, enn annar er skiri ok er sa liosgrenn" (*Alfræði íslenzk* 1:80.8).[30]

---

26. de Vries, *Altnordisches etymologisches Wörterbuch*, 174; Ásgeir Blöndal Magnússon, *Íslensk orðsifjabók*, 314.

27. See note 24 above, where 1-b is particularly relevant.

28. The sapphire is described as "any pure, transparent, gem-quality corundum other than ruby, specially the blue color variety of corundum. Blue color being due to traces of oxides of cobalt, chromium, and titanium. Sapphire color ranges from light-blue, to dark velvety blue (shades of blue)." Mohsen Manutchehr-Danai, *Dictionary of Gems and Gemology* (Berlin: Springer, 2000), 413.

29. Ásgeir Blöndal Magnússon, *Íslensk orðsifjabók*, 569.

30. Concerning the color of the topaz, D. B. Hoover points out that "prior to the tenth century the name 'topaz' in the Western world was generally restricted to describing a

Ljósgulr (LP: "lysegul") is attested once, in a verse in *Hjálmþérs saga*, and the referent is a *lokka frón* (a kenning for a head [of human hair]).[31]

Ljósjarpr (ONS: "lysebrun"; CV: "light chestnut") is common, and in all instances the referent is human hair. Examples include "Helgi var . . . lios-iarpur a har" (*Fljótsdœla hin meiri* 31.20) and "Þordr var . . . lios-iarpr á hær" (*Sturlunga saga* 1:434.9).

Ljósrauðr (ONS+: "lyserød"; CV: "light red") is attested once, and the referent is the fur (*hamr*) of a dog: "sýndist hann [hundrinn] . . . stundum sem hann væri með myrkbrúnum lit, ok þegar, sem hann sé í ljósrauðum ham" (*Saga af Tristram ok Ísönd* 130.23).

Rauðljóss (LP: "lyserød") is attested once, in Hallvarðr háreksblesi's *Knútsdrápa*, and the referent is *baugjǫrð* (a *heiti* for a shield).[32]

2.6 Color terms with the prefix *myrk-*.

Myrkr, which is derived from Germanic **merkwia* and means "dark,"[33] is also a tonal color word and unspecific as to hue. It appears as a prefix to three color terms.

Myrkblár (LP: "'mörksort,' kulsort"; ONS: mørkblaa") is attested once in poetry, in a *lausavísa* by Sigvatr Þórðarson, and the referent is *meiðir drasils tjalda* (a kenning for a warrior).[34] In prose, the term is used primarily about clothing, the referents being *kyrtill* (DN 3:95.12; DN 4:423.12; *Sagan och rimorna om Friðþjófr* 31.11), *dýki* (DN 2:189.16), *kápa* (*Biskupa sögur*

---

green stone which most authorities identify as peridot (olivine) . . . . However, by the eleventh century . . . it has a golden color. From this date onwards topaz is more often described as golden or yellow . . . . It seems most probable that this change in the colour description of the topaz is due to a translation or copying error, rather than the result of empirical evidence. One wonders what confusion this might have caused among gem merchants of the world, but, unfortunately, no texts exist to shed light on this. This must be the period during which the name 'topaz' began to be associated with the mineral we know today." *Topaz* (Oxford: Butterworth Heinemann, 1992), 13.

31. "Hver ert þú / hýrlund með kinn fagra / ok ljósgult lokka frón?" (1.3; *Skjaldedigtning* 2:358).

32. "Rauðljósa sér ræsir / (rít brestr sundr en hvíta) / baugjǫrð brodda ferðar / (bjúgrend i tvau fljúga" (5.1; *Skjaldedigtning* 1:294).

33. de Vries, *Altnordisches etymologisches Wörterbuch*, 398.

34. "Hlýð mínum brag, meiðir / myrkblás, þvít kank yrkja, / alltíginn—mátt eiga / eitt skald—drasils tjalda" (2.2; *Skjaldedigtning* 1:246).

2:108.30, 168.24; *Diplomatarium Islandicum* [henceforth DI] 2:691.29), and *olpa* (*Ectors saga* 124.9). In three instances, the adjective describes the color of a stone: "er hann [ADamantes] eigi sva skiR at hann lati iarðlit ok er hann því myrkblar" (*Hauksbók* 228.1); "Adamantis . . . er eigi sva skiR, ath hann lati iarligt ok er þi myrkblar" (*Alfræði íslenzk* 1:82.3);[35] "Konradr tok þa þann steinn [ametistus] er hann stak fyr or bordskutlínum hann var myrkblár ath lítt" (*Konráðs saga keisarasonar* 165.12).[36] Once the term is used about the color of a shield ("skjǫldr": *Eyrbyggja saga* 32.29). *Myrkbrúnn* (ONS+: "mørkebrun"; CV+: "dark brown") is attested three times. Twice the referent is a tunic ("kyrtill": *Clarus saga* 7.24, 21.29–30), and once it is the fur (*hamr*) of a dog (*Saga af Tristram ok Ísönd* 130.22).

Myrkgrár is attested once and describes a calf (*kvíga*): "Þetta haust var Andríði vant kvígu þrévetrar myrkrar [var. myrkgraarar: AM 560 c 4°; myrkgrär: AM 164 h fol.] (*Kjalnesinga saga* 5.11).

2.7. Color terms with the prefix *lit-* and the suffixes *-leitr*, *-litaðr*, and *-litr*.[37]

Litr is derived from Germanic **ulitu-z* and related to Middle English *lit*, Gothic *wlits*, Old Saxon *wliti*, and Old English *wlite*.[38] Its primary meaning is "color"; secondary meanings include

---

35. Adamant is a synonym of diamond and coronium. The word is derived from Greek "invincible" and is an old name for a hard stone.

36. The amethyst is described as being "a pale violet to purple or violet, transparent variety of quartz, the color being due to presence of Fe^{+2} or Fe^{+3} and traces of manganese, owing to irregular color zoning" (Manutchehr-Danai, *Dictionary of Gems*, 16). See also Biggam: "The hues involved are red-purple and violet" (*Semantics of Colour*, 134).

37. There is one term consisting of a noun + *-litr*, another consisting of an adjective + *-leitr* and a third consisting of an adjective + *litaðr*. The first is *dǫgglitr* (LP: "duggfarvet, dugget"; ONS: "dugfarvet"; CV: "dew-besprinkled"), which is attested once, in *Helga-kviða Hundingsbana II*, and describes Odin's hawks (*haukar*). Here *litr* seems to reflect the secondary meaning, as suggested in LP and CV, which disqualifies the adjective as a color term. The second is *fǫlleitr* (ONS: "bleg af Ansigtsfarve"; CV: "looking pale"), which is attested ten times (*Njáls saga* 70.14, 298.21, 301.6; *Byskupa sǫgur* 307.21; *Flateyjarbók* 1:545.31; *Heilagra manna sǫgur* 2:641.29; *Jómsvikinga saga* 67.2; *Mágus saga* 2.65; *Óláfs saga Tryggvasonar en mesta* 1:172.26; *Sturlunga saga* 2:125.16; *Vápnfirðinga saga* 63,15). In all instances, the referent is human complexion. The third is *fǫllitaðr* (ONS: "bleg af Farve"; CV: "pale"), which is attested five times (*Njáls saga* 302.1; *Byskupa sǫgur* 378.9; *Rómveriasaga* 82.29; *Þiðriks saga* 1:340.14–15). In all instances the referent is human complexion.

38. de Vries, *Altnordisches etymologisches Wörterbuch*, 359.

"appearance," "character," "gloss," and "beauty." The suffix *-leitr* is derived from the verb *líta*, meaning to "look," "behold," "see."[39] In terms of meaning, the color terms seem not to differ from their monolexemic parallels and should perhaps be regarded as basic color terms, although their semantic range differs somewhat.[40]

Bláleitr (LP: "med blåsort ansigt"; ONS: "blaa eller sort af Ansigts-farve"; CV: "blue-faced"; ONP: "[om person] mørk, blå/sort at se på / [of a person] dark, blue/black in appearance") is found once in poetry, in Einarr Gilsson's *drápa* about Guðmundr Arason, and the referent is a woman (*brúðr*).[41] In prose, it is attested three times and describes human facial color (*Islendzk æventyri* 283.19; *Karlamagnúss saga* 54.33; *Sigurðar saga þǫgla* 108.6).

For *ljósbrúnleitr*, see section 2.5 above.

Hvítleitr is attested twice; in both instances the referent is the amethyst: "Amatistus . . . er hvit-leitr, sem vin se dreypt i vatn" (*Alfræði íslenzk* 1:81.2), "Ematistvs . . . er ok hvitleitr sem vindreyp með vatni" (*Hauksbók* 227.1).[42]

Jarplitaðr (LP: "brunfarvet, rødbrun") is found once, in Einarr Skúla-son's *Geisli*, and describes the color of an eagle (*ǫrn*).[43]

Litrauðr (LP: "rød af farve") is found once, in Einarr Skúlason's *Geisli*, and describes the color of gold (*blik unnar*) in a kenning for king.[44]

Rauðleitr (ONS: "rødmusset, rødlig i Ansigtet eller Kinderne"; CV: "ruddy") is attested eight times and used exclusively about human complexion (*Jóns saga leikara* [AM 588 f 4° 3ʳ]; *Laxdœla saga* 235.19; *Leifar* 90.25; *Mágus saga* 7.59; *Maríu saga* 253.31; *Tróju-manna saga* 66.20, 67.18; *Þiðriks saga* 1:334.30).

Rauðlitaðr (ONS: "farvet rød"; CV: "red-coloured, dyed red") is found only in prose. In most instances, it is used about human complexion (*Alfræði íslenzk* 3:98.3; *Fljótsdœla hin meiri* 31.20; *Sturlunga saga* 1:518.13); where there is a referent, it is human

---

39. Ásgeir Blöndal Magnússon, *Íslensk orðsifjabók*, 554.

40. See Brückmann, *Altwestnordische Farbsemantik*, and Wolf, "Some Comments."

41. "aptr kom brúðr til beiðis / bláleit ok dauð hneitis" (21.8; *Skjaldedigtning* 2:424).

42. See note 36 above.

43. "Lét (japrlitaðs) ǫtu / (arnar jóðs) enn góði / (munn rauð malmþings kennir) / Magnús hugin fanga" (29.1; *Skjaldedigtning* 1:434).

44. "Ǫld hefr opt enn mildi / unnar bliks frá miklum / (Krists mærik lim) leysta / litrauðs konungr nauðum (33.4; *Skjaldedigtning* 1:435).

flesh and body parts: "augu" (*Eirspennill* 437.25), "kinnr" (*Reyk-jahólabók* 2:152.26), "líkami" (*Stjórn* 161.7), and "skinn" *(Flóres saga konungs* 132.13). Twice the referent is hair ("hár": *Flóres saga konungs* 132.13; *Saga Óláfs Tryggvasonar* 173.25), twice it is blood ("blóð": *Karlamagnúss saga* 505.25; *Þiðriks saga* 1:25.9), and once it is the branches ("greinar") of a balsam tree (*Old Icelandic Medical Miscellany* 61.6).

Svartleitr (LP: "sort af udseende"; ONS: "mørk af Ansigtsfarve"; CV: "swarthy") appears twice in poety, in a verse by Jórunn skáldmær, where the referent is a verse (*bragr*),[45] and in a verse in *Hjálþérs saga*, where it is a man (*seggr*),[46] In prose, it is attested once, in *Gríms saga loðinkinna*, where it is used about the complexion of a woman (149.17).

2.8 Compounds of two color terms.

A problem with these mixed colors or one color plus an achromatic (as in *gráblár* and *svartjarpr*) is that it is often difficult to ascertain the balance of their elements (though in the case of achromatic terms, *hvítr*, *grár*, and *svartr*, they would seem to represent degrees of saturation from "pale" to "medium" to "dark" along with the color name).[47] Should *rauðblár* be defined as "reddish-blue" (blue being dominant) "red-blue" (neither being dominant), "bluish red" (red being dominant) or "purple"? And should *rauðgulr* be described as "reddish-yellow" (yellow being dominant), "yellow-red" (neither being dominant), "yellowish-red" (red being dominant), or "orange"? Only the referents can provide possible answers.

Blábrúnaðr (ONS: "blaabrun"; CV: "dark blue coloured"; ONP: "?farvet sortbrun / ?coloured blackish-brown") is attested once. The referent is a female tunic ("kvenkyrtill"; *Guðmundar saga A*, 175.8).[48]

---

45. "Haralds frák Halfdan spyrja / herðibrogð, en logðis / sýnisk svartleitr reyni / sjá bragr, ens hárfagra" (2.3; *Skjaldedigtning* 1:53).

46. "Hjálmþér, ek heiti; / hverr spyrr at því, / seggr enn svartleiti, á sædýri" (2.3; *Skjaldedigtning* 2:354).

47. See Biggam, *Semantic of Colour*, 123.

48. Interestingly, the same tunic is referred to in the B-redaction of *Hrafns saga Svein-bjarnarsonar*, where it is described as being "brúnaðr" (56.21–22).

Bláhvítr (LP: "sort-hvid, vistnok hvid med sorte striber"; CV: "white-blue") appears in poetry only, in *Guðrúnarhvǫt* ("bœcr . . . inar bláhvíto," st. 4) and *Hamðismál* ("Bœcr . . . inar bláhvíto," st. 7). Hollander, Terry, and Larrington translate *bláhvítr* as "bluish-white," "blue-white," and "blue and white," respectively;[49] the last-mentioned translation would render *bláhvítr* ineligible as a color term.

Blásvartr (LP: "blåsort, sort"), too, is found only in poetry, in *Helgakviða Hundingsbana I*, where the referent is *brimdýr* (a *heiti* for a ship),[50] in Þórarinn stuttfeldr's *Stuttfeldardrápa*, where it is *byrvargar* (a *heiti* for ships),[51] and in a *lausavísa* by Einarr Skúlason, where it is *Muninn* (a *heiti* for a raven).[52]

Brúnrauðr (ONP: "rødbrun / reddish brown") is attested twice. The referents are a stone ("steinn": Veturliði Óskarsson 22.17) and a small implement for carving or cutting ("krít": Veturliði Óskarsson 22.30).

Gráblár (ONS: "graablaa") is attested once, and the referent is a frock ("hekla": *Laxdœla saga* 234.14 var).

Gulbrúnn is attested once, and the referent is eye-brows (*brýnn*: AM 764 4° 17ᵛ).

Gulgrár (CV: "yellow-gray"), too, is attested only once, and the referent is a tunic ("kyrtill": *Laxdœla saga* 233.13 var. [AM 123 fol. 38]).

Gulgrœnn (ONS: "gulgrøn"; CV: "yellow-green.") is attested twice, in *Laxdœla saga* (233.13), where the referent is a tunic (*kyrtill*), and in *Jarlmanns saga* (26.32 var. [AM 167 fol. 53ᵛ]) where it is the sea (*sjór*).

Hvítjarpr (LP: "lyse-rødbrun"; CV: "white-brown, blond") is found once, in a *lausavísa* by Magnús berfœttr, and the referent is *svanni* (woman).[53]

---

49. Lee M. Hollander, trans., *The Poetic Edda* (Austin: University of Texas Press, 1962), 312, 317; Patricia Terry, trans., *Poems of the Vikings* (Indianapolis: Bobbs-Merrill, 1969), 233, 238; Carolyne Larrington, trans., *The Poetic Edda* (Oxford: Oxford University Press, 1996), 235, 239.

50. "liggia hér í grindom fyr Gnipalundi / brimdýr blásvort oc búin gulli" (st. 50).

51. "Bað gramr guma / gunnhagr draga / byrvarga á bjarg / blásvarta tvá" (4.4; *Skjaldedigtning* 1:462).

52. "En við hjaldr, þars hǫlðar, / hugþrútit svellr, lúta, / (Muninn drekkr blóð ór benjum / blásvartr) konungs hjarta" (7.4; *Skjaldedigtning* 1:452).

53. "sá kennir mér svanni, / sin lǫnd es verr rǫndu / (sverð bitu Hǫgna hurðir) / hvítjarpr sofa lítit" (3.8; *Skjaldedigtning* 1:402).

Rauðblár (ONS+: "rødblå") is attested once and describes the color of an amethyst: "Amatista heitir eirnn ærligur steirnn. ok hefir ʀaudblann lit suo sem uiole eda ʀosa. enn sumir hafa bleikan lit" (*Old Icelandic Medical Miscellany* 110.7).[54]
Rauðbleikr (ONS: "lysrød"; CV: "reddish") is attested four times.[55] Twice the referent is human hair ("hár": *Eyrbyggja saga* 21.5; *Stjórn* 460.11—here a translation of "rufus"; "skegg": *Þiðriks saga* 1:336.3), and twice it is a gem stone. One is a sardonyx: "æ ofan-verdum hvitleikanum þickir hann raudbleikr, ok ero þo allir litir samblandnir" (*Alfræði íslenzk* 1:79.6).[56] The other is a jacinth, and here one particular kind, the "garnatus" is described: "sa er raudbleikr ok fafundare" (*Alfræði íslenzk* 1:80.18).[57]
Rauðbrúnn (LP: "rødbrun"; ONS: "rødbrunfarvet"/"rødbrun"; CV: "red-brown") / *rauðbrúnaðr* (ONS: "rødbrunfarvet"; CV: "red-brown, dark-red, reddish") is found once in poetry, in Sigvatr Þórðarson's *Erfidrápa Óláfs helga*, where the referent is a sword (*hjǫrr*).[58] In prose, the referents are cloth ("blíaz": *Elis saga ok Rosamundu* 53.10; "klæði": *Sturlunga saga* 1:151.8 and var.), a tunic ("kyrtill": *Biskupa sögur* 2:55.17, *Eirspennill* 235.13; *Laxdœla saga* 242.7), and blood ("blóð": *Hauksbók* 181.18).
Rauðgrœnn (ONS: "rødgrøn"; CV: "reddish green") is attested once, in *Flóvents saga*, and describes the color of a mantle (*mǫttull*).[59] According to Ashlee C. Bailey, red-green and blue-yellow color terms should not exist, since such terms would confuse or fail to distinguish opponent colors.[60]

---

54. See note 36.

55. Susanne M. Arthur argues that all the referents "may be perceived as orange-colored." "Are Oranges Yellow? *Appelsínugulur* as a Basic Color Term in Icelandic," *Orð og tunga* 15 (2013): 28.

56. The sardonyx is "a gem variety of reddish-brown colored sand with white or black banded chalcedony or onyx used to make cameo with the raised black, red or brown background" (Manutchehr-Danai, *Dictionary of Gems*, 415).

57. The jacinth is "a term applied to a transparent yellow to reddish-brown variety of zircon" (ibid., 260).

58. "auk, at ísarnleiki, / Innþrœndum lét finnask, / rœkinn, gramr í reikar / rauðbrúnan hjǫr túnum" (14.8; *Skjaldedigtning* 1:242).

59. "skiɴ þav voro vndir, er engi maðr vissi hvaþan af voru; þav voro gvll savmvt; en þat etlvðv menn hellzt, at þat vęri af sialldsenvm fvglvm, ok sva atagz sem skiɴ. Þaı voro bla ok brѵ́n, raıðgren ok með alllzkyns litvm" (142.33).

60. "The theory [of color opponency] is based on the idea that there are four unique hues: red, green, yellow, and blue. These form opponent pairs, with red and green being one pair and yellow and blue the other pair. When we perceive one of the pure hues in

404 New Norse Studies

Rauðgulr (ONS: "rødgul"; CV: "yellow-red, orange") is used about human hair ("hár": *Karlamagnúss saga* 113.19; *Sturlunga saga* 2:125.20) and cloth (*pallklæði*): "eitt pallklæde raudgult" (DN 3:148.23).[61]

Svartblár (ONS+: "mørkeblaa"; CV: "dark blue") is attested twice and describes a rare-earth magnet: "Magnes . . . er svartblar, hann dregr iarn" (*Alfræði íslenzk* 1:81.17) and "Magnetis heitir sa steinn er finnr a India landi sv þioð er Trogodi heitir, hann er svartblar (*Hauksbók* 227.16).[62]

Svartbrúnaðr (ONS: "farvet sortbrunt"; CV: "dyed black-brown") is attested once and describes the color of fabric (*klæði*): ".ix. aalnar af swartbrunadu klæde" (DN 1:195.24).

Svartjarpr (ONS: "mørkebrun"; CV: "dark-brown") is attested twice (*Byskupa sǫgur* 307.19; *Laxdœla saga* 235.19) and describes the color of human hair (*hár*).

2.9 Compounds of a noun and a color term.

Biksvartr (ONS: "begsort, sort som Beg"; CV: "black as pitch"; ONP: "begsort / pitch-black") is attested once, and the referent is water (*vatn*): "Vatn er þar sialldfengit, en biksvart ok beiskt bæde þat er

---

a particular region of the visual field—say, pure green—we cannot perceive the other in the same area, in this case pure red. The same holds true for blue and yellow. All other colors are mixtures of these four. Thus, if 75% of the chromatic response received by the retina in a given area were green and 25% were yellow, the resulting color would be a yellowish-green. However, there can be no reddish-green or bluish-yellow because the same neural mechanism signals red in one state and green in the other (or yellow in one state and blue in the other), thereby not allowing for mixtures of members of each opponent pair . . . It is impossible for blue to overlap with yellow to create a 'blellow' or for red and green to combine to create a 'gred.'" "On the Non-existence of Blue-Yellow and Red-Green Color Terms," *Studies in Language* 25 (2001): 187.

61. Arthur argues that "the most frequently used term for the color orange in Icelandic (besides the now prevalent term *appelsínugulur*) is *rauðgulur* 'red-yellow,' which appears three times in *ONP* and fifty-three times in *ROH* [*Ritmálasafn Orðabókar Háskólans*] . . . . As with *rauðbleikr*, these instances describe objects that can be conceived of as orange-colored" ("Are Oranges Yellow?" 128).

62. This is presumably magnetite. Its color and transparency are described as "black" and "opaque," respectively, and its lustre is defined as being "metallic, shining; to submetallic, dull." It has a strong metallic character and has "by reason of its strongly magnetic properties . . . attracted attention since early times." W. R. Hamilton, A. R. Woolley, and A. C. Bishop, *A Guide to Minerals, Rocks and Fossils* (London: Hamlyn Publishing, 1970), 40.

fæz" (*Heilagra manna søgur* 2:471.8); it translates the Latin "quasi bituminea."

Bleikhárr (ONS: "hvidhaaret, lyshaaret"; CV: "auburn"; ONP: "lyshåret, blond / fair-haired, blond") is attested six times (*Heimskringla* 3:220.1, 286.16; *Hulda* 99.16, 185.4; *Trójumanna saga* 69.23; *Þiðriks saga* 2:336.2), and in all instances the referent is human hair.

Blikhvítr (LP: "lysende, hvid, lyst glattet"; ONS: "blinkende, lysende hvit"; CV: "white-gleaming") appears once in a verse in *Hervarar-saga*, and the referent is *lind* (a *heiti* for a shield).[63]

Blóðrauðr (ONS: "rød af eller som Blod"; CV: "blood-red"; ONP: "rød pga. blod, rød som blod / red on account of blood, blood-red") is attested nine times:

Classification	Referent	Number of examples
Animals	*hundr*	1 (*Saga af Tristram ok Ísönd* 130.31)
	gangari	1 (*Flóres saga ok Blankiflúr* 29.9—here translating "rouges")
Cloth	*dúkr*	1 (*Maríu saga* 872.14—here a cloth stained with wine)
	silkiklæði	1 (*Thomas saga erkibiskups* 458.38–459.1)
Hail (tears)	*hagl*	1 (*Vilhjálms saga sjóðs* AM 577 4° 41ʳ17)
Human complexion	—	2 (*Alexanders saga* 3.27; *Valvers þáttr* 388.3)

In two instances, it is used in an abstract meaning: "man olafr lata hring bloðrauðan vm hals þer ef þu kemr til hans . . . hann man lata af höfða þik (*Óláfs saga Tryggvasonar* 1:236.14) and "mun Óláfr láta hring blóðrauðan um háls þer, ef þú finnr hann" (*Heimskringla* 1:354.6).

Blóðroðinn (LP: "'blod-farvet,' blodig"; ONS+: "farget rød av blod"; CV: "blood-stained"; ONP: "farvet rød af blod / red with blood") is found three times in poetry, in Þjóðólfr Arnórsson's *Magnúsflokkr*, where the referent is shields (*skildir*),[64] in Ívarr Ingimundarson's

---

63. "Bresta mun bróðir / en blikhvíta lind" (10.2; *Skjaldedigtning* 2:272).

64. "Spurði einu orði / (ǫld blóðroðna skjǫldu) / satt's at mǫrg (átti) / Selunds mær hverr vé bæri" (17.2; *Skjaldedigtning* 1:336).

Sigurðarbǫlkr, where it is shafts (*skǫpt*),[65] and in Rǫgnvaldr jarl
and Hallr Þórarinsson's *Háttalykill*, where it is swords (*benja
rœði*).[66] In prose it is attested once, and the referent is the cross
(*kross*) of Jesus Christ (*Íslenzk æventýri* 1:150.15). It is questionable
whether the adjective should be considered a color term.

Blómhvítr (ONP: "hvid som en blost, blosterhvid / white as a flower")
is attested once, in *Karlamagnúss saga* (332.39), and the referent
is a horse (*hestr*).

Bráhvítr (LP: "med lyse öjenvipper"; ONS: "som har hvide Øien-
haar"; CV+: "white-browed) is found once, in *Vǫlundarkviða*, and
the referent is Bǫðvildr, a maiden (*mey*).[67]

Brandrauðr (LP: "ildrød") occurs once, in a verse in *Ragnars saga
loðbrókar*, and the referent is *baugr* (a ring).[68]

Brúnhvítr (LP: "med lyse öjenbryn"; ONS: "som har hvide Øjen-
bryn"; CV: "white-browed") is found once, in *Hymiskviða*, where
it describes a giantess: "Enn ǫnnur gecc, algullin, fram, / brúnhvít,
bera biórveig syni" (st. 8).

Dreyrrauðr (ONS: "blodrød"; CV: "blood-red"; ONP: "blodrød,
rød som blod [i ansigtet; af ophidselse, etc.] / blood-red, red
as blood [in the face; from agitation, etc.]") is found in prose
only: *Njáls saga* 39.20; *Egils saga* 37.3; *Flateyjarbók* 3:266.39;
Gibbons saga 44.14; *Heimskringla* 3:145.6; *Hulda* 210.12, 213.16;
Laxdœla saga 113.5; *Morkinskinna* 224.30; *Orkneyinga saga*
134.23; *Sagan ock rimorna om Friðþiófr* 31.22 and 57.4; and
Sturlunga saga 2:255.2–3. In all instances, it describes facial color
due to emotion.

Drifhvítr (LP: "hvid som sne"; ONS: "drivhvid, snehvid"; CV: "white
as driven snow"; ONP: "hvid som sammenføget sne / white as the
driven snow") appears in a verse in *Víglundar saga*, and the referent
is *dúkr* (cloth).[69] In prose it is attested four times:

65. "skarða skjǫldu / skǫpt blóðroðin, / veðrblásin vé / of vegǫndum" (34.6; *Skjaldedigtning* 1:473).

66. "vann blóðroðin benja / benflœðr skolat rœði, / sóknbára gat sára / sárvǫrm þvegit
árar" (33b6; *Skjaldedigtning* 1:504).

67. "bið þú Bǫðvldi, meyna bráhvíto" (st. 39).

68. "ilt er í borghhlið baugi / brandrauðum framm standa" (VI.1; *Skjaldedigtning*
2:257).

69. "strauk drifhvítum dúki / drós um hvarminn ljósa" (7.7; *Skjaldedigtning* 2:489).

Classification	Referent	Number of examples
Cloth and fabric	dúkr	2 (*Gibbons saga* 11.12; *Islendzk æventyri* 1:41.29)
	skrúðr	1 (*Karlamagnúss saga* 549.32)
Food	himnamjǫl	1 (*Postola sögur* 494.29)

Dumbbleikr (ONP: "?mat/grålig bleg / ?dull/greyish pale") is attested only once, and the referent is a chalcedony: "Calcedonius heiter eirn ærligr Stein hann hefur dumbleikann lit" (*Old Icelandic Medical Miscellany* 220.21).[70]

Fannhvítr (LP: "snehvid"; ONS: "snehvid"; CV: "white as driven snow") occurs once in poetry, in a *lausavísa* by Bjǫrn Breiðvíkingakappi, where it is used to describe the appearance of a woman (*fǫldu Fold*).[71] In prose, it is attested twice; the referents are human flesh ("hǫrund": *Bærings saga* 101.60) and horses ("hestar": *Stjórn* 206.8).

Fífilbleikr (ONS: "lysegul, med en Løvetand lignende Farve"; CV: "dandelion-yellow") is attested three times and describes the color of a horse ("hestr": *Víglundar saga* 77.6; "stoðhross": *Finnboga saga* 44.5; *Vápnfirðinga saga* 46.3).[72]

Físbleikr (ONS: "ɔ: fiskbleikr") is attested once: "Eigi vilda ek svá verða við blóðlátið físbleikr" (*Heimskringla* 3:416.19). *Eirspennill* has the variant *fullbleikr* (218.5) and Codex Frisianus has *fiskbleikr* (355.33).

Fiskbleikr (ONS: "hvid, bleg som Fisk"; CV: "pale as a fish") appears in Codex Frisianus (see above) and Hulda (300.21).

Fótgulr (LP: "'fod-gul,' med gule fødder") is attested once, in *Krákumál*, and the referent is an eagle (*fogl*).[73]

---

70. The chalcedony is "a translucent, crypto-crystalline variety of quartz. It is commonly microscopically fibrous, massive, and has a nearly wax-like luster, it has a lower density and is lower than ordinary quartz . . ., uniform tint, white, gray, pale-blue, brown, or black, many of the hues are known by a variety of names" (Manutchehr-Danai, *Dictionary of Gems*, 16).

71. "Þá mun þǫll en mjóva / Þórodds aðalbjóra / (Fold unni mér fǫldu) / fannhvít getu sanna" (3.4; *Skjaldedigtning* 1:125).

72. Cf. Wilhelm Heizmann, who translates the term as "hellgelb, löwenzahngelb." *Wörterbuch der Pflanzennamen im Altwestnordischen*, Ergänzungsbände zum Reallexikon der germanischen Altertumskunde 7 (Berlin: de Gruyter, 1993), 19.

73. "ok fótgulum fogli / fingum vér, þars sungu / við háseymða hjalma / hǫrð jǫrn, mikils verðar" (2.5; *Skjaldedigtning* 1:649).

Glóðrauðr (LP: "ildrød"; ONS: "glodrød, rød som en Glod"; CV: "red as embers") is found in poetry only, and the referent is gold or treasure (*goll, fé, eldr álfoldar*): "gull glóðrautt" (*Guðrunarkviða II*, st. 2); "gulli . . . glóðrauðo" (*Atlamál*, st. 13); "iþ/it glóðrauða fé" (*Fáfnismál*, st. 9 and 20); and "lýstiz hrein hæstum / hǫfn af skipstǫfnum / eldi álfoldar / auðar glóðrauðum" (Sturla Þórðarson's *Hrafnsmál*, st. 5.8; *Skjaldedigtning* 2:127).

Gollhvítr (LP: "lys som guld") appears once in poetry, in *Hárbarðsljóð*, and describes a woman (*mær*).[74]

Gollroðinn/gullroðinn (LP: "rød af guld"; ONS: "forgyldt"; CV: "gilt") is used in *Krákumal* about a spear (*geirr*) and in *Atlakviða* about helmets (*hjalmar*).[75] In prose, it is common, though it is questionable whether it should be considered a color term:

Classification	Referent	Number or examples:
Armor and weapons	*hjalmr*	22 (*Ágrip* 10.1; *Alexanders saga* 41.1; Codex Frisianus 577.33; *Egils saga* 159.19; *Fagrskinna* 327.3, 352.21; *Hálfdanar saga Eysteinssonar* 137.14; *Heimskringla* 1:211.5 and 441.2–3, 3:386.18; *Islendzk æventyri* 1:37.7; *Konráðs saga* 57.28; *Laxdœla saga* 67.14; *Morkinskinna* 455.21; *Óláfs saga Tryggvasonar en mesta* 1:42.8, 2:262.6; *Partalopa saga* 103.4; *Saga Óláfs konungs hins helga* 1:70.7; *Saga af Tristram ok Ísodd* 10.14; *Sǫgur Danakonunga* 136.23; *Þiðriks saga* 1:178.2; *Yngvars saga víðfǫrla* 6.10)
skjǫldr		1 (*Saga Óláfs Tryggvasonar* 225.17)

Grasgrœnn (ONS: "græsgrøn, grøn som Græs"; CV; "grass-green") is attested twice. The referents are foliage ("lauf": *Konungs skuggsjá* 9.15) and a helmet ("hjalmr": *Karlamagnúss saga* 311.8 var).[76]

---

74. "gladdac ina gullhvíto, gamni mær unði" (st. 30 var).

75. "Hǫ sverð bitu skjǫldu, / þás gollhroðinn glumði / geirr við Hildar nœfri" (21.3; *Skjaldedigtning* 1:654), "Scioldo knegoð þar velia oc scafna asca, / hiálma gullroðna oc Húna mengi" (st. 4).

76. The main text has "grœnn sem gras."

Hárarauðr (LP: "rødhåret"; ONS+: "rødhåret") is found in a verse in *Grettis saga*, and the referent is Grettir's head (*hǫfuð Grettis*).[77]

Helblár (CV: "black as death") is attested once, and the referent is (injured) bodies (*líkamir*): "þeirra lijkamer voru aller hudfletter og helblaaer" (*Dínus saga drambláta* 35.7).

Himinblár (CV: "sky-blue") is attested once, and the referent is a cloth (*klæði*): "eitt klædi . . . er himenn blatt var at lith" (*Reykjahólabók* 2:350.32).

Hrafnblár (LP: "ravnsort"; CV: "raven-black") is found in Bragi Boddason's *Ragnarsdrápa* and describes the appearance of Erpr's brothers, Sǫrli and Hamðir.[78]

Hrafnsvartr (LP: "ravnsort"; CV: "raven-black") is found in a verse in *Hjálmþers saga ok Ǫlvis*, and the referent is a man (*halr*).[79]

Hvarmrauðr (LP: "med røde öjelågs kanter"; CV: "with red eyelids") appears in a *lausavísa* by Kormákr Ǫgmundarson, and the referent is *frenju fœðir* (feeder of cows).[80]

Hǫrundshvítr is attested once and describes human complexion: "Leifur var hvitr [var. hórundz huijtur]" (*Skarðsárbók* 58.24).

Hǫrundsvartr, too, is attested once, and the referent is spirits (*andar*): "horundsuartir anndar stodu yfir henni" (AM 764 4° 22ʳ).

Ilbleikr (LP: "med bleg, d.v.s. gul, fod") is found in Einarr Skúlason's *Geisli*, and the referent is an eagle (*orri*).[81]

Indiblár (ONS+: "indigo") is attested once: "pund sinopur fyrir 6 aura, meniu fyri 2 aura ok brunt ok indiblatt, hvit fyri aura, gult 3 aurum" (*Alfrœði íslenzk* 3:74.6).

Járngrár (LP: "jærn-, stål-grå"; ONS+: "jerngrå; om naturlig farget ullstoff"; CV: "iron-gray") appears once in poetry, in Snorri Sturluson's *Háttatal*, and the referent is byrnies (*serkir*).[82] In prose, it is used about cloth ("klæði": DI

---

77. "Flutta ek upp ór eyju / ómett hǫfuð Grettis, / þann grætr nála nauma / nauðig hára-rauðan" (52.4; *Skjaldedigtning* 2:476).

78. "þás hrafnbláir hefnðu / harma Erps of barmar" (3.7; *Skjaldedigtning* 1:1).

79. "halr enn hrafnsvarti, / í hrævarskrúði" (2.7; *Skjaldedigtning* 2:363).

80. "Spurði frenju fœðir / fréttinn, hvé mér þœtti / (hann sýnisk mér heima / hvarmrauðr) ketilormar" (13.4; *Skjaldedigtning* 1:72).

81. "Hneitir frák at héti, hjaldrs at vápna galdri, / ǫðlings hjǫrr, þess 's orra / ilbleikum gaf steikar" (43.4; *Skjaldedigtning* 1:438).

82. "styrs rýðr stillir hersum / sterkr járngrá serki" (7.8; *Skjaldedigtning* 2:62).

3:418.33; *Islandske originaldiplomer* 71.4), a bull ("naut": DI 3:430.26), and a tent ("tjald": *Fljótsdœla hin meiri* 76.4). *Kinngrár* (LP: "grå, bleg om kinden"; CV: "gray-cheeked") is found in a *lausavísa* by Máni, and the referent is a man (*karl*).[83]
Kolblár (ONS: "kulsort"; CV: "'coal-blue,' dark blue, livid") is common:

Classification	Referent	Number of examples
Injured human body or body parts	*bak*	1 (*Isländska handskriften* N° 645 4° 30.21)
	fótr	1 (*Grettis saga* 252.6)
	líkami	3 (*Karlamagnúss saga* 54.29; cf. also *Eyrbyggja saga* 166.26, 253.5)
	kinn	1 (*Sturlunga saga* 1:139.19)
Sea and waves	*haf*	1 (*Isländska handskriften* No. 645 4° 73.16)
	sjór	9 (*Áns saga bogsveigis* 355.21; *Bósa saga* 49.4; *Njáls saga* 35.16, 78.6; *Færeyinga saga* 135.10; *Laxdœla saga* 103.10; *Jarlmanns saga* 26.32; *Maríu saga* 98.1, 271.19)

Kolsvartr (LP: "kulsort"; ONS: "kulsort"; CV: "coal-black, jet-black") is also common:

Classification	Referent	Number of examples
Animals	*hestr*	1 (*Partalopa saga* 103.1)
	kǫttr	2 (*Rómverja saga* 187.4; *Flateyjarbók* 1:26.9)
	sauðr	1 (*Konungs skuggsjá* 134.13)
	vargr	1 (*Gibbons saga* 87.17)
Clothing and cloth	*klæði*	1 (*Membrana regia deperdita* 230.5)
Human skin and body	*andlit*	1 (*Gibbons saga* 44.20)
	auga	1 (*Ívens saga* 10.10)
	maðr	1 (*Heilagra manna søgur* 1:84.28)

---

83. "Hvat munt hafs á otri / hengiligr með drengjum / karl, þvít kraptr þinn fǫrlask, kinngrár mega vinna" (5.1; *Skjaldedigtning* 1:520).

Once, the term is used in an abstract meaning: "alldri hefir orðit jafn kolsvart um mitt efni, síðan faðir minn miðlaði mér fé" (*Gautreks saga* 9.15).

Kverkhvítr (LP: "lys-, hvidhalset") is found in Þórbjǫrn hornklofi's *Haraldskvæði*, and the referent is a valkyrie (*valkyrja*).[84]
Laufgrœnn (LP: "løvgrön, grön som løvet"; ONS: "grøn som Løv"; CV: "leaf-green") is found in *Rúnakvæði*, which says about the runic letter ᛒ (*bjarkan*) that it is "laufgrœnstr lima" (25; *Skjaldedigtning* 2:249). In prose, it is attested four times:

Classification	Referent	Number of examples
Armor	*hjalmr*	1 (*Elis saga ok Rosamundu* 5.13)
Cloth and clothing	*klæði*	1 (*Sturlunga saga* 2:144.20)
	kyrtill	1 (*Hrafnkels saga* 1403.41)
	segl	1 (*Saga Óláfs konungs hins helga* 1:428.1 var.)

Lifrauðr (CV: "liver coloured, dark red") is used exclusively about clothing, more specifically a blouse ("stakkr": DI 8:801.20) and hose ("hosur": DI 10:488.20, 597.20).

Línhvítr (LP: "'linnedhvid,' hvid ved det brugte hovedtöj af lin"; ONS: "hvid som Lin? hvid under Lin, iført hvidt Linned?"; CV: "white as linen") occurs twice, in *Hárbarðsljóð*, to describe a woman (*mey*).[85]

Mansvartr is attested once: "Gestr scifti við hann sverþe oc oxi oc feck honum hesta ij knockotta [marginal note to 'hesta ij knockotta: h<n>ockottir ᴐ: mansvartir. sva avðþectir væri. þvi Gestr vildi hann feigann']" (*Skarðsárbók* 79.9).

Margrár (ONS+: "gråfarget [om naturlig farget ullstoff]") is attested once: "hesta madr V. alner margratt" (DI 3:414.33).

Mjallhvítr (LP: "hvid som nyfalden sne"; ONS: "hvid som nyfalden tør Sne"; CV: "white as driven snow") appears only in poetry. In

---

84. "kvaddi en glæhvarma / ok en kverkhvíta / Hymis hausrofa, / es sat á horni vinbjarga" (2.6; *Skjaldedigtning* 1:22).

85. "léc ec við ina línhvíto oc launþing háðac" (st. 30), "Liðs þíns væra ec þá þurfti, Þórr, at ec helda þeiri inni línhvíto mey" (st. 32).

412   New Norse Studies

Alvíssmál the referent is a woman (here *maðr*),[86] and in *Víglundar saga* the referent is *mundar jǫkla* (a kenning for silver).[87]

Móbrunaðr/móbrúnn (ONS: "graabrun"; CV: "dark brown") is attested once, and the referent is a tunic ("kyrtill": *Eyrbyggja saga* 48.8 and var).

Mórauðr (LP: "brunrød"; ONS: "rødbrun"; CV: "yellow brown") is found in a *lausavísa* by Kormákr Ǫgmundarson, and the referent is sheep (*sauðir*).[88] In prose, it is attested five times. In *Mágus saga* (34.37, 39.41), it describes the color of a man's one eye (*auga*) and likened to the color of cat's eyes, the one side of his nose (*nef*), and the one side of his body (*líkami*). In *Njáls saga* (59.14 var.) it is used about a tunic (*sǫluváðarkyrtill*), and in *Gǫngu-Hrólfs saga* (252.20) the referent is a hood (*hetta*).

Mosrauðr (LP: "rød, brun som mos, eller: 'farvet i mosfarve'"; CV: "moss-red) is attested once, in a *lausavísa* by Steinarr Sjónason, and the referent is a single pair of hose (*hosa*).[89]

Razhvítr is found once, and the referent is a horse (*hestr*): "gialla hessta, enn eigi merar, graðann hest, enn ecki gelldan, þann hvern er ecki sie rá: (ɔ: raz) hvitur" (*Gulaþingslǫg* [Fragments] 10.35).

Sauðsvartr (ONS+: "'sauesvart,' naturlig svartfarget [ullstoff]"; CV: "'sheep-black'") is attested twice, and the referents are cloth: "karfua m[enn]. form[aðr] x. alner saudsuart" (DI 3:406.21), "gizeri vij alner saudsuartar (DI 3:418.19).

Silfrhvítr (ONS: "hvid som Sølv"; CV: "silver-white") is found only in prose:

Classification	Referent	Number of examples
Armor	*brynja*	2 (*Karlamagnúss saga* 328.7, 342.31)
	herklæði	1 (*Karlamagnúss saga* 309.11)
	hjalmr	1 (*Karlamagnúss saga* 306.31)
	hringabrynja	1 (*Islendzk æventyri* 1:36.22)

Silkibleikr (ONS: "gul som Silke") is attested seven times. In four

---

86. "eiga vilia, heldr enn án vera, / þat iþ miallhvíta man" (st. 7).

87. "Mjǫk hefir mundar jǫkla / mjallhvít numit allan" (17.2; *Skjaldedigtning* 2:492).

88. "makara 's mér at mæla, / an mórauða sauði / of afréttu elta, / orð mart við Steingerði" (9.6; *Skjaldedigtning* 1:72).

89. "Lifðak lengi, / létk ráða goð, / hafðak aldri / hosu mosrauða" (1.4; *Skjaldedigtning* 1:89).

instances, the referent is human hair ("hár": *Heimskringla*
3:253.13; *Hulda* 152.13; *Jóns saga Hólabyskups* 133.5; *Ǫrvar-
Odds saga* 169.24), and in three instances it is horses ("hross":
Hrólfs saga Gautrekssonar 41.6–7; "merhross": *Gautreks saga*
35.9, 66.7).

Silkigulr is attested once, and the referent is human hair ("hár": *Ágrip*
6.17)

Skauðhvítr (ONS: "som har hvidt skauð"; CV: "sheath-white") is
attested once: "giallda hesta. en eigi marar. graðan hest. oc eigi
gelldan. þann hvern er eigi er raðzhvervingr. ne skauðhvitr. ne
skauðmigr. ne valldægðr. æða aðrer kauplestir a" (*Gulaþingslǫg*
75.21).

Skinnhvítr (ONS: "hvid af Hudfarve"; CV: "white-skinned") is
attested once, and the referent is a leg (*leggr*): "sæa menn þann
hennar leᴳ miora ok skinn huitara ok oþrymlottara eptir vadil
i frosti . . . en hinn sem fullkomliga var iafnan adr vsakadr"
(*Byskupa sǫgur* 368.15).

Skjallhvítr (LP: "hvid som *skjall*, d.v.s. som den hvide hinde i et æg")
is found in Árni Jónsson's *Guðmundardrápa*, and the referent is a
lily (*lilja*).[90]

Snjáhvítr, snjóhvítr, snæhvítr (LP: "snehvid"; ONS: "snehvid"; CV:
"snow-white") appears three times in poetry, in *Atlamál*, Árni
Jónsson's *Guðmundardrápa*, and in an anonymous skaldic verse;
the referents are silver (*silfr*), a dove (*dúfa*), and blood (*blóð*),
respectively.[91] In prose, it is common:

Classification	Referent	Number of examples
Animals,	*dúfa*	1 (*Heilagra manna sǫgur* 1:413.29 var.)
birds, fish	*fugl*	1 (*Heilagra manna sǫgur* 1:275.16)
	gangari	1 (*Flóres saga ok Blankiflúr* 29.9)
	hestr	4 (*Adonius saga* 201.7, 123.11; *Alexanders saga* 22.3; *Postola sögur* 502.24)
	hvítingr	1 (*Konungs skuggsjá* 15.22)

90. "Skírlífis með skýru prófi / skjallhvít lilja máttu kallaz" (68.2; *Skjaldedigtning* 2:458).

91. "mani mun ec þic hugga, mætom ágætom, / silfri snæhvíto, sem þú siáalf vilir" (st. 70); "snæfurt sýndiz snjóhvít dúfa / snara í gegnum ræfur þegni" (13.5; *Skjaldedigtning* 2:444); "Seggr sparir sverði at hǫggva, / snæhvítt er blóð líta" (*Skjaldedigtning* 2:147).

Classification	Referent	Number of examples
	kálfr (of a hart)	1 (*Strengleikar* 14.7)
	lamb	1 (*Heilagra manna søgur* 1:21.3, var.)
	sauðr	1 (*Heilagra manna søgur* 1:273.32)
Clothing,	*dúkr*	1 (*Thomas saga Erkibyskups* 494.14)
cloth, skin	*Klæði*	3 (*Gamal norsk Homiliebok* 82.7; *Heilagra manna søgur* 1:278.9; *Óláfs saga Tryggvasonar en mesta* 2:235.16)
	motr	1 (*Óláfs saga Tryggvasonar en mesta* 2:209.11)
	skinn	1 (*Karlamagnúss saga* 302.1)
Flowers	*leggr*	1 (*Heimskringla* 1:93.14)
and trees	*lilja*	2 (*Bærings saga* 122.52; *Nitida saga* 3.9)
Food	*brauðhleifr*	1 (*Maríu saga* 329.11)
	manna	1 (*Stjórn* 294.6)
Human hair	*hár*	3 (*Konungs skuggsjá* 22.26, 134,15; *Sverris saga* 10.9)
	skegg	1 (*Stjórn* 225.22)
Human skin	*líkami*	2 (*Mágus saga* 34.41; *Þiðriks saga* 2:51.14 var.)
and body		
	nef	1 (*Mágus saga* 34.39)
Snow and hail	*haglkorn*	1 (*Stjórn* 292.17)
	mjǫll	2 (*Erex saga*, 23.4, 17)
Stone or stone objects	*steinn*	1 (*Sverris saga* 2.15)
	steinþró	1 (*Heilagra manna søgur* 2:127.1)
Teeth and ivory	*tǫnn*	1 (*Duggals leiðsla* 73.16)
	fílsbeinn	1 (*Saulus saga* 13.21)
Other objects	*kistill*	1 (*Maríu saga* 199.21)

In addition, a man is said to be "sniahvitr af likþra" (*Stjórn* 618.22), and once the adjective is used in an abstract meaning: "meðr patriarchum ok dyrleghum guþs postolum meðr purpurleghum pislarvattum ok sniohuitum iaturum" (*Thomas saga erkibiskups* 282.10).

Sólbrúnn (ONS+: "brun av sol, solbrent") is attested once, and the referent is people (*menn*): "þau [smyrsl] eru god þeim monnum er solbrunir eru eda fialkomnir vid allz konar ryiu. oc ef ut þytur a manne" (*Old Icelandic Medical Miscellany* 98.10).

Sólhvítr (LP: "hvid, lys som solen"; ONS: "hvid som Solen"; CV: "sun-white") is found in *Hávamál*, and the referent is a woman (*mey*).[92]

Sótrauðr (LP: "'sodrød,' mörkerød"; ONS: "sodbrun"; CV: "'soot-red,' dark-red) occurs in *Vǫluspá*, and the referent is a cock (*hani*).[93]

Steingrár is attested twice, in *Ectors saga*, and the referents are cloth ("klæði" [139.17]) and a lock of wool ("lagðr" [166.2]).

Svanhvítr (LP: "svanehvid"; ONS+: "hvit som en svane"; CV: "Swan-white") is found in a verse in *Orms þáttr Stórólfssonar*, and the referent is Ásbjǫrn's mother.[94]

Tandrauðr (LP: "ildrød"; ONS: "ildrød"; CV: "fire-red") occurs three times in poetry, in Þjóðolfr Arnórsson's *Sexstefja*, in Einarr Skúlason's *Geisli*, and in a verse in *Harðar saga*; the referents are all *heiti* or kennings for gold (*ormtorg, vala strætis fasti*, and *nad Nílsandr*, respectively).[95] In prose, where it is attested five times, the referent is also gold ("gull": *Bragða-Mágus saga* 13.7; *Bærings saga* 95.35; *Clarus saga* 13.52–53; *Kirialax saga* 66.3; and *Partalopa saga* 23.3).

Úlfgrár (LP: "ulvegrå, grå som ulvens hår"; ONS: "graa af Farve som Ulven"; CV: "wolf-grey") occurs once in poetry, in Egill Skallagrímsson's *Arinbjarnarkviða*, where the referent is a human head (*hattar staup*).[96] In prose, the term is used about human hair ("hár": *Egils saga* 86.21, *Grettis saga* 110.4), a brown bear

---

92. "Billings mey ec fann beðiom á / sólhvíta, sofa" (st. 97).

93. "enn annarr gelr fyr iǫrð neðan, / sótrauðr hani, at sǫlum Heliar" (st. 43).

94. "Segið þat minni móður, / mun eigi syni kemba / svarðar láð í sumri / svanhvít í Danmǫrku" (IV.1.4; *Skjaldedigtning* 2:365). *Svanhvít* appears as the name of a valkyrie in *Vǫlundarkviða* st. 2).

95. "Tøgu má tekna segja / (tandrauðs) á Serklandi / (ungr hætti sér) átta / (ormtorgs hǫtuðr) borga" (2.2; *Skjaldedigtning* 1:339), "Tolf mánuðr vas týnir / tandrauðs huliðr sandi / fremðar lystr ok fasta / fimm nætr vala strætis" (25.2; *Skjaldedigtning* 1:433), "Víst mun Torfi treystaz / tandrauðra Nílsanda, hæðinn hǫldr, at ríða / heim í Botn at Gotnum" (15.2; *Skjaldedigtning* 2:480).

96. "þás ulfgrátt / við Yggjar miði / hattar staup / at hilmi þák" (7.5; *Skjaldedigtning* 1:38).

("viðbjǫrn": *Færeyinga saga* 28.13), and a boar ("galti": *Hrólfs saga kraka* 120.3).

Ullhvítr (ONS: "hvid som Uld"; CV: "white as wool") is attested twice, and in both cases the referent is human hair ("hár": *Óláfs saga Tryggvasonar en mesta* 212.16; *Saga Óláfs Tryggvasonar* 161.22).

Váðablár (ONS: "saa dyb, at den er udsat for fare") is found in *Þjalar Jóns saga*, and the referent is the sea (*sjór*): "þeir verda hræddir og felmz fullir, og villdi huer giarnan leita sier lijfz; enn þad er þó ecki hoglegt, þuiad vǫtn voru tueimmeigin, enn vǫda blár siór fijrir framann" (29.22). Although *váði* is compounded with a color term, it seems that color is not a primary meaning of the adjective (cf. *bládjúp*).

Valrauðr (LP: "blodrød, rød af blod"; ONS: "meget rød"; CV: "blood-red, crimson") occurs in *Atlakviða*, and the referent is tunics (*serkir*).[97]

Vetrgrœnn (LP: "vintergrön") appears in the superlative in *Rúnakvæði*. The referent is the runic letter *ýr* (ᛦ) which is said to be "vetrgrœnstr viða" (31; *Skjaldedigtning* 2:249). The meaning would seem to be "green(est) in winter," which disqualifies *vetrgrœnn* as a non-basic color term.

Ǫskubleikr (ONS+: "askebleik, askefarget") is attested once: "tok Sigurdur þǫgle fyrr sagt gler . . . og lijtur nu j þann hlut glersins sem hann synndizt <þegar hann þar j leit meðr> oskubleikum lit og storskorinne æsionu sem eins bergbua" (*Sigurðar saga þǫgla* 194.1).

2.10 Color tems with the suffix *-ligr*.[98]

Blóðligr (ONS: "blodfarvet"; CV: "bloody"; ONP: "blodfarvet, blodrød / blood-coloured, blood-red") is fairly common but appears to refer to color in only three instances: "tungl fal geisla sinn undir blodligu skyi" (*Heilagra manna søgur* 1:284.5), "Sol mun svǫrt verða, en tungl mun hafa bloðligan [var. blodgan: Stock. Perg. 4° no. 19 13ᵛ12] lit" (*Postola sögur* 22.7), "Hafdi hann .iii.

---

97. "Scioldo knegoð þar velia oc scafna asca, / hiálma gullroðna oc Húna mengi, / silfrgylt sǫðulklæði, serki valrauða, / dafar, darraða, drǫsla mélgreypa" (st. 4).

98. It can, of course, be argued that these terms consist of only one lexeme, since *-ligr* is not a second lexeme. See also Biggam, *Semantics of Colour*, 23.

nǫfn . . . hann het Esau sua sem raudr . . . ok Edom þat er bleikr edr blodligr" (*Stjórn* 161.9).

Blyligr (ONS+: "blyaktig"; CV: "leaden"; ONP: "blyagtig, blylignende / leaden") is attested twice and describes the planet Saturn (*Alfrœði íslenzk* 2:241n19, 3:66.26).

Eirligr (ONS: "af Kobber"; CV: "brazen"; ONP: "kobberagtig, kobberfarvet / copper-like, copper-coloured") is attested five times, all in prose, though, as noted in ONP, it only seems to refer to color in two instances: "eirligr Mars" (*Alfrœði íslenzk* 2:241n17, 3:66.27).

Eldsligr (ONP: "ildagtig, ildfarvet / fire-like, with the colour of fire") is attested only once as a color term: "Elldzlligr skinzlitr med skinǫndum augum snyzt til ædi (*Alfrœði íslenzk* 3:103.4).

Gulligr/golligr (LP: "forgyldt"; ONS: "af Guld"; ONS+: "gullaktig"; CV: "golden") is found once in poetry and numerous times in prose, but it seems to refer to color in only a few instances:[99]

Classification	Referent	Number of examples
Feather	*fjǫðr*	1 (*Vǫlsunga saga* 61.15)
Heavenly bodies	*himintungl*	1 (*Trójumanna saga* 87.16)
	sól	3 (*Alfrœði íslenzk* 2:241n14, 3:66.28; *Elucidarius* 66.11)
Human hair	*lokkr*	3 (*Saga Óláfs konungs hins helga* 2:674.14; *Sigurðar saga þǫgla* 198.15, 244.4)

Messingligr (ONS+: "messingaktig"; CV: "brasen") is attested three times. Twice the referent is the planet Mercury (*Alfrœði íslenzk* 2:241n16, 3:66.24), and once it is the sun ("sól": *Alfrœði íslenzk* 2:ccxiii.16).

Purpur(u)ligr (ONS: "purpurfarvet, purpurrød"; CV: "purple") is attested seven times. In three instances, the referent is a martyr or martyrdom ("píslarváttr," "píslarvætti": *Magnúss saga* 272.19; *Postola sögur* 592.32; *Thomas saga erkibiskups* 282.10), once it is

---

99. In their analysis of color terms in folk tales, Ralph Bolton and Diane Crisp note that "golden" is the most common secondary color term, "being especially prominent in European folk tale collections." "Color Terms in Folk Tales: A Cross-Cultural Study," *Cross-Cultural Research* 14 (1979): 241.

a precious stone ("gimsteinn": *Jóns saga Hólabyskups* 106.28), and once it is blood ("dreyri": *Trójumanna saga* 130.1). In *Rómverja saga*, it is twice used about a ring (*hringr*) around the sun (251.15, 25), which is said to signify martyrdom.

Rósaligr/rósuligr (ONS: "rosenfarvet, rosenrød") is attested once, and the referent is blood (*dreyri*): "Eptir þat dro hun dukinn með rosaligum [var. rosuligum] dreyra runnin or faðmi ser" (*Postola sögur* 121.19).

Silfrligr (ONS: "bestaaende af, som har et Udseende af Sølv"; CV: "silvery"; CV+ "of silver, silvern") is common, but it seems to refer to color in only the following instances: "Luna silfrlig" (*Alfræði íslenzk* 2:241n13, 3:66.24) and "En þa er hon [sólin] tæcr at vitia austrsættaʀ mæð varmum oc biartum geislum. þa tæcr þar fyst dagr upp at letta austan vinnde silfrligar brynn" (*Konungs skuggsjá* 7.31).

Smaragðligr (ONS: "smaragdgrøn"; CV: "emerald-like") is attested once, in *Konungs skuggsjá*, and the referent is grass or herbage (*gras*): "því næst leiðer hon [sólin] fram ilmannde gras mæð smaraglegom lit" (9.12).[100]

2.11 Nouns with the suffix -*litr*.

Finally, attention should be drawn to nouns with the suffix -*litr*, since they are indicative of color.

Blóðslitr (ONS: "Farve af Blod"; CV: "blood-colour"; ONP: "blod-farve, farve af blod, farve som blod / colour caused by blood, colour of blood") is attested three times. The referents are Þórr's stone (*steinn*) on which men were sacrificed (*Eyrbyggja saga* 28.11), the rings (*hringar*) around the eyeball (*Alfræði íslenzk* 3:99.32), and the moon ("tungl": *Postola sögur* 287.39).

Brennusteinslogalitr (ONS+: "farge som svovelild"; ONP: "svovll-uefarve, farve som en svovlflamme / colour of a sulphur flame") occurs once to describe one of the colors of the rainbow: "A ʀegn

---

100. The emerald is "a brilliant, grass-green variety of beryl . . . highly favored as a gem. Green color is caused by trace of chromium (Cr+3 and vanadium (V+3) ions" (Manutchehr-Danai, *Dictionary of Gems*, 161).

boga ero þrir lítír. vatnz lítr oc ældz lítr oc brenno steíns loga litr" (*Hauksbók* 174.31).

Dauðalitr (ONS: "Farve som er eiendommelig for den dødes Legeme"; CV: "colour of death"; ONP:"dødsfarve / deathly pallor") is attested once: "engi var da/þalitr á andliti þeira" (*Heilagra manna søgur* 2:238.27).

Eldslitr (ONS: Farve som af Ild"; CV: "orbs of fire") is attested four times. Twice it is used about a color of the rainbow (*Hauksbók* 174.31; *Veraldar saga* 80.24). Once it is used about a ring (*hringr*) on the horizon: "leit hann í vestrættina, ok þóttisk hann sjá hring ok eldslit á" (*Njáls saga* 320.23). And once it is used in an abstract sense: "Eldz litr merkír firir gefníng synda i liflate firir guðs sakar" (*Hauksbók* 175.4).

Fǫstulitr (ONS+: "farge i ansiktet under faste") occurs once: "Þeir ryggvasc sva sem skimenn er fyrir manna augliti syna fǫstu lit a sér. til þes at þæir róse goð-gerninge sinum fyrir mǫnnum" (*Gamal norsk Homiliebok* 76.28).

Gull(s)litr (ONS: "Guldfarve"; CV: "gold colour") is common. The following describes its usage:

Classification	Referent	Number of examples
Dragons and	*dreki*	1 (*Rómverja saga* 238.8)
serpents	*ormr*	1 (*Þiðriks saga* 1:137.3)
	yrmlingr	1 (*Bósa saga* 62.10)
Feathers	*fjaðrar*	3 (*Blómstrvallasaga* 7.6, 53.14; *Yngvars saga víðfǫrla* 8.20)
Flesh	*hǫrund*	2 (*Flateyjarbók* 3:291.33; *Hulda* 102.21)
Glass	*gler*	1 (*Gamal norsk Homiliebok* 132.29)
Gravel	*grjót*	1 (*Ectors saga* 112.16)
Hair	*hár*	2 (*Flóvents saga* 186.36; *Gǫngu-Hrólfs saga* 266.14; *Kirialax saga* 1.3–4)
	skegg	1 (*Kirialax saga* 1,3–4)
	tagl	1 (*Vilhjálms saga sjóðs* 19.11)
Hilt	*hepti*	1 (*Flateyjarbók* 3:431.18)
Horns	*horn*	1 (*Gautreks saga* 61.35)
Leek	*laukr*	1 (*Flóamanna saga* 46.10)
Teeth	*tennr*	1 (*Sǫgur Danakonunga* 5.29)

In three instances, it is difficult to determine the referent: "Aðalkelda ein var þar, grœnt var alt umhverfis ǫhana, á því þikkir gulls litr vera" (*Karlamagnúss saga* 423.1); "Hofudit uar bollott sem eyiar þær er gullz lit hafa med skina<n>de birte som logannde elldr e(dur) solar geislar" (*Sigurðar saga þǫgla* 100.11); and "Hann kom at þar sem upphæd uard fyrir honum, su er gullz litur var a" (*Yngvars saga víðfǫrla* 14.8–9).

Hermdarlitr (LP: "vredens farve, vredt ansigtsudtryk [blussende vrede]"; ONS: "Ansigtsfarve, Udseende som røber Misfornøielse, Forbittrelse") is found in *Helgakviða Hundingsbana I*: "Hví er hermðar litr á Hniflungom?" (st. 48).

Hǫrundarlitr/hǫrundslitr (ONS: "Kjødfarve") is attested seven times: "mosin var gróinn niðr í hausinn, svá sem múteraðr í beins náttúru, ok er frá leið tók jafnvel hörundslit, en var í þeim stað nǫkkuru linara átaks en í öðrum stað" (*Biskupa sögur* 2:180.30), "hálft hans nef ok enni ok haka hafði fagran hörundslit" (*Bragða-Mágus saga* 114.21), "haurunnz lit ok skinz hafdi hun miklu biartara enn nauckr madr annar" (*Dámusta saga* 51.28), "haurunz llit hefir hann suo biartann, at aunguann færr ek iafningia hans" (*Dámusta saga* 65.17), "Hon [Hel] er bla half, en half með haʀvndar [var. horundz] lit" (*Edda Snorra Sturlusonar* 35.8), "Þar er þer syndiz lėrín. ok hørundar [var. horvndz] litr a fagr" (*Saga Óláfs konungs hins helga* 2:679.5), "þer syndiz a baðum lėrunum hørundar [var. hǒrundz] lítr" (*Saga Óláfs konungs hins helga* 2:679.7).

Jarðlitr (CV: "earth colour, dark colour") is attested once: "er hann [Aᴅamantes] eigi sva skiʀ at hann lati iarðlit ok er hann því myrk-blar" (*Hauksbók* 227.28).[101]

Járnslitr (ONS+: "farge som jern, jernfarge"; CV: "iron colour") is used to describe a stone. One is asbestos: "Þar finnz ok sa steinn sem abeston heitir han hefir iarns lit" (*Stjórn* 86.2).[102] The other is

---

101. See note 35.

102. Asbestos is a mineral fiber. In terms of color, there are several types. One is amosite, which is known as brown asbestos. Another is crocidolite, which is known as blue asbestos. A third is tremolite, which can be white, green, gray, or even transparent. A fourth is anthophyllite, which displays a gray-brown color. See "Types of Abestos," accessed March 21, 2014, http://www.asbestos.com/asbestos/types.php.

an adamant: "Hann [adamas] er af kyne kristallo, iarns litr er æ honum" (*Alfrœði íslenzk* 3:84.7).[103]

Moldarlitr (ONS: "moldfarge, jordfarge") is attested once: "af altera es aþr hafþe legit sca/teN var þa oc non moldar litr á. sed var litr, sem ra/þr boca steíN" (*Isländska handskriften* N° 645 4° 11.17–18).

Náttúrulitr (ONS: "naturlig farge") is found once: "Er hun [calamentum] sodin med vin. þa dugir hun kvende at fa. sinn naturu lit" (*Old Icelandic Medical Miscellany* 67.26).[104]

Purpuralitr (ONS: "purpurfarve") is attested five times.[105] In three instances, it describes precious stones. One is a jacinth: "margar huitar byflugur sem snior flugu ok foru utan af seiminum. enn sumar af þeim hofdu raudan purpura lit sem iacinctus" (*Stjórn* 210.19).[106] Two are an amethyst, and in both *purpuralitr* is equated with the color of a drop of wine: "Ematistvs hefir pvrpvralit sem vindropi" (*Hauksbók* 227.1); "Amatistus hefir purpura lit sem vin-dropi" (*Alfrœði íslenzk* 1:81.1).[107] Once, the referent is the fold of a garment ("klæðafall": *Maríu saga* 113.22), and once it is the middle piece of a sword ("meðalkafli": *Islendzk æventyri* 1:37.3).

---

103. See note 35.

104. Cf. "Se hon sodin uít uín þa dugir hon kvende at fa sinn natturuligan lit" (*Gamalnorsk fragment av Henrik Harpestreng* 7.25).

105. *Purpuri* is a Latin (ultimately Greek) loan word. "Originally, purple derived from shells (Purpura) found on the coast of the eastern Mediterranean Sea. The animals gathered into shoals in spring time; abrasion produced a milky white fluid from which purple dye was obtained. When the shells were broken, the white substance oozed out. Upon exposure to the air and light this substance pased through a series of colours: first citron-yellow, then greenish yellow, then green, and finally, purple or scarlet. The juice obtained from Murex brandaris, a kind of Purpura, changed photochemically into a deep blue-violet, but that of Murex trunculus, another kind of Purpura, gave a scarlet red hue . . . . According to *OED*, in the Middle Ages *purple* applied vaguely to varous shades of red but now it applies to 'mixture of red and blue in various proportions.'" N. B. McNeill, "Colour and Colour Terminology" [Review of Brent Berlin and Paul Kay, *Basic Color Terms: Their Universality and Evolution* (Berkeley: University of California Press, 1969)], *Journal of Linguistics* 8 (1972): 27–28. See also Bailey: "The word *purpura*, originally from a blue-dye from seashells, was the name of a silk fabric which did not only represent the color purple, but also white, yellow, blue, black, red, and green . . . Not until the middle of the seventeenth century (at the earliest) did the term come to mean the hue purple" ("On the Non-existence," 203–204).

106. See note 57.

107. See note 36.

Silfr(s)litr is attested twice: "A góðo glere er bǽðe gullz lítr ok silfrs ok aller ener fægrsto litir" (*Gammel norsk Homiliebok* 132.19) and "syndíz þer niðr fra nafla allt um skøpín silfrs [var. silfr] litr a" (*Saga Óláfs konungs hins helga* 2:678.6).

Skinn(s)litr (ONS: "Hudfarve"; CV: "complexion of skin") is used about human complexion: "skinzliturin þrutnar. er allt yfirbragd af færizt" (AM 672 4° 15ᵛ); "hón var svá fögr ok hvít á skinnlit at . . ." (*Bárðar saga* 102.16); "Hann var . . . døkkr á hár ok svá á skinnslit" (*Njáls saga* 359.16); "Svartur skinnzlitur ok blandinn medur litlum blama synir hrygga menn ok i lunderni þunga" (*Alfræði íslenzk* 3:97.34); "Svartur skinzlitr segir mann slægan, en hvitur skinnzlitr ok nocud riodur segir styrka menn ok hugfulla. Akafliga hvitur skinnzlitr med bleikum merkir þrottnanda kraft ok ostyrckt af of kalldri natturu. Elldzligr skinzlitr med skinǫndum augum snyzt til ædi. Medal skinnzlitr hvitur ok svartr, ok bregdi a nocud brunu, synir mann med godu hugviti og godum sidum" (*Alfræði íslenzk* 3:102.32, 103.1, 2, 4, 5); "uenn madur ææ skins-lit og lidmannligur og kurteis" (*Jómsvíkinga saga* 32.20); "var hann hvítr á skinnsllit" (*Þorsteins saga bœjarmagns* 189.3).

Sænautalitr (ONS: "farge som på et 'sjønaut'") describes the color of a bull: "Þá reis upp í Krossavík þjórr nǫkkurr, ok var sænautalitr á" (*Vápnfirðinga saga* 48.27).[108]

Sævarlitr describes one of the colors of the rainbow: "Regnbogin . . . hefer a sier sævar lit" (*Veraldar saga* 80.24).

Vágslitr (ONS+: "materiefarge") is found once: "þa synom ver oc vágs lit utan a sciɴni" (*Leifar* 38.9). The noun *vágr* appears here in the secondary meaning of "medicinal fluid or salve."[109]

Vatnslitr (ONS: "farge som vann"; CV: "water-colour") is attested twice. Once, it describes one of the colors of the rainbow (*Hauksbók* 174.31), and once it is used in an abstract meaning: "vatnzs litr iartegnír fírír gefníng synda i skírn heilagre" (*Hauksbók* 175.2).

---

108. It is doubtful that the composer of *Vápnfirðinga saga* had seen a sea cow (*Hydrodamalis gigas*). It was first described by Georg W. Steller on his voyage of discovery in the North Pacific in 1741. It is now extinct, and its last known habitat was in the Commander Islands. Steller describes the hide of the sea cow as follows: "The hide of this animal has a dual nature. The outer hide is black or blackish brown, an inch thick, and with a consistency almost like cork." *Journal of a Voyage with Bering 1741–1742* (Stanford: Stanford University Press, 1988), 163.

109. Ásgeir Blöndal Magnússon, *Íslensk orðsifjabók*, 1150.

3. Conclusion.

By far the largest category of non-basic color terms is comprised of terms consisting of a noun and a color term. This is followed by the category of compounds of two color terms, terms with the suffix *-ligr*, and terms with the prefixes *døkk-, fagr-, glit-, heið-, ljós-, myrk-, lit-,* and the suffixes *-døkkr, -ljóss, -leitr, -litaðr,* and *-litr.* The smallest category is simplex terms.

Sixty-one non-basic color terms, about half of the ones listed, are attested only once. These comprise: *biksvartr, blábrúnaðr, blikhvítr, blómhvítr, bráhvítr, brandrauðr, brúnhvítr, dumbbleikr, døkkgrœnn, eldsligr, físbleikr, fiskbleikr, fótgulr, glitrauðr, gollhvítr, gráblár, gulbrúnn, gulgrár, hárarauðr, heiðblár, helblár, himinblár, hrafnblár, hrafnsvartr, hvarmrauðr, hvítjarpr, horundshvítr, horundsvartr, ilbleikr, indiblár, jarplitaðr, kinngrár, kverkhvítr, litrauðr, ljósbrún-leitr, ljósgrœnn, ljósgulr, ljósrauðr, mansvartr, margrár, móbrúnn/ móbrúnaðr, mosrauðr, myrkgrár, rauðblár, rauðdøkkr, rauðgrœnn, rauðljóss, razhvítr, rósaligr/rósuligr, silkigulr, skauðhvítr, skjallhvítr, skinnhvítr, sólbrúnn, sólhvítr, sótrauðr, svanhvítr, svartbrúnaðr, valrauðr, smaragðligr,* and *oskubleikr.* Of these, twenty-four appear in poetry only: *bráhvítr, brandrauðr, blikhvítr, brúnhvítr, fótgulr, gollhvítr, hárarauðr, hrafnblár, hrafnsvartr, hvarmrauðr, hvítjarpr, ilbleikr, jarplitaðr, kinngrár, kverkhvítr, litrauðr, ljósgulr, mosrauðr, rauðljóss, skjallhvítr, sólhvítr, sótrauðr, svanhvítr,* and *valrauðr.* In addition, the following five color terms are restricted to poetry: *blásvartr, glóðrauðr, hoss, línhvítr, mjallhvítr.* By far, most of the non-basic color terms in poetry serve alliterative purposes.[110]

Given the evidence, most of the remaining non-basic color terms are contextually restricted. These terms include *bláleitr, bleikhárr, blyligr, dreyrrauðr, døkkjarpr, eirligr, fagrgrœnn, fannhvítr, fífilbleikr, glóðrauðr, gollroðinn/gullroðinn, hárarauðr, hárr* (if indeed it should be regarded as a color term), *hvítleitr, horundarlitr/horundslitr, jarpr, lifrauðr, ljósblár, ljósbleikr, ljósjarpr, messingligr, rauðgulr, rauðleitr,*

---

110. Biggam comments that "a . . . potentially helpful consideration is the information which may arise from the role of certain color terms in alliterative, or other formulaic structures found in poetry. It is sensible to consider the possibility, for example, that a particular colour word had been chosen because it alliterates with other words in the same line of a poem. It is unlikely to be completely inappropriate semantically in such a position but its meaning may be weakened or slightly shifted" (*Semantics of Colour,* 150).

rjóðr, sauðsvartr, silfrhvítr, silfrligr, silkibleikr, steingrár, svartblár, svartjarpr, svartleitr, tandrauðr, and *ullhvítr.* The terms are especially prevalent in the context of human coloring (notably hair and complexion), animal colors (particularly horses), cloth and clothing, precious stones, and armor and weapons. Only *blakkr, bleikr, blóðrauðr, kolsvartr, snjáhvítr/snjóhvítr/snæhvítr* and to a lesser extent *drifhvítr, golligr/gulligr, járngrár, kolblár, laufgrœnn, mórauðr, myrkblár, rauðbleikr, rauðbrúnn,* and *rauðlitaðr* have a range of referents.

Of the terms consisting of two color adjectives, *blár* and *rauðr* are the most common. They are followed by *brúnn; gulr* and *svartr; grár, grœnn, hvítr, jarpr;* and *bleikr.* Of the terms consisting of a color term and a noun, *hvítr* is the most common color term. The nouns are primarily snow (*drif-, fann-, mjall-, snjá-/snjó-/snæ-*), metals (*goll-, silfr*), facial hair (*brá-, brún-*), and fabric (*lín-, ull-*). *Rauðr,* too, is common, and here the nouns are mostly blood (*blóð-, dreyr-, val-*), fire (*brand-, glóð-, tand-*), human facial hair (*hvarm-, hára-*), and vegetation (*mó-, mos-*). Most of the nouns have to do with vegetation (*blóm, fífill, gras, lauf, mór, mosi, rósa*); complexion, hair, and body parts (*brá, brún, fótr, grǫn, hár, hvarmr, hǫrund, il, kinn, kverk, lif, skinn*); and blood and fire (see above). Surprisingly few nouns are from the world of animals, birds, and fish (the only ones in evidence are *fiskr, hrafn, sauðr, skjall, svanr,* and *úlfr*). Of all the non-basic color terms that have a basic color term as one of its components, *rauðr* is by far the most common. It is followed by *hvítr, blár, svartr, brúnn, grár* and *grœnn* (which are equally common), and *gulr.* This is more or less in line with the frequency of the individual basic color terms in the sagas and *þættir* of Icelanders,[111] except that in non-basic color terms *brúnn* is more common than *grœnn* and *grár.*

Bibliography

Primary Sources and Translations

Adonius saga. In Loth, *Late Medieval Icelandic Romances,* 3:69–230.
Ágrip af Nóregs konunga sǫgum. Edited by Finnur Jónsson. Altnordische Saga-Bibliothek 18. Halle: Niemeyer, 1929.
Alexanders saga. Edited by Finnur Jónsson. Copenhagen: Gyldendal, 1925.

---

111. See Wolf, "Basic Color Terms," 156 (note 1 above).

Alfræði íslenzk 1: Islandsk encyklopædisk litteratur, Cod. Mbr. AM. 194, 8vo. Edited by Kristian Kålund. Samfund til udgivelse af gammel nordisk litteratur 37. Copenhagen: Møller, 1908.

Alfræði íslenzk 2: Islandsk encyklopædisk litteratur, Rimtǫl. Edited by N. Beckman and Kristian Kålund. Samfund til udgivelse af gammel nordisk litteratur 41. Copenhagen: Møller, 1914–16.

Alfræði íslenzk 3: Islandsk encyklopædisk litteratur, Landalýsingar m. fl. Edited by Kristian Kålund. Samfund til udgivelse af gammel nordisk litteratur 45. Copenhagen: Møller, 1917–18.

Áns saga bogsveigis. In Rafn, *Fornaldar sögur Nordrlanda*, 2:325–62.

Bárðar saga. In *Harðar saga*, edited by Þórhallur Vilmundarson and Bjarni Vilhjálmsson, 99–172. Íslenzk fornrit 13. Reykjavík: Hið íslenzka fornritafélag, 1991.

Biskupa sögur. Edited by Jón Sigurðsson and Guðbrandur Vigfússon. 2 vols. Copenhagen: Møller, 1858–78.

Blómstrvallasaga. Edited by Theodor Möbius. Leipzig: Breitkopf & Hærtel, 1855.

Die Bósa-Saga in zwei Fassungen nebst Proben aus den Bósa-Rímur. Edited by Otto Luitpold Jiriczek. Strassburg: Trübner, 1893.

Bragða-Mágus saga með tilheyrandi Þáttum. Edited by Gunnlaugur Þórðarson. Copenhagen: Páll Sveinsson, 1858.

Brennu-Njáls saga. Edited by Einar Ól. Sveinsson. Íslenzk fornrit 12. Reykjavík: Hið íslenzka fornritafélag, 1954.

Byskupa sǫgur. Edited by Jón Helgason. Editiones Arnamagnæanæ A13.2. Copenhagen: Reitzel, 1978.

Bærings saga. In Cederschiöld, *Fornsögur Suðrlanda*, 85–123.

Cederschiöld, Gustaf, ed. *Fornsögur Suðrlanda.* Lund: Berling, 1884.

Clarus saga. Edited by Gustaf Cederschiöld. Lund: Gleerup, 1879.

Codex Frisianus: En Samling af norske Konge-Sagaer. Edited by C. R. Unger. Christiania [Oslo]: Malling, 1871.

Dámusta saga. In *Þjalar Jóns saga / Dámusta saga*, edited by Louisa Fredrika Tan-Haverhorst, 48–108. Harlem: Willink & Zoon, 1939.

Dínus saga drambláta. Edited by Jónas Kristjánsson. Riddarasögur 1. Reykjavík: Háskóli Íslands, 1960.

Diplomatarium Islandicum: Íslenzkt fornbréfasafn. Edited by Jón Sigurðsson, Jón Þorkelsson, Páll Eggert Ólason, and Björn Þorsteinsson. 16 vols. Copenhagen and Reykjavík: Hið íslenzka bókmenntafélag, 1857–1972.

Diplomatarium Norvegicum. Edited by C. A. Lange, C. R. Unger, H. J. Huitfeldt-Kaas, and Gustav Storm. 22 vols. Christiania [Oslo]: Malling; Oslo: Kommisjonen for Diplomatarium Norvegicum, 1852–1992.

Duggals leiðsla. Edited by Peter Cahill. Reykjavík: Stofnun Árna Magnússonar, 1983.

Ectors saga. In Loth, *Late Medieval Icelandic Romances*, 1:81–186.

Edda Snorra Sturlusonar. Edited by Finnur Jónsson. Copenhagen: Gyldendal, 1931.

Egils saga Skallagrímssonar 1, efter forarbejder af Jón Helgason. Edited by Bjarni Einarsson. Editiones Arnamagnæanæ A19. Copenhagen: Reitzel, 2001.

Eirspennill. Edited by Finnur Jónsson. Christiania [Oslo]: Den norske historiske kildeskriftkommission, 1916.

Elis saga ok Rosamundu. Edited by Eugen Kölbing. Heilbronn: Henninger, 1881.

Elucidarius in Old Norse Translation. Edited by Evelyn Scherabon Firchow and Kaaren Grimstad. Reykjavík: Stofnun Árna Magnússonar, 1989.

Erex saga Artuskappa. Edited by Foster W. Blaisdell. Editiones Arnamagnæanæ B19. Copenhagen: Munksgaard, 1965.

Eyrbyggja saga: The Vellum Tradition. Edited by Forrest S. Scott. Editiones Arnamagnæanæ A18. Copenhagen: Reitzel, 2003.

Fagrskinna: Nóregs konunga tal. Edited by Finnur Jónsson. Samfund til udgivelse af gammel nordisk litteratur 30. Copenhagen: Møller, 1902–3.

Finnboga saga hins ramma. Edited by Hugo Gering. Halle: Waisenhaus, 1879.

Finnur Jónsson, ed. *Den norsk-islandske skjaldedigtning.* Vols. B1-B2, Rettet tekst. Copenhagen: Gyldendal, 1912–15.

Flateyjarbók. Edited by Guðbrandr Vigfusson and C. R. Unger. 3 vols. Christiania [Oslo]: Malling, 1860–68.

Fljótsdæla hin meiri eller Den længere Droplaugarsona-saga. Edited by Kristian Kålund. Samfund til udgivelse af gammel nordisk litteratur 11. Copenhagen: Møller, 1883.

Flóamanna saga. Edited by Finnur Jónsson. Samfund til udgivelse af gammel nordisk litteratur 56. Copenhagen: Jørgensen, 1932.

Flóres saga konungs. In *Drei lygisǫgur,* edited by Åke Lagerholm, 121–77. Altnordische Saga-Bibliothek 17. Halle: Niemeyer, 1927.

Flóres saga ok Blankiflúr. Edited by Eugen Kölbing. Altnordische Saga-Bibliothek 5. Halle: Niemeyer, 1896.

Flóvents saga. In Cederschiöld, *Fornsögur Suðrlanda,* 124–208.

Fóstbrœðra saga. Edited by Björn K. Þórólfsson. Samfund til udgivelse af gammel nordisk litteratur 49. Copenhagen: Jørgensen, 1925–27.

Færeyinga saga. Edited by Ólafur Halldórsson. Reykjavík: Stofnun Árna Magnússonar, 1987.

Gamal norsk Homiliebok: Cod. AM 619 4º. Edited by Gustav Indrebø. Oslo: Dybwad, 1931.

Gamalnorsk fragment av Henrik Harpestreng. Edited by Marius Hægstad. Videnskabs-Selskabets Skrifter. II. Hist.-Filos. Klasse 1906. Kristiania [Oslo]: Dybwad, 1906.

Die Gautrekssaga in zwei Fassungen. Edited by Wilhelm Ranisch. Palaestra 11. Berlin: Mayer & Müller, 1900.

Gibbons saga. Edited by R. I. Page. Editiones Arnamagnæanæ B1. Copenhagen: Ejnar Munksgaard, 1960.

Gísla saga Súrssonar. In *Vestfirðinga sǫgur,* edited by Björn K. Þórólfsson and Guðni Jónsson, 3–118. Íslenzk fornrit 6. Reykjavík: Hið íslenzka fornritafélag, 1943.

Grettis saga Ásmundarsonar. Edited by Guðni Jónsson. Íslenzk fornrit 7. Reykjavík: Hið íslenzka fornritafélag, 1936.

Gríms saga loðinkinna. In Rafn, *Fornaldar sögur Norðrlanda,* 2:143–57.

Guðmundar sögur biskups I: Ævi Guðmundar biskups, Guðmundar saga A. Edited by Stefán Karlsson. Editiones Arnamagnæanæ B6. Copenhagen: Reitzel, 1983.

Gulaþingslǫg. In vol. 1 of *Norges Gamle Love indtil 1387.* Edited by R. Keyser and P.A. Munch et al. Christiania [Oslo]: Gröndahl, 1846.

Gulaþingslǫg [Fragments]. In vol. 4 of *Norges Gamle Love indtil 1387.* Edited by Gustav Storm. Christiania [Oslo]: Gröndahl, 1885.

Gǫngu-Hrólfs saga. In Rafn, *Fornaldar sögur Norðrlanda,* 3:237–364.

Hálfdanar saga Eysteinssonar. Edited by Franz Rolf Schröder. Altnordische Saga-Bibliothek 15. Halle: Nirmeyer, 1917.

Hauksbók. Edited by Eiríkur Jónsson and Finnur Jónsson. Copenhagen: Thiele, 1892–96.

Heiðreks saga: Hervarar saga ok Heiðreks konungs. Edited by Jón Helgason. Samfund til udgivelse af gammel nordisk litteratur 45. Copenhagen: Jørgensen 1924.

Heilagra manna søgur. Edited by C. R. Unger. 2 vols. Christiania [Oslo]: Bentzen, 1877.

Heimskringla. Edited by Finnur Jónsson. 4 vols. Samfund til udgivelse af gammel nordisk litteratur 23. Copenhagen: Møller, 1893–1900.

Hjálmþérs saga ok Ǫlvis. In Rafn, *Fornaldar sögur Norðrlanda,* 3:453–518.

Hollander, Lee M., trans. *The Poetic Edda.* Rev. 2nd ed. Austin: University of Texas Press, 1962.

Hrafnkels saga. In vol. 1 of *Íslendinga sögur og þættir,* edited by Bragi Halldórsson, Jón Torfason, Sverrir Tómasson, Örnólfur Thorsson, 1397–1416. 2nd ed. Reykjavík: Svart á hvítu, 1987.

Hrafns saga Sveinbjarnarsonar: B-redaktionen. Edited by Annette Hasle. Editiones Arnamagnæanæ B25. Copenhagen: Munksgaard, 1967.

Hrólfs saga Gautrekssonar. In *Zwei Fornaldarsögur (Hrólfssaga Gautrekssonar und Ásmundarsaga kappabana) nach Cod. Holm. 7, 4to,* edited by Ferdinand Detter, 3–78. Halle: Niemeyer, 1891.

Hrólfs saga kraka. Edited by D. Slay. Editiones Arnamagnæanæ B1. Copenhagen: Ejnar Munksgaard, 1960.

Hulda: De norske kongers saaer 1030–1155 efter AM 66 fol. med varianter fra Gl. kgl. saml. 1010 fol. Edited by Jonna Louis-Jensen. Editiones Arnamagnæanæ A11–12. Unpublished manuscript.

Islandske originaldiplomer indtil 1450: Tekst. Edited by Stefán Karlsson. Editiones Arnamagnæanæ A7. Copenhagen: Munksgaard, 1963.

Islendzk æventyri. Edited by Hugo Gering. 2 vols. Halle: Waisenhaus, 1882–83.

Isländska handskriften N° 645 4° i den Arnamagnæanske samlingen på universitetsbiblioteket i København 1. Edited by Ludvig Larsson. Lund: Gleerup, 1885.

Ívens saga. Edited by Foster W. Blaisdell. Editiones Arnamagnæanæ B18. Copenhagen: Reitzel, 1979.

Jarlmanns saga ok Hermanns i yngre handskrifters redaktion. Edited by Hugo Rydberg. Åtföljer Eskilstuna realskolas och kommunala gymnasiums årsredogörelse. Copenhagen: Møller, 1917.

Jómsvíkinga saga (efter Cod. AM. 510, 4:to) samt Jómsvíkinga drápa. Edited by Carl af Petersens. Lund: Gleerup, 1879.

Jómsvíkinga saga efter Arnamagnæanske handskriften N:o 291. 4:to. Edited by Carl af Petersens. Samfund til udgivelse af gammel nordisk litteratur 7. Copenhagen: Berling, 1882.

Jóns saga Hólabyskups ens helga. Edited by Peter Foote. Editiones Arnamagnæanæ A14. Copenhagen: Reitzel, 2003.

Karlamagnus saga ok kappa hans. Edited by C. R. Unger. Christiania [Oslo]: Jensen, 1860.

Kirialax saga. Edited by Kristian Kålund. Samfund til udgivelse af gammel nordisk litteratur 43. Copenhagen: Møller, 1917.

Kjalnesinga saga. Edited by Johanna Arina Huberta Posthumus. Groningen: M. de Waal, 1911.

Konráðs saga. In Cederschiöld, *Fornsögur Suðrlanda*, 43–84.

Konráðs saga keisarasonar. Edited by Otto J. Zitzelsberger. American University Studies, Ser. 1, Germanic Languages and Literature 63. New York: Peter Lang, 1987.

Konungs skuggsiá. Edited by Ludvig Holm-Olsen. Utgitt for Kjeldeskriftfondet. Gammelnorske tekster 1. Oslo: Dybwad, 1945.

Larrington, Carolyne, trans. *The Poetic Edda.* Oxford: Oxford University Press, 1996.

Laxdœla saga. Edited by Kristian Kålund. Samfund til udgivelse af gammel nordisk litteratur 19. Copenhagen: Møller, 1889–91.

Leifar fornra kristinna manna frœða íslenzkra. Edited by Þorvaldur Bjarnarson. Copenhagen: Thiele, 1878.

Loth, Agnete, ed. *Late Medieval Icelandic Romances.* 5 vols. Editiones Arnamagnæanæ B20–24. Copenhagen: Munksgaard, 1962–65.

Magnúss saga. In *Orkneyinga saga and Magnus saga, with Appendices, Icelandic Sagas and Other Historical Documents Relating to the Settlements and Descents of the Northmen on the British Isles 1*, edited by Gudbrand Vigfusson, 237–80. Rerum Britannicarum medii ævi scriptores. Rolls Series 88. London: Eyre and Spottiswoode, 1887.

Mágus saga. In Cederschiöld, *Fornsögur Suðrlanda,* 1–42.

Mariu saga. Edited by C. R. Unger. Christiania [Oslo]: Brögger & Christie, 1871.

Membrana regia deperdita. Edited by Agnete Loth. Editiones Arnamagnæanæ A5. Copenhagen: Ejnar Munksgaard, 1960

Morkinskinna. Edited by Finnur Jónsson. Samfund til udgivelse af gammel nordisk litteratur 53. Copenhagen: Møller, 1932.

Neckel, Gustav, and Hans Kuhn, eds. *Die Lieder des Codex Regius nebst verwandten Denkmälern.* Vol. 1, *Text.* 5th ed. Germanische Bibliothek. 4. Reihe, Texte. Heidelberg: Carl Winter, 1983.

Nitida saga. In Loth, *Late Medieval Icelandic Romances,* 5:3–37.

Óláfs saga Tryggvasonar en mesta. Edited by Ólafur Halldórsson. 3 vols. Editiones Arnamagnæanæ A1–3. Copenhagen: Ejnar Munksgaard, 1958–2000.

An Old Icelandic Medical Miscellany. Edited by Henning Larsen. Oslo: Dybwad, 1931.

Orkneyinga saga. Edited by Sigurður Nordal. Samfund til udgivelse af gammel nordisk litteratur 40. Copenhagen: Møller, 1913–16.

Partalopa saga. Edited by Lise Præstgaard Andersen. Editiones Arnamagnæanæ B28. Copenhagen: Reitzel, 1983.

Postola sögur. Edited by C. R. Unger. Christiania [Oslo]: Bentzen, 1874.

Rafn, Carl Christian, ed. *Fornaldar sögur Nordrlanda.* 3 vols. Copenhagen, 1829–30.

Reykjahólabók: Islandske helgenlegender. Edited by Agnete Loth. 2 vols. Editiones Arnamagnæanæ A15–16. Copenhagen: Munksgaard, 1969–70.

Rómveriasaga (AM 595, 4°). Edited by Rudolf Meissner. Palaestra 88. Berlin: Mayer & Müller, 1910.

Rómverja saga. In *Fire og fyrretyve for en stor Deel forhen utrykte Prøver af oldnordisk Sprog og Literatur,* edited by Konrad Gislason, 108–252. Copenhagen: Gyldendal, 1860.

Saga af Tristram ok Ísodd. Edited by Gísli Brynjúlfsson. *Annaler for nordisk Oldkyndighed og Historie* (1851): 3–160.

Saga af Tristram ok Ísönd samt Möttuls saga. Edited by Gísli Brynjulfson. Copenhagen: Det kongelige nordiske Oldskrift-selskab, 1878.

Saga Óláfs konungs hins helga: Den store saga om Olav den hellige. Edited by Oscar Albert Johnsen and Jón Helgason. Oslo: Dybwad, 1941.

Saga Óláfs Tryggvasonar af Oddr Snorrason munk. Edited by Finnur Jónsson. Copenhagen: Gad, 1932.

Sagan ock rimorna om Friðþjófr hinn frækni. Edited by Ludvig Larsson.

Samfund til udgivelse af gammel nordisk litteratur 22. Copenhagen: Malmström, 1893.
Saulus saga ok Nikanors. In Loth, *Late Medieval Icelandic Romances,* 2:3–91.
Sigurðar saga þǫgla. In Loth, *Late Medieval Icelandic Romances,* 2:93–259.
Skarðsárbók. Edited by Jakob Benediktsson. Reykjavík: Hólar, 1966.
Stjorn. Edited by C. R. Unger. Christiania [Oslo]: Feilberg & Landmark, 1862.
Strengleikar. Edited by Robert Cook and Matthias Tveitane. Norrøne tekster 3. Oslo: Kjeldeskriftfondet, 1979.
The Two Versions of "Sturlaugs Saga Starfsama." Edited by Otto J. Zitzelsberger. Düsseldorf: Triltsch, 1969.
Sturlunga saga. Edited by Kristian Kålund. 2 vols. Copenhagen: Gyldendal, 1906–11.
Sverris saga etter Cod. AM 327 4°. Edited by Gustav Indrebø. Kristiania [Oslo]: Dybwad, 1920.
Sǫgur Danakonunga, 1: *Sǫgubrot af fornkonungum,* 2: *Knytlinga saga.* Edited by Carl af Petersens and Emil Olson. Samfund til udgivelse af gammel nordisk litteratur 46. Copenhagen: Ohlsson, 1919–26.
Terry, Patricia, trans. *Poems of the Vikings.* Indianapolis: Bobbs-Merrill, 1969.
Thomas saga Erkibyskups. Edited by C. R. Unger. Christiania [Oslo]: Bentzen, 1869.
Trójumanna saga. Edited by Jonna Louis-Jensen. Editiones Arnamagnæanæ A8. Copenhagen: Munksgaard, 1963.
Þiðriks saga af Bern. Edited by Henrik Bertelsen. 2 vols. Samfund til udgivelse af gammel nordisk litteratur 34. Copenhagen: Møller, 1905–11.
Þjalar-Jóns saga. In *Þjalar Jóns saga / Dámusta saga,* edited by Louisa Fredrika Tan-Haverhorst, 1–47. Harlem: Willink & Zoon, 1939.
Þorsteins saga bœjarmagns. In vol. 3 of *Saga Ólafs konúngs Tryggvasonar,* edited by Sveinbjörn Egilsson and Þorgeir Gudmundsson, 175–98. Fornmannasögur 3. Copenhagen: Popp, 1827.
Valvers þáttr, Ein Bruckstück des. Edited by Eugen Kölbing. *Germania* 25 (1880): 385–88.
Vápnfirðinga saga. In *Austfirðinga sǫgur,* edited by Jón Jóhannesson, 23–65. Íslenzk fornrit 11. Reykjavík: Hið íslenzka fornritafélag, 1950.
Veraldar saga. Edited by Jakob Benediktsson. Samfund til udgivelse af gammel nordisk litteratur 61. Copenhagen: Luno, 1944.
Veturliði Óskarsson. "Að mála upp á tré." *Árbók hins íslenzka fornleifafélags 1989* (1990): 21–33 [abbr. as *"Smíð(1990)x"* in ONP].

Víglundar saga. In *Kjalnesinga saga,* edited by Jóhannes Halldórsson, 63–116. Íslenzk fornrit 14. Reykjavík: Hið íslenzka fornritafélag, 1959.

Vilhjálms saga sjóðs. In Loth, *Late Medieval Icelandic Romances,* 4:3–136.

Vǫlsunga saga ok Rangars saga loðbrókar. Edited by Magnus Olsen. Samfund til udgivelse af gammel nordisk litteratur 36. Copenhagen: Møller, 1906–8.

Yngvars saga víðfǫrla jämte ett bihang om Ingvarsinskrifterna. Edited by Emil Olson. Samfund til udgivelse af gammel nordisk litteratur 39. Copenhagen: Møller, 1912.

Qrvar-Odds saga. Edited by Richard Constant Boer. Leiden: Brill, 1888.

Secondary Sources

Arthur, Susanne M. "Are Oranges Yellow? *Appelsínugulur* as a Basic Color Term in Icelandic." *Orð og tunga* 15 (2013): 121–39.

Ásgeir Blöndal Magnússon. *Íslensk orðsifjabók.* Reykjavík: Orðabók Háskólans, 1989.

Berlin, Brent, and Paul Kay. *Basic Color Terms: Their Universality and Evolution.* Berkeley: University of California Press, 1969.

Biggam, C. P. "The Ambiguity of *Brightness* (with Special Reference to Old English) and a New Model for Color Description in Semantics." In *Anthropology of Color: Interdisciplinary Multilevel Modeling,* edited by Robert E. MacLaury, Galina V. Paramei, and Don Dedrick, 171–87. Amsterdam: John Benjamins, 2007.

———. *Blue in Old English: An Interdisciplinary Semantic Study.* Amsterdam: Rodopi, 1997.

———. *Grey in Old English: An Interdisciplinary Semantic Study.* London: Runetree, 1998.

———. *The Semantics of Colour: A Historical Approach.* Cambridge: Cambridge University Press, 2012.

Bailey, Ashlee C. "On the Non-existence of Blue-Yellow and Red-Green Color Terms." *Studies in Language* 25 (2001): 185–215.

Bolton, Ralph, and Diane Crisp. "Color Terms in Folk Tales: A Cross-Cultural Study." *Cross-Cultural Research* 14 (1979): 231–53.

Brückmann, Georg C. *Altwestnordische Farbsemantik.* Münchner nordistische Studien 11. Munich: Herbert Utz Verlag, 2012.

Clark, A. M. *Hey's Mineral Index.* London: Chapman & Hall, 1975.

Cleasby, Richard, and Gudbrand Vigfusson. *An Icelandic-English Dictionary.* 2nd ed., suppl. William A. Craigie. Oxford: Clarendon, 1957.

Finnur Jónsson. *Lexicon Poeticum Antiquæ Linguæ Septentrionalis: Ordbog over the norsk-islandske skjaldesprog oprindelig forfattet af Sveinbjörn Egilsson.* 2nd ed. Copenhagen: Møller, 1931.

Fritzner, Johan. *Ordbog over Det gamle norske Sprog.* 4th ed. 3 vols. Oslo: Universitetsforlaget, 1973.

Hamilton, W. R., A. R. Woolley, and A. C. Bishop. *A Guide to Minerals, Rocks and Fossils.* London: Hamlyn Publishing, 1970.

Heizmann, Wilhelm. *Wörterbuch der Pflanzennamen im Altwestnordischen.* Ergänzungsbände zum Reallexikon der germanischen Altertumskunde 7. Berlin: de Gruyter, 1993.

Hoover, D. B. *Topaz.* Oxford: Butterworth Heinemann, 1992.

Hødnebø, Finn. "Rettelser og Tillegg" to Johan Fritzner, *Ordbog over det game norske Sprog.* Oslo: Universitetsforlaget, 1972.

Manutchehr-Danai, Mohsen. *Dictionary of Gems and Gemology.* Berlin: Springer, 2000.

McNeill, N. B. "Colour and Colour Terminology." Review *Basic Color Terms,* by Berlin and Kay (see above). *Journal of Linguistics* 8 (1972): 21–34.

Mead, William E. "Color in Old English Poetry." *PMLA* 14 (1899): 169–206.

Pokorny, Julius. *Indogermanisches etymologisches Wörterbuch.* 2 vols. Bern and Munich: Francke Verlag, 1959–69.

Steller, George Wilhelm. *Journal of a Voyage with Bering 1741–1742.* Edited with an Introduction by O. W. Frost. Translated by Margritt A. Engel and O. W. Frost. Stanford: Stanford University Press, 1988.

Van Deusen, Natalie M. "The Matter of *blár* in *Tristrams kvæði.*" *Arthuriana* 22 (2012): 109–15.

Vries, Jan de. *Altnordisches etymologisches Wörterbuch.* 3rd ed. Leiden: Brill, 1977.

Wolf, Kirsten. "Basic Color Terms in Old Norse-Icelandic: A Quantitative Study." *Orð og tunga* 15 (2013): 141–61.

———. "The Color Blue in Old Norse-Icelandic Literature." *Scripta Islandica* 57 (2006): 55–78.

———. "The Color Brown in Old Norse-Icelandic Literature," *NOWELE.* [Forthcoming.]

———. "The Color Grey in Old Norse-Icelandic Literature." *Journal of English and Germanic Philology* 108 (2009): 222–38.

———. "The Colors of the Rainbow in Snorri's *Edda.*" *Maal og minne* (2007): 51–62.

———. "Reflections on the Color of Esau's Pottage of Lentils (*Stjórn* 160.26–161.9)." *Gripla* 16 (2005): 251–57.

———. "Snorri's Use of Color Terms in *Gylfaginning.*" *Skandinavistik* 37 (2007): 1–10.

————. "Some Comments on Old Norse-Icelandic Color Terms." *Arkiv för nordisk filologi* 121 (2006): 173–92.

————. "Towards a Diachronic Analysis of Old Norse-Icelandic Color Terms: The Cases of Green and Yellow." *Orð og tunga* 12 (2010): 109–30.

Zanchi, Anna. "The Colour Green in Medieval Icelandic Literature: Natural, Supernatural, Symbolic?" In vol. 2 of *The Fantastic in Old Norse/Icelandic Literature: Sagas and the British Isles – Preprint Papers of the Thirteenth International Saga Conference, Durham and York 6th-12th August, 2006*, edited by John McKinnell, David Ashurst, and Donata Kick, 1096–104. Durham: Durham University, 2006.

CPSIA information can be obtained
at www.ICGtesting.com
Printed in the USA
FFOW04n1553180316
22430FF

9 780935 995237